PACIFIC RAMPART

A HISTORY OF CORREGIDOR AND THE HARBOR DEFENSES OF MANILA AND SUBIC BAYS

GLEN M. WILLIFORD

A formal portrait of the men of a battery of the 59th Coast Artillery Regiment manning Fort Drum in 1933. Bolling Smith Collection.

REDOUBT PRESS - MCLEAN, VIRGINIA — 2020

Library of Congress Cataloging-in-Publication Data
Library of Congress Catalog Number 2020-944001
Williford, Glen M.
Pacific Ramparts : a history of Corregidor and the harbor defenses of Manila and Subic Bays
— 1st Edition
p. cm.
includes index

ISBN 978-1-7323916-3-5
1. American seacoast defenses—history—20th century. 2. Manila and Subic Bays miltary—history
3. World War II Philippine battles
I—title

Front Cover Image: Battery Smith firing drill in 1932 – McGaraugh Collection
Rear Cover Images: Map of Manila Bay showing the fortified islands in 1905 – National Archives
Retreat on Corregidor's Mile-long Barrack in 1921 – Karl Schmidt Collection
Battery Crockett's 12-inch disappearing gun during target practice in 1932 – McGaraugh Collection
Paratrooper of 521st Regiment walks on Battery Crockett's 12-inch disappearing gun during the retaking of Corregidor in 1945 – National Archives
Lower two photos were colorized by author
Symbols on Spine: Insignia for 59th Coast Artillery Regiment and the Insignia for 91st Coast Artillery Regiment

Cover design by Mark Berhow

Redoubt Press is a division of McGovern Publishing, which along with Three Sisters Press, publishes books on subjects of historical interest. Under the Redoubt Press label, we have published *The American Defences of the Panama Canal* by Terrance McGovern, *The Concrete Battleship - Fort Drum, El Fraile Island, Manila Bay,* by Francis J. Allen, *A Legacy in Brick and Stone,* by John R. Weaver II, and *Pacific Rampart* by Glen M. Williford. Under the Three Sisters Press label, we have published *The Chesapeake Bay at War! – The Coastal Defenses of Chesapeake Bay During World War Two* by Terrance McGovern, *Seacoast Cannon Coloring Book* by Brian B. Chin, and *The Delaware Bay at War! – The Coastal Defenses of Delaware Bay During World War Two* by Terrance McGovern. McGovern Publishing is interested in new titles, especially those dealing with fortifications, please contact Terry McGovern at 703/538-5403 or at tcmcgovern@att.net if you have a title that you are seeking to have published. Visit www.mcgovernpublishing.com

Redoubt Press
A Division of McGovern Publishing
1700 Oak Lane, McLean, Virginia 22101 USA
tcmcgovern@att.net

Dedicated to:

William C. Gaines

PREFACE

The fortification term "Rampart" refers to a wall or barrier on the exterior of defensive works. When America obtained the Philippine Islands after the Spanish-American War, military officers were tasked to recommend defenses for the new possession. Realizing that the navy could not be regularly stationed here, these officers recommended building a defensive strongpoint at the major Manila and Subic Bays. This is the technical and historical account of this rampart.

Following World War II most of the material written about Corregidor and the other fortified islands in Manila and Subic Bays focused on the combat of 1941-1942 and especially the islands' retaking in 1945. Beyond articles written in the army's professional journals, very little has been published regarding the events that transpired on the "Rock," as the "Corregidoros" called it during the years that preceded World War II. Many official histories and secondary accounts are available on the two combat campaigns. While the author has summarized these battles, they are not the primary focus of this work. The larger part of this history is devoted to the story of Corregidor and the other fortified islands in the years during which these fortifications were constructed and garrisoned. The Harbor Defenses of Manila and Subic Bays were, between the two world wars, one of the few locations where the men of the U.S. Army Coast Artillery Corps could carry out comprehensive training. Most coast artillery career officers would serve one or more tours of duty on the "Rock" during this period. Many of these officers would rise to senior rank in that corps and several would serve in the course of their careers as Chiefs of Coast Artillery, while still others would attain general officer rank.

This work started as one of William (Bill) Gaines's series of histories about various fortification sites of the United States. Bill quickly found that it had grown beyond the size and format of that series. The sheer size of the defenses, their importance to the service, and the fact that they were just about the only modern American defense to actually see action led him to a book-sized work and necessitated the assistance of a co-author to fill in different historical perspectives. I accepted the offer to share the work from Bill in late 2011. Unfortunately, Bill's long struggle with his health led to his untimely loss in 2014. It has been my privilege to rewrite this history with appreciation to my collaborator and dear friend of over thirty years. In respect for his early efforts, this book is dedicated to him.

The research is heavily sourced with primary archival documents. Thankfully textual, cartographic, and photographic records for the construction and service of these defenses are available, if requiring knowledgeable mining techniques, at public-access repositories. The U.S National Archives in both Washington, D.C., and College Park, Maryland, have the most critical holdings of coast artillery, corps of engineer, ordnance, medical, and quartermaster army departments, along with pertinent navy and marine corps records. Unit records are held in army care in St. Louis, Missouri. The U.S. Army's Heritage and Education Center in Carlisle Barracks, Pennsylvania, holds personal accounts and photo records, an essential source for first-person accounts, particularly during the siege of the garrison. Also, many of the prisoners of war from the first campaign and veterans of the second campaign have left us valuable accounts of what they experienced. Accumulating the records supporting this work has required many hundreds of hours, dozens of trips, and over twenty years of effort.

The undertaking of a project of this magnitude would be almost impracticable without the assistance afforded by our fellow members of the Coast Defense Study Group. Bolling Smith was especially helpful in the obtaining some of the initial archival materials from the National Archives. He also made his collection of period photos available for this project, as well as assisting me in editing the final drafts. I also thank Col. Shawn Welch, who made his photographic collection available. I was fortunate to gain access to Col. Riley E. McGarraugh's photograph collection. McGarraugh was an avid and prolific photographer, who left over 800 images from two tours of duty in Manila Bay. Similarly, I want to thank Karl Schmidt for the loan of his photographs and impressive postcard collection of Manila and Subic Bay. Thanks also to the MacArthur Memorial, Newport News, Virginia, and the Navy and Marine Corps Historical Commands for various documents and photographs.

I would be remiss to not thank my associate on all historical events in the Philippines, Anthony (Tony) Feredo. His reviews, inputs, and ceaseless responses to my inquiries are integral to the completion of this work.

A work of this size and complexity about a relatively obscure branch of military technology means only a small, select audience will appreciate it. Only the proactive assistance of Redoubt Press, managed by Terry McGovern and Mark Berhow, has made this publication possible; they are as much responsible for its ultimate appearance as anyone.

Glen Williford
Zionsville, Indiana
2020

ILLUSTRATION SOURCES

Alfonte Collection, USAMHI	William Alfonte Photographs, USAMHI, Carlisle Barracks
Ashton Collection, USAMHI	John Ashton Papers, USAMHI, Carlisle Barracks
Boston Public Library	Boston Public Library, Boston, MA
City of Olongapo	City of Olongapo, Philippines
Cornwell Collection, USAMHI	Cornwell Papers, USAMHI, Carlisle Barracks
Gaines Collection	William Gaines personal photograph collection
Jensen Collection	Walter Jensen Photographs, USAMHI, Carlisle Barracks
Jim Black	James Black personal sketch
Library of Congress	Library of Congress, Prints & Photographs Division.
Life Magazine, hosted by Google	http://images. google. com/hosted/life
MacArthur Memorial	MacArthur Memorial Research Center, Norfolk, VA
McGarraugh Collection	Riley McGarraugh Photograph Collection, with G. Williford
NARA	National Archives and Records Administration, Archives II, Still Picture Branch.
NHC	Naval History and Heritage Command, Washington D.C.
Ruhlen Collection	George Ruhlen Papers, USAMHI, Carlisle Barracks
Schmidt Collection	Karl Schmidt personal postcard and photograph collection
Smith Collection	B.W. Smith personal photograph collection
University of Texas	The University of Texas at Austin, TX
USAF Museum	National Museum of the U.S. Air Force, Wright-Patterson AFB, OH
USAMHI	United States Army Military History Institute, Carlisle Barracks, PA
USMC HC	United States Marine Corps, History Command, Quantico, VA
Welch Collection	Colonel Shawn Welch personal photograph collection
Williford Collection	Glen Williford personal photograph collection
Zink Collection	Robert Zink personal photograph collection

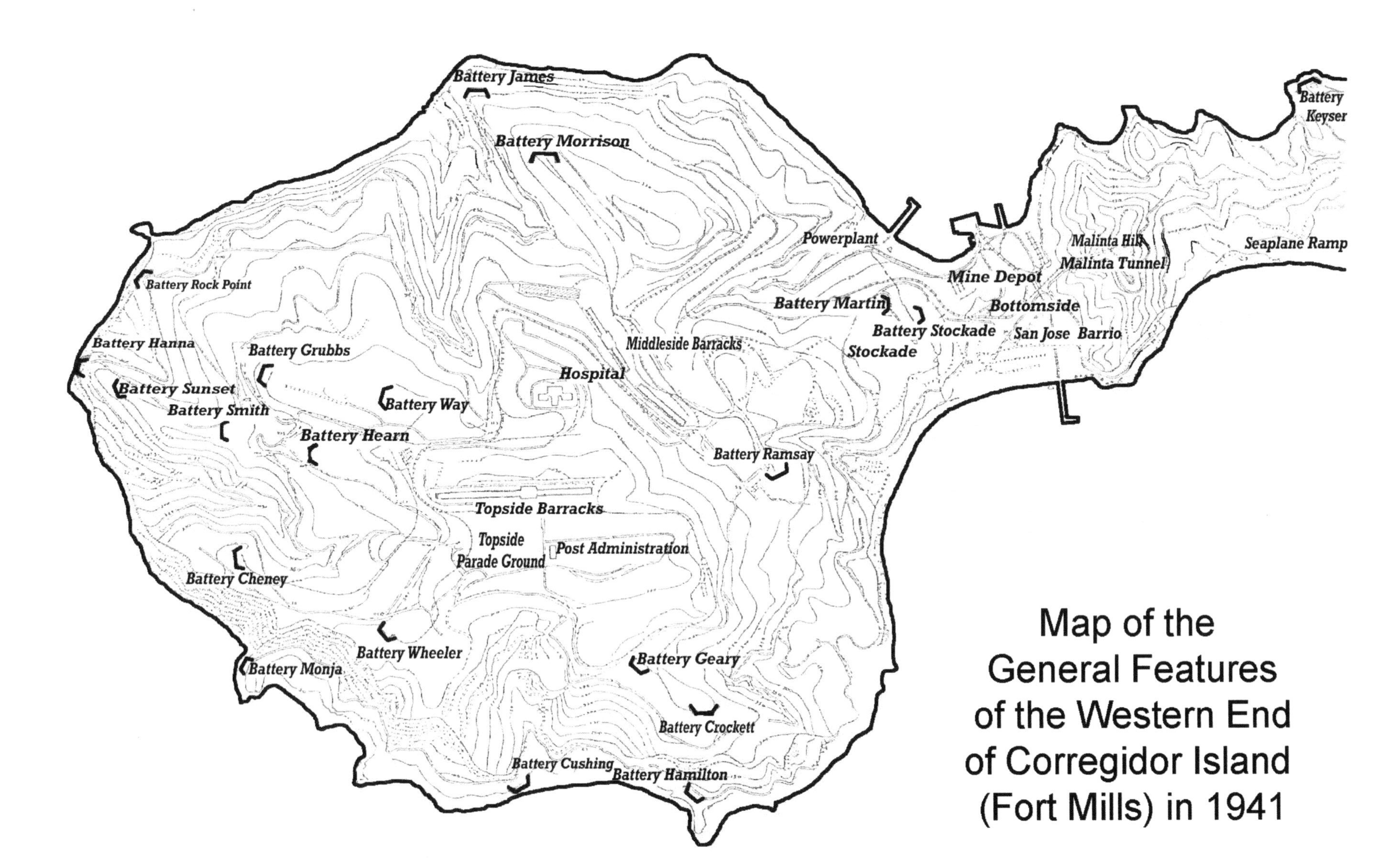

Map of the
General Features
of the Western End
of Corregidor Island
(Fort Mills) in 1941

CONTENTS

CHAPTER 1
THE SPANISH ERA

The Prevailing Geography

Manila Bay, on the west coast of Luzon Island in the Philippine Archipelago, is some 30 miles long and 12 miles wide. Its entrance is formed by the Bataan Peninsula to the north and the rolling terrain of Cavite Province to the south. Several islands of volcanic origin stretch across the bay's entrance. They range in size from the three and one-half mile long tadpole-shaped Corregidor Island of some 1,735 acres to islets such as La Monja that are little more than large rocks.

Two main channels pass from the South China Sea into Manila Bay. The Boca Chica (literally "small mouth") or North Channel lies between the west end of Corregidor and the mountainous Bataan Peninsula. The Boca Grande ("large mouth") or South Channel is the main entrance to Manila Bay. It passes between Corregidor's easternmost point and Caballo Island on the channel's north side, and passes the small but very rugged volcanic cone of El Fraile Island some two miles north of the Cavite shoreline. Another pair of rugged volcanic rocks, Carabao and similarly sized Limbones, hug the Cavite shore at the bay's south entrance. Thirty miles north and east at the head of the bay is the city of Manila and the mouth of the Pasig River, and to the city's southwest, the Cavite and Sangley Point peninsulas jut into the bay from the shore of Cavite Province. It is one of the finest protected harbors in Asia, and of sufficient depth and clearance to be of notable value for maritime commerce. It had long been used for commercial and military activity.

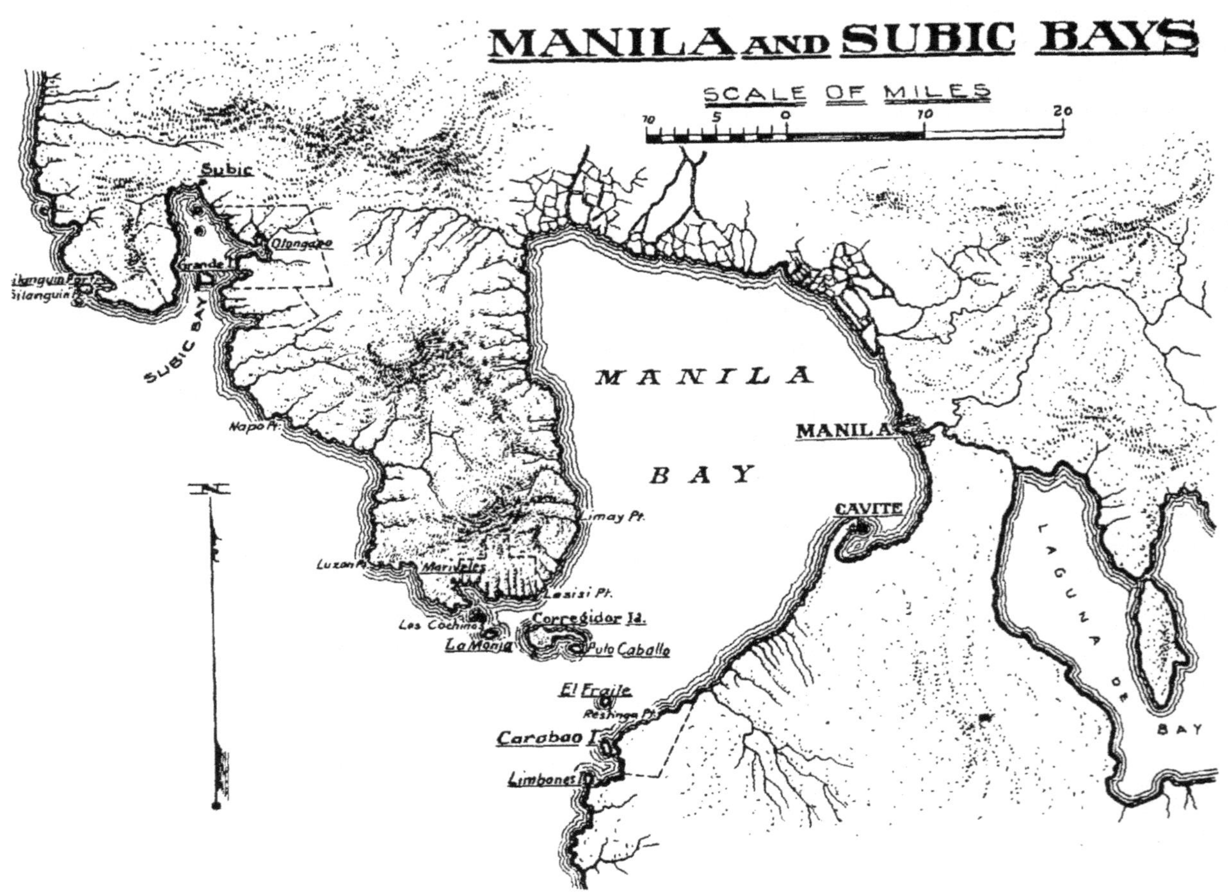

Manila Bay area in 1898. NARA.

A separate significant bay lies about forty miles north of Manila Bay, and also opens into the South China Sea. In the early days known as Subig Bay, the name Subic Bay eventually emerged in the early 20th century for this body. Somewhat smaller than Manila Bay, it is still a fine, deep-water bay. Surrounded by protective heights on both the northern and southern coasts, the main entrance to the bay is occupied by Grande Island (or also called Grande Isle). It lacked a large city or port but did open inland to a wide plane exiting to the southeast and eventually Manila. For development as a naval base it presented an interesting set of pluses and minuses versus Manila Bay and would present challenges for both the Spanish and American navies to consider.

The Spanish Colonization of the Philippines

At the head of Manila Bay is a delta formed by the Pasig River, the fertile land drained by a number of estuaries. Manila began as a small tribal settlement on the Pasig River banks near its entrance to Manila Bay. It took its name Maynilad, or where the nilad grows, from a white-flowered mangrove plant that grew in abundance in the area. Manila's indigenous inhabitants were the Tagalog or river people, who were actively trading with the Chinese long before Europeans arrived. By the 16th century Manila boasted an international community brought together by trade, represented were Chinese, Arabs, Borneans, Japanese, and Indians.

Maynilad was a fairly prosperous Islamic community ruled by Rajahs. The Rajahs were in turn related to the royalty of Brunei, a center of Islam, which in an addition to being a religion, shaped the development of political and social life. Bornean Rajah Sulayman Mahmud, descendant of a royal Malay family and a relative of the Sultan of Brunei, ruled the Sultanate of Maynilad. Rajah Sulayman made his palisaded residence on the Pasig River's southern bank, where the river empties into Manila Bay. Sulayman ruled the Maynilad Sultanate from a location now occupied by Fort Santiago, while his relatives Rajah Matanda and Rajah Lakandula ruled the adjacent Sultanate of Tondo, on the Pasig's north bank.

King Charles I of Spain, who was also Charles V, Emperor of the Holy Roman Empire, commissioned the Portuguese navigator Ferdinand Magellan to seek out the Spice Islands by sailing westward into the Pacific Ocean. Increased demands for spices in Europe made those commodities very profitable. Magellan sailed from Spain with five ships manned by 250 men on September 20, 1519. After an arduous voyage of sixteen months, Magellan sighted an island on March 17, 1521, and named it "Archipelago of St. Lazarus," known today as Samar Island. Subsequently, Magellan disembarked on Leyte Island, where the expedition celebrated the first Catholic mass in the Philippines on March 31, 1521. Magellan then sailed southwest, landing on Mactan Island off the Island of Cebu. There his reception by the natives led by their Rajah Lapu-Lapu proved less than cordial. The natives chose to fight to avoid submission. The famous Battle of Mactan took place on April 27, 1521. Although the Castilians were armed with muskets, crossbows, and swords, and had body armor and shields, they were defeated and the Lapu-Lapu slew Magellan.

After the disaster at Mactan, King Charles I sent other expeditions seeking the Spice Islands between 1525 and 1527, but these too failed to attain the desired goal. Finally, bankrupt, Charles I signed the Treaty of Zaragosa with Portugal on April 22, 1529, dividing the Pacific at 297.5 leagues east of the Moluccas Islands, an archipelago laying south of the Philippines between the Celebes Islands and New Guinea. Because of this treaty, the Philippine and Moluccas Islands became, at least temporarily, Portuguese colonies. Although the treaty was still in force in 1542, Charles I sent an expedition under Roy de Villalobos to establish a permanent hold in Islas de Poniente, (the present Philippines). Villalobos, accompanied by Augustinian priests, landed in Sarangani, Mindanao, in 1543. The Moros' aggressiveness and the island's poverty combined to drive the Spaniards from the island. En route, a member of the expedition named Bernardo de la Torre gave the archipelago the name Las Islas de Filipinas in honor of Prince Philip, the heir to the throne.

Philip II became king in 1556 and made it his policy to colonize the islands that now bore his name. Subsequently a colony was established on the island of Cebu in the central part of the archipelago and by the

1560s the colonization movement was spreading northward toward the island of Panay, where they learned of a capacious bay to the north on the island of Luzon. Philip ordered Miguel Lopez de Legazpi to leave Mexico for the Philippines on November 1564, landing on Panay Island on April 27, 1565.

In 1570, Legazpi dispatched his nephew Juan de Salcedo and Marshal Martin de Goiti to reconnoiter north. They reached Mindoro, where the inhabitants succumbed to Spanish guns. From there they moved on to Manila Bay. On May 24, 1570, a half-century after Magellan's discovery of the Philippine Islands, a Spanish expedition under Martin de Goiti anchored at a hook-shaped sandbar called Kawit (Cavite). Subsequently it became the Spanish staging point for their attack on Sulayman's palisaded fortification. Goiti dropped anchor off the Pasig River and claimed the region in the name of the King of Spain. Sulayman's palisade was heavily bombarded and severely damaged by the Spanish guns. On the following morning the Battle of Bangkusay, in the Sultanate of Tondo, took place between thousands of Macabebe warriors against 300 of de Goiti's Spanish soldiers. Defenseless against Spanish steel, and the fury of rival Christianized tribes, the sultans' armies were forced to capitulate. Because of continuing resistance by Rajah Sulayman and the other Muslim kings, de Goiti burned their villages.

Although 1570 marked the formal conquest of Manila by Spain, colonists did not arrive until May of 1571. By then Sulayman's palisade, damaged by the previous year's bombardment, was rebuilt. Another battle ensued, Sulayman again being forced to surrender and abandon his fortified residence. The following month on June 24, 1571, the feast day of the birth of John the Baptist, Manila was constituted as a city of the Spanish realm and designated the colony's capital. Thus began the 300-year Spanish colonization of the Philippines.[1]

Manila's Spanish Colonial Defenses

Although Manila received its royal charter in 1571, the city remained for decades without the wall, or the buildings of mortar and adobe with which the Intramuros (Spanish for inner walls) is associated. From 1571 to 1574, Manila's only defense was a wooden palisade, reinforced with earth laid out along the trace of Sulayman's fortification. In September 1574, news was received of an impending attack by the Chinese pirate and warlord Limahong, with a fleet of some 65 vessels. Limahong with 3,000 men anchored in the Boca Chica between Corregidor and the small port of Mariveles at the foot of the Bataan Peninsula. Legazpi's successor as the colonial governor general, Guido de Lavezares, ordered the building of makeshift defenses that consisted of "board, stakes and boxes and barrels filled with sand." Two attacks against Manila were launched by Limahong, and he almost overran the city. Only the timely return from north Luzon of troops on an expedition saved the city. Limahong was forced to retreat to the north and was finally defeated at Pangasinan. Realizing the need to fortify, Lavezares began surrounding Manila with a palisade that was completed under the third governor general, Francisco de Sande. In 1581, Jesuit Priest Antonio Sedeño, who had some knowledge of architecture, was tasked with designing a fortification for Manila's southern and most vulnerable flank. Sedeño designed a roofed circular fortification in the style of medieval towers, dedicated to Nuestra Señora de Guia.

Construction of a stone wall was begun in earnest in 1591 and was continued until 1594, under Governor General Gomez Perez Dasmariñas. He had Sedeño's tower redesigned and integrated into a new walled system that became known as the Intramuros. Over the next century, the Spanish increased their hold and control over the Philippine Archipelago. By 1600 the European struggles for empire saw the Dutch attempt incursions into the Philippines. In November and December of that year, the waters off Corregidor Island were used by Dutch Admiral Olivier van Noort. His two ships, *Mauritius* and *Hendracht,* were engaged in pirating on the sailing route to and from Manila. Van Noort with his two vessels had attacked several Chinese junks and Spanish ships in the waters off Corregidor. After December 14, 1600, the colonial government in Manila sent Don Antonio de Morga, a Colonial Supreme Court justice, down the bay with a pair of old Spanish galleons to drive off Van Noort. De Morga engaged the Dutch in Boca Chica off Mariveles and in the naval battle of Fortune Island south of Manila Bay managed to capture the Dutch *Hendracht*, although at the cost of the galleon *San Diego* that sank with considerable loss of Spanish lives. Van Noort managed to escape with *Mauritius*.[2]

Sinking of the Spanish flagship in battle with Oliver van Noordt, near Manila, December 14, 1600. T. de Bry's *Peregrinationes*, Amsterdam 1642. Boston Public Library.

In 1609, the Dutch returned to the Philippines with a fleet commanded by Admiral François de Wittert. After an unsuccessful raid on the island of Panay, Wittert sailed north to Manila Bay, where he intercepted and captured several trading vessels. The Spanish governor with a small squadron of six ships sailed down to Mariveles where he engaged Wittert on April 23, 1610, in a second battle of Mariveles. The battle raged for six hours, finally ending with Wittert's death, the Dutch fleet's defeat, and the capture of all but one of the Dutch vessels.[3]

The struggles between the Dutch and Spanish over the Philippines continued. In 1617 a third sea battle, the Battle of Playa Honda, was fought off the shores of Corregidor and in 1624 a fourth engagement off Mariveles again resulted in the Dutch being driven off, thus preserving Spanish possession of the islands. In 1638, while the governor general was attempting to subdue Mindanao and Sulu in the southern reaches, Spanish soldiers were recalled to Manila in anticipation of another pending Dutch invasion. Once the Dutch invasion threat had passed, Spain decided to refortify the Southern Philippines with forts in Zamboanga, Sulu, and Palawan in 1718. The Moros were alarmed and prepared for the impending presence of Spanish forces. A 1751 royal decree known as "Privateer System" encouraged enlisting individuals to join the expeditions against the Moros. The Moros retaliated by raiding Spanish territories and taking captives to be sold in slave markets.

Corregidor Island was actually occupied by the Dutch in June 1647 and from there they launched an offensive against Cavite that destroyed the fort at Porta Vega on June 10, 1647. While the attack on Cavite was eventually repelled by the Spanish garrison, the Dutch remained on Corregidor for an additional seven months. The island served as an operating base from which they intercepted Chinese merchant traffic in the vicinity of Luzon and Cebu. Finally, they withdrew with little of their expectations fulfilled.

Fortifications Are Enhanced

Because of the threat posed by the Dutch, Governor General Alfonso Fajardo de Tenza had a moat dug along the Intramuros' eastern flank. The fortifications of the Intramuros were regularly repaired and improved under successive governors until 1872, when the last work on the fortifications was reported. As a consequence of the events during the 17th century's first three decades, a watch vessel was positioned at Corregidor to control the entrance to the bay and prevent a sneak attack by Muslims from Mindanao. According to data from 1637, this vessel had a crew of 20 men, each paid 540 pesos a year.

The Spanish discovered that Cavite la Punta (the point of Cavite) was a good location for the construction and repair of ships and galleons. It was staffed with shipwrights and engineers who were transferred to the Philippines from the Spanish shipyard at San Blas, Mexico. Puerto de Cavite was an integral part of world trade. A galleon sailed every July to Acapulco, Mexico, and a second galleon sailed from Acapulco to Manila, each loaded with goods valued at 250,000 pesos. Between 1609 and 1616 the galleons *Espiritu Santo* and *San Miguel* were constructed in the Cavite shipyard. In 1590 Puerto de Cavite's surrounding walls and Fort Guadalupe on the south side of the peninsula were built. The last galleon built at Cavite for the trade between Mexico and Manila was the *Magallanes*, which left Manila in 1811, ending a long line of stately ships of Spanish design but built almost wholly by Chinese and Philippine labor and craftsmanship. This venerable galleon trade between the Philippines and Mexico continued as a government monopoly until 1815, when the last official galleon from Acapulco docked at Manila.

Under Governor General de Corcuera, the moat around the Intramuros was expanded and covered ways constructed during 1635 to 1644. The moat was also extended around the citadel's eastern and southern flanks. A *contra foso* (outer moat), was excavated and separated from the principal moat by the island formed between the two. The moats were linked at the Baluarte de San Nicolás by a narrow canal. A bridge across the inner moat linked Puerta Del Parian with the island, where a small tenaille was built to protect the gate. Puerta Real, which at this time was at the end of Calle Real del Palacio, was also protected by an outer fortification, a demilune.

The 18th century brought a change of dynasty to Spain, the Bourbons succeeding the Hapsburgs and instituting a more efficient modern government. Among the monarchy's concerns was the fortification of the Philippines, because of its strategic location in the western Pacific. In 1705, they sent the military engineer Juan Ramirez de Ciscara to examine the Philippine fortifications and to plan improvements. He worked on the defenses of Manila, Cavite, and other locations in the colony. In 1734, under Governor General Fernando Valdez Tamon, Manila's fortifications were improved further. Responding to the king's directive to supply information as a fire had damaged the royal archives, Tamon sent a report on the status of colonial fortifications in the Philippines in 1738. Not content with what he considered a hasty report, the following year he sent a fuller and more complete version. This report, elegantly presented in handsome calligraphy and illustrated with a Philippine map and plans of the fortifications arranged from north to south, is a valuable 1730's snapshot of the Philippines' defenses, including the Intramuros. While awaiting a new governor general, Fray Juan Arechederra, Archbishop of Manila, took charge of the government. Upon assessing the danger of a possible

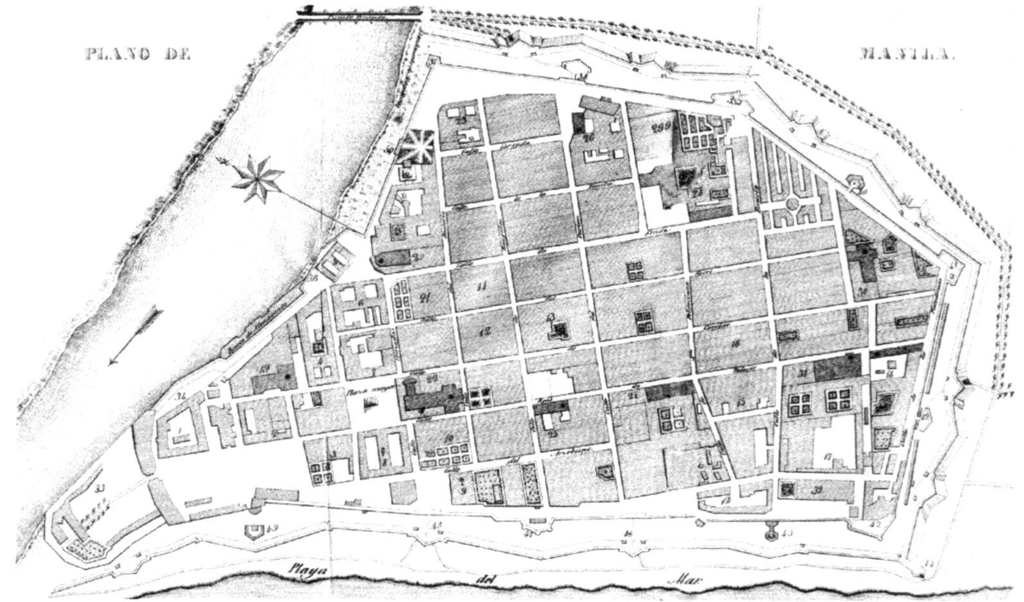

Map of old Manila in 1851, encompassing the walls of the Intramuros.
Diccionario Geografico-Estadistico-Historico de Las Islas Filipinas, Madrid. University of Texas, Austin Library Map Collection.

Quartel de Espania infantry barracks complex of the Intramuros.
The Baluarte de San Diego formed the southwest corner of the Intramuros. Colonel Welch Collection.

British attack, he ordered the consolidation of the city walls, reconstruction of the Pasig River gate, restoration of the foundry, and an inventory of the city's stock of ammunition and weapons, greatly improving the Manila defenses. By now the city's walls were 50 feet thick and 20 feet high and fronted by a deep moat.[4]

The British Capture Manila

What the Dutch had failed to achieve in the 1600s, Great Britain was able to accomplish in 1762. During the Seven Years' War between Great Britain and France, Spain aligned herself with the French. The British promptly declared war on Spain and developed plans to seize the Philippines. Sir William Draper, colonel of the 79th Regiment of Foot, sailed to India, where he assembled an army of some 6,839 men - 2,000 British East India Company Sepoys (native troops) from Madras bolstered by 500 British troops of the 79th Regiment of Foot, about 270 Royal Marines from the fleet, two small detachments of artillery, a battalion of sailors numbering about 250 French deserters, nearly 500 unarmed lascars to perform labor, and a collection of African slaves, native Christian Indians who claimed to be of Portuguese descent, and European infantry in the employ of an Indian Nawab.

After more than six months of preparation, sailing against foul weather, and the loss of two of his supply ships, Rear Admiral Samuel Cornish's small fleet of some 13 sail entered Manila Bay on September 23, 1762, and anchored off the Spanish shipyard of Cavite, much to the consternation of the Spanish. Corregidor was used as a sort of auxiliary anchorage for warships, particularly HMS *Panther,* a fourth rate, 60-gun ship of the line, and Spain's Manila galleon *Santisima Trinidad y Nuestra Señora del Buen Fin,* during November 1762. The 54-gun full-rigged ship *Santísima Trinidad,* with her treasure cargo valued in the millions, had been captured by *Panther* and the 28-gun frigate HMS *Argo,* October 31, 1762.

Manuel Antonio Rojo del Rio y Vieyra, Archbishop of Manila and Philippines Governor General, was unaware of a declaration of war with Great Britain and was completely unprepared for war. The understrength Royal Regiment (recruited in Mexico) made up the Spanish garrison at Manila, consisting of a bare 600 men distributed among 20 companies along with an 80-man detachment of Filipino artillerists and four small infantry companies of Filipino militia. After reconnoitering the Spanish defenses, Draper managed to land his troops through heavy surf between Manila and Cavite near the town of Malate. Covering fire from three British frigates rendered the weak Spanish defenses ineffectual.

Fort San Antonio Abad at Malate was used as gunpowder storage by the Spanish. After the British arrival in the bay, Archbishop Rojo decided to hold the fort and began removing the powder after Draper's men landed, and he sent 100 men to defend the fort. However, the fort guarding the route to Manila from Cavite was quickly captured by the British and used in their assault against Manila. After bombarding the southern flank of the Intramuros walls for almost a week, a breach was made and the city fell. For two years, the British occupied Manila. Efforts to expand their control of the archipelago beyond Manila and Manila Bay, however, were unsuccessful. In 1764, possession of the Philippines was returned to Spain in accord with the 1763 Treaty of Paris. With the British departure, the Philippines would remain Spanish for another 135 years.[5]

The British occupation emphasized the need to improve the defenses of Manila. In September 1766 a Spanish fleet, led by General Ignacio Mario de Alava, arrived with the mission to placethe Philippine Islands on alert. He established a naval station adjacent to Fort San Felipe de Neri on the Cavite Peninsula. The principal defensive works for Manila Bay continued to be located along the Manila waterfront and at Cavite, the primary Spanish naval base in the Philippines. Shaped somewhat like pincers of a crab claw, the Cavite Peninsula projects into Manila Bay; the longer of the two "pincers" formed Sangley Point, and Cañacao Bay lay between the claw's two pincers. The other pincer, Cavite proper, was the location of a naval shipyard capable of constructing galleons and other vessels. Forts San Felipe Neri, whose granite scarps rose 30 feet above the peninsula, and Porta Vaga were begun in 1595 and completed in 1602. Although the naval base's primary fortification was Fort San Felipe de Neri, additional batteries would be built at the Cavite naval base with a battery on adjacent Sangley Point before 1898. The Spanish also established a naval hospital at Cañacao at the Sangley Peninsula's head and in 1871 built a coaling station across Cañacao Bay from Cavite on Sangley Point.[6]

Cavite City suffered from unhealthy living conditions, with malaria and other diseases rampant, and its harbor and naval base were vulnerable during bad weather. Because of Cavite's shortcomings, a board of officers was assigned to investigate a new location for the primary naval station. A military expedition was sent to Subic Bay in 1868 with orders to survey the bay and determine if a suitable site for a naval base existed there. From their camp at the mouth of the Cawag River on Subic Bay's northern shore, the Spanish officers explored the entire bay and concluded that the area at Olongapo held the most promise. Upon returning to Cavite the board informed the naval command that Subic Bay, with its deep water and healthy environment, was superior to Cavite and an ideal place for a naval installation. This report, however, was not well received in Manila. The Spanish command was reluctant to give up the social life of Manila for the provincial isolation of Subic Bay. Nearly two decades would pass before plans for a naval station would be prepared and submitted for the king's approval. Finally, in 1884, Subic Bay was declared by Royal Decree a "naval port and the property appertaining thereto set aside for naval purposes."[7]

The Spanish commission authorized construction of an arsenal at Olongapo on March 8, 1885, with walls and markers to fence off the location. The following September Filipino laborers were employed dredging the area and filling in low spots. The Spanish planned to make their naval station and the village of Olongapo an "island," protected against attack by *insurrectos*. A harbor and inner basin were dredged and a drainage canal constructed. The canal served the dual purpose of draining the swampy area around the naval base and forming a line of defense. Gunboats of shallow draught could enter the waterway at the inner harbor, proceed via the drainage canal and the connecting Kalaklan River, and emerge into the bay. The circuit would then be completed by sailing parallel to the beach until coming back to the inner harbor. The gunboats *Caviteno, Santa Ana,* and *San Quentin* were assigned to the arsenal for its defense. In addition, shore batteries were planned for the station's eastern and western sides and on Grande Isle, to complete the naval arsenal's defenses.[8]

A narrow road lined by large mango trees led from the small fishing village of Olongapo across tidal flats to the West Gate (Spanish Gate), the main entrance to the newly completed navy yard. Defenders could fire small arms through the loopholes, while remaining protected in two small keeps, one on either side of the entrance way, which also served as prison guardhouses. A high wall constructed of locally kilned brick connected the West Gate to the South Gate near the waterfront. Inside the wall, the Spanish constructed a foundry and other shops necessary for ship repair and construction. The buildings were laid out in two rows on a sandy spit that projected into Subic Bay, named for the captain general of the Philippines, Fernando Primo de Rivera. The ship *Marques de la Victoria* initially provided electric power and steam for the yard. The station hospital was of unique construction; built of iron and brick on a radically different plan from any previously structures. The brick walls were supported in place by huge iron posts cast in Barcelona. Handrails and other grilled ironwork were fabricated locally. The hardwood flooring consisted of large hand-sawn, trimmed, and finished mahogany boards. The arsenal commandant's office was considered the naval station's showpiece. It was a one-story building constructed of native hardwood, with colored glass windows. The garrison consisted of about 30 marines in addition to the ships' crews, as well as civilian workers.[9]

Fort Santiago circa 1899 prior to American alterations. A 24 cm Hontoria breechloading rifle was emplaced in one of the batteries in front of the Baluarte de San Diego of the Intramuros. Library of Congress

Modernizing the Defenses of Manila

Deteriorating relations between Germany and Spain over possession of the Caroline Islands in the early 1890s prompted an increase in the armament of Manila and the Cavite and Olongapo naval stations. Four 24 cm breechloading rifles (BLR), nine 16.5 cm muzzle-loading rifled (MLR) mortars; four 14 cm converted BLR, and 15 old design 16 cm bronze MLR were shipped to Manila from Spain and were emplaced by 1897. These guns were mounted facing Manila Bay in front of the Intramuros in well-screened earthen batteries. One 24 cm gun was emplaced in front of the north bastion of Fort Santiago, while another was emplaced in front of the Baluarte de San Diego. Four 14 cm guns were emplaced near the center bastion Baluartillo (small bastion) de Plaria. Four 16.5 cm mortars were emplaced along the flank of the south wall. Additional armaments augmented the city's defense in the latter part of 1897 and early 1898. Two modern 15 cm BLR siege guns were added to the 14 cm BLR guns fronting the city wall, and two 12 cm siege guns were added to the pair of bronze 16 cm smooth-bore guns in Fort Santiago's circular redoubt on the south mole at the Pasig River's mouth. The two remaining 24 cm rifles were emplaced on the bay's waterfront to the east in the town of Ermita.[10]

The Cavite naval station's defenses were also enhanced. A new casemated earthwork battery was erected on Sangley Point for six 15 cm Ordoñez rifles. At the Cavite Arsenal itself there were three 16 cm Armstrong MLR guns mounted in Forts Guadalupe and San Felipe. Anticipating that additional armament would arrive from Spain in time for emplacement at Cavite, four 15 cm rifles from the battery on Sangley Point were sent to Subic Bay in early March 1898 for emplacement on Grande Isle.[11]

18th century Spanish smoothbore bronze pieces were still in position on the ramparts of the Intramuros outside the Manila Arsenal in 1900. Neely, *Fighting in the Philippines.*

Spain Establishes a Presence on Corregidor at the Entrance to Manila Bay

Corregidor, the largest island at the entrance to Manila Bay was, along with Caballo Island, an extinct volcanic crater rim. Corregidor is tadpole-shaped with its westward-facing, bulbous end (later known as "Topside") rising some 500 feet above sea level and its narrow tail extending to the east curving slightly to the south. Numerous naval engagements had been fought within sight of Corregidor and it had been occupied briefly by several European powers during the early colonial period. The island was initially used by the Spanish as a signal station, where bonfires were lit to notify Manila of the arrival of a galleon. A small barrio, San Jose de la Corregidor, was established about 1779 at the island's lowest, central part (later known as "Bottomside") between heights to the west (later known as "Middleside") and Malinta Hill to the east. The Spanish established a small naval dockyard, storehouses, and a naval hospital on Corregidor in 1795. In 1836, a lighthouse was built on Topside, replaced in 1853 by a stronger light. This light was replaced again in 1897. At the island's mid-point, 400-foot-high Malinta Hill separated the island's two parts. On "Topside," a signal station was built adjacent to the lighthouse to provide notice to Manila and the naval station at Cavite of commercial shipping arrivals as well as to warn of the appearance of an enemy squadron.[12]

The widest channel leading into Manila Bay was Boca Grande, between Corregidor and the Cavite mainland. No measures were taken to fortify Corregidor or the other islands at the entrance to the bay until the last years of the 19th century. Up until that time the channels were simply too wide for the era's short-ranged smoothbore weaponry. During the last half of the 19th century, improvements were made in rifled breechloading artillery. With the arrival of more modern artillery from Spain in the late 1800s, it finally became possible to attempt to bar passage of a hostile fleet.

Entry to Fort San Felipe de Neri, Cavite Arsenal. Gaines Collection

Cavite Arsenal ca. 1890s. Arnaldo Dumindin, *Philippine-American War 1899-1902.*

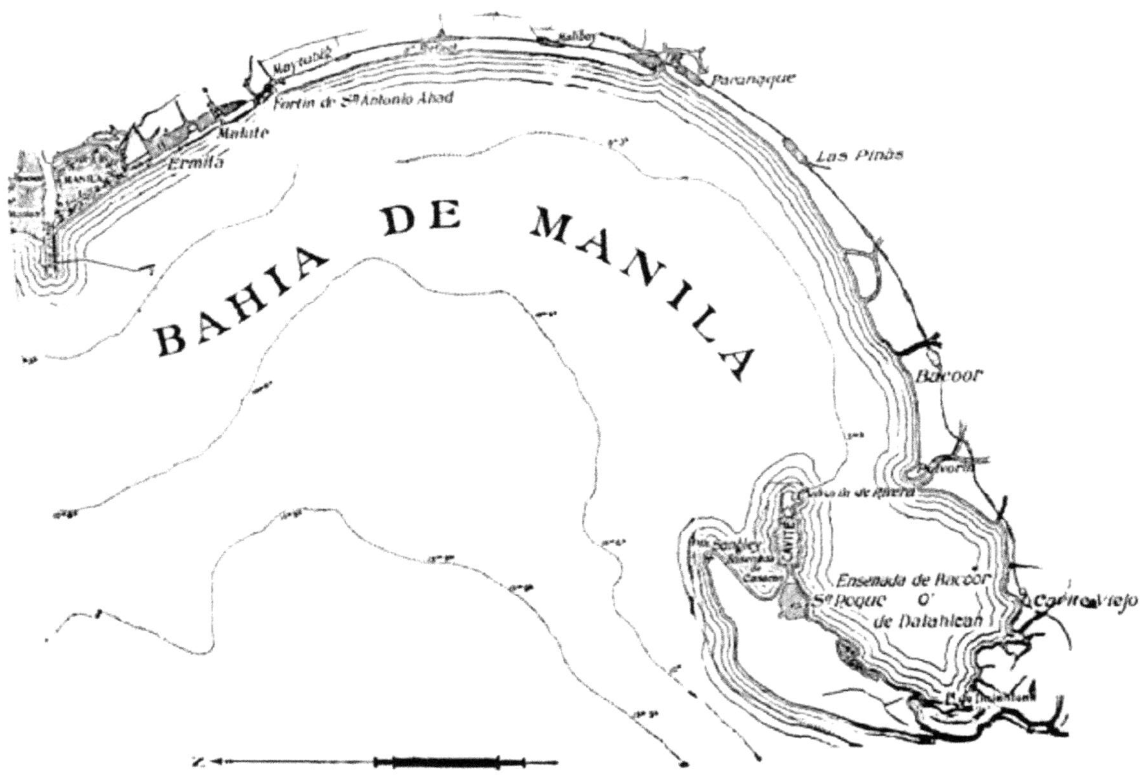

Upper part of Manila Bay showing the location of the Spanish Arsenal at Cavite. NARA

Spanish Preparations for War in 1898

Relations between Spain and the United States had festered for several decades over Spanish colonial policies in Cuba. These relations deteriorated rapidly following the destruction of the USS *Maine* on February 15, 1898, in Havana Harbor. The presence of an American naval squadron in the western Pacific constituted a potential threat to the Spanish in the Philippines. Faced with the probability of war with the United States, preparations for the defense of Manila Bay were called for and the Spanish Colonial War Board issued directives to the navy in February 1898 to fortify the islands at the bay's entrance. Ordnance from batteries at Manila and from a few naval vessels at Cavite was moved to Corregidor and Caballo Islands.[13]

The Spanish War Board, in session at Manila since early March, attempted to devise a means of defense for the colony. About March 10, the board sent a commission to Subic Bay to determine the best positions for four of Fort San Felipe's 15 cm Ordonez guns. The commission decided that no guns could be mounted on the almost perpendicular west coast and that it would only be possible on Isla Grande or Maquiling. Additionally, one channel into the bay could be blocked by sunken hulks and the other by 14 Mathession electrically-controlled mines available at Cavite's naval arsenal. Orders were given for the work to proceed with all energy. Almirante Patricio Montojo y Pasaron, commanding the Spanish fleet, was informed from time to time that the work was progressing rapidly. However, this seems an overly optimistic, as Montojo later noted: "Del Rio informed him by telegraph that when he was not disturbed by insurgent parties from Bataan, he worked with two hundred men and never stopped a minute. Arizmendi, assistant inspector of ordnance, reported that as long as the engineers had not finished the cement work he could do nothing, and Rizzo, assistant inspector of engineers, stated that he could not just say what the status of the work was; that he was waiting for an official report from Commander Sidrach, who had charge of the work, before he could answer."[14] composed of

After directing that batteries be erected at the entrances to the two bays and submarine mines be laid, the board called for the fleet's mobilization. Meanwhile, the board's members were locked in dispute as to where

Spanish Naval Station at Subic Bay in the 1890s. City of Olongapo.

the fleet should make its stand. The land force's commandant at Manila wanted it in front of the city, where it could be supported by the numerous waterfront batteries, but Admiral Montojo wished to go to Subic Bay. The War Board had also ordered the main channel into Manila Bay mined, however the waters at the entrance to the bay were too deep for effective mining. There were only 14 mines available in the Cavite Navy Yard, so mining of Manila Bay would be limited to contact mines.

At the entrance to Manila Bay only eight contact mines had been planted in the Boca Chica Channel. These had been carelessly placed at depths too great to be effective and accounts indicate that that all eight had been simply dropped overboard and had gone straight to the bottom in 80 feet or more of water. The sunken mines were no threat by the time the American fleet arrived off Manila Bay. Apparently, none were planted in the Boca Grande Channel. The board also ordered the lights at the Corregidor and Caballo Lighthouses extinguished on April 23, 1898.[15]

In late April, the transport *Isla de Mindanao* arrived from Spain with a large cargo of coastal artillery, ammunition, automobile torpedoes, and submarine mines. Some of these guns were intended to replace those sent from the batteries at Sangley Point to Subic Bay and the mines were slated to be planted in Boca Grande. However, these munitions arrived only the day before the American squadron and played no role in the forthcoming battle.[16]

On March 15, 1898, Spanish naval Lieutenant Rafael Benavente, captain of the 2nd-class iron gunboat *General Lezo,* laid out a plan for the defense of Manila and Cavite as well as the islands of Corregidor, Caballo, and El Fraile, and the headlands on the bay's north and south side. The work was carried on with an unusual and most praiseworthy energy; two cranes, six launches of the harbor works, two gunboats, and two hundred men from the Cavite Navy Yard, *General Lezo, Don Antonio de Ulloa*, and laborers from Corregidor being used. The shore batteries that were installed at the entrance of Manila Bay, were ready to fight 24 days after work commenced.[17]

Corregidor had a shoreline more than eleven miles long, mostly composed of precipitous cliffs. The barrio's north and south shorelines offered the most practicable landing locations. As the 20th century neared, locations on Corregidor and other islands at the bay's mouth were finally provided with coastal fortifications. On a small plateau (that would come to be termed the "Stockade," or "Scout Level") about 100 feet above Barrio San Jose the Spanish placed a small battery for a handful of smoothbore guns that covered the landing places from San Jose Bay on the south to Corregidor Bay on the north. This fortification became known as "Spanish Fort" after the American arrival. At Punta Talisay on Corregidor's north coast, later known as "Battery Point,"

Postcard view of Barrio San Jose on Corregidor Island, ca. 1890. Gaines Collection.

Corregidor lighthouse on Topside in 1901. NARA.

three 180-pounder (6-inch) Armstrong MLRs were emplaced to cover the Boca Chica Channel. This battery crossed its fire with a battery of three 17.3 cm Palliser MLRs on Punta Gorda and two 16 cm Hontoria BLRs at Punta Lasisi on the Bataan Peninsula.[18]

In addition to the Punta Talisay battery, a single gun of about 6-inch caliber was mounted on a "stationary carriage" at Battery Bocana, just west of Malinta Hill on Bottomside's south shore. Another cannon, an old 6-inch brass piece on a stationary carriage, was positioned on Bottomside's north shore of Corregidor Bay near the wharf. Three or four more muzzle-loading guns of about 4-inch caliber on wheeled garrison carriages were positioned between the naval hospital and the shoreline of Corregidor Bay. The shore of San Jose Bay was guarded by two smaller guns on wheeled carriages.[19]

Caballo Island. NARA.

The 12 cm guns from the Spanish gunboat *Lezo* were mounted in Battery Lezo in El Fraile Island just before war in 1898. NARA.

Dismounted Armstrong muzzle loading rifles on the timber gun platforms of the battery at Point Talisay, Corregidor (later named Battery Point) in 1898. NARA.

The batteries on the three fortified islands and those on Bataan and the Cavite mainland were each garrisoned by a company of the 1st Regiment of Spanish Marine Infantry. The entire command at the entrance to the bay consisted of only five companies, some 392 men, commanded by Colonel Garces. A detail to communicate with both Manila and the Cavite Naval Base was located in the signal station at the lighthouse near the summit of Corregidor's west end. This location also served as Colonel Garces's command post.[20]

Adjacent to Corregidor was Caballo Island, which consisted of two principal geographic parts. The terrain of the island's eastern half was comparatively flat and unimpressive, with a freshwater lake occupying nearly a quarter of the island's eastern end. The topography sloped gradually from an elevation of less than 10 feet on the eastern shore to about 50 feet at the foot of the cliffs near the island's mid-section. The shoreline of the island's western half was occupied by rugged sheer cliffs that rose to a hogback rim some 300 feet above sea level. The batteries on Caballo and El Fraile Islands guarded the Boca Grande passage into Manila Bay. Three 15 cm Armstrong breech-loading rifles were removed from the laid-up, unprotected cruiser *Velasco* undergoing repairs at Cavite. These guns were emplaced behind a low 12-foot-thick stone parapet on the south side of Caballo Island, some 10 feet above the water. Although manned by crew members of *Velasco* and named Battery Velasco, these guns were so far from ready for service that the Spanish had abandoned all hope of getting them prepared when the American squadron arrived. Carabao Island just off Restinga Point on the coast of Cavite Province was left unarmed. Three l6 cm converted Palliser muzzle-loading rifles were emplaced near Cainipa Point on the Cavite mainland.

El Fraile, a rugged rock jutting up from the bay about midway between Caballo and Carabao Islands, was hastily armed with three 12 cm quick-firing Hontoria guns. Two of these guns were taken from the Spanish gunboat *General Lezo* and one from the cruiser *Don Antonio de Ulloa.* The guns were emplaced about 10 feet above the water only days before the Americans arrival. The battery was named Battery Lezo and manned by members of that gunboat's crew.

Montojo was convinced that Subic Bay would make a better base of operations against any American naval force and on the night of April 25, 1898, he took his squadron to Subic Bay. The cruiser *Castilla* was taken to Grande Island to defend the western entrance, since the eastern entrance had already been closed with the sunken hulks of the *San Quintin* and two old merchant vessels. From this almost landlocked bay at the north end of Bataan Peninsula, the admiral believed that the Spanish squadron could fall on the American fleet's rear if it attempted to blockade Manila Bay. Upon arriving there he discovered that the floating dry-dock he had previously sent to the small port of Olongapo was there and available for use. The four guns he had previously ordered moved from Fort San Felipe to Grande Isle, while present, had not been emplaced, and had been left lying on the ground near their proposed emplacements. Only a handful of the 14 electrically controlled mines that were to have been planted in the harbor had been laid.[21]

Because of Subic Bay's inadequate defenses, and the Spanish Army's preference to defend the Philippines from Manila, Montojo ordered his fleet back to Cavite. The move was delayed, as *Castilla* had developed a leak around her shaft that required repairs. Once these repairs were completed, the Spanish squadron returned to Manila Bay on April 29. Montojo prepared to fight the Americans, when they came, from the Spanish Naval Base at Cavite and from in front of Manila itself.[22]

U.S. Navy's Asiatic Squadron Engages the Spanish Fleet

Soon after the news of an expected war with Spain reached the American Asiatic Squadron at Hong Kong, Commodore George Dewey began preparations to conduct operations against Spanish naval forces. Prior to any movement to the Philippines, Dewey had ordered a reconnaissance of Subic Bay to ensure that the Spanish squadron was not anchored there. As the American squadron entered Manila Bay through the Boca Grande Channel on the night of April 30, 1898, it left Corregidor and Caballo Islands on its port hand, Carabao, and El Fraile Islands to starboard. As the American warships steamed past Corregidor's tail, the signal detail at the Corregidor Lighthouse lit a torch as a signal that the enemy fleet was approaching and a signal gun was fired to attract the attention of the Bataan and Cavite batteries. Only a few rounds were fired from the Punta Restinga battery, and these soared high over the American squadron and landed farther out in the bay. As the U.S. Revenue Cutter *Hugh McCullough* steamed past El Fraile, unburnt coal soot in her funnel flamed, alerting the Spanish gunners to the cutter's position, resulting in the firing of about three rounds by the quick-firing guns of Battery Lezo as the squadron passed. *McCullough* and cruisers *Raleigh, Concord,* and *Boston* returned a furious fire on the outgunned Spanish battery. One round landed in the middle of the battery, quickly silencing it. Although this firing did no damage to the American squadron, it was clearly heard further up the bay at Cavite, alerting Montojo.[23]

Commodore Dewey entered Manila Bay with a squadron of seven vessels, of which six were engaged in the Battle of Manila Bay. Included were cruisers *Olympia* (flagship, 5,870 tons displacement), *Baltimore* (4,413 tons), *Boston* (3,000 tons), and *Raleigh* (3,213 tons). In addition to *McCullough* were gunboats *Concord* (1,710 tons) and *Petrel* (892 tons). The engaged Spanish squadron under Admiral Montojo also consisted of seven ships: cruiser *Reina Cristina* (flagship, 3,250 tons), old unarmored cruiser *Castilla* (3,260 tons), and small cruisers/gunboats *Isla de Cuba* (1,045 tons), *Isla de Luzon* (1,045 tons), *Don Juan de Austria* (1,160 tons), *Don Antonio de Ulloa* (1,160 tons), and *Marques del Duera* (500 tons). While seemingly matched in numbers, the American squadron consisted of more modern ships, with about double the tonnage and much better weaponry and training.

Although signals were shown from the Corregidor signal station, neither the Corregidor nor Caballo Island batteries opposed the passage of Dewey's squadron into the bay and did not fire on the passing American vessels. In all probability, the ships had steamed past the Spanish batteries and were beyond the range of their guns before they could be manned. Additionally, the three muzzle-loading guns on Corregidor's Talisay Point were ill positioned to oppose the American warships in Boca Grande and the guns at Bottomside had been emplaced primarily to oppose landings. Similarly, the Caballo battery may not have been properly manned or able to see the vessels after they had passed into the bay. One account states that the major commanding the Spanish troops on Caballo said that he believed the American warships were commercial vessels. Some of those

Manila Waterfront, 1898. NARA.

Protected cruiser USS *Raleigh* in Manila Bay 1898. NHC.

"Battle of Manila Bay," contemporary halftone print after an artwork by W.G. Wood. NHC.

serving in that command said the major was drunk. On the morning of May 1, 1898, Dewey steamed up the bay and engaged Montojo's flotilla and the batteries along Manila's shoreline.

Fort San Felipe, a masonry and earth fortress on the Cavite Peninsula, mounted a number of obsolete iron smoothbore pieces. Montojo had ordered the fort's two remaining 15 cm Ordonez breechloading rifles at the fort moved to Sangley Point. Augmenting the Cavite fortifications were two 12 cm guns from the disabled Spanish cruiser *Don Antonio de Ulloa*'s port battery. One gun bore on the waters of Manila Bay while the other covered the waters of Cañacao Bay; a single 12 cm Canet BLR was emplaced in an earthen battery further up the narrow peninsula. These guns, commanded by Lieutenant Valentine de Valera of the Spanish Artillery, proved to be the only shore batteries to inflect any damage on the American squadron. Their fire, however, attracted the special attention of Dewey's squadron that soon drove de Valera and his 17 cannoneers along with the 26-man infantry platoon back up the Sangley peninsula toward the town of Cavite.[24]

The naval action off Manila's waterfront ended by noon with the Spanish fleet completely destroyed. Around two o'clock that afternoon a launch arrived at Corregidor from Cavite bearing news of the Spanish defeat. Colonel Garces, and the island's governor, Lieutenant Miranda, were urged to come to terms with the Americans. Garces held a meeting of his officers and decided to await developments. Following the Spanish fleet's destruction, USS *Baltimore* and *Raleigh* were ordered to return to the islands at the bay's entrance and obtain the surrender of their batteries. On May 2, *Baltimore* anchored off Corregidor, and Garces and Miranda surrendered. Garces, his officers, and 292 men with their weapons and ammunition were transferred to Mariveles. From there they marched to Manila via Bataan and Pampanga provinces, arriving in Manila on May 5. Miranda remained on the island with 100 Spanish Marine Infantry and the Spanish Flag flying. *Baltimore* landed sailors and marines who dismounted the Spanish batteries on Corregidor and El Fraile, while *Raleigh* performed the same duty at Caballo.

Upon leaving Caballo, *Raleigh* proceeded to Subic Bay, where they found the cruiser SMS *Irene* of the German Far East Squadron providing support for the small Spanish garrison on Grande Island then under siege by Filipino insurgents. *Irene* departed when *Raleigh* and gunboat USS *Concord* arrived. After a short bombardment of Grande Island, the American cruiser accepted the Spanish garrison's surrender. A few days later *Concord* returned to Manila Bay, where it sent a party ashore on Caballo Island to remove the breech plugs of the Spanish guns. The guns on El Fraile and Caballo later disappeared, according to some into the hands of General Emilio Aguinaldo's insurgent army. Some of Corregidor's muzzle-loaders were eventually trophies gracing the grounds near the Fort Mills administration building.[25]

On May 6, 1898, two companies of U.S. Marines were put ashore on Corregidor, where they carried out a search for Spanish stragglers. They then dynamited the signal station flag hoist mast to prevent its use. The marines raised the American flag in the barrio and then departed.[26]

Almost immediately after the May 1, 1898, victory of Manila Bay, the American military began considering a defensive scheme for the city. The Spanish were still capable of organizing a substantial relief fleet, and several other foreign nations were snooping around the Philippines with naval forces anxious to try and obtain territorial scraps from the conflict. Commodore Dewey was able to land light forces from his ships and secure the Cavite naval station and disable the coast defense guns on Corregidor and the bay's other entry points, but he had to wait for an expeditionary force to be sent from the U.S. before attempting to confront the Spanish defenders of Manila. A sort of peaceful stand-off followed between the American fleet occupying Manila Harbor and the Spanish Army occupying the city (and most of the rest of the archipelago). It was not until three months later — August 13, 1898, — that the city surrendered to American and insurgent forces.

On May 20 Dewey was told that Spanish Admiral Cervera's squadron had left Spain for a presumably Cuban, but still unconfirmed destination. On that same day in Washington the chief of ordnance and chief of engineers met to suggest emergency armament for the new possession's defense. Presuming that the city would soon be occupied, the branch chiefs looked at sources for barbette guns that could be mounted in place of Spanish weapons in already existing emplacements. They recommended that two 10-inch barbette carriages intended for Puget Sound (and actually on the wharf in Seattle) be taken to San Francisco, to be joined with 10-inch gun tubes to be taken from Fort Winfield Scott. Furthermore, 8-inch guns and barbette carriages should be shipped as quickly as possible from the U.S. east coast rather than removed from batteries already armed at Fort Columbia on the Columbia River. Mortars were to be taken from the San Francisco defenses, to be married with a surplus of mortar carriages on hand at the manufacturer in St. Paul, Minnesota. However, events moved favorably for the Americans, ending the war with Spain after only a few months and derailing these proposals.[27]

The Battle of Manila Bay spurred the Spanish government to organize a second relief expedition to support and reinforce Spanish forces in the Philippines. Rear Admiral Manuel de la Camara was given Spain's only modern battleship, *Pelayo*, her largest cruiser, *Carlos V*, three modern torpedo boat destroyers, and two large auxiliary cruisers to confront Dewey's Squadron. Six steamers carried soldiers, coal, and supplies. On June 15, 1898, Camara's squadron steamed eastward, arriving at the Suez Canal June 26. Egyptian authorities' strict enforcement of neutrality laws hindered Camera's transit of the canal. The Battle of Santiago on July 3 destroyed Spanish maritime power in the Western Hemisphere, freeing the large U.S. fleet for action elsewhere. Faced with the likelihood that the Americans would cross the Atlantic and begin operations against Spain herself, Camara was ordered to return home July 6.

The American occupation of the Philippines moved ahead smoothly, significantly aided by the Spanish army's decision not to fight. There is some evidence that some initial steps were taken to provide seacoast defenses. The mortar carriages from St. Paul were indeed sent first to San Francisco before being returned to their original routing destination of Fort Stevens, Oregon. Following the annexation of the Philippines, the regiments of state volunteers were returned to the U.S. and replaced with Regular Army and US Volunteers. Between 1899 and 1901 nearly two dozen batteries of field artillery were assigned to the Philippines. While a number of these batteries saw service in the field, most were posted at Manila to form the city's garrison and to man the seacoast batteries there. After 1901 a small force of four coast artillery companies was retained at Manila to man the armament mounted at the Intramuros: the 25th, 27th, 31st, and 36th Companies, Coast Artillery, Artillery Corps. These four companies were replaced by the 10th, 38th, 85th, and 108th Companies in 1903. However, the need to continue manning the defensive armament in Manila ultimately evaporated, particularly in view of the heavier fleet units dispatched there. The coast artillery contingent was eliminated entirely by June 1904, when the companies were returned to the U.S. For the next four years of occupation, the Philippines would remain undefended by coast artillery.

Corregidor 1898-1903

Corregidor was included in the Military District of Cavite when the interim American military government was established in 1898. A convalescent hospital was established by the Army Medical Corps in San Jose Barrio in November 1898. This 250-bed hospital initially occupied the old stone Spanish *Infirmaria de Conception* and a few other old masonry buildings, as well as tents. In September 1899, with activity against the Filipino nationalists intensifying, the first of several new wood-frame hospital structures was completed to replace the tents and old Spanish buildings. One of these new structures was a two-story building and by June 1900, the facility held 220 beds. As described by the surgeon in charge of the Corregidor facility, the hospital also boasted "The first dental office ever fitted out officially by the United States government." It was managed by a hospital corpsman who in private life had been a professional dentist. Plans to expand this hospital had to be suspended because of high construction costs resulting in part from a conspiracy among lumber dealers. By May 31, 1903, the hospital staff of three doctors, 50 medical corpsmen, and six female nurses had treated 1,229 patients. The hospital was discontinued June 10, 1905. [28]

Although the Philippine Islands were declared a United States possession on January 4, 1899, the matter of an insurrection by a sizeable faction of Filipino nationalists led by Emilio Aguinaldo de Famy occupied the army's attention. On March 23, 1901, Aguinaldo was captured. His followers continued the fight however, until the insurrection was finally declared curbed April 16, 1902, and a universal amnesty proclaimed July 4, 1902, whereupon a civil government was established in Manila.

The 10th Pennsylvania Volunteer Infantry Regiment, part of the initial army expeditionary force, provided the first garrison for Corregidor. In April 1899, companies A and B were sent to Corregidor to provide a station force. A tent camp named Camp Jesse Noss was established at the mouth of what would later become

Barrio San Jose de La Corregidor. The bay is at right showing the old wharf and part of the town.
The two masonry buildings at the foot of Skipper Hill (center) served the Spanish government on the island.
They were later utilized by the U.S. Army when they occupied the island in 1899. Schmidt Collection.

known as Engineer or Power Plant Ravine. Noss, of Company E, had been killed in an early conflict near Manila. Companies A and B remained at Corregidor for only about a month when they were replaced by Companies E and H that camped at Corregidor from mid-May to the end of June 1899, when they too were recalled with the volunteers' return to the United States. The 10th Pennsylvania shipped out for the United States in July.[29]

Various U.S. troops from the Cavite or Manila Districts were posted to Corregidor during the remainder of the insurrection until the arrival of a battalion of Philippine Scouts in 1904. On January 14, 1899, the chief of engineers requested that the commanding officer of Company A, Battalion of Engineers, be instructed to prepare a description of existing defenses in the Philippine Islands. On July 9, 1900, First Lieutenant Sherwood A. Cheney forwarded this succinct report on Corregidor: "Corregidor Battery. Three 8-inch Armstrong M.L.R. on point just west of Corregidor Bay. There is a low earthen parapet 16 feet thick. The guns are now dismounted."[30]

In November 1899 a detachment of army engineers arrived to conduct initial surveys, continuing into the 20th century. The engineer troops were quartered in the Cuartel de San Rafael that had once housed the Spanish Marine garrison. The army NCOs occupied a large frame building and one of stone that had formerly served as the Spanish medical officers' residence and offices. A detachment of 12 men of Company E, 2nd Engineer Battalion, commanded by 2nd Lt. George B. Pillsbury, was still conducting surveys for the projected fortifications in late 1903.[31]

Corregidor Bay shore near San Jose in 1899. Gaines Collection.

Corregidor was included in the land reserved for military purposes by a U.S. executive order of April 11, 1902. Civilian landowners (mostly at San Jose barrio) had their deeds extinguished by condemnation. Compensation procedures dragged out for some time but were eventually settled for a cost of $13,606.23 in 1909. [32]

The Army Reorganization Act of February 1, 1901, abolished the U.S. Artillery's regimental structure and substituted an Artillery Corps composed of 126 companies of coast artillery and 30 batteries of field artillery. The act also changed the army's old Battalion of Engineers and created three new engineer battalions. Each battalion was to consist of four companies organized from the old battalion. The 2nd Engineer Battalion, Companies E, F, G, and H, was sent to the Philippines, where it relieved the 1st Engineer Battalion late in 1901.

The engineers were heavily involved in the fortification plans on Corregidor. Establishing the branch's quarters and offices became the first task at hand. As there were only a few structures in Barrio San Jose that could accommodate the engineers' needs, they selected the ravine between Skipper Hill and the uplands of Middleside as the location for their workshops and storehouses. Eventually more than 40 structures would be constructed in "Engineer Ravine" that in more recent times became known as Powerhouse Ravine. Here also was a shelter for the three locomotives used on the island's narrow-gauge railway during construction. Powder and fuze magazines were built, along with 10 storehouses that sheltered construction materials initially and later became warehouses for fortification and war reserve materiel. Most of these buildings, classed as temporary structures, would be built between 1904 and 1925. In 1934 several more structures were authorized and added to those in the ravine. Other than those built to house the civilian employees, they were for the most part constructed with concrete floors and corrugated galvanized iron (G.I.) siding on wood frames with G.I. roofs. Others which might be classed as even more "temporary" were built at Topside near the gun and mortar battery construction sites. These structures, quarters for the foreman and 10 mechanics, a mess house and kitchen, and a wash house had walls built of suali and nipa with bamboo lattice to anchor the nipa roofs. A machine shop and a storehouse were built a bit more sturdily and had concrete floors and G.I. roofs.

The U.S. flag flying over Corregidor Island in 1899. NARA.

CHAPTER 2
EARLY EMERGENCY DEFENSES & CONSTRUCTION ON GRANDE ISLAND

Early Defenses

The second emergency armament plan for the Manila and Subic Bay defenses was proposed in mid-1904. There does not appear to be a specific incident triggering this plan; perhaps the study was just a routine effort to have a document written and approved if a true emergency occurred prior to the construction of permanent defenses — which was just about to begin. In July 1904 artillery Capt. LeVert Coleman and Lt. William I. Westervelt submitted a thorough report for the emergency defense of both Manila and Subic Bay. It was based on the assumption that all or most of the defensive equipment must already be on hand, as any new emergency would probably develop too quickly for matériel to be obtained from the Continental U.S.[33]

They found that the army had 14 5-inch siege guns, 12 7-inch siege howitzers, 14 field guns, 29 mountain guns, and 13 miscellaneous light guns available either in storage or with local artillery units. The navy had 14 6-inch and seven 4 or 4.7-inch deck guns and four 3-inch landing guns in storage at Cavite. The plan was to distribute these guns to provide coverage of the main channels. Corregidor, El Fraile, and Caballo Islands were to get the majority of the armament. However, the 10,000-yards between Corregidor and El Fraile was just too much for these short-ranged guns to cover. The officers rejected the potential sites of Lasisi, Bataan, and Restinga (Ternate) Points as too vulnerable. Also, La Monja Island was in a fairly good position to fire on the entrances to the Boca Chica and Boca Grande channels, but was too isolated and not supportable from Corregidor. Interestingly, these were exactly the same conclusions the engineer officers would arrive at when permanent construction began a couple of years later.

The submarine mining problem was also daunting. The Philippines had adequate stocks of cable, but only four old boilers that could be used for mine cases and just a small amount of high explosive. Requirements for Manila Bay ran to 856 mines and 42 tons of explosives. It was thought that by skimping on the explosive charges and increasing the distance between mines, at least some coverage could be obtained. The navy had just 36 mines available, but there was also a torpedo battery available for mounting that would be useful on Caballo Island. A new mine control casemate at El Fraile Island was strongly advocated, apparently a recommendation that was soon implemented. It was thought that altogether five days would be needed to transport and set-up these defenses. There would only be enough time available to mount guns either in old Spanish positions (particularly in Manila and Cavite), or in simple rock or earthen clearings. There would be no time or material to build new concrete emplacements. This emergency scheme was of course, never actually implemented.[34]

War Scare of 1907

The stunning Japanese military successes in the Russo-Japanese War of 1904-05 and the controversial San Francisco School Board segregation issue of 1906 considerably enhanced perceptions of a possible American and Japanese conflict. While appropriations had been made for defenses in the 1904 and 1905 Fortification Acts, there would be a gap of several years before much would actually be serviceable. In mid-1907 hurried steps were taken to provide at least some protection to the fledgling naval base and coaling station at Olongapo in Subic Bay.

On June 4, 1907, President Theodore Roosevelt asked Assistant Secretary of War Robert S. Olson what the plans were for Philippines defense in case of worsening troubles. This request triggered a Joint Board meeting four days later. The Joint Board advised that the fleet be sent to Philippine waters as soon as possible and for the deployment of existing armament to protect Subic Bay. A further meeting with the president at his summer home at Oyster Bay, New York, on June 27, led to more definitive action. A large supply of coal was arranged for shipment to Subic Bay, two monitors and several torpedo boats were ordered moved from Cavite to Subic, and the fleet's movement to the Philippines was changed to just a token visit to Pacific coastal waters for the following October. Additionally, the navy was ordered to have their advanced base material in storage at Cavite moved to Olongapo. The army was also to move mining material to the post, along with field rations for five months, and to push battery construction on Grande Isle. What is interesting is that these commands occurred precisely during the same period that the debate raged over whether Subic or Manila would become the major naval base in the territory.[35]

The Advanced Base Force was an interesting concept. As developed in 1900, it was the navy's attempt to prepare a defensive force for an expedition in advance. The navy went on to collect the matériel for two such forces, one to be kept in storage in the Pacific and the other in the Atlantic. Marines for the defensive echelon would be assigned at the time of activation, but the guns, mounting plates, timber, concrete construction cement, crushed stone, minefield materials (including two steel scows), and 3000 emergency rations were to be stored in a separate warehouse at each primary location. The Atlantic Ocean unit was initially kept at League Island, near Philadelphia. The Pacific unit was originally stored at the Cavite Naval Station but was soon transferred to the new base at Olongapo. The units were primarily expected to be sent to any new coaling base established during combat operations and protect this base from raids by light enemy forces. They were not to be used to defend existing bases, which was the role of the army. The Advanced Base Force ordnance at Cavite included 10 6-inch/30-caliber Mk III guns and gravity return mounts, complete with platforms, 10 6-pounder Hotchkiss rapid-fire guns, and five double platforms, along with ammunition for the guns. This ordnance was provided by 1902. By about 1904 both "kits" for these advance base forces were complete.[36]

After careful consideration, the navy had selected the 6-inch gun as the primary heavy weapon for the Advanced Base Force. They realized that the local force would not generally have time or heavy equipment to get larger guns up hillsides or onto isolated islands. Also, the 6-inch had proven to be an effective size for dealing with cruisers and destroyers, and while it could not penetrate battleship armor, rapid-fire 6-inch guns could inflict a lot of damage to upper works. Guns of this size came from two sources. A large number of older

The protected cruiser USS *New Orleans* in 1898. This ship was assigned to the Asiatic Fleet between 1899 and 1917. When the vessel was re-armed in the early 1900s, its 6 and 4.7-inch British guns were used to augment the navy's Advanced Base Force. NHC.

6-inch/30 guns from cruisers dating from the 1880s were becoming available as ships were either modernized with new guns or decommissioned. Also, two British-built protected cruisers building for Brazil had been recently acquired during the Spanish-American War and renamed USS *Albany* and *New Orleans*. Each had been armed with six 6-inch and four 4.7-inch Armstrong quick-firing guns. As the navy was in the process of rearming the ships with standard, American-made 5-inch guns, the Armstrong guns had become excess to naval needs. Their performance and simple pedestal mounts with wrap-around shields were considered perfect for use by the Advanced Base Force.

In December 1902 a naval exercise was conducted in Subic Bay. Part of it involved a simulated attempt to seize an undefended harbor on an enemy's coast and then defend it utilizing Advanced Base equipment stored at Cavite. For the exercise the new base was to be on Grande Isle. Buoys representing submarine mines were laid in the channels east and west of the island beginning on December 26 and 27. A force of 200 marines was landed on Grande Isle on the afternoon of December 27 and a signal station was established in the abandoned lighthouse. Two battery sites were selected to cover Grande Isle's east and west channels, and a camp named Camp Evans was established on the island. Advanced Base materiel, which included four 4-inch guns and four 6-pounders with mounts, platforms, tools, accessories, and ammunition, along with 500 yards of industrial railway track and three steel railway cars was landed successfully by dusk. No attempt was made to land any 6-inch guns, as their mounts and platforms were too heavy to be handled without special equipment. The same was true of the dual platforms for the 6-pounders. They could not be floated on their own, so they were rafted ashore on top of the 4-inch gun platforms. The 4-inch gun platforms proved to be satisfactory; so much so that the Commander in Chief on Asiatic Station recommended the Advanced Base Force's 10 6-inch guns at Cavite be replaced by four 4-inch guns and six 5-inch guns; the 6-inch guns being reserved for permanent emplacements at Cavite or at Subic Bay.

The sites selected for these temporary batteries were very good. The West Battery covering the 2,000-yard-wide main channel consisted of three 4-inch guns on a ridge with a pair of 6-pounders about halfway down the slope and clear of the 4-incher's blast effect. The other battery was on a ridge on the island's east side to cover the narrow reef-strewn east passage. It was armed with one 4-inch gun and the other pair of 6-pounders.[37]

When the mid-1907 war crisis developed and the president requested emergency defenses for Subic Bay, the army and navy together agreed to temporarily release the nearby guns of the Pacific Base Force for local defense. By September 23 all but one gun were emplaced. They were placed on temporary wooden grillage platforms, and had adjacent wooden, earth-covered magazines. The most heavily developed site was Grande

One of the Advanced Base Force 6-inch guns sent to Grande Island to be manned by the Marine Corps until the army fortifications were completed. View dated April 14, 1909. NARA.

Island itself, care being taken to make sure the structures did not interfere with pending permanent battery construction, which was going on simultaneously. At the end of October, it was reported that all intended 6-inch guns were mounted, as were all four smaller guns. Guns were also installed at Macmany and Binanga Points on the mainland. While there were some armament adjustments and shuffling during 1907 to 1910, in February 1910 the navy reported the temporary defenses of Subic Bay as:[38]

Grande Island
- ten 6-inch/50 Armstrong
- four 6-inch/30 Navy
- four 4-inch/40 Navy
- four 6-pounder Hotchkiss

Macmany Point
- three 6-inch/30 Navy
- four 4.7-inch Armstrong
- three 6-pounder Hotchkiss

Binanga Point
- three 6-inch/30 Navy
- three 6-pounder Hotchkiss

True to intentions, after the army guns were installed at Fort Wint, orders were issued on February 11, 1909, for dismounting the Advanced Base Force weapons and returning them to storage. However, the marines found it useful to leave them in place for training purposes for some time. The army requested the guns be moved to Carabao Island pending the completion of batteries there, but the navy demurred. It appears that the guns were gone from Grande Island by early 1911, but some 6-inch were still mounted on Kalaklan Ridge above Olongapo as late as 1913 for practice purposes. Also in 1913, the General Board substantially revised the Advanced Base Project. There was a desire to modernize the equipment and move the Pacific unit storage to either Honolulu or Mare Island near San Francisco, with the latter site being selected on May 17, 1913. Most of the material at Olongapo was either abandoned or re-distributed. Ultimately most of the guns were sent to Guam and used as temporary defenses by the navy on that island.

U.S. Army Plans for the Defenses

On September 12, 1901, Brig. Gen. George Lewis Gillespie Jr., chief of engineers, recommended that a board of engineer and artillery officers be appointed to report on the defense of the important harbors of the Philippine Islands. Lt. Col. Charles L.B. Davis was dispatched to the Philippines in February 1902 as chief engineer of the Division of the Philippines, arriving there March 12. He served as senior member of the board of officers to devise projects for fortifying the islands. The board, composed of two engineers and two artillery officers, submitted their report February 4, 1903. For Manila Bay, the board recommended heavy gun and mortar batteries covering the Boca Chica Channel from Bataan Peninsula and Corregidor, and for the Boca Grande Channel, Caballo Island and the shore of Cavite Province. Rapid-fire guns were projected for emplacement on Carabao Island. The board initially recommended the bay's primary defenses be built on Corregidor: four 12-inch guns, two 10-inch guns, and six 6-inch guns. The projected costs were estimated at $1,608,000 for the entire project; of which $398,000 were for the projected works on Corregidor.[39]

On April 11, 1902, the islands of Corregidor, Caballo, Carabao, La Monja, El Fraile, and Santa Amalia, along with an unnamed rock (later named Razor Island) off Corregidor's southeast point in Manila Bay, and lands on either side of the bay's entrance at Calumpan Point, Cavite Province, and at Mariveles, Bataan Province, were set aside by Executive Order as military reservations.[40]

An initial appropriation of $700,000 was made on April 21, 1904, to be expended in the construction of batteries at Corregidor in Manila Bay and on Grande Isle in Subic Bay. The local board's initial plans for the fortifications underwent considerable modifications during the early 20th century, but in general terms most of the major sites and types of ordnance to be used were true to the plans proposed.

U.S. Navy Selects Subic Bay as its Primary Station in the Philippines

The prospect of sending a considerable-size naval force into Asian waters led the US Navy's General Board in 1901 to call for a base in the Philippines. In 1903, the secretary of the navy added his support in urging the development of a strong naval base in the Philippines and recommended locating this major repair and supply facility in Subic Bay. Later that year a joint army-navy board also recommended the base be developed at Subic Bay. The Cavite Naval Base that had been Spain's chief naval base in the Philippines until the late 1890s was continued in American service after the occupation of Manila Bay. While not an elaborately equipped facility, the wharves, magazines, and shops were immediately occupied and began to serve American naval vessels. This site, about eight miles by water from Manila, had not been held in high esteem by the Spanish colonial authorities and certain elements in the Spanish Navy, because of its various natural disadvantages, including shallow water and vulnerability in time of war. From the late 1880s the Spanish Navy had tried to transfer their naval emphasis from Cavite to Olongapo in Subic Bay, where it intended to develop its principal far eastern naval and coaling station. The Spanish believed Subic Bay had the natural advantages of both deep water and defensibility. However, the local navy command in the Philippines, like many of its predecessors, preferred Manila Bay to the isolation of provincial Subic Bay. Manila Bay was the archipelago's principal port, where labor, commercial, and administrative services could be more easily obtained. The cost-effective facilities at Cavite were convenient, and the defense of Manila Bay was already deemed a high priority.[41]

Between 1900 and 1908 the navy in Washington preferred to see a major new facility built at Subic Bay for the recently constituted Asiatic Fleet. The navy thought the high surrounding hills that in some cases attained an elevation of more than 1,000 feet, could provide excellent protection for this base. The relatively flat

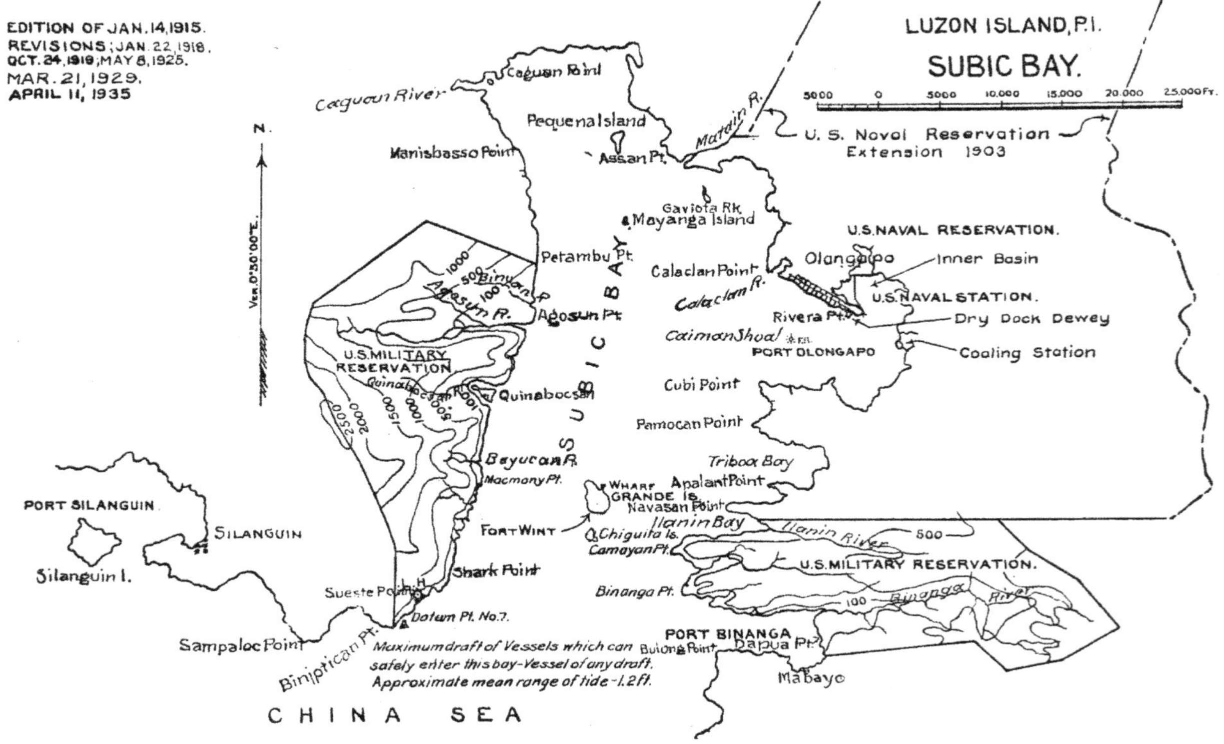

Subic Bay map dated 1935. NARA.

trajectory of the period's naval ordnance prohibited an enemy from firing over these heights into the bay. Only from directly outside the bay's mouth could a hostile warship engage a fleet anchored within. Grande Isle was situated inside Subic opposite the bay's entrance. If Grande Isle were properly fortified, hostile vessels firing into the bay would have to contend with heavy counter-battery fire from this island.[42]

The local military defense board met in mid-January 1902. They immediately recommended that a portion of the new U.S. Navy reservation in Subic Bay be turned over to the War Department for military defense purposes, and that a detailed survey of likely emplacement sites be undertaken. The situation proved difficult for the army, charged with providing the coast defense for naval bases. The army engineers were torn between Manila and Subic Bays. In their opinion both locations had good positions to site guns for defense against direct naval attack — actually Subic Bay was narrower and was dominated by the central location of Grande Isle. However, when considering defense against land attack, the situation was considerably different. Subic Bay could not be adequately defended from land attack. If an enemy landed elsewhere in the Philippines and approached the bay from land, the heights surrounding both the northern and southern shore were for all practical purposes indefensible. An enemy could easily capture the proposed gun sites on either the north or south entry into the bay, and then turn the guns on the American base. One study placed the size of a necessary defending force as great as 100,000-120,000 armed men, at that time an obvious impossibility. On the other hand, Manila Bay could have its seaward defenses entirely placed on the bay's islands, vastly improving their resistance to land attack. The army preferred the defense of Manila Bay but would be forced to defer to the navy's decision on where it located its naval station.

Later in 1902, the navy's General Board concluded that Subic Bay should be their principal naval establishment in the Philippines and already 4-inch and 6-pounder guns manned by marines had been temporarily emplaced on Grande Isle. Subsequently in late 1903, the Joint Board in Washington requested $1.5 million for Subic Bay defenses and $1.0 million for Manila. Envisioned for Subic were 11 big guns, eight mortars, 20 rapid-fire guns, two groups of buoyant mines, and 30 ground mines.[43]

Despite the back and forth, nothing could actually be done until funds were appropriated. That finally came about with the Congressional Act of April 27, 1904. That act provided $725,000 for continuing work on a large floating steel dry dock for the Philippines, and $862,395 for the establishment of a coaling station and other naval station facilities at Olongapo. For the next several years the navy began a subtle juggling act between the two locations. Both had their advantages. Subic Bay was certainly less crowded with a deep an-

Armored cruiser USS *Pennsylvania* in the floating dry dock *Dewey* at Olongapo Naval Station. Gaines Collection.

chorage and could be used by the navy almost exclusively. However Manila Bay already had the former Spanish facilities, was the country's principal port, and skilled labor was more easily obtained there.[44]

The same April 1904 act also appropriated $700,000 for seacoast batteries in the Philippines. A decision of May 26 directed, however, that it all be spent on the Subic Bay defenses. Realizing that they would eventually be required to defend both ports, there was a strong desire by the army engineers, with limited staff and labor available, to begin work on the easier of the two. Local engineer Maj. Harry Taylor began by inspecting the proposed sites.

Detailed surveys were to follow, and Taylor asked for a staff of four engineer officers and 20 enlisted men to begin work. He hoped to start this work in October 1904. Also in that month, he began preparing for preliminary construction on Grande Isle. Thus work soon began on both Corregidor and Grande Isle during much of 1905-1907, with Subic Bay the lead location for both harbor defenses. The army acquired Grande Isle in 1905 and began preparing a detailed project for the projected naval installation's defense. The Japanese naval blockade of Port Arthur and the Russian fleet's subsequent annihilation by Japanese forces in 1905 focused much of America's attention on the Pacific and especially on the Philippines Islands' vulnerability. It also brought about reconsideration of the primary base location in the Philippines.

Perhaps in light of the Russo-Japanese War, President Theodore Roosevelt directed Secretary of War William Howard Taft to appoint a body of army and navy officers and civilian personnel to a National Coast Defense Board, known unofficially as the Taft Board and chaired by the secretary. Taft was well acquainted with the Philippines, having served as its first civilian governor general 1901-1903. The board appointed on January 31, 1905, was charged with the task of making recommendations regarding what "armament both fixed and floating, mobile torpedoes, submarine mines, and all other defensive appliances that may be necessary to complete the harbor defense with the most economical and advantageous expenditure of money." While this was a review of national scope, Taft directed the board's primary efforts toward the development of defenses for the newly acquired overseas possessions and considerable attention was assigned to the defense of Manila and Subic Bays. The fortification construction program developed was the product of the Taft Board's deliberations from 1905 to 1906.[45]

On February 1, 1906, General John P. Story submitted the National Coast Defense Board's final report to Secretary Taft, outlining a proposed coastal defense system for the United States and its possessions. Ten stateside and one overseas port, Subic Bay, were classed as "ports of first importance" for armament with modern coastal defense weapons. Fortification of Subic Bay along with Guantanamo Bay in Cuba were considered the highest priority overseas defenses. In its recommendations the board noted:[46]

> Subic Bay occupies the same position in relationship to the control of the Philippines (As Quantanamo [sic] does to the Panama Canal) and its protection by fixed defense is of the greatest importance, not only in order that the fleet may protect Manila. But that it may have facilities for docking, repairing, and provisioning in those distant waters.

The Taft Board initially recommended four 12-inch disappearing guns, 12 3-inch rapid-fire guns, and 12 12-inch mortars be emplaced to defend Subic Bay. This armament would be distributed around the shores of the bay and on Grande Isle. Still, army leaders began a conscientious effort to persuade the navy and the administration of Manila's advantages over Subic Bay. Chief of Engineers Brig. Gen. Alexander MacKenzie maneuvered to obtain a White House conference on the evening of October 26, 1907. At that meeting President Roosevelt ordered a suspension of construction pending a review and recommendation of a Philippine Naval base site by the Joint Board. That report brought about a decision in favor of Manila Bay on November 1. General Leonard Wood, relying on the board's report and the findings of a survey conducted in person by Brig. Gen. Abbot, argued persuasively that Subic Bay was impractical to defend. When it was later decided that the Cavite Naval Base in Manila Bay was to be retained as the U.S. Navy's principal naval facility in the Philippines and Subic Bay would serve primarily as a coaling station and ammunition depot, the allotment of seacoast artillery for the bay was pared down. The Fortifications Board in Manila altered Subic Bay's defenses to a single battery for two 10-inch disappearing guns to engage cruisers and destroyers, four 6-inch disappearing guns, and eight 3-inch guns to cover submarine mine fields controlled from a mine casemate on Grande Isle. While the navy would spend a little more time weighing alternative sites within Manila Bay, and the facilities built at Subic Bay were never totally abandoned, no further serious attempts were made to locate the main Philippine base in Subic Bay. What *did* happen later in 1908 was a wider decision to ultimately build the main Pacific naval base at Pearl Harbor in the Hawaiian Islands instead.[47]

In the Taft Board's report, eight harbors in the continental United States and six overseas were designated as sites of "secondary importance" for the new armament. Of these harbors of secondary importance, the recommendations for the defenses of Manila amounted to more than $8.5 million even though Manila Bay ranked seventh of the eight secondary harbors. A total of eight 14-inch, two 12-inch, four 6-inch, 12 3-inch guns, and eight 12-inch mortars were initially recommended to protect Manila Bay. Most of these weapons were to be emplaced on Corregidor's Topside. These initial recommendations would in succeeding weeks undergo considerable alteration. By February 23, the Corregidor defenses had been increased by two 3-inch guns and four more mortars. When appearing before the Fortifications Appropriation Sub-Committee of the Congress in 1906, Secretary Taft was asked if he thought Manila needed to be protected; he responded: "Yes, I think it is a weakness we have there — that any nation could just enter there and take them. You know, if you take Manila, you take the Philippines."

Following the decision to base the Pacific fleet in Hawaii, both the army and navy reversed their previous positions on August 24, 1908. They jointly agreed that Manila Bay, with Corregidor as the main defensive work, should receive priority over Subic Bay. The decision was also made to develop Corregidor as a "keep" that could be held "indefinitely" in the event Manila should be in imminent danger of being captured. The "government officials, government archives and the garrison will be withdrawn to Corregidor Island, that island having been placed in a state of preparedness prior to the outbreak of war." This concept would guide the U.S. military policies in the Philippines for the next four decades.[48]

Grande Island Gun Batteries

Congress authorized funds for the army's purchase of 96-acre Grande Isle (the terms Isle and Island were used interchangeably in these early documents) and its subsequent fortification. The lands on the Bataan and Zambales Province sides of Subic Bay's entrance were set aside by Executive Order and designated as military reservations on May 1, 1905. Subic Bay soon became viewed, however, as something of a "rat trap" rather than a safe haven for the Asiatic Fleet. The army engineers completed a study that indicated that an enemy force occupying the heights on either side of Subic Bay's entrance with artillery could bottle up and destroy any naval squadron in the bay with plunging fire. This fire could probably not be returned, as the period's naval guns would not be able to attain sufficient elevation. In the summer of 1906, the dry dock USS *Dewey*, capable of accommodating a 20,000-ton battleship, arrived via the Suez Canal. By 1907, Subic Bay had become a ship repair and replenishment facility and was being operated as a substation of the Cavite Naval Base.[49]

The relationship between the United States and Japan in the early 20th century was marked by increasing tension and corresponding attempts to use diplomacy to reduce the threat of conflict. Each side had territory and interests in Asia that the other might threaten. U.S. treatment of Japanese immigrants, and competition for economic and commercial opportunities in China also heightened tensions. Relations reached a flashpoint in 1907 over Japanese actions in northeast China and immigration to the United States. In 1905, the Japanese had begun establishing more formal control over South Manchuria by forcing China to give up ownership rights to the South Manchurian Railway. The Japanese used this opening to make further inroads into northeast China, causing the Roosevelt Administration concern that this violated the ideals of free enterprise and the preservation of China's territorial integrity. Simultaneously, leading Japanese officials expressed frustration with the treatment of their immigrants in the United States. An 1894 American-Japanese treaty had guaran-

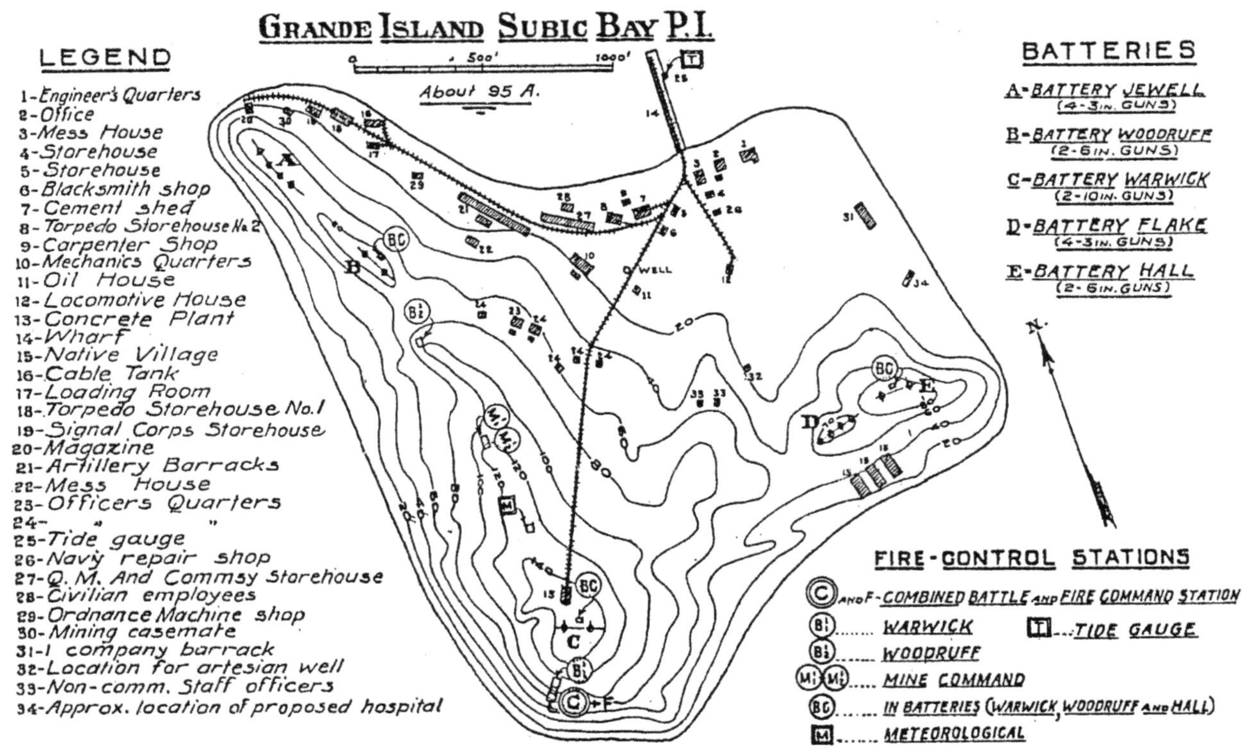

Map of Grande Island and Fort Wint, circa 1920. NARA.

teed the Japanese the right to immigrate to the United States, and to enjoy the same rights in the country as U.S. citizens. In 1906, however, the San Francisco Board of Education enacted a measure to send Japanese and Chinese children to segregated schools. The Government of Japan was outraged by this policy, claiming that it violated the 1894 treaty. In a series of notes exchanged between late 1907 and early 1908, known collectively as the Gentlemen's Agreement, the U.S. Government agreed to pressure the San Francisco authorities to withdraw the measure, and the Japanese Government promised to restrict the immigration of laborers to the United States. In this atmosphere defensive work in the Philippines appeared even more urgent.

Maj. John Millis, in charge of fortification engineering at Manila from Oct. 14, 1905, to Oct. 5, 1907, ordered the commencement of works on Grande Isle. First Lt. Henry H. Robert was initially placed in charge of the project. He was soon joined on the island by Company D, 1st Engineer Battalion, commanded by Capt.

Waterfront of the Olongapo Naval Station, Subic Bay, ca. 1915. Former Spanish gunboat *Pampanga* visible at center. NHC.

Meriwether L. Walker, tasked with site preparation and commencement of fortifications. Soon Companies A and B were also assigned to the project on Grande Isle. Although actual construction did not commence until late in 1906, once started it was prosecuted diligently over the next four years.[50]

Among the engineer's first tasks was the construction of quarters and mess rooms. Oregon pine shipped from the U.S. was used for framing the quarters, offices, and mess room structures, and used as flooring and doors. Suali (a local matting made from woven bamboo strips) was used for partitions and ceilings and nipa (a type of palm) for the exterior siding. Windows were of the sliding shell variety and roofs were of corrugated galvanized iron. Storehouses and workshops were of similar construction, with either dirt or concrete floors.[51]

On May 12, 1908, the new fort on Grande Isle was named Fort Wint for Brig. Gen. Theodore J. Wint, USA, who had died on March 21, 1907. In this era, typically both forts and batteries were provided names published in general orders by the army. Almost inevitably they celebrated either significant senior officers or soldiers who had died with notoriety in combat. General Wint entered military service during the Civil War as a private in the 6th Pennsylvania Volunteer Cavalry and was promoted to lieutenant in 1864. He was appointed a second lieutenant in the 4th U.S. Cavalry in 1865, advancing in that regiment until 1892, when he was promoted to major in the 10th Cavalry and in 1899 to lieutenant colonel, 6th Cavalry. In 1901, he was promoted to the colonelcy of the 6th U.S. Cavalry, and on June 9, 1902, prior to retirement, he was advanced to brigadier general.[52]

The first two permanent gun batteries were commenced in 1906 and transferred in the latter part of 1910. Transferring was the official act of handing the battery over from the constructing engineers to the artillery troops that would subsequently man the battery. Both of these new batteries were to be armed with pairs of M1905 6-inch guns on M1905 disappearing carriages. Battery Woodruff was built on the northwest end of Grande Isle at about 90 feet above sea level. Battery Hall was erected on the island's east end, about 80 feet above the water.[53]

As the first of the gun batteries on Grande Isle were commenced in 1906, plans for providing a garrison for the new Philippine forts were developed by the War Department. It was not until construction in Subic Bay neared completion, however, that the initial coast artillery companies (at least since the temporary assignment of a couple of companies right after occupation) were dispatched from the United States to the Philippines. Capt. Robert E. Wylie's 57th Company, a submarine mine company stationed at Fort Wadsworth, NY, had the distinction of being the first coast artillery company alerted for "Foreign Service" in a coast defense role. On July 24, 1907, the company left New York by train for San Francisco, arriving there July 30. On August 5, the company boarded U.S. Army Transport (USAT) *Warren* and sailed for the Philippines, arriving in Manila Bay September 4. Upon arrival in Manila the company was dispatched to Fort Wint. There the 57th company manned the 6-inch Armstrong guns provided by the navy and, as the first of the army's batteries on that island were brought to a near state of completion, began the process of mounting their armament.[54]

With the construction of the two 6-inch gun batteries well underway, the engineers next turned to construction of the battery that would serve as Grande Isle's primary armament. This battery was positioned on the island's southwest point at an elevation of 140 feet. Construction commenced in 1907 and continued into 1909. The battery was armed with a pair of 10-inch M1895M1 guns on M1901 disappearing carriages. Wylie's company mounted the 10-inch guns shortly before the company boarded USAT *Buford* September 15, 1909, for transportation back to San Francisco. Construction was still underway when the emplacement was named Battery Warwick to honor Capt. Oliver Barnette Warwick. The battery was transferred to the Fort Wint garrison on November 26, 1910.[55]

After the larger batteries were underway in 1908, the engineers began constructing two batteries of M1903 3-inch rapid-fire guns for the defense of the projected minefields. One was sited atop a ridge on the northwest corner of the island near Battery Woodruff. The second was just to the west of Battery Hall on the ridge that extended along the island's south side. On May 12, 1908, both batteries were named. The one on the island's northwest point was named Battery Jewell for 2nd Lt. James McDonald Jewell, 14th U.S. Cavalry Regiment. The second rapid-fire battery was named for 2nd Lt. Campbell W. Flake, 22nd US Infantry. Both batteries were completed in 1910 and Battery Jewell was transferred to the Fort Wint garrison on November 9, 1910, while Battery Flake was transferred on December 7, 1910.[56]

Concurrent with the construction of the gun batteries, a mine depot was constructed on the island's northwest corner. A large concrete cable tank (20 by 60 feet) with traveling bridge cranes for the storage of 27 reels of submarine cable and an 81 by 34-foot mine storehouse and a 23 by 46-foot mine loading room, both of corrugated iron, were built. Also constructed was a concrete magazine with earthen cover for the storage of gun cotton used as explosive in the submarine mines, as well as a 1,720-foot 36-inch-gauge tramway from the wharf to the mine facilities. These structures were transferred to the garrison December 29, 1908, as was a four-room temporary mine casemate measuring 10 feet by 21 feet of corrugated iron on a concrete floor and a double primary mine observation station (M'M") located on the ridge between Batteries Warwick and Woodruff. A concrete plotting room was also finished. In 1910 a second cable tank and a mine storehouse were added. The mine casemate itself was a most impressive structure. Transferred on February 14, 1910, for $22,136.36; it was far larger and better protected than the independent casemates built in Manila Bay. The mine wharf and boat house were added in 1911-1912. Other tactical structures dating from the first couple of years at Fort Wint included a combined battle commander and fire commander station. A protected switchboard room, radio station, and two protected shelters for 60-inch searchlights were also transferred May 12, 1911. About 650 feet east of Battery Warwick was a central power plant. This plant, which supplied electric power to the post and the tactical structures, was transferred August 25, 1911, at a cost of $67,170.30. It was backed up by a 25 kW generator at Battery Warwick and three more sets in an auxiliary power house.[57]

Between 1908 and 1911 primary fire control stations were built for Batteries Warwick, Woodruff, and Hall, a meteorological station, and a tide station, all of concrete. The batteries on Grande Isle formed a fire command. The fire commander's station that also served as the fort's command post was south of Battery Warwick.[58]

As this is the first set of tactical structures encountered in this account, some description of their purpose is probably appropriate. Emplacement construction was always supervised by the army's professional Corps of Engineers. Officers were well trained and had access to standardized emplacement plans on which to base their designs. However, they were also urged to adopt these plans to local terrain and tactical considerations. Once notified that funds were available, the local engineer would be authorized to draw up a plan for an already-approved element (battery or batteries, casemate, etc.) of the defense. This engineer would make the ultimate decision as to the precise placement and various design features, though his submission would have to be approved by Washington.

Batteries were intended to be succinct structures holding and protecting gun or mortar armament. As the usual guideline assumed that they would receive return fire from the same size gun they mounted, the guns and their ammunition magazines were massively protected by a recommended thickness of concrete and earth. In the 1900s the primary heavy guns were mounted on "disappearing carriages." These were mechanically complicated devices that raised the gun preparatory to firing and then used the recoil to lower it back behind the protective parapet for cleaning and reloading. Of course, in the early 1900s there was no need for protection from aerial bombardment, and the trajectory of ship guns meant that the major danger was from direct frontal impact, not plunging fire. Each larger emplacement had heavily protected separate magazines for powder and shell, usually a set for each individual gun. Ammunition service for the larger guns was from lower-level magazines serviced by mechanical chain hoists. Gun crews were not expected to live in their batteries, rather they were quartered nearby in barracks and assigned to man the emplacements only during use. Still they had minimal support features—such as latrines, storerooms, an emergency generator for power if combat cut the underground cables from the central system, and a command and plotting room where firing solutions were calculated.

Heavy batteries (10, 12, and 14-inch guns) were expected to engage large enemy ships. Mortar batteries were intended to fire salvos of plunging 12-inch rounds onto the same type of targets. Because of the arching fire by mortars, they were not required to have an actual line-of-sight view of their opponent, and they were usually emplaced in groups within a pit rather than individually mounted in their own protected platform. Light guns (3 and 6-inch) generally protected mine fields and searchlights. They would engage light enemy craft trying to sweep the mines or put out the lights. Also, at many locations they could command possible landing beaches and be used to help repel boats attempting to bring parties ashore. The 3-inch guns were emplaced in the smallest emplacements, on pedestals that left the guns exposed but also allowed rapid traverse to follow fast targets close offshore.

Controlled mines were an important part of the defenses. The coast defense operated their own types of mines and had the infrastructure to lay and control them. In times of peace the unloaded mines (usually in this era spherical cases) were stockpiled ashore in "torpedo storehouses." (Torpedo was the original term used for underwater explosives, and only later became restricted to just the automotive torpedo type.) Usually the storehouses were lightly constructed structures, mainly just providing protection from the weather. Explosive charges were kept in separate "storage dynamite rooms." Prior to planting, the mines were moved and loaded at the "mine lading room." Then, usually by a rail track, they were moved to a special mine wharf where they were loaded onto dedicated army ships (army mine planters or smaller mine yawls) and taken out to pre-selected locations to be laid in groups. They could be either placed on the seafloor (if shallow enough) or anchored at a pre-determined depth to give maximum effect. Mines were connected to the shore by electrical cables and detonated on command by a signal from a protected "mine casemate." Unlike the familiar navy mines with contact "horns," usually coast defense mines were detonated only by a specific signal, unless purposely set to contact.

Both guns and mines required direct observation of the target in order to calculate range and azimuth, although mines could be set to fire at any vessel striking them, especially at night or in bad weather. This requirement was fulfilled by a network of concrete fire control stations. These were observation stations equipped with optical instruments to identify azimuth and distance to targets. They were tied into a system of mechanical plotting boards and used to calculate range for firing. Often two or more stations were assigned to each major battery, as well as a similar "battery commander's station" with a clear view of the field of fire. Later even an emergency system of stations was built, though not as elaborate as the primary system. Other structures considered tactically important (and thus usually heavily protected) were the main power station, the fire control switchboard room, searchlight positions, reserve magazines, and the command station.

While not "tactical structures," no fort could function over time without the living structures to support a garrison. Adjutant General Fred C. Ainsworth sent a cable to Gen. Leonard Wood, commanding the army in the Philippines, on August 17, 1907, urging Wood to send an estimate of costs for construction of the post buildings necessary for a garrison of four companies on Grande Isle. Wood replied that the cost for post buildings of a type similar to those built at Fort McKinley near Manila would be $121,400 and that the requisite roads and wharves would run an additional $41,000. Sewage and water systems would be additional.[59]

While some of these structures were completed, the gradual abandonment of the Subic Bay defense had begun by the time it came to considering permanent garrison quarters. Only a very few concrete garrison buildings were built in 1910-1912: the power plant, bakery, three sets of married officer quarters, the post laundry, and the ice plant. These were complemented with the usual lightly constructed (wood walls, corrugated iron roofs on concrete piers) barracks for companies of 109 men, commanding officer's quarters, offices, mess facilities, and hospital. Nothing like the three-story concrete barracks and hospital structures such as those at Fort Mills was ever constructed on Grande Isle.

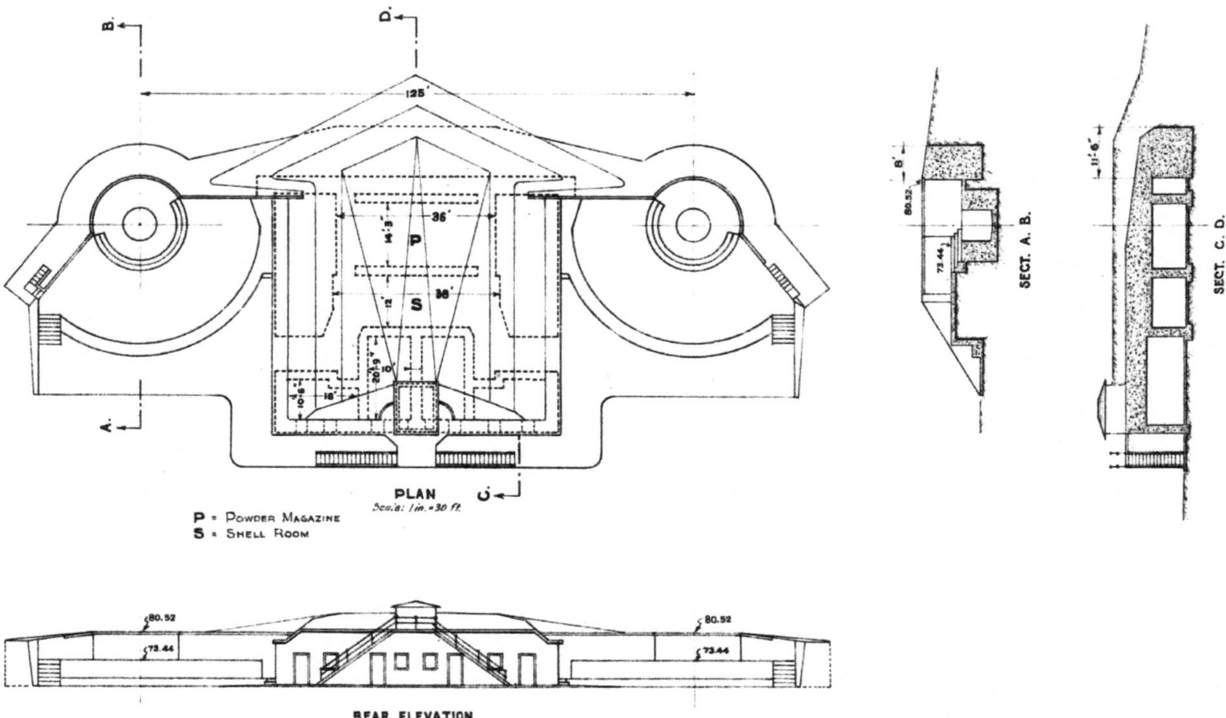

Plan, elevation, and sections of Battery Woodruff, Fort Wint in 1920. NARA.

2-8 Battery Woodruff with both of its guns emplaced and ready for emergency service as construction continues in 1908. NARA.

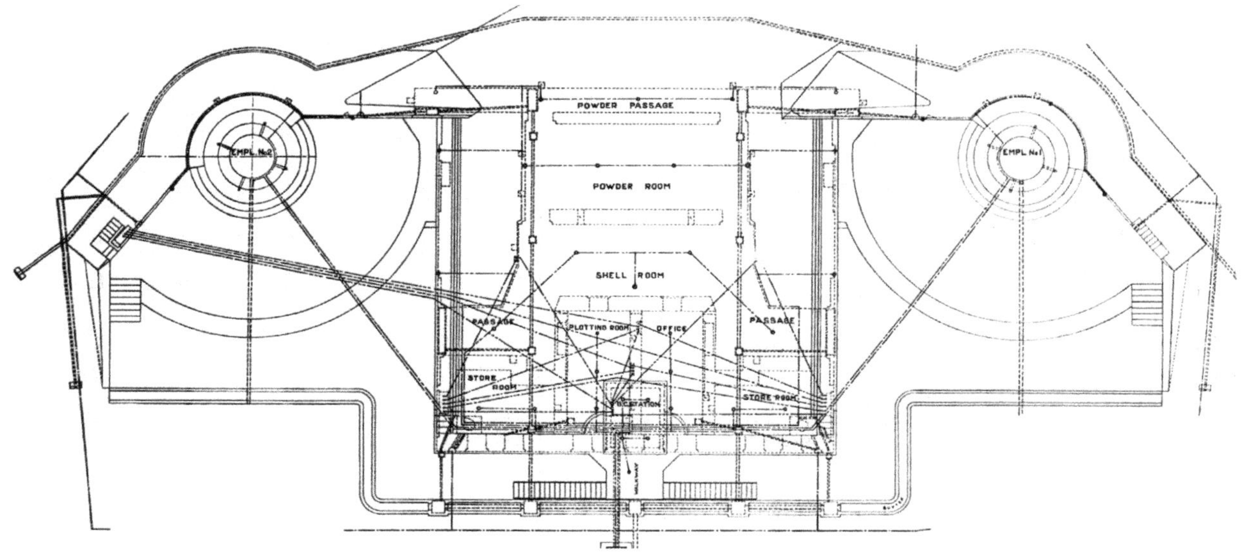

Overhead plan for 6-inch disappearing guns Battery Hall, January 1911. NARA.

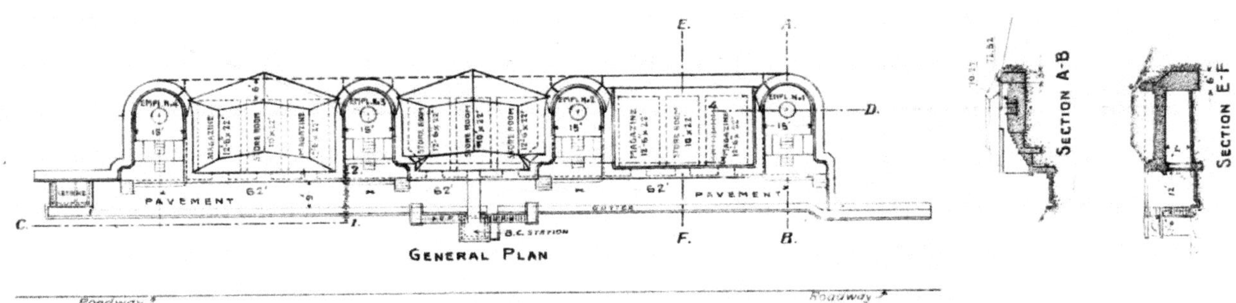

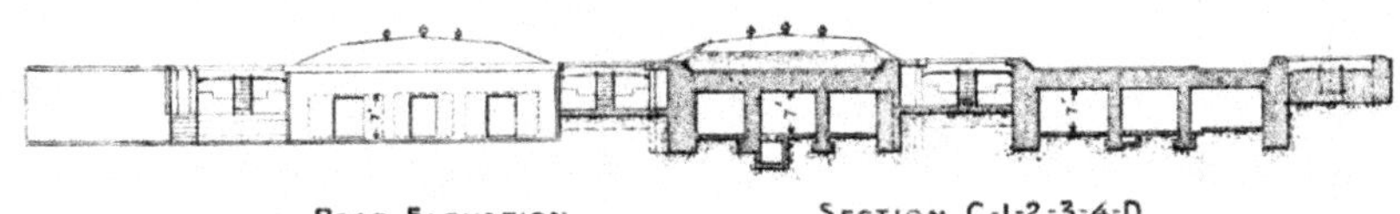

Plan, elevation, and sections of Battery Flake, 1920. NARA.

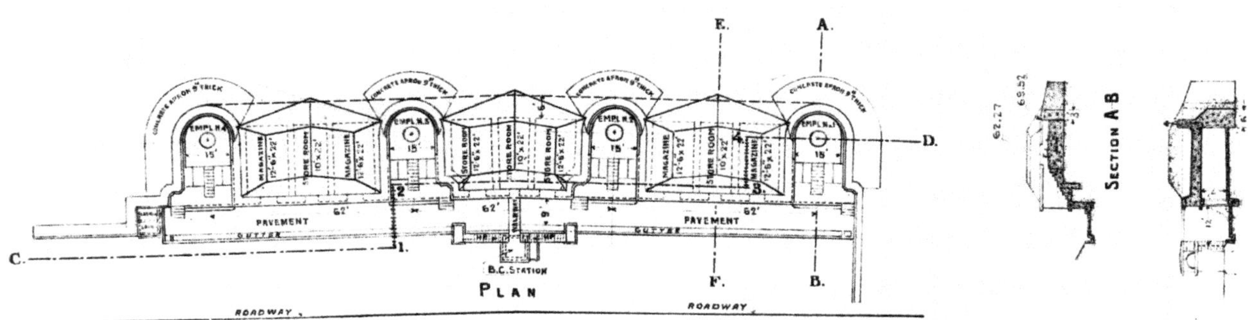

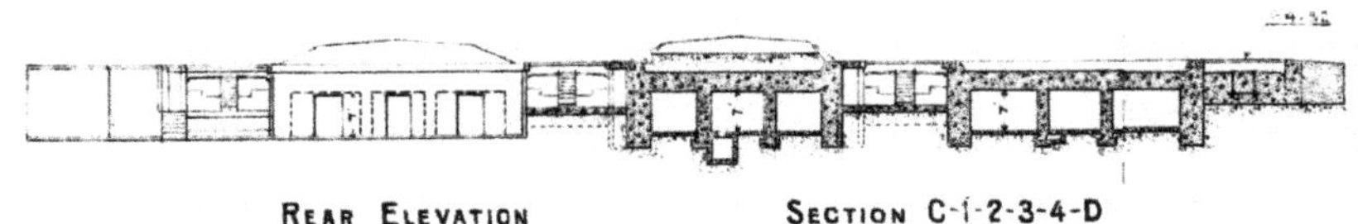

Plan, elevation, and sections of Battery Jewell, 1920. NARA.

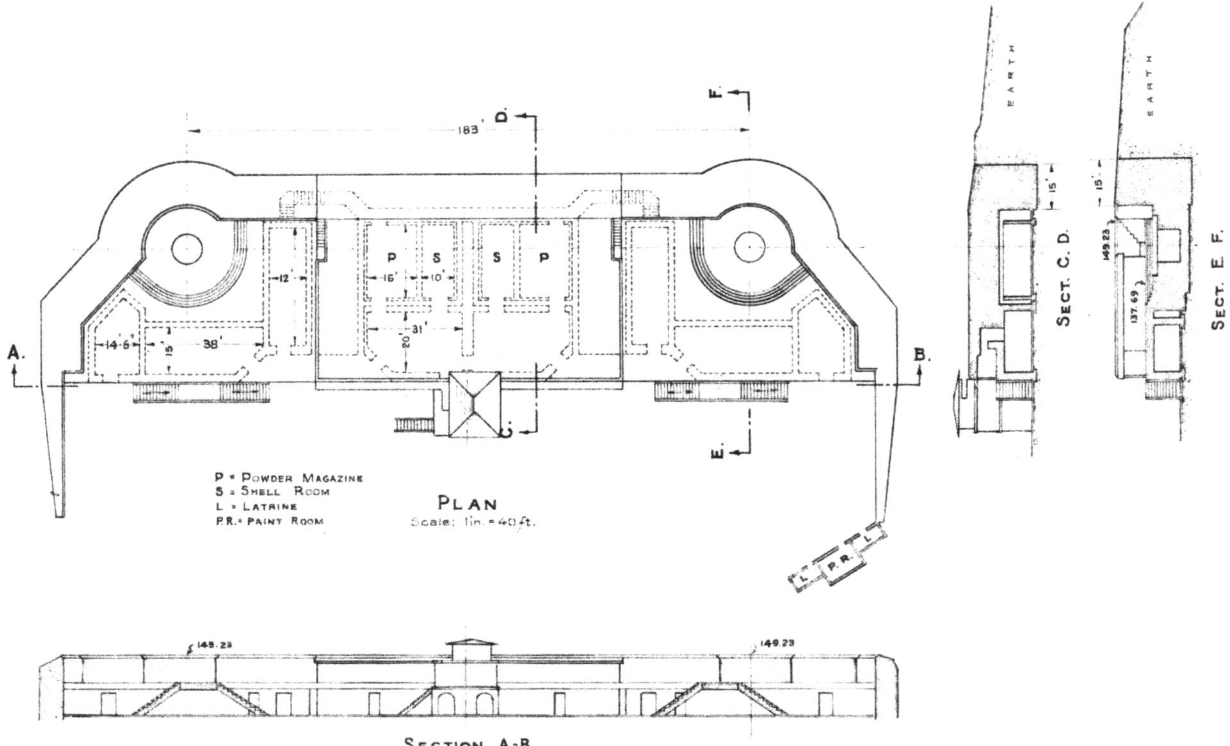

Plan, elevation, and sections of Battery Warwick, 1920. NARA.

Construction of Battery Warwick nears completion. Note the inclusion of the battery commander's station (BCS) in center. NARA.

10-inch Battery Warwick after completion. This was why they were called "disappearing batteries" – from surface level the gun and carriage (and crew) could not be observed by enemy forces. NARA.

In addition to its gun batteries, Fort Wint received extensive submarine mine facilities. This is the interior of the operating room of the mine casemate on April 14, 1909. NARA.

CHAPTER 3
SELECTING AND BEGINNING THE POSTS IN MANILA BAY

Defense Planning for Manila Bay

Realizing that they would eventually be required to defend both ports, there was a strong desire on the part of the army engineers to begin work on the easier of the two. Local engineer Major Harry Taylor began by inspecting the proposed sites. Sea conditions prevented Major Taylor from getting immediately to Subic Bay, but in Manila Bay he was impressed with what he found:[60]

> At Corregidor I found conditions much more favorable than I anticipated. The growth on the island is not as heavy as I expected to find. I was shown a spring on the side of the hill, at an elevation of perhaps 200 feet above sea level, or 300 to 350 feet below the sites of the batteries, which I as informed flowed at the rate of about 15,000 gallons a day all the year. The water supply was something I had been very anxious about. The tops of the hills are thickly covered with boulders of trap, varying in size...they are hard and when crushed will form excellent material for concrete, the best in fact that I have seen in these islands.

Also in that month he began preparing for work in Subic Bay, though he had difficulty in finding adequate gun battery sites on the mainland for these defenses. The project for the defense of Manila Bay was significantly modified in 1907. A board composed of Lt. Col. Fredric V. Abbot and Capt. Stanley D. Embick recommended that the seacoast defenses then under consideration be situated only on the four islands at the bay's entrance and consequently the batteries of 6-inch guns proposed for Lasisi Point on Bataan be constructed on Corregidor instead.[61]

The series of preliminary surveys of Corregidor were begun and soon a substantial amount of preliminary work was accomplished. The major decisions regarding the armament for the defense of Manila Bay were not outlined, however, until 1906. The principal gun batteries were to be sited on the western high ground of the island. After a careful study of the island's rugged terrain, the engineers concluded that the shortest route from the bottom to the top of the island could best be attained by constructing a combination railway and cable incline system. Company H of the 2nd Engineer Battalion was eventually assigned to begin construction on Corregidor in September 1904, initiating a project that would ultimately convert Manila Bay into one of the United States' most heavily fortified harbors.

The "Taft Board's" initial recommendations for the defenses of Manila Bay called for a total of eight 14-inch, two 12-inch, four 6-inch, 12 3-inch guns, and eight 12-inch mortars. However, this allocation fluctuated up and down as various boards and surveys were completed. On August 24, 1908, the army and navy jointly agreed that Manila Bay and Cavite would become the navy's primary base in the Philippines with Corregidor as the main defensive work. The navy's Subic Bay installation at Olongapo would be relegated for use as a dry-docking and repair facility. A naval magazine for reserve ammunition and a reserve coal depot would also be maintained there.[62]

Corregidor's Construction Plant

Before fortification construction could begin, it was necessary to establish facilities for the receiving and temporary storage of vast amounts of construction materials as well as to erect the plants that would be used to build the necessary tactical structures. Water and food, as well as construction supplies and materials, had to be brought from either Manila or Cavite. The antiquated earth and timber wharf on Bottomside's north shore was totally inadequate to handle the material arriving on the island. Consequently, one of the first projects undertaken was the construction of a new wharf and pier. This was ultimately designated the Engineer Wharf. Materials, equipment, and other supplies could be landed from small ships. Various buildings and warehouses were built at the foot of the pier in support of the construction project. The engineers also built housing fa-

Quartermaster camp in Corregidor's Camp Avery post. Early buildings were often built of suali and nipa palm leaves typical as native construction materials. NARA.

U.S. Army engineers on Corregidor about 1906. Gaines Collection.

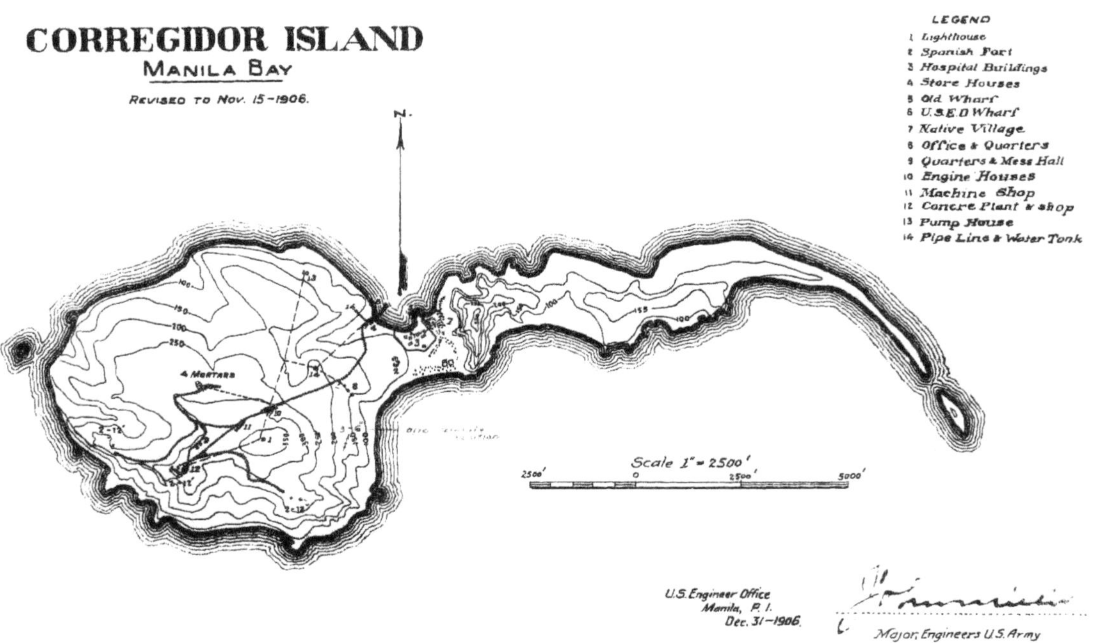

Map of Corregidor in 1906 showing the location and development of fortifications and other facilities on the island. NARA.

Members of the U.S. Army 1899 Corregidor survey crew use the roof of the old Spanish lighthouse water tank as a good spot to set up their heliograph. NARA

The first American hospital on Corregidor erected in 1901 near the island's northern pier. NARA.

cilities for army personnel, civilian employees, and Filipino construction workers. A number of structures in San Jose Barrio were taken over by the army and adapted for the use. Bottomside eventually became a major storage area for the matériel to be used in the submarine mine defenses of Manila Bay.[63]

When the engineers arrived on Corregidor, only a single roadway wound its way from Barrio San Jose at Bottomside up to the Spanish lighthouse. Space for the storage of construction material soon became a premium as the engineers took up nearly all the available space at Bottomside. The island was covered with thick vegetation and extensive clearing was required before a construction plant could be set up. A 36-inch gauge railway and cable car system were built to connect the wharf and the construction sites. The batteries were to be built at elevations from 300 to 500 feet at the island's western end that would become known as Topside. Saddle tank 0-4-0 steam locomotives pulled carloads of material along the engineer railway from the wharf through the barrio's edge and up the western slopes of Corregidor to an elevation of about 100 feet near the Spanish Fort. This area, which later became known as the Stockade or Scout Level, became the lower terminus of a cable car incline that ascended further, passing the 300-foot level that would become known as Middleside. From Middleside the incline continued on to Topside some 500 feet above Manila Bay. The cable car tramway was powered by a steam engine located at the cableway's upper terminus. From this upper terminal, more 0-4-0 locomotives conveyed the trainloads of building materials to the battery construction sites. Conveying the construction plants, railway trestles, and storehouses for cement and other materials to the battery sites and then erecting them consumed considerable time. Along the railways that led to the battery sites, land was cleared for the numerous storehouses, offices, quarters for the mechanics and other employees, as well as water tanks, mess halls, a machine shop, and a carpenter shop. Many of these temporary structures occupied the area that would later become the Fort Mills parade ground.[64]

The 2nd Battalion, Philippine Scouts, composed of about 450 officers and men under Maj. James N. Munro, were sent to become Corregidor's initial garrison in January 1908. The battalion set up their camp on the plateau overlooking Barrio San Jose. The Scout battalion's four companies set up a tent encampment near the old Spanish fort and occupied a few huts. The walls and roofs of these huts were constructed using the fronds from nipa palms attached to wooden frames. In some instances, the walls were formed by weaving the nipa fronds or suali grasses into large panels that were then secured to the wooden frames to form the hut walls. Many of these huts had raised wooden floors founded on wooden poles.[65]

Adjacent to the battalion campsite was a barbed wire enclosure formally designated the Corregidor Branch of the Bilibid civilian prison in Manila. This first prison stockade was built to house the Filipino convicts who performed the majority of the manual labor required in the massive construction effort on the island. It consisted of a rectangular enclosure 226 feet wide and 426 feet long, enclosed by a 20-foot-high double barbed wire fence. Inside the enclosure were three large nipa huts, each of which measured 120 feet long and 32 feet wide, in which the convicts were housed. Also within the enclosure were the hospital, a kitchen, and other auxiliary buildings, also of nipa construction, that were necessary for the care of the hundreds of convicts. The "Bilibids" were initially guarded by personnel from the main prison in Manila with the Philippine Scouts on hand as a backup if necessary. The number of convicts employed on Corregidor's various projects averaged between 600 and 1,000 during the primary construction period 1904-1914. This Scout Level between Bottomside and Middleside also became known as the Stockade Level.[66]

The Post on Corregidor Is Named Fort Mills

Spain ceded Cuba, Puerto Rico, Guam, and the Philippines to the Americans under the Treaty of Paris, signed December 10, 1903. Corregidor was designated as a U.S. Military Reservation in 1907. The regular army post was established in 1908 and named Fort Mills on May 12, 1908, after Brig. Gen. Samuel M. Mills, chief of artillery, U.S. Army 1905-1906, who had died September 8, 1907. Samuel M. Mills was an 1865 graduate of West Point, appointed second lieutenant in the 19th Infantry. Mills transferred to the 28th Infantry in 1866 as a first lieutenant but returned to the 19th in 1869. On May 10, 1870, Mills transferred to the 5th U.S. Artillery and was promoted to captain in April 1883. On March 8, 1898, he was promoted to major of the newly organized 6th U.S. Artillery and participated in the army's siege train organization at Tampa, Florida, during the war with Spain. Major Mills commanded the 6th Artillery when the regiment was deployed to the Philippines in 1899. He accompanied General Chafee to China as an observer during the expedition to relieve Peking in 1900, and was advanced to lieutenant colonel, Artillery Corps, on February 2, 1901, while

Brig. Gen. Samuel M. Mills, chief of artillery. NARA.

commanding Fort Wadsworth, New York, and to colonel September 11, 1902, when he was transferred to Fort Barrancas, Florida. Colonel Mills commanded the Artillery Districts of Portland and Boston in 1903 and 1904 and was promoted to brigadier general and chief of artillery on June 20, 1905. General Mills retired September 30, 1906, and died at Monmouth Beach, New Jersey, September 8, 1907, at the age of 64. [67]

In 1904 army engineers were ready to begin in earnest building the fortifications. Within a short period, construction was begun by the Constructing Quartermaster on four company-size temporary barracks for the scouts made of the usual combination of nipa and wood. Guardhouse and headquarters structures were also built. The headquarters was a one-room structure 28 feet long and 15 feet wide with its wooden floor on the ground. The walls were of suali panels and the roof of nipa leaves. The guardhouse was built with corrugated galvanized iron walls and roof on a wooden floor raised above ground on wooden posts. The temporary Scout camp remained unnamed until July 1908, when it was declared a sub-post of Fort Mills and named Camp Avery in honor of 1st Lt. Moron L. Avery, Philippine Scouts, who died February 2, 1905, of wounds received in combat.

The construction project on Corregidor was not without its setbacks. Work was being rapidly advanced on the gun and mortar batteries in late 1908 on the night of November 24, when a fire broke out in the stockade. A Camp Avery sentry fired a shot to give the alarm and set in motion the response to the emergency. Within five minutes after the alarm sounded, the fire had spread rapidly through the dry nipa structures and was totally out of control and beyond the feeble firefighting apparatus available on Corregidor. Capt. Edwin R. Stuart was aboard the engineer vessel *Mindanao* anchored just offshore from Corregidor. He quickly arranged to go ashore and requested *Mindanao*'s captain to illuminate the wharves and roads leading to them with the vessel's searchlights. Upon reaching the mine wharf he gave instructions for the two steam launches moored there to get underway to prevent their use in the event any of the 975 convicts then on the island made an

One of the convict dormitories in the stockade level built after the fire that destroyed the initial buildings. NARA.

unauthorized decision to leave. By this time the nipa huts inside the enclosure had been completely consumed by the flames. Some 200 convicts had been secured by the Philippine Scouts outside the enclosure with chains and the remaining prisoners retained within the barbed wire fence. Some prisoners kept inside the enclosure suffered from the heat and smoke, but none were seriously injured and none escaped.[68]

Captain Stuart arranged for additional tentage for the convicts and before the month's end began construction of Camp Avery's new stockade. Two weeks later, a typhoon struck Corregidor, taking the roof off a partially rebuilt stockade building and destroying the convict laborers' tents. After the typhoon, Stuart resumed rebuilding the stockade buildings, which continued through the first half of 1909. The new stockade would consist of 11 single-story buildings with walls and roofs constructed of corrugated galvanized iron on timber frames founded on concrete piers with cement floors. The stockade was enclosed within a double barbed wire fence. The structures were ventilated by awning-type shutters along the buildings' length and width. Five of these buildings served as dormitories for the convicts while the others functioned as a lavatory and workshop, a kitchen and storeroom, an office, and a combination hospital and dispensary with a separate isolation ward. During World War I, two dormitories as well as the office and the isolation ward were rebuilt. When the island underwent another spurt of construction in 1919 following the war and the number of convicts on the island was increased, four more dormitories were enlarged to accommodate the increased number. These stockade buildings would last until they were destroyed early in 1942 during the Japanese siege.[69]

The typhoon that struck Manila Bay in December 1908 also dealt a devastating blow to the engineering efforts on Corregidor. Although the Coast Artillery Corps establishment got off lightly from the storm, the Engineer Department's steamer *Natchez* and one Quartermaster Department launch were wrecked, along with a floating derrick. Ten engineer buildings were also destroyed in the storm, along with one of the nipa barracks occupied by the Scout Infantry on the Stockade Level.[70]

Another example of local construction utilizing native suali and nipa fronds. This is one of the island's early scout barracks. NARA.

Planning Corregidor as a Keep

The War Department developed a sort of general war plan, or "state of preparedness" for the military in the Philippines. One of its provisions was the movement of most of the troops in the Philippines to the harbor forts if the loss of the city of Manila was considered likely. This plan called for the accumulation of sufficient stores, ammunition, and water for 20,000 men for a year to be stored on Corregidor for such a contingency. These plans for preparing Corregidor as a "keep" were approved by the secretary of war, but no funds for actual construction or accumulation of supplies were forthcoming. In addition to serving as a keep for the defense of Manila and Manila Bay, measures were also considered to move certain functions from the U.S. Navy Base at Cavite to Corregidor in the event Cavite should become untenable. By October 1910 it was determined that the island could not accommodate 20,000 men and the garrison's projected size was reduced to 10,000 in October 1910 and to 7,500 in February 1911. The question of bombproofing the storehouses and other vital structures arose in 1910 and it was decided that the power and pumping plants, the cold storage plant, machine shops, and reserve storehouses should be protected where their locations did not provide secure natural shielding from siege gun and mortar fire. The bombproofing project was delayed pending appropriation of the requisite $154,000; a sum that was not allotted until August 1914. By September 1914, a total of more than $456,000 had been appropriated for defenses in Manila and Subic Bays.[71]

The vault for the Philippine Treasury was dug into the cliffs near Ramsay Ravine. Schmidt Collection.

Philippine Government Reservation

In the event Manila came within imminent danger of being captured, the secretary of war issued a declaration in 1908 "that if at any time during the investment of Manila the capture of that city appears imminent, the civil government officials, government archives and the garrison will be withdrawn to Corregidor Island... that island having been placed in a state of preparedness prior to the outbreak of war to serve as a keep that can be held indefinitely."[72] It should be noted that between 1908 and 1936 "the government" meant the American civil government headed by the High Commissioner.

To accommodate the civil government, a roughly triangular-shaped reservation on the slope southeast of Topside, adjacent to Ramsay Ravine, was set-aside for this purpose. A 1916 report makes it clear that the approval and presence of the government refuge was not the rationale for Manila Bay defenses, but as long as the island was heavily fortified, it was a perfectly acceptable location to host such a facility. The reservation was titled the "Philippine Government Reservation," and subsequently the ravine was naturally dubbed "Government Ravine."

While there may have been elaborate plans to eventually construct buildings meant to house government functions, only one permanent structure was built. A treasury vault of concrete was built into the hillside. A wooden guard station and small quarters were positioned nearby, all built in the early 1920s. The planned additional facilities were never approved. However, the plan to move the government persisted. The 1932 Philippine Islands Defense Project reiterated that the commanding general or his subordinate officers were still the judges with regard to the granting of asylum within the defensive areas to civil government officials in times of emergency. In the late 1930s, provisions were extended to include the Commonwealth Government in addition to the commissioner's office. Without the necessary protected buildings, when the move did come at the very end of 1941, except for the treasury funds, the government moved into the laterals of Malinta Tunnel.[73]

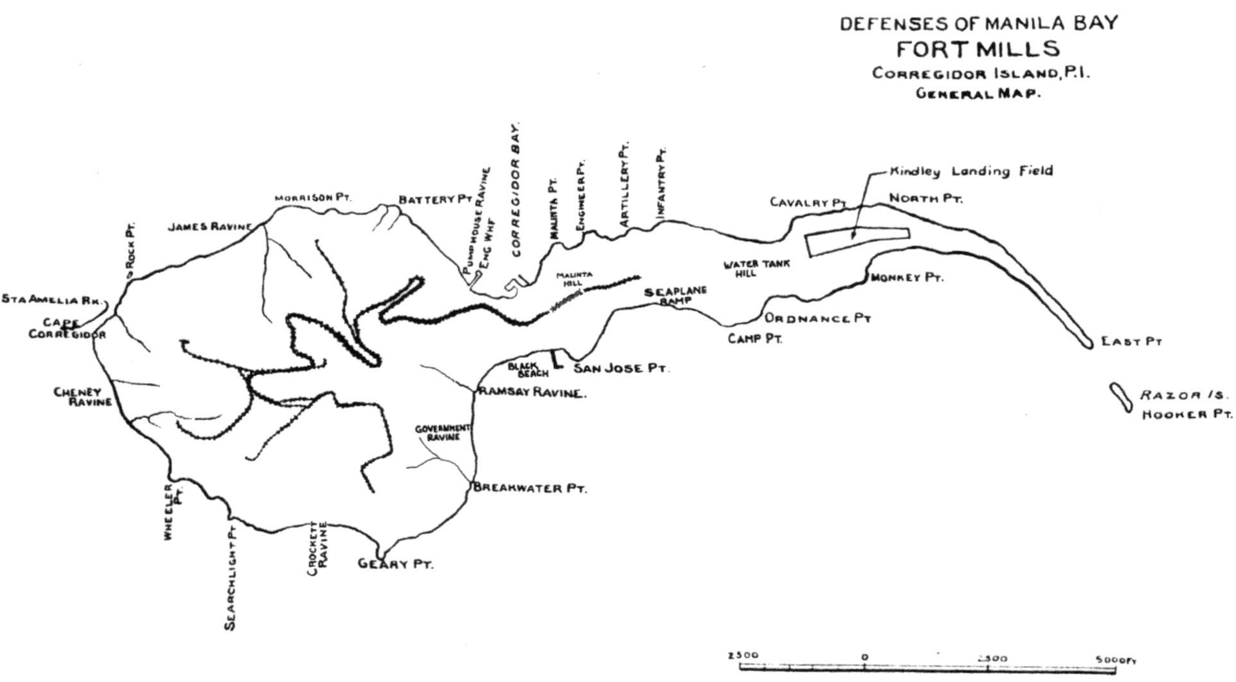

Outline map of Fort Mills on Corregidor, Major geographical points, adjacent islands and ravines illustrated along with the main lines of the island's trolley system. NARA.

CHAPTER 4
CONSTRUCTING AND ARMING CORREGIDOR'S BATTERIES

The First Batteries

The initial plans for Corregidor called for batteries of three guns each. Two batteries of three 12-inch guns on disappearing carriages and one of three 10-inch guns, also of the disappearing type, were projected for Corregidor early in the 1900s. Six 12-inch guns and six 10-inch guns were duly fabricated and shipped for use in the Philippines. However detailed site inspections revealed that few, if any good sites existed where lengthy battery emplacements could be located. The steep volcanic ridges of Corregidor (and eventually also of Carabao and Caballo) simply did not allow that length of construction without disproportionate expenses for excavation. In fact, at one point during the early planning, the other extreme was anticipated — it was thought that only single-gun emplacements could fit onto the western edges of Topside.[74] With some creative planning, eventually room was found to site four large, two-gun batteries.

Once the limited funds were prioritized, the heavy gun and mortar batteries were begun. Engineer officers completed site surveys. As for materials, it was found that adequate aggregate for concrete and sand was locally available on Corregidor. A visit to Hong Kong turned up acceptable cement sources. Surprisingly, quality wood for pier pilings and concrete forms was a problem; much of this had to be imported from the United States and often projects had to be suspended pending the arrival of the next lumber load. In January 1908 a special board of officers chaired by Maj. Gen. J. Franklin Bell, the army chief of staff, confirmed all the major Corregidor batteries projected to be built with pending appropriations had been commenced. These would ultimately consist of six 12-inch disappearing guns, 12 12-inch mortars, two 10-inch, five 6-inch, and four 3-inch guns.[75]

All of the initial seacoast guns and carriages (however, not the mortars required) mounted in Manila and Subic Bays were made anew specifically for these emplacements. Of course, it did take some coordination in timing, as large pieces took a year or more to fabricate. In 1904-1916 Congress was very careful about authorizing and tracking specific expenditures for the new possessions gained in 1898. Individual expenditure bills were authorized for battery construction and for ordering their individual armament and ammunition. General authorizations for the ordnance or engineer departments could not be expended for the "Insular Possessions."

Bilibid convicts and army engineers on the island in the early 1902. Gaines Collection.

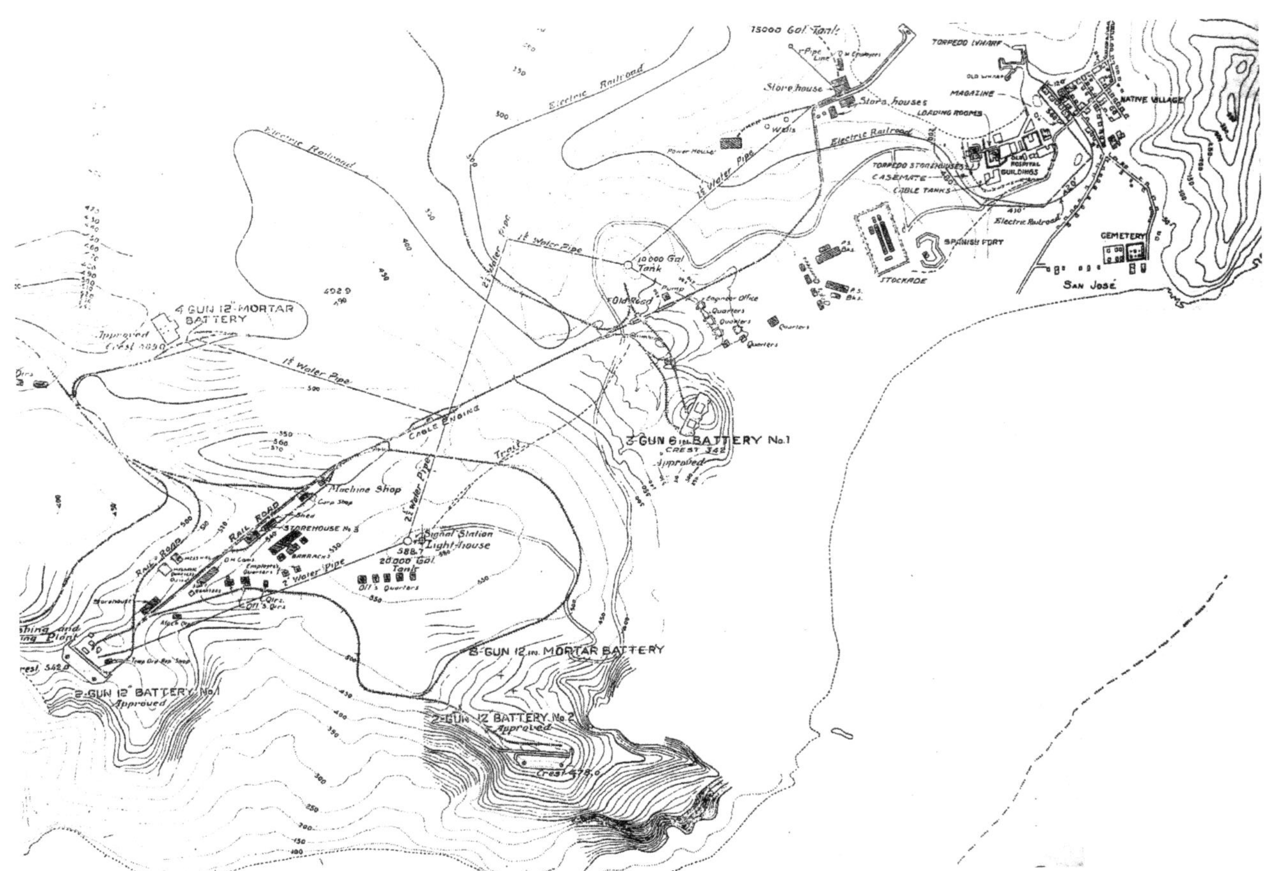

Engineer drawing of part of Corregidor showing the construction railroad lines in July 1909. Locations for what would become batteries Crockett, Ramsay, and Geary are easily spotted. NARA.

Battery Wheeler (Battery No. 1, two 12-inch Guns)

The first of the three 12-inch batteries to be constructed on Corregidor was begun in September 1904 with the clearing of land and excavation. This important battery atop the cliffs on the southwest coast of Topside was to receive two 12-inch guns on disappearing carriages. The battery was considered in the best location possible, with coverage extended on both flanks so that some of both channels could be covered. Because of the intense rainfall during the "Monsoon Season," the top surfaces of the loading platforms and traverse covers were designed with slight slopes and channels to run off the rainwater and prevent internal leaks. Known initially just as "Battery No. 1," this first emplacement was named Battery Wheeler on May 12, 1908, for Capt. David P. Wheeler, 22nd U.S. Infantry Regiment.[76]

Battery Wheeler was armed with a pair of 12-inch M1895M1 guns on M1901 disappearing carriages, which arrived on Corregidor in 1907. Ordnance and engineer personnel mounted the first 12-inch gun and its disappearing carriage in 1907 while the 35th Company, Coast Artillery Corps, mounted the second gun and carriage in 1908 after that company's arrival. By May 25, 1908, the pair of guns had been mounted on their carriages. The magazines of Battery Wheeler were, however, still full of engineer material and the trolleys for moving projectiles had not been installed. Consequently, the moving and sorting of projectiles had to be done by hand with the help of pinch bars.[77]

It is interesting to note the breakdown of the cost estimate for this "typical" two-gun emplacement. Estimated at an engineer expenditure of $252,000, the major items of expense were pegged at:[78]

Concrete supply and placement	$103,000
Construction plant	$ 40,000
Contingency expenses	$ 26,000
Excavation of the site	$ 23,600
Engineer office overhead	$ 13,000
Ammunition hoists	$ 6,000
Doors	$ 4,000
Steel rebar	$ 3,000
Waterproofing	$ 3,000
Transport services	$ 3,000
Share of wharf	$ 3,000

By mid-June 1908, considerable work remained to bring the battery to completion. The fire control instruments had not yet been installed, and about half the concrete work on the battery commander's station remained to be completed. The pavement in rear of battery was not yet done and the grading and filling of the parapet on the right flank was still incomplete. Grading on the hill behind the battery that formed a natural parados (a protective earthen mound) also remained to be done. While two of the four ammunition hoists had been installed, the trolleys, steel doors, and electrical fixtures were still on order from the U.S. With all these deficiencies, the opinion was that it could be fought in an emergency using the "Navy method" of spotting. Finish work including installation of two Taylor–Raymond back-delivery projectile hoists and two Type "A" powder hoists continued over the following months. The battery was finally proof fired on January 17, 1909. Battery Wheeler's construction work was completed in July 1910. The battery was transferred from the Corps of Engineers to the 13th Company, C.A.C., on July 23, 1910, having cost $244,600 up until that time.[79]

Concrete work on Battery Wheeler nearly complete in January 1908. NARA.

Battery Wheeler was, in Brig. Gen. Charles E. Kilbourne's estimate, well positioned but poorly sited. Shortly after his arrival on Corregidor, Kilbourne wrote to Capt. Stanley D. Embick, a close friend then serving as assistant to the chief of coast artillery in Washington, noting that while this battery was located at the highest 12-inch site, it was also placed to the rear of many of Topside's fire control stations, interfering with their operations when the battery fired.[80]

Calibration firing of Battery Wheeler was delayed due to absence of clinometers and lack of an artillery boat. A temporary horizontal fire control system was laid out by Kilbourne using the battle commander's station and Battery Grubbs' station. Kilbourne believed that the battle commander's station and the Wheeler battery commander's station (BCS) would suffer the blast effects of Wheeler's firing. The artillery officer at the Philippine Division, Capt. William Chamberlaine, did not think so and wanted to fire four rounds directly over the stations to test results. Chamberlaine noted that if the sites had to be abandoned it would be hard to secure better ones. The consensus was that Wheeler should have been built at the foot of the coastal cliff, at only about 50 feet elevation. There it would be able to cover the dead space created by the height of the other batteries. However, by December 1908 agreement had been reached that moving Wheeler was not practical, but the traverse of its guns could be limited so as not to endanger any fire control station.[81]

As Battery Wheeler was then the only battery on Corregidor capable of firing, Kilbourne was irritated at the lack of progress on making this battery operational and was still waiting to complete Wheeler at the end of 1908. Calibration and record practice for Wheeler was finally set for January 26, 1909. Kilbourne had invited the governor general and other politicians to witness the firing. As the governor general was a close friend of the President and would soon be returning to the United States, Kilbourne hoped the visit to Corregidor and the firing would reflect well on the efforts to date. While the shoot was viewed favorably by the governor as well as Captain Chamberlaine and others on the Philippine Division staff, Kilbourne himself was not as impressed with it.[82]

By March 8, 1909, Battery Wheeler was complete except for the gasoline tank room and some grading of the parapet in front and on right flank that still had not been completed. The guns had been calibrated and proof-fired and were being used for service and sub-caliber practices by the 35th Company. Some overhead trolleys had been partly installed and the others were on hand except for their switches. The lighting system and railings had finally been installed, but the steel doors and speaking tubes were still awaiting delivery. Early on the decision had been made that the relatively long distance between batteries and the main powerhouse in the protected ravine at Bottomside argued in favor of alternating current, supported by local generating plants

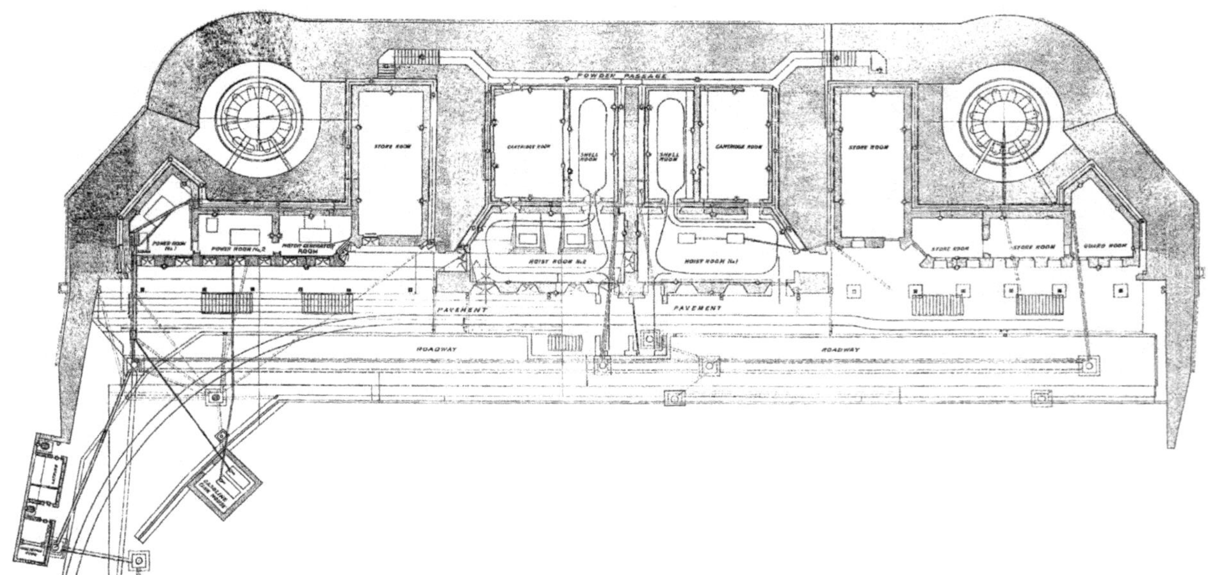

Original construction plan for Battery Wheeler, 1910. NARA.

housed in the rear portion of the individual batteries' traverses. For an entirely different purpose, but basically the same reason, each major battery also got its very own latrine. All three 12-inch batteries were provided with a substantial amount of storage space. Two large storerooms measuring 43 feet by 18 feet, 6 inches; and three more rooms measuring 32 by 10 feet, and a guard room measuring 18 by 10 feet were provided inside the structure. All of these could be converted into bombproof officers' quarters, dormitories, kitchens, and messing spaces in wartime.[83] By the time the 12-inch batteries on Corregidor were being completed, the age of the improved *Dreadnoughts* had arrived, with battleships mounting 14-inch and 15-inch guns that outranged American 12-inch disappearing guns. On Corregidor, because of Topside's elevation, the range of the 12-inch guns was slightly greater than the 13,200-yard range of the same type guns in the US coastal defenses. The 12-inch guns were, however, limited by their disappearing carriages that did not permit elevations greater than 10°. By 1913 projected new disappearing carriages for 14-inch guns in the defenses permitting 20° elevation were underway and measures to modify the 12-inch disappearing carriages in American coastal defenses to attain a greater range had begun.[84]

In September 1917, shortly after the U.S. entered World War I, Batteries Wheeler, Cheney, and Crockett's range was increased from 13,500 yards (eight miles) to 18,300 yards (ten miles) when the guns' maximum elevation was increased from 10° to 15° by modifying their carriages. The Corregidor batteries' elevation above the water enabled the guns to attain an additional 1,000 yards range beyond the typical 17,300 yards afforded by these adjustments.[85]

Battery Way (Four 12-inch Mortars)

Soon after construction began on Battery Wheeler, site clearing started in October 1904 for a battery of four 12-inch mortars using the same appropriations. Use of heavy mortars, offering advantages of plunging fire on enemy decks, was an integral part of American seacoast defense of this era. Virtually every major American harbor featured a mix of both direct-fire heavy guns and pits for multiple clusters of heavy mortars. On January 15, 1905, the engineers submitted their design for what was to become Battery Way. This battery was constructed near the central point of Topside some 700 yards north of Battery Wheeler, at about 450 feet above sea level. Unlike most American mortar batteries, this battery consisted of a single pit containing four mortars flanked by concrete structures containing the shell rooms and powder magazines. No plotting room or battery commander's station was included in the battery design. These facilities were to be located elsewhere on the island. The mortars on Corregidor could obtain all around fire and their range of more than 15,000 yards, coupled eventually with the mortars at Fort Hughes and Frank, enabled them to cover both the Boca Chica and Boca Grande Channel entrances to Manila Bay. Battery Way's secondary mission was to provide counter-battery fire against any enemy on the Bataan Peninsula.

Storage space on Corregidor was at a premium and the initial use of the battery's magazine spaces was as a place to store the large amount of coast artillery material being accumulated on the island. All of Battery Way's ordnance matériel was received and cleaned in preparation for mounting as soon as the railway line was laid to the battery site.[86]

Writing to Captain Embick in January 1909, Kilbourne noted that he expected to have all mortars mounted by the end of February 1909. This proved overly optimistic, however, as mounting the armament was delayed when changes in the railroad route were made. The mortar battery's construction was generally complete in March with the exception of installing steel doors that were still on order. Trolleys were installed and two mortars had been mounted by early March with two more mounted by March 29, 1909. Even before the battery was completed and its armament in place, Captain Chamberlaine, artillery officer for the Philippine Division in Manila, was planning the battery's projected firing at land targets at Mariveles to determine what coast artillery could do to control the Bataan Peninsula's south face. This counter-battery test firing was not conducted, however, until January 1911.[87]

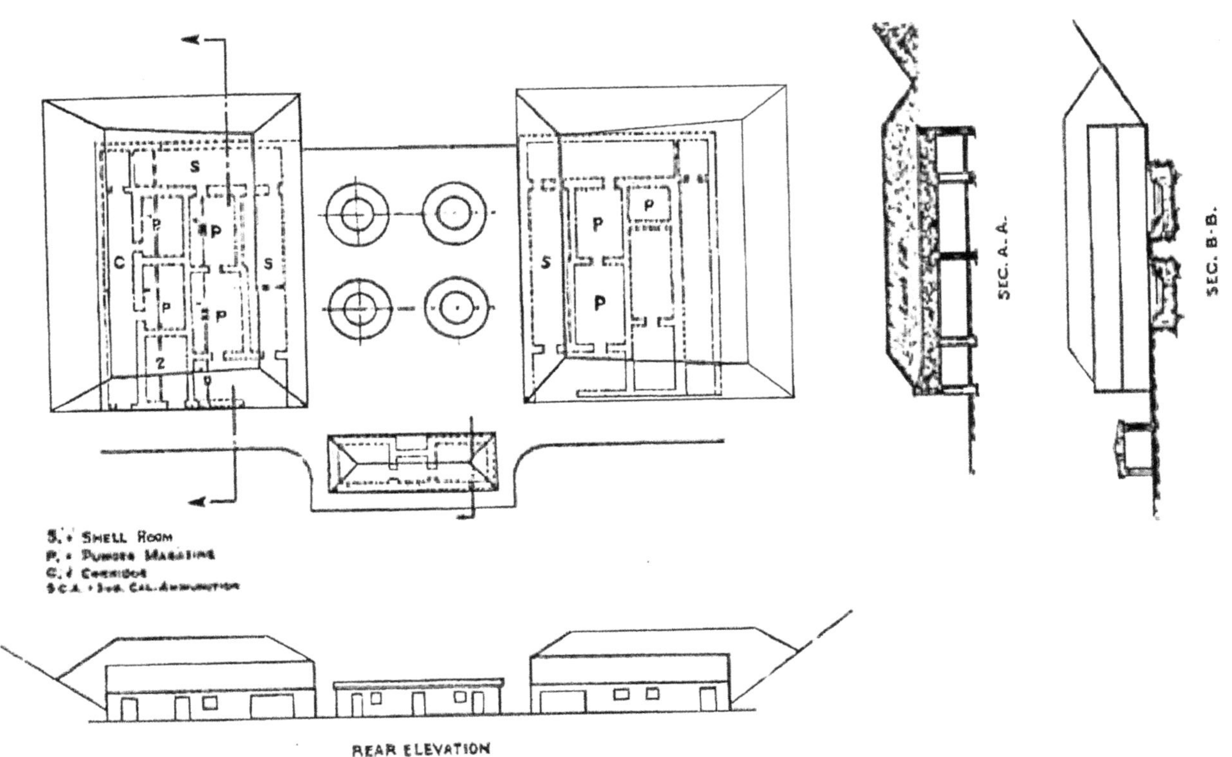

Plan, sections, and elevation of Battery Way. NARA.

The battery was brought to completion and transferred to the coast artillery garrison on July 26, 1910. It was named on May 12, 1908, for 2nd Lt. Henry Newell Way, 4th U.S. Infantry.[88]

Battery Way was armed with four M1890MI 12-inch breech-loading mortars on M1896MI mortar carriages. The emplacement front was protected by an earthen parapet. When built, the roofs of the magazine structures flanking the mortar emplacements were not provided with the usual earthen bombproof cover found in works of this type elsewhere. It was thought that the battery would never be attacked except by direct shipboard gunfire. The battery site was considered sufficiently defiladed because of its high elevation of more than 400 feet and the relatively flat trajectory of naval armament of the day. As a result, overhead protection was not considered necessary. Consequently, the concrete walls and roofs of the shell and powder magazines were only 30 inches thick, much less than the type plans of similar batteries in the continental United States. Dependence on the battery's naturally protected position proved overly optimistic, as heavy land-based artillery fire observed from the Mariveles heights could be brought down on the battery. By early 1911, the need for additional overhead protection for the magazines was increasingly evident. The estimate for increasing the protection of magazines of Battery Way was $74,554.50. Funding availability proved to be a major obstacle and it was not until early 1914 that bombproofing consisting of additional reinforced concrete and a heavy covering of earth was finally placed over the magazine traverses and planted in vegetation. This additional covering also helped to camouflage the battery's location.[89]

The mortars needed for Fort Mills — Batteries Way and Geary — were to be of the exact same type that had been purchased and employed by the hundreds with the Endicott forts in the continental U.S. On July 29, 1907, the chief of ordnance recommended the transfer of mortars and carriages from Atlantic coast forts to insular possessions. They could either be replaced later with newly ordered units or even deemed surplus to needs and never replaced. Twelve were recommended for the Philippines. At this time it was suggested that four be sent from Fort McKinley in Maine to Corregidor, and eight from the Newport defenses to Subic Bay. However, ultimately other sources were used for these pieces. Battery Way received four recently produced mortar tubes. For carriages it got one not previously used from an ordnance facility, one recently repaired

Battery Way's 12-inch Model 1890 mortars in 1933. McGarraugh Collection.

after accidental breakage at Battery Stoneman, Fort Terry, and two from Battery Whitman, Fort Andrews. At the latter post the mortar batteries were being rebuilt. The existing armament was reshuffled, in part because one pit of Battery Whitman was to get the most modern M1908 mortars and carriages — which freed a like number for assignment elsewhere. Battery Geary received four of its eight mortars from Fort Andrews, along with three carriages. The final carriage was also a repaired item, most recently having been damaged at Fort Casey in Puget Sound.[90]

Battery Cheney (Battery No. 3, Two 12-inch Guns)

The next construction project undertaken was for Topside's second battery of 12-inch disappearing guns. This was commenced in November 1906, some 500 yards west of Battery Wheeler. Like the first battery of this type, this battery was arranged to receive a pair of 12-inch M1895M1 guns on M1901 disappearing carriages. Concrete work was expected to be completed by September 1908. The armament was already on hand by July

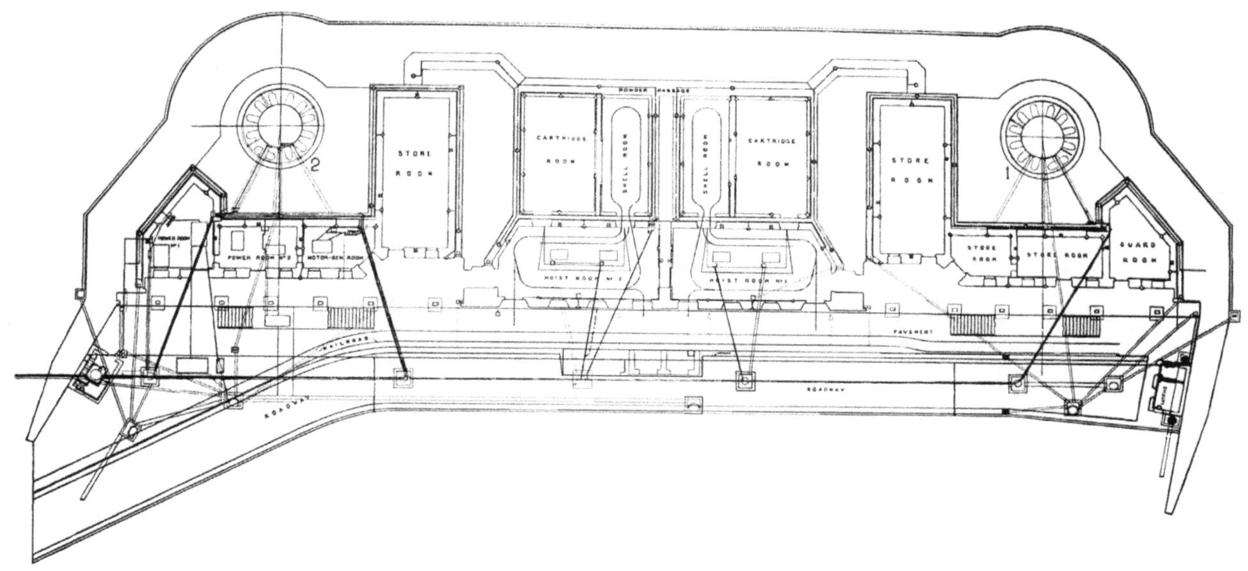

Overhead plan of Battery Cheney from 1912. NARA.

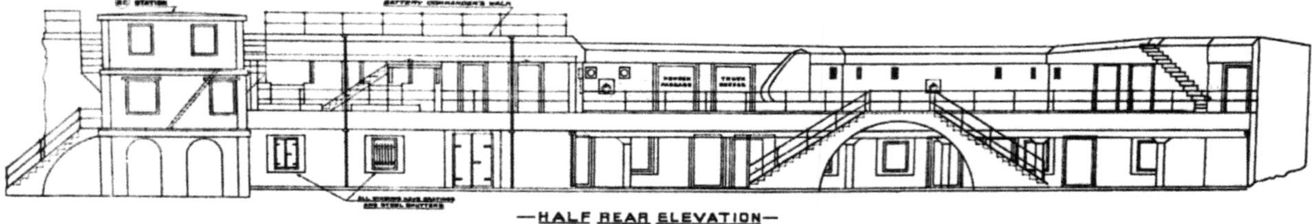

4-8 Front view of Battery Cheney. NARA.

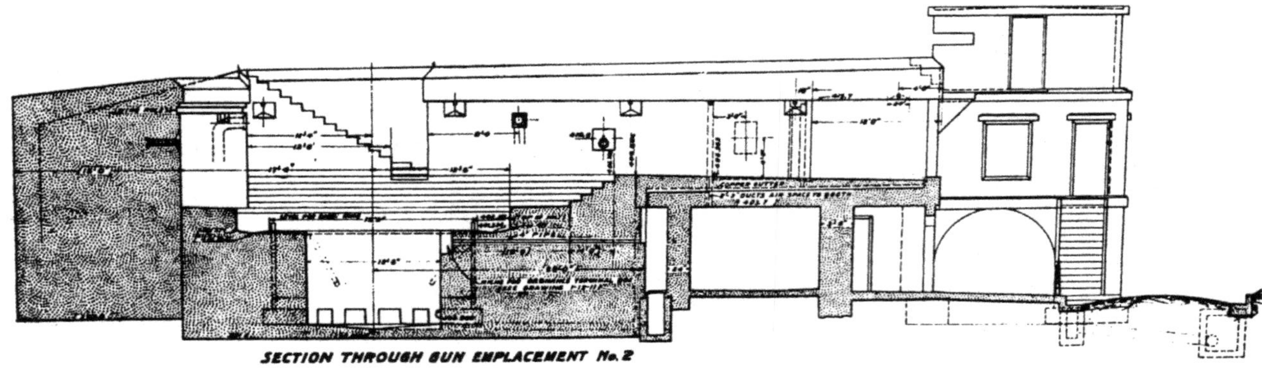

DEFENSES OF PHILIPPINE ISLANDS
ENTRANCE TO MANILA BAY
BATTERY CHENEY
(2 GUN 12 in BATTERY)

Cross section view of Battery Cheney. Note massive thickness of magazine protection. NARA.

One of Battery Cheney's 12-inch guns. McGarraugh Collection.

1908 and it was anticipated that mounting the ordnance could begin as early as January 1909. The electrical equipment had been ordered and doors, etc. were ready to be ordered. As the battery's construction neared completion in 1908, it was named Battery Cheney to honor 1st Lt. Ward Cheney, Co. C, 4th U.S. Infantry Regiment.[91]

Mounting Battery Cheney's guns got underway in December 1908. This task was finally completed in mid-March 1909. Two Taylor–Raymond projectile hoists and two Type "A" powder hoists were provided and scheduled for installation in March. Concrete work was complete except for walkways. Electrical fittings, doors, and railings were on order. Parapet grading and filling on the battery front and flanks, and the parade ground in the battery's rear still remained to be done. The battery was declared completed by the engineers in 1910 and was transferred to the garrison on July 23, 1910, having cost $267,200.[92]

Battery Crockett (Battery No. 2, Two 12-inch Guns)

The third 12-inch disappearing gun battery on Topside was begun in March 1907 some 700 yards southeast of Battery Wheeler. By July 9, 1908, excavation had been completed and the concrete plant was being erected. After construction had been underway for about a year, it was named Battery Crockett to honor 2nd Lt. Allen Taylor Crockett, 21st Infantry.[93]

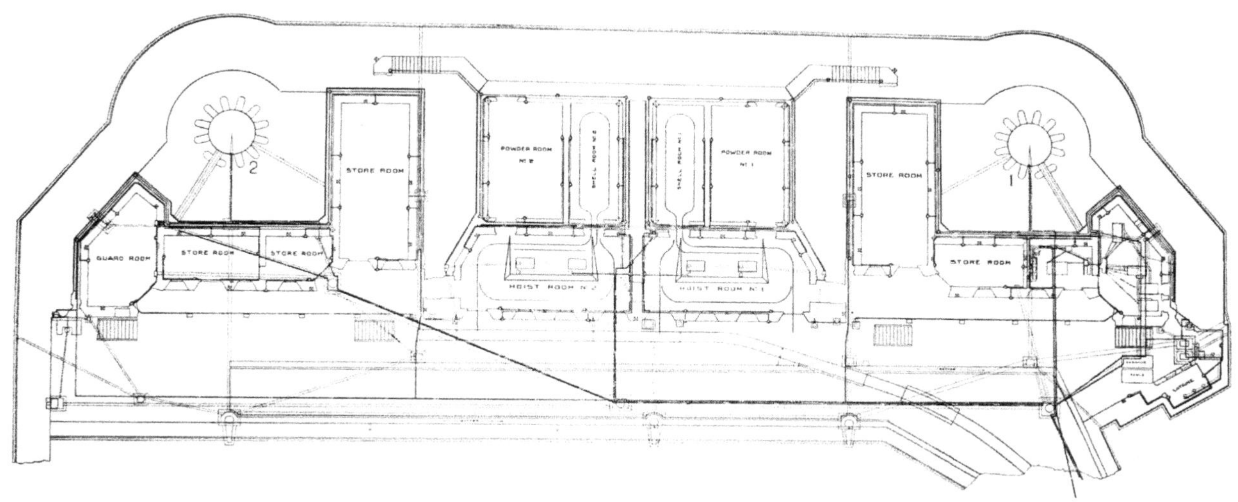

Plan of Battery Crockett, March 7, 1911. NARA.

The battery's armament was already on hand and Captain Chamberlaine estimated that they could be mounted by July 1909. Like the other two large-caliber batteries, Battery Crockett was to be armed with a pair of 12-inch M1895M1 guns on M1901 disappearing carriages. As with the other 12-inch gun batteries, Battery Crockett had a pair of Taylor-Raymond back-delivery projectile hoists and two Type "A" powder hoists.[94]

Work continued into 1909, when concrete work on the gun blocks was completed and the magazines were finished. The earthen part of the parapet was raised to the level of the gun blocks. By March 1910, a few finishing touches by the engineers were required but Battery Crockett was capable of being used in an emergency. On February 2, 1911, the battery was transferred to the Fort Mills garrison and assigned to the 90th Company. At the time the battery was completed, it had cost $290,046.76. In December 1917, shortly after the U.S. entered World War I, Battery Crockett's range was increased from 13,500 yards (eight miles) to 18,300 yards (ten miles) by increasing the gun's maximum elevation from 10° to 15° by modification of the disappearing carriage.[95]

The 12-inch batteries received combined plotting rooms and battery commander stations late in their construction. These were not the only early modifications for these important works. In 1912 each battery received mechanical range indicators that transmitted range settings from the plotting room to a display indicator mounted on the edge of the loading platform for the gun crew to see. These devices cost only a couple of hundred dollars each to install, and all three 12-inch batteries had the devices transferred on March 13, 1912. Between 1910 and 1912 all three of the 12-inch batteries were modified for long-point projectiles and provided with modified Taylor-Raymond back-delivery projectile hoists. The modifications to allow greater range were made to the guns and carriages in 1917-1918. In later years additional traverse of the 12-inch guns was obtained by gadding out concrete pockets to the sides of the front parapet for the guns' recoil. This enabled a few precious degrees increase in coverage to the north and south.

Battery Ramsay (Three 6-inch Guns)

In the same month Battery Crockett was begun, construction of 6-inch secondary gun batteries was also started. From atop the steep cliffs of Middleside's south shore the first 6-inch battery site overlooked San Jose Bay. This battery's three emplacements were designed to sweep the waters between Corregidor and Caballo Islands. Upon completion of the extensive excavation work, concrete pouring commenced until October 1908. By July 1908, one magazine was completed. By 1909 most of the concrete work was finished, with only the latrine and transformer rooms remaining to be completed. The battery was armed with three 6-inch M1905 guns mounted on M1905M1 disappearing carriages. The magazine between emplacements No. 1 and No. 2 served only gun emplacement No. 1, while the traverse magazine between emplacements No. 2 and No. 3 was larger, to serve gun Nos. 2 and 3.[96]

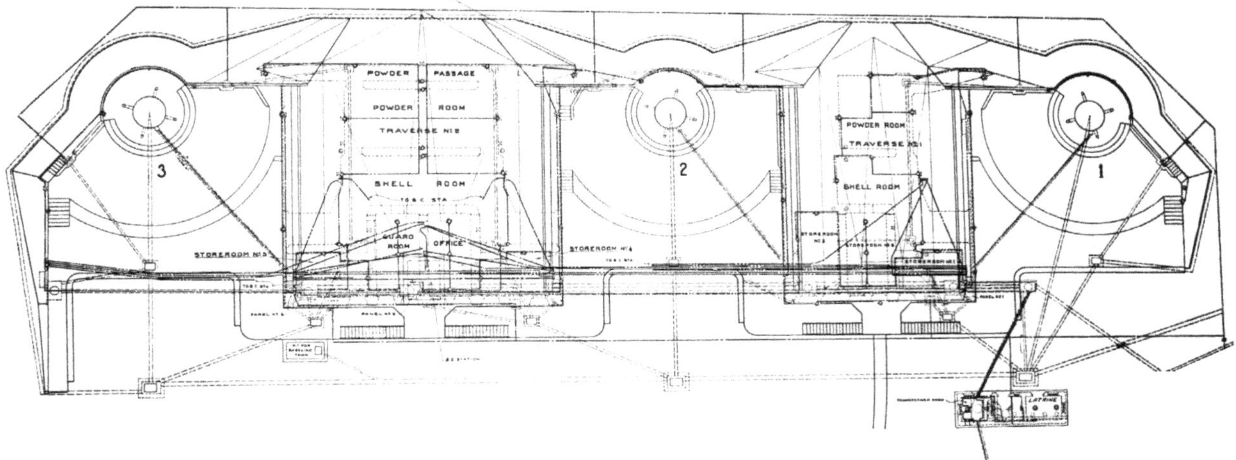

Plan of Battery Ramsay dated December 1910. NARA.

Battery Ramsay's No. 1 6-inch disappearing gun. Smith Collection.

On May 12, 1908, the battery was named for 1st Lt. Charles Rufus Ramsay, 21st U.S. Infantry. On January 20, 1911, Battery Ramsay was transferred to the 42nd Company that was also assigned to 6-inch Battery Morrison.[97]

Battery Grubbs (Two 10-inch Guns)

Of the six 10-inch M1895 guns sent to the Philippines early in the 1900s three were slated for a battery of 10-inch guns planned for Macmany Point in Subic Bay. The other three were intended for emplacement on the western part of Topside above Cape Corregidor to cover the Boca Chica Channel to the northwest of Corregidor. Before construction was even planned, the Corregidor battery was canceled in favor of a third battery of 12-inch guns (Battery Cheney). Later, a defense needs reassessment resulted in the reauthorization of a battery of two 10-inch guns for Corregidor. The battery site was moved further inland to a higher elevation of 470 feet above sea level. While now intended as a standard two-gun emplacement, one gun and mount became available earlier than anticipated when the planned three-gun battery of 10-inch guns for Macmany Point in Subic Bay was canceled. Two of these guns went to Fort Wint on Grande Isle, where they were subsequently emplaced in Battery Warwick. The third gun became available for Corregidor's 10-inch battery.[98]

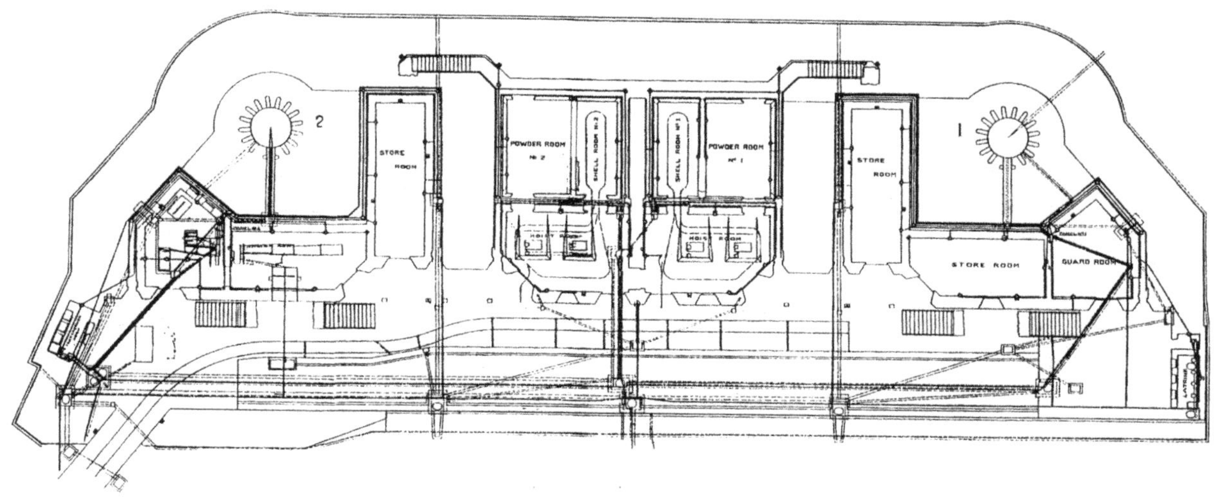

Plan of Battery Grubbs in 1911. NARA.

Battery Grubbs' combined BCS and plotting room on September 9, 1909. NARA.

Corregidor; May 7, 1908
10" Battery. Ordnance on the R.R. track

Carriage counterweights awaiting installation at Battery Grubbs. NARA.

Relations between the United States and Japan deteriorated in 1907-1908, and work was hastened on the Corregidor defenses. Work on the foundation and gun block for one 10-inch gun was initiated in November 1907 with the intent to add the second emplacement and complete the battery when additional funds were provided. The battery was begun in the new location with construction of a single gun block, and a combined battery commander's station and B' station. This combined station sat on a slight elevation directly to the rear of what was anticipated to be the central traverse for the twin-gun battery. By June 19, 1908, the first 10-inch M1895M1 gun was mounted on its M1901 disappearing carriage. On May 12, 1908, the battery was named for 1st Lt. Hayden Young Grubbs, 6th U.S. Infantry. No adjustment in the revised plan was made in the relative location of the battery's combination battery commander's station and primary fire control station (B'), a bare 50 yards to the rear of the battery and only about 10 feet higher in elevation.[99]

It was soon discovered that locating the combined BCS and B' station so close to the battery was a miscalculation. Consequently, the original BCS and B' Station was demolished, and a new combined station built to the rear of the battery's left flank with a plotting room directly behind it. The new BCS and B' station and plotting room was completed by January 1911 and transferred to the garrison on February 11, 1911.[100]

Within seven months after the battery's construction commenced, authorization came for the battery's completion, when Congress appropriated almost a million additional dollars for Philippine seacoast defenses — thus enabling completion of the 10-inch battery to proceed. Once funding became available, work was quickly begun on the second emplacement and the remainder of the battery. Concrete work on Grubbs' gun blocks and ammunition rooms were finally brought to completion in March 1909. At that time, the parapets had been raised to the height of the gun blocks. Ultimately, the second 10-inch gun was mounted in the battery. Battery Grubbs' armament consisted of two M1895M1 10-inch guns on M1901 disappearing carriages, the only armament of that caliber in the Manila Bay defenses. A spare gun tube was also provided for the battery. Work proceeded until it was finally declared finished in late 1910. On February 2, 1911, Battery Grubbs was transferred to the 18th Company, having cost $212,397.86 up until that time.[101]

Battery Morrison (Two 6-inch Guns)

Battery Grubbs had barely been commenced in December 1907 when the engineers began construction of emplacements for the second battery of 6-inch guns. This battery was to cover the waters between Corregidor and the Bataan Peninsula. It had been approved as a substitute for a once projected battery on Lasisi Point near Mariveles on the Bataan Peninsula, which had been canceled when the decision was made to concentrate all of Manila Bay's defenses on the islands. This 6-inch gun battery was at an elevation of some 360 feet above sea level on Topside's north side overlooking a deep ravine. This elevation would eventually take the battery's name and be called Morrison Hill. The ravine would be named James Ravine for the rapid-fire battery located near the ravine's mouth. Construction continued from December 1907 until the middle of 1909.[102]

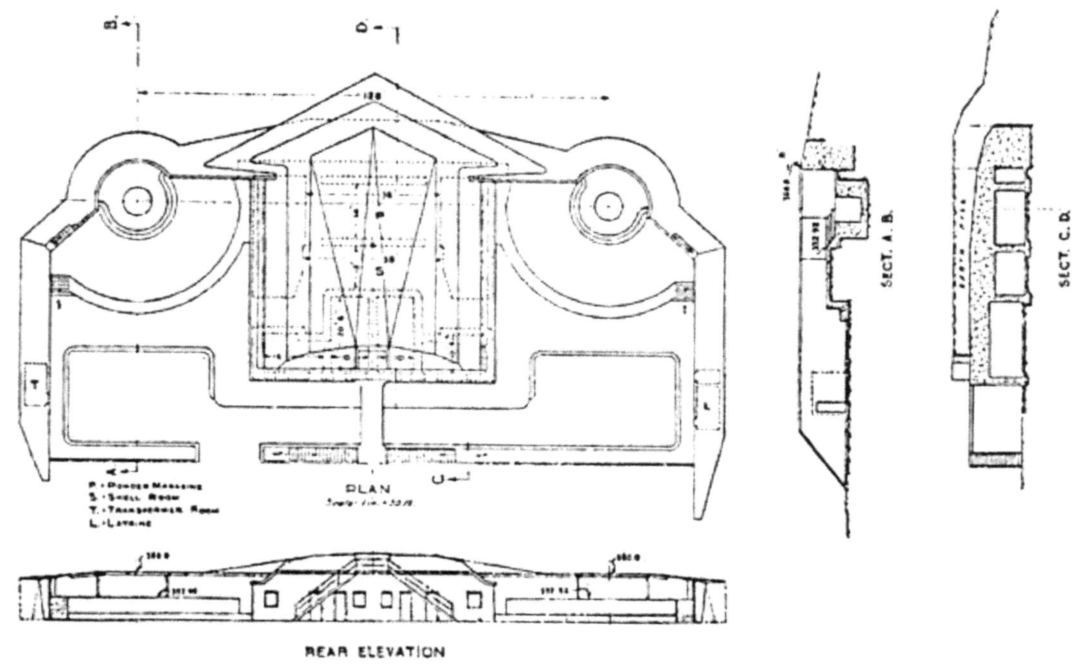

Plan of Battery Morrison, December 3, 1910. NARA.

Newly completed Battery Morrison, August 2, 1909. NARA.

Excavation work was generally complete by July 1908 and concrete work commenced shortly thereafter, with the expectation that it would be completed by January 1909. Both gun blocks were completed and the remainder of concrete work was about two-thirds complete by April 30, 1909, and the battery's armament was on hand and ready to be to be mounted. The battery was named May 12, 1908, for 1st Lt. John Morrison Jr., 4th Cavalry. The battery was armed with its pair of 6-inch M1905 guns on M1905M1 disappearing carriages. Finish work was carried out over the next 18 months and on November 10, 1910, it was transferred at a cost of $79,845.99 to the 42nd Company that was also assigned to Battery Ramsay.

Battery Geary (Eight 12-inch Mortars)

In late 1907 the engineers suggested that a battery for eight mortars could be sited near 12-inch disappearing Battery No. 2 (Battery Crockett), construction of which had just started. Funding and armament for the battery would come from the mortar battery once projected at Subic Bay and subsequently deleted. The second Fort Mills mortar battery was begun in November 1907 just northeast of Battery Crockett, the project sharing the same construction plants and storehouses. To facilitate that sharing, a cut was made through a low ridge between the two battery sites. Unlike Battery Way, this battery was a standard two-pit design built for eight 12-inch mortars. A data booth was positioned in the rear of each mortar pit. The battery was still far from complete when it was named on May 12, 1908, for Capt. Woodbridge Geary, 13th U.S. Infantry. Excavation work at the battery site was completed at the end of June 1908. The concrete work that followed advanced rapidly and by March 1909, concrete work and the drains had been completed. The four gun blocks and the magazine rooms of Pit B had also been completed except for their roofs. No armament, however, had yet been received. The battery was designed, and base plates installed, for eight of the newest M1908 mortars and carriages. Shipment of the new mortars and carriages was delayed and the first four did not arrive until about November 1910.[103]

Construction was completed by the middle of 1909, but there was a shortage of the new M1908 mortars and carriages. In light of the strained relationship with Japan in 1910, there was an immediate need to fully arm Corregidor's batteries; therefore on August 12, 1910, the secretary of war ordered four older type M1890M1 mortars and their M1896M1 mortar carriages removed from Battery Frank Whitman at Fort Andrews in Boston Harbor and shipped to Corregidor as replacements for four M1908s. Eventually the four delayed M1908 mortars went into Battery Whitman, when it was found desirable to have at least one battery of these guns for training and evaluation in the continental U.S.

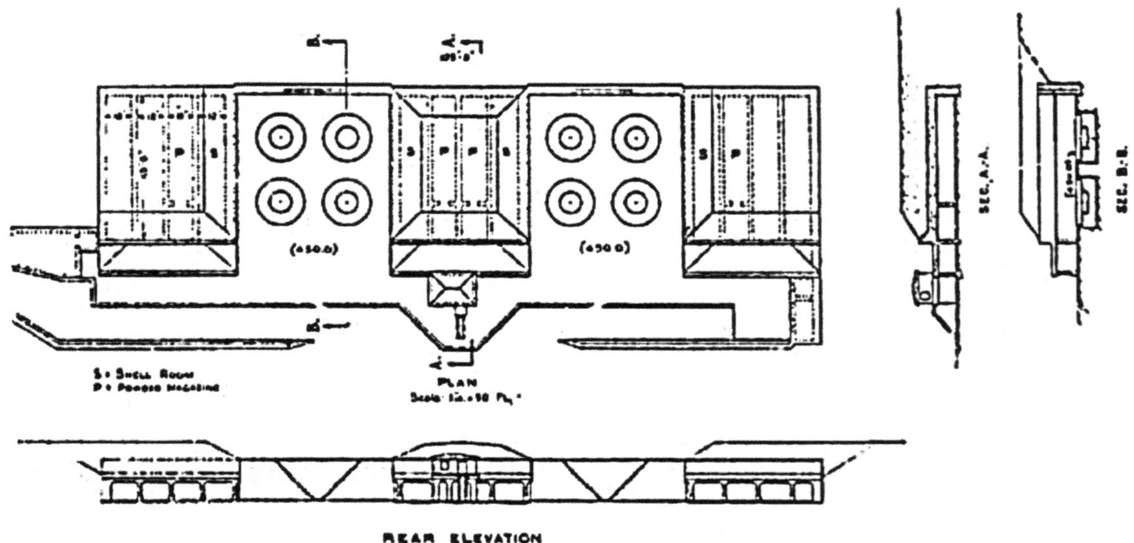

Plan, elevation, and sections Battery Geary. NARA.

Battery Geary as it neared completion, January 1, 1910. NARA.

The four older type mortars were emplaced in Pit A, requiring removal and changing of the carriage foundation bolts. Pit B was finally armed with four M1908 12-inch mortars on M1908 mortar carriages. Battery Geary was transferred to the coast artillery garrison on June 6, 1911. The mixing of armament type in the same battery created problems in maintenance and particularly fire control that would persist for many years.[104]

Because Battery Geary, like Battery Way, was considered fully protected from naval bombardment by its defiladed site, steel reinforcement of the concrete was not provided and, the tops of the magazine traverses were not initially bombproofed to the same extent as similar batteries built in the United States. However, that was soon regretted, and an estimate of $103,241.25 for increasing the protection of magazines of Battery Geary was prepared in 1911, but the actual cost of the bombproof cover of the battery only came to $31,827.91. This work was not completed until 1914.[105]

Battery James (Four 3-inch Rapid-Fire Guns)

As construction of Battery Morrison was ending in April 1908, a new battery was commenced nearby. This battery was located in front of and about a hundred feet below Battery Morrison, adjacent to the mouth of a deep ravine that would become known as James Ravine. It was designed to receive four 3-inch rapid-fire guns on barbette carriages to protect the Boca Chica's northern minefields. Work was still in progress in May 1908 when it was named Battery James, honoring 1st Lt. John F. James, 8th U.S. Infantry.[106]

Excavation work drew to a close in September 1908 and the concrete pouring followed with that work projected for completion in three months. The concreting lagged, however, and was not finished until March 31, 1909. Battery James was completed except for the retaining wall behind the battery, the telephone booth, and the battery commander's station. The battery's armament of four 3-inch M1903 rapid-fire guns and barbette carriages were already on hand and ready to be mounted. Finish work continued until early 1910, when it was declared complete and on November 10, 1910, Battery James was transferred to the 95th Company at a

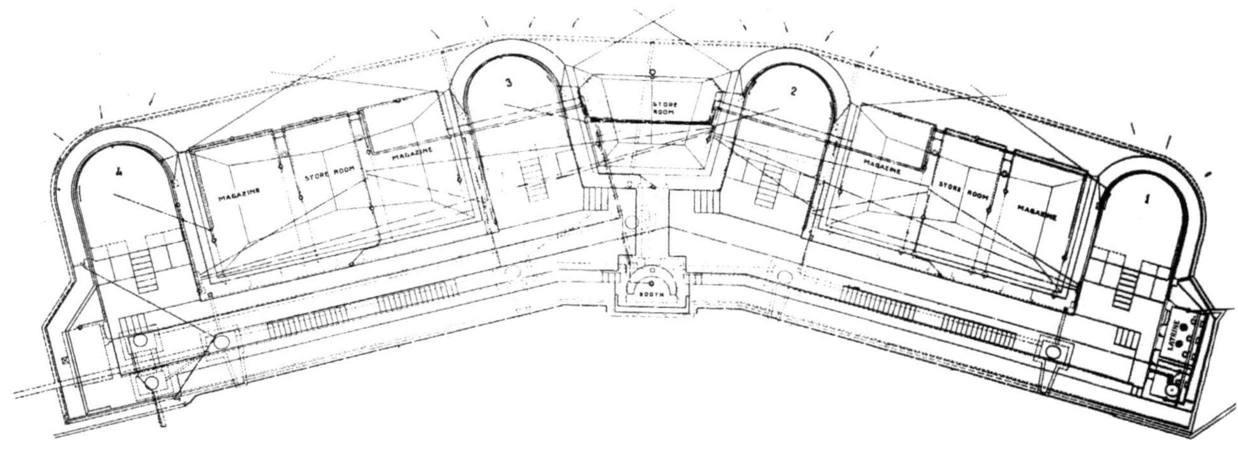

Approved overhead plan for Battery James, September 30, 1910. NARA.

cost of $50,537.95. With the completion of batteries on Corregidor in 1913, there was a short lapse in battery construction on the "Rock." By this time, however, plans had been developed and fortification construction begun on other islands in the bay. Battery James's armament remained in place until 1917, when two of its guns were removed and re-emplaced to protect Searchlights No. 3 and 4.[107]

A couple of accidents occurred while mounting and proofing new guns on their carriages. One of the 10-inch guns recently mounted at Battery Warwick at Fort Wint was damaged in December 1908. The tube had to be removed and sent stateside for repairs. Fortunately, there was an extra gun available that could be quickly mounted as a replacement. Then at Battery James the 3-inch guns were mounted in late April 1909. While being proofed by the 54th Company on May 10, 1909, Gun No. 4 developed a longitudinal crack in the jacket's lower exterior, requiring it be sent to Watervliet Arsenal for repair.

Emplacement No. 1 of Battery James, May 25, 1909, as the battery neared completion. NARA.

Ammunition Allowances

Constructing the emplacements and then receiving and mounting the intended ordnance were only the first steps in preparing a battery for service. Another important task was to acquire and properly store the ammunition supply. In fact, the cost of a typical battery's ammunition stockpile roughly equaled both the initial construction expense and the gun and carriage costs. Normally American seacoast batteries of this era were supplied with 80 rounds for 14-inch guns, 90 rounds for 12-inch guns, and 120 rounds for 10-inch guns. Lighter 6-inch batteries got 200 rounds per gun, and rapid-fire guns like the 3-inch typically received 800 rounds/gun. Mortar batteries were given 120 rounds per mortar. All of the ammunition was routinely stored at the batteries, though in special circumstances some extra supply could be kept at a reserve magazine on a post. Much of the original ammunition stock for the Harbor Defenses of Manila and Subic Bay was obtained through a specific appropriation of March 3, 1911, "Ammunition for Insular Possessions."[108]

Due to the Philippine Islands' remote location, and the likelihood that in the event of war they might have to endure a lengthy campaign before being resupplied, the batteries in Manila Bay were allocated ammunition supplies above the standard adopted stateside. After an exchange of letters from 1909 to 1911, it was decided to equip the mortar batteries with 200%, or double, the normal allocation. While the timing of the approval came before completion of Frank's and Hughes's batteries, enabling enlarged magazines, extra room had to be found at Batteries Way and Geary to accommodate these additional munitions. At Battery Way that was accomplished at the same time the battery was given overhead protection; and at Battery Geary a special separate magazine had to be built behind the battery in 1911. This two-room concrete structure was 63 feet long and 32 feet wide, centered on a concrete slab measuring 69 feet long by 38 feet wide. Calls were subsequently made to secure quantities of high-explosive rounds for the mortars. They were considered of value for use in counter-battery firing against the Bataan or Cavite shores. Although authorized in 1916, the additional ammunition was never adequately supplied; only very limited numbers of HE rounds ever made it to the Philippines for the 12-inch mortars (or any other seacoast gun for that matter).[109]

Even in 1911 Fort Wint received only a relatively small allocation of ammunition per gun. Compared to the above figures for Fort Mills, Battery Warwick was supplied just 100 rounds/gun, the 6-inch just 140, and the 3-inch only 200. In the latter case that was only 12.5% of Corregidor's allocation.

A Fort Mills magazine, fully-stacked with 12-inch shells. Note the chain hoist being attached to a shell for transfer and instructional diagrams on the wall. Life Magazine.

CHAPTER 5
CONSTRUCTING THE MILITARY POST ON CORREGIDOR

Active coast defense posts were much more than just the batteries and other tactical structures built within their confines. An entire infrastructure to adequately house and care for their substantial garrisons was needed. Storehouses and workshops for weapons, ammunition, and supplies of all types were required, along with a network of transportation knitting them all together. At Fort Mills in particular many more structures and dollars were expended on this infrastructure than on the batteries themselves. Before serious work could begin on either type of construction, temporary facilities for engineers, labor gangs, and storehouses for construction material had to be erected, along with accumulating or processing adequate stockpiles of timber, stone, and cement. In the early years on Corregidor all of these functions were conducted simultaneously.

On August 17, 1907, U.S. Army Adjutant General Brig. Gen. Fred C. Ainsworth sent a cablegram to Maj. Gen. Leonard Wood, commanding the Philippine Division at Manila, requesting cost estimates for construction of a post for four companies of coast artillery at Subic Bay and of eight companies at Corregidor. A few days later, Wood responded to Ainsworth that general plans for a coast artillery post on Corregidor had been completed for temporary quarters and barracks in 1906 and recommended details of the construction types that should be used. The first structures built on Corregidor by the American engineers and the Quartermaster Department to house and support the growing numbers of American military and civilian workers on Corregidor were temporary ones of timber and galvanized iron. The Filipinos, both military and civilian, were temporally quartered in structures built of nipa and suali. As the initial seacoast gun and mortar batteries neared completion in 1908, the chief of coast artillery called for funding barracks and quarters for 10 companies on Corregidor and four more companies on Grande Isle.[110]

Building the Temporary Post on Corregidor: 1906-1910

Pending permanent structures, a temporary post was timed for completion by the time the first garrison troops arrived. The preliminary post at Topside called for three sets of officers' quarters, a barracks, a small hospital, four storehouses, an ordnance repair shop, ordnance storehouse, artillery engineer storehouse, and an artillery district headquarters. Overall cost estimates for construction of the post buildings anticipated Bilibid convict labor being available. However, the constructing quartermaster had little in the way of funds. As it turned out, insufficient funds had been appropriated to maintain the existing quarters elsewhere in the Philippines that were already falling down, much less to fund construction of new posts. Consequently, the quartermaster built only one barracks, one officer's quarters, and one combined commissary and quartermaster storeroom. These temporary structures were completed just before the first permanent garrison arrived in May 1907. A few days following their arrival, one end of the enlisted barracks was demolished by a typhoon and the officers' quarters were wrecked to such an extent that it had to be abandoned. The entire command took shelter in the commissary and quartermaster storeroom until the storm passed.[111]

Following the typhoon, the garrison lived under canvas until the barracks and officer's quarters were repaired. Repairs were still underway when orders were received by the quartermaster authorizing the immediate construction of ordnance and artillery storehouses as well as two additional sets of officers' quarters and two sets of noncommissioned officers' quarters. In addition, $12,000 was made available for a concrete hospital authorized by the chief surgeon of the Philippine Division.[112]

When Col. John B. Bellinger, the constructing quartermaster, arrived on Corregidor in September 1909 he found that nearly all the convicts were being utilized in fortification construction and other engineer projects. This set back the post construction program almost a year. Construction costs were increased further when it was discovered that the original plans had to be changed due to inaccuracies discovered in the early surveys of the dense jungle-covered island. Appropriations totaling $1,650,000 for non-tactical post structures were ob-

Temporary NCO quarters built in 1909 continued in service in the late 1930s. NARA.

Enlisted barracks in 1909 occupied by the coast artillery companies that arrived early the following year. NARA.

tained between 1908 and 1913. In late 1910 the War Department tasked the garrison to quarter a regiment of infantry to provide mobile infantry support, a company of engineers, and five more coast artillery companies to adequately man the land defenses and its artillery.[113]

Work crews, plagued with shortages of funds and building materials, pressed on with the temporary post's initial construction in anticipation of the increased garrison. By December 1908, three more sets of officers' quarters and two double sets of NCO quarters were under construction, another storehouse had been framed, and the frames for a combination barrack, kitchen and mess hall, and sinks, etc. put up. A house for the superintendent of construction had also been built along with a small quartermaster office, a garbage incinerator, and a storehouse at the foot of the hill. Quarters were also built for the civilians employed by the army on the island, and the water supply was improved. From his office at Manila, Captain Chamberlaine's concerns regarding the sluggish pace of construction increased as the date for the next garrison augmentation grew closer. He noted that the expected companies would not even have a temporary hospital.[114]

The temporary post being built at Topside by the quartermaster at Fort Mills was being advanced only as fast as matériel could be made available, much of it having to be delivered from the mainland U.S. By the end of January 1909, the ordnance storehouse had finally been completed, along with the two double sets of NCO quarters. Two barracks were nearly complete, and eight new sets of officers' quarters were almost finished. Grading of sites for two more barracks was underway. The arrival of Maj. Clint C. Hearn as the new senior coast artillery officer would bring a bit more "horsepower" to be used in expediting the post development. The temporary post was still far from complete when Hearn arrived in April 1909. While Bellinger continued to feel confident that the quarters for the four additional companies scheduled to arrive in July would be ready in time, Hearn was not as optimistic. He noted that July marked the height of the typhoon season and if barracks were not completed when the troops arrived, the men would have to live in tents that would not stand up to even the mildest of tropical storms.[115]

Hearn's fears that the companies would have to quarter under canvas during the typhoon season when they arrived continued to plague the new post commander. Little progress had been made on new structures. No additional work had been done on officers' quarters, although grading of sites for two more barracks had been completed and a few piers put down. It was found necessary to request a delay in the departure of the four additional companies from the United States until September because of construction delays.[116]

Between 1909 and 1916, scores of temporary structures were erected on Corregidor to serve as quarters and barracks for officers, NCOs, enlisted men, and both American and Filipino civilians. Also mess halls, quartermaster, commissary, and engineer storehouses, guardhouses, oil storehouses, a pumping plant, crematoriums, stables, a dispensary, and a power plant to name were fabricated, just a few. Nearly all Filipino civilian employee quarters were constructed of impermanent materials; sometimes provided with galvanized iron roofs as a substitute for nipa, or in other cases these quarters were simply adapted from existing structures in the barrios on the island. Those built for the American civilian employees were of generally better materials, wood-frame buildings with galvanized iron roofs and concrete or wood floors founded on concrete piers. Many of these structures would undergo numerous changes in function as needs changed and more permanent structures were built. Construction of temporary buildings would continue into the early 1930s and their use extended to the early days of 1942. Interestingly, considerable material from these temporary structures would be repurposed in tunnel shelters during the war.

Permanent Post Construction: 1910-1919

The initial phase of construction of permanent garrison structures was well underway by March 1910 and continued to 1918. Initially, the capacity of each permanent barracks was limited to 109 men. Hearn, realizing that the personnel needs on Corregidor differed greatly from the situation in the United States, wanted barracks that would accommodate 140 men, pointing out that there was no National Guard coast artillery available in the Philippines to augment the peacetime garrison in the event of a war. Additional personnel would be required to provide reliefs for the batteries. In this the command of the Philippine Department in Manila fully concurred.[117]

Colonel Bellinger was hard pressed to make the limited funding of the $550,000 available for permanent barracks and quarters construction stretch as far as was needed. The Quartermaster Department believed that they could build a 10-company post with this initial appropriation, an assumption that would ultimately prove false. Congress' Sundry Civil Bill did, however, contain an additional $230,000 requested for the permanent post needed to accommodation the troops on Corregidor called for by Hearn.[118]

Among the initial permanent tactical structures built were the first of nearly a dozen large powder magazines. The magazines in the various gun and mortar batteries were susceptible to dampness and long-term storage of powder charges at the batteries was not recommended. The initial pair of reinforced concrete magazines was built into the south slope of Morrison Hill, where an extensive ordnance storage area would be developed by the early 1920s. Progress was also being made on a massive permanent concrete barracks to quarter 11 coast artillery companies, a band barracks, and include a post exchange in its center. This barracks would be built on cleared land near Topside's summit. Most of concrete was in place for the ground floor, and steel and forms ready for concrete pouring on the upper walls and floors by August 1910. By then the projected number of coast artillery companies required in the Artillery District of Manila had risen to 14, while the number of companies in the Artillery District of Subic Bay still numbered four.[119]

The first eight three-story sections of Topside's massive artillery barracks were completed in April 1914. Each section was designed to house a company of about 150 coast artillerymen, although most companies at the time had less than 100 men. The remaining four sections were completed in August 1914. The central section of the 1,516-foot-long reinforced concrete barracks structure contained a combination post exchange and gymnasium, barracks and practice rooms for the band, a barbershop, bowling alley, mess room and kitchen, a swimming pool, billiards, and reading rooms. Each company section was laid out the same. The company mess and kitchen, along with a company office, the company storeroom, and the room for the Quartermaster Sergeant were on the ground floor. The second and third floors each had a room for two company NCOs and a

Field officers' quarters constructed in 1914 as part of the permanent post. NARA.

Senior non-commissioned staff quarters for eight families. NARA.

This bombproof magazine was built into the slope of Morrison Hill and completed September 10, 1913, at a cost of $34,445. It had 50,000 cubic feet of storage space. NARA.

113-foot by 31-foot dormitory for the privates. The companies not housed in the "mile-long" barracks at Topside were initially accommodated in the temporary frame barracks and quarters elsewhere on the post.[120]

The Fort Mills Hospital was completed in December 1913 as the initial construction phases of the permanent garrison structures at Topside drew near a close. This three-story, 39,340-square foot, 150-bed medical facility was, like the other permanent structures on the island, constructed of reinforced concrete and designed to resist splinters from bombardment.

Coast artillery barracks at Topside viewed from the lighthouse. Williford collection.

Interior of dormitory for privates 1938. Cornwell Collection, USAMHI.

Library and reading room in Topside barracks 1938. Cornwell Collection, USAMHI.

As soon as the barracks were underway, the quartermaster began building housing for the garrison officers across the parade ground from the main artillery barracks. The initial officers' quarters were built to accommodate a single officer and his family. Two field officers and eight company officers' quarters were built in 1914. All were concrete one-story, single sets that had the dining room, four bedrooms, and two bathrooms in the building's main part, with a wing at the rear containing the kitchens, laundry, servants' quarters, etc. Once the single sets were commenced, 12 double sets of concrete two-story company officers' quarters were started and were finished in June 1914. These quarters were each arranged to accommodate two officers and their families: one family to each floor of the building. Each set of these quarters had a living room, three bedrooms, two closets, a bathroom, pantry, kitchen, and dining room, as well as two servants' rooms, a servant's bathroom, a storeroom, and a drying room. All of the Topside officers' quarters were built near the lighthouse or on the south side of the newly laid out parade ground and athletic fields across from the artillery barracks. Six more single sets of concrete field officers' quarters and six more single sets of concrete company officers' quarters were built between 1915 and 1918 and were added to the row of quarters fronting the parade ground.[121]

By November 1914, a second complex of permanent barracks was nearing completion at Middleside, about 150 feet downhill from and some 600 feet northeast of the Topside artillery barracks. These barracks consisted of four company sections, each of approximately the same arrangement and dimensions as those in the Topside barracks. These sections would accommodate the last four coast artillery companies to arrive before World War I.[122]

Fort Mills hospital in 1921. Smith Collection.

As construction wound down on the Middleside artillery barracks, work was commenced in August 1915 on a concrete three-story structure to house the infantry garrison. Six companies of the 24th U.S. Infantry Regiment were posted to Corregidor in 1913. They were initially quartered under canvas and provided with temporary buildings constructed in early 1914 of nipa and suali that housed NCOs and served as a headquarters, a dispensary, and a combination corral and stables for the regimental animals. In an effort to accommodate the infantry in proper quarters, an additional range of barracks similar to those occupied by the coast artillery was built to the west of the Middleside barracks in 1914 and 1915. This barracks complex, similar in design to the artillery barracks, consisted of a regimental headquarters section and two sections to accommodate two 150-man companies. Two more company sections were begun on the infantry barracks in 1916 and were completed in January 1917. By June 1917, four additional sections of barracks, each designed to accommodate an infantry company, had been built immediately west of the initial infantry barracks. These barracks were, however, wood frame on a concrete foundation and were two stories instead of three. The first floors of these sections accommodated the NCOs, the kitchen, mess hall, company offices, commissary, and lavatory, while the second floor had a large dormitory room and a day room.[123]

Guard station at Middleside infantry barracks. Jensen Collection

Splinter-proof quartermaster storehouse. NARA.

In 1919, the stockade itself received 10 additional structures, some of which replaced older buildings. Among these were a bathhouse, a two-story 60 by 22-foot cell house for 50 prisoners, a prison office and commissary storehouse, a morgue and laundry building, mess hall, and a special confinement structure for the some thirty "Bastoneros" or "tough guys."[124]

Fort Mills' role in a prolonged siege was not ignored. Relatively early in the consideration of permanent garrison facilities provision was made for storage of large quantities of stores. These were manifested by a series of five substantial concrete storehouses built on a slight shelf off Topside, southeast of the lighthouse and officers' row. Under the care of the quartermaster, these were well-protected by both their location and construction. Like the concrete barracks at Topside and Middleside, they were not strictly "bombproof," but certainly they were resistant to light shelling and fragments. Four quartermaster storehouses, measuring 42 by 151 feet and numbered Storehouses No. 75 through 78, were used for bulk storage of subsistence, clothing, and equipment. The fifth warehouse for the storage of supplies for the Medical Department/Signal Corps was smaller at 42 x 62 feet. The buildings were completed in 1913, though it took a while and additional appropriations to stock them adequately. During the course of World War I, four 175-foot-long and 50-foot-wide, galvanized iron roofed, single-story, wood-frame barracks on concrete footings were constructed to house quartermaster troops near their storehouses. These barracks, each of which accommodated 150 men, were completed April 30, 1918.[125]

Housing the Garrison: 1920-1940

Most of Fort Mills' coast artillery garrison was housed at or near Topside. The main artillery barracks at Topside known as the "mile-long barracks" housed most of the separate coast artillery companies until 1922. The barracks at Middleside initially housed some of the coast artillery companies assigned to Corregidor during the World War. When the 59th Artillery Regiment arrived from the United States in 1921, it briefly occupied a portion of the barracks at Middleside. The reorganization of the garrison and the departure of most of the infantry in the early 1920s saw much shuffling around by the remaining garrison elements. Philippine Scout infantry occupied the Middleside Infantry Barracks and were succeeded by the Philippine Scout coast artillery companies by the end of 1922. By the summer of 1924 the 59th Coast Artillery Regiment had moved up to the Topside Artillery Barracks and the newly constituted 91st Coast Artillery Regiment and the 1st Battalion, 92nd Coast Artillery Regiment, had taken up quarters in the Middleside Artillery Barracks. The 2nd (Guard) Battalion, 92nd C.A. occupied the new barracks at the east side of the stockade. After the Air Service contingent on Corregidor was reduced in the mid-1920s, the 1st Battalion, 92nd C.A., moved into the vacated Air Service quarters and barracks on Corregidor's tail. When the 60th Coast Artillery Regiment arrived on the island in 1928, they occupied the Middleside Barracks that had been vacated by the scouts a few years before. Eventually, the 60th C.A. would also move into the Topside Barracks.

Quarters and Barracks on the Stockade Level

The Philippine Scouts occupying Camp Avery at the stockade level on Corregidor were assigned to guard the post's primary labor force of convicts from Manila's Bilibid prison. These troops had lived under canvas and then in nipa huts, before being moved into temporary barracks adjacent to the stockade. The scout headquarters was begun in 1913 and completed January 23, 1914. In 1916, four barracks were constructed for the scouts at the stockade level. These 137-foot-long and 50-foot-wide wood-frame structures had pitched roofs of galvanized iron. Each was arranged to accommodate 113 men. A pair of latrines was also constructed for the scouts. Each served two companies and had three bathing rooms and three latrines. The barracks were completed in July 1916 and the latrines a month later. Also built were a bodega and a headquarters, also of wood frame. All were founded on concrete pier footings and provided with galvanized-iron pitched roofs, the eves

Fort Mills administration building, ca. 1920. Schmidt Collection.

Middleside artillery barracks, 1939. Schmidt Collection.

Officer's quarters stockade level. Gaines Collection.

of which extended beyond the verandas that surrounded the buildings. Smaller structures of the same basic construction were provided for Filipino NCOs. Many married scout NCOs lived in the nearby barrio of La Concepción. An additional pair of 150-man barracks and a latrine was built in April 1918 in accordance with a similar design, but much sturdier and more comfortable. The three older barracks were demolished and the fourth converted into a schoolhouse. The two new scout barracks were built east of the stockade that stood just to the north of Spanish Fort. These new 150-man barracks were occupied by the 2nd Battalion, 92nd C.A., after its organization in 1922.[126]

The American officers assigned to the 92nd C.A. lived at the stockade level's western edge. Initially the quarters for American officers were of temporary frame construction. The old temporary structures were knocked down and new concrete quarters with wide verandas were built about 1915. The quarters differed slightly in layout from those at Topside and Middleside in that they had a fourth bedroom in lieu of the kitchen that was relocated to a semi-detached wing with the servants' quarters. Field officers were provided with single-story bungalows, while company/battery grade officers were generally housed in double sets of quarters. Unmarried officers were housed several to a set of quarters. Maj. Fred M. Green described the officers' housing in early 1922:[127]

> All quarters are of practically identical pattern, and there is very little choice between them. A central living room in front, opens into a dining room in the rear. Two bedrooms are on one side of the house, with a bathroom between them. There is a single bedroom on the opposite side of the house with a separate bath. In the rear of the latter, the kitchen, butler's pantry, servants' quarters, etc. The walls are concrete [with timber floors]. Large sliding shell windows provide ample ventilation. No cellers [sic] or attics; storage space except a small trunk room is wanting. Closet space somewhat restricted.

Middleside Officer Quarters

Double sets of two-story junior officers' quarters of a type of cement-plaster known as "Sewell construction" on elevated concrete bases were constructed at Middleside. Field officer's quarters were single-story bungalow-style buildings. The first six sets were constructed with concrete floors, but post World War I cost-cutting measures soon resulted in the remaining 27 double sets of quarters being given wooden floors. All quarters had wide porches and nearly identical floor plans and had generally the same overall design as the officers' quarters at the stockade level.[128]

Topside Officer Quarters

The quarters occupied by the commanding general and by the numerous senior field grade officers on Corregidor were located on Topside near the parade ground and the lighthouse. A small number of senior ranking officers and their families lived in the handful of single-story bungalows. Two dozen concrete two-story double sets of quarters for field grade officers were ranged around the south side of the combination parade ground and athletic field at Topside. The remaining sets of quarters occupied by battery and company grade officers were similar to those at Middleside except all were concrete. In March 1916, a large concrete set of quarters for nine bachelor officers was completed adjacent to the Fort Mills administration building.[129]

Constructing the posts was just the first step. Maintaining them would be a major challenge in the years following. The expense of keeping the structures in good repair was a constant, and costly, task. While the barracks, quarters, hospitals, and many tactical structures were built of permanent materials, many storage buildings and other support structures were timber buildings roofed with galvanized iron. Other structures had been constructed by the troops using salvaged materials. The weather conditions were harsh, and more than 200,000 square feet of surfaces required annual painting with costly, high-quality paint, a goal more frequently unmet than achieved.[130]

Some of the double sets of officers' quarters at Topside. NARA.

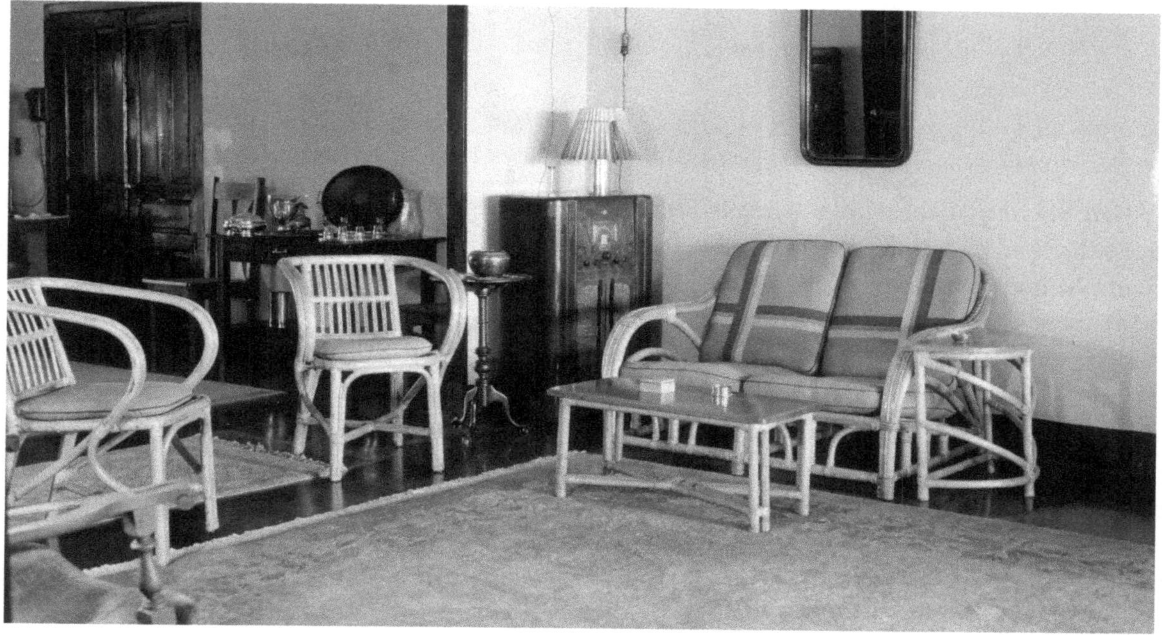

Rattan and bamboo furniture was highly recommended for the officers' quarters on Corregidor. Ruhlen Collection.

The weather was also a factor in dealing with the road and trail network on Corregidor. There were over 26 miles of roads and trails on the island, constructed through rank vegetation along hillsides with deep cuts and fills, steep grades, and sharp turns. The typhoon season's torrential rains caused frequent landslides and excessive erosion. Only about 17 miles were ever lightly surfaced with crushed stone and afforded a width of nine to 12 feet. By 1941, only five miles had been rehabilitated and macadamized, most of these in the early 1930s.[131]

War Scare of 1913

Several diplomatic disputes erupted between the United States and Japan in the early 1900s. In 1913 one developed that, at least for a while, threatened military consequences. On April 15, 1913, the lower house of the California State legislature passed a bill forbidding foreign aliens (at least those ineligible for citizenship — like Japanese and other Orientals) from owning property. While the Wilson administration sent Secretary of State William Jennings Bryan to the state to prevent the bill's passage, that effort failed and the Webb bill

One of the hairpin turns on the North Shore Road. Williford Collection.

was passed on May 4. Japanese response was immediate and negative. They felt it contrary to the spirit of the negotiations that had ended the 1907 dispute, and distinctly racial in nature. There were vocal demonstrations in Tokyo and heated diplomatic exchanges.

Both the navy and army wished to take steps to prepare for possible hostilities. The navy wanted to move their three cruisers of the Asiatic Squadron to Manila from Shanghai, and to prepare and concentrate the six armored cruisers of the Pacific Fleet in Hawaiian waters. General Funston in Hawaii appealed for reinforcements. In the Philippines, General Bell found that the Corregidor defenses were well advanced, but he had no guns in service at the other Manila Bay forts yet. However, the administration refused to approve the most visible steps on the grounds that they might provoke even more dangerous responses. The two services could not openly cooperate. In the Philippines some deployments were carried out under the guise of maneuvers—but the army was refused the cooperation of navy ships. Bell reported to General Leonard Wood that we "Have full Corregidor garrison well in hand and enough on island to prevent any surprise."[132]

Under the impression that war was imminent (apparently the Americans believed so, though the crises was never taken that seriously in Japan), quick steps were taken to prepare the garrison and defenses at Fort Mills. Gun battery crews were temporarily quartered at their positions. Action stations were manned day and night. The controlled mines were deployed. For six weeks (much of May and June 1913) the defenses were on high alert. Of course, no hostile action occurred, but the panic did serve to constructively accelerate the building of defenses on the outer islands.[133]

CHAPTER 6
CONSTRUCTING THE OUTPOST FORTIFICATIONS

While the powerful batteries on Corregidor could effectively bar passage into Manila Bay in clear weather, a stormy night or morning haze prevented full observation of the southernmost channels. The board of engineer and artillery officers that submitted their report on the defenses of Manila and Subic Bays in February 1902 had recommended additional defenses on the south shore of Manila Bay, as well as the islands of Carabao, Caballo, and El Fraile, to effectively close the Boca Grande between Corregidor and the Cavite shore. The secretary of war approved the board's recommendations as modified by the chief of engineers. Subsequent studies would cancel the projected construction of fortifications on the mainland and concentrate the Manila Bay defenses on just the fortified islands.[134]

Plans for Carabao Island

Carabao, a rugged island a scant 500 yards off the Cavite shore, consisted of a rocky 44.5-acre north-south ridge of volcanic rock a half-mile long. Its sheer cliffs rise some 100 feet to a somewhat less precipitous, but no less rugged, slope that continue upward for another 85 feet before terminating on a narrow north-south hogback crest that extended most of the island's length.

With respect to the 1902 board's recommendations regarding Carabao Island, the initial plan called for placing only rapid-fire guns on the isle. President Theodore Roosevelt's Executive Order setting aside the islands at the entrance to Manila Bay as military reservations had included a sizable area in the vicinity of Restinga Point on the Cavite Mainland at the southern entrance to Manila Bay, as well as Carabao Island. It was on that tract designated the Cavite Military Reservation that the emplacement of major gun and mortar batteries were initially projected while retaining smaller-caliber rapid-fire guns on Carabao. As a temporary measure, the War Department requested that the navy's 6-inch guns on Grande Isle in Subic Bay be tempo-

Carabao Island, site of Fort Frank. Note the proximity of the Ternate mainland and the Pico DeLoro Hills. NARA.

rally moved to Carabao and emplaced there pending the construction of the projected batteries. The navy demurred, noting that when the army batteries on Grande Isle were completed the Navy Department would reconsider the army's use of navy guns in Manila Bay. Subsequently, consideration of Carabao as the site for primary gun and mortar defenses was undertaken. Capt. William Chamberlaine, while serving as Philippine Division Artillery Officer in the summer of 1908, noted in a letter to Capt. Stanley Embick, then an assistant to the chief of coast artillery, that Carabao was not a "suitable place" for the bay's southern flank defenses. He noted further that:[135]

> Carabao will be very hard to protect from the mainland. It is a bad island from a geological point of view, full of cracks, etc... Furthermore, it will be hard to locate two 14-inch guns and eight mortars so as to not have mutual interference. If to be located here, I think it would be better to put the 14-inch rifles in separate emplacements, giving each practically an all-around fire, rather than put them together in a normal type of emplacement. I know that this is a departure from the general rule, but so is Carabao.

Staff officers made a careful reconnaissance of Restinga Point on the Cavite mainland and they generally agreed that it was "much less vulnerable than Carabao and can be made impregnable from the land side. There are no domineering heights anywhere near (within four miles) while the same is not true of Carabao. Carabao is likely to be beaten in detail by ships to the south out of range of Corregidor, which is not true of Restinga."[136]

The island's tactical situation was problematic, the Pico DeLoro Hills with heights reaching 2,223 feet on the Cavite mainland completely dominated Carabao. Hostile artillery in the hills could quickly render the exposed seacoast batteries top surfaces on Carabao untenable. In 1906, retired Maj. Gen. John P. Story recommended that the 1902 board's position as well as the recommendations of Chamberlaine and the Philippine Division staff that placing batteries on Carabao would be inadvisable, be overruled. However, despite this opinion, the National Coast Defense Board and War Department directed that batteries be constructed on both Carabao and El Fraile Islands. Building proper defenses on Carabao would prove a severe challenge for the engineers.[137]

As the construction of Fort Mills' batteries on Corregidor was well advanced by 1908, and the construction work at Fort Wint in Subic Bay was drawing down, the engineers' attention turned to Carabao Island and the defense of the bay's southern passage. Preliminary site selection for the proposed batteries was followed by establishing a wharf and landing near the island's middle on the eastern shore in the latter months of 1908. Surveys of the island were then conducted. Setting up of a construction plant followed and construction sites

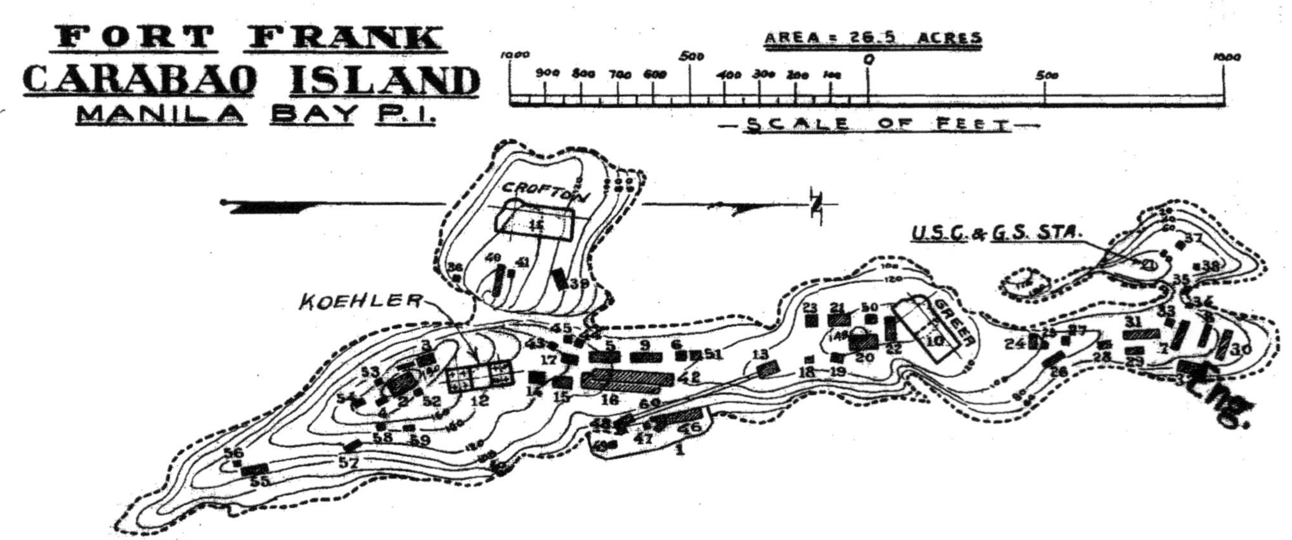

Layout of Fort Frank on Carabao Island, circa 1920. NARA.

Construction plant at site of Battery Koehler on Carabao Island, May 1920. NARA.

Tramway of the construction plant at Fort Frank. NARA.

for the batteries consisting of two 14-inch disappearing guns, and eight 12-inch mortars were selected. Site preparation was interrupted by a typhoon that ripped through the bay in early December 1908. The storm wrecked the engineer's steamer *Natchez*, a quartermaster launch, and a floating derrick at Corregidor, generally setting back progress on the fortifications for several weeks.[138]

The choice of 14-inch guns for the primary armament at Carabao Island is interesting, as the batteries here and at Fort DeRussy in Hawaii were the first of this size in U.S. coast defense. A new gun of this caliber had been recommended by the Taft Board in 1906. Several motives were behind this: including a worry about the increasing size of foreign battleship main armament and problems with the final generation of high-velocity 12-inch guns. The M1900 12-inch 40-caliber gun was very powerful but sacrificed barrel life due to the erosive effects of its high velocity. It was hoped that a lower-velocity 14-inch gun of 34-calibers (designed to "fit" the same sized emplacements, at least from a tube length standpoint) would solve these problems. The initial two guns for Carabao were ordered in late 1907. However, teething problems ran the gamut from modifications of the powder chamber, to changes in breech design, to mechanical problems with the intended new disappearing carriages. Seven years passed without the guns being finished for issue. While ultimately a successful gun (once emplaced, these original guns lasted through the 1942 campaign), they were not shipped to the Philippines until June 5, 1915.[139]

First Lt. Henry H. Robert arrived in January 1909 on Carabao Island from Subic Bay, where he had been building batteries on Grande Isle. Robert continued in charge of the Carabao works until April 1909. First Lt. John J. Kingman subsequently took up supervision of the construction, which continued to advance slowly but steadily toward completion. He supervised the works until September 16, 1910. Between Kingman's departure and the arrival of a successor engineer, the fortifications on Carabao fell to engineer officers at Corregidor. In his Annual Report to the War Department for 1913, Brig. Gen. Erasmus Weaver, chief of coast artillery, reported:[140]

> On Carabao Island the emplacements for the 14-inch batteries and mortar batteries are practically completed. The guns and carriages will be shipped in the fall [of 1912] and mounted probably before the close of the fiscal year [June 30, 1913]. With the installation of this armament, the strength of the defenses of Manila Bay will be greatly increased. The fire control and searchlight installations for Carabao have proceeded simultaneous with the battery construction, and the mounting of the guns will complete the defense at that point.

Weaver's expectations proved to be quite optimistic and while the carriages were finally received, assembled and emplaced in early 1914, the 14-inch gun tubes had not arrived at the beginning of 1915, delaying the mounting of the fort's primary armament.[141]

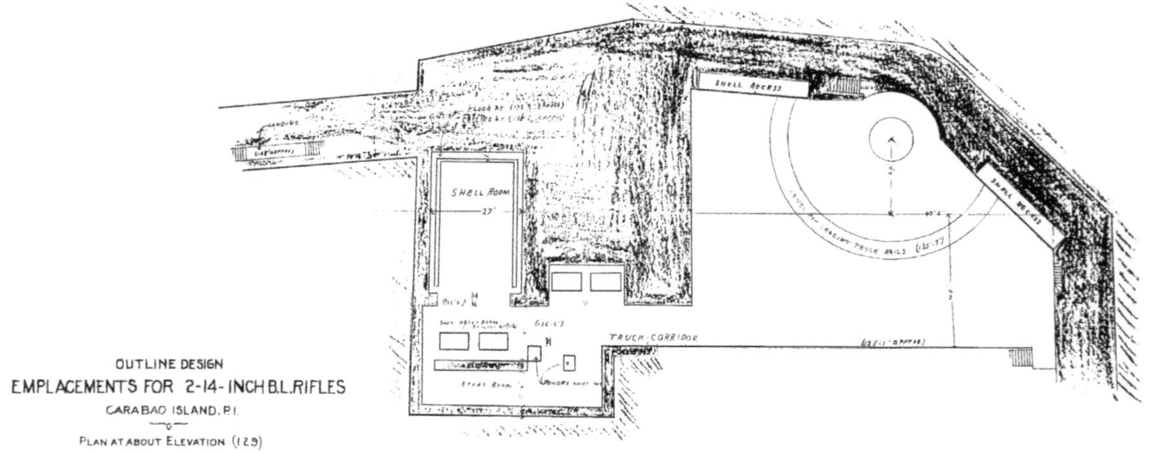

Example of field notes composed by engineers surveying gun sites on Carabao Island. This shows the general outline for a single emplacement, though ultimately not of the orientation eventually built at Fort Frank. NARA.

For the relatively small amount of artillery emplaced on the island, the construction costs of nearly $1.4 million were large. Most of these costs were necessitated by the difficulty of construction on the rugged island, coupled with the need to provide bombproof underground facilities for the supporting defense elements and the garrison that would be otherwise exposed to hostile fire from the Cavite mainland. In common with Corregidor, labor was carried out by Bilibid convicts, under the supervision of engineer personnel and guarded by a detail of Philippine Scouts.

Battery Greer (One 14-inch Disappearing Gun)

Lieutenant Robert promptly commenced work preliminary to construction for a 14-inch disappearing gun emplacement on the island's spine, where some initial work had been begun in December 1908. To provide space for the massive emplacement, considerable blasting and excavation were required that decreased the elevation of the hogback ridge and widened the battery site. This 14-inch battery on the ridge at the island's center was named Battery Greer in honor of Col. John Edwin Greer, Ordnance Department, January 28, 1909.[142]

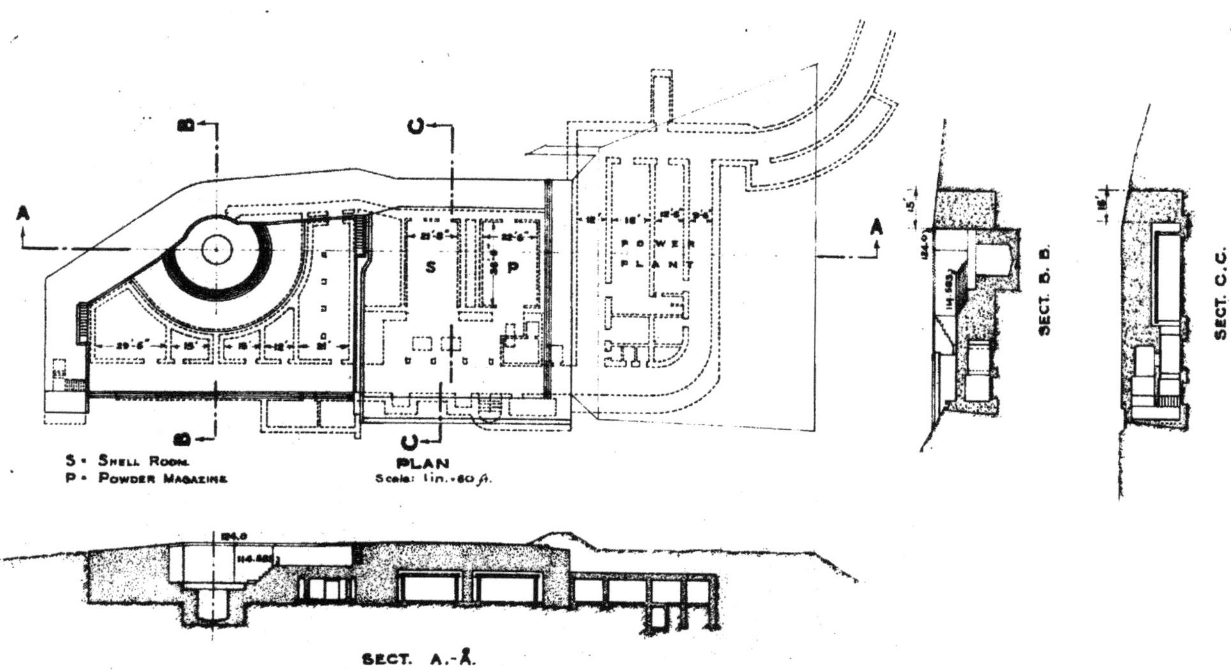

Plan, elevation, and section of Battery Greer. NARA.

Target practice with the 14-inch gun of Battery Greer. McGarraugh Collection.

The emplacement and its supporting tunnel complex were slowly advanced. The battery's concrete work progressed and was generally complete by 1913. Its M1907 disappearing carriage had been received and was installed awaiting the delivery of its M1907M1 gun. Prior to the 14-inch gun's arrival, the disappearing carriage was modified; its elevation was increased from 15° to 20° and the gun's range from 19,200 yards to 22,800 yards. The unarmed battery was transferred to the garrison October 24, 1913. In May 1915, the gun was finally delivered to the emplacement and mounted.[143]

Battery Crofton (One 14-inch Disappearing Gun)

The second 14-inch disappearing gun emplacement was also commenced in January 1909 by Lieutenant Robert, who began clearing space for the battery site on an outcropping from the main part of the island's west shore about 1,200 feet to the southwest of the first gun battery. Again, considerable blasting, excavating, and leveling of the rocky outcropping were necessary to gain sufficient space for the large concrete gun emplacement, its magazines, and support facilities. Soon after construction commenced this emplacement was named Battery Crofton to honor Capt. William Moore Crofton, 1st U.S. Infantry, January 28, 1909. Like its sister battery, it was also brought to completion in 1913. Although it had received its M1907 disappearing carriage, this emplacement too was awaiting delivery of its gun when Battery Crofton was transferred to the coast artillery on October 24, 1913. Like Battery Greer, Battery Crofton had its carriage modified to increase elevation and range. The 14-inch M1907 gun tube was received 20 months later.[144]

Both batteries were the two-story, or horizontal crest type, in which their ammunition was raised from the magazines by back-delivery vertical hoists that opened onto delivery tables in a gallery at the rear of the battery traverse/magazine structure. Projectiles and powder charges were conveyed to the guns' loading platforms on ammunition carts. Both batteries were equipped with Taylor-Raymond back-delivery projectile hoists installed in April 1914 and March 1916, while the "Type D" back-delivery powder hoists were not installed until February of 1916. A second Taylor-Raymond back-delivery projectile hoist was installed in both of Fort Frank's 14-inch batteries in March 1917, which improved the rate of fire of the two guns.[145]

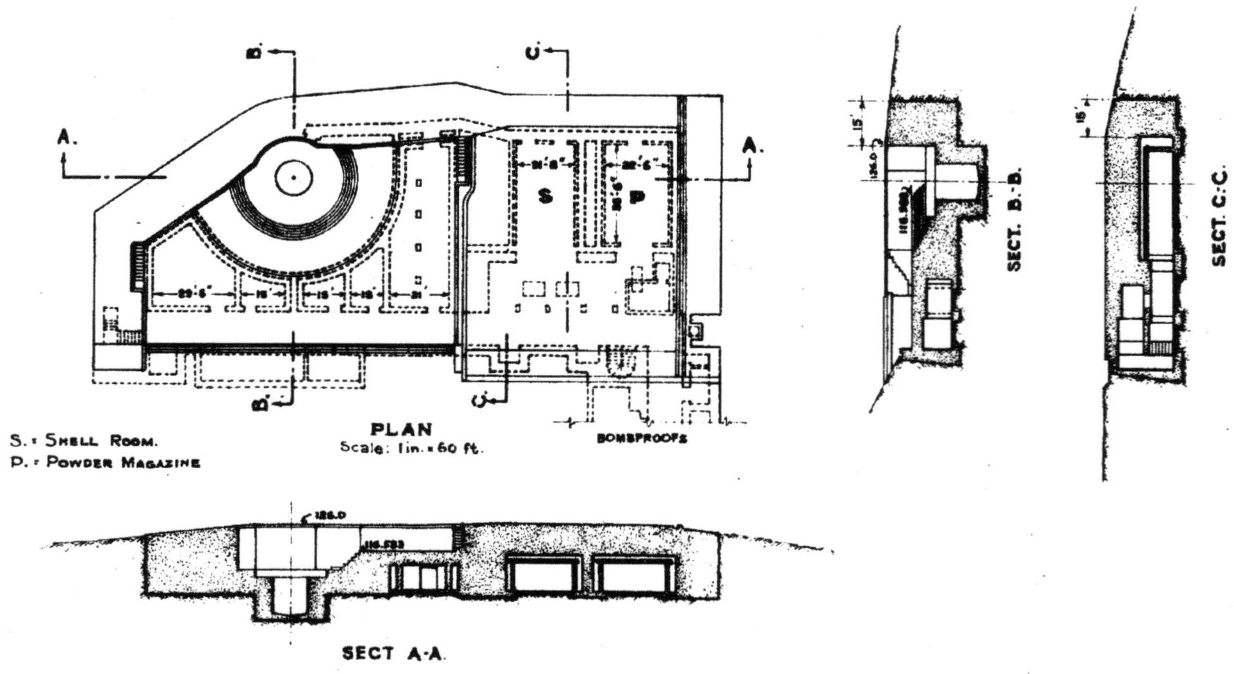

Plan, elevation, and section of Battery Crofton. NARA.

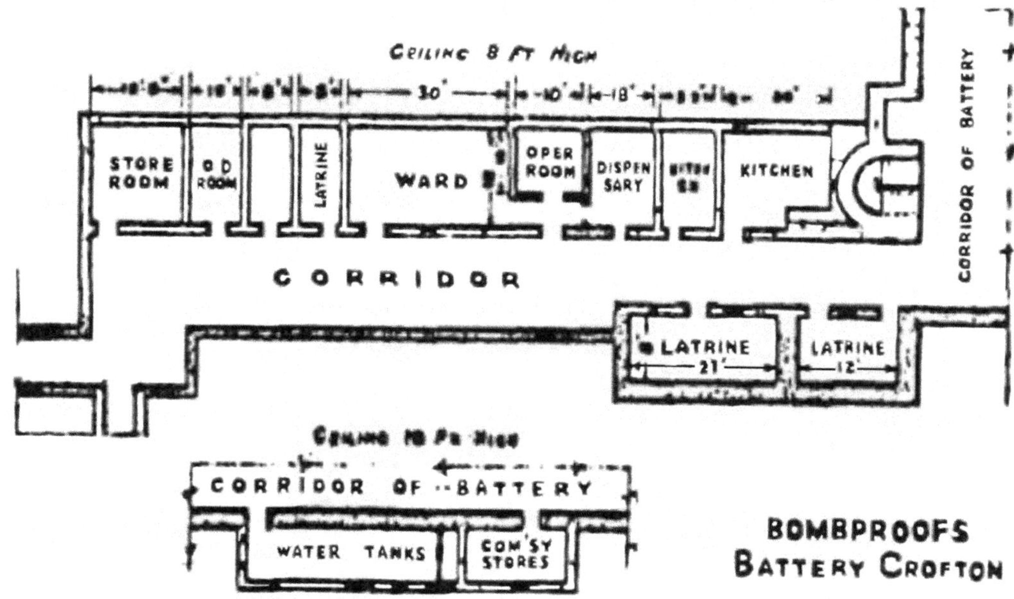

Layout of Crofton tunnel. NARA.

Battery Koehler (Eight 12-inch Mortars)

About 600 feet east of Battery Crofton, Lieutenant Robert started blasting out a site for the mortar battery in January 1909. It was situated atop the hog-back ridge that ran nearly the island's length and again considerable earth moving and rock crushing was required to make a place for the two large pits in which the powerful mortars would be emplaced. Like both gun emplacements, the two mortar pits and magazines were advanced

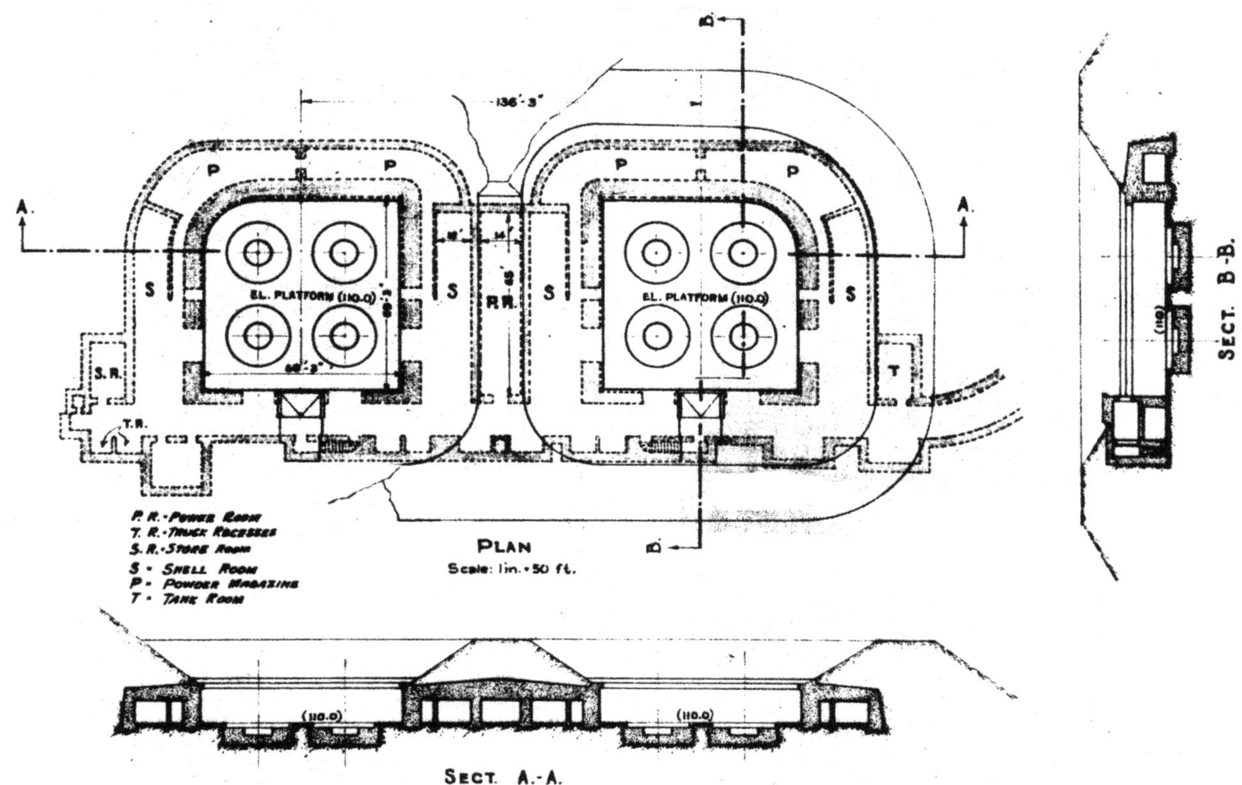

Plan, elevation, and section of Battery Koehler. NARA.

Model 1908 mortars of Battery Koehler. McGarraugh Collection.

to completion in 1913. The battery was built in general accordance with the 1912 standard plan with the powder magazines located to the battery's front and the shell rooms on the mortar pits flanks. The two pits were separated by a large traverse in which shell rooms and the power generator room was located. Storerooms and tool rooms were arranged around the sides and rear of the two pits. Like one pit at Battery Geary at Fort Mills, it was armed with eight 12-inch M1908 mortars on M1908 mortar carriages.[146] The mortar battery was named for 1st Lt. Edgar Frederick Koehler, 9th U.S. Infantry.[147]

Carabao's Fortifications Named Fort Frank

Work had scarcely commenced on Carabao when the island's fortifications were named Fort Frank by War Department General Orders, No. 15, January 28, 1909. Fort Frank was named for Brig. Gen. Royal Thaxter Frank of Maine. An 1858 West Point graduate, Frank initially served with the 5th Infantry and after promotion to captain he was assigned to the 8th Infantry with which he served through the Civil War. For his gallant and meritorious service, Frank was brevetted major for his service in the Peninsular Campaign of Virginia, and lieutenant colonel for service at Fredericksburg, Virginia. On December 15, 1870, he transferred to the 1st U.S. Artillery and by October 1894 had been advanced to colonel of the regiment. He was promoted to brigadier general, U.S. Volunteers, May 4, 1898, and to brigadier general in the Regular Army, October 17, 1899. General Frank retired October 18, 1899, and died in 1908 at age 72 in Washington, D.C.[148]

Officer quarters at Fort Frank built in 1915. NARA.

Temporary enlisted barracks, Fort Frank. NARA.

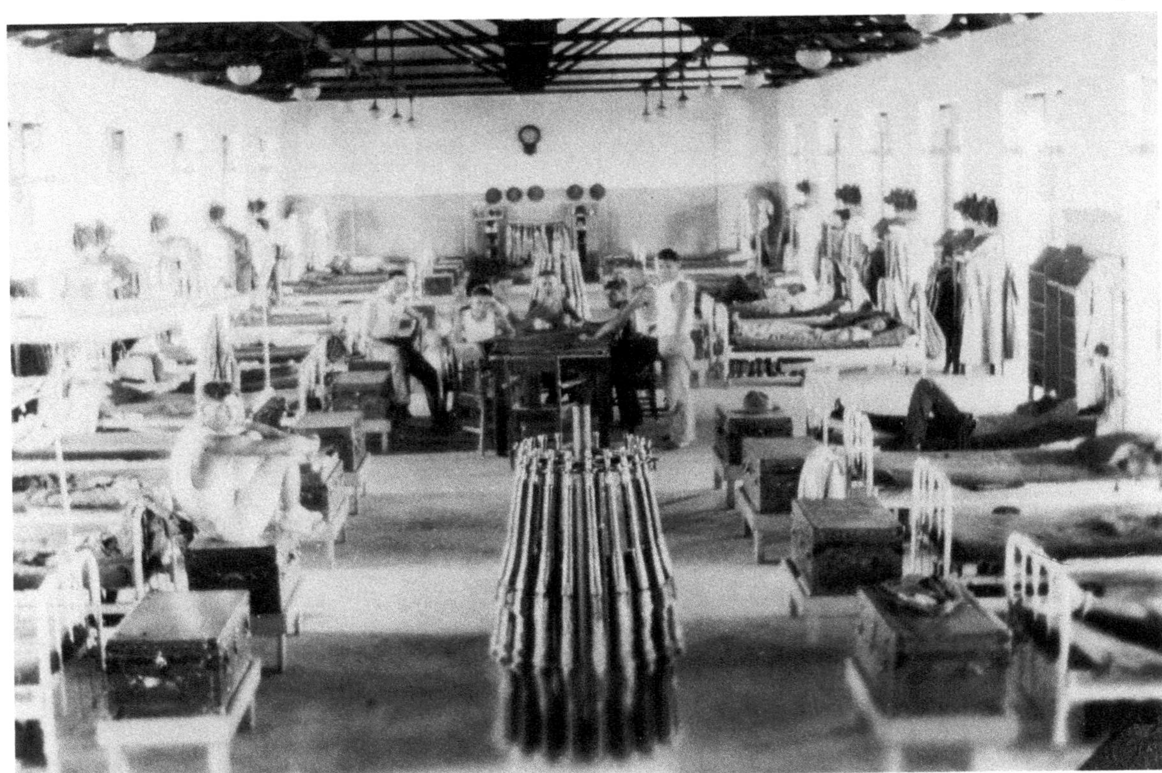

Fort Frank barracks. Interior view of one of the fort's barracks when manned by Battery D, 91st Coast Artillery, in 1930. Schmidt Collection.

Carabao Island's Vulnerabilities Addressed by Bombproofing Support Facilities

Even before construction was completed on the island's powerful gun and mortar batteries, the Philippine Islands Defense Board concluded that Carabao Island was near defenseless. It noted on June 24, 1910, that: "The nearest point on the mainland (to Carabao) is about 1,000 yards to the east. At a somewhat greater distance are concealed battery positions from which fire from mountain guns and small field mortars can be brought to bear on Carabao. To the south at right angles to the line of fire are commanding heights from which this fire can be observed and corrected." Under such circumstances, the heavy armament would soon be out of action. On November 27, 1912, as the batteries on Carabao neared completion, the board reiterated its concern: "An energetic enemy would have no difficulty in finding concealed and well protected positions in which to emplace mortars and howitzers. The extent of front available would permit him to widely disperse his armament and at the same time by means of many excellent viewpoints to concentrate his fire on any point on Carabao Island." The board further noted that heavy fire from the Cavite shore could force the garrison to seek shelter in the tunnel complex while a landing force approached the island unopposed.[149]

Almost every board or inspector who visited Carabao recognized the exposed nature of the island's emplacements and urged the provision of overhead cover or traverses to protect the gunners from defilade fire from the mainland. The 1912 Defense Board believed that just four mortars in Battery Koehler were sufficient and recommended that two mortars in each of Battery Koehler's pits be removed and the space used to provide overhead protection for the remaining mortars, but this recommendation was not favorably considered by the War Department.[150]

Nonetheless, considerable efforts were made to provide bombproof protection to the garrison and the fort's support facilities. While it was initially thought that this protection could be provided using the island's ridgeline as a natural parados, it soon became clear that the batteries would still be vulnerable to high angle fire. Approval was granted in June 1913 to modify the Carabao project by improving the garrison's protection. Additional protection centered around the narrow-gauge cargo tramway that began at the island's wharf and extended upward to the island's mid-point where it intersected with the fort's main tunnel. Rail cars powered from an engine room at the tramway's upper terminus carried supplies and other cargo up from the wharf. The island's 700-foot-long main tunnel was also provided with a narrow-gauge track that extended through the central part of the island north to Battery Greer, from which a short branch led further to the north and the outside. The main tunnel extending southward from Battery Greer (though a portion was left unprotected) to a branch where one gallery continued on for an additional 100 feet into Battery Koehler's Pit "B" while the another branch also of about 100 feet led to a short bridge over a narrow ravine onto the outcropping and on to Battery Crofton's galleries. This provided a network of bombproof galleries or tunnels offering a place of refuge for the fort's personnel, and connected the batteries, with their additional magazines, plotting rooms, fire control switchboards, quarters, and messing facilities, latrines, power generator rooms, as well as a dispensary and supply facilities. All were under an average of 20 feet of concrete and rock.[151]

As early as 1912, planning for the land defenses of Fort Frank had been undertaken, but it was not until the United States entered the World War in 1917 that work was done to implement the land defense system. Eight emplacements and small service magazines for 7-inch siege howitzers and a pair of emplacements for 6-pounder rapid-fire guns were built on the island's west and north peninsulas. The choice of 7-inch howitzers for this post reflects the continuing worry over bombardment from the shore just to the south. By the time the emplacements were completed, the armament contemplated for them was almost obsolete and replacement by more modern armament was projected in the years following the war.[152]

Although the island would require a minimum of two coast artillery companies to man its armament in wartime, it was not contemplated that in peacetime the island would be occupied by more than a small caretaking detachment to perform maintenance and guard the government property. A combination barracks, post exchange, and office was built near the island's middle point above the wharf area to house the peacetime

Water distilling plant at Fort Frank. NARA.

Calumpan dam on the Cavite shore in 1933. This dam collected fresh water for Fort Frank and supplied it by undersea pipe. A small, but sharp action was fought over the site's possession between the Americans and Japanese in early 1942. NARA.

garrison. The exchange was converted to a mess hall and kitchen in 1915. Two sets of officer's quarters were erected; one was a nipa and suali structure that had been occupied by the engineers while constructing the fortifications, the second of wood and galvanized iron on a concrete footing was not built until 1926. Quarters for eight NCOs were built in 1919. Two storehouses for quartermaster supplies were also built, one in 1910 and the other in 1919. A distilling plant was installed in 1917. An initial freshwater tank with a capacity of 58,344 gallons was built in 1909 and a second 3,196-gallon tank was built later. A 54,753-gallon reservoir filled by rainwater augmented the freshwater storage on the island.[153]

The 5,260-acre Calumpan Military Reservation on the mainland of Cavite Province east of Carabao was established by Executive Order April 11, 1902, to guard the harbor defenses' left flank land approaches. The reservation was to be occupied in wartime by field forces providing added protection to Fort Frank by occupying terrain that an enemy could otherwise use for artillery bombardment. No action was taken, however, beyond reserving the tract for military purposes until the late 1920s. In November 1929, a report was received in harbor defense headquarters that civilian natives had been trespassing on the reservation. Brig. Gen. Charles E. Kilbourne Jr., the harbor defense commander, recommended that a resident civilian guard be established on the reservation to prevent trespassing and to protect government property. This recommendation was not approved and finally after considerable discussion and further difficulties, including a destructive fire on the reservation, another request was submitted. The commander asked for permission to build a house for the use of guards, stating that the house was also expected to form the nucleus of a barrio to be constructed for the use of Filipino soldiers stationed at Fort Frank. Approval of this project was received in June 1931. Shortly after this, Kilbourne designated the limits of the "Calumpan Barrio" and vested its administration and control in the commanding officer, 91st C.A. Residence was restricted to enlisted personnel of Fort Frank and civilian government employees. Subsequent to that approval the 91st C.A. cleared, graded, and drained the land for the barrio, constructed the Sinalam River Dam, and the quartermasters built the first of nine projected double sets of wood-frame family quarters. Also projected was a combined schoolhouse and residence for a schoolteacher. At least one double set of quarters was occupied by the small detachment of the 91st C.A. that provided security to the reservation.[154]

Fort Frank turned out to be the least favorably placed of the harbor forts. Its closeness to the bay's southern shore was an inevitable product of geography. The fort's armament and garrison could not avoid being pummeled during any foreseeable siege. Indeed, this is what ensued, during the 1942 campaign it was the most damaged of the forts. Even with later efforts at bomb-proofing, the decision to emplace older style, exposed mortar pits and disappearing batteries on this heavily exposed location seem obviously debatable. Also, the location on the extreme southern flank of the bay meant that while the heavy guns here could (and did) certainly add to the defense of the harbor's entry, they could add far less to the land siege that eventually emerged. Army correspondence during the 1930s on several occasions suggested that the armament on Carabao could be better utilized by moving it to either Caballo or Corregidor.

Plans for Caballo Island

Located off the southern end of Corregidor's tail, Caballo Island was the geological extension of an extinct volcano rim. The terrain of Caballo's eastern third had an elevation of a scant ten feet above sea level. Nearly a quarter of the island's relatively flat eastern portion was occupied by a freshwater lake. The island's remainder was rugged with sheer cliffs rising to elevations in excess of 300 feet above the waters of Manila Bay terminating in a hog back rim. Although some preliminary survey work and clearing of sites for projected batteries commenced as early as 1904, planning for the island's armament was altered several times. The island was projected initially to consist of a pair of 10-inch disappearing guns and four 12-inch mortars, but appropriations earmarked for Caballo in the amount of $769,000 were not forthcoming until 1910. During the years prior to the commencement of construction, the 10-inch guns were dropped in favor of 12-in guns and these designs were eventually upgraded to 14-inch guns. Initially, six 6-inch guns were projected for the island, but plans were finally reduced to two guns. Early plans also called for two 3-inch guns. Ultimately the armament on Caballo Island would consist of two 14-inch guns, four 12-inch mortars, two 6-inch guns, and two 3-inch guns, with three searchlights.[155]

The projected work for Caballo Island was named Fort Hughes on December 13, 1909, to honor Maj. Gen. Robert P. Hughes, who died October 27, 1909. Hughes entered military service during the Civil War as a private in the 12th Pennsylvania Infantry on April 24, 1861, and after being discharged in August 1861, he

Caballo Island. NARA.

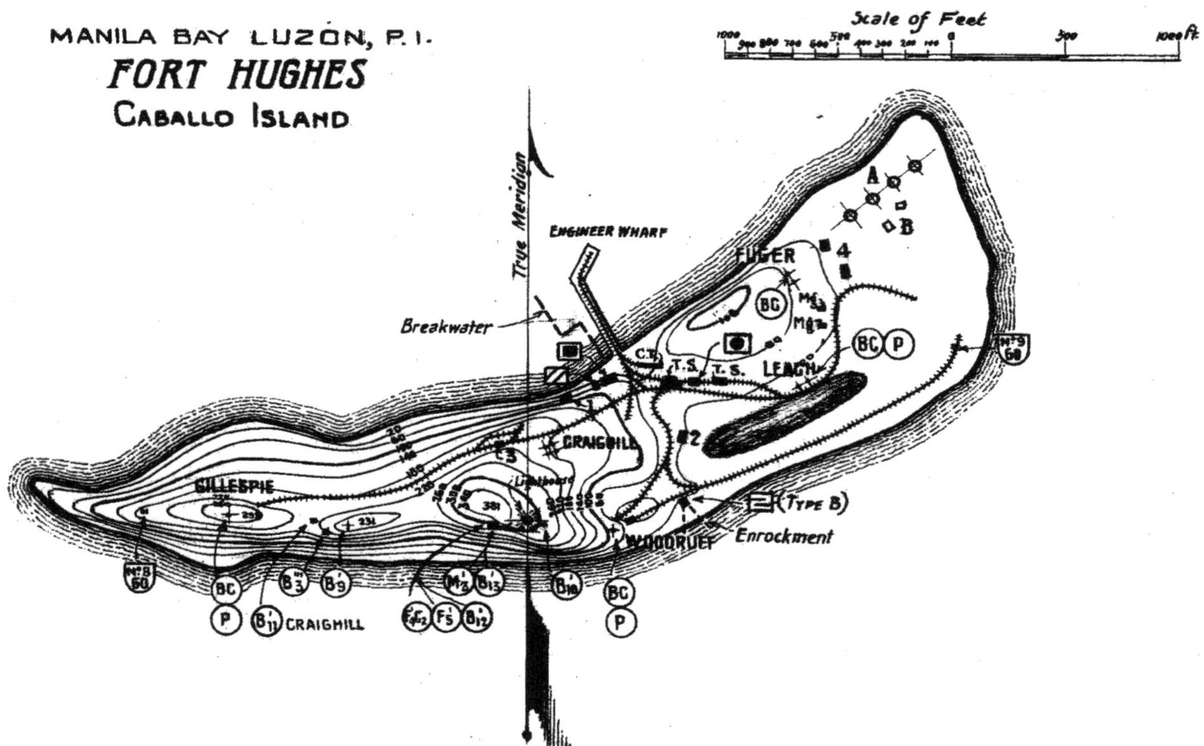

Fort Hughes map circa 1920. NARA.

was appointed a lieutenant the 85th Pennsylvania. On December 7, 1864, Hughes was appointed lieutenant colonel, 199th Pennsylvania Volunteer Infantry. For his gallant and distinguished service at Fort Gregg, near Richmond, Virginia, April 2, 1865, Hughes was promoted to brevet colonel, USV. After his mustering out at the war's end, Hughes was appointed a captain in the 18th U.S. Infantry. He was reassigned to the 3rd U.S. Infantry July 5, 1870. In 1885, he was transferred to the Inspector General's Office and promoted to major, February 19, 1885. A month later, he was advanced to lieutenant colonel and in August 1888 to colonel. On June 3, 1898, Hughes was appointed a brigadier general of volunteers. He attained that rank in the Regular Army February 5, 1901. On April 1, 1902, he was promoted to major general. General Hughes retired April 11, 1903, after 42 years of service.[156]

Maj. Charles W. Kutz, who had arrived in the Philippines September 2, 1911, oversaw the construction project on Caballo Island until January 1914. As work wound down on Caballo, engineering supervision on the island was turned over to 1st Lt. Charles J. Taylor, who arrived in the Philippines at the end of October 1914.[157]

Due to being the final installation of armament for the initial Manila Bay defenses, Fort Hughes received the most modern and advanced suite of coast artillery weapons. The 14-inch guns selected for emplacement were 14-inch/40-caliber M1910 guns, more powerful than the M1907 guns at Fort Frank. The island also received M1912 12-inch/15-caliber mortars; with a considerably improved range of 19,319 yards compared to the 15,291 yards of the previous M1890M1 and M1908 mortars at Forts Mills and Frank. This armament was similar to that installed at the final continental U.S. harbor to be armed, at Los Angeles, along with the defenses of the newly completed Panama Canal.

Battery Gillespie (One 14-inch Disappearing Gun)

Not until 1911 were funds finally made available to permit actual construction to commence on the first 14-inch disappearing gun emplacement. This first emplacement (Battery Gillespie) was situated on the west end of Caballo Island at an elevation of some 200 feet. Construction began in October 1911 and was advanced steadily to completion in 1914. The battery was pronounced complete from an engineering standpoint and transferred to the coast artillery on December 31, 1914.[158]

The increasing probability that the United States would become involved in the World War hastened the arming of Caballo Island's 14-inch batteries. The ammunition service for the 14-inch guns had not been fully installed when the battery was transferred, although Battery Gillespie had received its first Taylor-Raymond back-delivery projectile hoist. The Type A powder hoist was also received and installed in 1916 and transferred January 29, 1917. A second projectile hoist was received and installed during the summer of 1917. The M1910M1 14-inch gun for Battery Gillespie also arrived in early May 1917 and by July 30, 1917, had been mounted on its M1907MI disappearing carriage. The 14-inch batteries were soon modified to give additional range with increased elevation in a matter similar to that used on the 12-inch batteries at Fort Mills.[159]

On September 2, 1914, Caballo's four batteries were named in War Department General Orders, No. 63. The 14-inch disappearing gun emplacement atop the cliffs on the west end of the island was named Battery Gillespie for Brig. Gen. and former Chief of Engineers George Lewis Gillespie Jr.[160]

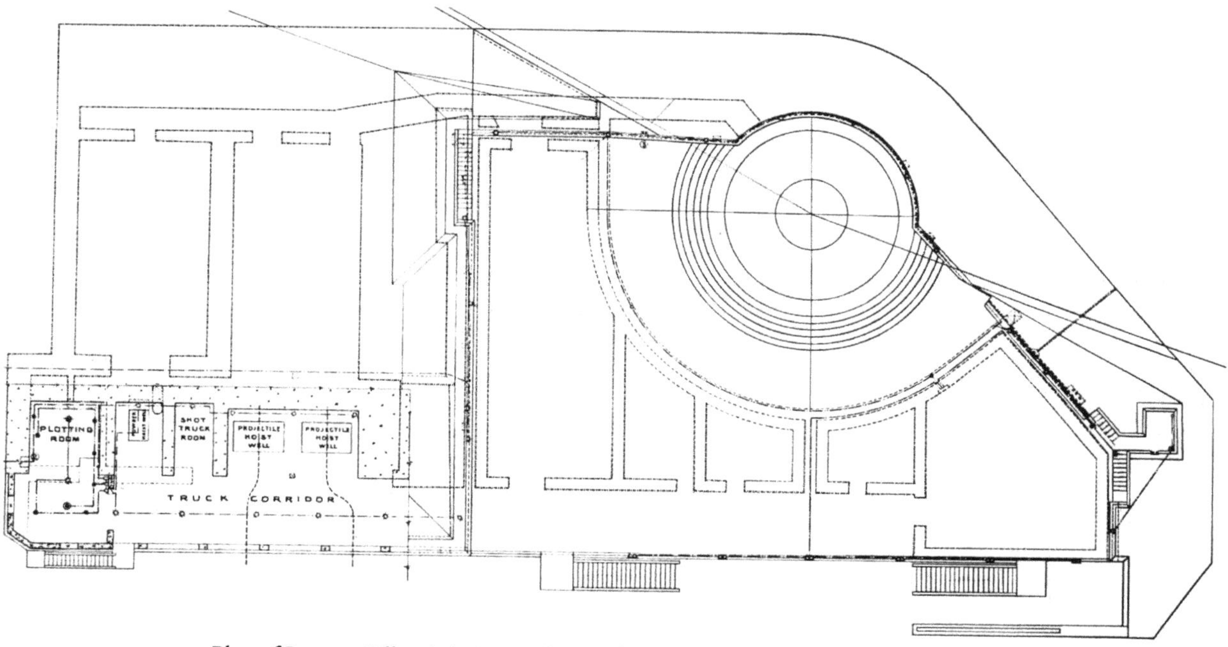

Plan of Battery Gillespie in 1925, after modifications of the plotting room. NARA.

Artillery drill at Battery Gillespie. Ruhlen Collection.

Battery Gillespie was a two-story, or horizontal crest battery similar to the batteries built on Carabao Island. Its projectiles were raised from the magazines by a Taylor-Raymond vertical back-delivery hoist transferred December 31, 1914. The hoist shaft opened onto a delivery table in the gallery at the rear of the battery structure, from which the ammunition was conveyed to the loading platform on ammunition carts.

Battery Woodruff (One 14-inch Disappearing Gun)

The second 14-inch emplacement was begun in November 1911 on the south side of the island about 50 feet above the water at the foot of the steep western slopes. On September 2, 1914, the battery was named to honor Brig. Gen. Carl Augustus Woodruff. While from a construction standpoint the two 14-inch gun batteries had been completed by 1914, they had not been armed. Battery Woodruff was transferred to the coast artillery in December 1914.[161]

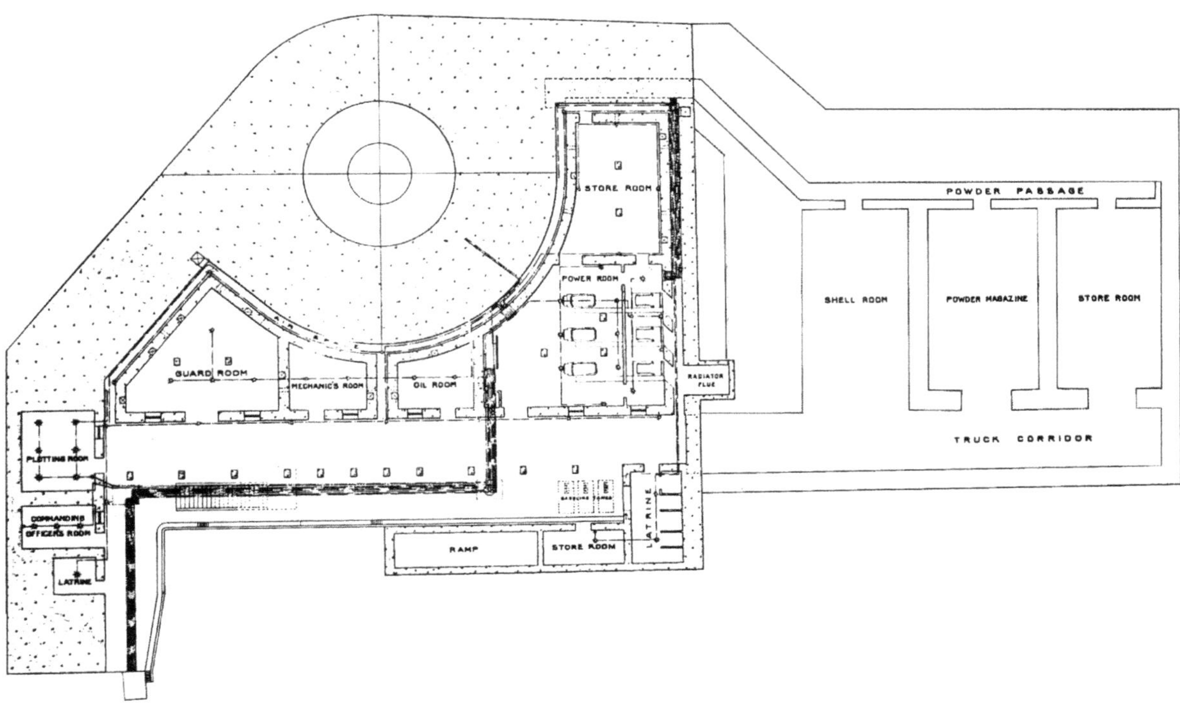

Lower level plan of Battery Woodruff, as completed in 1915. NARA.

Artillery drill at Battery Woodruff by Battery G, 59th Coast Artillery, in 1933. McGarraugh Collection.

Battery Woodruff's design differed from that of Battery Gillespie. It was a one-story battery where the magazine floor and loading platform were on the same level and the projectiles and powder charges were loaded onto the ammunition carts in the magazines and moved directly to the gun. Evidently, salt water was used in the making the battery's concrete. This caused the reinforcing railroad iron used to strengthen the concrete to corrode and weaken the structure that in later years resulted in the considerable flaking of the concrete when the gun was fired. Rather large chunks of concrete broke off the battery walls and fell onto the loading platform, creating a hazard to the gun crew. Consequently, the battery was taken out of service in the late 1930s (although restored during the 1941-42 campaign). The last M1910MI 14-inch gun for Fort Hughes arrived May 5, 1917, and was emplaced on its M1907MI disappearing carriage in Battery Woodruff.[162]

Battery Leach (Two 6-inch Disappearing Guns)

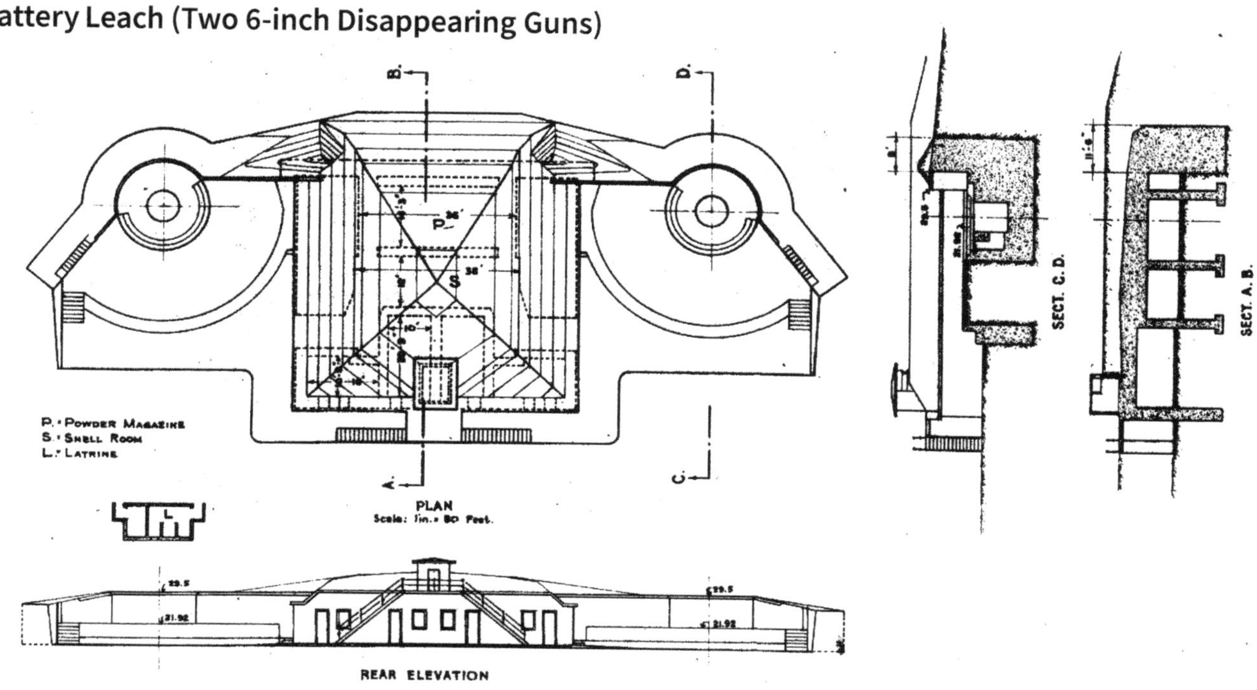

Report of Completed Works plan, elevation, and section for Battery Leach. NARA.

No. 1 6-inch disappearing un of Battery Leach in its retracted (loading) position. USAMHI.

This battery's site was on the island's "flat" portion north of the lake. Its field of fire bore to the south to cover the Boca Grande Channel. This battery was begun in May 1912 and was completed by December 1914. It was armed with a pair of 6-inch M1908 wire-wrapped guns on M1908MII disappearing carriages. The battery was transferred to the garrison June 30, 1919, along with the 14-inch batteries. The battery was named for Col. Smith Stallard Leach.[163]

Battery Leach was built in accordance with the approved 1903 standardized type plan for 6-inch seacoast guns on disappearing carriages. The two M1908 guns were shipped to the Philippines in July 1917. The projectiles were delivered to the loading platform by a projectile cart from the magazine exits at the rear of the central traverse located between the gun emplacements. The powder charges were delivered to the guns manually through a corridor at the front of the magazine traverse that exited to the loading platforms adjacent to the front parapet. Its only subsequent modification appears to be the installation of a coincidence rangefinder in 1917.[164]

Battery Craighill (Four 12-inch Mortars)

On September 27, 1913, the secretary of war directed the project for the defense of Manila Bay revised to include a battery of four mortars on the eastern slopes of Caballo Island above Battery Woodruff. The plans for this battery called for two pits, each armed with a pair of M1912 12-inch mortars. Plans were approved on April 4, 1914. Fort Hughes' mortar battery was a considerably modified version of the standard Type 1912 mortar battery. This departure from the standardized plan was required by the topographical constraints imposed by the island. Its two mortar pits were each to be armed with a pair of mortars with the forward pit being some 10 feet above the rear pit. The powder magazines were at the front of the pits with shell rooms on either

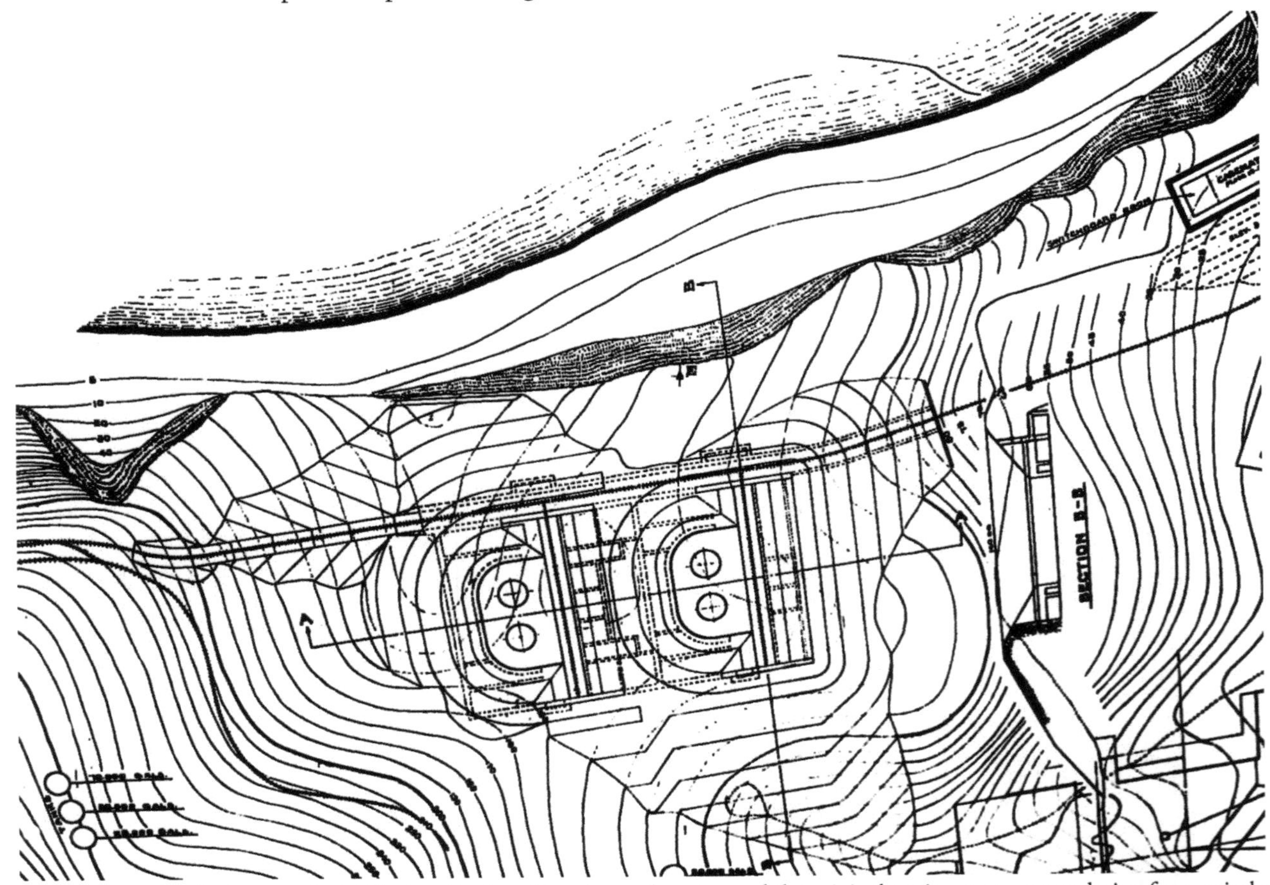

Site selection plan for Battery Craighill, Fort Hughes. Plan shows elevation and the original engineer recommendation for precisely where the battery was to be located. NARA.

side of the pits. Plotting rooms and storerooms were arranged along the rear of each pit. Later that year the type mortar carriages for the battery were established as M1896MIII. Although construction began in 1914, it was not completed until 1919, when its four M1912 mortars were emplaced. The battery was transferred to the garrison June 30, 1919.[165]

Battery G, 59th Coast Artillery, personnel in Battery Craighill (left) and firing one of the Model 1912 mortars of Battery Craighill at Fort Hughes, about 1934 (right). McGarraugh Collection.

On April 25, 1916, the battery was named for Brig. Gen. William Price Craighill.[166] Like Fort Frank, measures were taken to provide bombproofing protection for the garrison in the form of tunnels that connected Battery Craighill with the wharf. The various fortification elements were served by a sheltered narrow-gauge railroad that extended the length of the island. As work wound down on the gun and mortar batteries at the end of the World War, measures were taken to provide for the island's land defenses. Emplacements were prepared for eight 7-inch siege howitzers on the island's east end. Machine gun emplacements were also built to cover the wharf, and concrete revetted infantry trenches were constructed on the island's eastern slope.[167]

As at Fort Frank, garrison accommodations at Fort Hughes were minimal. The quarters used by the engineers during the battery construction phase were eventually turned over to the quartermaster and served as one of two sets of officers' quarters, home to the junior officer on the island outpost. A second and far more suitable set occupied by the senior officer on the island was built in 1919 of wood with a galvanized-iron roof and concrete foundation. In 1920 a 60 by 190-foot wood-frame barracks for 132 men that also housed a kitchen, mess hall, and quartermaster storerooms was erected on the island. It was set on a concrete foundation atop concrete piles, had wood floors, and a galvanized iron roof. Two single sets of quarters of galvanized iron construction built to accommodate civilian employees during the building of the fort were adapted for use as single sets of NCO quarters. While Fort Hughes had no water distillation plant, the island fort received regular supplies of fresh water barged over from Corregidor or from Sisiman Cove on Bataan, pumped into an 80,000-gallon freshwater tank. A saltwater tank with a capacity of 48,000 gallons provided water for the sanitary system.[168]

Junior officers' quarters at Fort Hughes. NARA.

Barracks at Ft. Hughes. NARA.

El Fraile Island Chosen for Fort Drum

El Fraile, about halfway between the islands of Caballo and Carabao, only measured about 350 feet by 150 feet and was surmounted by a 90-foot rock pinnacle. The 12 cm guns on that small isle had been one of the few Spanish batteries to fire on Dewey's squadron when it entered Manila Bay in 1898. Initially El Fraile was considered by the United States as a potential location for observation, fire control, and as a torpedo (submarine mine) casemate. Two structures were initially slated for construction on the site formerly occupied by the Spanish battery of quick-firing guns.[169]

The first U.S. defensive structure built on El Fraile Island was a mine casemate, part of the initial mine project for Manila Bay proposed in 1904. Work was funded either by the Fiscal Year 1904 or 1905 appropriations. Excavation into the volcanic rock to the west or rear of the old Spanish gun platform on the island's eastern end got underway in 1907. The casemate was connected to the platform by a short tunnel. Also planned, but not built, were two double mine observation stations almost directly above the casemate. This mine casemate was the most short-lived of the American defenses of Manila Bay. It probably served for less than two years and was never completely equipped. A new plan emerging in 1908 for an entirely new defensive work on the island preempted this work.[170]

El Fraile rock September 1909. NARA.

Because of Fort Frank's vulnerability to fire from the Cavite mainland, closure of Boca Grande channel took on an even greater importance as the already strained relations between Japan and the United States worsened during the 20th century's first decade. A concept was put forward for construction of an artificial island on a shoal just south of El Fraile. When considered by the Coast Artillery Board at Fort Monroe the proposal was judged too costly and its effectiveness questionable. First Lt. John J. Kingman, serving on Corregidor in connection with the construction of its fortifications, proposed on July 18, 1908, that El Fraile be utilized instead as it would be a more effective defense and be far less costly to construct than an artificial island. Kingman's initial proposal called for reducing the island to near water level and building an elliptical two-story concrete structure mounting two pairs of 12-inch guns in turrets on the structure's roof. The turrets were originally to have 21 to 24 inches of nickel steel on the sides and 8 to 10 inches of armor on their tops. The structure itself was to have exterior walls 30 feet thick and the roof or top deck 10 feet of concrete. The magazines were to be built to accommodate 200 rounds of ammunition for each gun. The fort's electric power would be provided by gasoline generators producing 350 kW of electricity for interior lighting, searchlights, and powering the motors that would traverse and elevate the guns, operate the power rammers, run the navy-type ammunition hoists, fans, air compressors, pumps, and even the stoves in the galley. This proposal would undergo a number of changes over the next several months, but Kingman's basic concept would be adopted.[171]

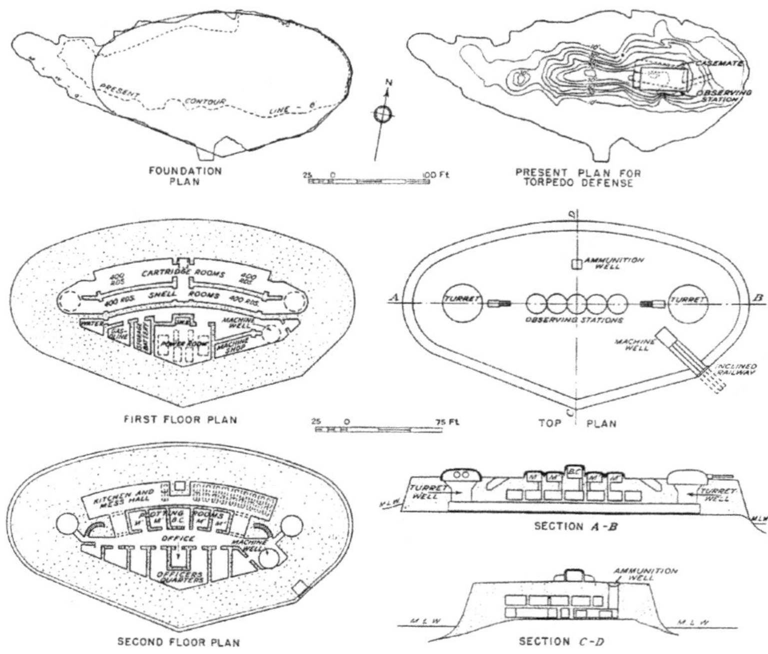

Kingman's original concepts for a fort on El Fraile island. USAMHI.

Final Design for Fort Drum

The final design for the projected fort on El Fraile was eventually completed and its construction authorized. The revised plan saw the work's original trace altered from an ellipsis to one composed of straight lines in the form of an irregular octagon that gave the structure the general shape of a ship. During the early planning, it was determined that the island's area was too limited to permit construction of the standard size emplacements for four 12-inch guns on disappearing carriages (the next progressive change to Kingman's turret

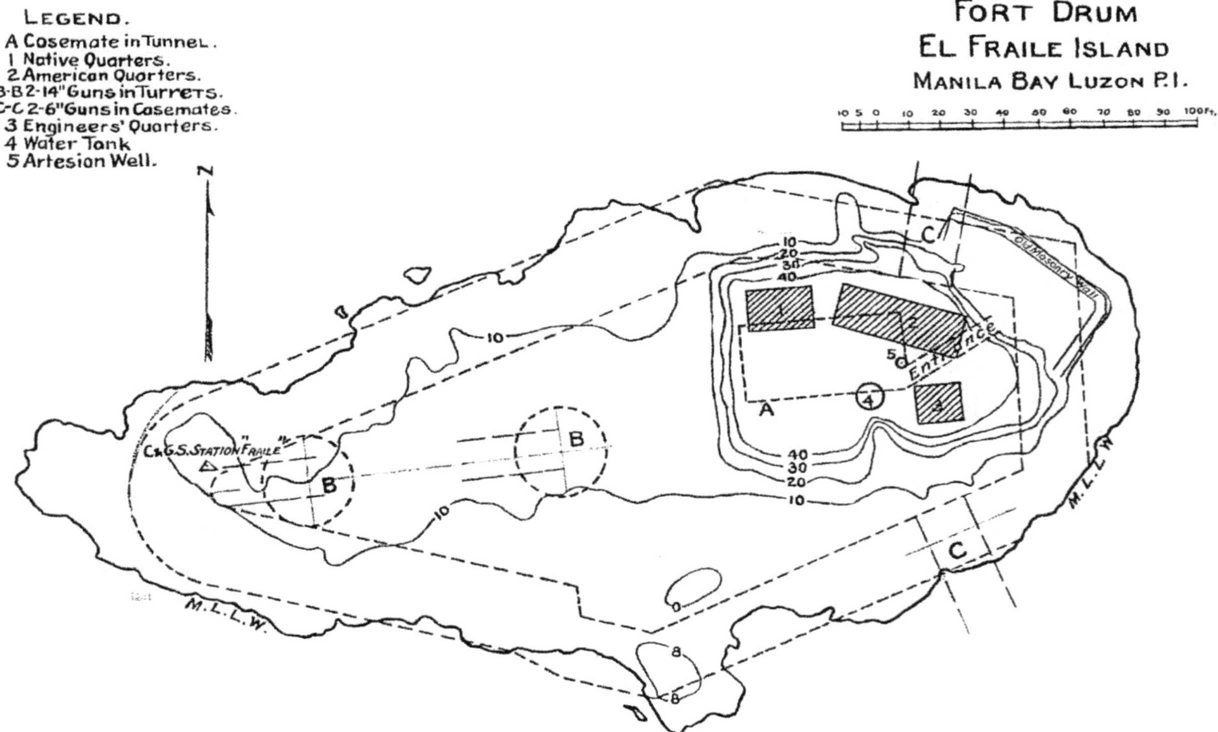

Proposed fortification plan for El Fraile rock about 1910; note early decision to concentrate the armament in two turrets. NARA.

plan) as were projected for the other fortified islands. Ultimately, the primary armament would be increased from four 12-inch disappearing guns to four 14-inch turret-mounted guns at the fort's western end, with the rear turret firing above the forward turret. Although the Endicott Board had envisioned turrets for use in the American coastal defenses as early as 1886, turrets had proven twice as expensive to produce as standard disappearing gun batteries. The pair of turrets authorized for El Fraile became the first and only such turrets to be manufactured for American fixed coastal defenses. In addition, two secondary batteries, each consisting of two 6-inch guns, were added to the fort's defenses. These guns would be emplaced in casemates on the fort's port and starboard sides; one gun mounted above the other behind sponsons reminiscent of the secondary batteries on turn-of-the-century warships.[172]

Landing for the mine cable and location of a proposed mine casemate on El Fraile, 1908. Note the partially demolished brick masonry work of Spanish Battery Lezo. NARA.

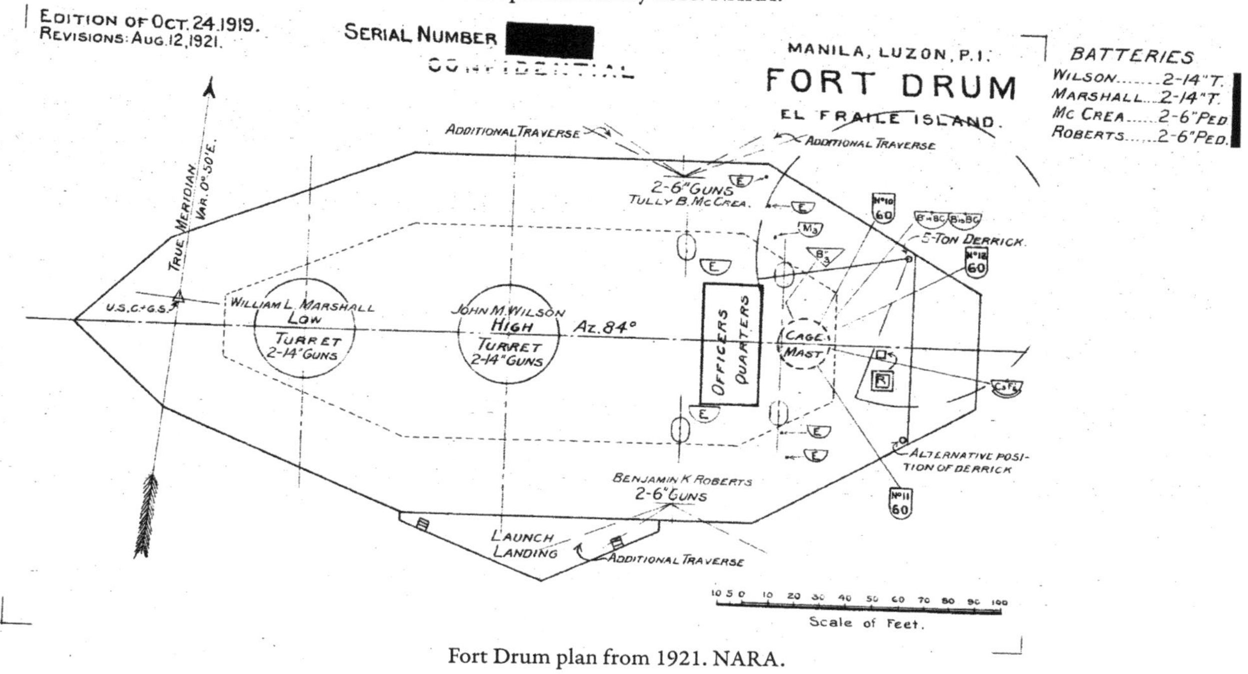

Fort Drum plan from 1921. NARA.

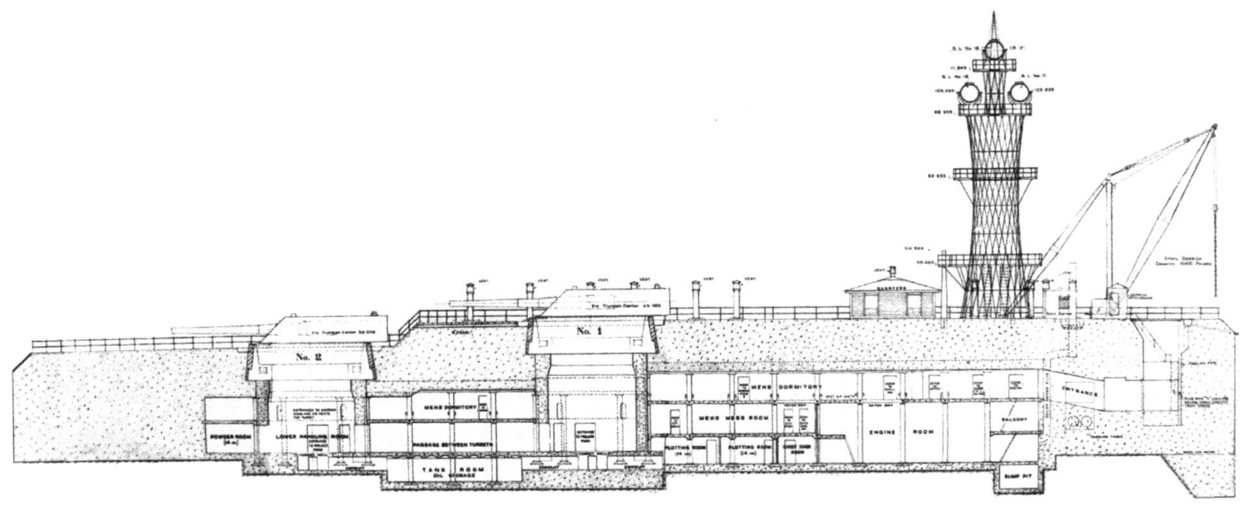

Cross-section plan for Fort Drum. Plan dates from 1919, about the time of the fort's completion. This view clearly reveals the interior subdivision with the ammunition storage and handling rooms forward, below the turrets, and the accommodation and power plant in the large spaces toward the aft portion of the structure. NARA.

Once approved for construction, $1,408,000 was appropriated for the four 14-inch guns and the two turrets. They were begun in 1911 and completed in 1915. The M1909 turrets were manufactured at the Newport News Shipbuilding and Dry Dock Company, Newport News, Virginia. The four M1909 14-inch guns were built at Watervliet Arsenal, New York, while their M1909 turret carriages were fabricated at Watertown Arsenal, Massachusetts.[173]

El Fraile Military Reservation Named Fort Drum

On December 13, 1909, the El Fraile Military Reservation was renamed for Brig. Gen. Richard Coulter Drum. General Drum entered military service as a private in the 1st Pennsylvania Infantry December 16, 1846, during the War with Mexico. He was appointed second lieutenant of infantry in the Regular Army February 18, 1847, and assigned to the 9th U.S. Infantry Regiment. For his gallant and meritorious service at the Battle of Chapultepec, Mexico, during the War with Mexico, he was given the brevet rank of first lieutenant. Drum transferred to the 4th U.S. Artillery March 8, 1848. During the Civil War Drum was brevetted colonel and brigadier general in 1864 and 1865 respectively. He was promoted to Brig. Gen. and Adjutant General of the Army June 15, 1880. He retired May 28, 1889, and died October 15, 1909.[174]

Construction of Fort Drum

On March 8, 1909, authority was granted to commence the works on El Fraile. The process of excavation began the very next month. A cofferdam in the form of a breakwater of timber cribs filled with stone was erected around the projected fort's perimeter. The island's leveling began in 1910 and continued into 1911. With the breakwater complete, pouring the concrete foundation began in 1912 and gradually the structure rose above the bay. Work progressed until June 1918, when the fort was completed. During those nine years, the island was transformed into a warship-shaped reinforced concrete structure some 350 feet long and 144 feet wide, arranged to carry two twin 14-inch gun turrets and their barbettes. The fort's interior contained a large engine room, offices, plotting rooms, magazines for powder and projectiles, storerooms, barracks, mess rooms, a kitchen, and fuel and water tanks.[175]

Construction underway at Fort Drum in 1914. Note barbette at left with a part of the construction plant at right. NARA.

One of the 14-inch turrets during testing at Sandy Hook Proving Ground prior to delivery in the Philippines. NARA.

Fort Drum's Armament

The fabrication of the massive turrets of Fort Drum's main battery of 14-inch guns that were about twice the size and weight of American naval turrets of that era was completed in 1915. One turret was forwarded to the Army Proving Ground at Sandy Hook, New Jersey, where it underwent tests for several weeks before being declared ready for shipment to the Philippines. The mounts for the gun were completed by 1916 and two were shipped from the Watertown Arsenal to Manila on February 29, 1916. The second pair was forwarded from Watertown March 6, 1916, and arrived in Manila along with the M1909 turrets on May 16, 1916. The four 14-inch M1909 wire-wrapped guns were specifically developed and produced for this fortification, and delivered by the army's regularly scheduled transports to Manila. One gun was received on June 10, 1916, two were received November 27, 1916, and the final tube on May 5, 1917. The turrets were delivered disassembled and transported to the fort for reassembly. By June 1918, the assembly of the gun carriages and turret assemblies had begun and the armament installed. The fort was transferred to the Coast Artillery on June 17.[176]

In addition to the Corps of Engineers professional staff and the labor provided mostly by Bilibid prisoners, American contract workers were frequently needed for specific skilled tasks. A good example of this was for the assembly and erection of the massive 14-inch gun turrets at Fort Drum. The contract proposal the army's Ordnance Department offered to a Mr. Harry Whitely in Newport News, Virginia, in mid-1915 is illustrative of both the business arrangement and conditions at the work site. The salient points of this offer were:[177]

> Monthly pay of $130, from the day the journey starts to El Fraile to the day you return to Newport News. Quartered in or near the work in government buildings. There are no quarters available for a family—those are only available in Manila and would be entirely at the worker's own expense. There is no charge for quarters.
>
> Subsistence will be provided free of cost. There will be a travel allowance during transit to and from El Fraile. Meals taken in Manila or other locations away from the work site will be at your own expense.
>
> Medical care provided by a hospital steward. There is no physician or surgeon at the work site, serious cases will be provided carefree of charge at Corregidor Island. Pay for sickness will be at a maximum for 60 days/year. If injured during work, full pay will be given during disability not to exceed one year.
>
> Transportation to site will be furnished. Includes railway sleeping car accommodations to San Francisco and then army transport to Manila.
>
> Governed by army regulations as regularly in force. Previous employer (Newport News Shipbuilding and Drydock Company) expected to retain a place for you in their employment upon return.

The turret's armor was 18 inches thick in the front and 14 inches on the sides and rear, while the turret tops were from 4.5 to 6-inch thick. Each turret had four levels. The uppermost was the gun compartment that was 10 feet 3 inches long and was divided longitudinally down its centerline by a fireproof bulkhead. This compartment contained the guns, the sighting and command equipment, gun crew, and loading mechanism. Below the gun compartment was the upper handling room. Here the lower ammunition hoists receiving ends were located. The munitions were removed from the lower hoists and transferred to the upper hoists for delivery to the loading mechanism in the gun compartment. The upper handling room was also divided along its length. Below the upper handling room was the electrical compartment, where the switchboards that controlled the power for the various mechanisms in the turrets, the ventilation fans, motor generators, and air compressors for the guns were installed. The hoist shafts were enclosed on this level. Below the electrical compartment was the lower handing room, where the concrete walls of the barbette opened onto the passages to the projectile and powder magazines. Projectile service from the magazines to the lower handing room was provided by overhead rail system common in large-caliber gun batteries. Powder was moved by hand to the lower hoist. The lower M1909 14-inch gun turret had a traverse of 230° with its capital bearing 270°. The upper turret had a 360° traverse.

Port quarter view of Fort Drum. Note the sally port near the fort's stern and the temporary barrack at the upper deck. Ruhlen Collection.

Fort Drum batteries Wilson (lower) and Marshall (upper). Ruhlen Collection.

Fort Drum's secondary armament consisted of four 6-inch M1908MII guns and their M1910 barbette mounts and sponson type casemate shields that arrived from 1914 to 1916; by early 1917 all had been mounted in their casemates. One pair of guns was emplaced in the fort's port (north) side; the second pair on the fort's starboard (south) side. In each case, one gun was emplaced above the other in a semicircular armored casemate behind 6-inch-thick armored sponson shields in separate casemates.[178]

The 6-inch ammunition service was similar to that of the main battery in that they were supplied with projectiles and powder charges by M1914 Crocker-Wheeler electrically operated hoists that raised the munitions from magazines located below the casemates.[179]

The batteries at Fort Drum remained unnamed until 1922, when General Orders, No. 13, March 27, 1922, named the lower 14-inch turret Battery William L. Marshall for Brig. Gen. William L. Marshall and the upper turret Battery John M. Wilson for Brig. Gen. John M. Wilson. The two 6-inch batteries at Fort Drum were also named in G.O. No. 13. The guns on the fort's northern side were named in honor of Brig. Gen. Tully McCrea, the southern battery was named for Brig. Gen. Benjamin Kearney Roberts.[180]

Fort Drum Garrison Facilities

With the fort and its batteries completed, a company of coast artillerymen would be earmarked as Fort Drum's garrison. During peacetime, the assigned company, quartered on Corregidor, would provide a small caretaking detachment, periodically rotated, to maintain the fort. The constrained size of Fort Drum presented real challenges in planning for a garrison. As projected in early 1911 the full wartime complement of two full-strength companies would total about 300 men. The wartime garrison was broken down as:[181]

72	14-in gun crews	6 men/gun x 3 relief crews
60	Ammunition detail	5 men/gun x 3 relief crews
36	6-in gun crews	3 men/gun x 3 relief crews
60	Ammunition detail	5 men/gun x 3 relief crews
60	Fire control	5 men/observing station x 3 relief crews
60	Plotting Room	5 men/observing station x 3 relief crews
9	Searchlights	
6	Meteorological Station	
9	Dynamo Room	
6	Engine Room	
9	Switchboard	

387 Subtotal, reduced to 258 if only two reliefs (recommended)

4	Cooks
12	Hospital Corps
20	Extras

294-300 men and allow for 20 officers

Following World War I the garrison was reduced to a single company housed on Corregidor. Allowance for rations was pegged at supplies for 60 days. That translated to 500 square feet of storage. Included in that storage were coolers for supplies of fresh vegetables and 30 days' worth of fresh beef in cold storage. The magazines were to hold a total of 444 rounds for the 14-inch guns, and 2,016 rounds for the 6-inch guns. This calculated to a 50% additional overage for 14-inch, and 100% for 6-inch versus regular emplacement guidelines. After some debate, the mining casemate incorporated 29 cable connections—sufficient for that number of groups.

Interior of barrack at Fort Drum. Note the bunks at right and the rifle rack on the left. Colonel Welch Collection.

Fort Drum was initially provided with seven high-compression General Electric diesel engines. This type was a relatively new innovation—they ran at a higher speed and theoretically generated more horsepower than the older, slower style. But as often happens, all the mechanical problems had not yet been worked out. The engines and generators were purchased under a contract of September 17, 1912, delivered in 1915 and installed by the end of 1916. The plant was run for the first time on October 25, 1916. They never lived up to expectation and were very prone to mechanical failure. Finally in 1924, the army asked for $200,000 for replacing these engines with three more conventional low-speed engines. This was done, and finally a dependable electrical power system was available for this important post. In the tank room off the engine room were tanks with a capacity of 60,000 gallons of diesel fuel.[182]

Completing the list of internal rooms were a complete machine shop, a water distillation plant, an ice plant, commanding officer's office, bedroom, and toilet. Subordinate officers had a dormitory with bunks and toilet. The enlisted men's barracks on the barrack floor contained 336 bunks and a latrine. Officer's had their own mess, as did enlisted men. The kitchen was equipped with three ranges, a steam coffee urn, two steam kettles, and sinks. Commissary storerooms, a laundry with 21 tubs, and a centrifuge dryer were included. Finally, the small hospital had its own toilet, operating room, storeroom, and a ward with 24 bunks. A timber one-story 24 by 48-foot dormitory type building with a galvanized iron roof was built on the fort's upper deck for the engineers during construction. The dormitory was retained as quarters for the caretaking detachment because it was cooler and could accommodate 12 men. This building was provided with a 12-foot-wide awning around

Kitchen at Fort Drum was equipped to serve more than a hundred men. NARA.

Fort Drum mess hall. Colonel Welch Collection.

its four sides. As a further shield from the sun, two 66-foot-long and 28-foot-wide tents were positioned on either side of Battery Wilson. [183]

Fort Drum became the pride of the American defenses. The robustness of the design — a virtually impregnable citadel with powerful guns fully protected by stout turrets of wide traverse - was both impressive to any observer and held up well during the campaign. Despite the heavy aerial and gun bombardment in 1941-42, its service was never interrupted. The guns were firing, the ammunition still adequate, the garrison still full of fight when the fort was ordered to surrender in 1942. Unlike Fort Frank, the design of Fort Drum seems to have been a much wiser concept — though obviously at the cost of time (it took nine years from start to finish) and immense expense. It was so expensive it was never duplicated by American engineers anywhere else.

Originally built to house the engineers during construction, this temporary building was later adapted for use as a barracks for Fort Drum's caretaking detachment. NARA.

Fort Drum rear view. NARA.

CHAPTER 7
FIRE CONTROL AND ELECTRICAL SYSTEMS, MANNING THE FORTIFICATIONS

Planning the Fire Control System

Between 1908 and 1909 the Philippine engineer division developed and submitted ideas for the fire control plans to go with the batteries being constructed. Organizationally there were to be two separate artillery districts for Subic and Manila Bays. In Manila Bay the Artillery District Headquarters would, when all batteries were built, have two "Battle Commands" — a northern battle command made up of the batteries at Forts Mills and Hughes, and a southern battle command composed of the batteries at Forts Frank and Drum. Nearly all the fire control stations possessed adequate elevation to enable utilization of vertical position finding systems with range and azimuth data provided from depression position finder (DPF) instruments. The horizontal baseline system employed in the harbor defenses in the continental U.S. would only be used in the Philippines in special cases.[184]

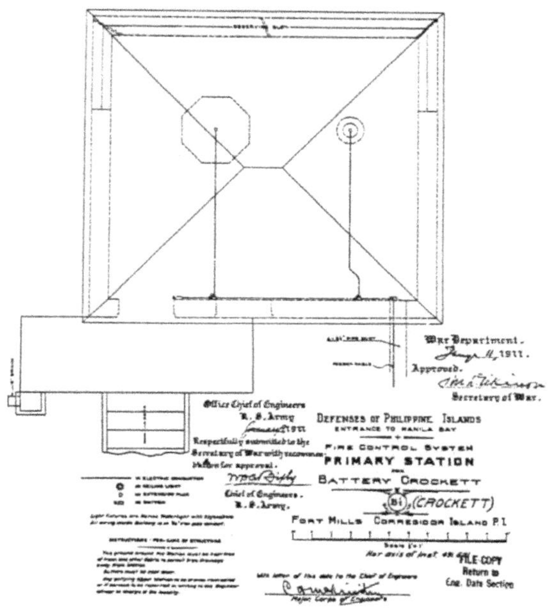

This station was originally constructed as B' Station for Battery Crockett and was transferred on February 9, 1911. It was abandoned as such on February 21, 1912, when a new replacement station was built for the battery. The building was later included in the Fire Control Project for 14-inch guns at Fort Frank and Hughes and transferred once again as part of that project on April 20, 1922. NARA.

Each major battery would have a primary station (B') equipped with a DPF instrument. These primary stations would be a safe distance from the battery itself and have a good view of the battery's field of fire. Each battery would also receive a battery commander's station (BCS). At least at the large-caliber disappearing gun batteries, the BCS would also have a DPF instrument. Plotting rooms were typically located at the battery, often directly adjacent to or below the BCS. There were exceptions to this general plan. At Fort Frank, the plotting rooms were located at the primary stations; at Fort Drum the plotting room was located deep within the "concrete battleship."[185]

The mortar batteries had a differing problem and solution. Because they were located in remote, protected positions, it was not possible to see targets from the batteries. Consequently, the primary stations for the mortar batteries would be combined with the BCS and plotting rooms. Additionally, as they could place fire on both the north and south channels, separate facilities had to be built to cover either, and in turn each location would have fire control stations for both Battery Way and Geary; as well as an additional room for their separate fire command. Eventually even a west and east mortar station was built in order to have a sort of baseline to use for firing at land targets on Bataan.[186]

Rear view of B' Station for Battery Wheeler. NARA.

Original three-story North Mortar Station before its demolition. NARA.

Problems with the Initial Fire Control Stations

Within days of his arrival on Corregidor, Captain Kilbourne began discovering shortfalls in the fire control station locations built concurrent with the batteries. Apparently, the stations built in 1908-1909 were either done improperly or were situated at poorly selected sites. As mentioned previously, the combination BCS and B' station for Battery Grubbs was built at an inappropriate location, placing its position finding station 50 yards to the battery's rear and only about 10 feet higher than the battery's superior crest. It had to be torn out and replaced.[187]

While the fire control stations for Topside's 12-inch batteries were sited to provide good observation of the north and south channels, the same could not be said about the batteries themselves. Battery Wheeler was so positioned that when it fired at targets in the Boca Chica channel, its shots passed over its own station as well as the position-finding stations of the other two 12-inch batteries. It was doubtful that the fire control stations of Batteries Cheney and Crockett could do any work when Battery Wheeler was in action. Even Battery Wheeler's own BCS was threatened. Kilbourne elaborated: "If guns were pointed that way at 3,000 yards range they would knock the station off the bluff...I don't believe any personnel could work in there if we were firing toward the North Channel along a stretch of 2000 yards. The battle comdre [sic] station is threatened also. At five degrees depression a projectile would strike about 2000 yards out [and] it would pass about eight feet over the battle comdrs [sic] station." It proved necessary to start over again and provide a new BCS for Battery Wheeler.[188]

Ultimately, at least five stations had to be torn down and rebuilt, or at least replaced in function by a new station in a new location. The north station for Batteries Geary and Way were found to be too tall and obvious to enemy fire, in another case, Battery Wheeler's primary station, the station was supposed to be 30 feet lower than actually constructed, leaving it in the field of friendly fire. In at least two other cases they simply were not pointed in the optimal direction. Perhaps this all was a little embarrassing, but at least the cost of correction was affordable within the overall project's scope. By mid-1913 it was reported that Fort Mills had 13 concrete fire control stations, one double mine station, and five battery commander stations at their batteries. Fort Frank had five separate stations, and another five were under construction at Fort Hughes. Typically, the primary stations were single story splinter-proof, covered concrete structures partially dug into the cliffs at Topside and provided with a pedestal for a single DPF. However, this instrument was in chronic short supply, and some perfectly acceptable stations served years before being adequately equipped.

The navy loaned the former Spanish gunboat *Pampanga* to the army for use as an artillery boat from 1908 to 1910. NHC.

Although fire control station construction progressed apace with the batteries, equipping the stations lagged considerably. Even the initial calibration firing for the guns following their emplacement was delayed because of fire control instrument shortages. As all the Corregidor stations were above 400 feet in elevation, only the Warner-Swayze DPF of the vertical fire control system would work at that elevation. Compounding these deficiencies, there was no artillery boat available for use in conjunction with target practices. Kilbourne was finally successful, after many weeks of wrangling and pleading, in getting the former Spanish gunboat *Pampanga* overhauled for use as an artillery boat for Fort Mills. *Pampanga* was refitted in mid-December 1908 and sent to Corregidor, loaned to the army by the navy for use as a patrol boat and ferry about the fortified islands on December 31, 1908, and was returned to the navy November 11, 1910, after the army mine planters arrived.[189]

Kilbourne maintained frequent communication with Capt. William Chamberlaine, the artillery officer in the Philippine Division headquarters in 1908. The two worked closely in developing Corregidor's fire control system and defenses. Although lacking suitable range-finding instruments, Kilbourne established a horizontal base fire control system using the battle commander's station and the battery commander's station (BCS) of Battery Grubbs as base end stations at either end of a base line. By the end of 1908, a preliminary fire control system had been established on Corregidor. While Chamberlaine described it as being a bit backward, it consisted of two fire commands. The First Fire Command was composed of 6-inch gun Batteries Ramsay and Morrison. Kilbourne's Second Fire Command consisted of the 12-inch guns of Batteries Cheney and Wheeler. Many stations still lacked the necessary telephones and fire control equipment to make them operational and what communication lines existed were strung on overhead wires, rather than buried.[190]

The Provisional Fire Control System

The fire control system developed in 1909 consisted of a battle commander's station for the First Battle Command (C_1), also known as the "C" Station. This battle command controlled the fire of the First (F_1), Second (F_2), and Third (F_3), Fire Commands and the First (M_1) Mine Command at Forts Mills and the Second (M_2) Mine Command at Fort Hughes. The C_1 command post was a large two room concrete structure to the left front of Battery Wheeler on the cliffs overlooking Searchlight Point at an elevation of about 484 feet. The "C" Station was transferred to the coast artillery on January 6, 1911.

The primary station for the First Fire Command (F_1') was housed in the same structure as the "C" Station near Battery Wheeler, and transferred on the same date. The First Fire Command controlled the fire of Batteries Wheeler, Crockett, Cheney, and Grubbs. No secondary stations were provided to this fire command as its gun batteries used the vertical base line system with DPFs.

Battery Wheeler's BCS and plotting room were transferred to the artillery on July 23, 1910. The BCS was equipped with a Warner-Swasey azimuth instrument. The battery's primary station (B') was a one-room concrete structure built at an elevation of 444 feet atop Searchlight Point. This station was transferred to the coast artillery on July 27, 1910. As previously mentioned, it was necessary to move the primary station's to Cheney's original station on a promontory 444 feet above the water at Wheeler Point. Nearly 100-feet lower than the battery, the effect of projectiles passing over the station was diminished. This new station was also a one-room concrete structure. Battery Crockett's BCS and plotting room were part of the battery structure. Its B' Station was north of the battery in a one-room concrete building at an elevation of 486 feet. The station was transferred February 9, 1911.

Battery Cheney's BCS and plotting room were also located at the battery. Its B' station was to the right of Battery Wheeler at an elevation of 461 feet in a one-room concrete structure of the same standard type built for Batteries Wheeler and Crockett. The station was also transferred July 27, 1910.[191]

Construction of plotting rooms for Batteries Way and Geary was held up by the engineering officer pending the decision as to whether to build two or four plotting rooms. Eventually each mortar pit received its own primary station and plotting room.[192] The initial fire control stations for the mortar batteries were completed except for minor details in 1907-08. The south station had two observing stations, the upper station behind and directly above the lower station. The south station's exterior ground level was brought to about a foot below the lower station's observation slot, reducing its visibility from seaward. On the other hand, the north station was a large three-story concrete structure built entirely above ground level on one of the island's highest sites. This station could easily be seen by an enemy at sea or on Mariveles Heights. As the upper station's instrument was over 540 feet high, this building was entirely unshielded from view or fire. The top observing station was an entire level above its second-story companion; a plotting room occupied the first floor. A stairway was provided on one side of the station's exterior. Whatever the reason for the error in design, it was quickly recognized, though not until after completion and considerable expenditure of money and effort. Maj. Charles H. McKinstry, the Philippine Division's fortification engineer, wrote a letter to the chief of engineers concerning fire control arrangements for the mortars shortly after north station's completion, noting the need to include two full plotting rooms at both the north and south station locations. This would allow both mortar batteries to fire on either the Boca Chica or Boca Grande channels.[193]

Among McKinstry's various recommendations was calling for the demolition of the three-story north mortar station and its replacement on the same spot with a dug in station similar to the south mortar station. Although the instruments in the new north station would be 11-feet lower than in the old station and would increase the dead space in front of Battery Grubbs by about 600 yards, McKinstry believed the tradeoff of reducing the size of the station as a target would be worth it. The new north station had its two observing stations much closer to the earth slope, and one large plotting room equipped with a 360° M1911 plotting board for Batteries Geary and Way. The new station was transferred on March 29, 1911, at a cost of $5,964.37.

The fire control system for the mortar batteries on Corregidor was established as follows: Each mortar pit functioned as a separate tactical battery. Battery Way's system consisted of its (B') station at the north mortar station while its secondary station (B") was located in the south mortar station. The B' for Pit "A" of Battery Geary was located in the north mortar station while its B" station was in the south mortar station. As the

Interior of Battery Grubbs's BCS observing room manned by the 91st Coast Artillery. NARA.

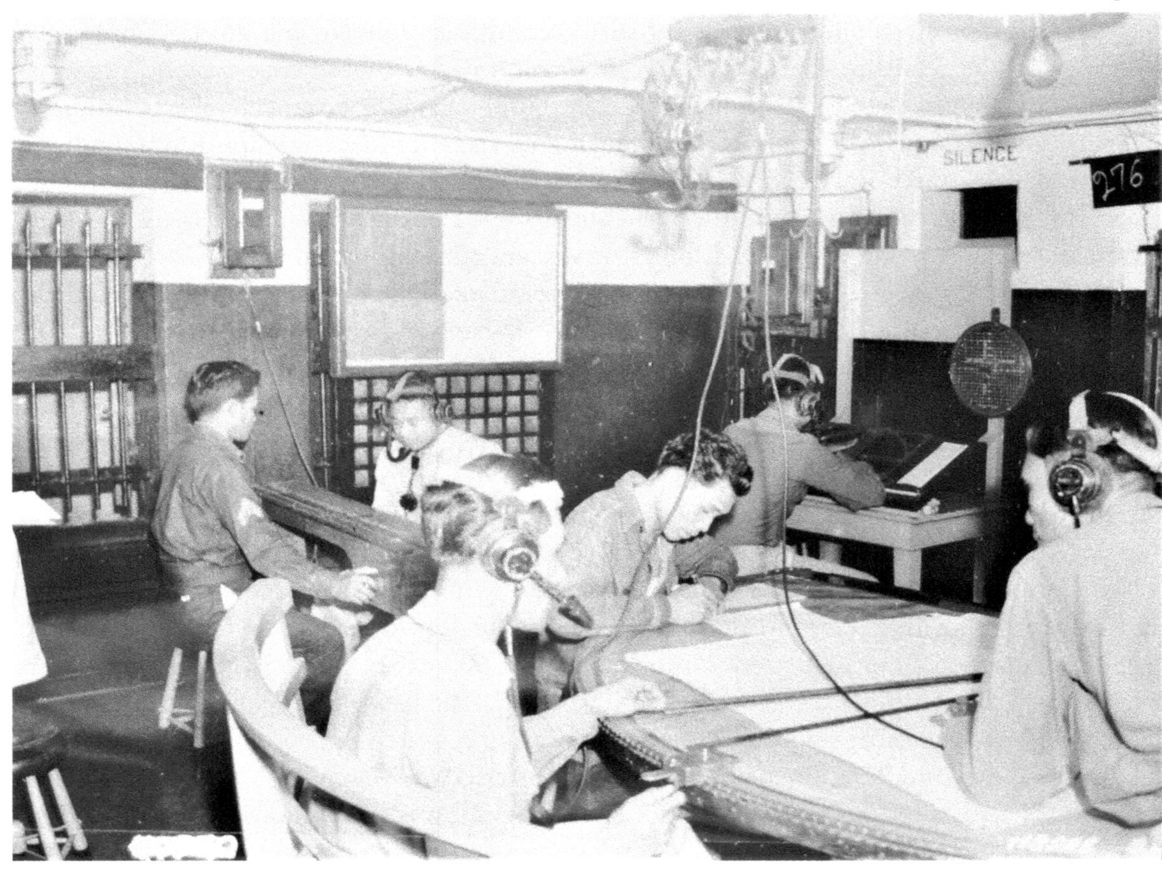

The plotting room at Battery Grubbs, the large half-circle table on the lower right is the plotting board. NARA.

mortars for Pit B of Battery Geary had not yet been received, no plotting board had been provided. Upon the mortars' arrival and mounting, a 110° M1915 plotting board was installed in the plotting room.[194]

Other important tactical buildings were built to facilitate the fire control system. Probably most important was the combined fire control switchboard and post telephone exchange. This was a two-story concrete building built on Topside east of the parade ground. It had three major rooms, one for the post telephone exchange, one for the fire control switchboard, and one for a storage battery. The building was transferred on July 27, 1910, for a cost of $6,631.13. While of heavy concrete construction, it was not strictly bombproofed, though that lack would be remedied in just a short time. A concrete meteorological station was built north of Battery Way, and a tide station erected at Bottomside's north mine wharf. Both of these rooms collected important inputs for adjusting the solutions to the firing equation.[195]

In 1913, the fire control scheme for the newly completed batteries at Forts Frank and Hughes was implemented, along with the final reassignments for the stations serving the 12-inch batteries at Fort Mills. The primary fire control stations and plotting rooms of Batteries Cheney, Wheeler, and Crockett, initially transferred 1910-1911, were relocated from their original sites to new ones. Battery Cheney's B' station was moved to a new station built between its old station and Battery Wheeler. Battery Crockett's B' station was abandoned in 1912 and shifted to a new station built above Geary Point. Battery Wheeler's B' station was relocated to Battery Cheney's original B' station. The stations left unoccupied were eventually taken over in 1922 as secondary stations for Batteries at Forts Frank and Hughes. Fort Frank's Battery Crofton's B" Station was located at the original Crockett B' site and Battery Craighill at Fort Hughes was located at the original Wheeler B' site.

By 1915, the original fire control system had been further modified by the addition of the two new mortar stations. The primary station for Pit "B" of Battery Geary also functioned as the primary emergency station for the Second Fire Command (F'''_2) and was located above Cheney Ravine. The secondary emergency station (F''''_2) was located atop Malinta Hill. A month before the U.S. entered World War I in April 1917, Capt.

George W. Cocheu devised a plan that would enable all mortars in the harbor defenses to concentrate their fire on specific targets through improved communications between command posts, plotting rooms, etc.[196]

When Fort Drum was transferred to the garrison June 17, 1918, it had its own fire control problem. At this location (at least initially) range finding was to be provided by 15 ft coincidence rangefinders (CRF) and azimuth instruments placed on the fort's cage mast. Later, conventional primary DPF stations for the 14-inch turrets of Drum were installed on the cage mast and secondary stations projected at Fort Frank. However, by 1920 CRF instruments had proved so useful (and accurate) that the stations at Fort Frank were not completed, and no additional fire control instruments were assigned to support Fort Drum. Fort Drum's 14-inch and 6-inch guns would be served only by their CRF instruments.[197]

Electric Power on Corregidor

The gun and mortar batteries, their fire control and direction, and the projected searchlights on Corregidor were dependent on electric power. While 25 kW independent power plants were installed in the batteries and later at some searchlight positions, these were projected for use only in an emergency as reserve sources of electricity. The projected electric trolley line that served Bottomside, Middleside, and Topside also required considerable electric power. When the permanent post was built, that too would also require electrical service. Until then mineral oil lamps continued to be relied upon to light post interiors.

Central Power Plant Built at Bottomside

Early 20th century American seacoast fortifications were typically provided with electricity to operate the motors used to maneuver guns, illuminate their emplacements and fire control stations, power their ammunition hoists, and light their observation instruments, as well as powering the telephone system and searchlights. The early method was to use direct current electrical generating plants as the coastal fortification elements were typically positioned close to one another. Consequently, there was little "line loss" of electricity using direct current. But as the distance between the defense's tactical elements increased, the probability of line loss in electrical transmission grew and use of alternating current systems at locations such as Corregidor became necessary.[198]

To provide the requisite electrical power a central power plant was projected for Corregidor. Plans for the plant were finalized about 1907 and a site selected in the Engineer's Ravine (later named Power Plant Ravine) in the northwest section of Bottomside. Here a wood-frame building was erected on a concrete slab, sheathed, and roofed with corrugated galvanized iron.

The American-owned Manila Street Railway Company was at that time in the process of updating its outdated power plant. In an effort to conserve funds, the Philippine Division quartermaster arranged to purchase a portion of the older civilian plant for installation as Corregidor's plant. The purchased plant consisted of two coal-fired Altman-Taylor 250 h.p. water tube boilers and the two tandem-compound Buckeye steam engines, each of 250 h.p., and 150 kW, 2,300-volt alternator engines. The plant acquired from the railway, however, was already pretty much worn out when it was installed at Fort Mills. This plant was supplemented with a 150 kW, 600-volt, General Electric Company railway generator, one 150 kW, 370 volts A.C. 600-volt D.C. General Electric rotary converter, one 150 kW 2,300 to 370-volt step-down transformer for use with the rotary converter, and one 7½ kW 125-volt exciter for the alternator. The converter was essentially a mechanical device used to convert between alternating and direct current, since transformers could not be used with direct current. Upon installation, the plant supplied electric power to the batteries, the fire control stations, and the mine defense installations, as well as the trolley line. The central plant was transferred to the garrison on February 1, 1910. Almost from the start, the plant was inadequate to supply the requisite current for the searchlights, which remained dependent upon the direct current 25 kW generator sets at the lights or nearby gun or mortar batteries. Post lighting continued to be provided by mineral oil lamps.[199]

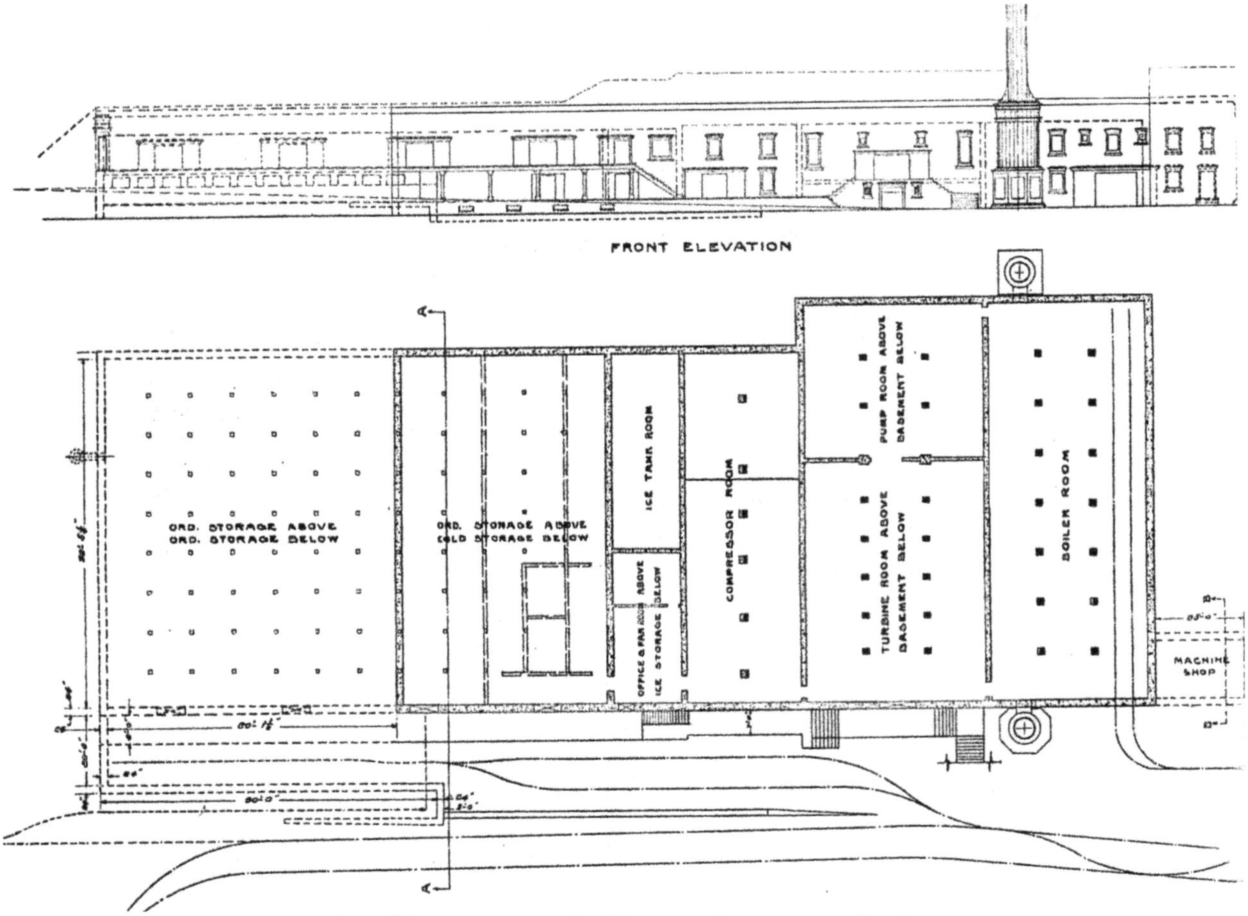

Plan of the new power and cold storage plant at Fort Mills. NARA.

Power plant and cold storage facility about 1917. NARA.

Turbo-generators in the Fort Mills power plant. NARA.

The demands for electric power continued to mount on Corregidor as more facilities were built requiring electricity; soon two new engines were ordered and plans prepared for upgrading the power plant to enable post lighting. It was estimated that at least three 500 kW generators would be needed to meet all the electrical needs on the island (At that time consideration was also afoot to establish a brigade-size camp for infantry on Corregidor's tail).[200]

By 1914, construction was complete on a 23,660 square foot bombproof reinforced concrete combination central power plant and cold storage plant in Power Plant Ravine. Once the structure was built the steam power plant was upgraded with five 300 h.p. water tube boilers manufactured by the Heine Safety Boiler Company, three 462 KVA, and one 156 KVA turbine-driven 2300-volt AC generating sets, two 300 kW synchronous converters, and a 150 kW rotary converter, which were installed by October 1915. Corregidor's reserve generating system consisted of six 25 kW generating sets located in the three 12-inch batteries, the 10-inch gun battery and the two mortar batteries.[201]

The new cold storage part of the plant had three freezing rooms that operated on the principal of compressed ammonia. The plant featured an ice plant, compressor room, pump room, and a butcher shop, in addition to the power plant's turbine room and boiler room, all on its first floor. The second floor contained a storeroom, fan room, and office. The building was also provided with a basement containing latrines for officers and enlisted men and a large open room which could be used for storage or as a personnel shelter. When completed the new power plant cost $355,828.21.[202]

The 1914 power plant was later supplemented by a new 6,821-square-foot reinforced-concrete diesel-generator plant just south of the cold-storage plant in Powerhouse Ravine. Construction commenced June 29, 1929, and was completed September 13, 1930. The plant was equipped with three powerful 8-cylinder, 4-cycle Air Injection Worthington 17 x 25 diesel engines, directly connected to 600 kW Westinghouse alternators and exciters. A 500,000-gallon fuel oil tank was built nearby and completed May 22, 1930. Although heavily bombarded by the Japanese, this plant remained in service well into 1942.[203]

Corregidor's Trolley Line

In 1907, even before the first gun and mortar batteries were completed, plans for a new permanent 36-inch gauge trolley system powered by electricity from the central electric light and power plant through overhead wires was being developed. This new 13,200-foot-long trolley line would use part of the construction railroad system right of way, with spurs providing access to the various gun and mortar batteries and many other locations. The 56-pound rails were laid on Australian jarrah wood ties. The main trolley line was a single track that ran from the Mine Wharf at Bottomside through San Jose Barrio and then by a circuitous route up to Middleside and thence on to Morrison Hill and Topside. Each trolley car could be controlled from either end, and at the end of the line the backs of the seats were on slides that could be changed so that the passengers would be facing forward as the car reversed. Spur lines were used to bring munitions to the batteries. Those portions of the lines that served the batteries were set up so that electric power could be shut off on the spurs when that part was not in use.[204]

Bilibid prisoners working on the trolley line with an engineer and Philippine Scout guard detachment in 1909. NARA.

The trolley system was beset with problems from the first. Line construction was sluggish as funding became increasingly difficult to come by and appropriations for Corregidor were used up. There was also a squabble between the coast artillery and the quartermaster over who would run the trolley line. Gen. Arthur Murray, the chief of coast artillery, wanted the Quartermaster Department to do it. The Quartermaster Department was not opposed to running the car system, but it wanted the coast artillery to provide the engineers and firemen and electrician sergeants to operate the electric power components. In the end, the Quartermaster Corps operated the trolley system. The dispatchers were quartermaster personnel, while many motormen and conductors were initially detailed from the coast artillery companies on the island. After 1921, the details came from Headquarters Battery, 59th C.A. Whenever they encountered significant problems and needed technical assistance, the Manila Street Railroad Company came in to help.

The trolley system saw frequent electrical service problems early on. Some of them were caused by power interruptions and failures of the over-burdened steam power plant. The plant was barely able to provide the requisite electricity, and there was difficulty in getting a competent chief engineer for the power plant because of the low wage of $150 per month offered by the department. In the view of Major Hearn, the job demanded a salary of $200 dollars and the Quartermaster Department was unwilling for some time to provide the additional funds.[205]

The line was generally run without serious accidents until February 20, 1925, when a trolley car accident killed eight people. Col. Valentine P. Foster, a captain at the time, recalled the wreck in 1963:[206]

> I believe it was the 7:00 a.m. trolley from Topside which made connection for the Manila boat leaving at 7:30 a.m. Also the harbor boat going to Ft. Hughes and other islands which carried military and Johnson, and myself were on our way to Ft. Hughes preparing upper pit Craighill for target practice. The trolley appeared to function normally until we left the Middleside Barracks station. Then after we passed the Ordnance warehouses, I noticed the car speeding up, glanced around toward the motorman Private Fagan and observed that he got no response from his air brake operating lever. We were now approaching [the] first hairpin curve which we rounded safely, though we listed badly. Now we were on long steep run toward Washerwoman's Ravine (Not sure of the name). The motorman was trying to reverse his motors for braking action. The circuit breaker tripped several times then Lt. Hayden held the breaker lever in thereby causing the fuze to blow. Lt Hayden, & W.O. [warrant officer] Carter was trying to tighten up the hand brake. I also reached thru and tried to help but immediately realized it was useless. We were now rounding the sharp left curve and the high stone retaining wall loomed up before us. I thought we would hit it head on but by some miracle we still held the rails. We were now headed for San Jose barrio and I realized that we could not make it around the curve. I then decided the floor was the safest place as the frame of the car was the strongest part. From testimony later I must have voiced my thoughts. The car was rushing toward the barrio by now and as we struck the first part of the curve the car leaned over to the right far enough to slide along one of the iron poles holding the trolley wire. After it slid past it went violently on its right side sliding until it hit the next iron pole bending it at right angles.
>
> After the car came to rest I slid down to the ground or rather rubble, landing on some pieces of wood and there right in front of me was Mrs. Herring lying on her back. I leaned over and raised her up to standing position and carried her out through the front part of the car. She was able to stand and kept calling for her husband. I went back into the car and helped get Colonel Herring out. He had a compound fracture of one leg, bones protruding. We found a floor inspection cover and gently moved him on to it and carried him to the road where he could be loaded into an ambulance. From the ashen color of his face, [I] was sure that he had internal injuries as well. He survived several hours only. Those who were on the right running board were ground and horribly mangled. The most pitiful sight was W.O. Carter; His legs were twisted round and round. Though still conscious he realized he would never walk again and repeatedly begged me to shoot him. We seemed and were so helpless as we could not raise the car by hand it wasn't until a work train arrived on the other track and a steel cable was attached to [the] wrecked car and it was tilted back to upright position that we were able to get all the injured out. As I recall we had a mass funeral on the Topside Parade Ground that same afternoon.

One of those killed in the accident was Sgt. James T. Davidson who, while assigned to the 59th C.A., had charge of work on the American enlisted men's tennis and handball courts at Topside, later named Davidson Park in his memory. The 1925 accident notwithstanding, the trolley system served Fort Mills very well. The service was free and provided convenient access to nearly all locations on the post. When the tunnel was completed through Malinta Hill in the mid-1930s, the trolley system was extended with a track through the tunnel to the garrison area west of Kindley Field.[207]

The trackage and electric power that the trolley system operated on was only part of the system. In addition to the car barn or roundhouse and its tool house, there were three dedicated freight checkers stations, a dispatcher's office, and 14 car stops along the trolley line with a freight and passenger station at the east end of the line. Built between 1916 and 1924, most of these structures associated with the trolley system were of timber construction, sheathed and roofed with corrugated and galvanized iron. Some car stops, especially those around Topside, had a less utilitarian appearance.

Electric car stopping at Middleside Station. Schmidt Collection.

Trolley car maintenance barn, on the western side of Topside. Smith Collection.

35th Company Receives Orders for the Philippines

In 1901 the regimental system of the U.S. Artillery was abolished. An Artillery Corps composed of 126 separate sequentially numbered companies of coast artillery and 30 sequentially numbered batteries of field artillery was constituted in its stead. It soon became apparent that the two types of artillery were rapidly moving farther apart in their training and mission goals. Within five years, technological advances had become even more rapid, further separating field and seacoast artillery. No longer was an officer considered qualified to command both light and heavy artillery. The techniques had become too different, and increased specialization was required. The field artillery batteries were provisionally reorganized into regiments of field artillery and by 1905 the secretary of war had authorized what eventually became a bill to reorganize the field and coast artillery components into separate branches. This act was passed January 25, 1907, and the six provisional field artillery regiments became "legal." In an effort to provide garrisons for the insular possessions of Puerto Rico, Hawaii, and the Philippines, the act also authorized the Coast Artillery Corps an additional 44 companies, bringing the total number of companies to 170.[208]

With the 57th Company garrisoning Fort Wint at Subic Bay, and the batteries at Corregidor nearing completion, the War Department issued movement orders for a second coast artillery company to provide the garrison for the defenses being developed at the mouth of Manila Bay. On March 29, 1908, the 35th Company, posted at Fort Monroe, entrained and traveled cross country to San Francisco, where it boarded USAT *Sherman* for transportation to the Philippines, arriving at the small harbor of Mariveles on May 7.

Barracks of 146th Company at Fort Wint. Schmidt Collection.

From Mariveles, the company was transported across the Boca Chica Channel to Corregidor. Upon arrival at the Corregidor wharf, Capt. Charles Kilbourne's company fell in with full packs and commenced a march up to the island's highest level. Kilbourne later recalled that by the time the men had reached the Middleside level they "collapsed when they saw that they had still another hill to surmount before they reached Topside". [209]

After its arduous hike up to Topside, the company occupied the single-story wooden frame barracks about 300 yards west of the lighthouse. Quarters for the officers and offices were built at the western edge of Middleside some 175 feet above Camp Avery occupied by the scout garrison and the Bilibid convicts' stockade. Had it not been for the efforts of the scout battalion to obtain adequate rations for the company upon their arrival, the company would have been without food, as the higher command had made no arrangement for providing the company's commissary supplies. To make matters worse, three days after their arrival, the troops were welcomed by a typhoon that struck the island, tearing off the newly completed barracks roof. Both officers and enlisted men sought shelter in the combined commissary and quartermaster storehouse that proved to be of sturdier construction. With the typhoon's passing, the 35th Company moved into tents pending repairs to their barracks. Subsequently, new quarters were built for the officers at Topside near the enlisted men's barracks. [210]

Only a single gun, the No. 1 Gun of 12-inch Battery No. 1 (Battery Wheeler), had been mounted when Kilbourne's company arrived. They found the state of affairs among the various commands on Corregidor in flux with little cohesive organization. When Kilbourne arrived on Corregidor, Major Munro of the Philippine Scouts commanded the island. Kilbourne, as a coast artillery district commander, did not view with favor the precedent of a coast artillery officer being accountable to a Philippine Scout infantry officer, but noted that Munro had been very helpful to him and considered the Scout commander as a fine man personally. Although a major in the Philippine Scouts, Munro held the rank of captain in the 3rd US Cavalry and was junior to Kilbourne. The engineers based at Bottomside were independent of both Kilbourne and Munro. The Quartermaster Department being almost without resources of its own had to borrow materials from the engineers for any but the most minor construction projects it undertook. Further, it operated pretty much as the Chief Quartermaster saw fit and seemed uninfluenced by any other army elements on the island, not to mention Division Headquarters in Manila.[211]

Apparently, Kilbourne's views regarding the matter of Corregidor's command situation were shared by the higher command in Manila and within a week of Kilbourne's arrival Major Munro had been relieved of island command and Kilbourne appointed in his stead. With the change in command, the coast artillery captain's responsibilities expanded greatly. Kilbourne assumed command of the entire island and its population of Americans and Filipinos, both civilian and military. As daunting as this task was, the War Department had chosen well in selecting Kilbourne as the first coast artillery commander on Corregidor.

Charles E. Kilbourne as a Captain in 1910 (left) while serving as superintendent of the officer's school of the Philippine Constabulary, and as a Major General (right) in 1936. Gaines Collection and NARA Still Pictures.

Kilbourne's initial duties were to take custody of and care for the ordnance as it arrived on the island, see to its mounting in the batteries as they neared completion, and once mounted, to man the emplaced armament. In addition, as a company commander he was also responsible for the good order and discipline of his men and their training as well as the establishment of a coast artillery post on Corregidor.

Kilbourne described the daily routine for the coast artillery company soon after his arrival on the island:[212]

> We turn out at five have fatigue call for general police at six—first call art'y drill at 6:40 drill till eight — there is no dummy ammunition so we made some out of a tree we cut down. From eight to 11 we work at mounting guns, moving ordnance etc. We turn in at 11 so that the men can reach barracks in time to cool off and wash up before dinner.

Kilbourne tried not to work the troops in the early afternoon as the summer months were "something fierce for heat." Occasionally, however, when the wharf became congested with heavy ordnance, Kilbourne had to work the company in reliefs during the afternoons in order to clear the wharf to permit the landing of other supplies. The company worked day in and day out, rarely with a day off. The day ended with a half-hour of infantry drill consisting of the manual of arms and "squads right and left," as very little area had been cleared at Topside for anything more. Taps were at 2200.[213]

Storage facilities were practically nonexistent. The engineers had taken over nearly all battery magazine spaces for storage of their materials, leaving many projectiles outside. There the ants ate off all the stenciling on the boxes, making their sorting more difficult. Those projectiles stored in the batteries were in spaces where there were no trolleys and their movement could be achieved only by the use of pinch bars and physical strength. There were precious few resources available to Corregidor's first coast artillery company. Kilbourne's company managed to mount only one additional gun before the end of 1908, but during the ensuing months as their experience increased, that pace increased. Kilbourne's men would mount thirteen more guns and mortars at Fort Mills before returning to the United States on May 18, 1910. In 1909 Kilbourne left Fort Mills for Baguio City to assume his duties as inspector, and later as superintendent, of the officer's school of the Philippine Constabulary.

31st Infantry on the rifle range in 1938. By the 1930s, department infantry units visited the harbor defenses only for occasional training exercises. NARA.

Corregidor's Coast Artillery Garrison Augmented

From May 1908 until April 1909 the 35th Company served as Corregidor's sole coast artillery garrison. Although most of the seacoast batteries on Corregidor had been completed or were nearing completion, barracks and officers' quarters for the 10 companies of coast artillery that were projected to man the defenses had not been built because of lack of Congressional funding. This drew Chief of Coast Artillery Brig. Gen. Arthur Murray's attention in October 1908 when he discussed this funding shortfall in his annual report to the secretary of war:[214]

> More rapid progress has been made in the completion of the fortifications authorized heretofore for those places than had been anticipated, and the situation now confronting the War Department with providing for the care and preservation of the armament is serious. With the completion of the other batteries now under construction, this condition will become worse and relief cannot be obtained until barracks and quarters are provided. The armament completed or to be completed before the close of the present fiscal year on Corregidor Island will require 10 companies for its service; that on Grande Island, 4 companies. Due to the lack of available funds for the construction of quarters, it has been possible to station but one company of Coast Artillery on Corregidor Island and but one company on Grande Island.
>
> Failure to obtain funds at this session of Congress will mean that for the next three years these defenses will be in a state of almost complete unpreparedness for war, due to the lack of personnel to man the armament and receive proper training in handling the same. The distance of the Philippine Islands from the United States renders it improbable that sufficient time will be available when a war appears imminent and before its outbreak to enable coast artillery troops sent from the United States to reach these islands. For this reason it is considered useless to install fortifications in the Philippine Islands unless a sufficient garrison of coast artillery is maintained there at all times to fully man them.
>
> It is therefore recommended that Congress be asked to provide at its next session for a 10-company post on Corregidor Island, Philippine Islands, a 4-company post on Grande Island, Philippine Islands, and it is further recommended that in the hearings before the congressional committees the urgency of the early commencement of this work be pointed out and Congress be asked to make the appropriation for this purpose available immediately upon the approval of the act of appropriation.

The Fort Mills garrison was finally increased to four companies in April 1909 when a major augmentation of the coast artillery garrison was implemented. The 50th, 51st, 54th (Mine), and 55th Companies from forts in New York Harbor received movement orders transferring them to the Philippines. On February 17, 1909, these four companies boarded USAT *Kilpatrick* in New York Harbor and sailed for Manila, arriving there on April 22. The 51st, 54th, and 55th Companies were assigned to Fort Mills while the 50th was sent to Fort Wint, where it joined the 57th Company. As the increased garrison rated a field officer to command Fort Mills, Maj. Clint C. Hearn arrived to relieve Captain Kilbourne as the post's senior officer.[215]

The 146th Company, commanded by Capt. Gordon Robinson was constituted and organized as a mine company in 1907 at the Presidio of San Francisco. The company remained at the Presidio only until 1909, when it too received orders for the Philippine Islands. The 146th Company boarded USAT *Sheridan* on August 5, 1909, and departed the same day for the Philippines via Honolulu. Upon arrival in Manila on August 31, the company was transported across Manila Bay to Fort Mills. Shortly thereafter the company moved to Fort Wint, briefly bringing the Fort Wint garrison up to three companies as the 57th Company departed from Manila for San Francisco aboard USAT *Buford* on September 15, 1909.[216]

The 13th Company, commanded by Capt. Frank J. Miller, arrived at Fort Mills from Fort Monroe in 1910 and was assigned to Battery Wheeler. By the middle of 1910, the first mortar battery was completed and those gun batteries still incomplete on Corregidor were nearly finished. By January 1910, additional companies were being alerted for transfer to Corregidor. In May 1910, the War Department began implementation of plans to increase the number of coast artillery companies in the Philippines to 20 companies as the gun and mortar batteries were brought to completion. The 11th and 18th Companies at Fort Schuyler, New York, and the 42nd and 138th Companies at Fort Mott, New Jersey, were also alerted for transfer to Fort Mills in May 1910. Their departure was initially scheduled so that they would arrive in Manila about July 1, 1910. Major Hearn soon discovered that delays in the construction of quarters for the additional companies had lagged so badly that little choice remained but to request a delay in the troop's departure until September after the worst of the rainy season. They would now be transferred to San Francisco to embark on or about September 5, 1910, for passage to Manila. Also sailing aboard the September transport was the 9th Coast Artillery Band that arrived from Key West Barracks, Florida, in response to Hearn's urging for a Regular Army band to replace the band of volunteer musicians who had to provide their own instruments.[217]

The coast artillery companies in the Philippines in June 1910 were generally assigned at least three commissioned officers. Frequently this required the attachment of officers from other companies to fill out the officer ranks for foreign service and on occasion a fourth officer was attached to a company for overseas deployment. The same situation existed for enlisted personnel, as other companies on the post were used as manpower sources to fill out the ranks of companies being transferred.

Officers' families accompanied the four companies transferred to the Philippines in 1909, all of whom were reportedly enthusiastic about the venture. Although the intent was to provide a full peacetime complement for the overseas garrisons, this goal was rarely met due to personnel shortfalls in the coast artillery. The diminished size of the companies' enlisted component as they were transferred resulted in a lack of reliefs for the gun crews and ammunition parties. These reliefs were to be filled by using the infantry on the island as ammunition details, thus freeing up coast artillerymen for gun detachments and fire control range sections.[218]

With the additional companies' arrival, Hearn was able to provide manning detachments for all of the completed batteries. At the end of 1911, Fort Mills' garrison still numbered only eight coast artillery companies. The 13th 51st, and 54th Companies were rotated back to the United States and the 55th Company to Fort DeRussy, in Hawaii. The 86th Company from Fort Wadsworth, New York, the 90th Company from Fort McKinley, Maine, and the 95th Company from Fort Hancock, New Jersey, replaced these companies. Only one additional company: the 70th Company from Fort Winfield Scott, California, was forwarded to the Philippines in 1912, replacing the 13th Company. As a result, the number of companies at Fort Mills was maintained at eight until 1913, when the 99th Company from Fort Morgan, Alabama, marched up the Fort Mills wharf on December 4, 1913, bringing the number of companies up to nine. The companies that left in 1913 would be the last to leave the Philippines until after World War I.

Manning the Philippine defenses proved to be a daunting task and many alternatives were considered to provide the manpower needed to man the guns on Corregidor and the other fortified islands. A minimum of 10 full-strength coast artillery companies were required for Corregidor, three companies each for Forts Frank and Hughes and four more for Fort Wint. The nine coast artillery companies on Corregidor at the end of 1913 fell short of meeting the manpower needs. The concept of using the infantry on the island to serve as ammunition details was not considered acceptable to the chief of coast artillery, who insisted that men well trained in the artillery service man the batteries. Finally in 1914, after the outbreak of war in Europe, the secretary of war authorized the movement of additional companies to Corregidor in an effort to build up the garrison to nominal peacetime levels.[219]

In addition to the coast artillery garrison, infantry was also posted on Corregidor. The 2nd Battalion, Philippine Scout Infantry, consisting of four companies was posted at Fort Mills in 1904 under Maj. James N. Munro. The 2nd Battalion, 15th U.S. Infantry, arrived in Manila from the U.S. in December 1911. In the early months of World War I, the 2nd Battalion, 15th U.S. Infantry, in company with the 4th Battalion (Provisional), constituted the fortified islands' land defenses and were posted at Fort Mills. The remainder of the 15th Infantry arrived in early 1912, but its headquarters, band, and the 1st and 3rd Battalions were forwarded on to China. The 2nd Battalion never rejoined its parent regiment; it was inactivated (less Co. G at Fort Mills which remained active until 1932), on August 1, 1916, and its personnel transferred to the 1st Battalion, 31st U.S.

Infantry, upon that regiment's organization later that month. In June 1917, the 1st Battalion, 31st Infantry, assumed infantry garrison duties on Corregidor. It was joined in July by the regiment's 2nd and 3rd Battalions and by the headquarters, machine gun, and supply companies that arrived in August. One of the regiment's roles on Corregidor was manning the land defense field pieces. The entire 31st Infantry remained at Fort Mills only through the early months of World War I. By September 1917 all but the 3rd Battalion had returned to Fort McKinley. The 3rd Battalion remained on Corregidor until August 10, 1918, when it moved into Manila's Cuartel de España, where it prepared for deployment to Vladivostok, Russia, as part of the Allied expedition. [220]

To maintain contact with Manila and beyond, Fort Mills had a powerful radio.
In the 1930s the main antenna was just to the west of the parade ground. NARA.

CHAPTER 8
MINES, SEARCHLIGHTS, LAND DEFENSE AND AVIATION PROJECTS

Submarine Mine Defenses Established

Congress actually made the initial appropriation of $150,000 for submarine defenses of Manila Bay during the Spanish American War on June 8, 1898. The first submarine mine project report in 1901 called for mines only in the Boca Grande channel between Caballo Island and the southern (Cavite) shoreline. No action was taken, however, until the Artillery Torpedo Board at Fort Totten, New York, prepared a project for the Taft Board in 1906. This project called for construction of a mine wharf, two double torpedo storehouses, four cable tanks, a mine casemate, two loading rooms, and a tramway at Bottomside, as well as a second mine casemate and double primary and secondary mine stations at Topside. A second appropriation for torpedo defenses in Manila Bay was made in the Act of March 2, 1907, and work in accord with the 1898 project as modified in the early 1900s was finally begun.

The first casemate, a single-story 53-foot-long and 24 feet wide concrete structure containing an accumulator room, engine room, battery room, and a dormitory for the manning detachment, and the loading rooms that were converted from the old Spanish masonry structures near the north shore of Bottomside were reported in operation as early as April 1908. Also included were mine casemates and double primary mine observation stations on El Fraile and Caballo Islands. The Artillery Torpedo Board's project called for 26 grand groups of mines and estimated the project's cost at $161,000. Prior to 1912, a grand group consisted of three groups of seven mines each, a total of 21 mines.

In May 1909, the chief of coast artillery recommended more changes to the project that were approved August 5, 1910: an increase from 26 to 56 grand groups; and an increased number of mine support structures including two more torpedo storehouses, two additional cable tanks, and a storage magazine, all at Bottomside, and a second mine casemate on Corregidor on the west side of James Ravine. An additional mine casemate was projected for Carabao Island. Following the Philippine Defense Board's declaration on September 8, 1911, the chief of coast artillery agreed that the James Ravine casemate be bombproofed. While the increase in the number of operational grand groups of submarine mines was not approved, the infrastructure to support 56 grand groups was eventually provided.[221]

There was substantial professional opposition during this early planning for storing and loading mines at Caballo Island. It was thought that the island was too small to allow adequate protection for such structures, even though the island was to be the site for a casemate to control mines in the Boca Grande's northern half. Instead it was proposed to simply enlarge the facilities on Corregidor's Bottomside, and connect these to a new mine wharf on the south side of the island. The connection would be by tramway with a tunnel running under the road to Middleside with protective sidewalls. Ultimately the wharf was built, but savings were made by re-routing the tram line further to the east, avoiding the necessity for a tunnel. The savings thus made in the November 1, 1911, allocation was used to pay for the new James Ravine mine casemate's bombproofing that was finally undertaken in 1913.[222]

In August 1911 the projected increase in the number of mine grand groups was cancelled and thus the two double mine storehouses, the four mine loading rooms, as well as the Carabao casemate were to be deleted. Providing mine wharves on the north and south side of Bottomside along with a tramline connecting them with the various mine facilities was also arranged by simply expanding the existing wharf on Corregidor Bay so that it could be used as a combined mine and quartermaster wharf.[223]

The entrance to Manila Bay was seven miles wide and had depths attaining 30 fathoms (180 feet), thought to be a prohibitive depth for submarine mines. These initial mine defense plans called for mines to be planted in Boca Grande, but if this proved to be impractical, radical changes would be required. In his 1908 report to the chief of coast artillery, as well as through less formal channels, Captain Chamberlaine recommended that a mine company be assigned to plant an experimental minefield in Boca Grande. Quarters for this company were unavailable, however, and it was proposed that initially the company be quartered temporarily at Bottomside near the mine facilities rather than at Topside.[224]

Constructing the Bottomside mine cable tanks in 1908. These tanks were used to keep the cables for the army's controlled mines constantly wet during storage. The shallow concrete "pools" or tanks were provided with overhead cover. NARA.

Bottomside mine casemate near the North Mine Wharf as it neared completion in 1907. When control of the minefields shifted to other casemates the room building was converted to an instrument testing room. NARA.

Building the Mine Facilities

Building the first mine facilities on Corregidor began in 1907 at Bottomside. These consisted of a 53 by 24-foot mine casemate, transferred on February 18, 1910, a double torpedo (mine) storehouse of corrugated iron on concrete floors, and four concrete cable tanks surmounted by houses of corrugated iron, each able to house 27 reels of submarine cable. Each cable tank was equipped with a 5-ton traveling bridge crane. Two masonry buildings dating from the Spanish period were converted for use as mine loading rooms and equipped with 1,500-pound traveling bridge cranes. The loading rooms were completed in June 1908. By March 1909, a mine testing room was under construction and the excavation had been completed on a site 265 feet above sea level on Morrison Hill above Morrison Point for a double mine primary station providing observation of the Boca Chica Channel.

A second mining casemate was authorized to control the Boca Chica minefields. This 53 by 24-foot structure, commenced in 1908, located near sea level in James Ravine was a temporary unprotected galvanized iron building. It contained a battery room, engine room, closet, storeroom, transformer room, operating room, and an officers' cot room. The casemate was connected with a cable terminal hut on the shoreline by a 2-foot-square concrete cable gallery tunnel. By November 1, 1911, the District Engineer had submitted a revised project to bombproof the casemate. In 1913, the James Ravine casemate was rebuilt of bombproof concrete and transferred to the garrison on September 19, 1913.[225]

Corregidor's first mine practice was carried out on March 10, 1911, when three Type 42 mines were planted by the 54th Company. One mine developed a leak and could not be fired. It was taken up, the leak repaired and when the mine was replanted on March 12 it was successfully fired. Another mine practice was conducted December 22, 1911. The 95th and 138th Companies planted and successfully exploded three spherical M1910 Type 32 mines.[226]

In addition to the James Ravine casemate, the District Engineer's project called for construction of an extension to the concrete mine wharf on Corregidor Bay so that it could be used as a joint mine and quartermaster wharf. He also called for construction of a second mine wharf on the San Jose Bay (south) shore of Bottomside; construction of connecting tramways to all the mine facilities; and providing rip raps along the roadside to the three gun-cotton magazines at Malinta Cove. This latter project was eventually dropped. The two wharf projects were completed in 1914 and transferred to the coast artillery on December 31, 1914.[227]

Mine Planters Arrive

Submarine mines (originally called torpedoes) were by the early 1900s an integral part of the United States coastal defenses. In 1904 four mine planting vessels were built and placed in service along the east coast. These planters of 447 gross tonnage were 150 feet long, twin-screw steel steamers, built under contract at Philadel-

Mine planter *General Henry J. Hunt* in the United States prior to its departure for the Philippines. The 447-ton vessel was built in Philadelphia and delivered to the army in 1904. She journeyed to the Philippines in 1910 via the Mediterranean, Suez Canal, and Indian Ocean. NARA.

Mine planter *General Henry Knox* at the Fort Wint wharf. A sister ship to *General Hunt*, she also made the voyage to the Philippines in 1910. In service, these ships doubled as local passenger and freight transports to the island forts. NARA.

phia at a cost of $122,000 each. The Appropriations Act of May 27, 1908, provided $193,000 for construction of a steam-powered mine planter and four 32-foot gasoline-engine-powered distribution box boats: DB Boat Numbers *L-17, L-18, L-19*, and *L-20* were provided for the submarine mine service in Manila Bay and DB boats *L-21* and *L-22* for Subic Bay. Distribution box (DB) boats were small craft designed to work in the open sea and were used in the minefields for making up the joints of various submarine electrical cables into the distribution boxes and planting them as the mines were being planted. The DB boat was equipped with a large boom to hoist connected distribution boxes over the bow and lower them into the water.[228]

North Mine Wharf in 1937. The wharf (center of the three pictured) has two vessels tied up. To the west (furthest) is the Quartermaster Wharf, with its direct access to the powerhouse and quartermaster storehouses in the ravine. McCrary Collection, USAMHI.

South Mine Wharf seen from Concepcion Barrio, late 1930s. Almost due south on the opposite side of the island from the north wharf, mines and cables were fed to the wharf via a rail line from the bottomside depot. McCrary Collection, USAMHI.

Plan of the James Ravine Mining Casemate. The casemate was transferred to operating troops of September 10, 1913, for a construction cost of $12,736.08. The other structure was a two-by-two concrete tunnel connecting the casemate with the cable terminals. NARA.

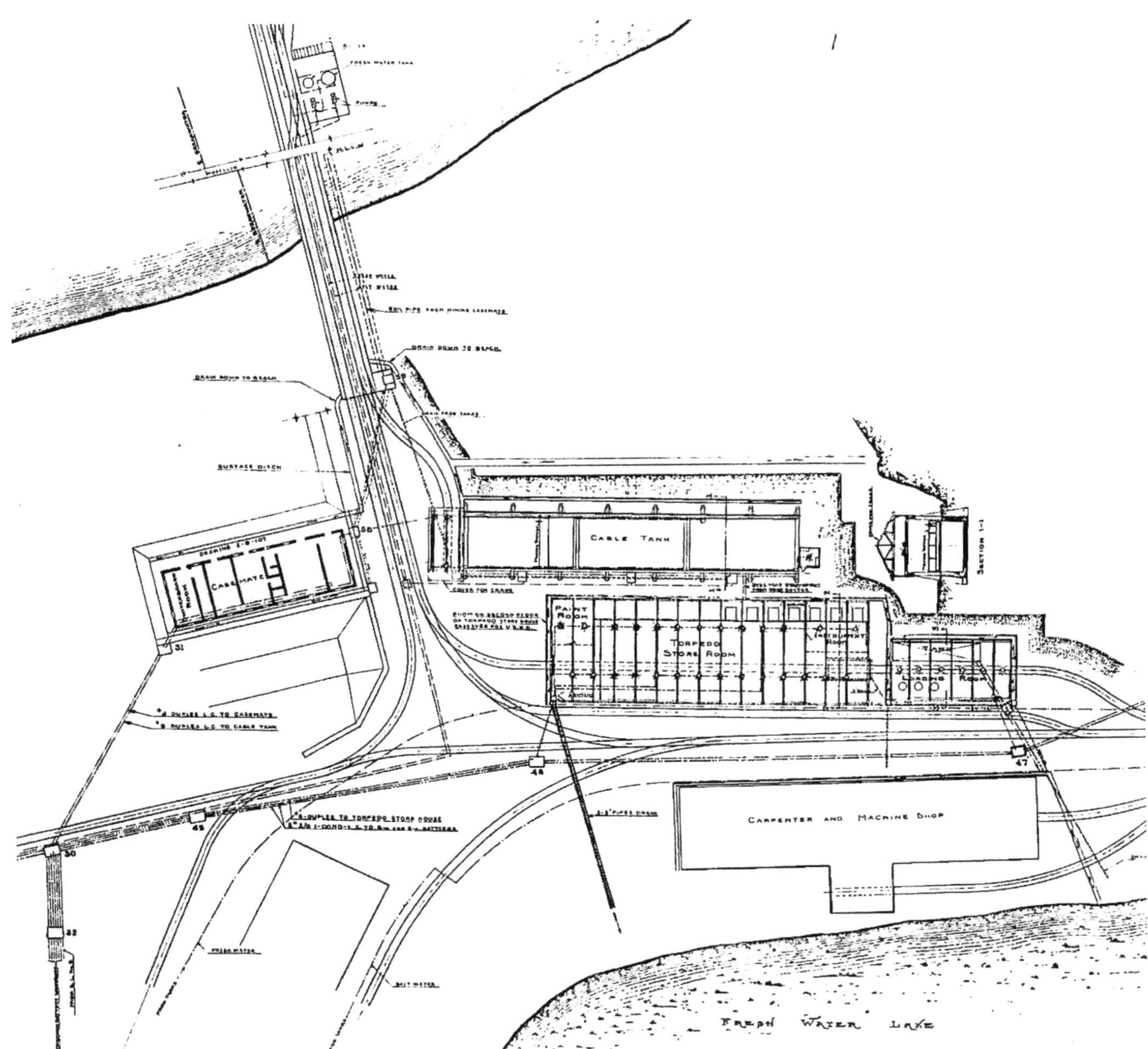

Fort Hughes mine casemate in 1917. The building was shared between the functions of mine casemate and post switchboard. It had been structurally completed in 1913, but there was a delay in outfitting it with all its electrical equipment. NARA.

The need for additional mine planters increased with the submarine mine program development on the Pacific Coast, the Philippines, and Hawaii. Four 1908-class mine planters with an overall length of 165 feet were authorized. These four were projected to replace the four 1904-class planters in service on the Atlantic Seaboard. Two 1904-class planters would then be freed up to provide planters on the Pacific Coast and the Hawaiian Islands and the other two would be assigned to Manila and Subic Bays. The urgency of these reassignments was such that movement of the four 1904 planters to their new stations was ordered even before all four 1908-class replacement planters were in service. The USAMP *Major Samuel Ringgold* and *Colonel George Armistead* sailed in company from the east coast for the west coast through the Straits of Magellan. USAMP *General Henry J. Hunt* and *General Henry Knox* departed Fort Monroe, Virginia, on December 2, 1908. The two Philippines-bound planters also sailed in company across the Atlantic, through the Mediterranean, and thence by way of the Suez Canal into the Indian Ocean and South China Sea to Manila Bay. All four planters proved very seaworthy and managed to make their voyages without major mishap, with *Hunt* and *Knox* arriving at Manila on March 25, 1909.[229]

The mine planters' arrival in Manila Bay reduced the pressure on Kilbourne's recently acquired artillery boat, the former Spanish gunboat *Pampanga*. After their arrival the planters needed about a month for refitting, setting up A-frames and un-housing the forecastle, as well as a general cleaning and painting after the voyage from the United States.[230]

Searchlights Provided for Manila Bay

As an enemy might try to sweep minefields at night, illumination to discourage this was important. With the mine planters' arrival, steps were taken to illuminate the minefields at night. Prior to acquiring the *Pampanga* in December 1908, development of a proper system of searchlight defenses had been a major problem, but with the availability of an *ad hoc* artillery boat, it was possible to conduct tests at night using portable searchlight outfits to select the best permanent positions. The first searchlight received on Corregidor was a 36-inch fixed Sperry-General Electric light received from Fort Totten, New York, on August 21, 1907. It was positioned on Geary Point and designated SL 1. Three more 36-inch GE lights were transferred to the Philippines in 1907 and 1908. Some of these lights went to Fort Wint initially, but all eventually ended up at Fort Mills. Four more 36-inch lights arrived on Corregidor in 1910.[231]

Plans were made to hold searchlight exercises in December 1909; by that time, it was expected that there would be available eight 60-inch and two 36-inch searchlights. It was January 1910 however, before the exercises were held. During the night exercises, one gasoline generator broke down, and before the engine could be stopped, it was wrecked. This placed one of the four searchlights out of commission (a fifth searchlight had not yet been sited). Using reserve generator sets to power searchlights was not deemed desirable and Major Hearn wanted the lights powered by the central power plant.[232]

Noting that placing the lights on tops of cliffs, as one plan called for, interfered with observation of targets and gun pointing, Hearn ordered that all positions for searchlights go down to about 60 feet above water. Eventually seven locations for 60-inch Sperry searchlights were selected around the perimeter of Topside. To operate effectively it was desirable to place the searchlights at elevations somewhat higher than 60 feet above the water to provide an adequate range and avoid having the beams becoming defused by spray created by wave action.[233]

The original plan for permanent searchlight positions in both Manila and Subic Bay defenses was approved in 1910. Work was begun for seven positions at Fort Mills and two at Fort Wint in late 1911 and completed by the end of 1912. The initial searchlight project called for two 36-inch and five 60-inch searchlights on Corregidor, one 60-inch French Sautter-Harlé light on Caballo Island, and three 60-inch General Electric lights and one 60-inch Sautter-Harlé light on Carabao Island. On Corregidor the seven initial searchlight positions were constructed and transferred:

SL No. 1 Geary Point (36-inch SL)
SL No. 2 Searchlight Point (60-inch SL)
SL No. 3 Wheeler Point (60-inch SL)
SL No. 4 Cheney Ravine (60-inch SL)
SL No. 5 Rock Point (60-inch SL)
SL No. 6 Crockett Ravine (60-inch SL)
SL No. 7 Battery Point (36-inch SL)

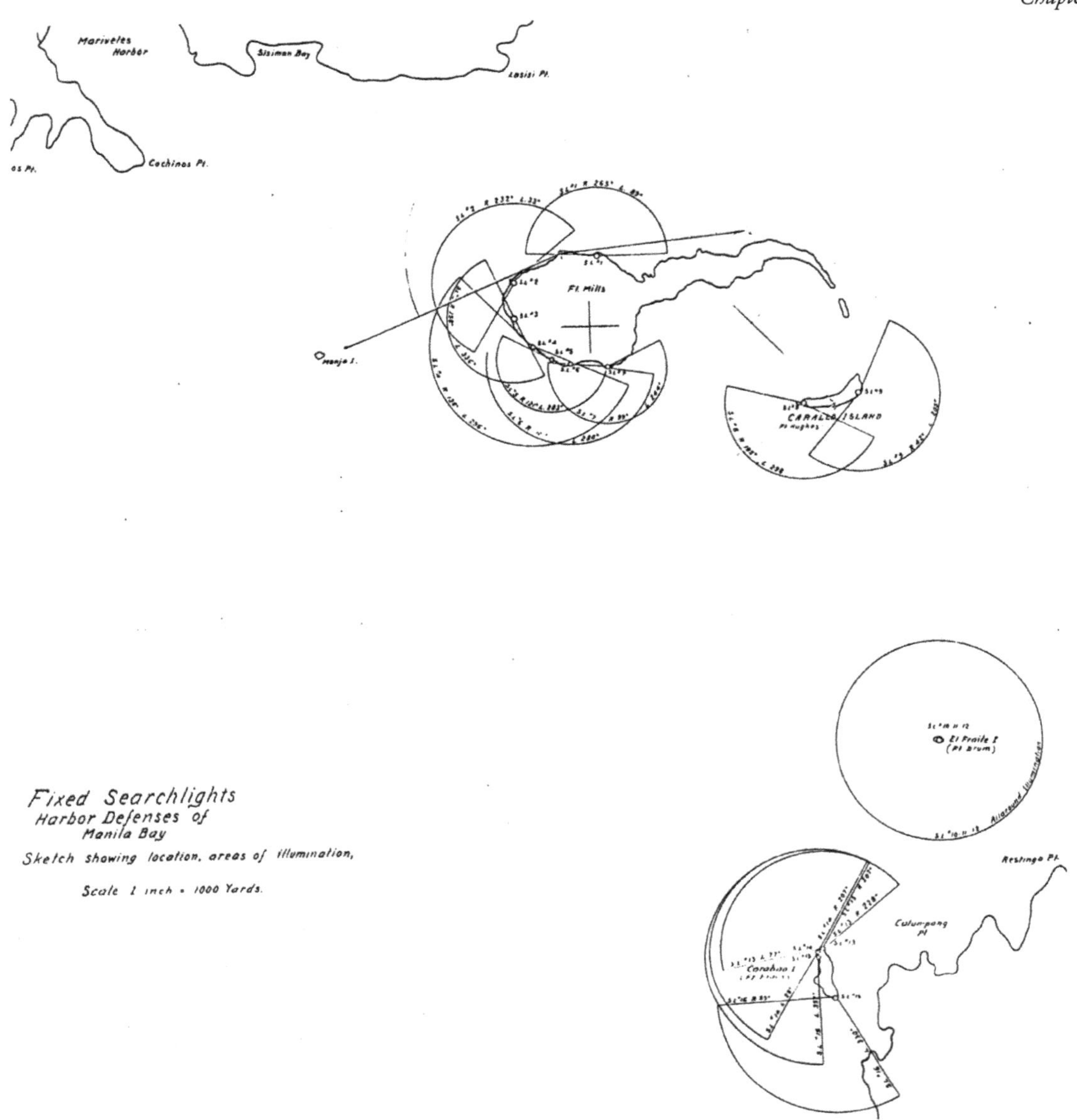

Map showing searchlight coverage and arcs for the Manila Bay Harbor Defenses. These were the light positions for the larger, fixed 60-inch lights. The 36-inch lights (coverage not shown) were intended primarily for temporary beach defense purposes. NARA.

In conjunction with the searchlight positions, plans were made to provide shelters for the lights in daytime. Letters were sent from the chief of coast artillery to the chief of engineers for Maj. Charles H. McKinstry, the Philippine Division's fortification engineer, to confer with Hearn and select sites at Fort Mills for permanent bombproof searchlight shelters and their short railways leading to their operating positions.[234]

The searchlights were kept in their shelters during daylight hours and when not in use. These shelters were similar in construction: a simple protective concrete shelter dug into the cliffs with an adjacent run-out platform with rails for the wheels on the mounting cart or "truck." Most cost around $12,000 each. Power for the searchlights was usually provided from the nearest battery generating set. Searchlight directors termed "distant electric controllers" were not located in separate structures but rather housed in nearby fire control stations. On Corregidor the 60-inch lights in Positions 2 through 7 were renumbered in a counter-clockwise order, beginning on Battery Point, and transferred to the garrison on March 7, 1912. The searchlights for Forts Frank, Hughes, and Drum were completed concurrent with battery construction on those islands.

Less elaborate shelters for some of the seven 36-inch searchlights used to illuminate the minefields and potential landing beaches were constructed in mid-1916. The shelters for these lights and their generator sets were less substantial than the shelters for the 60-inch lights, being wood frame with galvanized corrugated iron

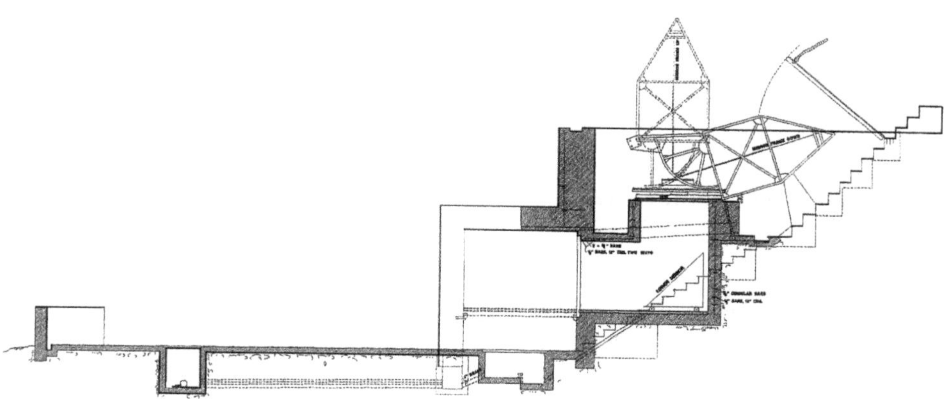

Section for Searchlight No. 1 at Battery Point, Corregidor. This was an experimental type of reflecting light, the light in the protected concrete shelter to the right was meant to project its beam to a mirror in the swiveling tower above it. NARA.

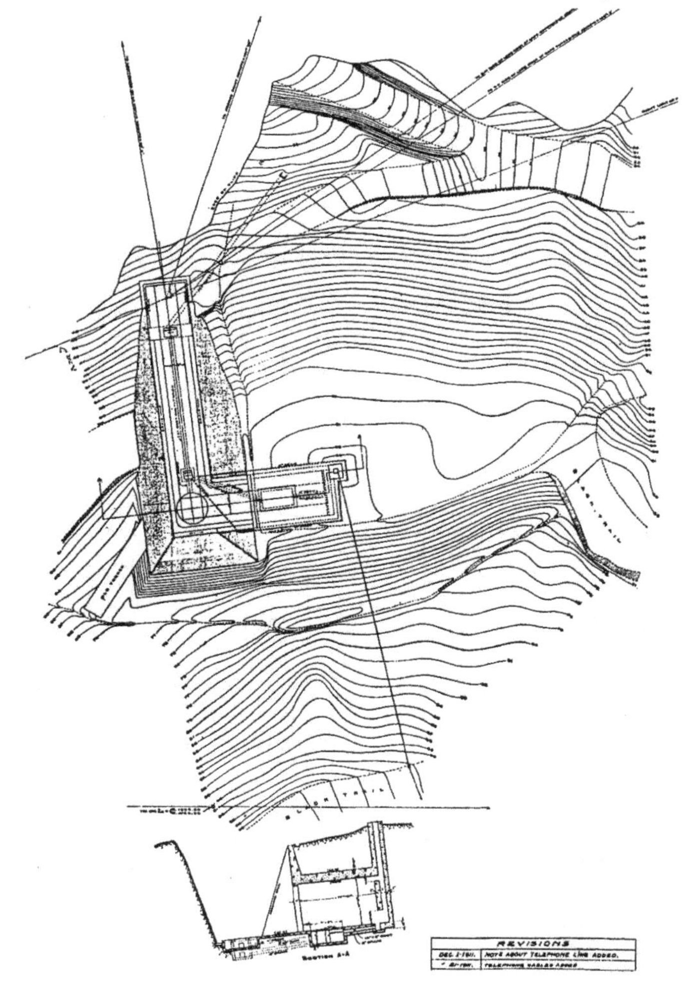

Plan for Searchlight No. 3 in Cheney Ravine. This position was completed on March 7, 1912, for a cost of $11,782.48. In service the light was powered from a 25 kw electric generating set in Battery Grubbs and controlled from Battery Grubbs's primary fire control station. NARA.

roofs. These seven 36-inch searchlights on Corregidor were situated to supplement the 60-inch lights and to cover the waters closer to the island. Of the initial three 36-inch lights provided, two had no specific location while the third was at Cavalry Point on the north shore of the island's tail. Four lights, received just before World War I, were positioned at Battery Point on Corregidor's north side overlooking Corregidor Bay, on Malinta Hill, on the south slopes of that hill overlooking the waters of San Jose Bay, and at Breakwater Point. The generator sets for these 36-inch lights were all mounted on Mack motor trucks.[235]

Searchlight No. 1 was initially a 36-inch searchlight built above James Ravine on Morrison Point and used as a minefield light. The original 36-inch unit did not have a permanent shelter, only a light galvanized-iron shelter over a slab platform accessed by a trail leading to the position. In July 1913 the coast defense commander recommended that the James Ravine light be replaced by a 60-inch light. This recommendation was approved in October 1913, the requisite power and controller cable and the 60-inch light itself were forwarded to the Philippines in 1914 and 1915. The construction and assembly of its parts, however, were prolonged well into 1916. The light was relocated to a new position at Battery Point, some 60 feet above the water atop the cliffs on Topside's north shore. Its primary source of power was a 25 kW generating set in Battery Morrison, but it could also be powered by the central power plant at Bottomside. This light was an experimental reflecting light built on an entirely different design principle.

All the other 60-inch lights in the harbor defenses of Manila and Subic Bays had lights mounted on four-wheeled rail tram carts or "trucks" that were moved out from a protected shelter for use. However, the light for Battery Point was designed to stay in place, shining its light onto a mirror mounted at a 45-degree angle. The beam of light would reflect upward into a tower that in turn had a mirror and could traverse. The tower could

Fixed 60-inch searchlight in February 1922. The position is No. 8 (later re-numbered), emplaced in a shelter on the high, western end of Fort Hughes. Note the tracks set in concrete for the wheeled "truck" transporting the light. NARA.

be folded down when not needed. The position also had an opening to allow the light also to be used in the conventional matter. Thus, it had two lives – it could be used at first in the reflecting mode, but if the mirror was destroyed by enemy fire, it could be subsequently used directly. This light was controlled from the primary mine observation station on Morrison Hill. It was turned over to coast artillery troops for a relatively high cost of $16,064 on March 15, 1917. Power continued to be supplied by a cable from the Battery Morrison 25 kW plant.[236] Searchlight No.1 was approved slightly later than the first six lights for Fort Mills (No. 2 through No. 7). In any event the design did not prove successful, so about 1930 the mirrored tower was removed but Searchlight No. 1 continued to function as a conventional light.

Searchlight No. 2 was located at Rock Point on the island's western extremity. At about 100 feet elevation this installation had two operating positions and the projector was mounted on a truck that enabled its movement from the shelter to either operating position. Its concrete shelter was well dug into the side of the cliffs of Rock Point. A 25 kW power plant at Battery Grubbs supplied its electricity. Searchlight No. 3 was some 75 feet above Cheney Ravine. Its truck-mounted projector was also powered from Battery Grubbs. Searchlight No. 4 was at Wheeler Point some 50 feet above the waters of Manila Bay. Its projector was truck mounted and its 25 kW power plant was at Battery Cheney. Searchlight No. 5 was on Searchlight Point, about 60 feet above the bay. The projector was truck mounted and its power was supplied from a 25 kW generator set initially located in a small room in the rear of Battery Wheeler. Later the power plant was relocated to the "H" Station, the harbor defense command post above Searchlight Point. Searchlight No. 6 was at Crockett Ravine between Searchlight and Geary Points. The projector was truck mounted and also received power from Battery Wheeler. Searchlight No. 7 on Geary Point replaced a 36-inch light. Its projector was truck mounted and also received its power supply from a 25 kW power plant at Battery Crockett. Later this power source was moved to a new location near the Topside parade ground.[237]

Two of the most elaborate searchlight shelters in the defenses were placed on the outer islands. One was cut perpendicular to the ragged cliff line at the extreme western tip of Caballo Island, becoming virtually a concrete-lined cave. Its transfer cost on December 31, 1914, of $14,028.55 made it one of the most expensive searchlight shelters built in the defenses. At the northern end of Fort Frank a dual shelter was built for search-

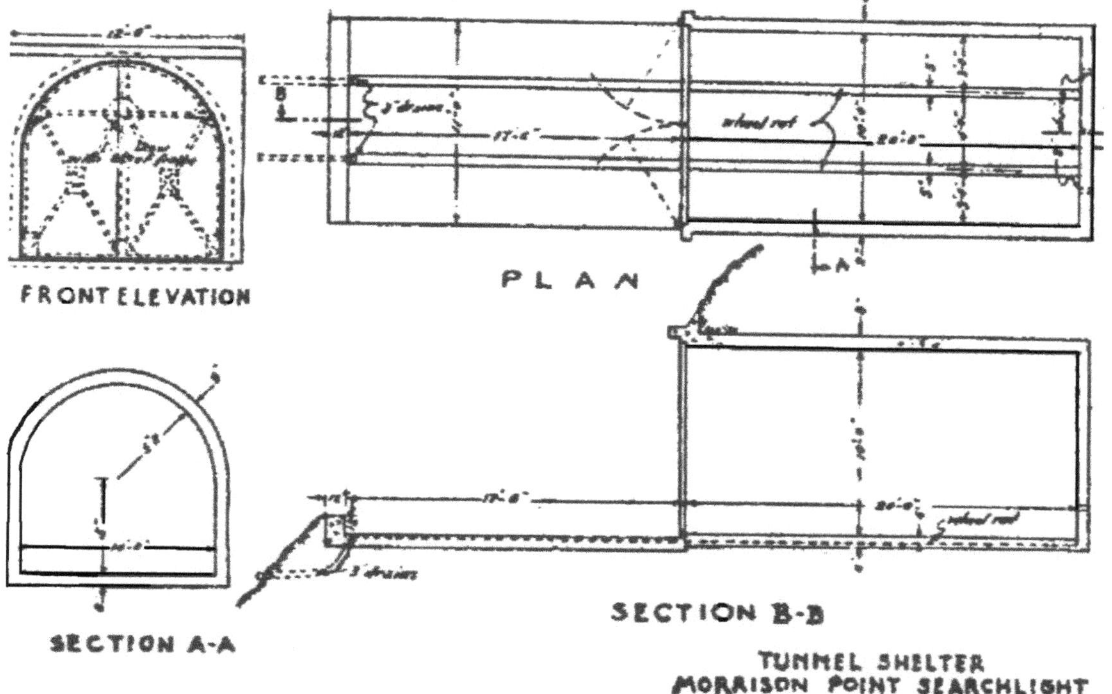

Tunnel shelter for one of the 36-inch beach defense searchlights. This shelter was built on the slope of Morrison Point below the 6-inch battery at that position. Note the simpler design of this type of shelter vs. those for the 60-inch seacoast variety. NARA.

Mack 36-inch searchlight truck. The searchlight was powered by the truck's motor. Six of these trucks were supplied to the harbor defenses as part of the post First World War augmentation. Gaines Collection.

lights Nos. 13 and 14. An enlarged protective shelter fed the two General Electric N-2 truck-mounted projectors through a common passage to two separate operating bays. This dual shelter and single emplacement for light No. 15 nearby cost a whopping $44,467.46 up to its 1913 transfer date. On the opposite extreme, the two lights mounted in the cage mast at Fort Drum incurred a negligible expense to install.[238]

After the United States entered World War I, six 5½-ton M1918 Mack motor trucks each with a 36-inch barrel-type GE type Sperry High Intensity Searchlight and their gasoline powered generators were delivered to Fort Mills (one of these was later moved to Fort Drum to power a 36-inch searchlight positioned there on a temporary basis). These lights mounted on a wheeled cart or "truck" were carried in the Mack truck bed and moved to the operating position. The Mack's engine ran the generator that provided the electrical power to operate the light. The ponderous Mack trucks proved less than satisfactory negotiating the roads over Corregidor's rugged terrain and the truck's engine could not be run longer than 20 minutes in continuous operation without overheating when powering the searchlight.[239]

Over the later years there were incremental changes and improvements made in the searchlight deployment. Originally the big 60-inch lights supplied were either General Electric or, in the case of those at Forts Frank and Hughes, French-made Sautter-Harlé et. Cie. lamps. In 1930 the old General Electric N-5 60-inch lights were replaced with new model N-10 projectors. In May 1932 Searchlight No. 12 on the cage mast at Fort Drum was authorized for removal to Fort Mills, where it was slated for permanent reinstallation in a tunnel shelter near the summit of Malinta Hill, to cover the island's east end and renumbered Searchlight No. 8. The searchlight was finally moved to Corregidor and stored in October 1935. Its power plant was built into an adjacent abandoned land defense battery magazine. The smaller 36-inch lights were also shifted in position during the 1930s.[240]

By 1941, there were 42 searchlights in the harbor defenses: 17 60-inch fixed searchlights in the harbor defenses, six 36-inch portable beach defense searchlights on Mack trucks, nine 60-inch portable beach defense lights on M1918 Cadillac trucks, and 10 60-inch portable beach defense lights on M1925 Cadillac trucks. There were also eight 60-inch G.E. lights and two 36-inch serviceable lights held in reserve and one steel and 16 glass mirrors in reserve, of which six had been re-silvered in 1939.[241]

Land Defenses

Construction had barely commenced on Corregidor in the early 1900s when the Philippine Department staff recognized that the army mission in the Philippines was far broader than its means and resources. Japanese successes during the Russo-Japanese War of 1904-1905, especially their siege and capture of Port Arthur, was considered ample proof that the Philippines, if attacked by Japan, would not be able to withstand and United States prestige and influence in the Far East would as a consequence be greatly diminished. If, however, the Americans could manage to hang on to Manila and Manila Bay, the American battle fleet would be able to steam out from the United States to the Philippines and relieve the U.S. possession as well as destroy the invading Japanese fleet. As early as 1908, plans were afoot to make Corregidor the "keep" of Manila Bay. Until the proposed additional defenses on Caballo, El Fraile and Carabao Islands were completed it was not believed that Manila would be secure from naval attack and capture. In preparation Corregidor was to be prepared with the requisite armaments, ammunition, and supplies for a siege of up to one year. Additionally, at least one-third of the total infantry force required for Corregidor's defense was to be maintained on the island at all times and its land defenses completed and armed. The full infantry garrison was to be moved to Corregidor upon the outbreak of hostilities. In the event of an invasion of Luzon, and if the fall of Manila seemed imminent the entire Manila Garrison would be relocated to Fort Mills.[242]

Corregidor and the other fortified islands in Manila Bay from the very beginning were considered especially vulnerable to attack, not from the sea, but from the mainland on either side of the bay. Enemy artillery fire from defiladed positions on the Bataan Peninsula directed from the Mariveles Heights posed the most serious threat. These heights looked down on the exposed top surfaces of Corregidor's and Caballo's seacoast batteries. Should hostile forces manage to land elsewhere on the Island of Luzon and take up positions on Bataan and on Cavite Province's shore, the fortified islands would be subjected to accurate plunging fire. This threat coupled with an enemy landing on Corregidor and the other fortified islands would quickly place the Philippine Islands in the hands of an enemy. Such a possibility caused the War Department to focus attention on the land defenses of Corregidor early in the development of the bay's defenses. Ideally, securing the flanks

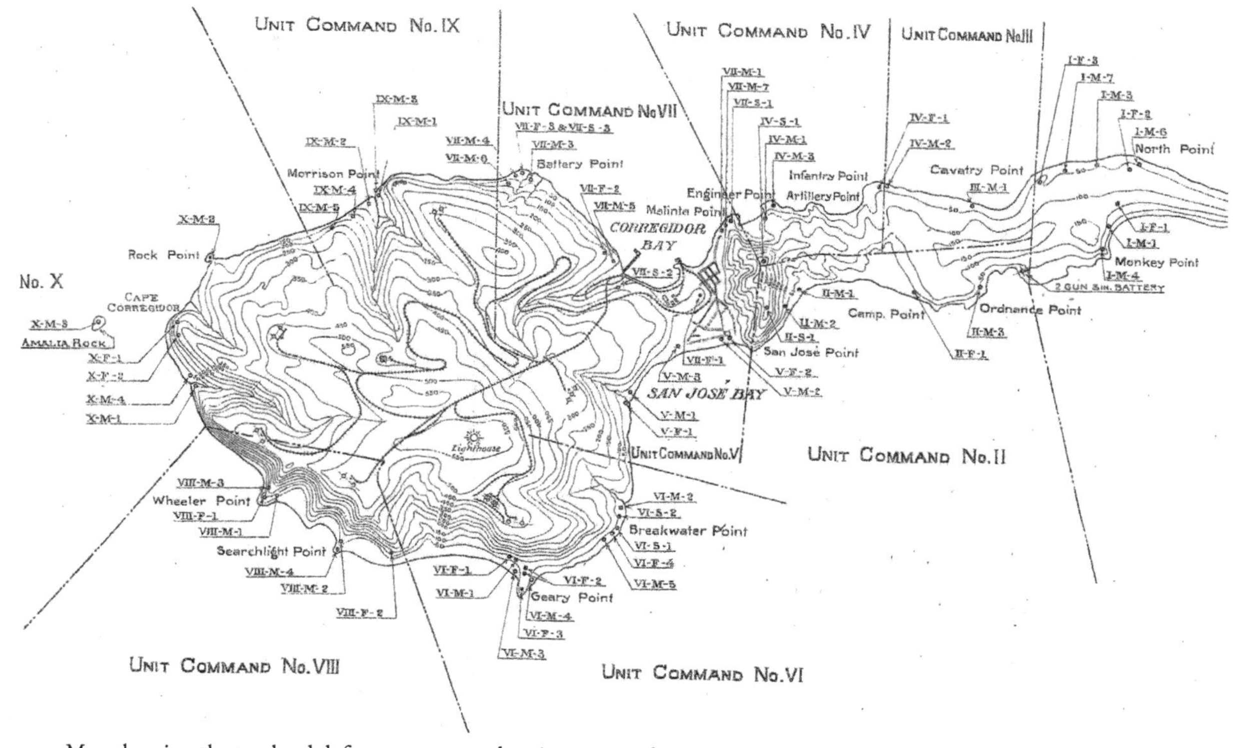

Map showing the ten land defense sectors and major prepared gun positions created by the 1910 project. NARA.

of the defenses by occupying the Mariveles Heights on Bataan and the Pico de Loro Hills of Cavite would have been the appropriate step to prolong the harbor forts defensibility. The cost in both treasure and personnel resources to secure the American flanks would, however, prove to be unsustainable, especially later when various administrations and congresses dealt with whether the United States' presence in the archipelago would be a permanent one. Although some preliminary surveys were conducted around the Mariveles area prior to World War I, the army's lack of detailed knowledge of the Bataan Peninsula would continue for many years.[243]

During the 20th century's first decade, relations between the Empire of Japan and the United States walked a rocky path. Although the U.S. had mediated a treaty between Russia and Japan at the end of the Russo-Japanese War, considerable anti-Japanese sentiments continued in the United States and anti-Japanese measures increased markedly over the years, especially in the western United States. By 1910, there were numerous examples of anti-Japanese legislation and riots egged on by a kind of "Yellow Journalism" that warned against Japan's expansionist policies in the Far East. Coupled with this was the still present threat of insurrection among the Filipino people which would receive, in the minds of many in the military, the full support of Japan. The U.S. War Department viewed this latter activity with alarm and bolstering the American military posture in its Pacific possessions acquired increasing importance. By May 1913, the situation had deteriorated to the point that war seemed imminent and instructions were sent from the War and Navy Departments alerting the various military and naval commands. On Corregidor, Col. John W. Ruckman, commanding the Artillery District of Manila, placed his command on alert and the garrison assumed an extended War Condition Period for some six weeks.[244]

When Major Hearn arrived in April 1909 to assume command, one of the major issues confronting him was the islands' land defenses. As relations with Japan continued to worsen, an emergency project for the land defense of Corregidor was recommended and the secretary of war authorized the Philippine Fortification Board to prepare an emergency project. The sum of $10,000 was allotted from the appropriation for seacoast

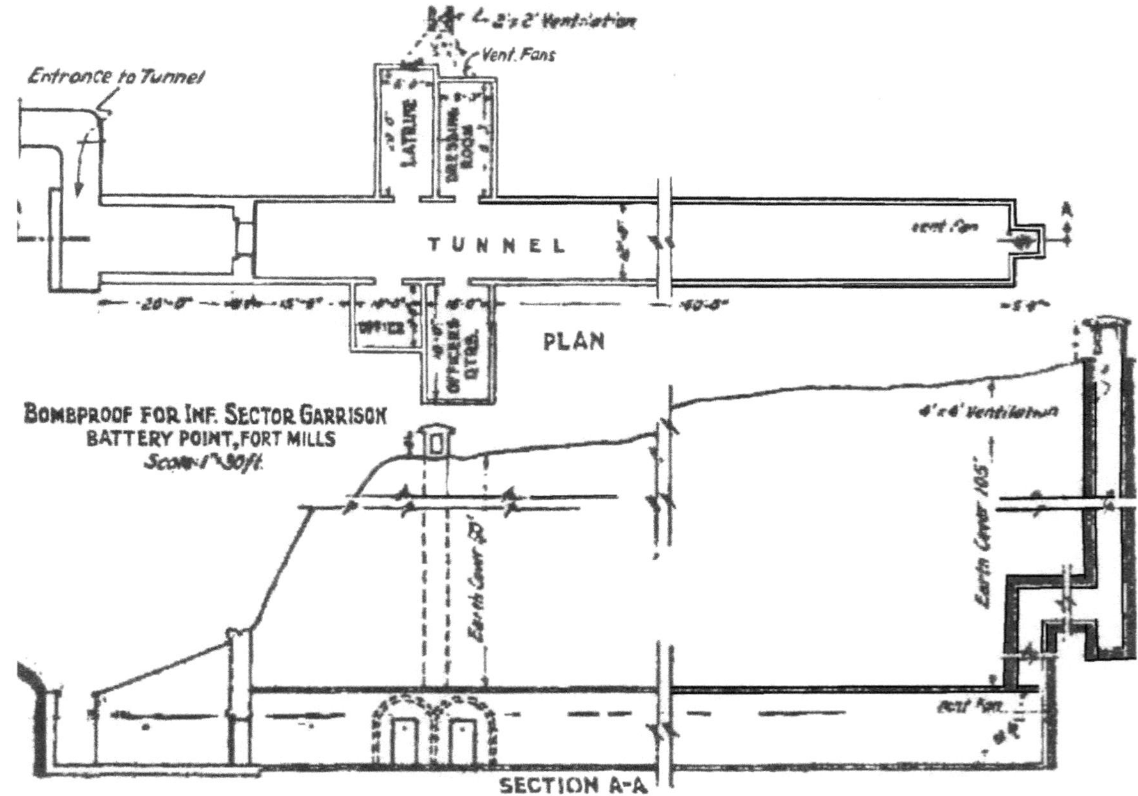

Plan for the bombproof for infantry sector at James Ravine. While many were planned, only the two roughly similar infantry bombproofs at James and Battery Point were actually built. They served up to the 1941/42 campaign, though the site of major casualties when damaged in the siege. NARA.

batteries, Philippine Islands, for the project. First Lt. Henry A. Finch, CE, arrived in the Philippines early in 1910 and was assigned the task of developing Corregidor's land defenses.[245]

The project initially called for 30 field guns and 42 machine guns. The funds allotted for land defense "far from solved" the problem in January 1910. There were still an insufficient number of smaller-caliber guns available. No 3-inch guns had been provided to cover the proposed searchlight position on Geary Point. Infantry support was also in such short supply that the Fortification Board on the Land Defense of Corregidor recommended posting 500 of the 1,200 marines then in the Philippine Islands on Corregidor. The board also

A 75 mm M1917 field gun on fixed firing stand. Since the 1920s a number of these "British 75s" had been allocated to the harbor defenses for beach defense. Over time a number of fixed emplacements like this one were prepared, some of which were even given overhead shelters as late as early 1942. Schmidt Collection.

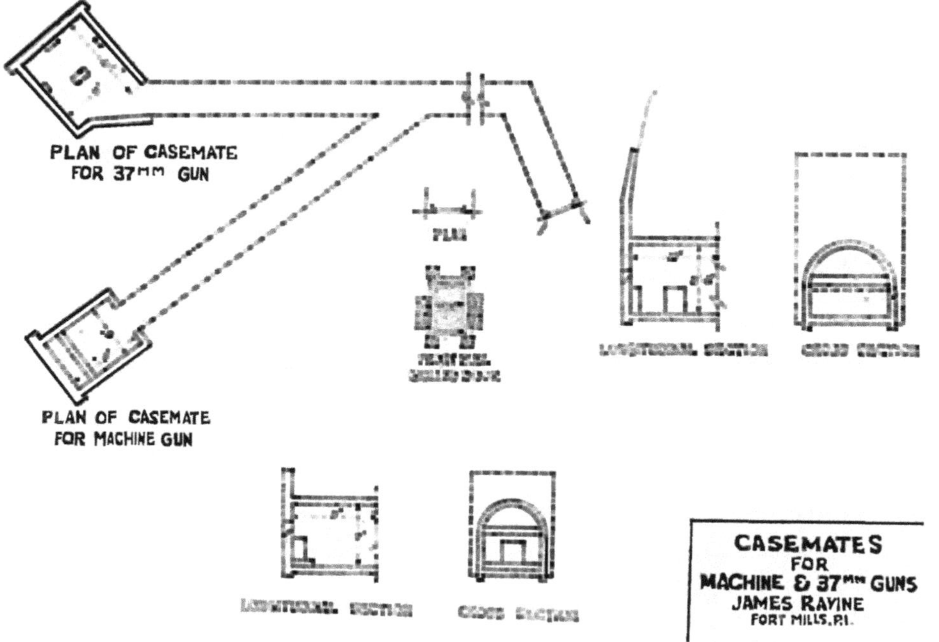

Casemates for 37 mm guns and machine guns of the beach defense unit assigned to James Ravine. While many of the beaches on Corregidor had protective defense positions, these casemates were among the most elaborate constructed. NARA.

recommended removing the navy's Advanced Base Force 6-inch Armstrong guns from Fort Wint and re-emplacing them on Corregidor to be manned by the marines until permanent land defense armament could be put in place and army personnel provided to man them. Major Hearn, commanding at Fort Mills, considered the land defense armament that had been proposed for the islands generally obsolescent, noting "Its use in the defense is scarcely of any value." However, he added, what was on hand was "better than none at all."[246]

Infantry trenches were also projected for the land defenses. On Corregidor, 3,520 linear yards of concrete-lined trenches were planned. The excavation work was to be done by the troops and their revetting to be by the engineers. Other trenches were excavated for the burial (finally) of the island's fire control cable system. The Corregidor commander reported as early as January 1910 that the infantry defenses on the island were "progressing satisfactorily." The James Ravine defenses consisting of bombproofs and other field fortifications were in "pretty fair condition." The shoreline defense plan in 1910 ran around Topside from Geary Point to James Ravine and trails and temporary trenches had been developed leading to all the defenses in that area. A supplementary project was developed in 1910 and reports were submitted September 8 and December 16, 1910. The secretary of war approved this project on February 29, 1912, subject to the modifications deemed appropriate by the commanding general, Philippine Department.[247]

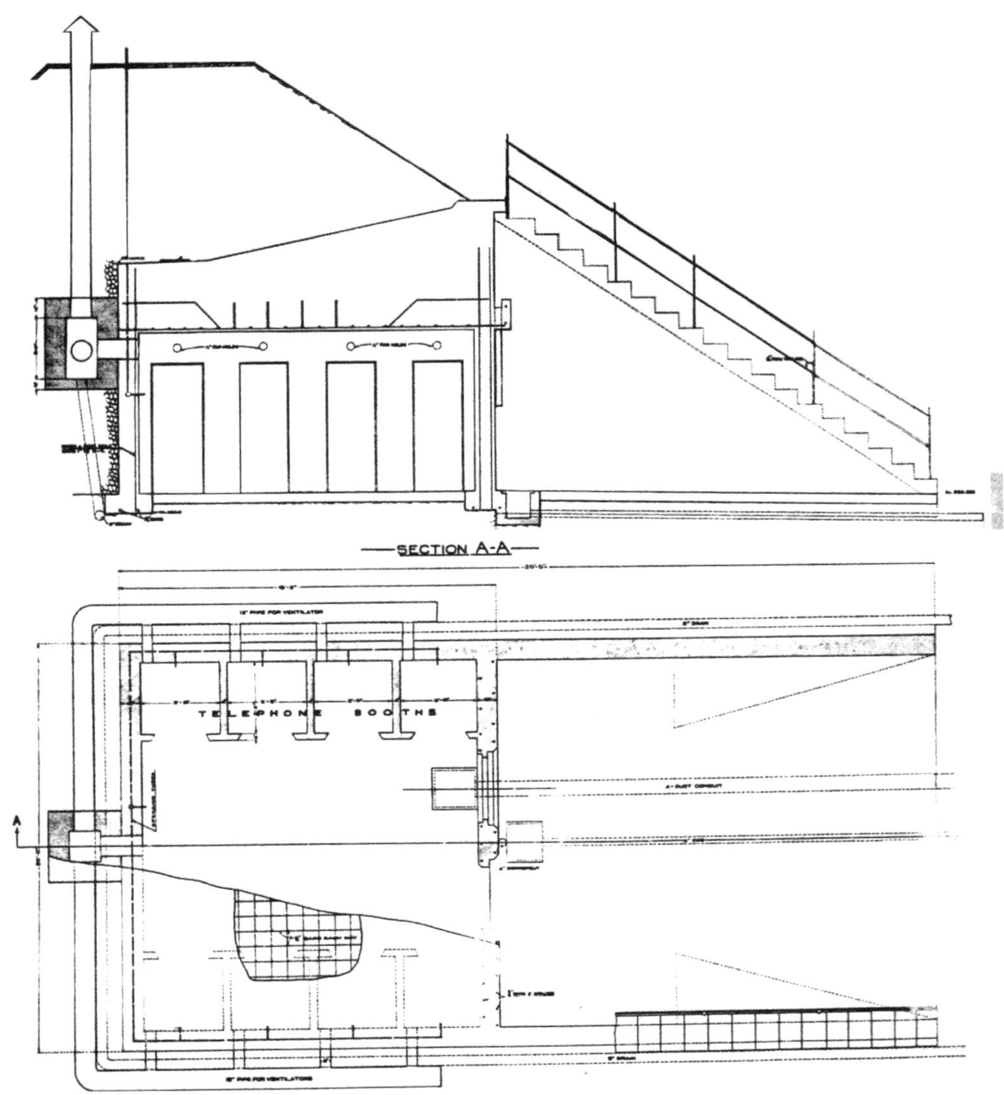

Plan and section for the East Sector Defense Officer's command post on Malinta Hill. A similar but slightly smaller station was also built on Morrison Hill for the Western Sector. The officer here was to coordinate land defense of his six defense sectors through direct phone connection to each. It was completed in 1913. NARA.

An extensive road and trail project was undertaken on Corregidor as well. Thirty-four miles of roads and trails affording access throughout the island facilitated the rapid movement of troops to threatened points. Preliminary work on land defenses was about complete by March 1910. Writing to Assistant to the Chief of Coast Artillery, Lt. Col. Charles J. Bailey, Major Hearn noted: "The preliminary work on the infantry defenses is about completed, trails are in to all infantry positions and a great deal of the battery position has been done for the land defenses. The land defense needs only elaboration and to be made permanent. With plenty of supplies and troops to man the place we can put up a strong defense. In fact the plan now is to build temporary quarters for the infantry at work on the land defenses to house them during the typhoon season." Trails to most of the infantry and artillery positions had been completed and needed only to be made permanent. Major Hearn noted in a July 1910 letter "We have trails all over the island now and one can ride to almost any point of the island."[248]

An additional $180,000 was appropriated from the Fortification Act of March 4, 1911, for land defenses on the fortified islands. On November 22, 1911, the Fortification Board on the Land Defense of Corregidor recommended adoption of a sub-project for completion of the land defense project on Corregidor and the other fortified islands. This sub-project, approved on February 29, 1912, included construction of emplacements for 29 M1897 3.2-inch field guns, four emplacements for 3-inch M1902 field guns, emplacements for two 3-inch M1903 seacoast guns (Battery Maxwell Keys), emplacements for 33 M1909 machine guns, and 11 M1890 5-inch siege guns and 7-inch siege howitzers. In addition, 37 miles of trails, a wagon road around Malinta Hill's south slope, 13 bombproof command posts, infantry trenches, obstacles, and storage for armament and searchlights were planned. Ten 36-inch portable searchlights to illuminate various landing locations were authorized for Corregidor, of which eight were on hand. To implement this phase of the project 1st Lt. John W.N. Schultz, CE, was assigned to Corregidor.[249]

There was considerable disagreement between the Philippine command and Washington about the selection of guns for this project during 1911-1912. The locals strongly preferred the modern M1902 or M1905 3-inch field gun (with its relatively quick traverse and firing fixed ammunition). The older 3.2-inch gun used separate ammunition with bagged powder. Ordnance only had available the older 3.2-inch field guns on non-recoil carriages firing separate ammunition. Eventually the Philippines were bluntly told that the old 3.2-inch guns were being shipped, which was better than nothing. Forty guns arrived on December 18, 1911. Also shipped were numerous older coast artillery 6-pounder (2.24-inch) guns on wheeled carriages and in 1913 the 7-inch howitzers for siege gun emplacements were supplied for Forts Frank and Mills.[250]

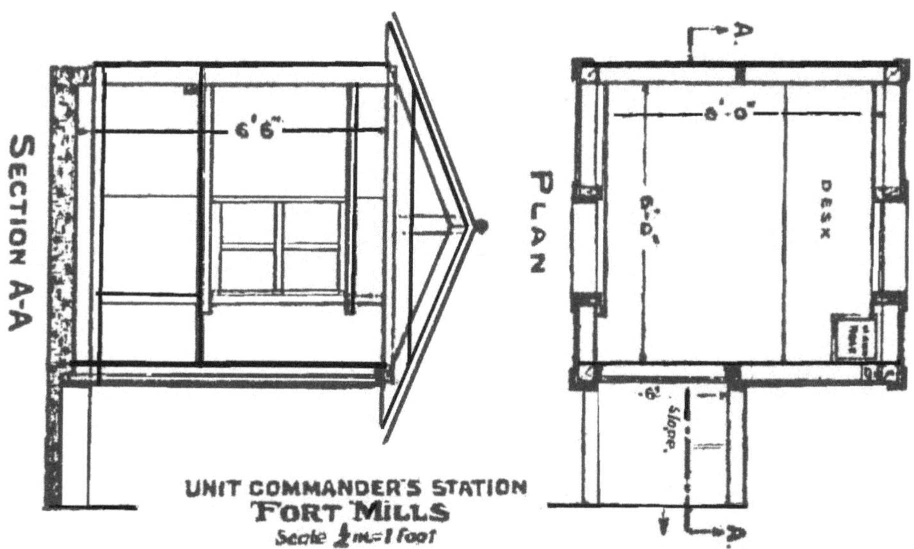

Standardized plan and section for the unit commander's station. There were ten of these at Ft. Mills, one per sector. Basically, they were just a simple wooden building with corrugated iron roof 6x6 feet to hold a telephone and small desk. They were completed in 1913 as part of the Land Defense Project. NARA.

At this stage, at least on Fort Mills, the land defense organization was well established. Each of 10 "sectors" (designated by Roman Numerals I – X) were established to defend a defined geography. They in turn reported to either the Western (six sectors) or Eastern Land Defense Command (four sectors). Buried telephonic cables ran from each Defense Officer's bunker to a sector unit command. The former was a well-protected bombproof bunker, the unit sector command just a wooden building on a slab with a telephone on a desk. Within the sector unit were concrete machine gun ("M"), field gun ("F") or siege gun ("S") emplacements. Usually these were prepared concrete-walled open-topped bunkers with adjacent ammunition magazines. Each sector also had a siege material storehouse (SMSH), a corrugated iron building on a concrete slab. It stored material such as empty sandbags, barbed wire, and *chevaux de fries* (a frame with projecting spikes used to block roads and trails).

By September 1914, the Philippine Defense Board had modified the project. The project's armament now consisted of 11 siege guns and four 15-pounder (3-inch) seacoast guns, 29 M1897 3.2-inch field guns, four 3-inch M1902 field guns, and 33 Hotchkiss machine guns distributed among Corregidor, Caballo, and Carabao Islands. On Corregidor, concrete bombproof command posts for the commanding general and for the east and west defense sector commanders were planned and built; the Western Defense Sector command post was established on Morrison Hill and the command posts for the commanding general and for the East Defense Sector commander were atop Malinta Hill. Infantry trenches and bombproof personnel shelters for the gun detachments exposed to artillery fire from Bataan Peninsula along with shelters for searchlights and mobile armament were also planned. A large supply of wire entanglements supported on concrete beams and *chevaux de frise* were also to be provided. These latter items were to be stored on Corregidor until needed. In light of a plan to utilize the tail of Corregidor as an encampment for an infantry brigade, construction of a wagon road around the south side of Malinta Hill advocated in 1909 was still in anticipation.[251]

The first generation of field gun allocated to the harbor defenses had been the old 3.2-inch gun, Model of 1890/98. While being replaced with more modern 3-inch guns with recoil mechanisms in the field army, these older weapons were provided as part of the land defense program to the defenses. NARA.

The outbreak of world war in 1914 gave new impetus to the land defense preparations. In the early weeks of 1915, Maj. John McAuley Palmer, 24th U.S. Infantry, commanding the infantry garrison on Corregidor, carried out a comprehensive study of the island's land defenses and a detailed plan of actions was prepared. The 24th Infantry companies participating in the study were assigned a specific sector and the company officers studied the sectors after their enlisted personnel carried out preliminary clearings.[252]

Palmer's plan consisted of multiple parts. First, the land defenses were to prevent an enemy landing on Corregidor's vulnerable tail. To accomplish this, the medium and smaller caliber artillery, both fixed and mobile, would concentrate their fire on the enemy landing parties while still offshore aboard their small boats. Should the enemy manage to affect a landing they would be placed under an enfilading fire of machine guns in strong points on the shoreline outcroppings in positions defiladed from enemy artillery fire directed from the Hill 935 ridgeline at Mariveles. Field artillery on Morrison Hill could sweep the tail's northern shoreline with both direct and indirect shrapnel fire. The effect of this fire would be observed and corrected from the East Defense Command Post on Malinta Hill.

From the heights above Government Ravine on the south side of Middleside, field artillery there would also be defiladed from fire from Mariveles Heights. This field artillery and more machine guns could cover the entirety of island's tail, as could armament on Caballo Island, which in addition could cover Corregidor's south shore from Hooker Point on the tail to Geary Point at Topside. Fire from Middleside and Caballo would also be directed from Malinta Hill's East Defense Command Post. Thus, the tail and its long beaches were fully covered from positions outside of the defended area.

Concrete-revetted infantry trenches were also established at the ravines around Topside and on the tail just east of Malinta Hill and it was from these positions that the defense of the tail would be fought if the enemy affected a landing. Typical of the projected defenses at the ravines were those at Cheney Ravine:[253]

The largest of the land defense guns allocated to the Philippines was the 7-inch siege howitzer, Model of 1898. Special emplacements for this gun were built in 1910-1914 at both Fort Mills and Fort Frank. Guns were held in special artillery storehouses until the situation demanded their distribution—however they were removed after the First World War and never utilized in combat. NARA.

With the 7-inch howitzer were also a number of Model 1898 5-inch siege guns, of longer range but used in a matter similar to their larger companion. They only served, and then just in storage for emergencies, for 6-8 years before being permanently removed and disposed of. NARA.

The most useful mobile gun supplied to the harbor defenses was the 155 mm Model 1917 (French manufactured) or Model 1918 (American manufactured) gun. Several dozen were made available in the 1920s, 1930s, and 1940s to the harbor defenses, field artillery, and Philippine Coast Defenses. Fortunately, large stocks became available after the First World War, such as this piece supplied to the Philippines in the early 1920s. McGarraugh Collection.

> With the exception of the immediate vicinity of the mouth of the Cheney Ravine, the shore between these points is high, precipitous, and unscalable. The opening at the mouth of Cheney Ravine is not over 50 yards in width of scalable shore. The configuration of the ground on the south side of the ravine affords sheltered day positions for the defense. We recommend the construction of barbed wire fences and entanglements across the mouth of the ravine with rife pits for one platoon of infantry on the north side of the ravine and trenches for three platoons on the south side. One machine gun emplaced on the south side of the ravine on a natural bench will command the mouth of the ravine. In this position it will be concealed and protected from fire from the water.

The defense of Corregidor's tail would be based on a system of concrete-revetted trenches on Malinta's eastern slope supported by artillery fire. For the tail's defense Major Palmer estimated that a battalion should be assigned to the task but that only two of its companies would be assigned to the outposts' further out on the tail and the main line of resistance would be at the infantry trenches. The battalion's remaining two companies would be held in immediate reserve in the ravines between Malinta Hill and the trench.

To cover the area to the immediate west of Bottomside, a position armed with 6-pounder rapid-fire guns on wheeled carriages was in a ravine on Malinta Hill's west slope where it was defiladed from Mariveles. This position also flanked the approaches to Battery Point on Corregidor's north shore. A similar position for 6-pounder (2.24-inch) rapid-fire guns on the south slopes of Malinta Hill above San Jose Point covered the southern shoreline from Bottomside to Geary Point.[254]

For the western defenses, six sectors, each defended by a company of infantry, made up the defense of the main body of the island:

Corregidor Bay Sector
Battery Point Sector
James Ravine Sector
Cheney Ravine Sector
Wheeler Point-Geary Point Sector
Breakwater Point-San Jose Point Sector

A general reserve of six companies was to be provided, a total of sixteen 150-man companies, or one regiment and one battalion of infantry, 2,400 men for the land defenses of Corregidor. Work would continue on variations of the land defense project throughout World War I.[255]

Bombproof Protection Project

The realization that the island defenses were vulnerable to bombardment from an enemy-held mainland led to two related but separate solutions. A major land-defense project envisioned defenses not only against a potential enemy invasion, but also provision of high-angle guns to fire counter-battery against hostile siege batteries on the mainland. At the same time, it was realized that a multitude of lightly built structures on Corregidor would have to be better protected from howitzer fire. Not only new structures, but existing buildings were going to need better overhead protection from plunging fire. Some batteries (particularly the mortar emplacements) and important garrison buildings were given additional bombproofing. In 1911 that degree of protection was described as:[256]

> The question of the thickness and resisting power of overhead protection for bombproofs was then considered. It was decided that all bombproofs be constructed of sufficient strength to withstand the destructive effect of 7-inch howitzers requiring 5 feet or the equivalent, except the bombproofs for magazines, power houses, switchboard rooms, and the stations for the General Commanding, the East and the West Defense Officers. That these latter be protected so as to withstand the destructive effect of 12-inch mortar fire, requiring 9 feet of concrete or the equivalent.

Funds were appropriated and work was done to modify or entirely rebuild the following structures to the bombproof standard from 1911 to 1914:

1. Battery Way (four 12-inch mortars)
2. Battery Geary (eight 12-inch mortars)
3. James Ravine mining casemate
4. Post and fire control switchboard room

By February 19, 1919, all work authorized by the prewar land defense project had been completed with the exception of a bombproof hospital and bombproofs for mobile reserves that were to be tunneled into the ravines on Corregidor. The bombproof hospital was to be tunneled under the post hospital that had been completed in December 1913. On May 6, 1918, the Philippine Department had recommended that the bombproof hospital be larger than that recommended by the chief of engineers, however, the original project of an 800-bed facility was confirmed and $350,000 was provided in the 1920 estimates for the construction of a bombproof hospital and bombproofs for the mobile reserves. The former was never approved — though the concept survived and would eventually be implemented as the hospital tunnel annex to the Malinta Tunnel. Work proceeded on the bombproof infantry sector garrisons at James Ravine.[257]

Additionally, the following structures were either planned anew or had their plans modified for bomb-proofing to the new standard in the same time period:

1. The West Defense Officer's Station (Land Defense Project)
2. The East Defense Officer's Station (Land Defense Project)
3. The Commanding General's Station (Land Defense Project)
4. The post power plant and cold storage facility
5. The pumping station
6. The ordnance machine shop
7. Ordnance magazines not at gun batteries

The other post that benefited from the bombproofing initiative was Fort Frank on Carabao Island. Plans were modified to provide greater length to the access tunnels at all the major batteries. The road between Battery Koehler and Battery Greer was reconfigured as a sunken road with side protection. The tunnel interiors would provide bombproof protection for the fort's garrison along with various tactical and support functions.

Bombproofs for Mobile Forces

Late in the land defense project the idea arose of providing protected bombproofs for troops assigned to either the beach defenses or to the concentrated mobile reserves. These were places where company-sized or larger units could be protected during any bombardment but be positioned close to potential landing beaches to repel amphibious assaults. In 1916 plans were drawn up for five large underground bombproof stations. The two smallest were essentially long concrete-revetted tunnels to house a full company (120 men) in a barracks along with office, latrine, a dressing station, and a storeroom. They were not meant for long-term occupancy, but as temporary protected quarters pending immediate action. Two larger 3-bay bombproofs were planned, one each for Cheney Ravine and above Power Plant Ravine near the ordnance storehouses on the backside of Morrison Hill. The final, largest work had six bays and was to be placed on the only road leading to Topside from Ramsay Ravine.[258]

Work was authorized and the two smaller tunnels were built in 1917-18. One was at Battery Point not far from Searchlight No. 1; the second was on the southwestern flank of James Ravine. The Battery Point tunnel was about 100 feet above and to the rear of Searchlight No. 1. The James Ravine bombproof was dug into the ravine's west slope near the mine casemate. Both were about 250 feet long and 20 feet wide. At about three-fourths of the tunnel length there were two short laterals opposite one another that were used as dormitory spaces. There was a delay in final completion; neither was transferred until March 8, 1921, at a cost of about $26,000 each. While the local command continued to push for funding for other protected bombproofs in both the FY 1919 and 1920 budgets, no additional authorizations were forthcoming. Finally, Article XIX of the Washington Treaty put an end to any further development of the program. The two bombproofs built were not occupied until the war conditions of the 1942 campaign. Unfortunately, heavy casualties were sustained by the Philippine Scout unit when the James Ravine bombproof took a devastating artillery hit.[259]

Aviation Comes to Corregidor

By about 1910, the Army Signal Corps had begun experimenting with the aeroplane. The Philippine Air School was established at Fort William McKinley near Manila in March 1912. In May 1913, 2nd Lt. Herbert A. Dargue was detached from the 138th Company and detailed to aviation training at Fort McKinley, flying the Wright "B" and "C" aircraft. There in July 1913 he became Expert Pilot No. 16 and the 15th army officer to be awarded the Military Aviator badge. The Wright "B" was severely damaged in August 1913 and in September the Wright "C" crashed on its first flight after being equipped with pontoons for water operations.

In September 1913, a Burgess I hydroplane was delivered to the Philippines for service with the coast defenses and began flying operations. They tested a system of air to ground communication using small message parachutes and firing a series of red and green flares from a flare gun. A makeshift hanger and other facilities were constructed near Barrio Concepción on San Jose Beach at Bottomside.

Army aviation was initiated at Fort McKinley near Manila as early as 1912. Both Wright "B" and "C" Flyers were used for early training schedules. This is the Wright B Flyer being launched at Corregidor in 1913. USAF Museum.

Fort Mills's first aero plane facilities were located at Bottomside's south shore. This is the only image available of the original hangar with track for seaplanes connecting to the water. USAF Museum.

After various experiments and adjustments during test flights between September and November 1913, a new and very simple wireless sending and receiving set was developed. A switch was developed to rapidly change the antenna between sending and receiving modes. During the operations in 1913 and 1914 at Corregidor, landings and takeoffs were conducted in the water on the island's south side. As Dargue's airplane was the only one left in the Philippines, the aviation school was closed in the autumn of 1913. On December 11, 1914, the first wireless message was successfully received from the ground on Dargue's airplane. On December 16, the first two-way communication was finally made in the skies over Corregidor. These tests ended on January 12, 1915, when Dargue wrecked the Burgess hydroplane, and flying in the Philippines came to a temporary halt.

The 1st Company, 2nd Aero Squadron, was organized on December 1, 1915, in San Diego, California. In January 1916 it was assigned to the Philippine Department. Upon arrival in Manila on February 3, the company was posted at Fort McKinley. On February 14, 1916, the squadron traveled across Manila Bay from Fort McKinley to Fort Mills. The Air Service Company brought with it several Martin "S" hydroplanes that it would operate from the location formerly used by Lieutenant Dargue at San Jose Beach at Bottomside. On July 17, 1917, the company was expanded and on July 20, redesignated as the 2nd Aero Squadron. The squadron was subsequently transferred to Kelly Field, Texas.[260]

Balloons for coast artillery observation arrived at Corregidor in 1920. This photo captures both one of the hydrogen-filled balloons and its hangar located at the beach southeast of Malinta Hill. NARA.

A Martin "S" hydroplane in 1916 in the Philippines - probably at Cavite. NHC.

CHAPTER 9
THE FIRST WORLD WAR AND IMPROVEMENTS IN THE AFTERMATH

Liggett Board Reviews the Defenses

In January 1915 Maj. Gen. Thomas H. Barry, commanding the Philippine Department, convened a board of officers to enquire into and report on various questions affecting the Manila and Subic Bay coast defenses and the department's mobile forces. The board, chaired by Brig. Gen. Hunter Liggett, consisted of Brig. Gen. Charles J. Bailey, commanding the Coast Defenses of Manila and Subic Bays; Lt. Col. Ernest Hinds, Chief of Staff, Philippine Department; Maj. Frank K. Ferguson; Maj. John Palmer, 24th U.S. Infantry; and Capt. Harrison Hall. The Liggett Board met frequently between mid-January and mid-May 1915. In February and March 1915, the War Department also directed the board to report on the Land Defense Project status and what additional seacoast armament was deemed necessary for the defenses.[261]

Upon completion of their coast defense study, the board submitted their report on May 14, 1915. Summarizing the situation, they reasserted the long-recognized weakness of Corregidor. While Manila Bay could be defended from attack by a hostile fleet, once an enemy gained possession of the mainland and established hidden siege batteries on Bataan and the Cavite mainland, medium-caliber artillery could quickly silence the batteries on Corregidor, Caballo, and Carabao Islands. As there was no first-class American naval base in Manila Bay before the World War, the location in and of itself possessed little strategic value. Manila and the Philippines in general served primarily as "bait" for a foreign power, but in moving against the American possession an enemy would be required to be ready to meet an offensive movement of a superior American naval force. The United States holding Manila, however, would have no influence on the mission of an American fleet in Asian waters. The fall of Corregidor would have no adverse effect on the operations of an American fleet.

The board further noted that maintaining the defenses as a "keep" was not reason enough to have such defenses but that if the defenses were to be maintained, the fortified islands might well be considered as a place of refuge for the civil government officials, the treasury, and archives. Thus, the mission of the Coast Defenses of Manila and Subic Bays was primarily to contribute to the defense of Manila until it fell and thereafter for sentimental and political reasons to keep the flag flying over some part of the Philippines and providing "assurances to the Filipino people that their interests were being safeguarded." The board also recommended that in time of war the naval facilities at Olongapo and Cavite not be transferred to Corregidor, but to a naval reservation protected by the Coast Defenses of Manila Bay. Noting the necessity for naval forces to maintain security between the fortified islands and the shore of Manila Bay, this requirement would ultimately lead to the establishment of a naval installation in Mariveles Bay. The board's conclusions would influence military thinking about the fortified islands over the next quarter century.[262]

In response to the War Department directive regarding the armament necessary to strongly defend Manila Bay, the board recommended the removal of the four 6-inch and eight 3-inch guns from Fort Wint, as that armament was no longer needed and should be relocated to the north shore of Corregidor where, from concealed and defiladed positions, it could bear on the Bataan Peninsula and provide effective counter-battery fire. The board also believed that after the completion of the new fortifications on El Fraile, Fort Frank on Carabao would have insufficient military value to justify its retention as it was subject to enemy fire from the Cavite mainland. Its armament should be removed to Corregidor as well. The board also called for the replacement of the 10-inch and 12-inch guns on Corregidor by new positions defiladed from land bombardment from Bataan, and the allocation of another 16 12-inch mortars to Corregidor. This would require the removal of four mortars from Carabao to Corregidor. Caballo Island's (Fort Hughes) projected armament would remain unaltered. Carabao (Fort Frank) would continue to be armed with two 14-inch guns and four 12-inch mortars until the fort on El Fraile was completed; then both the guns and mortars were to be removed to Corregidor and its garrison moved to El Fraile. The new fort on El Fraile was to be armed upon completion with four 14-inch guns in turrets and four 6-inch guns in casemates. Although four 3-inch guns were initially slated for Caballo Island, the number was reduced to two before any guns were provided.[263]

The board also recommended that non-disappearing carriages be installed at all elevated sites not on the skyline. In the board's opinion, a barbette type carriage could be developed that was simpler in construction and operation and ample protection could be afforded in the form of a newly developed shield similar to that provided for British 9.2-inch guns. For sites such as those on Corregidor that were exposed to overhead fire from hostile guns on Bataan or Cavite, the board strongly recommended that they be mounted in turrets similar to those projected for El Fraile. In addition to the reallocation of armament, the garrison would also be reassigned: 15 companies on Corregidor and five companies on Caballo. The three companies on Carabao would be moved to El Fraile when that fort was completed. While making the above recommendations, the board also noted that if the War Department accepted the limited mission of maintaining the coast defenses merely to show the flag and function as a point of refuge for the civil government, then the present armament assigned to the Coast Defenses would be deemed adequate. The board further noted that in peacetime only one company would be needed at the outlying posts, as the space on the smaller islands was too constricted for more than one company.[264]

When considering the war garrison for Corregidor, the board recommended that one regiment and one additional battalion of infantry, a total of 16 companies, and one company of engineers be assigned to the island's land defenses. While this number reflected a reduction from the earlier estimate of two full regiments of infantry, it required an upward adjustment in the number of machine guns for Corregidor. Land defense of Forts Hughes, Frank, and Drum was to be provided by their coast artillery garrisons. While field guns were provided for the islands' land defenses, they were mostly situated in fixed emplacements and were to be manned by coast artillery personnel. No field artillery units were recommended for Corregidor. The fort's infantry support should be stationed on the island in peacetime and be provided with special fortress warfare training.[265]

The board noted that the land defense project commenced in 1910 and steadily advanced in the succeeding years had been "practically completed." A detailed study of Corregidor's land defenses had been completed and the locations of trenches and other field works selected. Additionally, modifications had been made to cover all potential landing places with sweeping machine gun fire from defiladed positions. These modifications also consisted of a defense line on the island's tail supported by a strong defensive trench system east of Malinta Hill. The tail's defense was to be augmented by field artillery fire from Corregidor and Caballo. The project consisted of:[266]

Sixteen machine gun emplacements for 31 guns
Eighteen field gun emplacements for 30 3.2 in. and 4 3in. guns
Seven siege gun emplacements for 11 guns
One emplacement for 2 15-pdr (3-inch) seacoast guns (Battery Keys)
Three bombproof stations for the Commanding General and the East and West Defense Sector commanders
Approximately 25,000 feet of telephone cable installed connecting defenses and unit commanders' stations and the reserve positions with the permanent telephone system
Two thousand pointed steel stakes fabricated for high wire entanglements and seventy-seven reels of barbed wire provided

Other improvements suggested included bomb and splinter-proofing protection for the searchlights and procurement of six reserve searchlights. The Boca Grande (south) and Boca Chica (north) minefields were also considered inadequate.

While the 12-inch seacoast mortars primary mission was seacoast defense, they also had a secondary capability of counter-battery fire against hostile batteries on Bataan and the Calumpan area of Cavite. The requisite high-explosive ammunition, however, was never supplied in the quantities that would be needed.

After almost 10 years of incremental expansion, the land defense program was finished. To January 1920; there had been built:

> Fort Mills: 68 armament positions, 2 defense officer protected positions, 10 siege material storehouses, 10 unit command stations, numerous trench lines.
> Fort Hughes: 16 armament positions, 3 siege material storehouses, several trench lines.
> Fort Frank: 18 armament positions.

Fort Drum, on account of its unique construction, was not involved in the plans, and Subic Bay's reduced status simply did not justify any land defense projects.

In October 1916, the Liggett Board's report was reviewed by Brig. Gen. Montgomery M. Macomb of the War Department and the Army War College. These reviews resulted in a reiteration of the War Department's mission of defending Manila and Manila Bay and ordered a further joint army-navy study to develop a plan to oppose an enemy invasion of the Philippines. With regard to Corregidor, no changes in the current armament would be made, except to supplement it with a battery of two 12-inch guns on long-range barbette carriages. However, an increase in the allotment of ammunition for the armament was authorized. The existing defenses at Fort Wint were to be retained, as were those of Fort Frank on Carabao Island.[267]

Reinforcing the Garrison on the Eve of World War I

When war between the Central Powers and the Allies erupted in 1914, the War Department authorized an augmentation of the Manila coast defenses. Eight companies were alerted in 1915 for a permanent change of station from the continental United States to Manila Bay. This last prewar augmentation would bring the coast artillery garrison up to 16 companies by October 1915. The companies alerted were:[268]

4th Company, transferred from Fort Mott, New Jersey
17th Company, transferred from Fort Washington, Maryland
23rd Company, transferred from Fort McKinley, Maine
33rd Company, transferred from Fort Columbia, Washington
36th Company, transferred from Fort Mott, New Jersey
95th Company, transferred from Fort Hancock, New Jersey
111th Company, transferred from Fort Dade, Florida
142nd Company, transferred from Fort Howard, Maryland

The War Department's policy regarding the garrison had called for the regular rotation of troops between posts in the United States and the possessions. The typical tours of coast artillery companies on "foreign service" were about 24 months, although the time lapse between the time a company departed from a stateside post until it returned to one was usually more like 27 months on average. This policy remained in force until about 1910, when it was determined that unit proficiency suffered when the company was transferred from post to post and frequently from one type of armament to another. Therefore, most coast artillery company transfers after 1910 were permanent changes of station. Although officers would continue to be rotated between posts in the United States as well as the overseas stations, enlisted personnel when recruited were either assigned to a mainland post or sent to overseas posts in Panama, Hawaii, or the Philippine Islands. At the end of their term of enlistment, those posted overseas could reenlist at the same station or be shipped back to the U.S. for discharge or reenlistment at a mainland post.[269]

With an imminent entry by the United States into World War I, the Manila Bay harbor defenses were moved to readiness in early 1917. An inspection period of March 6-14, 1917, gives a good picture as of that date. All drills had been well conducted and morale was high. Each battery had a permanent detachment actually living at the battery, and all fire control stations were manned around the clock. Full allocations of ammunition were at each battery.

No further transfers of coast artillery units to the Philippines were made during the World War. Any companies that could be spared outside the continental United States were used to reinforce the units being deployed to France or to the newly completed Panama Canal Zone defenses. Newly recruited personnel would continue, however, to be sent to the Philippines after 1910. In August 1916, the coast artillery companies were renumbered as serially numbered companies of the post to which they were assigned:[270]

138th Company redesignated the 1st Company, Fort Mills
95th Company redesignated the 2nd Company, Fort Mills
142nd Company redesignated the 3rd Company, Fort Mills
17th Company redesignated the 4th Company, Fort Mills
36th Company redesignated the 5th Company, Fort Mills
86th Company redesignated the 6th Company, Fort Mills
70th Company redesignated the 7th Company, Fort Mills
90th Company redesignated the 8th Company, Fort Mills
11th Company redesignated the 9th Company, Fort Mills
23rd Company redesignated the 10th Company, Fort Mills
42nd Company redesignated the 11th Company, Fort Mills
18th Company redesignated the 12th Company, Fort Mills
4th Company redesignated the 13th Company, Fort Mills
33rd Company redesignated the 14th Company, Fort Mills
111th Company redesignated the 15th Company, Fort Mills
9th Company redesignated the 16th Company, Fort Mills

9-1 Col. James M. Williams commanded the coast defenses at Manila Bay during various times. He supervised the preparation of the defenses when America's entry into the First World War was announced. Gaines Collection.

Thus, when the United States entered World War I, 16 "firing" companies of coast artillery were posted on the fortified islands.[271]

First World War Starts

War broke out in Europe in August 1914, and while the War Department took note of the event and undertook to bolster America's readiness, the official posture of the United States was neutrality. The Philippine Islands were a long way from the seat of the war, so beyond the modest augmentation of the Philippine garrison, little was done initially to strengthen the Manila and Subic Bay defenses.

By the time hostilities commenced between the Central Powers and the United States in April 1917, the threat of a German attack on the Philippine Islands had already become remote. Japan, the presupposed "enemy" during the previous decade, had joined with the Allies against the Central Powers. Great Britain's Royal Navy had disposed of the China Squadron of the German High Seas Fleet early in the war when it engaged the German squadron in the eastern Pacific and later destroyed it in the South Atlantic Ocean. Swift action early in the war by Japan, allied with Great Britain, Australia, New Zealand, and France against the Central Powers, had quickly reduced a German threat in the Pacific by seizing the German territories of New Guinea and the Palau, Caroline, Mariana, Samoa, and Marshall Islands. The threat of naval attack on harbors like Manila ceased.[272]

Manila Bay was a long way from the war and the primary attention of the U.S. War Department was focused on Europe. Beginning in 1917 and continuing through the war, the more experienced coast artillery officer personnel, both commissioned and non-commissioned, were rotated back to the United States for reassignment to the continental coast defenses, or more typically to units being readied for service in France with the A.E.F. These men were replaced more often than not with less experienced officers or in many cases untrained or partially trained enlisted personnel. Consequently, basic training of recruits absorbed much time that would have been used for maintenance of coast defense matériel. By the war's end, the maintenance and care of the seacoast armament had suffered severely.[273]

On April 5, 1917, President Woodrow Wilson signed an Executive Order establishing a Defensive Sea Area at the entrance to Manila Bay. USS *Elcano*, a former Spanish gunboat captured in 1898, and USS *Wilmington*, both operating out of Mariveles, were assigned to patrol off Manila Bay. Brig. Gen. Charles J. Bailey, who had assumed command in 1914, was still in command when war was declared on April 6, 1917. Shortly thereafter, Bailey was briefly assigned to command the Philippine Department and by August 1917, he was en route to the United States to assume command of the 81st Division. Bailey was succeeded at Corregidor by Lt. Col. Clint C. Hearn. During this time an order was issued closing Manila Bay to coastwise shipping between sunset and sunrise. A patrol vessel would escort all coastal vessels through the minefields.

April 1917 found the majority of the coast artillery companies quartered at Fort Mills. However, the 2nd Company garrisoned Fort Hughes and the 14th Company was posted at Fort Frank. On March 1, 1917, the district engineer in correspondence to the chief of engineers referred to the discontinuance of work and even maintenance for the coast defenses at Fort Wint. With the outbreak of hostilities, the 4th Company was sent to Fort Wint, where it served as a mine company until May, when it returned to Fort Mills, leaving the Subic Bay post to caretakers. In August the 5th Company was sent to garrison the fort on Grande Island, which then remained manned and operational throughout the war.[274]

By July 1917, sufficient filler troops in the form of new recruits and some experienced personnel from the United States had arrived on Corregidor. This augmentation enabled the coast defense command to reactivate the 17th Company and constitute and organize the 18th through the 21st companies, whose cadres were provided by detailing personnel from the 16 active companies in the defenses. This bolstering of the coast artillery companies in mid-1917 was the principal wartime step taken to increase Manila Bay's defenses.[275]

The Mine Defenses in the World War

In reviewing the mine defense plans and material the Liggett Board had discovered that about 70% of the 19-conductor mine cable on hand was unserviceable and there was not a single mile of the 66 miles of cable that did not have defective cores. The board called for the replacement of the cable, noting that establishing an effective submarine mine defense would otherwise be impossible. The board also noted that as there were no suitable vessels such as lighthouse tenders available for use as emergency mine planters, two additional mine planters and distribution box boats would be necessary if the four separate minefields were to be promptly planted in the event of hostilities. The new planters design could, however, be different from USAMP *Knox* and *Hunt*, in that they would not need elaborate fittings and quarters, but be of the simple twin-screw steam lighter type with an abundance of open deck space and equipped with powerful hoisting and cable laying gear. Additional storehouses and cable tanks for submarine mining matériel adjacent to Corregidor's south mine wharf and at Caballo Island were considered an absolute necessity to provide a proper state of preparedness.[276]

With the outbreak of World War I, a new emphasis was given to the Philippine defenses and the mine project underwent another modification. Developed in May 1915, the new submarine mine project received quick approval and authorization by Washington in August 1915. Construction of two cable tanks was begun, a double track tramway between the two mine wharves, and a new storehouse on the north mine wharf. Rather than build new structures, it was decided to disassemble and remove the torpedo storehouse, Loading Room No. 1, and the houses and traveling cranes from two cable tanks at Fort Wint and bring them to Fort Mills, where they would be reassembled at Bottomside. The wood-frame torpedo storehouse with its 4,000-pound traveling crane from Fort Wint was reroofed and sheathed in galvanized corrugated iron and renumbered Torpedo Storehouse No 3. Torpedo storehouse No. 4, a wood-frame building sheathed in galvanized corrugated iron, was built on the north mine wharf. Fort Wint's wood-frame Loading Room No. 1 was also sheathed and roofed in galvanized corrugated iron, its 1,500-pound traveling crane reinstalled, and the structure renumbered as Loading Room No. 3. The wood-frame houses and 5-ton traveling cranes from Fort Wint's cable tanks were installed at Bottomside atop two newly constructed concrete cable tanks, Nos. 5 and 6. These were concrete structures topped with a wood-frame house sheathed and roofed in corrugated galvanized iron. The structures were completed and transferred to the coast artillery on June 30, 1916. The original concrete mining casemate at Bottomside was converted into an instrument room by the end of 1916.[277]

Minefields were planted in both Boca Grande and Boca Chica Channels of Manila Bay by USAMP *General Henry J. Hunt.* The quartermaster harbor boat *San Pedro* was pressed into service as an auxiliary mine planter and worked in conjunction with *Hunt,* 65-foot distribution box boats *L-1* and *L-2,* and 32-foot distribution box boats (*L-17* through *L-20)* in maintaining the Manila Bay minefields. Minefields in Subic Bay were planted and maintained by USAMP *General Henry Knox* and 32-foot distribution box boats *L-21* and *L-22.* The mine planting fleet was fully occupied over the following two years towing targets for the gun and mortar batteries in addition to maintaining the minefields. The planters, having seen hard service since their commissioning in 1904, were well-worn vessels by the end of World War I. Long before the end of the war, *Knox* was in a ruinous state and by the summer of 1918, it became necessary for her to undergo a complete overhaul in Olongapo Naval Station, which would require many months.[278]

Manning the Batteries in the World War

The bolstering of the garrison in mid-1917 was the principal step taken during the World War to increase Manila and Subic Bay's defenses. In September 1917, the 1st through 21st Companies that had been numerical companies of Fort Mills were redesignated respectively as the 1st through 21st Companies, Coast Defenses of Manila and Subic Bays.[279]

Once the new companies' basic training was completed, it became possible to rotate the various companies between the outposts of Fort Hughes and Fort Frank from Fort Mills.[280]

When Fort Drum was finally completed in June 1918, its first garrison was assigned when the reactivated 2nd Company was sent to the "concrete battleship." In September 1918 the 2nd Company was joined by the 18th Company. Those two companies operated the new fort until November 1918, when the 2nd Company returned to Fort Mills, leaving Fort Drum in the hands of the 18th Company at war's end. Fort Wint was manned by the 4th Company until May 5, 1917, when the fort was briefly placed in caretaking status. The 6th Company was posted at Fort Wint from November 2, 1917, until February 5, 1918, when it was relieved by the 7th.[281]

When the Armistice was signed in France on November 11, 1918, the coast artillery garrison in Manila and Subic Bays was posted as follows: the 1st, 3rd 4th, 5th, 6th, 8th, 11th, 12th, 14th, 15th, 16th, 17th, 19th, and 20th Companies garrisoned Fort Mills. Fort Frank was manned by the 10th Company; Fort Hughes was manned by the 9th Company; Fort Wint was manned by the 7th Company; and Fort Drum was manned by the 2nd and 18th Companies.[282]

Infantry Support

In addition to the coast artillery, the 2nd Battalion, 31st Infantry, and Co. G, 15th Infantry, were assigned to the coast defenses and posted at Fort Mills when the United States entered World War I. In accordance with pre-war planning, the 3rd Battalion, 31st Infantry, moved from Fort McKinley to Fort Mills in June 1917 to serve in the land defenses as coast artillery support. In July the regimental headquarters company, machine gun company, and supply company, 31st Infantry, joined the 2nd and 3rd Battalions on Corregidor. The infantrymen occupied the newly constructed frame barracks at Middleside that became known as the "Infantry Barracks" for several years to come. In September 1917 the 31st Infantry with the exception of the 3rd Battalion, returned to Fort McKinley, due to a diminished likelihood of attack, the island's overcrowded state, and the inability of supply and water resources to support such a large force. The Philippine Scouts underwent a complete reorganization and redesignation in April 1918, as per instructions contained in General Orders, No. 21, Headquarters Philippine Department, Manila, dated April 5, 1918. The 4th Philippine Infantry (Provisional), was formed from Scout companies at Fort Mills, providing an infantry garrison on Corregidor by replacing the elements of the 31st Infantry that had returned to Manila.[283]

The 3rd Battalion, 31st Infantry, was withdrawn at the end of hostilities and the sole infantry left in the coast defenses was the 4th Provisional Regiment. By July 1919, the infantry presence on Corregidor increased to Company G, 2nd Battalion, 15th U.S. Infantry, the 4th Regiment Philippine Scouts (Provisional), the 5th Battalion (Prison Guard) Battalion, and four separate companies of scouts.

Changes in the Coast Defenses Command

The Coast Defenses saw frequent changes in commanders during World War I. On August 3, 1917, Brig. Gen. Clarence P. Townsley arrived to assume command of the coast defenses. His tour of duty proved to be short, as he was soon promoted to major general. He was relieved August 11 by C.C. Hearn, who had been promoted to brigadier general on August 5. Hearn's tenure as coast defense commander lasted only to September 14, 1917, when he too received orders transferring him back to the U.S.[284]

Lt. Col. William R. Doores was promoted to full colonel in 1918 and commanded until August 10, 1918, when Col. Samuel E. Smiley, commanding the 4th Philippine Infantry Regiment (Provisional) then serving as the infantry garrison at Fort Mills, as senior ranking officer assumed command of the CDM&SB until February 1919. Col. Samuel E. Allen arrived in the Philippines January 20, 1919, to take command of the Philippine Department until February 16, before proceeding to Corregidor to assume command of the harbor defenses. Colonel Smiley continued to command the infantry garrison at Fort Mills and the 4th Philippine Infantry Regiment (Provisional) until March 6, 1920. Colonel Allen continued in command until he was relieved May 15, 1919, by Brig. Gen. Richmond P. Davis.[285]

The Outposts are Placed in Caretaking Status

Following the war, the coast defense garrison was reduced as enlistments expired and companies inactivated. As a result, the outposts were reduced to caretaking status. Frequently a single platoon from the company assigned as an outpost's garrison carried out the maintenance of matériel and armament as well as serving as the outpost's guard detail. These platoons were rotated periodically between the outpost and Fort Mills. Fort Wint was garrisoned by a small caretaking detachment made up of an officer and about 27 enlisted men. As the fort was the most isolated in the fortified islands, all fire control instruments were removed and placed in storage at Fort Mills. The guns breechblocks were also removed and stored inside the emplacements. The steam power plant and the steam-operated utilities were taken out of commission. The only power source on the island consisted of four 25 kW gasoline generating sets. Meanwhile, the rapid-fire batteries' had been reduced to two guns each. Subsidence that caused the breaking away of Battery Warwick's right flank traverse and its parapet had continued for several years. By 1925 it was in serious threat of breaking off completely in the event of an earthquake or erosion caused by several days of heavy rainfall, as was common during the monsoon season. [286]

Additional Rapid-Fire Guns for Land Defense

As the battery construction program's initial phase wound down at Topside, attention was directed to the land defenses. By March 30, 1911, authorization had been received to utilize four 3-inch seacoast guns as part of the Manila Bay Land Defense Project. A four-gun battery of 3-inch M1903 guns was projected for the eastern part of Caballo Island from which it could fire on hostile forces landing on Corregidor's tail. Before construction could be started, the plan was reduced to only one pair of the guns on Caballo. The second pair would be emplaced on Corregidor.

Batter

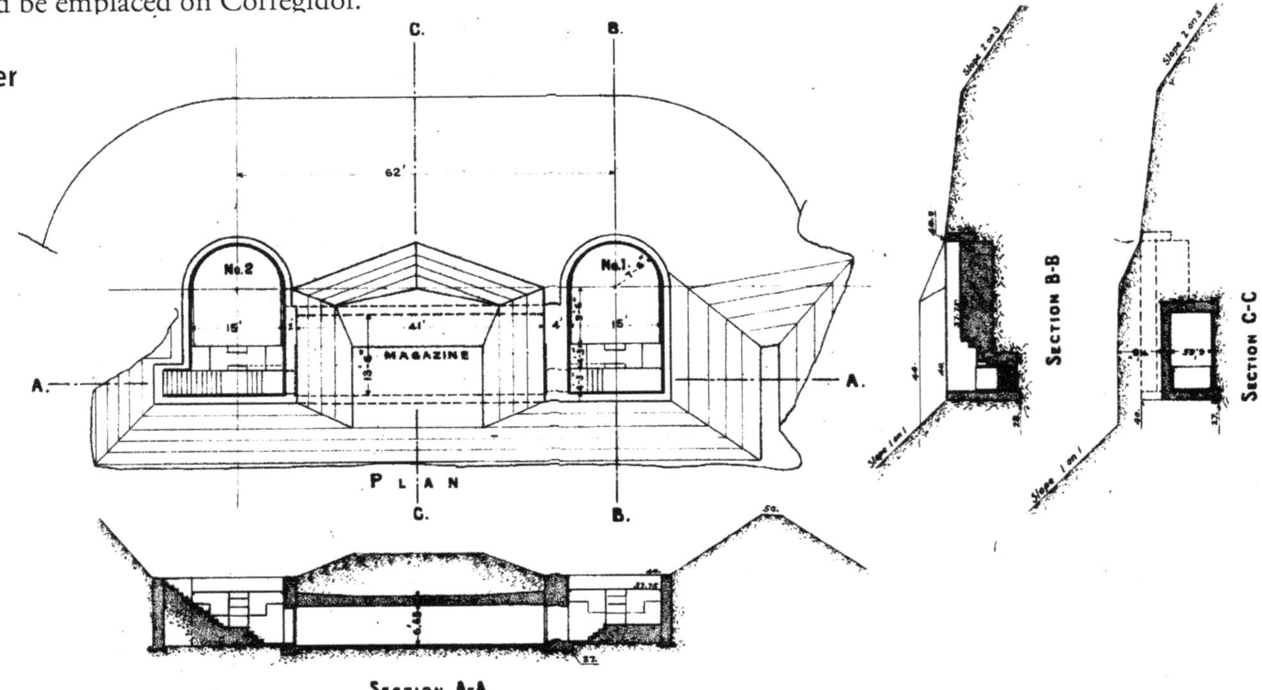

Design sketch for Battery Fuger. Funded and built at the same time as Battery Maxwell Keys, it was emplaced on the eastern side of Caballo Island's Fort Hughes, covering the waters to the north and east. NARA.

Gun drill by soldiers of the 59th Coast Artillery (HD) at Battery Fuger. The photo dates from about 1934 and was probably taken during the annual activation and practice of the batteries at the outpost forts. McGarraugh Collection.

The first 3-inch "land defense" battery was planned for Fort Hughes on the low-lying northeastern end of Caballo Island. The battery covered the tail of Corregidor and the waters off Corregidor's southern shore. Although intended as a land defense battery, Battery Fuger was constructed in accord with the advanced 1903 design for 3-inch seacoast gun batteries. In order to reduce the blast effect on the manning detachment of the other gun, the guns were emplaced 62 feet apart and the magazine was placed between the two guns. The magazine roof was covered with a gently rounded mound of earth that also served to enhance the magazine's bombproof protection. Unlike the standardized plan of 1903, the entire space between the guns was utilized as a magazine. It was armed with two 3-inch M1903 guns mounted on M1903 barbette carriages. Construction was commenced in January 1912 and completed that same year. The battery was transferred to the coast artillery on December 31, 1912. On September 2, 1914, this battery was named in honor of Lt. Col. Frederick Fuger. After the World War, the guns were removed and stored on Corregidor until shortly before World War II, when they were remounted in Battery Fuger.[287]

Battery Maxwell Keys (Two 3-inch guns)

At a point about halfway between Malinta Hill and the island's eastern most point, Corregidor's second battery of two 3-inch M1903 seacoast guns on M1903 barbette carriages was laid out early in 1912. Construction commenced in February 1912 and continued until September 1913, when it was completed at a cost of $4,140.64. On September 10, 1913, the battery was transferred to the Fort Mills garrison. Its design was simple, consisting of two gun blocks behind low parapet walls, separated by a small traverse magazine. The battery remained unnamed until April 25, 1916, when it was designated Battery Maxwell Keys (for some reason historians and even occasional official documents spell this at times "Keyes") to honor 2nd Lt. Maxwell Keys.[288]

In December 1917, plans were in development to remove some of the smaller-caliber obsolescent seacoast ordnance from their emplacements in the continental United States for arming transports. Arming the local transports plying the islands was also a Philippine Department concern. At that time the only small-caliber armament available in the Philippines were the 3-inch RF guns and the only ones considered releasable to service on the transports were those in Batteries Flake and Jewell at Fort Wint. On December 12, 1917, four of

Battery Flake's and two of Battery Jewell's 3-inch M1903 RF guns were dismounted and prepared for mounting on local transports. Following the war on January 13, 1919, all six guns were removed from the transports. Two of Battery Flake's and two of Battery Jewell's guns were remounted in their respective batteries. The third pair, from Battery Flake, was earmarked for relocation to Fort Mills.[289]

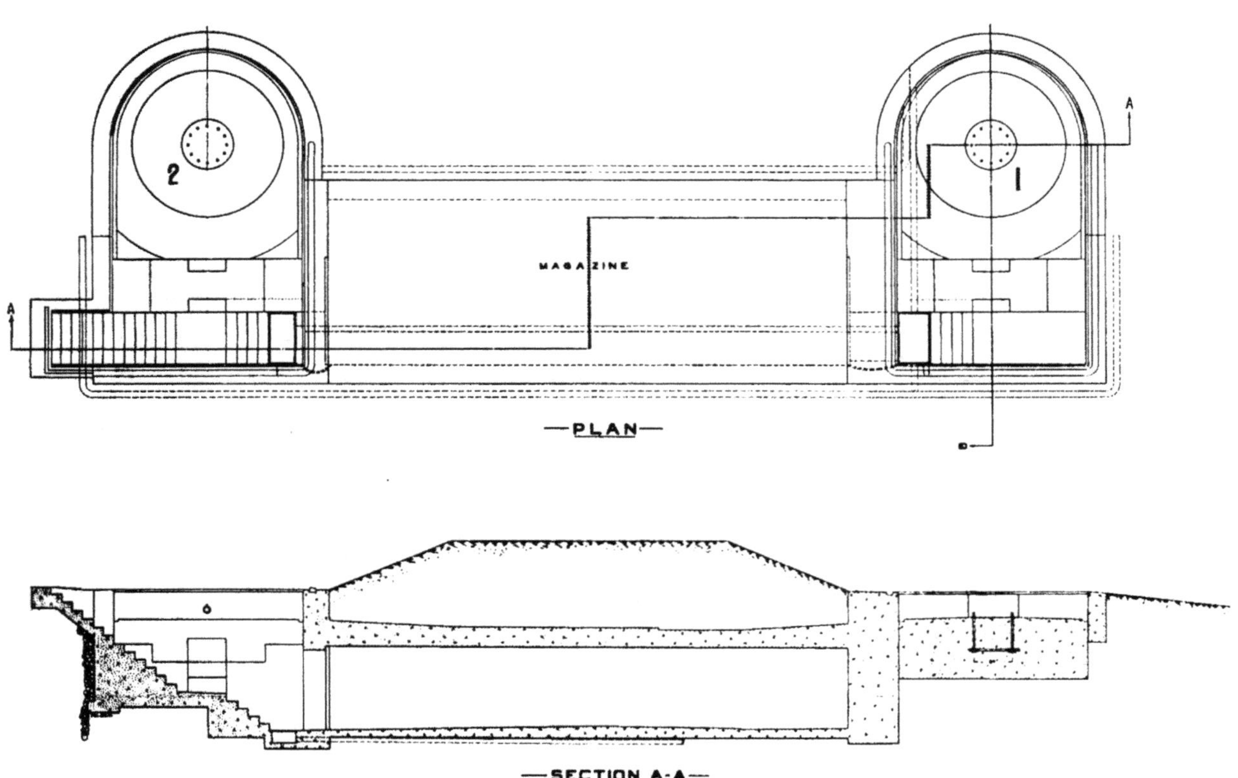

Design sketch for Battery Maxwell Keys. Funded as part of the Land Defense Project of 1910, it followed a design somewhat simpler than that previously used for 3-inch batteries. Maxwell Keys was located on Corregidor's eastern tail to cover the waters between Fort Mills and Hughes. NARA.

The two 3-inch Model 1903 pedestal guns of Battery Maxwell Keys.
In this view of the mid-1930s they are being exercised by troops of the 91st CA (PS). McGarraugh Collection.

Minefield and Searchlight Protection Increased

After the commencement of World War I in Europe in 1914, an expansion of the Boca Chica Channel submarine mine field to seaward was considered and approved. Existing Batteries Morrison and James were no longer adequate to cover the relocated minefield and new gun blocks designed for 3-inch RF guns were recommended to prevent minesweeping vessels from clearing the minefields and to protect the seacoast searchlights covering the expanded fields. These two new RF batteries (utilizing guns to be taken from existing emplacements at Fort Mills and Fort Wint) were to be built on Corregidor; each to be armed with a pair of 3-inch M1903 guns on M1903 barbette carriages. An additional battery armed with guns from Fort Wint was to be built on Carabao Island.[290]

Battery Guy B.G. Hanna (Two 3-inch Guns)

The first of the two searchlight protection batteries on Topside was sited just south of Cape Corregidor where it could protect Searchlight Nos. 3 and 4. Actual construction did not commence until November 1917, and work progressed slowly until late in 1918, when it was finally completed. Battery Guy B.G. Hanna was armed with two 3-inch M1903 guns on barbette mounts; one removed from Battery James, the other being a spare gun at Fort Mills. The magazine service was manual and the battery's fixed 3-inch ammunition was housed in a 17-foot-long and 8-foot-wide concrete cut-and-cover building between the two guns. The battery was transferred to the Fort Mills garrison on March 29, 1919. Initially named Battery Johnson, (perhaps unofficially), the battery was subsequently named on March 27, 1922, for Capt. Guy Ben Gad Hanna, 78th C [291]

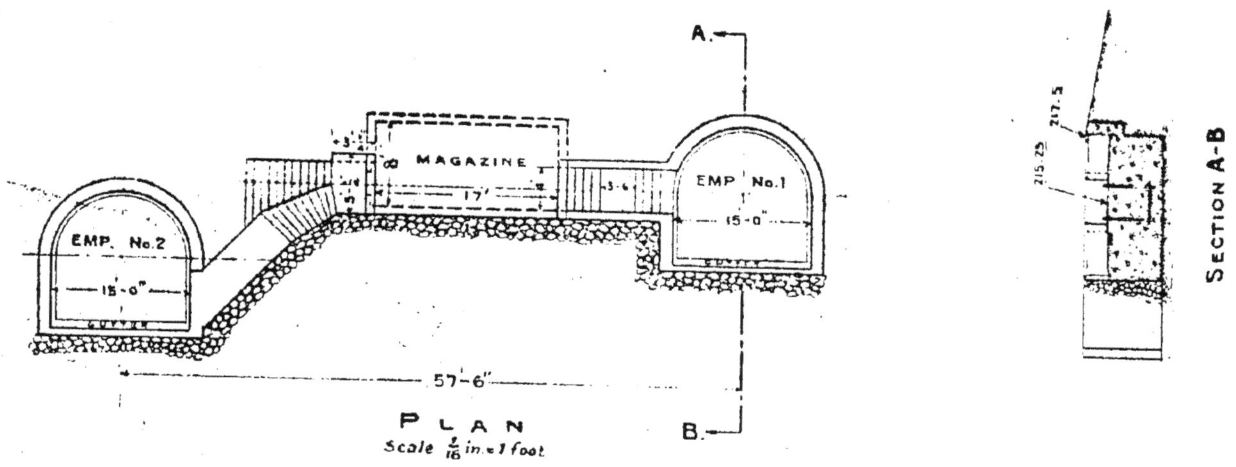

Plan sketch for Battery Guy B. Hanna. Built to protect Searchlights Nos. 2 and 3, Hanna was the first of the new 3-inch batteries. It was started in late 1917 and completed in 1918. Its guns originated at Battery Jewell, Fort Wint. NARA.

Battery Alonzo H. Cushing (Two 3-inch Guns)

The second new battery, later named Battery Alonzo H. Cushing, was just to the southeast of Searchlight Point on the cliffs about 80 feet above the south shore of Corregidor. The battery's two emplacements were built on Corregidor's southwest coast to protect searchlights Nos. 5 and 6. It was begun in January 1919 and completed in December. The battery's armament consisted of two 3-inch M1903 guns on pedestal mounts transferred from Battery Flake at Fort Wint. Both emplacements were relatively simple affairs consisting of a concrete gun block and loading platform sunk into the ground and provided with a low concrete retaining wall around the loading platforms' front and sides. No magazine was constructed for Battery Cushing. The battery was transferred to the Fort Mills garrison on December 19, 1919. Battery Cushing was named on March 27, 1922, for 1st Lt. and Brevet Lt. Col. Alonzo Hersford Cushing.[292]

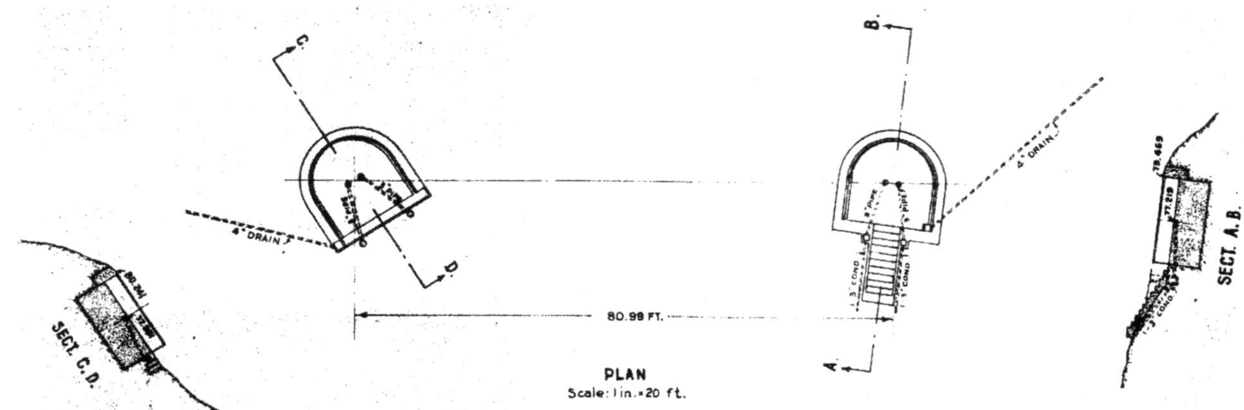

Plan sketch for Battery Alonzo H. Cushing. The two emplacements for this battery were placed on Corregidor's southeast coast to protect Searchlights No. 5 and No. 6. The simple battery was composed basically of just two gun blocks, with no protected magazine. NARA.

One of the 3-inch RF guns of Battery Alonzo H. Cushing. The two guns for this battery, completed in 1919, were originally emplaced at Battery Flake, Fort Wint, Subic Bay. Photo taken September 20, 1920. NARA.

Battery Eli Hoyle (Two 3-inch Guns)

The battery of 3-inch guns authorized for Fort Frank was commenced in January 1919 and completed by December 19, when it was transferred to the garrison. A pair of 3-inch M1903 guns and M1903 pedestal mounts were dismounted from Battery Jewell at Fort Wint and moved to Fort Frank. The battery's emplacements were composed of a pair of simple open gun blocks. The battery was located near searchlight Nos. 13, 14, and 15 at the island's north end. The gun block for the No. 1 Gun was a simple flat slab without the traditional parapet, while the No. 2 gun received a low concrete parapet. Ammunition was stored in Carabao's tunnels. The battery protected the searchlights and covered part of the narrow passage between the island and the Cavite mainland.

The battery was named for Brig. Gen. Eli Du Bose Hoyle, March 27, 1922. In the spring of 1938 the decision was made to place two pairs of 155 mm GPF guns on Carabao Island. As the GPFs fields of fire and those of Battery Hoyle's guns were essentially the same, both of Battery Hoyle's guns and carriages were dismounted and moved to storage on Corregidor about 1940. In January 1942, one of Battery Hoyle's guns was moved from storage to Fort Drum to cover that fort's rear approaches.[293]

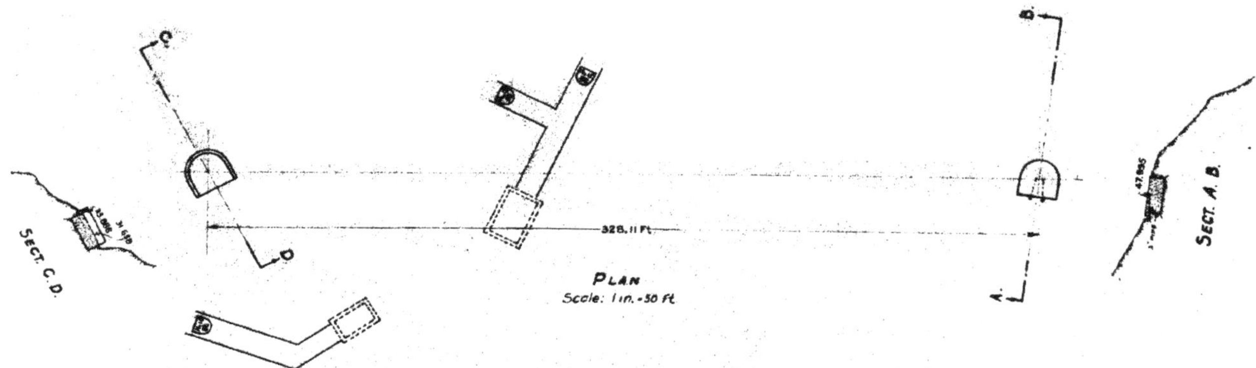

Plan and section of Battery Eli Hoyle. Hoyle was intended to protect Searchlights Nos. 13, 14, and 15 at the northern end of Fort Frank at Carabao Island. Like Cushing it had no integral magazine, ammunition being stored in the tunnels of the larger batteries of the for NARA.

One of the 3-inch RF guns of Battery Eli Hoyle of Fort Frank. Because of their exposed position, the two guns of this battery were usually kept in storage—except when it was necessary to practice firing with the troops assigned to the battery. Schmidt Collection.

Long-Range Gun Batteries Planned and Built on Corregidor

There were substantial improvements in naval design and ordnance (including development of the "dreadnought" type of battleship with its heavier armor) during the 20th century's first decade. These improvements continued into the World War era. In March 1915, the War Department established a Board of Review to study the nation's defense needs partially in light of the outbreak of war in Europe and partly as a follow up to the Taft Board 1906 findings. The board was instructed to review the seacoast defense requirements of the mainland United States as well as its overseas possessions. On November 26, 1915, the Board of Review submitted its findings, calling for increased numbers of heavier, longer-range seacoast guns and mortars in many of the nation's harbors. The report also called for increasing the seacoast armament of the overseas and insular possessions.

For the defense of Manila Bay, the board recommended that two 12-inch guns on long-range barbette carriages be emplaced at Fort Mills, along with the requisite fire control structures, equipment, and power plants as a "means of defense against long range artillery that may be established by an enemy on the Mariveles Peninsula and to supplement the existing defenses in fire to the seaward." Further, the board recommended that additional submarine mines be provided. The two 12-inch guns, their emplacements, and supporting facilities were estimated to cost $538,150 and the submarine mines an additional $138,100.[294]

A new long-range carriage was developed by the army's Ordnance Department; followed by the planning for a new type of concrete gun emplacement. At Fort Mills the site selected for the battery was some 350 feet west of the Topside garrison area. The No. 2 Emplacement was a scant 900 feet from the parade ground while the No. 1 Emplacement was another 990 feet farther west. With the sites selected for the guns, Bilibid convicts began excavations on the first of Corregidor's pair of 12-inch long-range gun emplacements in September

New long-range 12-inch Battery Smith had its emplacements on Topside directly west of the main garrison compound. Ruhlen Collection.

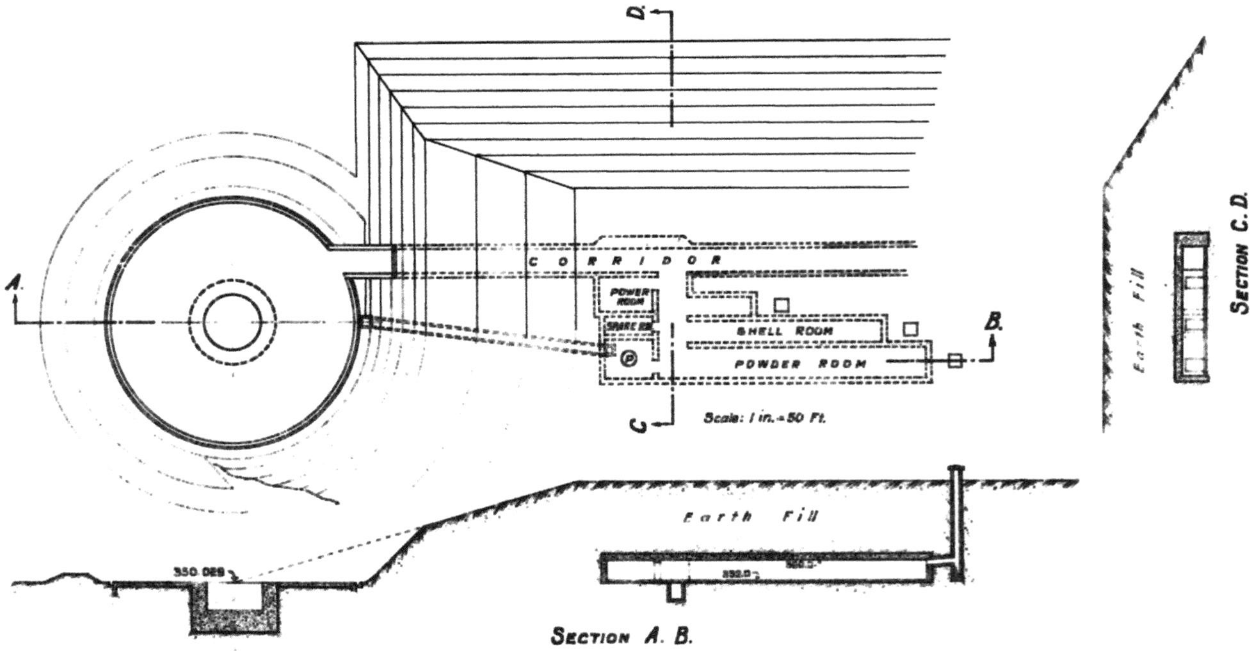

Plan and section for long-range Battery Smith No. 1. Unlike all other American batteries of this generation, the Philippine unit was constructed of two fully separated guns and emplacements rather than a single two-gun emplacement. NARA.

1918. The second emplacement was started in January 1919. Both were brought to completion in 1921 and were transferred to the garrison on June 27, 1921. They were each armed with an M1895M1A1 12-inch seacoast gun mounted on an M1917 long-range barbette carriage.[295]

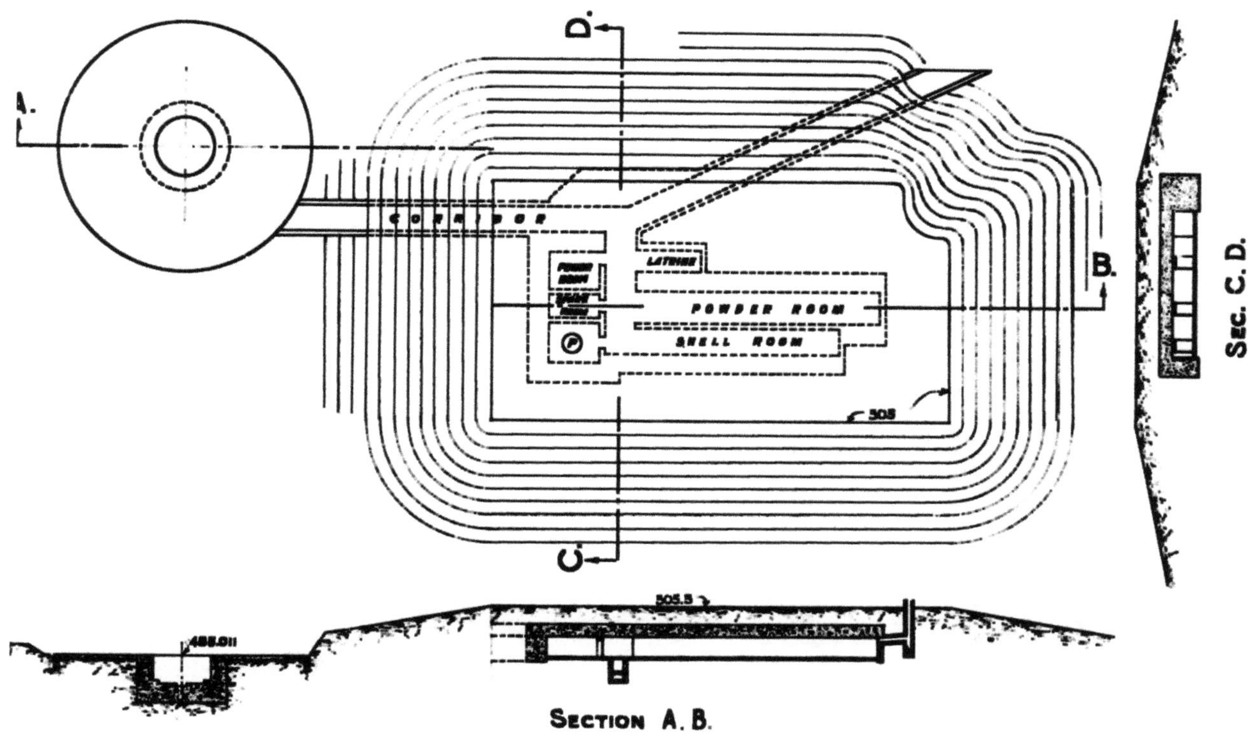

Plan and section for long-range Battery Smith No. 2. Shortly before World War II this emplacement was renamed Battery Hearn. The two sister batteries mounted Model 1895 12-inch guns on long-range barbettes capable of firing to 29,300-yards. NARA.

Work was underway on the two 12-inch long-range gun emplacements in early 1920. The No. 1 Emplacement, not yet complete, is shown in this photograph on June 3, 1920. NARA

The overall design for these new emplacements on Corregidor differed markedly from those built in locations in the continental United States, Panama, or Hawaii. While the gun emplacements themselves were virtually identical, consisting "of a gun-well surrounded by a circular concrete pavement on the same level as and continuous with the metal loading platform of the gun carriage and forming therefore the loading platform of the emplacement," the magazine and power plant arrangement was at variance with the batteries of this type built elsewhere. In the Philippines the guns were not paired, but instead mounted in entirely separate, one-gun emplacements.[296]

Mounting Gun No. 1 at the new 12-inch long-range battery on February 16, 1921. NARA.

The sister battery No. 2 was virtually complete on the same date. Beside the gun in its open emplacement is the entry to the bombproof and magazine. The exposure of the gun to aerial bombardment is obvious—both Smith and Hearn had to be heavily camouflaged during the Second World War. NARA.

The gun emplacements on Corregidor were 1,000 feet apart and designed to function separately with their own plotting rooms and magazines. Their magazines varied only slightly in design but were at variance with the standard design adopted for the batteries of this type. Each magazine was located directly behind the gun emplacement and consisted of a shell room and a powder room as well as a generator room equipped with a pair of 25 kW generator sets and a storeroom. This reinforced concrete magazine/support structure was rendered bombproof and had a covering of earth several feet thick that blended into the surrounding terrain. A concrete paved corridor passed through the bombproof magazine "hillock" out to the gun's loading platform. The powder charges and projectiles were moved from the magazines to the gun by means of a combination trolley and shell cart system.

There was one major difference between the two emplacements. The No. 1 emplacement (Battery Smith) magazine was much better protected by being in a natural terrain cut. That meant it could have minimal overhead concrete protection and much more earth coverage. Unfortunately, in the case of Battery Smith's Emplacement No. 2 (Battery Hearn, 1937) the magazine was more exposed, and had to rely on a much thicker (and expensive) proportion of concrete in its overhead cover. Another problem in the battery's initial design was the location of the battery power plant close to the plotting room. The noise created by the generators, coupled with the ventilating fan and motor noise in the plotting room itself, made accurate reception and transmission of data by voice or telephone impossible. The plotting room was also ill-equipped. The plotting board's vertical baseline was inadequate as its plotting board could only plot ranges out to 18,000 yards, about half the battery's range. A long horizontal base was considered necessary to render the fire control system effective.[297]

The battery was named in 1922 for Brig. Gen. Frank Guest Smith, USA, who died October 7, 1912. The guns were known as Battery Smith No. 1 and Battery Smith No. 2 until gun emplacement No. 2 was renamed Battery Hearn September 17, 1937.[298]

La Monja Project

Throughout the years a great number and variety of seacoast defense plans were discussed with Manila Bay in mind. One of the more interesting of these would seem to be the plan to emplace a dual 16-inch/50-caliber army turret on La Monja Island. This small island west of Corregidor contained a lighthouse but had never been fortified by the Americans. A surviving plan of November 6, 1919, gives a few details. The proposal was to emplace an enclosed, combined magazine, powerhouse, and garrison quarters. Only the turret and a cage mast somewhat reminiscent of Fort Drum would be above ground level. The battery would be accessed from a landing on the island's east shore and through a tunnel. Ultimately, this plan ran into both the realities of army budgets in the 1920s and the terms of the Washington Treaty, and never advanced beyond the drawing board.[299]

Fire Control System Is Expanded and Improved

During the World War I years there were three initiatives that required additional fire control stations. First, the 1915 Program's 12-inch long-range guns required new observing stations and a combination battery commander's station and plotting room. Then the increase in range resulting from the carriage elevation modifications on the 14-inch disappearing guns at Fort Frank and Hughes required new stations to exploit the greater range. And in 1918 a new program to build emergency stations for all the major batteries in the Manila Bay Harbor Defenses was approved. All three of these programs overlapped in time. Over 40 new concrete stations were constructed and transferred to troops from 1918 to 1922.[300]

For the 12-inch long range battery, a local board on fire control met at Fort Mills on May 28, 1917. They recommended building a combined BC station and primary B' station in a new concrete structure near the

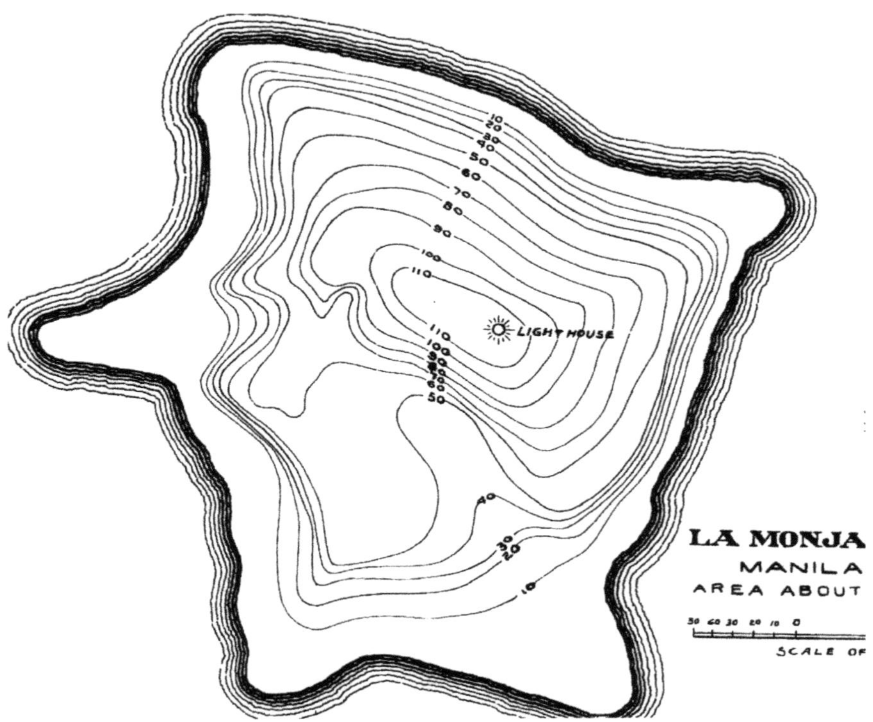

La Monja Island. While acquired as one of the military's fortified islands, it was never developed as a site for gun armament. NARA.

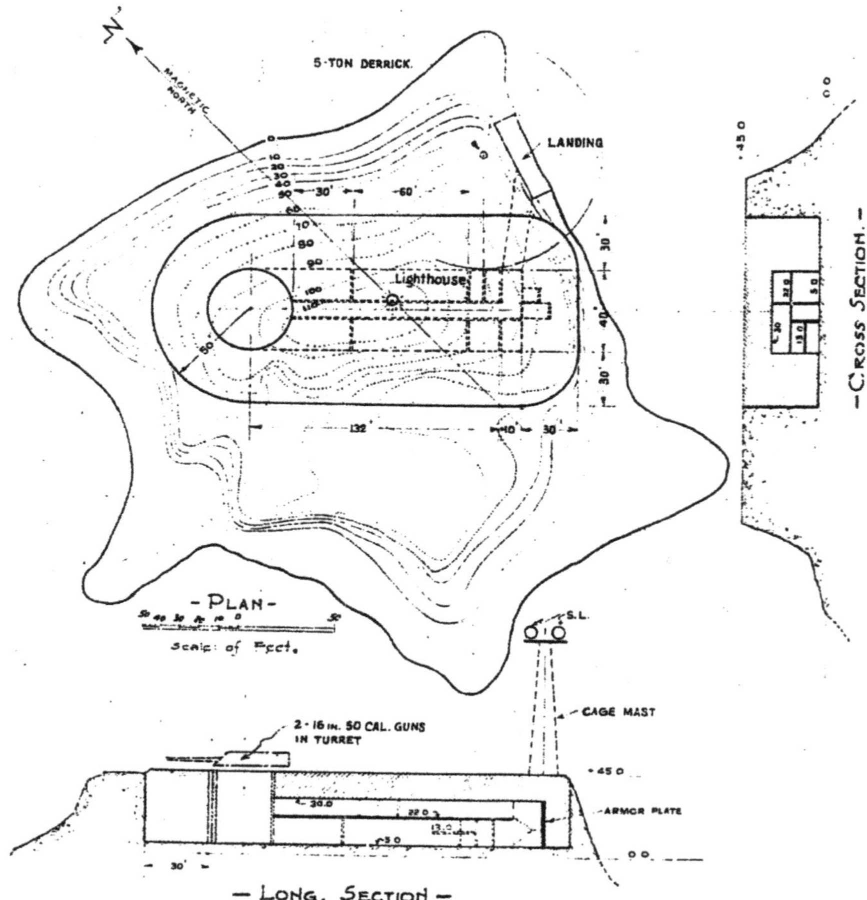

Project for 16-inch turret for La Monja Island. The design for a heavily armored dual turret mounted over underground magazines with a cage mast above is somewhat reminiscent of Fort Drum's design. With the reduced budgets of the postwar-era, projects of this scale were never approved. NARA.

north mortar station northwest of the ordnance machine shop. It was equipped with both an azimuth and DPF instrument. That battery's B" station was to be in the cage mast at Fort Drum. A tertiary (B"') station was to be built on the hogback at Fort Hughes. Finally, a standard concrete manhole-type B^{iv} station was built on a 300-foot knoll at Cochinos Point on the Mariveles shore of Bataan. For the first time in the defenses, the distance and cost were too great to put in a normal underwater telephone cable, so communication from the station to Fort Mills was by radiotelephone. Slightly later the battery got a new fire command station about halfway between the battery's two emplacements, with a deep underground plotting room specially built to hold the large 110-degree plotting board. These B' stations and the F' station allowed the plotting rooms in the batteries to be abandoned.[301]

Increases in the 14-inch guns' range about 1919 resulted in the fire control system's expansion and development of a horizontal base line system in addition to the original vertical system for the 14-inch guns employing additional fire control stations. New stations were established at Fort Frank for the 14-inch guns at Fort Hughes, and Fort Frank's 14-inch guns were authorized two additional stations on Limbones Island. This island southwest of Carabao Island was already military property but had not been previously used. Roughly the same size and topography as Carabao, it lay to the southwest. Two square concrete stations were erected on the northern end of Limbones Island. These two stations were eventually provided with instrumentation and communications and placed in service in 1940.[302]

At Fort Hughes both single-gun emplacements had their own BCS and plotting rooms at the battery and their primary stations (B') on the island's steep hogback ridge. New secondary stations were constructed at Fort Mills. However, just one station was actually built — it was found economical to re-use the abandoned primary station for Battery Crockett as the new B" for Battery Crofton. These manhole stations were transferred on April 20, 1922, for $1,145 each. Another pair of new stations was built at Fort Frank to become the anchor for the southern baseline. Both B"' stations for Batteries Woodruff and Gillespie were located off the main tunnel leading into Frank's Battery Greer. They were also transferred on April 20, 1922, having cost $4,666.90 each.[303]

The designation of tactical numbers for the batteries in Manila Bay went through several changes during the 1920s and 1930s. While there were no new observing stations built after 1922, there were frequent reassignments of the existing stations. For example, the tertiary stations (B"') at Fort Frank for Batteries Gillespie and Woodruff were later assigned as secondaries (B") for long range Batteries Smith and Hearn, while the "original" long-range secondaries at Fort Hughes were relocated to the Limbones locations by early 1940. Some of this relocation was prompted by the tactical division of Battery Smith and the subsequent need for separate fire control stations.[304]

The final generation of new stations sprang from a different concept. The idea was that in times of siege or prolonged combat, some regular observing stations might be knocked out by enemy fire, or in 1918, the threat of aerial bomb damage was now being considered a distinct possibility. It was considered wise to have a substitute station for many, if not all, of those already existing. This would involve a pre-selected spot already tied into the plotting boards and communications network. A spare instrument would be in storage, as it would be unlikely that the original DPF, azimuth, or CRF instrument would survive in a knocked-out station. The new position itself would be just an open fixed concrete stand with a light protective parapet. The program was unique to the Harbor Defenses of Manila Bay. No other American harbor defense got such a network of emergency stations, and by 1918 the future of Fort Wint was such that no investment was made to provide emergency stations for Subic Bay.

The actual number of stations built was driven by the number of new instruments being authorized, financed, and fabricated. Deducting the new DPFs intended for the new long-range stations, the engineers calculated their assignment. Spread between the four existing fortified islands, there would be 25 emergency stations for Lewis DPFs. All of these were to go on concrete bases, all but one having a shallow, surrounding concrete wall. To hold down costs, many of these featured a curved forward wall, immediately creating the

The primary observation station for long-range Batteries Smith Nos. 1 and 2 in 1921. Built on Way Hill, just below the North Mortar Observation Station. Note the brackets to hold the hinged windows when raised to clear the view for the range-finding instruments. NARA.

Fire command station for the long-range 12-inch Battery. It was almost exactly between the two gun emplacements. This observation room sits atop an exceptionally large plotting room - the range and coverage of the guns was so great that the corresponding plotting table in the underground room had to have a room of specially-enlarged dimensions. NARA.

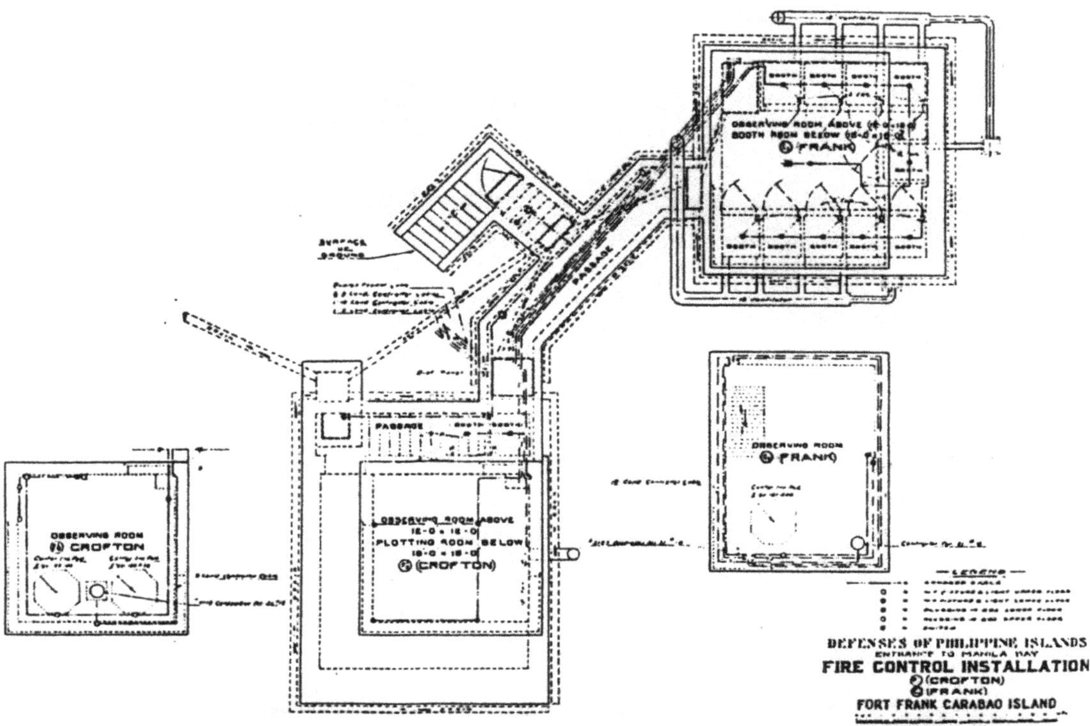

Plan of the complicated "nest" of observing rooms, plotting rooms, and telephone booths at Fort Frank. As part of the reorganization of the fire control system in the early 1920s, extensive changes were made to the assignment of stations for the 14-inch batteries. NARA.

Small shelter for the crew manning the new Limbones Island fire control stations, built in 1921. NARA.

unofficial designation of "bathtub" stations. In addition to the DPFs, eight coincidence rangefinders were obtained. Mostly used for mine stations or as large battery emergency BCSs, these were placed in similar type emplacements, but with a different base. A total of 15 azimuth instruments were also obtained. However, in this case, all that was needed was a pre-selected benchmark or concrete marker on a level piece of ground; the instrument could be erected on its tripod base directly above the locator.[305]

By late 1918 33 new emergency stations had been provided for the DPF and CRF instruments. Three were built at Fort Frank, six at Fort Hughes, and 21 at Fort Mills. Fort Drum was allocated three stations, but as there was no space to build new emplacements, the instruments were simply stored inside the concrete battleship and were to be taken onto the deck when needed. Transfer of the emergency fire control system was on January 13, 1921, for an engineering cost of $12,007.58. Communication cables were provided buried trenches only if the station was within 100 yards of an existing structure or cable. The more remotely located were to get temporary cable communications only at time of need. A new protected storage facility was built at Fort Mills to house the expensive newly obtained fire control instruments.[306]

A few other last-minute additions were made to the fire control situation. For example, in 1921 a new plotting room was built specifically for Battery Morrison. It was dug out of the hillside directly below the battery commander's station at the rear overlooking Battery Morrison. Later in the 1930s, lightly-constructed galvanized-iron battery commander stations were also provided for Batteries Guy B.G. Hanna and Alonzo H. Cushing, along with several semi-permanent 155 mm Panama mount batteries.[307]

Also in the 1920s an extensive network of emergency stations was constructed at Fort Mills and Hughes. Just simple, open emplacements, they were pre-selected foundations for ranging instruments already anticipated on various plotting boards. This is the alternate station for the coincidence rangefinder (CRF) for 6-inch Battery Morrison. NARA.

More numerous were emergency stations for depression position finders (DPF) to be used as alternates for most of the larger battery primary stations. This is the one for the primary station of mortar Battery Geary. NARA.

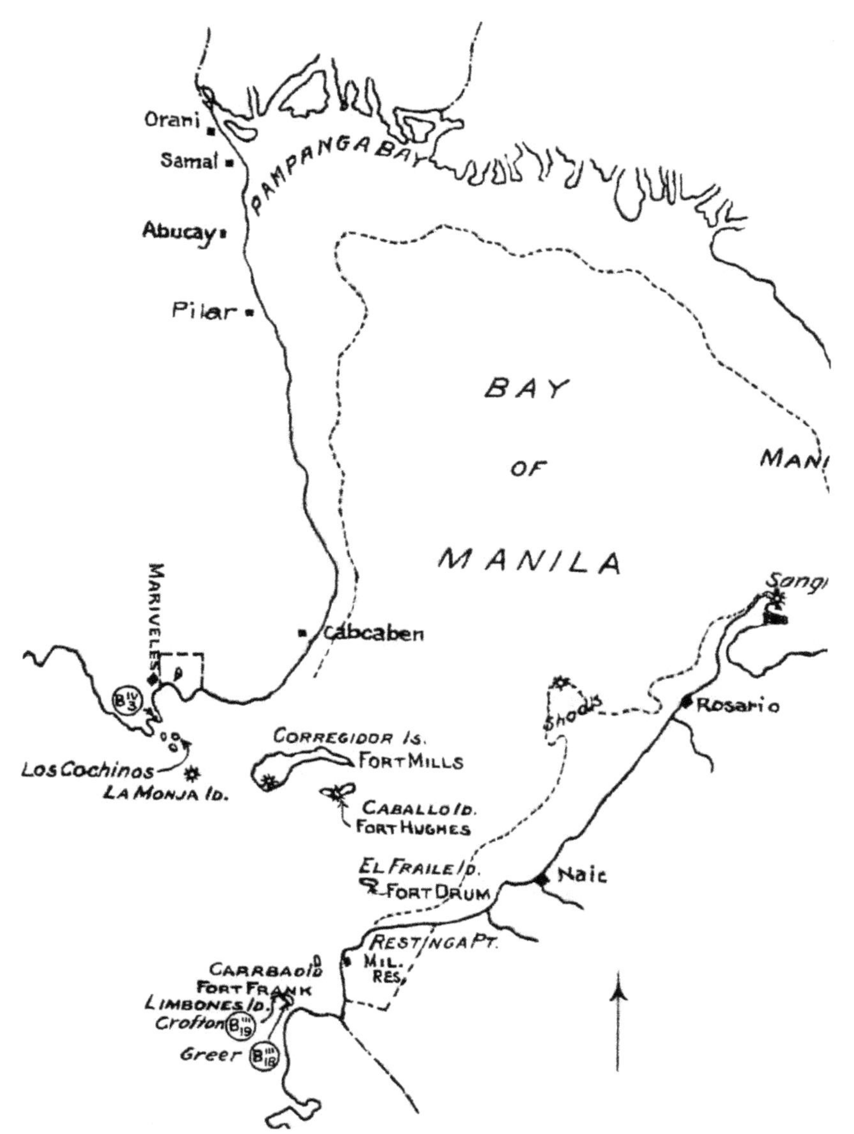

Map of the fire control reservations provided for the 1920s assignment. Note the new reservation at Los Cochinos Point, Bataan, for a station to observe for Battery Smith, and in the opposite direction new stations on Limbones Island to allow a baseline for horizontal range-finding for the 14-inch guns of Battery Crofton and Greer. NARA.

CHAPTER 10
THE HARBOR DEFENSES BETWEEN THE WARS

General Richmond P. Davis Takes Command

On May 16, 1919, the day after Brig. Gen. Richmond P. Davis arrived in the coast defenses, his predecessor prepared a voluminous report for the general on the command's state that included an inspection report. Among the deficiencies found were:[308]

- Serious shortages of commissioned officers
- Shortages of enlisted specialists
- Movable armament in only fair condition, generally obsolete and unsuitable for the mission
- Fire control stations and instruments in good condition, but insufficient in number and poorly concealed
- Ammunition found to be in excellent condition but insufficient in quantity and number of powder charges, projectiles, and fuzes
- War reserve supplies were found to be in good condition but insufficient in quantity
- Mine matériel on hand found to be in very good condition, but insufficient in terms of the number of minecases, submarine cables and dynamite
- Small craft were found to be in good condition, but two large distribution box boats needed
- Mine planters in serious need of overhauling and requiring replacement
- Storehouses and magazines were found in excellent condition, but far short in numbers of what was required
- Quarters for the garrison were found to be in excellent condition but far short in quantity
- The Air Service was no longer present on the post and a presence was recommended
- Gas defense matériel was absent
- Motor transport was very deficient

Maj. Gen. Richmond P. Davis. Gaines Collection

Several recommendations were made as a result of this appraisal of the defenses:

That modern mobile artillery be provided at once:
- 48 pieces of light field artillery for beach defense
- 24 6-inch guns as a secondary armament
- 24 medium and heavy howitzers along with all accessories and ammunition

That magazines, storehouses and inexpensive gun sheds be constructed as soon as possible

That the infantry regiment assigned to the defense be replaced by a heavy artillery regiment reinforced by a machine gun battalion, or that such quantity be supplied to the artillery regiment

That the mine defense of the South Channel be planted with automatic (contact) mines and the North Channel be planted with controlled mines

Garrison Deficiencies Addressed

General Davis, who had commanded a field artillery brigade in France in 1918 before getting orders for the Philippines, followed up the report with one of his own in July 1919. By early 1920, the concerns regarding the deficiencies in the coast defenses had reached the office of the chief of coast artillery, and action was being taken to address them. Reductions in the Regular Army and the Coast Artillery Corps in 1920, however, prevented the maintenance of Manila Bay's defenses at even a full peacetime level.

Because the Panama Canal Zone, Hawaii, and the Philippines were at great distances from the mainland United States and reinforcement of the overseas possessions might not be immediately possible, it was considered vital to provide adequate garrisons for their defense. In the aftermath of the World War the U.S. Army was reduced annually until by 1924; the Coast Artillery Corps that had numbered over 147,279 men in World War I was reduced to a mere 12,000 enlisted men. There were not enough coast artillerymen in the post-World War I army to man both the continental and the overseas coast defenses, even on a peacetime basis. Consequently, it became necessary to abandon a number of continental harbor defenses and place others in caretaking status in order to maintain the overseas garrisons at even 75 percent of peacetime strength. The army's goal was to maintain the Manila Bay garrison at 136 officers and the enlisted strength (excluding bands and non-commissioned specialists) was set at 2,146, or about 75 percent of peacetime strength. The garrison was also to receive a company of engineers, an aero squadron, and two balloon companies as well as the usual supply and service personnel. In addition to Regular Army personnel, a regiment of Philippine Scouts would continue as infantry support. While many of these measures were implemented, manpower issues continued to plague the coast defense command.

By the end of 1919, there were only 16 active companies of coast artillery in the Philippine defenses. In spite of attempts to maintain Corregidor's garrison at 75% strength, even this goal could not be realized and as enlistments expired, manpower shortages required the inactivating several under-strength companies in the early 1920s; their remaining personnel were transferred to active companies in the defenses to maintain effective personnel levels.

The coast defense garrison's organizational structure changed as troop levels rose and fell. Companies were inactivated and reactivated depending upon the number of men assigned to the coast defenses. By January 1920 there were 18 companies active in the coast defenses, assigned as follows:[309]

Fort Mills – 1st, 3rd, 4th, 5th, 7th, 8th, 11th, 14th, 15th, 16th, 17th, 18th and 20th Companies.
Fort Drum – 2nd and 19th Companies
Fort Wint – 6th Company
Fort Hughes – 9th Company
Fort Frank – 10th Company

In May 1920 the number of active companies was briefly raised to 21. Other tactical units stationed on Corregidor were the Army Air Service's 4th Aero Squadron; Company A, 3rd Engineers; the 4th Philippine Infantry Regiment; and the 5th Infantry Battalion.[310]

During the early 1920s companies were frequently deleted, added, or merged. The detailed changes are not relevant to the account presented here. In this period the coast artillery officer complement in 1920 and 1921 ranged between 25 and 45, frequently giving a coast artillery company only one, or at best, two officers. The officer strength remained considerably below the goal of 136 total officers well into the 1920s. By August 1921, the coast defenses still had only about 50% of its authorized company-grade officers.[311]

Personnel shortages were not the only travails faced by the coast defenses in the early 1920s. While typhoons were a frequent event during the monsoon season each year, they rarely came close enough to Manila Bay to do serious damage. On August 31, 1920, however, the fortified islands were struck by a powerful typhoon that did considerable structural damage to Fort Mills, destroying many of the temporary garrison buildings; $239,740 was requested for repairs. Considering the downsizing of the army and budget constraints, coupled with uncertainty as to whether the United States would even retain possession of the Philippines, it is doubtful that the requested sum was provided as permanent structures had replaced the functions of many temporary buildings demolished by the typhoon.[312]

Corregidor Receives Antiaircraft Defenses

Prior to the World War the principal threat to Manila Bay's defences came from naval guns, which at that time had generally flat trajectories. The high elevation of Topside's seacoast batteries provided secure positions unlikely to suffer serious damage from the shipboard artillery. A greater threat came from shore-based high-angle fire from howitzers emplaced in defilade on the Bataan Peninsula and Cavite mainland. From the Mariveles Heights on Bataan and the Pico De Loro Hills of Cavite, the seacoast batteries were clearly visible and subject to heavy damage if not countered by fire from the fortified islands. To provide this counter-battery

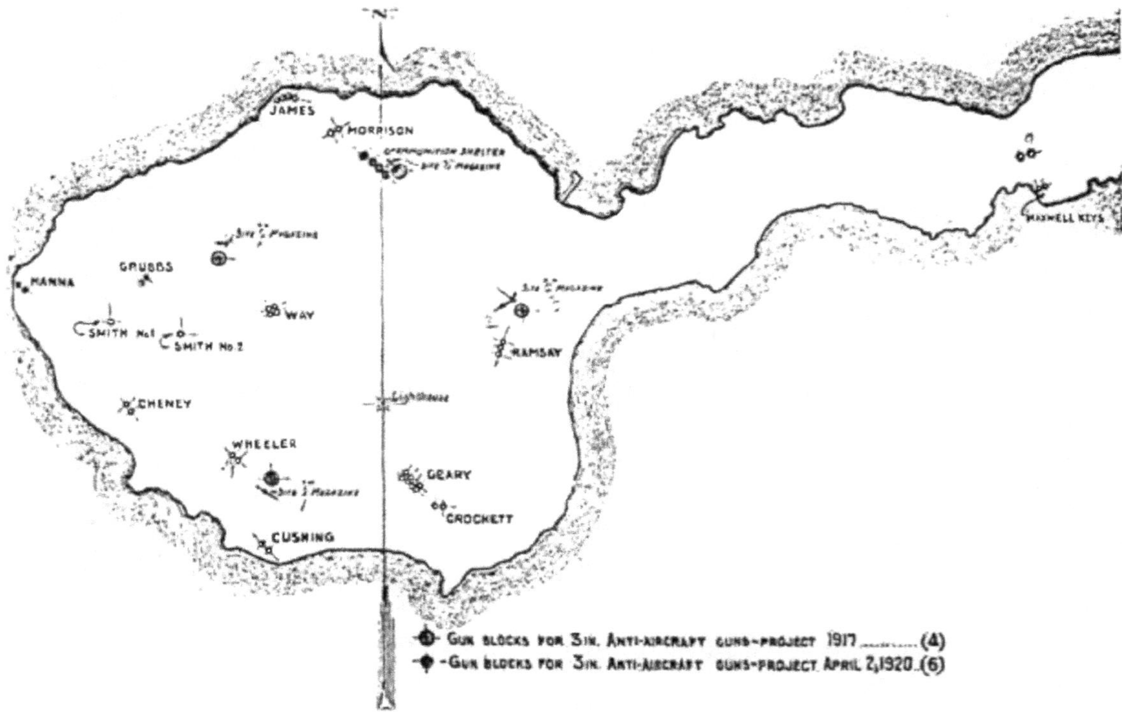

Map of projected antiaircraft battery emplacement positions. Shows proposed locations for the four emplacements of the 1917 project and an additional six for the 1920 project. NARA.

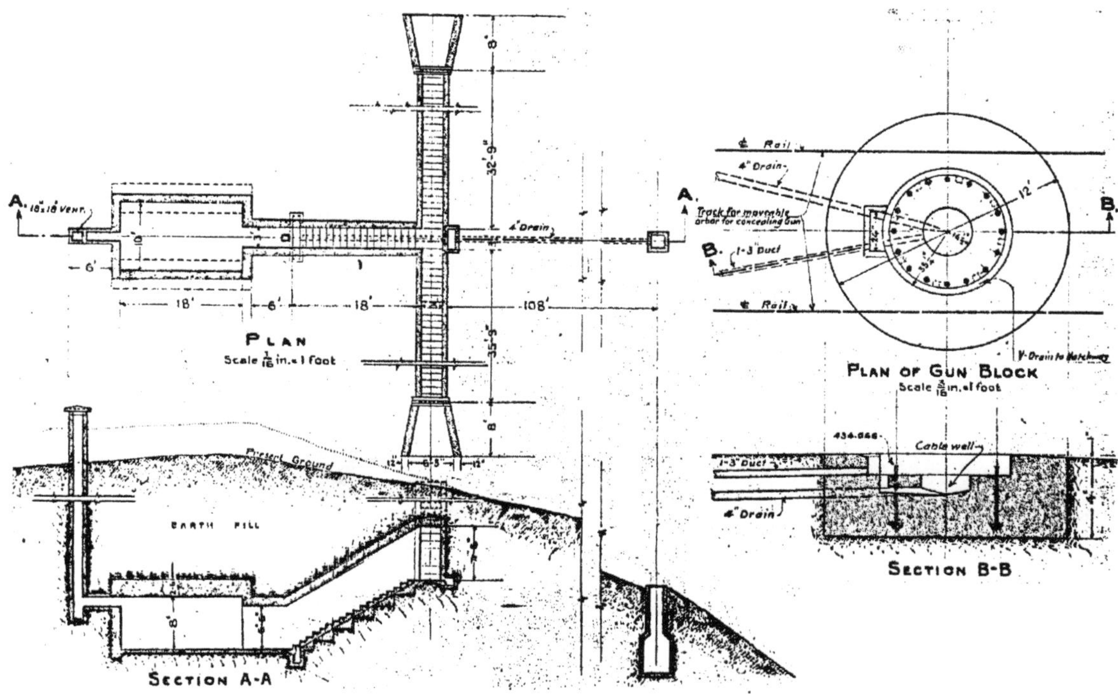

Plan, elevation, and section of a magazine and gun platform for antiaircraft Site D. After construction, this magazine and platforms was known as Battery No. 2 and located on Morrison Hill. It was an important AA battery site through the 1941/42 campaign. NARA.

fire, the coast defenses relied upon the twelve 12-inch mortars on Corregidor and the additional mortars on Forts Hughes and Frank. The airplane's advent as a weapon in the World War and the experience of bomb-carrying rigid framed airships, or dirigibles, created a third potential threat to the seacoast batteries. From the air, the massive concrete batteries were readily visible and made excellent targets. Provision of antiaircraft guns to oppose a potential enemy air attack had increased in importance by the World War's end.

The first attempts to provide an antiaircraft defense for the fortified islands came early in the war. Responding to a request from Washington in 1916, the Philippine Department put together its first project for the coast defenses' antiaircraft defenses. The recommendation for Fort Mills was for five 4-gun batteries. The fixed gun emplacements were projected to be roughly placed around a rectangular form, with two shared magazines — one for each pair of guns. It was recognized that the lack of available armament meant that it was likely only two of the four emplacements for each battery might be armed at first. Additionally, one 4-gun battery was envisioned for Fort Hughes, three guns for Fort Frank, and two for Fort Drum.[313]

This action was taken partially in response to the potential threat posed during the World War by German dirigible airships. These airships had a proven capability to travel long distances on bombing raids and there was the possibility, slim as it may have been, that airships fitted with bombs and staged out of the German protectorates or from vessels in the Pacific could carry out attacks on allied possessions in the Pacific. This risk was reduced early in the war when the Allies seized the German Asian and Pacific territories.

The U.S. War Department embarked on a widespread construction program of AA gun emplacements at its coast defense installations both at home and in the overseas possessions soon after the declaration of war with Germany. What was actually constructed in the Manila Bay defenses during the war was considerably less than the project envisioned in 1916. Just four gun blocks were constructed for 3-inch Model 1917 AA guns on fixed pedestal mounts, one at each of just four of the five recommended battery sites at Fort Mills. (The fifth site on Corregidor's tail was not immediately developed). These four emplacements, Sites "A," "B," "C," and "D," located around the perimeter of Topside near seacoast Batteries Wheeler, Grubbs, Ramsay, and Morrison, respectively, were commenced in June 1917. Upon completion in 1918, two 3-inch M1917 antiaircraft guns on fixed pedestal mounts were received and emplaced near Battery Morrison. These emplacements as well as the unarmed emplacements of Batteries A, B, and C were transferred to the garrison on August 4, 1919.[314]

One of the two 3-inch Model 1917 antiaircraft guns actually delivered to the Manila Bay harbor defenses. For a while it served on Morrison Hill (as here in early 1921) but was eventually moved to Fort Drum and was there during the final campaign. NARA.

The improvement of aircraft during the World War resulted in a reappraisal during the postwar years of the necessity to counter faster, higher-flying planes carrying heavier bomb loads. In 1920, six additional emplacements for 3-inch M1917 antiaircraft guns on fixed carriages were constructed: four were built near the original pair of emplacements on Morrison Hill some 600 yards to the rear of Battery Morrison; and two more on the tail astride the low ridge behind Battery Maxwell Keys. These new emplacements were begun in May 1920 and completed by March 4, 1921. All six were transferred to the garrison on March 25. However, despite the relative abundance of emplacements, the coast defenses in Manila still had only two AA guns. While 14 more fixed M1917 guns had been authorized for the Philippine coast defenses, it was not until early 1922 that the guns were actually ready for shipping from Aberdeen Proving Ground.

Of the 10 emplacements on the island in 1921, only two on Morrison Hill were actually provided with their armament. Shipment of additional M1917 AA guns continued to be hoped for in the following months and planning of emplacements continued. By the mid-1930s, after undergoing a series of redesignations, the fixed AA battery emplacements on Corregidor were renumbered as follows:[315]

Battery No. 1 (Tail of the island) Two 3-inch M1917 AA guns
Battery No. 2 (Morrison Hill) Five unarmed emplacements for 3-inch M1917 AA guns
Battery No. 3 (Adjacent to Batteries Grubbs) Two unarmed emplacements for 3-inch M1917 AA guns

Emplacements for M1917 AA guns were also authorized in 1920 for the other fortified islands. Two fixed emplacements were built at Fort Wint on Grande Island in Subic Bay; four emplacements were constructed at Fort Hughes, and four more at Fort Frank. From the early 1920s until 1924, the two M1917 AA guns on Corregidor were used by the various separate companies for their annual antiaircraft service practices. From the 1924 reorganization until 1934 the firing batteries of the 59th Coast Artillery Regiment manned the AA guns as an alternate assignment. Fort Drum did not receive its AA emplacements until 1934, when positions were established on either side of the main deck for 3-inch M1917 antiaircraft guns. The two guns were removed from Morrison Hill and moved to Fort Drum between August and October 1934 and designated AA Battery Number 7.[316]

Even after the 60th Coast Artillery Regiment's arrival at Fort Mills in 1928, the 59th C.A. continued to man the two fixed antiaircraft guns in the harbor defenses as a secondary assignment even after they were moved to Fort Drum.

Revising the Submarine Mine Project

Soon after taking command of the coast defenses in 1919, General Davis noted that the minefields planted during the war were "imperfect, indefinite, and is now not capable of affording effective mine defense." While the "mine matériel on hand was in good condition, [the] amount of submarine cable was insufficient and what was available was in poor condition." Davis felt the lead-covered, seven conductor submarine cable was unserviceable. Replenishment of matériel was badly needed. The distribution box boats were considered in good condition but two more of the larger 65-foot vessels of this type were considered necessary because of the bay's open waters.[317]

The hard service of both the mine planters and the distribution box boats during the war had taken a toll. The 72-foot *L-61* and *L-62* DB boats were out of service because of unsatisfactory engines, leaving only the 32-foot *L-20* and *L-22* DB boats available for service with the mine command. Both the 32-footers were very old with rotten hulls, and while still useful as mine yawls; they were inadequate as distribution box boats in the choppy waters of Manila Bay. Three new DB boats, *L-58*, *L-59*, and *L-60* built at Gulfport, Mississippi, were still at San Francisco awaiting shipment to Manila in January 1922. Gasoline-powered mine yawls were small craft used to ferry ropes, cables, etc., from the mine planter to the DB boat or shore as needed during mine laying operations and for transportation of men and matériel to and from the mine planters at sea.[318]

Following the World War, the mine project was revised once again. On January 9, 1920, the secretaries of war and navy approved transferring the Boca Grande Channel Minefield to the navy, who would assume responsibility for planting and maintaining a field of about 3,000 navy contact mines in the wide channel, laid between Caballo Island and Restinga Point, Cavite. Until there was a sufficient number of contact mines available at Manila and the navy was prepared to carry out the new project, the army controlled ground mine project for Boca Grande that was controlled from Fort Hughes and Fort Drum remained in effect.

The army would retain control of the grand groups of controlled ground mines that composed the Boca Chica minefield (In 1912, the number of mines composing a grand group was reduced from 21 to 19). The army minefield would consist of three lines of mines. The outer line was to be composed of five grand groups of mines (95 mines); the middle line was to consist of six grand groups (114 mines), and the inner line would also consist of six grand groups. All of these mines were to be controlled from the James Ravine casemate. The original galvanized-iron casemate initially transferred January 25, 1911, was replaced by a bombproof concrete structure containing seven rooms and transferred on September 10, 1913. The 62-foot-long and 22-foot-wide casemate contained an operating room, switchboard room, storage battery room, two storerooms, an engine room, and a dormitory for the manning detail. The army minefield was to be supplemented by navy contact mines that were to be available after the Boca Grande field was laid, to be laid at the local commander's discretion. At Subic Bay, the army minefield would be planted in three lines with the outer and middle lines composed of four grand groups (76 mines) each and the inner line having two grand groups (38 mines).[319]

The seven operating panels for the Boca Grande (south) minefield at the Fort Hughes and Fort Drum casemates were projected for removal and reinstallation in the James Ravine casemate after the navy assumed responsibility for mining the Boca Grande Channel. The single casemate in James Ravine would control all mine operations in the Boca Chica (north) Channel.

Air Service Returns to Corregidor

A sizable army air service installation for hydroplanes had been established during World War I on the south shore of Bottomside, where the original wooden hanger had been built before the war. But then the tail's southern portion between Malinta Hill and Ordnance Point was briefly designated a U.S. Naval Reservation. Requiring more space, the Air Service showed an interest in expanding its operations at Barrio Concepción, where the air service installation would become an extension to the main post. This site had, however, been tabbed by the coast artillery as the location for wartime storage facilities. Because it required a location where the waters would be calmer during the typhoon season, the air service accepted the coast artillery's offer of a tract on Corregidor's tail as the location for a new installation. Thus the "brigade-sized" development on Corregidor's tail envisioned by Clint Hearn in 1910 came, after a fashion, to fruition following World War I.

The tail's southern side in the area once reserved for navy use was reassigned to the Army Air Service. There, service hangers, a repair hanger, a motor repair building, a testing platform, a storage hanger for wireless communication aerials, a dope shed, and a photo laboratory were projected for construction. A concrete apron area was to be provided between the hangers and two concrete ramps built for the seaplanes along with a small wharf for the small craft that tended the aircraft. By 1919, clearing land on the northern part of the tail near Cavalry Point and North Point for an aircraft landing area was undertaken.

The prospect of using captive balloons for fire control and direction was considered by the War Department and in August 1919, a site for the balloon installation was selected between the proposed seaplane facility

Aerial photograph of a section of Corregidor's tail in the early 1920s. It shows the recently built additions to the aviation detachment. Note the large hangars to the left (south) near the shore. NARA.

Balloon hangar on the tail of Corregidor. The coast artillery balloons had a surprisingly short service life considering all the effort and expense invested in constructing their infrastructure needs. NARA.

and the landing field. An Air Service officer assumed charge of the projected facilities on the tail. Some grading of the area east of the seaplane installation for the balloon facilities was required. There were erected two large balloon hangers, a fabric and carpenter shop, a sodium hydroxide storage tank, a ferro-silicon storage building, and a hydrogen generating plant, at a cost of $98,959. Also constructed was an Air Service administration building, three barracks for enlisted men, three bachelor officer's quarters, one bungalow-type set of family quarters for a field-grade officer and eight double sets of bungalows for company-grade officers and their families. All of these buildings were wood frame on concrete foundations with shingle roofing and wood floors. These structures extended from near Infantry Point on the island's north side across the tail to the seaplane service area near Camp Point on the island's south shore. The construction costs of the barracks and quarters came to $39,272.[320]

The Air Service installations were to be built by the constructing quartermaster who arrived from the U.S. in September 1919. Planning of these facilities was still in process and it was not until December 31, 1919, that the final approval of the hangers' layout at the seaplane facility was received. Obtaining sufficient numbers of skilled workers to build the Air Service installations proved a serious problem. Manila and much of the Philippine Islands were undergoing a building boom at that time and artisans and other workers were in short supply. Wages paid in Manila were substantially higher than those authorized on Corregidor. The skilled labor and white supervisors that could be obtained in Manila could only be hired when the government agreed to pay some 20% more than the prevailing wage in Manila. All of these factors contributed to delays in the overall project.[321]

To further complicate matters, Fort Mills was a difficult place for a contractor. The army was very security conscious and required close supervision of laborers, thus requiring larger numbers of overseers and supervisors. The Air Service was pressuring the Quartermaster Division to advance the project and a shortage of contractors who were already overburdened with civil projects resulted in the decision to build the Air Service installations using the "purchase and hire" process of construction. Fortunately, the transport that had brought the constructing quartermaster from the U.S. had sailed by way of Vladivostok, where it took aboard a large number of soldiers from the Siberian Expedition who were being returned to the U.S. for discharge. The quartermaster canvassed the men and secured 12 with experience in construction, had them discharged at Manila, and hired them to initiate construction. The project was consequently plagued with rapid turnovers in work force. Building materials were difficult to obtain and premium prices were paid for materials that were sometimes of poor quality. Deliveries were irregular and frequently mismanaged, so shortages occurred frequently. Water transportation also proved to be a frequent problem as there was a shortage of suitable vessels for the movement of materials to the island from Manila and government vessels were usually fully utilized for other purposes. The work was advanced in fits and starts as one project supervisor followed another until January 1921, when Maj. Wilmot A. Danielson, "an officer of good judgment and technical knowledge," took charge of the project. Thereafter "the work was administered very satisfactorily until it was completed," May 23, 1922, and transferred to the Air Service."[322]

The 2nd Aero Squadron (Observation) was reassigned to the Philippine Department on December 24, 1919, and posted at Fort Mills. On March 10, 1920, it was reassigned to the 1st Observation Group (successively redesignated the 4th Observation Group and later the 4th Composite Group). The 2nd Aero Squadron was redesignated 2nd Squadron (Observation) on March 14, 1921, and the 2nd Observation Squadron on January 25, 1923.[323]

While operating from Corregidor, the squadron was initially equipped with Curtiss JN-4 "Jenny" aircraft equipped with Burgess Floats for water operations. On October 15, 1920, the 1st Squadron was moved to Corregidor's tail where a landing field and hydroplane ramps and hangers were being built. The field was named Kindley Field, for Capt. Field Kindley, the first American member of the 148th Aero Squadron to down a German aircraft in the World War. He became an ace with 12 "kills" during that war. At age 23, he died in a flying accident at Kelly Field, Texas, on February 1, 1920. The squadron received De Havilland DH-4 planes to operate from the landing field replacing, or at least supplementing the Curtiss JN-4 floatplanes that operated out of the seadrome off Corregidor's south shore. The squadron remained at Kindley Field until October 15, 1920, when it moved to Nichols Field near Manila, leaving a small detachment on Corregidor.[324]

Army Air Service Captain Field Kindley. Kindley was a famous American ace during the First World War. He was killed in a flying accident in Texas in 1920. Kindley Field on Corregidor was named for him. Gaines Collection.

In September 1922, a portion of the 28th Bombardment Squadron from Nichols Field at Manila also occupied Kindley Field with its DH-4 aircraft. The detachment of this squadron was joined by a detail of eight officers and 100 enlisted men of Flight "A," 2nd Observation Squadron, with four Curtiss DS2L hydroplanes that arrived on Corregidor from Nichols Field on February 9, 1923.[325]

The role of Flight "A" was to carry out support operations during the annual coast artillery target practices from mid-March to mid-April 1923. By March 1924, the six seaplanes of Flight "A" operating from the ramps on Corregidor's tail had become increasingly obsolete and except for a Loening Sea Yacht seaplane, none could be kept in service without excessive cost. Further, the Curtiss DS2L seaplanes were becoming unsafe to fly. Following a tactical inspection of the defenses in March 1924, it was recommended that Flight "A" be removed to the airstrip at Camp Nichols near Manila and be reequipped with DH-4 planes. Because the seaplanes were of some value to the coast artillery on Corregidor, a small detachment of the squadron could be retained on the island as long as the seaplanes could be safely flown.[326]

Twenty-two missions were flown by the detachment in conjunction with coast artillery operations. Nineteen of these were adjustment of fire problems and three were with battery commanders tracking problems with the seaplanes flying an imaginary battery target line.

Although the DS2L aircraft were obsolete, mechanical problems were few and air to ground and ground to air communications using navy CP-1110 transmitter and the specially installed army SCR-75 receivers worked well. Radios were provided at each battery in preparation for the firing practice to facilitate air to ground communication. While communication proved effective in one set of target practices, the gun fire was less effective than anticipated. Nine of Battery Cheney's 10 rounds fell far from the target. A malfunction in one of Battery Marshall's 14-inch guns required Fort Drum's garrison to change turrets to Battery Wilson; only the rounds fired by the newly emplaced Battery Smith were judged satisfactory. In addition to the radio communications, colored panels were also used in some target practices with varied success. Units of the air detachment remained at Kindley Field until June 1929, when they moved to Nichols Field.[327]

The Air Service continued to operate a facility at Fort Mills through most of the 1920s. The 17th Balloon and the 27th Balloon Companies sailed from San Francisco on April 5, 1920, aboard USAT *Sherman* for the Philippines. Upon arrival in Manila on May 4, the two companies were transported to Corregidor, where they took up quarters in the new Air Service facilities on the tail. The companies' mission was to carry out experimental observation and fire adjustment for the coast defense batteries. They remained at Corregidor until the 27th Balloon Company was demobilized September 6, 1920, and the 17th Company was eventually demobilized February 28, 1927.[328]

Army DH-4 airplane in 1921. This type of aircraft supplanted the JNs and served from 1921 from the new landing strip on Corregidor Island. USAF Museum.

Water Supply on the Fortified Islands

The plans to garrison and defend the five fortified islands for a prolonged campaign or siege encountered problems when it came to a fresh water supply. Both Forts Wint and Mills had some, but not enough, water through wells or springs. The other islands had none. Each island required a carefully configured plan to assure a water supply necessary for a prolonged defense. Much was in place by 1916 when major construction ended, but incremental additions continued to be made up until almost the start of the Second World War.

Fort Wint had several small freshwater wells available to serve its garrison. Also, some buildings were designed to collect rain water on roofs as a supplement. In 1913 two large 150,000-gallon storage tanks were completed to act as the general post reserve. As Fort Wint was soon reduced to caretaker status, water supply never became a significant issue.[329]

Corregidor had 9-10 fresh springs or wells, concentrated in Ramsay, Powerhouse, and James Ravines, but the capacity was not equal to the demand. Well into the 1920s and 1930s fresh water had to be rationed. In the early 1920s fresh water was only turned on for three half-hour period per day. Units hoarded water in barrels, troughs, and ponds; a practice that aggrevated the on-going attempt to eliminate disease-carrying mosquitoes. All potable water had to be boiled first, as there was no filtration or chlorinators present. At Fort Mills the primary storage of water was entrusted to two 3-million gallon reservoirs. There was one at Topside and one at Middleside. While planned for quite a while, the garrison increase of World War I accelerated the reservoirs' completion. They were completed in 1918 and cost about $35,000 each. In both cases the reservoirs' flat ground-level top surface was creatively used as the post's tennis and handball courts. The Japanese, being unaware of the reservoir beneath the courts, tended to ignore them in their bombing, according to a German journalist who visited the island soon after its capture by the Japanese. In addition to the two big reservoirs, a network of tanks for fresh water was distributed at other key points around the island. Four large, concrete tanks totaling over 750,000 gallons would be built from Topside to the aptly named Water Tank Hill on the island's tail by 1926.[330]

Two of the four large water storage tanks near the Topside Lighthouse. Saltwater was used for firefighting and wherever it could be conveniently substituted for fresh water. Fire control stations were also located atop the towers. Ruhlen Collection.

Water wagon on Corregidor. Most water at Fort Mills was obtained at fresh springs and stored in reservoirs or tanks. Besides a pipe pumping system that delivered it to major facilities, water wagons were used well into the 1930s for construction or remote sites. Cornwell Collection, USAMHI.

As a supplement and potential back-up, the fresh-water springs in James and Ramsay Ravines were also developed. In particular, James Ravine's freshwater wells proved to be a fortuitous source. Though not finished until after 1931, this program saw the careful development of the three best wells in the ravine with a new pump house, a 100,000-gallon holding tank, and a secondary pump and pipeline directing the water to the Topside reservoir. On November 1, 1939, a fourth well 225 feet deep was begun in James Ravine by a crew from the Philippine Commonwealth Government's Bureau of Public Works in a further effort to increase the supply of fresh water for the post. The project was completed January 30, 1940, and had a 90-gallon per minute capacity. Corregidor also had a considerable system for saltwater intake with pumps and tanks also completed about 1920. A major system of intake pipes and pumps was constructed below Battery Point. The most famous tanks on the island, the four adjacent to the old Spanish lighthouse, were for salt water in the firefighting system, and for toilets, the swimming pool and other functions that did not require scarcer fresh water.[331]

Fort Drum was supposed to obtain its water from evaporators. But true to the trend of perpetual mechanical problems at Drum, it was found more convenient (and less expensive considering fuel cost) to barge water to the post in peacetime. Fresh water storage was in internal steel tanks; six in the tank room had a combined capacity of 27,300 gallons. Storage was enhanced during peacetime with two large wooden tanks on the deck. When war approached, the larger of these was disassembled and moved inside. Throughout the 1941-42 campaign, water was strictly rationed, and the supply was adequate until the surrender. The fort was supplied with fresh water by a water barge that obtained its water at Sisiman Cove on Bataan. Following the fall of Bataan, the barge filled up at Corregidor's north wharf. One other emergency innovation was to use empty 14-inch powder cans for water storage.

Fort Hughes also used water delivered by the army in barges. No facilities were ever built for the fort to distill or otherwise obtain its own water, though there had been a thought in 1916 to move the Fort Wint distilling plant to Hughes and employ it there. Storage for water was built between 1914 and 1925. Four freshwater tanks with a capacity of up to 80,000 gallons were constructed part way up the slope to the hogback for local storage, where it was subsequently distributed by gravity. The post also had a saltwater system, starting with a pumping station on the wharf.[332]

The proximity of Carabao Island to the Cavite shore offered a different solution. In 1903 a concrete dam was erected on the Sinalam River where it passed through the Calumpan Military Reservation, just inland from Sinalam Cove. A 6,200-yard 3-inch pipe was run to a shoreline booster pump, and a settling tank. From the tank a 2-inch pipe ran underwater another 5,800-yards to Fort Frank. The usual concrete tanks were built to hold a ready water supply on the island. The system worked well enough, although it had to be rebuilt in 1932. During wartime this arrangement was assumed to be vulnerable, and Fort Frank was equipped with a desalination plant in 1916, and a reservoir also held a 10-day supply of water.[333]

Medical Services Between the Wars

Administratively part of the Philippine Department, the command's medical services were supplied as much as possible from Manila and the large regional Sternberg General Hospital. On each post facilities were needed for the medical care of the garrisons. This was particularly true at Fort Mills, with the fine post hospital built before the First World War. While the numbers of medical staff fluctuated as much as the garrison numbers, in a typical year like 1921 there were 18 medical offers assigned to the harbor defenses. One at Fort Frank also serving Forts Hughes and Drum, one at Fort Wint, and the other 16 at Fort Mills. Twelve were various doctors, three dentists, and one administrative/property officer. They were accompanied by 15 female nurses and 153 enlisted men — the majority being Philippine scout orderlies and assistants. In fact, the staff outgrew the meagre quarters on the second floor of the hospital; an entirely new bombproof concrete medical staff barracks was built adjacent to the hospital for $60,000 in 1927-29.[334]

Typically, about 200 patients from the garrison were seen daily; the hospital might have 100-125 cases resident. Long-term or more difficult surgical patients were transferred to Manila for more complete care. The top six reasons for treatment in 1921 were reported as: digestive disorders, Dengue fever, injury, respiratory problems, venereal disease, and malaria. The last was almost entirely due to the return of survey teams from Bataan, malaria itself being extremely rare on the islands; in some instances no new cases were reported for up to three years. About 20-30 births occurred a year at the Fort Mills hospital. The report for 1921 also lists eight deaths: four drownings, two accidents, and two suicides (by side arms). In addition to the garrison hospital, a smaller facility was maintained for the Bilibids at the stockade. There was little for the civilian population at the barrios. In 1924 a trained nurse was employed by the town of San Jose who also operated a baby clinic. Army medical staff did inspect the sanitary conditions of the barrios, and repeatedly urged the replacement of earth-closet toilets with water closets.[335]

In the early 1920s, at least until the virtual shut-down of the post, Fort Wint had an assigned doctor and one enlisted staff member. There was no real facility besides an office; the army sent any cases requiring hospitalization to the navy facility at Olongapo. Fort Frank had a small dispensary and 15-bed wooden hospital manned by one doctor and a full-time private first class. Fort Hughes and Drum had small aid stations, but no assigned staff — though during annual firing and training periods staff members would accompany the unit involved. Always aware of possible emergency wartime needs, the posts were kept stocked with medical supplies.

Additional duties of the medical staff were sanitation inspections. At times they tested water supply and frequently had to shut down certain wells or springs as supply sources. They conducted lectures on hygiene — the dangers of contracting venereal disease during the monthly trips to Manila seemed to be of great interest to everyone concerned. Up until the mid-1930s veterinarians were a regular part of the staff; they inspected and cared for mules and other draft animals, and also inspected the storing and status of meat supplies.

Additional War Matériel is sent to the Philippines

Massive amounts of ordnance and supplies were manufactured during the World War and upon its conclusion, much of this matériel along with some French and British ordnance was brought back to the United States from France and stockpiled in arsenals in the United States. By the early 1920s, some of this matériel was being distributed to various army posts around the country and arrangements were being made to ship considerable amounts of these military goods to the overseas stations as well.

Following World War I, Brig. Gen. Richmond P. Davis noted in a July 1919 communication to the chief of coast artillery that Corregidor still lacked modern mobile artillery. He called for the provision "at once" of 48 pieces of light artillery (75 mm), 24 6-inch guns, 24 medium (8-inch) and heavy (240 mm) howitzers, along with all their accessories and ammunition.

The supplying of the requisite ordnance was not long in being approved. By January 1920, the first installment of 32 75 mm M1917 British-type field pieces had been received from the Philadelphia Arsenal. In May 1920 the remaining 16 of the requested 48 75 mm guns arrived in the Philippines. Sixteen of these field pieces were provided by mid-September 1920 for the beach defenses of Corregidor and the other fortified islands. Twenty-four 155 mm GPF guns were shipped to the Philippines from the Ordnance Department's Erie Proving Grounds, Ohio, arriving in Manila September 1, 1920, aboard USAT *West Caddon*. Additional shipments of 155 mm GPF guns arrived in the harbor defenses between 1925 and 1933. Plans were also underway to send 12 240 mm M1918 howitzers to Corregidor for counter-battery use in case hostile forces occupied positions on the Bataan Peninsula or the Pico Del Loro Hills on the Cavite mainland. Also planned for shipment were 14 3-inch M1917 AA guns. In December 1920 a substantial amount of ammunition was shipped to Corregidor: 90,000 75 mm rounds and 24,000 155 mm rounds.[336]

The 59th Artillery is Transferred to Fort Mills

While the garrison strength on Corregidor saw a considerable reduction at the end of the World War, reductions in the Regular Army as a whole were equally substantial. The 31st Artillery Brigade: the 55th, 57th and 59th Artillery Regiments, organized during the war, had been one of three brigades of railway (Ry) and tractor drawn (TD) artillery retained in active status at the end of the war for training purposes. Initially posted at the Presidio of San Francisco, the brigade was later moved to Camp Lewis, Washington, where more maneuver room was available. The brigade consisted only of a training nucleus. All three components of the 31st Brigade were tractor-drawn regiments equipped with either French or American-built 155 mm M1917 or M1918 guns. During the World War, the 59th Artillery (CAC) had been equipped with 8-inch howitzers. This armament had been exchanged for the 155 mm GPF guns when the regiment was transferred to the U.S. West Coast. The original M1917 and M1918 mobile carriages, were intended for slow speeds, with two steel-bodied wheels carried on bronze hub liners. Each wheel had two solid rubber tires. These medium caliber artillery pieces had been used extensively in France in support of the American field army during the World War.[337]

All three of the postwar retained brigades were inactivated and all but four of the 10 regiments that had constituted those brigades were inactivated as well in the summer of 1921. The 52nd Artillery (Railway) and the 51st, 55th and 59th Artillery (TD) Regiments, while retained, were reduced to skeletal organizations. Subsequently the 55th and 59th Artillery, received movement orders. The 55th would go to Hawaii, while the 59th would be transferred to the Philippines.

After juggling personnel assignments, the 59th would move to Corregidor as the requested "heavy artillery" regiment. Efforts to bring the active batteries of 59th up to near peacetime strength were only marginally successful. Only enough men were transferred on June 30 to enable the unit to bring the regimental headquarters company and Batteries A and B up to nominal peacetime strength levels. The headquarters batteries of the 2nd and 3rd Battalions and Batteries C, D, E, and F remained inactive. The following weeks were spent preparing for "foreign service," as duty in the insular possessions and Panama Canal Zone were termed. The 59th Artillery departed for the Philippines aboard USAT *Sherman* in the latter part of July 1921 on a nearly a month-long voyage.[338]

Upon arrival in Manila, 59th Artillery personnel, their baggage, and matériel were offloaded from *Sherman* and ferried 30 miles across Manila Bay to Corregidor aboard the Quartermaster Corps harbor boat *San Pedro*. Disembarking at Bottomside's north mine dock, the 59th's officers and enlisted men were transported on trolley cars up to Middleside, where they moved into the quarters and barracks vacated by the recently departed infantry regiments. The coast defense staff officers and company grade officers of the remaining separate companies occupied concrete officers' quarters on Topside and the main barracks was still occupied by the handful of separate companies manning the fixed gun and mortar batteries. The 59th's field grade officers occupied Middleside's single story bungalows, and battery grade officers lived in two-story double sets of quarters. When the 59th arrived, the concrete quarters were only five or six years old. The 4th Battalion of Philippine Scouts was quartered in Middleside's other barracks. The 59th Artillery's arrival increased the number of active coast artillery company or battery organizations in the coast defenses to 15, counting the headquarters batteries. Most of these units were, however, at considerably less than nominal strength levels.[339]

When the new artillery unit arrived in the Philippines, the continued presence of the U.S. in the Philippines was under reevaluation in Washington. The original plan was to assign the scout coast artillery companies to man the fixed gun and mortar batteries, thus permitting the American personnel manning the fixed defenses to be transferred to the 59th Artillery. At that time all but six of the serial-numbered American companies had been inactivated, and during 1923 the 59th Artillery absorbed these six remaining separate companies. This enabled the activation of the 2nd and 3rd Battalions and the four inactive firing batteries and brought all regimental components up to nominal peacetime strength. However, the plan was only partially implemented; about half of the newly organized scout companies continued on the same duties they held previously, that of manning the land defense field artillery pieces, operating the Fort Mills stockade, and providing guard details for the Bilibids engaged in the numerous construction projects on the islands. The 287th and 288th Companies were initially assigned to the 59th Artillery as Batteries G and H respectively, for training on the 155 mm guns. [340]

The Washington Treaty and USAT *Wheaton*

The President of the United States ratified the "Treaty between the United States of America, the British Empire, France, Italy and Japan" on June 9, 1923. The delegates to the Conference on the Limitation of Armament had finalized the treaty in Washington, D.C., on February 6, 1922, and the Senate ratified the treaty on March 29. Also known as the "Five-Power Treaty," it is now generally referred to as the "Washington Treaty." The treaty's primary intent was to limit the numbers and power of major naval combatants. An important adjunct to these limits was a provision that limited the fortifications and base infrastructure in the Pacific Ocean. Insisted upon by the Japanese, their rationale was that the treaty was more acceptable if coastal defenses in their potential theatre of operations were also limited. The three Pacific powers agreed in Article XIX to: [341]

> The United States, the British Empire, and Japan agree that the status quo at the time of the signing of the present treaty with regard to fortifications and naval bases shall be maintained in their respective territories and possessions specified hereunder:
>
> 1. The insular possessions which the United States now holds or may hereafter acquire in the Pacific Ocean, except (a) those adjacent to the coast of the United States, Alaska and the Panama Canal Zone, not including the Aleutian Islands, and (b) the Hawaiian Islands;
> 2. Hong Kong and the insular possessions which the British Empire now holds or may hereafter acquire in the Pacific Ocean, east of the meridian of 110° east longitude, except (a) those adjacent to the coast of Canada, (b) the Commonwealth of Australia and its Territories, and (c) New Zealand;
> 3. The following insular territories and possessions of Japan in the Pacific Ocean, to wit: the Kurile Islands, the Bonin Islands, Amami-Oshina, the Loochao Islands, Formosa and the Pescadores, and any insular territories or possessions in the Pacific Ocean which Japan may hereafter acquire.
>
> The maintenance of the status quo under the foregoing provisions implies that no new fortifications or naval bases shall be established in the territories and possessions specified; that no measures shall be taken to increase the existing naval facilities for the repair and maintenance of naval forces, and that no increase shall be made in the coast defenses of the territories and possessions above specified. This restriction, however, does not pre-

clude such repair and replacement of worn-out weapons and equipment as is customary in naval and military establishments in time of peace.

The geographical description purposely left the various sovereign homelands out of the agreement, along with the major Pacific bases of Britain (Singapore) and the United States (Hawaii). The Philippines were, however, specifically included within the treaty's "no new fortifications" caveat. Enhancements to the coastal defenses of Manila and Subic Bay were no longer possible under the terms of this treaty. From 1923 until the end of 1936 every major decision concerning improvements in the harbor defenses in the Philippines was subject to the terms of the agreement.

The most immediate implication of the treaty's enforcement was on a pending shipment of fortification matériel destined for Manila. The most significant manifest item was a regiment's worth of 12 new 240 mm M1918M1 howitzers. This was the army's new heavy siege artillery piece developed for World War I but delayed in production so that they first became available in 1919. The very first unit scheduled to receive the new piece was the Philippine Department. These guns were intended to replace the harbor defenses' obsolete 7-inch siege howitzers, and act as counter-battery weapons against any enemy artillery on the shores of the bay. By all accounts, their 345-pound projectiles ranging over 16,000-yards would have been highly effective in this role. On April 28, 1920, the 12 new pieces were given expedited status for proofing at the army's Erie Proving Grounds. However, these guns were delayed due to the lack of suitable ammunition — shipping of which was not projected to be available until December.

On January 15, 1921, with ammunition now available, the ordnance department began to assemble the guns, carriages, ammunition, spare parts, and tools for the Philippines. Only the guns were to be shipped to the Philippines, where they no doubt would have been issued to the defenders (likely the 59th Artillery) for manning. But once again the shipment was suspended. On March 30 a delay was imposed due to the desire to include other ordnance supplies in the same shipment. This time it was the additional 14 3-inch M1917 AA guns needed to complete the requirement of 16 such guns in the Philippines. Finally, the USAT *Wheaton* was scheduled to leave Boston on December 15, 1921, after loading ordnance supplied from Watervliet and Watertown Arsenals.

Army transport *Wheaton*, in November 1918, under construction at the Bethlehem Shipyard at Sparrow Point, Maryland. *Wheaton* was transporting important ordnance material in 1922 to the Harbor Defenses when her delivery was cancelled by the signing of the Washington Treaty and its provision against further fortification of Pacific bases. NARA.

At sea east of Hawaii in mid-February, USAT *Wheaton* carried a varied quantity of ordnance supplies for the Philippines. Onboard were:[342]

12 x 240mm M1918M1 howitzers with appurtenances
8000 rounds of HE shells for 240 mm howitzers
2 x 3-in M1903 seacoast guns and pedestal mounts
14 x 3-in M1917 antiaircraft guns and mounts
Electrical equipment for 2 x 3-in M1917 AA guns already in the Philippines
Fire control instruments from the Frankford Arsenal
Shot trucks for 12-inch BCLR M1917 carriages from the Poole Engineering Co.
Watersheds for 14-in M1909 turret mounts carried at Fort Drum
Parts from Watertown Arsenal for 12-in M1917 BCLR carriages and M1908 12-inch mortar carriages
Miscellaneous articles, tools, and parts for seacoast defenses, Manila Bay
59 propelling charges for 10-inch seacoast cannon.
Chemical Warfare Service materiel

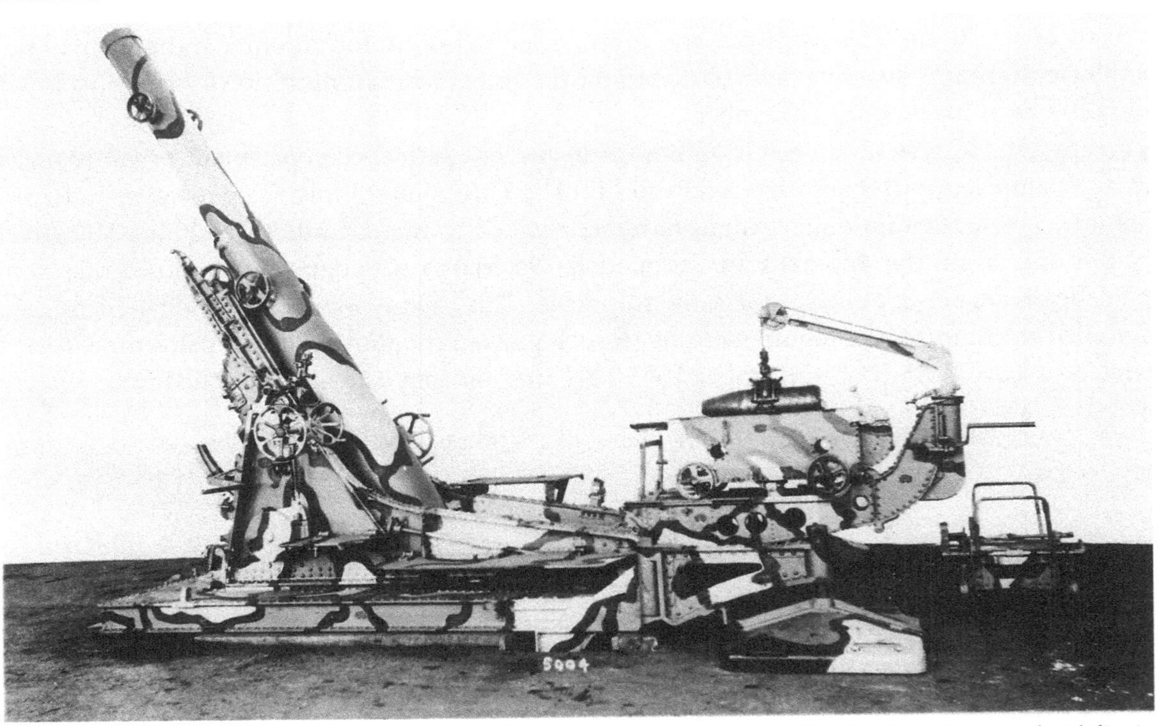

US 240 mm howitzer Model 1917. Twelve of these powerful counter-battery guns were scheduled for delivery to the Philippine garrison in 1922. Their delivery was cancelled, and the guns offloaded in Hawaii instead. They would have been extremely valuable in the siege of 1942. NARA.

As mentioned above, the treaty had been signed by the American representative, but not yet ratified, on February 6, 1922. A week later, on February 13, the army chief of staff approved a memorandum on "The Interpretation of Article XIX." Two days later, *Wheaton* was scheduled to arrive in Honolulu. The secretary of war cabled the Hawaiian Department concerning the ordnance supplies: "circumstances now render these unnecessary in the Philippines."[343]

Honolulu was offered the chance to remove what ordnance they needed, with the understanding that in no circumstance would there be any increase in personnel to man it. Hawaii grabbed the howitzers and their ammunition, the two 3-inch seacoast guns, and the antiaircraft guns, as well as a considerable supply of gas warfare matériel. The ordnance and chemical warfare matériel were absorbed into the Hawaiian Department's War Reserves. Then on February 17, the secretary of war made a blanket announcement informing the branch chiefs that all shipments to the Philippines should be suspended except those for peacetime needs.[344]

There was a problem with the balance of the Philippine-bound cargo on *Wheaton*. The 10-inch powder charges were taken to Puget Sound on *Wheaton*'s return trip to the Pacific Coast. The electrical equipment for the two 3-in AA guns, the 12-inch shot trucks, and the urgently required watershed for the Fort Drum turrets were deemed "essential for peacetime needs" and scheduled for re-shipment on the next available transport going west to the Philippines. If not delayed (twice!) in 1920 and 1921, the howitzers would have been in the islands and retained as existing armament under the treaty terms. The Philippine defenses, by poor timing, had lost their one opportunity to obtain an effective means to counter a siege from Bataan.[345]

It is easy to apply too much negative credit to the Washington Treaty's Fortification Clause for the lack of modernization in the Manila Bay. While unpopular with many coast artillery officers (even more so with key naval officers), there were many benefits of the treaty for America. It certainly curtailed a massive naval construction program the country could ill afford. Without it, America would have had a navy bloated with heavy ships that were soon proven to be obsolete, probably resulting in a slow-down of development for the aircraft and naval aviation that in fact "won" the Pacific War. The Japanese would have been able to heavily fortify their own possessions, making them even more costly to ultimately take. While some specific weapon deliveries and underground tunnels were directly stopped by the treaty, in the long run it was financial constraints that prevented modernization. The army's rapid postwar downsizing followed by the crippling depression simply meant there never was the budget to implement most of the modernization schemes, regardless of the treaty's provisions. Hawaii and the Panama Canal's defenses were not affected by the treaty, yet they were as inadequately defended (understaffed and using many obsolete weapons in emplacements unprotected from air or howitzer attack) as the Philippines. Of course, the Philippine Department had also to contend with the nagging thought that expenditures might be wasted when the Philippines ultimately obtained full independence. From an historical perspective, the ultimate effect of the Fortification Clause counts for little. It did not impact MacArthur's ground army, the air force, the supply of food, or a very well-conducted Japanese siege.

Postwar Reorganizations

From the earliest days of the Philippine Islands becoming an American possession, the United States Army had relied upon Filipino nationals to augment the Regular Army's operations in its efforts to put down the independence movement known to the Americans as the Philippine Insurrection. These Filipino troops would over time evolve into the now famous Philippine Scouts.

Initially posted on Corregidor as a stockade guard and guard details for the Bilibid work parties engaged on various construction projects at Fort Mills and the other fortified Islands, by America's entry into World War I, 52 companies of scouts had been formed into 13 battalions stationed throughout the Philippine Islands. In April 1918, these battalions were further consolidated to form four provisional regiments, designated the 1st through 4th Philippine Infantry (Provisional) and the provisional 1st Philippine Field Artillery, 1st Philippines Signal Battalion, and the 1st Philippine Engineers. On Corregidor scout units served along with American regiments during the World War as part of the defenses.

The Philippine Scout infantry posted on Corregidor was organized into the 4th Philippine Infantry Regiment (Provisional). The 4th consisted of a headquarters company, supply company, machine gun company, and three battalions, each composed of four rifle companies. With the departure of American infantry the scouts assumed overall responsibility for the land defenses of the islands as well as providing guard details for the Bilibids. The Philippine Scouts were in the process of being reorganized as the war ended.[346]

Following that war, Congress approved reorganization of the Philippine Scouts and their induction into the Regular U.S. Army. An enlisted strength of 6,000 was authorized and tactical units were created with Regular Army designations, but with a suffix indicating "Philippine Scout."[347]

The four provisional regiments were in turn formally incorporated into the numerical structure of the Regular Army, when, in 1920, they were consolidated (on paper) with several inactivated Regular Army regiments formed during World War I and redesignated the 43rd, 45th, 57th, and 62nd Infantry Regiments and the 24th and 25th Field Artillery Regiments. By the latter part of 1920, the War Department had embarked upon a program of organizing division-sized units in the territorial and insular possessions. To achieve this goal in the Philippines the regimental records and colors, and officer cadres for the four infantry regiments were transferred to the Philippines. Upon arrival these regiments were to be reorganized as Philippine Scout Regiments. The 45th and 57th U.S. Infantry arrived in Manila December 2, 1920. In February 1921, the 62nd U.S. Infantry was transferred from Camp Lee, Virginia, to Fort Mills and the 43rd Infantry arrived on April 3, 1921. Three of these regiments, the 43rd, 45th, and 57th Regiments, were to be used in the organization of the Philippine Division while one battalion of the 43rd and the 62nd would be assigned to the coast defenses as its land defense force.

As personnel shortages increased in the years immediately following the World War and made it necessary to inactivate five more companies of American coast artillery, efforts were made to provide manning detachments for the numerous seacoast batteries from the scouts. Philippine Scouts from the several scout infantry companies on Corregidor were reassigned to these otherwise American companies in early 1922. These scouts were for the most part men with considerable prior service who were well disciplined and regarded capable of being trained to a high degree of efficiency as coast artillerymen.

Coast Artillery Reorganization of 1922

The numerous reorganizations and redesignations of the coast artillery units in the World War had, in the estimate of the senior levels of the corps, resulted in a loss of esprit de corps and unit traditions. In an effort to reverse this situation the decision was made to reorganize and return to the system of organization prior to the 1916 reorganization. In May 1922, the serially numbered coast artillery companies in existence in 1916 returned to their old numbers. Companies still active that were organized after the 1916 reorganization were assigned numbers from 171 upward. The several regiments organized during the war were to retain their designations but would also receive an additional serial number designations.

The American units partially organized with scouts proved troublesome when the 1st, 7th, 8th, 9th, and 16th companies reverted to their pre-1916 designations in the June 1, 1922 reorganization. They were largely composed of scouts, with the American personnel generally being composed of senior NCOs and officers. Later in 1922 the Coast Artillery Corps was allotted 1,600 Philippine Scouts to be organized into Scout coast artillery, their personnel to come from scouts already manning the fixed guns and mortars augmented with personnel from the various scout organizations on Corregidor assigned to the land defenses.[348]

Reorganizing the 59th Artillery

On June 30, 1922, in accordance with War Department G.O. 21, May 18, 1922, the 59th Artillery's headquarters and lettered firing batteries received additional designations as serially numbered companies.[349]

HQ Battery Additional Designation: 246th Co.
Service Battery Additional Designation: 247th Co.
HQ Battery, 1st Battalion, Additional Designation: 248th Co.
Battery A Additional Designation: 251st Co.
Battery B Additional Designation: 252nd Co.
HQ Battery, 2nd Battalion, Additional Designation: 249th Co.
Battery C Additional Designation: 253rd Co.
Battery D Additional Designation: 254th Co.
HQ Battery, 3rd Battalion, Additional Designation: 250th Co.

Battery E Additional Designation: 255th Co.
Battery F Additional Designation: 256th Co.

On October 1, 1922, the active coast artillery companies were stationed as follows:[350]

Fort Mills: 4th, 15th, 36th, 42nd, 70th, 90th, 93rd, 99th, 111th, 138th, 187th, and 190th Companies, and 9th C.A. Band
Fort Wint: 86th Company
Fort Frank: 11th Company
Fort Hughes: 23rd Company

Commissioning the new separate scout coast artillery companies numbered from 275 to 289 was accomplished by November 1922. It was not until December 18, 1922, that the actual organization could be implemented. Even then organization got off to a slow start as an anthrax outbreak in Central Luzon caused a dispersal of most of the scout companies to Pampanga and Rizal Provinces on quarantine enforcement operations until mid-January 1923.[351]

When the Washington Naval Treaty was ratified in February 1922, the coast defense garrison in Manila Bay had numbered 4,500 American officers and men. By the beginning of 1923, the garrison strength had been reduced to 3000, of which 50 percent were in the newly constituted companies of Philippine Scouts.

155 mm Firing Calibration

The 155 mm GPFs that had been shipped to the Philippines in 1920 had no reliable individual gun data available on the guns' shooting ability. The GPFs firing accuracy being considered an obvious necessity, approval to expend 390 rounds of ammunition was granted for their calibration. On April 10, 1923, the augmented 59th Artillery was finally able to undertake a wholesale recalibration of its 155 mm guns. The test was carried out at a firing point established on the south shore of Corregidor's tail. Twenty-four guns were lined up at 50-yard intervals, laid in the direction of the South China Sea, and prepared for the shoot. A pyramidal target was anchored at a range in excess of 10,000 yards to the west of Corregidor as a reference point for the observation stations established at the fort command posts at Fort Frank and Hughes, atop Fort Drum's cage mast, and at the right end of the GPF gun line at Fort Mills. The first shot was fired at 0850 and the firing continued until 1154, when the firing was suspended for the noon meal. Firing resumed at 1334 and continued until 1537, with each gun fired 16 times. The calibration shoot resulted in the shifting of the guns in the six firing batteries so as to reduce the average error variation in a given battery to a minimum.[352]

When a catastrophic earthquake, typhoon, and tsunami struck the densely populated area between Yokohama and Tokyo, Japan, on September 1, 1923, the 59th Artillery commanded by Col. Percy P. Bishop was alerted to provide a detachment to participate in a relief expedition to be made up from army units in the Philippine Department. Gradually order was restored to the devastated region and by mid-October the coast artillery relief elements expedition embarked on USAT *Somme* for a return to Manila Bay with the thanks of the Japanese government, arriving October 23, 1923.[353]

Although it was officially designated a 155 mm tractor-drawn gun regiment, having been augmented with personnel with substantial training and experience with fixed seacoast batteries, the 59th Artillery gradually took over some seacoast batteries while continuing to man the 155 mm guns. Most of the new scout coast artillery organizations remained on Corregidor completing their training, although some were assigned to Forts Hughes and Frank. Fort Wint remained in caretaking status with a small detachment of American coast artillerymen assigned to the Subic Bay fort. The scouts gradually took over most of the medium and small-caliber seacoast batteries, but ultimately they assumed the responsibility for the tractor-drawn armament as well as the land defense's light field pieces.

Organization of the Early 1920s

Brig. Gen. Malin Craig relieved Brig. Gen. Henry D. Todd Jr. as commander of the CD of Manila and Subic Bays on November 18, 1923. The station list of the coast artillery garrison indicated that Philippine Scouts manned Forts Wint, Frank, and Hughes, while the American troops provided manning detachments for the large-caliber seacoast guns on Corregidor and at Fort Drum. The garrison was distributed as follows:[354]

Fort Mills — 4th, 36th, 42nd, 95th, & 111th Companies and the 59th Regiment as well as 10 companies of Philippine Scouts: the 275th, 277th, 278th, 279th, 280th, 281st, 283rd, 284th, 285th, 287th, 288th, & 289th. Also posted were a detachment of Service Company No. 10, Signal Corps; and Detachments of the Finance, Ordnance, Medical, and Quartermaster Corps, and 2nd Aero Squadron at Kindley Field
Fort Drum — 23rd Co.
Fort Frank — 276th Co.
Fort Hughes – 286th Co.
Fort Wint - Caretaking Detachment

By March 1924, the coast artillery garrison had declined to 2,900 officers and enlisted men, of which 58% of the latter were Philippine Scouts. During the annual service target practices that month Manila Bay's active coast defense components proved to be highly proficient, obtaining 30 percent hits. Because of the large amount of seacoast artillery they were responsible for, the 276th at Fort Frank and the 286th Company at Fort Hughes were for all practical purposes only caretaking units and consequently were somewhat less proficient in their target practices compared to the companies posted at Fort Mills. The ammunition for the M1917 75 mm guns assigned to the land defenses and manned by the 59th Artillery was considered unfit for service in wartime. Of the 7,500 rounds fired in the 1924 annual service practice, only about 25% gave a full detonation. [355]

The Coast Artillery Reorganization of 1924

On February 20, 1924, still another reorganization was ordered to take effect on June 30 of that year. This time the entire corps would be reorganized once again along regimental lines. The serially numbered separate companies manning the fixed batteries were redesignated as either headquarters batteries or as lettered firing batteries of 16 newly constituted harbor defense regiments. The existing antiaircraft artillery battalions were expanded to regiments. These newly created organizations were redesignated as coast artillery regiments and the additional designations as separate companies applied in 1922 were abolished. The regiments dating from the World War such as the 59th Artillery were redesignated as either tractor-drawn or railway coast artillery regiments. The six remaining separate companies of American troops manning the fixed batteries in Manila and Subic Bays, and the 3rd Co. (Battery C, 59th Artillery) were inactivated and transferred, less their personnel and equipment, to coast artillery regiments in the continental United States or its overseas possessions. Less personnel and equipment meant that the only thing actually transferred were the unit records and the lineage. In the army, the expression was that the only thing transferred was the unit flag. The personnel of the transferred companies were then reassigned to the 59th C.A. which brought the regiment's strength up to near peacetime levels.

With the transfer of the last separate companies on June 30, 1924, and the reassignment of their personnel, the only American troops remaining in the Harbor Defenses of Manila and Subic Bays were those assigned to the 59th C.A., infantry support, or to the medical, finance, and quartermaster sections, etc. With the reorganization completed, those elements of the 59th C.A. still quartered at Middleside moved up to Topside and occupied the "mile-long" barracks. Basically this same structure of regiments and assignment of troop types persisted into the Second World War. The reassignment of all the American troops to the 59th C.A. enabled all the firing batteries to be maintained at nominal peacetime strength levels.[356]

During the general reorganization of 1924, the allocation of Filipino coast artillerymen was increased to 2,400. The 15 separate companies of Philippine Scouts would be organized into the newly constituted 91st and 92nd Coast Artillery (Harbor Defense) Regiments. The scouts temporally assigned to Batteries G and H, 59th Artillery, were reassigned to the newly organized 92nd. As was the case in the past, both scout regiments would be officered by Americans while the enlisted personnel would be composed solely of Filipinos, although by 1940 some officers of the scout regiments were Filipinos. Although the companies were all organized at Fort Mills, three were quickly deployed to the outpost forts in Manila and Subic Bays.[357]

This process was not seamless and the presence of Filipino troops in such large numbers on Corregidor disturbed some American officers who questioned the loyalty of Filipinos in general. Prejudice against Filipinos was strongly entrenched in the army's officer corps. When the scouts were first established in the early 1900s it had frequently been necessary to obtain the officers for the scout organizations by appointing American NCOs and volunteer officers to command them. Commissioned officers in the scouts were viewed by many Regular Army officers as inferiors and subordinate to officers assigned to Regular Army organizations. Many West Pointers considered assignment to a scout unit to be a career ender. When in June 1924, elements of the 57th Infantry Regiment and the 12th Medical Regiment at Fort McKinley near Manila mutinied, these prejudices were exacerbated. While generally limited to troops at Fort McKinley, the mutiny had no impact on the Corregidor scouts. There is no indication that any scouts on Corregidor were involved in, or even in sympathy with the mutineers.[358]

The authorized enlisted strength for Corregidor called for 3,600 men: 2,400 Philippine Scouts and 1,200 American troops. Chief of Coast Artillery Maj. Gen. Frank W. Coe, like many of his brother officers, had serious doubts as to whether the Filipino troops had the capability and the requisite qualifications to be trained to fill key positions in the coast artillery service. Coe was also uncomfortable with the number of Filipino troops outnumbering the Americans by a two to one margin in the coast defenses. He strongly recommended that the authorized defense plan for Corregidor of 3,600 troops be composed of only American troops and that no reliance be made on the scouts for the defense of what he termed the "keep" of the Philippine Islands. The coast artillery total enlisted personnel were reduced to only 12,000 in the post-World War I years and tripling the number of American troops on Corregidor in accordance with the Coe recommendation would have required more than 25 percent of the service's total enlisted strength, and would have also had the ultimate necessity of increasing overall authorized strength. In any event, General Coe's recommendations were not favorably considered by the War Department and the two regiments of Philippine Scouts continued to constitute about half the coast artillery garrison until the beginning of World War II. Over time, the scouts would be widely recognized as manifestly loyal, well-trained, and capable troops.[359]

The 91st Coast Artillery (HD)(PS) Regiment

The 91st C.A. was composed of a headquarters and headquarters battery and seven lettered firing batteries. Headquarters battery, and Batteries A and B were assigned to Fort Mills and occupied the barracks and quarters at Middleside. Battery A served as a mine battery and manned Battery Martin (two 155 mm guns) just east of Powerhouse Ravine overlooking Corregidor Bay. Battery B manned Batteries Morrison on Morrison Hill and James at James Ravine. Initially Batteries C, D, and E were assigned on a rotating basis to Fort Hughes on Caballo Island, but this was changed in 1928 when Battery G, of the 59th was assigned to Fort Hughes. Batteries F and G, 59th C.A., rotated in providing the peacetime garrisons for Forts Frank on Carabao Island and Wint at Subic Bay. In 1928, the harbor defenses were reorganized and the outposts of Forts Frank, Drum, and Wint were reduced to caretaking status. Batteries C, D, E, and G returned to Fort Mills and took up quarters in the former Air Service barracks on Corregidor's tail.[360]

After its return to Corregidor, Battery C, 91st C.A., was initially assigned to man one of Battery Geary's mortar pits in the early 1930s but when Battery B was assigned to the mine defenses, Battery C's assignment was changed to Batteries Morrison, James, and mobile 155 mm guns. Battery D also manned one of Battery Geary's mortar pits, but in the event of Fort Frank being provided with a full garrison, Battery D would man the 14-inch guns of Batteries Crofton and Greer at Fort Frank. Battery E manned Battery Grubbs after its return to Ft. Mills. Battery F that remained at Fort Frank served as a caretaking unit. It also manned the four 155 mm guns of Batteries Frank (north) and Frank (south) built in the summer of 1938 as well as the island's four searchlights. Battery G manned Battery Ramsay at Fort Mills and initially shared submarine mine duties with Battery A for a few years before being transferred to Subic Bay in the early 1930s to provide Fort Wint's caretaking unit.[361]

The 92nd Coast Artillery (HD)(PS) Regiment

The 92nd Regiment was composed of a headquarters battery and six lettered firing batteries. The 1st Battalion, Batteries A, B, C, and D, manned tractor-drawn 155 mm GPF guns. The battalion was quartered on Corregidor's tail in the former Army Air Service barracks and officer's quarters. Both the 91st C.A. and 1st Battalion, 92nd C.A., used the former aircraft and balloon hangers on the tail to house their tractors, guns, and other vehicles. The 2nd Battalion, 92nd C.A., Batteries E and F between 1924 and 1928, manned Batteries Ramsay and Morrison. When the 31st Infantry's departed Corregidor in 1928 to make room for the arrival of the 60th C.A. from Fort McKinley, the 2nd Battalion, 92nd C.A., was assigned the additional mission of supplying the guard detail for the Corregidor Branch of Bilibid Civil Prison, or "Stockade." The 2nd or "Bilibid Guard" Battalion, about five officers and 210 enlisted men, was garrisoned on the Stockade Level, or as it was also termed, the "Scout" Level between Bottomside and Middleside. Married enlisted scouts, about one-fourth of the regiment, lived in Barrio Concepcíón adjacent to the Stockade Level, while the remaining enlisted men were initially quartered in the pair of single-story scout barracks built in 1918 adjacent to the stockade. The Fort Mills stockade had an average combined population of some 800 civilian prisoners. The initial Batteries E and F were redesignated in late 1940 as the regiment's 3rd Battalion, as it was intended to organize a new 2nd Battalion to serve as an antiaircraft battalion. The reorganization was not fully implemented, and Batteries E and F retained their designations.[362]

The five American officers typically assigned to the Guard Battalion in the interwar period performed a number of collateral duties. The battalion commander served as the prison executive and as the stockade district fire marshal; he was also an instructor in officers' schools and served on a variety of boards, courts martial, etc. The battalion adjutant assisted the battalion commander and also served as stockade officer, in charge of the civil prisoners. Two more officers served as battery commanders and the remaining officer was in charge of the mess, police, athletics, etc. The tour of duty with the Guard Battalion for American officers was usually six months, after which they would be transferred to another regiment during the 1920s and early 1930s. This rotation of officers was to provide coast artillery officers with a variety of experience. By the late 1930s, however, the period of assignment to the various coast artillery units on Corregidor would be lengthened, in many cases upward to a full year or more.[363]

Several American non-commissioned officers were also attached to the Guard Battalion. The "Keeper" of the Stockade was an American sergeant detailed on special duty. Eight scout sergeants and eight scout corporals from the Guard Battalion were assigned as assistant keepers. Another American sergeant was detailed as the stockade mess sergeant. Three American enlisted men from the Medical Department were detailed to the stockade hospital.[364]

While the 2nd Battalion's primary duty was stockade guard, it also had its military duties. After the changing of the guard each morning, and the departure of the work gangs under a new guard of some 25 men, the remainder of the battalion was available for training. Each afternoon at 4:30 when the convicts returned to the stockade the entire battalion was present and this time was used for additional training. The battalion typically held one parade per month, two infantry drills, a battalion inspection, and a troop-leading problem. In addition, numerous drills concerning convict outbreaks, escape drills, and the evacuation plan were practiced. Batteries E and F functioned as a single firing battery when conducting target practices with seacoast armament. The battalion used nearby Battery Ramsay at Middleside to fire its annual seacoast service practices and fired .50-caliber AA machine guns as its secondary antiaircraft assignment.[365]

Battery Morrison, Fort Mills, showing one of the two 6-inch disappearing guns. This shot was taken during annual gun drill being conducted by 91st Coast Artillery (PS) in 1933. McGarraugh Collection.

Maj. Gen. George Grunert, commander, Philippine Department, presents the United States Coast Artillery Association award to Colonel Octabe DeCarre, 92nd Coast Artillery. Gaines Collection.

CHAPTER 11
GARRISON LIFE BETWEEEN THE WORLD WARS 1920-1940

Postwar Deficiencies

Although the Coast Artillery Corps as a whole was reduced to just over 12,000 men in the early 1920s, during much of the period between the two world wars, the garrison in Manila Bay was maintained at about 100 officers and some 1,200 enlisted men assigned to the 59th C.A., augmented by the 91st and 92nd C.A., whose enlisted ranks averaged about 800 men each. This number was less than an even nominal manning strength for the armament in the harbor defenses. Consequently, the outposts of Forts Drum, Frank, Hughes, and Wint were placed in caretaking status. The remaining troops were concentrated at Fort Mills.

Neglect of Manila Bay's harbor defenses, imposed by the disarmament treaties after World War I and strict budgetary constraints, remained an obstacle to improving the defenses on Corregidor and the other fortified islands through the 1920s. That neglect was worsened by indecision in Washington as to whether the Philippines were to be retained as a possession. A tactical inspection of the harbor defenses held at Fort Mills in 1925 provides a snapshot of the situation.

The combined central switchboard room and coast defense commander's station was not structurally sound enough to resist direct hits nor well located with respect to security from aerial bombardment or shelling from the sea or land. Even the reveille gun firing nearby shook the switchboard relays out of adjustment. Relocation of the station was deemed the best solution to the problem. The extensive vital utilities and the large amount of matériel stored on Corregidor and the other fortified islands created a high time demand on the enlisted component of the garrison. Fully 20% of the American enlisted personnel's time was consumed maintaining the storage facilities and their contents and running the various utilities. Consequently, their artillery training was drastically reduced.

There were other deficiencies. Protection from gas attack was inadequate. The gas masks available were so deteriorated from climate and age that they were no longer useable. Supplies of gas-protective clothing, neutralizing chemicals, and other gas defense matériel were nonexistent. The defenses were 800 scouts short of the 2,400 authorized in August 1924, resulting in an inadequate garrison to properly man the batteries and other defenses during the Joint Army-Navy exercises. Even radiomen and message center personnel had to be taken from other army posts in the Philippines to operate the communications during the annual exercises.[366]

By 1929 the authorized enlisted strength level for the coast artillery garrison in the Philippines had been increased to 1,539 Americans and 1,600 Philippine Scouts. On April 30, 1929, the actual strength was still only 1,333 American troops and 1,303 scouts. As the years passed, the strength of the harbor defense garrison gradually increased. By March 31, 1932, the garrison numbered 1,705 American, and 1,285 Philippine Scouts. The total enlisted strength of the coast artillery garrison, including both American and Filipino troops, continued to hover at, or just below 3,000 men through much of the 1930s. Although the corps was increased by nearly 50% or 5,918 men in 1935, the Philippines did not receive any of the augmentation.[367]

The vessels in the defenses were also inadequate and barely able to meet the garrison's artillery or supply requirements in the years following the World War. The USAMP *Knox* had finally been taken out of service by early 1923, leaving only USAMP *Hunt* available until the new mine planter USAMP *Colonel George F. Harrison*'s arrival. By 1925 only USAMP *Harrison* and the Quartermaster Corps harbor boats *San Marcos, Miley*, and *General John McE. Hyde,* along with one serviceable gasoline-engine distribution box boat were the sole vessels allotted to the garrison.

USAMP *Colonel George F. Harrison* was one of nine 1919 Class mine planters built by the Fabricated Ship Corporation of Milwaukee, Wisconsin, and placed in service between 1919 and 1920. The 704-groston planters were 172 feet in overall length, had a beam of 32 feet, and drew 17 feet when loaded. *Harrison* was a twin-screw oil-burning vessel, equipped to lay cable as well as plant mines. In 1921 all but three of the new 1919 Class planters were taken out of service and many were turned over to the U.S. Lighthouse Service. *Harrison* was one of those retained and was scheduled to replace both *Knox* and *Hunt*. When *Harrison* arrived in the Philippines March 11, 1923, it was necessary to moor her at the army's Manila docks, as additional dredging was required to access Fort Mills' north mine wharf. Soon after the dredging was complete, USAMP

US Army mineplanter *Colonel George F. Harrison*. When the ship first arrived in the Philippines in 1923, she had to station out of Manila until the waters around the mine wharf at Corregidor could be dredged to allow her to operate from Fort Mills. Schmidt Collection.

Quartermaster steamer *General John McE. Hyde*. One of several small transports that provided supply services to the outpost islands throughout the 1920s and 1930s. Smith Collection

Hunt was taken out of service and *Harrison* moved out to Corregidor by April 1924. *General John McE. Hyde*, a 144-foot Quartermaster Corps steamer, was used as a ferry between Manila and the fortified islands. It was built in 1921 by the Charles Ward Engineering Works, Charleston, West Virginia, and sent to the Philippines soon thereafter.[368]

Post Life

Between 1907 and 1917 Fort Mills was not considered one of the army's more desirable postings. The rugged, heavily wooded terrain coupled with the torrential rains of the monsoon season and the occasional typhoon did little to engender enthusiasm for duty on the fortified islands. Those assigned to the outposts faced primitive living conditions and an even greater isolation than that encountered on Corregidor. Even with the completion of Fort Mills' permanent barracks and quarters at the beginning of the century's second decade the place still had the rough "unfinished" appearance of having just been carved out of the woods. Many of the temporary structures built during the previous decade remained in use and threatened to become "permanent" unless destroyed by fire or the next typhoon. Only when the land upon which they were located was needed for some other purpose were these less substantial buildings actually dismantled and salvaged. Roads were mostly unpaved, narrow, and with hairpin curves that seemed to almost defy the use of gasoline-powered vehicles.

Officers assigned to "foreign service" were able to bring their families; the army operated a grammar school at Fort Mills' Middleside for the younger children while the older children went to Manila boarding schools to obtain their schooling. By 1932 the post school was able to provide classes for the first two years of high school.[369]

The arrival of an army transport at Manila was a signal event on Corregidor. The transports made a regular round trip from San Francisco by way of Honolulu, Guam, Manila, Hong Kong, Shanghai, and Japan every three months. In the early years before the World War, army transports *Sherman*, *Sheridan,* and *Buford* provided the transportation for military personnel between the U.S. and the Philippines. Following the World War, transports *U.S. Grant*, *Wheaton*, and *Republic* took over the Pacific runs. No matter which "boat" the officers and their families sailed on, the arrival in Manila was a welcome event for both those arriving as well as those who would be departing, a time for celebrating and renewing old friendships. Departing "despididas" were held for the officers and families who were leaving. During the period between the two world wars, those departing the Philippines would frequently travel part way home on the transport, stopping off at Hong Kong,

Topsides Officers' Quarters. Married senior officers were provided quarters near their unit's station on the island. Between the wars, the 59th Coast Artillery got the coveted topside barracks and officer's quarters surrounding the athletic field and on either side of the lighthouse. Schmidt Collection.

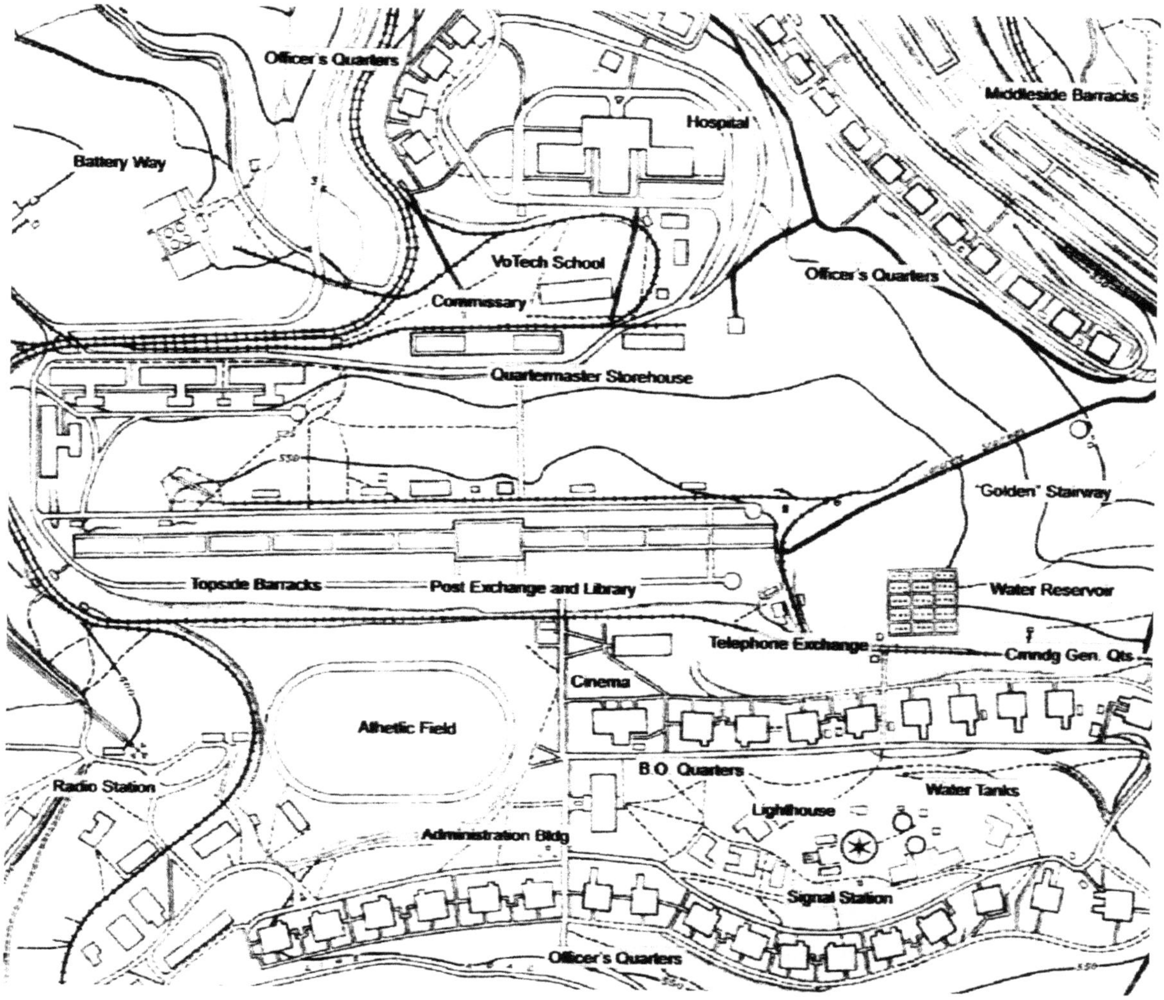

Map of Fort Mills' Topside garrison district in the late 1930s at the peak of the post's development. All the major permanent buildings, including barracks, officers' quarters and water storage facilities are completed and actively occupied. The "railroad" tracks are, of course, the electric tramway. NARA.

Enlisted troops on a transport to Manila in 1934. In the 1920s and 1930s many of the younger troops assigned to the harbor defenses experienced their first journey outside the country on such troop transports. U.S. Army transports operated on a regular schedule several times a year making Pacific troop and freight runs. Williford Collection.

Shanghai, or Japan to take leave before continuing on to San Francisco aboard the next transport. Personnel could also elect to utilize a month of detached service and four months leave in returning to the U.S. aboard a commercial vessel by way of India and the Suez Canal. They could also elect to extend their tour in the Philippines so as to return during India's cooler months of October to April. New arrivals were hosted and housed with one of the families on the "Rock" until their baggage arrived and their new quarters were ready for occupancy and set up for housekeeping. There was always a round of welcoming receptions for the new arrivals and when the new arrival was a regimental commanding officer, a regimental parade was held and in the case of a new harbor defense commander, a full-scale brigade review was held for the departing commander and his replacement.[370]

By the mid-1920s there were 114 sets of concrete quarters at Fort Mills for officers and their families, six sets for warrant officers, and another 18 for the senior non-commissioned officers and their families.[371]

Social life of the officers and their families at Fort Mills was centered on the Corregidor Club, the officers club located just south of the officers' row at Topside. The club boasted a nine-hole golf course, eight bowling alleys, tennis and badminton courts, as well as bar and dining facilities. Many wedding receptions were held at the Corregidor Club over the years. The Corregidor Club bar and its adjacent patio was a favored location of the "Sunsetters" at the end of the day. The Nipa Club at Middleside had a regular series of events, dances, and other celebrations each month.[372]

Only the two upper grades of enlisted men, Staff Technical, and Master Sergeants were allowed to bring their wives and families to the Philippines. The married senior NCOs assigned to Harbor Defense Headquarters were housed in two story 8-set concrete family quarters near the Topside Administration Building. Each set of quarters consisted of a living room, two bedrooms, a kitchen and two porches. Senior bachelor NCOs were housed in a building of similar construction accommodating 10 NCOs. Numerous additional sets for married NCOs, many of which were reconditioned temporary officers' quarters, were located on Corregidor. These quarters were for the most part single-story wooden double sets on concrete foundations with roofs of galvanized iron; similar quarters were provided for bachelor NCOs. [373]

The American and Filipino non-commissioned officers had their own separate clubs. The American NCO club was established in 1924 in an old wooden barracks building near the commissary. After being shunted around the post for nearly a decade, a new building was erected for the American club in 1932 at a cost of $10,000 in the Davidson Park area near the Topside radio towers and the Artillery Engineer's office. The

Corregidor Club. The primary officers' club for the garrison, it was just behind officers' quarters topside. Eventually it had a swimming pool, tennis courts, and a 9-hole golf course. Needless to say, it was the social center for most officer and family activities. Schmidt Collection.

Nipa Club at Middleside. Nipa is a local palm frond used to thatch roofs of native buildings in the Philippines. This was also an officer's club, less formal but more accessible to the quarters at Middleside. Schmidt Collection.

Enlisted men's service club at Middleside. When first opened it was managed by the YMCA, but later turned back to the army. It contained a bowling alley, basketball court, and post exchange, and was a very popular venue. NARA.

"Non-Com Club" boasted a large dance floor and assembly room, a bar where both draft and bottle beers were sold, and a restaurant operated by a Chinese concessionaire. By 1935 the club had some 300 members. The Philippine Scouts NCO Club was housed in a nipa and galvanized iron building at Middleside. A gigantic service club built at Middleside during World War I served the lower three ranks of enlisted men on Corregidor. Bowling alleys, basketball court, post exchange, and a beer hall were built by the Young Men's Christian Association (YMCA) with $50,000 in YMCA funds and $10,000 from the Fort Mills Cinematograph Trust

Fund. Initially it was administered by the YMCA under a sort of military contract, but on October 15, 1920, the YMCA passed maintenance and operation to the army while retaining title to the building.[374]

Recreational opportunities for enlisted personnel were largely limited to outdoor sports activities and were an important facet of garrison life in the harbor defenses. During the rainy season outdoor sports were limited, however, and other measures were needed to keep the troops from becoming discontented. A four-hole golf course was laid out at Topside for the enlisted men. Basketball and bowling took on increased importance. To compensate for the lack of athletic activities in the 60th C.A., Col. Frederick L. Dengler obtained use of an old unused barracks in 1933 and using salvaged material had the building converted into a regimental gymnasium containing a badminton court as well as well an indoor baseball diamond, a small-bore range, boxing and wrestling rings. The concept was expanded when a new athletic arena was opened on October 22, 1936. Economically built with limited funds of $5,000, the arena was a cooperative venture by all organizations at Fort Mills. The facility boasted a full-size basketball court that could be converted into tennis, volley ball, and

Grandstand and baseball game on the athletic field and parade ground. Note topside barracks behind the grandstand, which was later moved to the opposite corner of the field. Schmidt Collection.

Post golf course with its lovely view of Caballo Island. McGarraugh Collection.

boxing venues and could seat over 1,000 persons. The arena was open on its sides but had overhanging eves that provided protection from the sun and rain.[375]

There was intense competition for medals, cups, and trophies in basketball, boxing, track and field, baseball, softball, swimming, tennis, and bowling between the batteries of a regiment as well as between the regiments in the harbor defense and other military commands in the Philippines. For three years running in the 1930s the 60th C.A. won the Philippine Department basketball trophy before Battery G, 59th C.A., garrisoning Fort Hughes won the trophy in 1936. Battery G, 59th C.A., in the American Division and Battery B, 91st C.A. in the Scout Division managed to win the inter-battery bowling championships that year. Sports competitions were not limited to the men of the garrison. There was also a lively competition among the several ladies' leagues in tennis, bowling, and golf at Fort Mills.[376]

Under the direction of the commanding officer of the Guard Battalion the civil prisoners of the Stockade put on their annual Christmas program which was well attended by the Fort Mills' garrison. The program, which ran from Christmas Eve to New Year's Day, consisted of dramas, vaudeville acts, athletic events, special drills, and competitions. A large stage was set up in a corner of the stockade where plays and native dances and acrobatic events were held.[377]

Passes were granted on weekends and many enlisted men took one of the harbor boats or the mine planter to Manila. During 1926, a government boat left the Fort Mills mine wharf for the army dock at Manila at 0700 daily except Sundays making a return trip to Corregidor in the mid to late afternoon. On Saturdays the boat made two trips to Manila, departing from the mine wharf at 0700 and 1630. After staying in Manila overnight, the boat returned to Corregidor at 1930 on Sunday evening.[378]

Fort Mills's Cinémographs

Moving pictures were a popular source of entertainment on Corregidor. "Talkies" were first introduced to the island about March 1910. A theatre built at Bottomside was operated by a Mr. James A. Scott as a concession of the post exchange. It appears that Mr. Scott's connection with the moving picture business on Corregidor came to a close in November of 1911, when the Philippine Division commander, Maj. Gen. J. Franklin Bell, purchased with private funds the rights of Mr. Scott and paid off the claims of his many creditors. The theater continued in operation; reports being rendered monthly on financial status to Division (later Department) Headquarters by the "Officer in charge of the Theater." This control from Manila continued until August 1912, when General Bell turned the Cinémograph or "Ciné" over to the commanding general at Fort Mills, with the stipulation that any profits derived be expended for the benefit of the garrison. General Bell well realized the advantages of establishing the Ciné as an organization distinct from the post exchange, and the desirability of making available thereby to this isolated garrison what was in effect a "community fund." The Cinémograph Trust Fund was expended for the support of the schools; the maintenance of trained nurses; the provision of various forms of athletic facilities, and numerous other items. Of course, much of the profit from the Ciné went back into the business, enabling the purchase of new and better equipment for the theatres. Projectors were installed at Forts Hughes, Frank, and Drum so the men on duty at these small outposts might have amusement three nights a week.

In 1914 the Bottomside Ciné was destroyed by fire. The insurance carried, however, was sufficient to reconstruct the building. Late in 1914 the Topside Ciné was opened. While moving pictures were being presented, what Brig. Gen. Charles J. Bailey was pleased to call "Real High-Class Vaudeville" was also presented. At first, a room was fixed up over the post exchange. General Bailey noted in February 1915 that "even with these two theaters now the places are crowded every night and upon occasions hundreds of enlisted men stand in line outside to try and get seats." Apparently, movie fans were as rabid in 1915 as they are today. Trade became too heavy for this room, and a building was erected on the southeast corner of the parade ground. This building remained only until 1926, when it was torn down and a fine reinforced concrete building was constructed at the instance of Brig. Gen. Frank M. Caldwell near the east end of the Topside artillery barracks showing several movies each week, all well attended. By 1932 about 20 "talkies" were being shown at the two theaters each month.[379]

At the beginning of the First World War in Europe, the garrison at Fort Mills was being greatly increased and there was a considerable body of infantry stationed at Middleside. Accordingly, General Bailey approved construction of a third theatre, built about March 1915, just below the Middleside car station and close to where the post studio was located. That building was torn down about 1923 and not replaced, as the Topside and Bottomside Cinés' proved sufficient to care for the trade.

The Topside Ciné underwent a major renovation and updating in 1934. It was agreed to redecorate the interior in buff and ivory. Wash paint was used with a final result that greatly improved the appearance of the walls. Acoustic ceiling tiles were installed to enhance the sound and prevent echoes. An addition was built to the front, one story high, enlarging the lobby into what might be called a foyer. Two new ticket booths were constructed and best of all, facilities for entrance from the trolley line, through a station at one end of the new addition and from private automobiles via a *porte-cochere* at the other end: This *porte-cochere* was accessed by a U-shaped concrete drive from the main road. Due to the increased number of cars on Corregidor in the 1930s, and the consequent need for increased parking space, the main road was widened opposite the Ciné and a parking lot constructed. By mid-1941, when the reinforcement of the garrison was underway plans were implemented to build a new movie theater at Middleside.[380]

The theatre at Topside after renovation and addition of porte-cochere to the front of the building. Also note the tram station almost directly in front of the building and officers' quarters to the theatre's flank. Cornwell Collection, USAMHI.

Rest and Recuperation Camps and Cruises

About midway through their tour of duty all officers and enlisted men assigned to the harbor defenses were entitled to a month of detached service at Camp John Hay, the U.S. Army's popular rest and recuperation camp just outside Baguio in northern Luzon. As the time spent at Camp John Hay was considered "detached service," it did not count against an officer's leave or an enlisted man's furlough time. For many this entailed a trip up the "Zig Zag Road" through the mountains of "Igorot Country" and some of the most scenic parts of northern Luzon. At an elevation of about 5,000 feet, the air was clear and temperatures ranged between 50° at night and 75° in the daytime. It featured an 18-hole golf course and tennis courts. The area was also known for its excellent hunting for deer and wild pig. Other forms of recreation ranged from mountain hikes to poker and bridge games as well as the Army and Navy Club Annex just off post for those who took their exercise more philosophically.

Housing was provided in the forms of dormitories, cabins and bungalows for the guests. The camp, which served all of the services, also boasted a full-service restaurant. The cool temperatures of the region made Baguio the Philippine Commonwealth's summer capitol, somewhat akin to British "hill stations" in India. Also located at Baguio was Camp Henry T. Allen, the home of the Philippine Constabulary Academy. When the Philippine Commonwealth began establishing its own armed forces, Baguio was chosen as the site for the Philippine Military Academy. Some of the officers at Fort Mills chose to take up to a month's leave on a cruise aboard an army transport to China and Japan with a return by another transport, or by commercial vessels.

Camp John Hay in Baguio. View features the dormitory and mess hall. Today some of the old Camp Hay reservation is used for the Philippine Military Academy. Schmidt Collection.

Officer double-set bungalows at Camp John Hay. Due to its higher altitude, the post was a popular retreat during some months to escape some of the heat and humidity. Thus, it sort of served as the American equivalent of the British Indian Hill Stations. Gaines Collection.

It seems every post function fielded athletic teams. This is the Quartermaster Corps basketball team in about 1933. Smith Collection.

A second cruise opportunity was a 10-day detached service trip through the Southern Philippines visiting Mindanao, Zamboanga, Iloilo, and Jolo aboard a commercial steamer or by various government boats. Many of Corregidor's officers and their families took advantage of the opportunity. These trips through the southern isles were discontinued in the mid-1920s. They were reinstituted in February 1934 and continued until shortly before the Second World War. Another option was to take the army transport to an Asian country and after taking some leave time return to Manila.[381]

Manning the Outposts

The manning detachments for the outposts were provided by the 59th C.A. and 91st C.A. The 59th C.A. provided caretaking detachments for Forts Drum and Hughes, while the 91st C.A. provided caretakers for Forts Wint and Frank. The tours by the batteries on outpost duty were set at four months during the period from 1924 to 1931, when the tours were extended to eight or nine months. The 91st C.A. and the 1st Battalion, 92nd C.A., were responsible for manning and caring for the mobile batteries. Assignment of officers to the 2nd, or Guard, Battalion of the 92nd C.A. varied from three to six months depending upon the proximity of the annual target practice period.[382]

Battery E, 59th C.A., provided a platoon sized detachment to man Fort Drum that rotated periodically with another of Battery E's platoons about every six months. This detachment was housed in a prefabricated wooden barracks on the top deck of the concrete battleship. It was so constructed that the building could be disassembled when necessary or in an emergency simply pushed overboard. The Fort Drum detachment provided general maintenance as well as the necessary ongoing care of the ordnance and mechanical systems. The portion of Battery E remaining at Corregidor performed routine garrison duties and training at Fort Mills. When the annual target practices, harbor defense exercises, and war condition period were held, the entire battery went to Fort Drum.

Batteries C, D, and E, of the 91st C.A. were assigned on a rotating basis to Fort Hughes on Caballo Island from 1924 to 1928, when Batteries B and G of the 59th C.A. were assigned to Fort Hughes. The enlisted men of the battery occupied a small barracks on the ridge above Caballo Island's wharf while the officers of the battery (typically a captain and a lieutenant) each had a single set of quarters for themselves and their families. The initial quarters provided for the captain, while by no means luxurious, seemed so in comparison to the accommodations provided for his lieutenant. The set occupied by the battery commander was on a knoll overlooking the island's wharf. It was a roomy frame structure of three bedrooms with a porch around three sides. The lieutenant's quarters could best be described as a three room shack once occupied by the constructing engineer for his temporary quarters. Lt. Kai E. Rasmussen described these quarters on Caballo in 1931: "The back of the shack rested on the ground with a three-foot walkway along the back of the shack with doors leading into the two end rooms. The middle room had a sink with one cold water faucet, so it became the kitchen. We had an old fashion kerosene oil stove and a small ice box; the third room became our bedroom; it had a toilet in one corner. There was a shower at one end of the walk, cold water only, of course, though that wasn't too much of a problem in the tropics." In 1933, Battery B returned to Fort Mills and Battery G provided Fort Hughes' garrison for the remainder of the interwar period.[383]

Initially Batteries F and G of the 91st C.A. provided the peacetime garrisons for Forts Frank on Carabao Island and Wint at Subic Bay. In 1928 when the harbor defenses were reorganized and the troops concentrated at Fort Mills, the outposts were placed in caretaking status. Battery F assumed caretaking status of Fort Frank, maintaining a detachment at the island fort while the main body of the battery remained at Fort Mills. Battery G provided a small caretaking detachment for Fort Wint until 1934, when the Subic Bay fort was occupied by a small special composite detachment.

The 60th Coast Artillery (Antiaircraft) Regiment Arrives at Fort Mills

The Harbor Defenses of Manila and Subic Bays received another augmentation in December 1928 when the 60th Coast Artillery (AA) Regiment moved from Fort McKinley outside Manila to the "Rock." While the regiment had come to Corregidor on a regular basis for exercises since their arrival in the Philippines in May 1923, the antiaircraft unit had been posted at Fort McKinley. On December 22, 1928, the active elements of the 60th C.A. crossed Manila Bay and landed on Corregidor's wharf. The under-strength batteries were transported up to Middleside, where they occupied the barracks that had been recently vacated by the 31st Infantry when it moved to Fort McKinley. The regiment quickly settled into life at Fort Mills and assumed the primary responsibility for the antiaircraft defense of the Harbor Defenses of Manila and Subic Bays.[384]

American Four Wheel Drive trucks towing trailers with the 3-inch Model 1918 antiaircraft guns of Battery B, 60th Coast Artillery (AA). This is for a parade in Manila on July 4, 1923. Zink Collection.

When the 60th Artillery arrived in the Philippines in 1923 it came minus much of its organic equipment. While a portion of its guns, searchlights, sound locators, directors, AA machine guns, and motor vehicles were eventually received while the regiment was posted at Fort McKinley, the 60th C.A. seemed to fight a losing battle to obtain its full allotment of equipment during the 1920s. Much that was delivered to the 60th C.A. was already obsolescent when received. During the regiment's almost 14-year posting on Corregidor, that struggle would continue. The 60th C.A. had only a combined headquarters and service battery, and three active "firing" batteries when it came to Corregidor. Battery A, the regimental searchlight and sound locator battery, was equipped with eight M1917 60-inch portable searchlights and two T-1 type sound locators. Battery B was equipped with four M1918 trailer-mounted 3-inch AA guns, and Battery C was equipped with 12 .30-caliber M1917 AA machine guns. After the regiment's arrival on Corregidor, the War Department authorized the organization of the 2nd Battalion's firing batteries. On April 1, 1929, Batteries D, E, and F were activated at Fort Mills. Battery D was a gun battery, equipped with four new 3-inch M3 towed AA guns on M2A2 mobile carriages with the new M2 director, while Battery E manned 15 M1 60-inch mobile Sperry Antiaircraft Searchlights and M1 sound locator units. Battery F was equipped with about four M1917 .30-caliber and 12 M1921 .50-caliber AA machine guns.[385]

One of the 60th Coast Artillery (AA)'s T-1 Exponential Sound Locators in about 1928. The War Department purchased enough of the new T-1 locator so that each of the six regular AA regiments could be equipped with three each. Gaines Collection.

AA practice with a battery of four M1918 AA guns on trailers at the prepared exercise firing point near Battery Cheney in 1933. McGarraugh Collection.

Battery B established its positions near Battery Wheeler, while Battery D set up its battery position at the east end of Caballo Island. Battery C established its position near Monkey Point on Corregidor's tail. A platoon manned the pair of fixed 3-inch AA guns at the Morrison Hill AA position until they were dismounted and moved to Fort Drum in 1934. Although the regiment's strength was increased, the antiaircraft defenses of the harbor forts still required supplementing by antiaircraft detachments from the three seacoast gun regiments. Even with this assistance, the antiaircraft defenses at the harbor forts were still pitifully weak in 1940. As the M3 AA guns were provided to the 60th C.A., the older M1918 trailer-mounted armament was not scrapped, but was assigned to the 59th C.A. for use as secondary armament.[386]

The activation of the 2nd Battalion, 60th C.A., doubled the size of the unit, although initially Battery A had to share its nine 60-inch obsolescent truck-mounted searchlights pending the arrival of more modern lights and sound locators. The harbor defenses, however, remained largely reliant upon the outmoded trailer-mounted M1918 3-inch AA guns and their antiquated sound locators, directors, searchlights, and machine guns well into the 1930s. The regiment was armed with more than two dozen M1921 and M2 .50-caliber and 16 M1917 .30-caliber antiaircraft machine guns, hardly an adequate air defense for the five harbor forts. In April 1933, Battery B's old M1918 armament was placed in storage, having been replaced by the arrival of four more M3 3-inch AA guns mounted on M2A2 mobile carriages, towed by prime movers, and an M2 director.

Another view of 1933 antiaircraft practice firing at the field in front of Battery Cheney. In use are M1917 .30-caliber AA machineguns. Note the bamboo AA machinegun tower on the left. McGarraugh Collection.

Open-cab Cadillac trucks mounting 60-inch searchlights. These were initially supplied as equipment of the 60th Coast Artillery (AA). Schmidt Collection.

60-inch portable AA searchlight about 1930. When the 60th Coast Artillery arrived in 1923 it had eight M1917 60-inch lights, which were eventually replaced with a more modern model. Gaines Collection.

Two of the 3-inch M3 AA guns that began arriving on Corregidor in 1929. Eventually twelve were received for the 60th Coast Artillery (AA), replacing the older M1918 guns which went into storage. These are on display at Topside in 1933. McGarraugh Collection.

Another four guns arrived in 1935, enabling the 60th C.A. to equip its three gun batteries with modern armament. Also delivered in the summer of 1935 were four spare liners for the M3 guns and four M4 AA gun directors, along with basic spare parts for the 12 M3 guns delivered to that date. The regiment still lacked 12 modern 3-inch AA guns and five modern gun directors in March 1939. AA searchlights were also in short supply. In addition to the nine open-front 60-inch truck-mounted portable searchlights, there were 12 portable 36-inch AA searchlights in the harbor defenses, three dating from World War I. Another 15 were needed to complete the regiment's full allocation.[387]

The substantial vegetation and high trees on Corregidor presented an obstacle for the AA batteries of the 60th C.A. in combating low flying aircraft. High pedestal mounts built by Battery F, while satisfactory, did not solve the problem of the trees and in 1932, two 20-foot experimental towers were built at the regiment's AA firing point near Battery Cheney. One was constructed of four 6x6-inch wooden columns surmounted by a wooden platform. The second tower was built of rope lashed bamboo. While both proved satisfactory for their height, they still lacked promise in terms of steadiness at heights of 30 feet or more. Consequently, a single pole tower guyed with wire rope and set in a concrete footing proved to be cheaper than the frame towers and steadier than the wrapped bamboo towers. The poles were then fitted with outriggers at their tops upon which a platform was built to accommodate a gun crew of five men. Two of these pole towers were constructed near the summit of Topside north of Battery Smith No. 2 (Battery Hearn) adjacent to the fire control stations for Batteries Geary and Way. By 1936, however, these pole towers had proven unsatisfactory at heights of 30 feet and a new type tower built on steel angle irons and provided with steel-plate protection for the gun crews was designed. Between March and July 1936, two 35-foot steel machine gun towers were erected on Morrison Hill.[388]

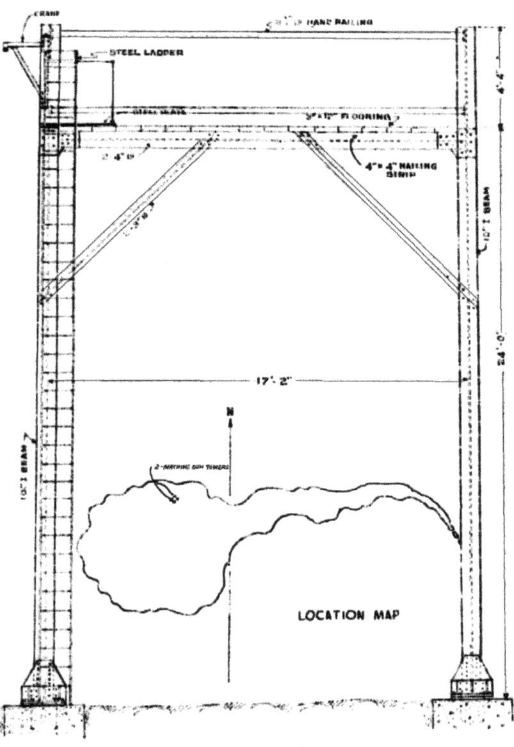

Machine Gun Towers of several different designs at several different locations were built in the 1930s. This is the plan for a pair of 28-foot high towers onMorrison Hill dated August 7, 1936. NARA.

By March 1939, antiaircraft defense had become a major concern. The 60th C.A. still had only three active AA gun batteries and it was necessary to train the 59th C.A.'s six firing batteries as AA batteries as an additional assignment using the M1918 armament. The antiaircraft matériel on hand in the Harbor Defense of Manila and Subic Bays was still in short supply and consisted of:[389]

12 - 3-inch AA guns M3
2 - 3-inch AA guns M1917 (fixed mount)
12 - 3-inch AA guns M1918M1A1
3 - Directors T8E3
3 - Height finders, T2
3 - Altimeters, M1917
14 - Altimeters, 1920

2 - Computers, data, M1917, R.A. type for M1917 guns
6 - Computers, M1917, R.A. type for M1918 guns
6 - Computers, wind and parallax, 1920
10 - 60-inch searchlights, M1925 (without comparators)
3 - 60-inch searchlights, M1917 (without comparators)
34 - .50 cal. AA machine guns (Browning) M2, water-cooled
15 - .50 cal. AA machine guns M1921, water-cooled
3 - Sound locators M1A2 with acoustic correctors and trailers
3 - Sound locators M1A3 with acoustic correctors and trailers
8 - AA BC observation instruments M1

Much of this matériel was generally obsolescent and Brig. Gen. Walter K. Wilson, commanding the Harbor Defenses of Manila and Subic Bays in the late 1930s, called for their replacement with modern directors, stereoscopic height finders, and related equipment, along with 15 modern portable 60-inch AA searchlights with sound locators and comparators. He also urged that an additional 12 modern 3-inch AA guns to be used with the modern directors and 16 BC M1 AA observation instruments be provided. Subsequently substantial amounts of AA matériel were eventually ordered for the harbor defenses. By August 1940, delivery of four more M3 3-inch AA guns was scheduled for delivery by October 1940 and delivery of 20 more in January 1941. Shipping the remainder of the needed matériel could not be scheduled and made available, however, until June 1942![390]

With the activation of a third battalion for the 60th C.A. in 1941, the gun battery firing positions were revised. Battery B was positioned near Battery Wheeler and the seaward defense command post, Battery C on Morrison Hill near the original 1920 fixed AA emplacements, D on the tail between Monkey Point and Kindley Field, Battery F near Battery Cheney at the prewar AA firing point, Battery G was projected to go to Bataan, and Battery H to be in front of Battery Ramsay at Middleside.

"Beautifying" Corregidor

Although much of Corregidor remained heavily forested, the areas where most construction had occurred still retained that relatively stark appearance typical of new building in the mid-1920s. Second Lt. Paul A. "Pablo" Leahe described Corregidor being "as beautiful as a bum oil painting." Water runoff from the summer rains frequently flooded the slopes of Morrison Hill and from Topside into the area occupied by Middleside's quarters and barracks. Erosion threatened the still primitive road system. It was not uncommon to receive 50 to 60 inches of rain during the rainy season. Sometimes as in August 1931, the rains came at the rate of as much as six inches per day; often for a week at a time, and on at least one occasion not associated with a typhoon, rainfall measured 19.69 inches in 24 hours.[391]

Many coconut palms, mango trees, and other ornamental plants had been planted during Brig. Gen. Henry J. Hatch's tenure as harbor defense commander in 1926 and by the early 1930s the palms had grown considerably, giving the post a more tropical appearance. Brig. Gen. Charles Kilbourne was at Madison Barracks, New York, on July 8, 1929, when he received orders transferring him to Corregidor for what would be a third tour of duty in the Philippines. He relieved General Hatch as harbor defense commander. During Kilbourne's and his successors' tours of duty in the 1930s, more trees and hedges would be planted around the post.[392]

Kilbourne may have done more perhaps, during his tours of duty in the 1930s to beautify Corregidor and to improve the quality of life on the "Rock" than any other harbor defense commander in the Philippines. Under his leadership, numerous improvements were made in the physical appearance of Fort Mills. The officers' saltwater beach located at the sandy Malinta Cove on the island's north shore between Artillery and Infantry Points was some two miles from Topside. At the beach, there was a bar and changing rooms. A raft

Field kitchen set-up near a battery during the War Condition period. Gun batteries were not meant as living spaces, even latrines were not installed until after most were constructed. They had no kitchens, resting areas, infirmaries, etc. Cornwell Collection, USAMHI.

Col. George Ruhlen, when commanding the 59th Coast Artillery (HD). Ruhlen amassed a considerable collection of photographs of the posts he served at as a coast artillery officer. Ruhlen Collection.

The War Condition Period typically lasted for about a week. It was a full-scale battle practice in which the seacoast gun regiments encamped under canvas in the rear of their gun and mortar batteries and the 60th C.A. deployed to their prepared AA battery sites across the fortified islands, setting up their bivouac areas and camouflaging their gun, searchlight, and sound locator positions. During this War Condition Period the garrison participated in tactical exercises and combat problems at their actual war stations. The seaward defense batteries tracked naval vessels and fired at towed targets. They fired their annual service practices and generally operated under wartime conditions. During this period, the Philippine Department's Commanding General and the Harbor Defenses Commander conducted their annual tactical inspections of the harbor defenses. The annual service practices were scored, and the battery's rankings officially recorded. Those units with the highest scores for their type of armament were rated excellent and for the next year permitted to wear the "E" Badge for excellence on their uniforms. If a given battery managed to turn in the best record in service-wide competition, it was likely to win the coveted Knox Trophy. In 1932 the trophy was awarded to Battery C, 91st C.A., for its 1931 annual service practice. In 1935 and 1937, the 59th C.A. received the annual U.S. Coast Artillery Association (USCAA) trophy awarded to the regiment with the most outstanding performance in target practice. The 92nd C.A. won the USCAA trophy in 1940, the final awarding of the trophy before war came to the Philippines.

Upon completion of the War Condition Period, the troops on Corregidor entered the seasonal small arms proficiency period in which the coast artillery units conducted target practice with rifles, pistols, and machine guns, and carried out beach defense problems. The Corregidor garrison then prepared the firing range as well as camp and supply facilities for the Philippine Division's various elements that would arrive between mid-April and the end of May to conduct their annual antiaircraft firings and beach defense exercises. With the onset of the monsoon season in June, activities retreated indoors once again.[403]

"Foreign service" tours of duty by the commissioned and non-commissioned officers were typically of two years duration during most of the years between the two world wars. About 1932, at the height of the depression, the tour was extended to three years for commissioned officers by the Economy Act. Implementation of this act reduced the expenditures for travel and had a stabilizing effect on officers and their families. Further, the extension enabled officers on foreign service to receive an additional year's training. During a typical tour in the early 1930s, a battery grade officer assigned to a coast artillery regiment on Corregidor could expect to serve in two or three units, such as a gun, searchlight, or battery, either within the same regiment, or to be

Streamer for best record service practice at Fort Mills, 1930.Gaines Collection.

Knox Trophy for 1930 awarded to Battery C, 91st Coast Artillery (PS), in 1931. This trophy was presented annually to the battery with the best performance in practice nationally. Gaines Collection.

transferred after a year to another coast artillery organization on the island to round out his experience. Field grade officers generally remained with the same organization throughout their tour until about 1933, when there was a tendency to move from one regiment after a year to another regiment or to the harbor defense headquarters staff. The changes in the length of foreign service tours eventually resulted in increased shortages of officers in the harbor defenses so that by the latter months of 1934 the defenses were short more than a quarter of its artillery officers. As many as half of the firing batteries were commanded by lieutenants. Some batteries had only a single officer and all activities were shorthanded. By 1935, however, the restrictions on travel imposed by the Economy Act had been reversed and the foreign service tour again became a two-year assignment.[404]

Only the two upper grades of NCOs were allowed to bring their wives to the Philippines. Newly enlisted personnel were recruited in the United States for service in the Philippines and would serve the term of their enlistment there. Their basic and subsequent training was conducted within their assigned regiment. Typically, upon completion of basic training a new enlistee would be assigned to a specific battery in which the training would be continued. Not until the nation neared war did the number of recruits increase dramatically. In early 1941 a separate recruit training unit was established on Corregidor. When an enlisted man's term of enlistment expired, he would be transferred back to the United States if he wished a discharge. If he preferred to reenlist, he could remain with the same regiment, or choose another outfit either in the Philippines or elsewhere within the army.

Brig. Gen. Walter K. Wilson, who assumed command of the harbor defenses February 26, 1937, noted early in 1940, "An acute shortage of officers existed on Corregidor in 1939 as the army began preparing for expansion." The shortage of experienced officers suitable for command of batteries was particularly serious. The War Department "… policy of furnishing enlisted replacements in equal increments throughout the years, although expected to be beneficial, did not come into effect in time to avoid the necessity of retaining, for the convenience of the government, a considerable number of soldiers who were needed to maintain the strength of the American regiments high enough to fire their record service practices."[405]

Japanese Espionage Efforts

Japan's interest in Corregidor began at the onset of the 20th century with the first fortification efforts in Manila Bay. By 1910 as the first seacoast batteries were brought to completion, U.S. Army counterintelligence elements caught Japanese Consulate General staff members in Manila attempting to bribe a soldier and a German-born Manila resident with $25,000 to photograph Corregidor. Although their initial attempt was frustrated, Japanese efforts persisted.[406]

In another incident that same year, a case of Corregidor fortification blueprints was stolen and later found on the streets of Calcutta, India. In 1912, a Filipino draughtsman in the office of the Philippine Division's chief engineer stole a confidential map of Corregidor. He was arrested, sentenced to one year in jail, and given a fine of $1,000, the then maximum penalty under American law. The Japan's quest to obtain the details of the American defenses on Corregidor continued. During the 1920s, fortification blueprints were again lost under suspicious circumstances. The subsequent investigation led to a Japanese agent. This time the papers were retrieved.

The value of information on Corregidor continued to rise. In September 1924, Pvt. Frank Costa, 31st Infantry Regiment (then posted at Manila's Fort McKinley), was charged with attempting to sell an army map of Corregidor for one million pesos (U.S. $500,000). In another instance during the 1920s, the Japanese colliers supplying coal to the harbor defenses would anchor off the North Dock and send in coal aboard lighters. On one occasion, the Japanese collier sent in an injured seaman who required hospitalization along with a petty officer as an interpreter. The officer of the day, Valentine P. Foster, became suspicious of the "petty officer" who had expensive shoes, hands unused to labor, and seemed an unlikely petty officer. Foster called harbor defense headquarters and said, "Look, they are trying to put one over on us. After dark, this fellow will slip out and case the joint." Soon afterward a guard showed up at the hospital and Foster, within hearing of the Japanese petty officer, instructed the guard: "You see this man? If he tries to leave this area, you shoot him, savvy?" The guard indicated he understood and the petty officer was unceremoniously escorted back to the collier.[407]

Japanese efforts to uncover Corregidor's secrets continued. In October 1940, West Point honors graduate Capt. Rufo Caingat Romero was arrested and subsequently convicted of attempting to sell classified maps of Bataan and Corregidor to an army-connected Mindanao Sultan with implied Japanese connections for $25,000. Romero, the regimental intelligence and topographic officer for 14th Engineer Regiment, was court martialed, sentenced to 15 years in prison and dismissed from the service July 10, 1941.[408]

Depression and Independence Impact the Harbor Defenses

While the army continued to diligently try to improve its strategic and tactical situation in the Philippines, the U.S. Congress was working to rid itself of its most distant possession. By the early 1930s, the United States was in a deepening economic depression and with it came increasing pressure on American farmers hit hard by imports of agricultural products from other countries. Imports of sugar and to some extent coconut oil from the Philippines, not subject to an import tariff, were considered contrary to domestic U.S. interests. Also, a growing Philippine independence movement led by political leaders such as Manuel L. Quezon and Sergio Osmeña soon prompted the passage in the U.S. Congress of the Hare-Hawes-Cutting Act of 1932 that would grant independence to the Philippines in 10 years. This act failed to receive ratification by the Philippine Senate, which was also required, and President Herbert Hoover vetoed the act in the waning weeks of his administration on January 17, 1933. The pressure to grant Philippine independence intensified as the depression deepened. Later in 1933, the Tydings-McDuffie Act was introduced with most of the same provisions as Hare-

Hawes-Cutting and was again passed by the Congress. The act among other things granted independence to the Philippines following a 10-year period in which the Filipinos would organize a government and adopt a constitution. It was this time ratified by the Philippine Senate and signed into law by President Franklin D. Roosevelt March 24, 1934. Among the major provisions of the Act was an article allowing the U.S. to maintain a military force and bases in the islands for two years following independence and another stipulating that all military forces of the Philippines be subject to call up by the United States until 1946.

As a result of the passage of Tydings-McDuffie, coupled with the staggering economy, the U.S. Congress was increasingly ill-disposed toward the expenditure of funds to bolster the Manila harbor defenses. Like previous administrations, the Roosevelt Administration's policy regarding to the Philippine Islands was in a state of flux through most of the 1930s. Requests for increased antiaircraft equipment as well as appropriations for funding bomb and gas proofing of vital command and tactical positions were rejected by a depression-conscious Congress that was disinclined to spend money on a territorial possession whose retention would soon end.

Between the wars the garrison for Fort Hughes was reduced to a single battery of the 59th C.A. Regiment. Here it is seen posing in one of the pits of Battery Craighill in 1935. McGovern Collection.

CHAPTER 12
PREPARING FOR WAR

Planning for War

Since 1903 a Joint Army-Navy Board composed of the military heads of those services and their chief planners had been established to formulate military policy. The Joint Board was intended to plan for joint operations and resolve problems of common concern to the two services. The board accomplished little, however, as its charter gave it no actual authority to enforce its decisions, it was denied the capacity to originate opinions, limited to commenting on problems submitted to it. After the First World War the board was revitalized and expanded to also include the deputies and both the chief of the army's War Plans Division and the director of the Plans Division of the navy. The new Joint Board could initiate recommendations on its own. However, the 1919 board was given no more legal authority or responsibility than its 1903 predecessor. Still it provided critical strategic thought and direction to future conflicts the nation should plan for.

From the first years of the 20th century most American officials and military planners considered war with the Empire of Japan likely. Relations between the U.S. and Japan remained rocky through much of the period preceding the World War and the U.S. military and civil governments of the Philippines planned for a defense against Japanese or German attempts to take possession of the archipelago. The threat of a German takeover in the Philippines had diminished by 1914, and it disappeared completely early in the World War. Japan on the other hand used the opportunities afforded by the war to establish herself as a major power and a strategic rival to the United States in the Western Pacific region. In the aftermath of the war Japan laid claim to Germany's Kiautschou Bay Concession in China and the former German possessions in the islands north of the equator (the Marshalls, Carolines, Marianas, and Palau Islands). Theseislands, some of which were a scant 1,000 miles from the Philippines, provided Japan with some of the finest anchorages in the Pacific and the capability to further project her power into the region. More significantly for the United States, these islands lay astride the most direct route for an American relief force to the Philippines from Hawaii.

War Plans ORANGE and RAINBOW 3

The Joint Board began developing secret color-coded contingency plans outlining U.S. strategies for various hypothetical war scenarios with other countries in 1904. These war plans became known by the color assigned them; a convention that would continue through World War II. In some instances, multiple colors were used for wars with more than one nation, i. e. BLACK-GRAY would have defined a war with Germany (BLACK) and Italy (GRAY). In all of these plans, the U. S. referred to itself as BLUE. Although the plans did not designate potential enemies by name or nationality, War Plan Orange was thecontingency plan for the U.S. fighting a war with Japan alone.[409]

As originally conceived in 1911, the plan for such a war anticipated stockpiling supplies in the Philippines and Guam in the Western Pacific that would enable them to hold out on their own for six-months while the Pacific Fleet mobilized at bases in California, and positioned itself to protect the Panama canal. After mobilization, the fleet would sail to the Western Pacific, and relieve American forces in Guam and the Philippines. Afterwards, the fleet would sail north to engage the Imperial Japanese Navy's Combined Fleet, in a decisive action and blockade the Japanese home islands.

War Plan ORANGE was regularly updated, and officially adopted by the Joint Board in 1924. It was the longest and most detailed of the colored plans. The plans developed by the Joint Planning Committee were updated regularly between 1924 and 1938 and ORANGE was substantially revised in 1928 and 1938. War Plan Orange governed strategic thinking with regard to the Philippines throughout the interwar period.

On May 25, 1923, the Joint Planning Committee "discussed in a logical progression that Japan was the primary threat and most likely source of a war in the Pacific and that most likely the war would strictly be between the United States and Japan. In order to effectively challenge the Japanese, an advanced base in the Western Pacific had to be established. As Manila Bay was the strongest location occupied by the U.S., it represented the best possible location for the base. Finally, projecting power in the Western Pacific would require repair and docking facilities for the fleet."[410]

Noting that it would require the maintenance of a standing army in the Philippines out of all proportion to the military policies of the United States, it was not practicable to provide a garrison in the Philippines strong enough to hold out against a determined attack by Japan for an indefinite period without relief from the United States. The initial emergency force sent would not be the only reinforcements the Philippines would receive; it only needed to be large enough to forestall a collapse and to secure the advance base for the navy. The Joint Board specified that the relief force must assemble in Hawaii within two weeks of the initiation of hostilities and that the forces already in the Philippines must be able to hold Manila Bay against Japanese capture for six months. It was upon this foundation that the War Plans Division built the 1924 version of War Plan ORANGE. [411]

While the Joint Planning Committee developed the 1924 plan, it was not without dissenters. Maj. John J. Kingman of the committee, and a member of the army's War Plans Division staff, proposed a reduction in the force levels in the Philippines commensurate with a mission solely supporting the authority of the Governor-General in maintaining internal order in the Philippine Islands. In his recommendation, Kingman felt that the conditions created by the Washington Naval Treaty meant that a half-hearted defense of the islands would be worse than all but conceding them in the early stages of a war. Kingman, who had played a significant role in the development of the fortifications at the entrance to Manila Bay, represented an early skepticism of the wisdom of holding the Philippines, and inclusion of his dissenting view in the official report shows that his ideas held weight in the discussions over the future of War Plan ORANGE.[412]

A change in the 1924 plan came after a finding in 1927 that the garrison was incapable of defending Manila and Manila Bay. In recommending the change to the mission, the garrison's efforts were to focus on just the defense of the Bataan Peninsula and the island of Corregidor for six months. With the reduction in scope of the mission of the garrison, it would appear that its capabilities would adequately support the goals envisioned in the 1928 plan.

The 1928 plan was based on several assumptions. The first was that the Philippines garrison would be able to hold for approximately six months. This assumption also relied upon the ability of the fleet to traverse the Pacific, fighting their way through the Japanese Mandates, refit in Manila Bay, then engaging the Japanese fleet on favorable terms. The 1928 plan changed the mission of the garrison from defending Manila and Manila Bay to a primary mission of holding the entrance to the bay, with a secondary mission of holding the Manila Bay area as long as possible, consistent with the primary mission.

The 1938 revision to ORANGE all but wrote off the Philippines in the event of war with Japan. The American garrison in the Philippines was incapable of preventing a Japanese invasion and seizure of the islands. A projected Philippine Army was yet to be organized and trained. Consequently, retreat into the Manila Bay defenses and Bataan to await relief remained the basic strategy in the years leading up to the American entry into World War II. That relief was becoming a false hope. The 1928 plan would have required the bulk of the Regular Army to relieve the Philippines garrison. The primary mission of the U.S. Army during the interwar period was training civilians. The U.S. in the 1930s was incapable of fielding a force of sufficient size to drive the Japanese out of the Philippines. After the outbreak of war in Europe in 1939, war planners realized that the United States faced the possibility of war on multiple fronts against a coalition of enemies. ORANGE was officially withdrawn in 1939, in favor of the "Rainbow Plans" developed to meet the threat of a two-ocean war against multiple enemies. To that end, the Joint Planning Committee developed a new series of war plans (the term "Rainbow" being a play on the multiple color plans that had been drawn up previously).[413]

Rainbow 1 was a plan for a defensive war to protect the United States and the Western Hemisphere north of 10 degrees south latitude. In such a war, the United States was assumed to be without major allies.

Rainbow 2 assumed that that United States would be allied with France and Britain.

Rainbow 3 was a basically a repetition of the Orange plan, with the proviso that the hemisphere defense would first be secured, as provided in Rainbow 1.

Rainbow 4 was based on the same assumptions as Rainbow 1, but extended the American mission to include defense of the entire Western hemisphere.

Rainbow 5, destined to be the basis for American strategy in World War II, assumed that the United States was allied with Britain and France and provided for offensive operations by American forces in Europe, Africa, or both.

Gas Proofing the Fortifications

Although advocated in the 1920s and reiterated in the Philippine Defense Projects into the early 1930s, approval of a gas proofing project was not forthcoming. Perceived for immediate priority in the 1930s was the gas proofing of plotting rooms, kitchens, messes, sleeping quarters, and latrine spaces of the heavy-caliber gun and mortar batteries, and the bombproof infantry garrison tunnels at Battery Point and James Ravine. No significant funding was authorized for gas proofing the gun and mortar batteries project until December 1937.

With the freeing up of $100,000 in additional funds for gas proofing defensive installations, a limited gas proofing project was finally embarked on late in 1937 that continued into 1938 to protect vital elements such as the post power plant and the water system from gas attacks. Among the facilities that received attention were the freshwater system, the perishable food storage and issue plant, the bombproof hospital in the North Malinta Tunnel, the post switchboard room and "H" Station, and the bombproofs at James Ravine and Battery Point. The plotting and switchboard rooms and rooms used for sleeping or as personnel shelters in the seaward defense batteries were also provided with gas proofing. Batteries Smith and Hearn received their gas proofing in 1938 when collective protectors and other Chemical Warfare Service (CWS) apparatus were installed. The following year Batteries Wheeler, Crockett, and Grubbs were gas proofed. Battery Gillespie's plotting room, Batteries Woodruff, Way, and Koehler also received their gas proofing equipment. In 1940 the roofed-over personnel shelter near Battery Geary was gas proofed, as was that battery's plotting room. The plotting rooms at both the north and south mortar observing stations received approval for their gas proofing in April 1940 and soon afterward were equipped with gas proofing apparatus. Battery Cheney was also gas proofed, but only with emergency material and wooden closures. As this proved to be unsatisfactory it was strongly recommended that a permanent installation be made. The AA Command Post, then located in Battery Way, received approval for gas proofing October 2, 1939.[414]

The Gun Replacement Initiative

Guns wear out, literally, with repeated firing. Larger coast artillery weapons might have just one or two typical engagements of barrel life before the bore erosion began to seriously affect accuracy. Prior to World War I, the effective life of a 12-inch M1895 gun tube was estimated at 600 rounds. By the end of 1918 the estimate varied between 300 and 900 rounds. The life of a 14-inch gun tube was estimated at 250 rounds and a 10-inch gun at 350 rounds. The smaller-caliber guns were rated at 600 rounds for the 6-inch guns, and 1,000 rounds for the 3-inch RF guns. Barrel life of the 155 mm GPF guns was estimated at 3,000 rounds. The re-supply of "fresh" barrels to a distant garrison likely to be under siege or blockaded, was a valid tactical concern. From the time of their emplacement, the 12-inch seacoast batteries on Corregidor had been fired on a regular basis using both sub-caliber and service ammunition. Consequently, by the late 1920s the gun tubes of several seacoast

Spare 12-inch M1895M1A2 gun tube near Battery Smith in 1938. Realizing that distances would prevent rapid replacement of worn or damaged gun tubes in time of war, the Manila Harbor Defenses were specially authorized to store replacement tubes for most of the large gun batteries on site. Coffin Collection, USAMHI.

guns required relining or replacement. Adherence to treaty limitations coupled with a penurious Congress and the indecision regarding the Philippines retention by the U.S. resulted in deferment of timely replacements of worn tubes.[415]

From the beginning of the defenses, the army's ordnance department had tried to maintain at least a few spare gun tubes in the Philippines. Gun carriages might break, or be damaged in combat, but otherwise they do not wear out from frequent usage, and no effort was made to make or keep spare carriages in the harbor defenses. As early as 1913 a 10-inch, 12-inch, and two 6-inch gun tubes were listed as spares at Fort Mills. At some point these were joined by an extra 12-inch M1890M1 mortar. In September 1919 another M1895M1 12-inch tube was forwarded to Fort Mills.[416]

By the early 1930s the coast artillery and ordnance officers had undertaken a serious effort to replace some of the most worn tubes in the Philippines and to locate a supply of newly relined tubes near the emplacements where they might be needed. These efforts were generally referred to as the Armament Replacement Program. The Philippines (by this time only the Harbor Defenses of Manila Bay) was the only American fortified location to benefit from such an ordnance replacement plan.

In 1932 it was found that the gun tubes of the three 12-inch disappearing batteries at Fort Mills had gone through about one-half of their accuracy life. The 14-inch guns of the defenses had only been fired occasionally and were not in bad shape. This was particularly fortunate as there was no domestic stock of spare 14-inch barrels. The 12-inch mortars fired at a relatively low muzzle velocity, and as such had a much longer service life. No problem was found with the various 10-inch and 6-inch batteries. However, some 3-inch rapid-fire guns were already worn well beyond their service lives. Four of these tubes were practically useless, and four others were fast approaching that description. As it took an estimated year to remove a gun tube, ship it to a major ordnance facility on the East Coast, reline it, and return and remount it, it was hoped that guns with serious wear could be replaced with new or newly lined tubes from the U.S. Thought was given to staggering any replacement so as not to seriously detract from the defenses all at once. It was recommended that four relined

12-inch M1895 tubes be sent to replace worn tubes. One was already on its way for Battery Hearn, one was to come from Battery Kirby at San Francisco, and the others were at Watervliet being relined.[417]

Before this could all be done, the army needed once again to consult the terms of the Washington Naval Treaty's Article XIX. It was decided that replacing guns already emplaced or storing replacement tubes that could not be fired until mounted was in accordance with the terms of the treaty's fortification section. The tubes for the Philippines were found as either spares at government arsenals, or from dismounting obsolete batteries. This program dragged out with time. In a second phase, six relined 12-inch tubes were to be sent. One of Battery Wheeler's two guns was dismounted in May 1934 and shipped to the Watervliet Arsenal, where it was relined and shipped back to Fort Mills and remounted. Wheeler's other gun was dismounted and sent to Watervliet for relining, replaced by a relined tube from the same arsenal. Battery Crockett, earmarked for relining since 1928, was finally rearmed with new tubes in 1939 and 1940, and a spare tube was received to be held in a close to the three 12-inch disappearing batteries, along with another spare for the two long-range batteries.

Even the relatively new battery of long-range 12-inch guns had been fired sufficiently by the early 1930s to require replacement of its tubes. Battery Smith's gun was changed in the mid-1930s, while Smith No. 2 (Hearn) was exchanged for a relined tube in 1936. Additionally, a spare tube was stored adjacent to Battery Smith. Eight 3-inch M1903 guns were also needed; four were found in the defenses of Long Island Sound (Batteries Pasco from Fort Michie and Henry Campbell at Fort Terry), two from Battery Trevor at Fort Casey in the HD of Puget Sound, and two more for use as spares were found in storage at Watertown Arsenal. With the receipt of these tubes by 1934, Batteries Cheney, Wheeler, James, Guy B.G. Hanna, and Alonzo H. Cushing were fully rearmed with reconditioned guns. Eventually the replacement program was accomplished, but the last relined 12-inch tube was not shipped until August 30, 1941, and delivered a bare six weeks before the war started. That tube (intended for Battery Cheney) never moved from its temporary unloading spot at Bottomside — and in fact is still there today.[418]

Positions for the 155 mm Guns

The 155 mm GPF guns had proven their value as a powerful element of the harbor defenses. While the gun dated from the First World War, it was a nice piece with good range, punch, and (with modern ammunition) accuracy. The gun was especially effective firing at stationary targets. The split trail carriage allowed for optimizing range and loading, while still being fairly mobile when coupled with an adequate truck or tractor.

The 155 mm guns received during the 1920s and 1930s were powerful pieces with a good range capability. However, they were heavy pieces. Here one is being towed by a Model 1917 Caterpillar tractor. USAMHI

It was used on three general types of emplacements in the defenses. As a mobile gun it could be (and as it turns out frequently was) used on just about any flat piece of terrain. Several locations on the fortified islands were selected as "semi-permanent" positions. This meant that the location was graded flat and often had a frontal berm to help protect the crew, a pit or excavation to allow the gun to attain maximum elevation and still have good breech clearance, and perhaps a pre-built magazine of wood or corrugated iron for ammunition or fuzes.

The 155 mm gun's most serious shortcoming from a coast artillery standpoint was its limited on-carriage traverse of 60°, which made it hard to track moving naval targets. Finally, by the early 1930s the army developed what was called the "Panama mount." This was a permanently concrete pedestal to support the central part of the carriage and a surrounding concrete ring (which could be 180, 240, or 360-degrees depending upon the desired field of fire) to support the trails and allow the entire gun to be traversed quickly. A 155 mm gun on a Panama mount also afforded a greater stability and improved accuracy. These emplacements also usually had protected magazines, although often that protection consisted of just wood and earth construction. In practice on Corregidor there were more emplacements than guns, the thought being that armament could be quickly sent to such a pre-prepared position at the time of need or threat. Also, shelters were scattered about Fort Mills to hold guns and their tractors, ready for movement to an appointed firing position when ordered.

Battery West

Various attempts were made at coast artillery posts in the late 1920s and early 1930s to develop a serviceable way to emplace the numerous 155 mm GPF guns on more stable, more quickly traversable emplacements. Ultimately the circular rail and central pivot developed in the Panama Department became standardized (hence the term "Panama mount"). Fort Mills attempted its own solution to the problem. Local engineers and ordnance personnel designed a simple concrete platform meant to hold the 155 mm gun and upper carriage. An experimental gun block was built on the slope to the west of Battery Cheney in 1930, at a cost of $140.26 for materials. It was extensively tested and proved quite adequate. However, its use involved a rather tedious (and time-consuming) process of removing the trails and then using heavy equipment to lift the gun and carriage onto its mount. In other words, it took too long to prepare a mobile gun for mounting and additional time restoring it to mobile status. The design was not reproduced in the Philippines or anywhere else. Named Battery West, the emplacement was not subsequently used in the war, though the unique gun block still exists today.[419]

155 mm gun mounted at Battery West. Prior to the adoption of the Panama Mount, the Manila Bay Harbor Defenses tried to develop its own type of emplacement capable of taking the 155 mm M1917 or M1918 gun. A prototype emplacement known locally as Battery West was built near the AA practice field in front of Battery Cheney. While it worked, it took too much effort to dismount the gun from its carriage to be practical. NARA.

Battery Monja

An emplacement for a single 155 mm M1918 gun on a semi-permanent emplacement enclosed within a concrete casemate was constructed on Wheeler Point at the south shore road's western terminus. Although authorized on February 13, 1929, this unique battery was not actually begun until January 1933. Construction was undertaken by troops with common labor supplied by Bilibid convicts and the casemated emplacement was brought to completion in November 1933 at a cost of only $495. Although the battery was to have an underground magazine and a tunnel connecting the emplacement with the magazine, funding was exhausted, and the tunnel and magazine's concrete lining was deferred. When funds were again made available in December 1936 the tunnel lining connecting the emplacement and magazine with the accessing roadway was resumed and brought to completion by the end of February 1937, having cost an additional $2,387. A second bombproof personnel shelter and connecting tunnel between the magazine and the casemate that did not require going out onto the roadway was also excavated and lined with concrete. The battery was named for the landmark of Monja Island directly offshore from Corregidor.[420]

A second M1918 155 mm GPF of Battery Monja was also was sited below and a little to the west of the casemate where a flat, relatively narrow, projection from Wheeler Point to the west is located. There a large cut was excavated in the promontory in 1940 and a 180° Panama mount built in the cut. Although the field of fire to the southwest was severely limited by the walls of the cut, the position afforded an excellent view of the shoreline west to Cheney Ravine. Both guns could also bear on the midpoint of Mariveles Harbor. Also constructed was a bombproof shelter at Battery Monja for an air compressor.[421]

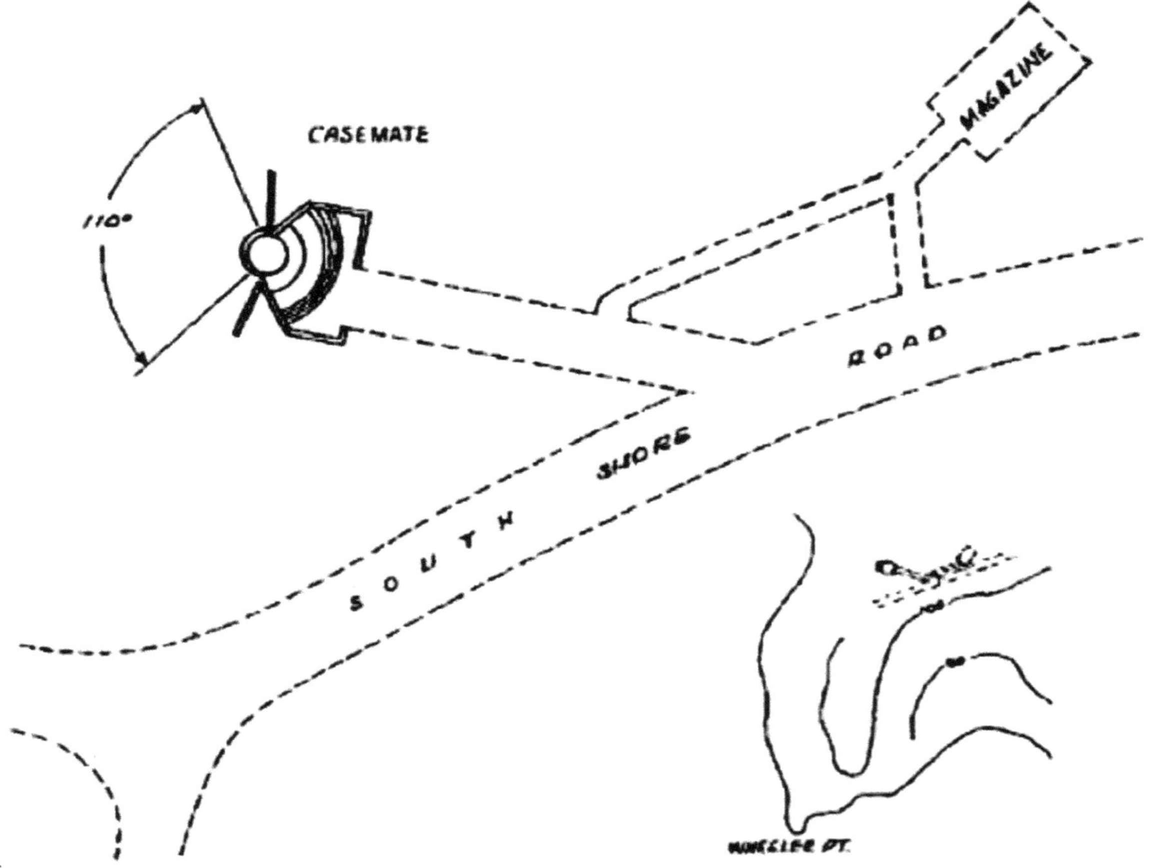

The final experiment for a 155 mm emplacement took the form of Battery Monja. A fully casemated gun position with magazine cut out of the rock to the rear was built near Wheeler Point on the far western Corregidor coastline. This plan shows the emplacement which was completed in 1940. NARA.

An exterior view of the small opening for the gun barrel of Battery Monja with its 155 mm gun. Note how well the emplacement would have been protected for incoming shell fire. USAMHI

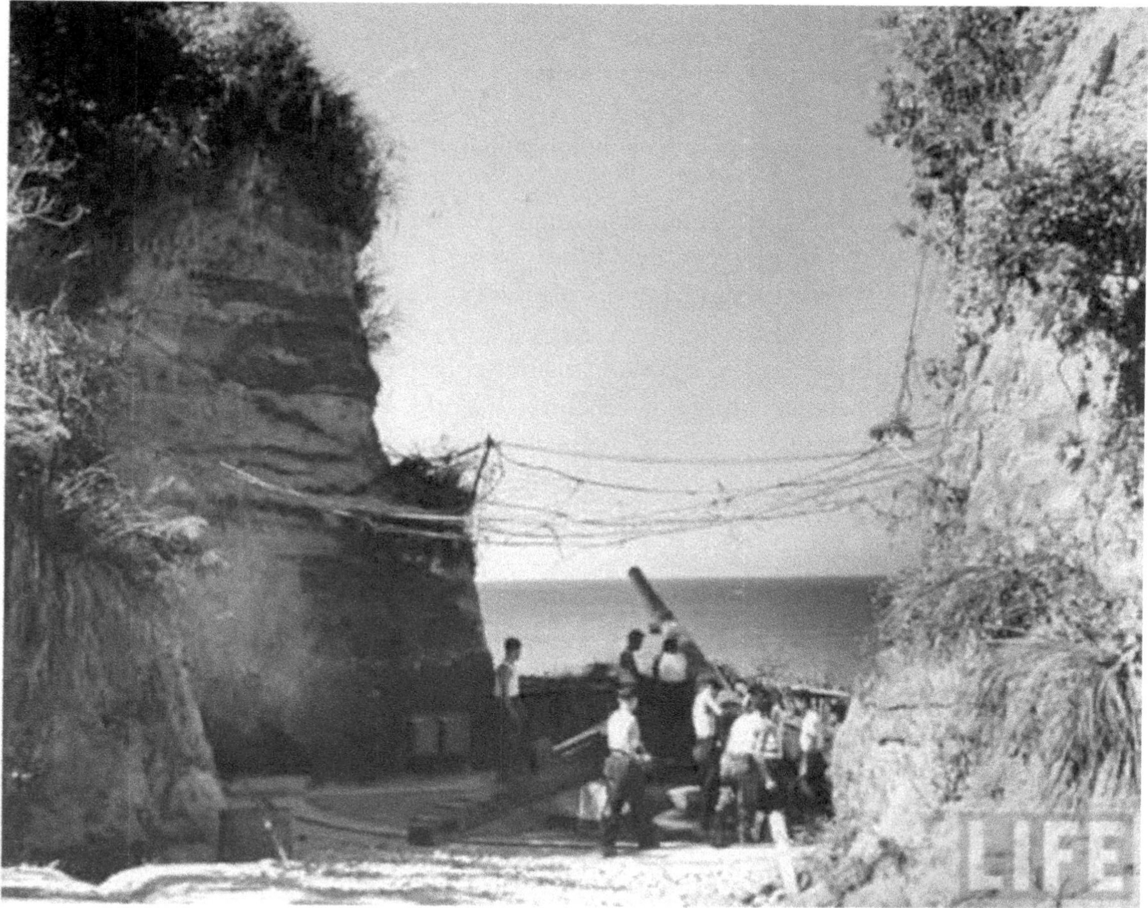

The second gun of Battery Monja was a Panama mount emplaced in a narrow cut at the base of Wheeler Point. This photograph from 1940 or 1941 shows the mounted gun and some of the overhead wires that would have supported camouflage in combat conditions. Life Magazine.

New 155 mm Emplacements Are Built

During the 1930s three-dozen firing positions, 12 consisting of Panama mounts, and the remainder semi-fixed emplacements for 155 mm guns, were constructed at 14 locations on Corregidor. Some of these Panama mounts had 360° traverse, while others had a traverse of only 240° or 180°. Fifteen 155 mm emplacements at nine battery locations were built around Topside's perimeter:[422]

Battery James Ravine - One semi-permanent field emplacement, Morrison Point
Battery Rock Point - Three Panama mounts, Rock Point
Battery Sunset – Two 180° semi-permanent emplacements, Wheeler point area
Battery Monja - One 110° casemated mount and one 240° Panama mount, Wheeler Point, built in 1940
Battery Lubang – one semi-permanent emplacement on a knoll midway between Wheeler and Searchlight Points
Battery South (New) - three authorized 180° field emplacements on Geary Point on the left front of Battery Crockett
Battery Searchlight Point - One field emplacement at Searchlight Point
Battery - Two semi-permanent emplacements on left flank of Battery Crockett

At the Middleside and Stockade Levels, there were three more battery positions:

Battery Martin - Two semi-permanent field emplacements
Battery Stockade - Two field emplacements
Battery Concepcíón - Three 180° Panama mounts

On Corregidor's tail, there were two more battery locations:

Battery North - Two 180° Panama mounts at Infantry Point
Battery Ordnance Point - Six prepared field positions for 155 mm gun drills between Camp and Ordnance Points. Panama mounts planned and one built prior to the war

Each of these batteries was projected to have one or more protected magazines. However, magazine construction was still underway when the United States entered World War II and several were never fully completed. Construction of about seven additional Panama mounts would be commenced at several existing battery locations on Corregidor after the war started.[423]

In the spring of 1938, the decision was made to place two pairs of 155 mm guns on Carabao Island. These emplacements, designated Batteries Frank (North) and Frank (South) were built in the summer of 1938. Each was to consist of two Panama mounts. The position at Battery Frank (North) was altered in the early summer of 1941 to accommodate four 155 mm guns on 360° Panama mounts and was provided with two concrete service magazines, a fuze magazine, and a galvanized iron observation station. Two of the battery's guns were those originally assigned to Battery Frank (North), while the third and fourth guns were transferred from Battery Frank (South). Because the field of fire for Battery Frank (North) was essentially the same as that of Battery Hoyle, its two 3-inch RF guns were dismounted and sent to Corregidor, where they were placed in storage.[424]

Funds were secured in 1940 to increase the efficiency of the mobile seacoast armament on Corregidor. Existing firing positions for 155 mm guns on Corregidor were improved and their armament increased. Battery South's pair of GPF guns in semi-permanent emplacements was relocated from the position on the cliffs in

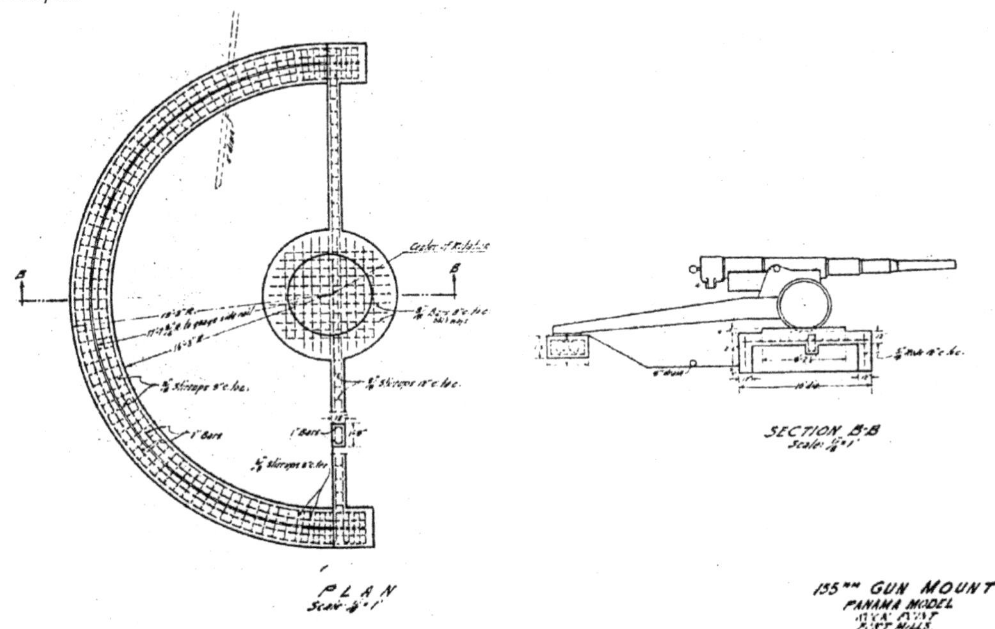

Panama mounts (developed in the harbor defenses of that command) were concrete circular or semi-circular forms holding a curved rail and center pivot. Once emplaced a 155 mm GPF gun could be easily traversed side-to-side to give it a level, fixed firing platform capable of tracking a fast-moving target. Many of these were built on several islands of the defense. This plan is for a 180° mount at Corregidor's Ordnance Point. NARA.

Battery Crockett's right front to a new position several hundred yards to the east at a point above Geary Point. There, three Panama mounts as well as two temporary magazines were built to provide improved coverage of San Jose Bay and the tail's south shore.

Additional construction of a second Panama mount was also carried out at Battery Rock Point, increasing that battery's armament to two 155 mm guns supported by a pair of cut and cover magazines.

At the 155 mm gun firing point on Ordnance Point on the tail's south shore three more field emplacements were constructed in 1940. On the tail's north coast at Battery North on Infantry Point, a Panama mount was authorized in addition to an existing field emplacement for a 155 mm gun.

Battery Sunset, four Panama mounts for 155 mm guns, was begun atop the cliffs at a point due west of Battery Smith and about midway between Cape Corregidor and Cheney Ravine.[425]

The 1940 Philippine Defense Project also called for additional 155 mm gun positions at Subic Bay and on the Bataan Peninsula. Two field emplacements were authorized for Olongapo and another pair on Grande Island itself. At Moron and Bagac on Bataan's west coast, field positions were built for 155 mm guns to cover the waters off the entrance to Subic Bay.[426]

Beach Defense Artillery Positions

In addition to the project for 155 mm guns, 15 emplacements for 75 mm and two for 37 mm beach defense guns were built during the interwar period, most of them along the island's northern shore. Several bombproof tunnels and personnel shelters were also built at locations judged to be potential landing places: James Ravine on Topside's north shore, Ramsay Ravine on Topside's south shore, and Infantry Point on the north shore of Corregidor's tail. These strong points consisted of underground shelters for the infantry supports of the beach defenses and splinter-proof emplacements for 75 mm and 37 mm guns, as well as .30 and .50-caliber machine guns. Additional splinter proof shelters arranged to receive one or two 75 mm guns were built at North Point, midway between North and Cavalry Points, at Infantry Point, on the east slope of Malinta Hill, Skipper Hill at Bottomside, on the Stockade level overlooking Corregidor Bay, Spanish Fort overlooking San Jose Bay, Battery Point, Rock Point, and Wheeler Point. At James Ravine an elaborate dual tunnel for true casemated 37 mm infantry guns and machine guns was also constructed.

Protected positions were also built at Malinta Point, at the foot of the Engineer Wharf, at James Ravine, Morrison Hill, Cape Corregidor, at either end of the AA firing Point near Battery Cheney, between Wheeler and Searchlight Points, at Battery Alonzo H. Cushing, at Battery Wheeler, Ramsay Ravine, at Battery Ramsay, and at San Jose Point. These small splinter-proof shelters typically had floors, sidewalls and roofs of concrete that were covered with earth. They were usually arranged to receive a 75 mm field gun, a 37 mm infantry gun, or a machine gun, and were typically located on the various points of land to cover the landing beaches and their approaches with both direct and enfilading fire.[427]

Wire entanglements on a Corregidor beach. The defenders took the possibility of hostile landings on the island seriously. Several small but usable landing sites were protected with barbed wire and covered by machine-gun emplacements. Sherr Collection, USAMHI.

Battery Smith No. 2 is renamed Battery Hearn

From the time Battery Smith had been completed, its guns had been viewed tactically as separate batteries and were provided with separate plotting rooms, base end stations, etc. Battery Smith No. 1 was formally separated from Battery Smith No. 2 on October 29, 1937, when the latter was renamed for the late Brig. Gen. Clint Calvin Hearn, who as a major in 1909 had been the first coast artillery field grade officer assigned to command Corregidor.[428]

Bombproofing on Corregidor

Improvements in naval artillery that included higher trajectories and greater ranges during World War I prompted the need for increased bombproof protection for the fortifications in the defenses of Manila and Subic Bays. The potential threat from German dirigibles had been recognized before the United States entered World War I and the development of airplanes as weapons increased Corregidor's vulnerability to aerial bombardment. The emplacement of a pair of antiaircraft guns on the island was a first step toward countering the threat from the air. The roadway around the south side of Malinta Hill was the sole means of communication between Bottomside and Kindley Field then under development as an Air Service installation. It is likely that General Davis, the coast defense commander immediately following World War I, saw the idea of tunnels as the first move toward establishing secure bombproof locations for the storage of supplies and for Corregidor's command operations. He advanced the concept of a tunnel through Malinta Hill to the Philippine Department in the annual estimates of 1921. Another tunnel at Middleside was proposed to serve as a new harbor defense command post (HDCP) to supplant the existing "H" station at Searchlight Point. This tunnel was projected to be some 600 feet long, 12 feet wide, and have a crowned arch 10 feet high. Work was actually commenced on the Middleside end of the HDCP Tunnel and had been excavated 235 feet into the ridge before the ratification of the Naval Armament Treaty of 1922. Accordingly, further work was halted. Near the "H" Station above Searchlight Point, it was also proposed in 1921 to build another tunnel for Fire Command 1 (later Gun Group 1), the seaward defense's large and medium-caliber seacoast guns. Work on this tunnel although planned had not begun when the 1922 Naval Treaty was signed in Washington.[429]

In 1926, bombproofing of the fortification structures on Corregidor and the other fortified islands was given additional study. A report by a board of officers recommended four types of dugouts for personnel and utilities and called for provision of drilling equipment to begin the construction upon the outbreak of war. The bombproofing project was the subject of continuous study and in 1931 the project was again submitted as part of the Harbor Defenses Annex to the Philippine Defense Project. This was a much-reduced project compared with the 1926 plan. However, it retained the following precepts: All batteries of 6-inch caliber and above as well as beach defense positions at Battery Point and James Ravine would have rest and sleeping accommodations for personnel. Fort Hughes was to have accommodations for 450 men in its existing tunnels and Fort Frank for 540 men in its tunnels. At Fort Wint, sleeping accommodations for the personnel assigned there would be provided in the batteries. Many bombproof structures recommended in earlier projects were omitted, it being believed that it would be possible to begin emergency and temporary construction upon receipt of information that war was imminent. This project was submitted with the proviso that the bulk of the major overhead protection (Malinta Tunnel) had been provided during the time of peace. The War Department,

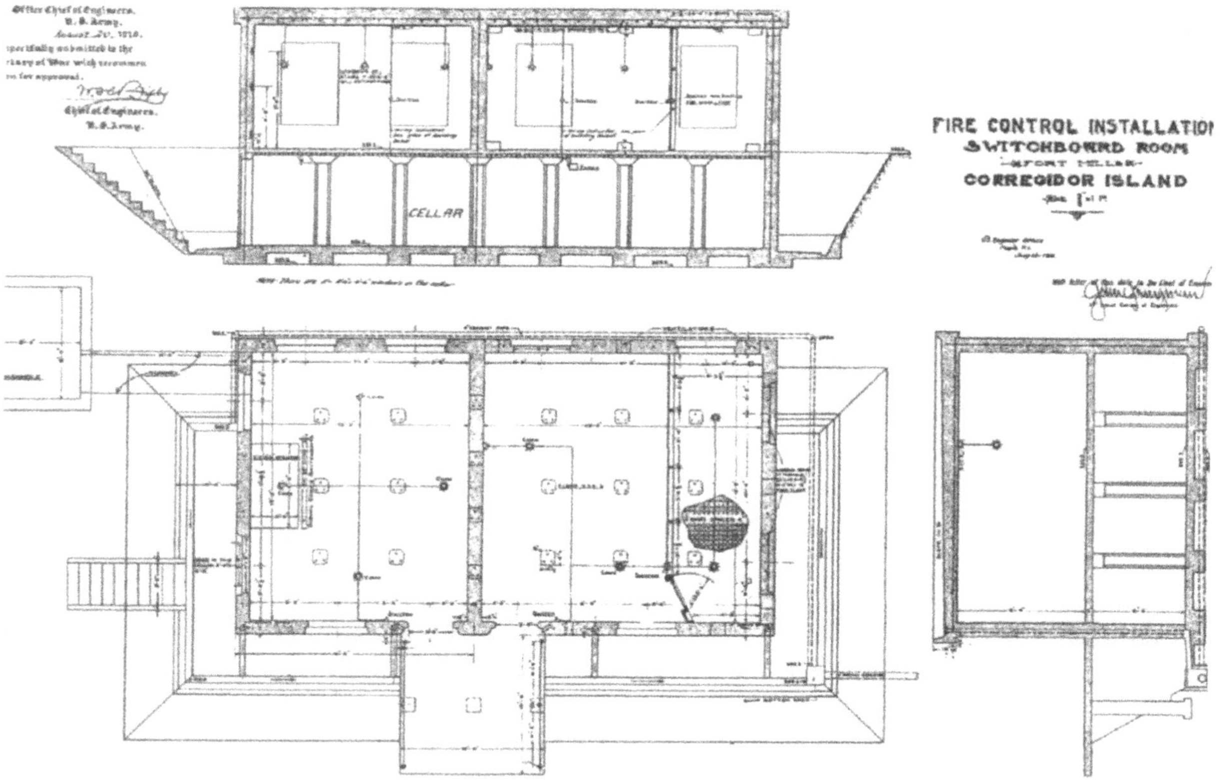

Plan, elevation, and section of the switchboard room at Fort Mills. The structure as built in 1910 did not last long like this. As part of the bombproofing effort for tactically important buildings, the lower-level moat was filled in to the upper floor and the building given a heavy concrete and earth overhead cover. NARA.

while appreciating the proposal's importance, felt it would be fruitless to pursue because of the "present uncertainty as to the future status of the Philippine Islands and because of unfavorable action that heretofore has been taken by the Bureau of the Budget and by Congress regarding other projects pertaining to the Philippine Department."[430]

The projects recommended in the Bombproofing Project on Corregidor were:[431]

Storage tunnels for fuels and lubricants
Wheeler Tunnel to the immediate Southwest of Battery Wheeler, begun as the HDCP in1920 but later abandoned in accord with the Washington Treaty, was to be repaired and relined as a shelter for the AA battery located there. Designed to accommodate the 123 officers and men of an AA battery, the tunnel had an overall length of 450 feet and was accessed from Cheney Road.
Splinter-proof shelter for 96 officers and men of an AA machine gun battery at Monkey Point
Tunnel on Cape Corregidor for beach defense detachment, and 155 mm gun crews and Battery Hanna
Tunnel at Ramsay Ravine for beach defense detachment of 63 officers and men
Tunnel at Government Ravine for beach defense detachment of 31 officers and men
Tunnel ordnance storehouse at Middleside
Tunnel reserve storage for eight searchlights and 14 mirrors at Topside
Splinter-proofs for water pumping plants at various locations on Corregidor
Steel doors and shutters for post steam and diesel plants at Power Plant Ravine
Tunnel at Cheney Point for 155 mm gun detachment and an AA platoon of 51 officers and men
Tunnel at Searchlight Point for 155 mm gun, Battery Cushing, and beach defense detachment
Tunnel at Infantry Point for 155 mm gun and beach defense detachment of 103 officers and enlisted men
Tunnel at Middleside for hospital for slightly wounded personnel with 100 beds, quarters for 65 officers, nurses, and men
Tunnel magazine at Battery Smith No. 1 for 12-inch powder charges
Tunnel magazine at Battery Smith No. 2 for 12-inch powder charges
Tunnel magazine at Battery Ramsay for 6-inch projectiles
Tunnel for two magazines for Battery Grubbs for 10-inch powder charges
Tunnel at North Dock for beach defense detachment of 93 officers and men
Tunnel at Geary Point for beach defense detachment of 73 officers and men
Tunnel for AA commander and staff, 34 officers and men
Tunnel for department commander and staff, 44 officers and men
Tunnel at Searchlight Point for seaward defense commander, 96 officers and men
Cut and cover bombproof at Topside for an enlarged HD command post and switchboard with 46 officers and men
Tunnel at Middleside for hospital with 410 beds and 255 officers, nurses, and men
Tunnel at Middleside for water reservoir with capacity of 50,000 gallons

The tunnels at Middleside proposed in 1921 were to be interconnected to the proposed HDCP and switchboard tunnel making a substantial underground bombproof that extended from below the hospital to beneath the existing Fort Mills administration building and post switchboard room and thence under part of officers row to emerge at the edge of the cliffs between Searchlight and Geary Points. Considerable changes were made in the 1930s that affected this large tunnel project that had fallen victim to the Washington Treaties of 1922 and had been abandoned shortly after it was commenced. However, the decision in the early 1930s to dig the tunnel through Malinta Hill, with its hospital annex, essentially removed much of the rationale for the expansive Middleside tunnel.

Projected at Fort Hughes were two gasproof tunnel magazines for storage of additional 14-inch shells and charges for Batteries Wilson and Marshall at Fort Drum and one gasproof tunnel magazine for 6-inch charges for Batteries Roberts and McCrea at Fort Drum. These three magazines would also accommodate excess ammunition allocations at Batteries Woodruff, Gillespie, and Leach at Fort Hughes. Also projected was a splinter-proof at the east end of Caballo Island to accommodate the Hughes AA Battery personnel of 103 officers and men. In the rear of Battery Woodruff, a tunnel for 106 officers and men was projected.[432]

At Fort Frank five tunnels were projected. One would provide storage facilities for six months of subsistence supplies. The second was a branch off Battery Greer's tunnel to house ammunition and additional protected access for the 155 mm guns. Also planned were gasproof tunnels to house the distillation plant and another near the Fort Frank wharf for the storage of gasoline and oil. A fifth tunnel was to be excavated from the rear of the fort commander's station and sleeping quarters and connected to the main tunnel. Also projected were new plotting rooms for Batteries Crofton and Greer.[433]

Although the bombproofing project developed in the 1930s was fully planned and priorities established within the harbor defenses and the Philippine Department, authorization and funding was withheld until the Roosevelt administration adopted a new defensive strategy for the Philippine Islands. By that time, additional projects had been developed in the harbor defenses and were only awaiting authorization and funding in order to proceed. A massive upgrading of the harbor defenses was projected during the budget preparation for F.Y. 1942; but before these improvements could be barely started the process was overtaken by events. Some bombproofing projects were commenced prior to the outbreak of hostilities with Japan: one was construction of the tunnel for the seaward defenses command post atop the cliffs of Searchlight Point. A second project developed in 1941 involved roofing with concrete and earth the revetted cut between Batteries Geary and Crockett for use as a personnel bombproof for the two batteries. The HDCP Tunnel was also restarted at Middleside after nearly 20 years, just a few days before the outbreak of hostilities. This tunnel, whose entrance was at Middleside, would become known as the "Middleside Tunnel." The HDCP itself would eventually be located in Malinta Tunnel.[434]

A Tunnel Is Excavated Through Malinta Hill

The concept of a tunnel through Malinta Hill was proposed in the waning days of World War I. Such a tunnel through the hill would avoid interruption of communication between the main part of the island and its tail and the inconvenience caused by storms washing out the roads on Malinta's slopes and causing landslides. In time of war, this communication could also be interrupted by hostile naval bombardment of the hill's south slope; and the roadway around Malinta's north side was equally vulnerable to hostile fire from the Bataan Peninsula. A tunnel would also be useful for the protected storage of critical supplies and matériel. The western entrance to the proposed Malinta Hill tunnel at Bottomside would be where a portion of the hillside had already been cut away as a source of rock for a nearby crushing plant. The tunnel as initially projected in May 1921 would extend through the hill for a distance of about 650 feet, be 16 feet wide, and have an arched crown of 19 feet. The walls, floor, and ceiling were to be lined with concrete and have a single trolley track running through it to the Air Service facilities on the tail. Four storerooms, each 40 feet long and 30 feet wide, were to be located off the main tunnel. These bombproof storerooms could be used as magazines or for storage of supplies; and in time of war the facility could be fitted out as an emergency hospital. The rock excavated from the tunnel would be used for construction on the island, providing an additional cost savings. The project's was estimated at $650,000. This proposal was eventually forwarded via the Philippine Department to the War Department.[435]

After several months, the idea was rejected in 1922 as being in contravention with the spirit of the Washington Armament Conference and the Harding administration's promises to the Japanese not to improve the Philippine Islands defenses.[436]

Although not met with favorable consideration by the War Department, the concept of a tunnel did not die. It may well have received tacit approval from Maj. Gen. John Gulick, the chief of coast artillery, when he visited General Kilbourne on Corregidor during the late 1920s. The United States officially continued to abide by the treaty provisions with regard to fortifications. The tunnel, identified by Kilbourne as a "civil project," and by others as "Kilbourne's Folly," involved excavation of a roadway and trolley tunnel through the hill to the Kindley Field area. Kilbourne had managed to prevail upon the gold mine owners at Baguio to make some of their older drills and compressors available for a modest rental fee. The Philippine mining matériel would be used to begin the small shaft through Malinta Hill. While started by General Kilbourne, it fell to his friend Brig. Gen. Stanley Embick who arrived on Corregidor June 17, 1932, as Kilbourne's successor as harbor defense commander, to advance the Malinta Hill project until January 31, 1935.[437]

When 1st Lt. Pashael N. Strong Jr. arrived in the Philippines in October 1932 for duty as an assistant to the departmental engineer, he was sent to Fort Mills where he was assigned to the Malinta Tunnel project. Lieutenant Strong was directed by Embick to take over work on the tunnel and informed that he was to do it with regularly allocated funds and use only equipment available on the island.

The scope of "Kilbourne's Folly" increased substantially in comparison with the original 1921 project. Once the small shaft was excavated, it was to be enlarged and 24 lateral tunnels excavated at about a 45° angle on both sides of the main tunnel to provide storage tunnels for "delicate parts" such as "searchlight mirrors, combustibles, and explosives." "Kilbourne's Folly" would now be 831 feet long and 24 feet wide with a 15-foot arched crown. The laterals were to be about 150 feet long with a width of 10 feet and crowns of 12 feet.

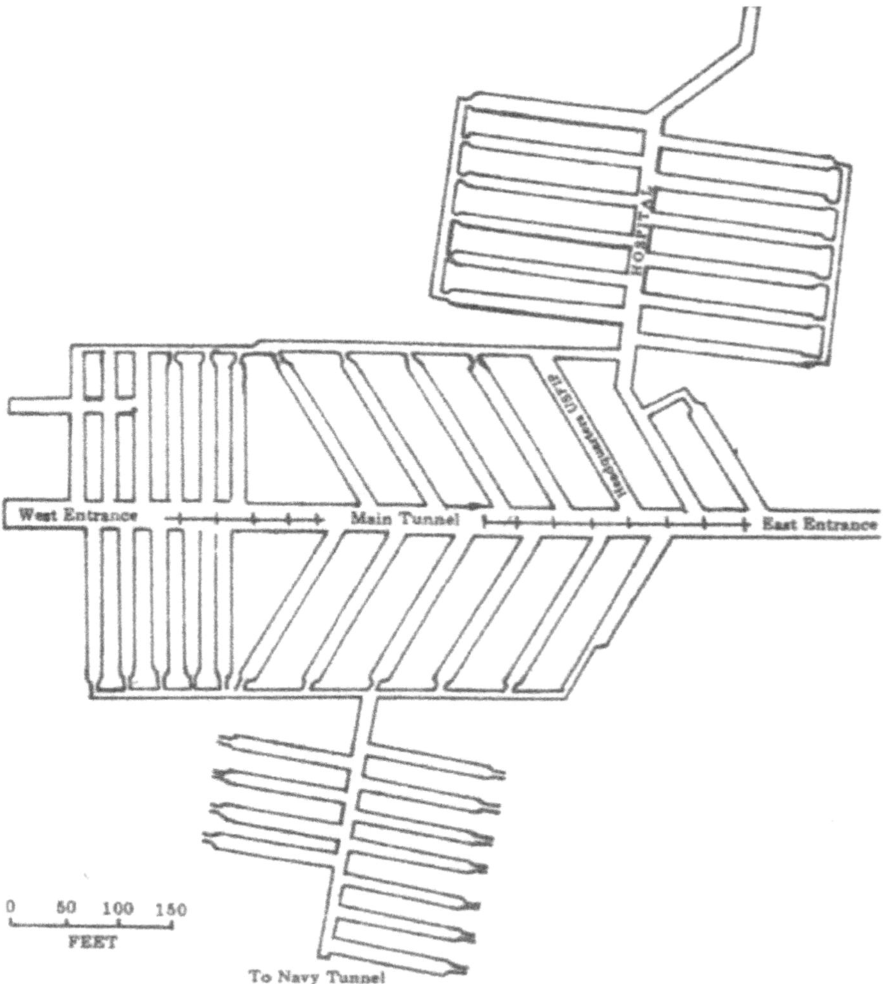

Malinta Tunnel as completed in the late 1930s, with hospital annex to the north, and storage annex to the south connecting to the future naval storage system. NARA.

Some 600 Bilibid convicts guarded by the 2nd (Guard) Battalion, 92nd C.A., provided the labor for the project. A company of engineers from the 14th Engineer Regiment provided foremen and clerks to oversee the Bilibid's work.[438]

The explosives for blasting were obtained from Ordnance Department stocks in the United States. This department provided tons of condemned powdered TNT that was shipped to Corregidor on an army transport. As the TNT was generally unusable in its powdered form for blasting, Fort Mills' ladies came to the rescue with old magazines that were used to wrap the TNT into makeshift cartridges that were inserted into the long holes drilled into the hill's volcanic rock.[439]

The blasting was to be conducted at night to prevent undue publicity. As Colonel Strong recalled many years later:[440]

> The midnight that we set off the first blast was a memorable one. We had a pattern of seventeen loaded holes in the heading each to be detonated by a short length of time fuze, Electrical caps were a luxury beyond our dreams. My mind was on engineering rather than military matters, and I overlooked certain trivia,_such as that I was working within a fortress whose guns and searchlights were perpetually manned by a skeleton alert and whose garrison was never allowed to forget that any Jap attack would be unheralded. So I failed to notify the defenders what to expect. At precisely twelve, the soft tropical night was rent by a series of explosions which sounded like the uneven salvo of attacking battleships. The echo had hardly bounced back from Bataan when a dozen alarms sounded, searchlights stabbed frantically into the China Sea and soldiers rushed to their stations in all clothing and no clothing. I was gratified to note this stirring example of a garrison that would not be caught napping but the commanding general summoned me and concealed his pleasure admirably. If I was mentioned in dispatches it was not the kind of mention to dwell upon. As the tunnel blasting proceeded the laterals were also excavated and crude blowers inside tunnels were used to expel the toxic gasses created by the TNT blasting.

The tunnel had been started at both ends and was to meet somewhere near the middle. Strong recalled:[441]

> The night we blasted the last remaining rock between the two approaching tunnels found me... confident. The Coast Artillery officers had placed bets on how closely the two headings would meet, a large crowd of them were present for the occasion. I was offered odds that the two headings would match in line or elevation by several feet, but being a man of honor, I would accept only even money. The headings matched by inches, a fact which I had previously determined by punching an exploratory drill hole through the rock wall.

Once the 24-foot-wide and 831.6-foot-long east-west tunnel was completed through the hill, it was discovered that the rock arches were too brittle to stand by themselves. It became necessary to line them with concrete. The 18-foot crown of the tunnel arch was slightly higher than the initial plan. Funding for the army during the "Great Depression" years was almost non-existent and was generally limited to military pay, food, and in the good years, a small allocation for a few rounds for target practice. To obtain funds for the tunnel's concreting it was necessary to use accounts earmarked for maintenance of the Fort Mills barracks, quarters, and other post buildings. About $10,000 was scraped up somehow and the cement was bought from a Japanese source at $.50 a barrel. The forms were built in post workshops and the concrete mixed and poured to line the tunnels. With the tunnel complete, a track for Fort Mills' trolley line was extended through Malinta Hill to the former air service facility at Kindley Field now occupied by the 91st C.A.[442]

Throughout the initial excavation phase, the tunnel complex was considered an "off the books" operation and annual inspections made no mention of its existence. It was not formally funded by annual appropriations and while it was known to exist by many high-ranking persons within the War Department and elsewhere, it did not show up in any official records until Lieutenant Paschal finished his work and returned to the U.S. in 1934. At that time, the tunnel complex consisted of the main east–west tunnel with a trolley track and roadbed running down the center. Twenty-three laterals branched off the main tunnel, 11 at a 90° angle and 12 more at an angle of 45°. These laterals varied between 112 and 165 feet in length, were 12 feet wide, and had crowns of about 10 feet. At the tunnel's west end, one of these laterals was initially designated for the storage of chemical warfare equipment and supplies, three others for the storage of gasoline, and 18 for use as ordnance magazines. When completed the tunnel had cost $104,720.45, not counting the "unofficial" expenditures made while Generals Kilbourne and Embick had commanded the defenses.[443]

On June 23, 1936, the Japanese cabinet formally decided to not renew the 1922 naval limitation treaties and their successors, including the London Naval Treaty of 1935. Japan believed that her prestige and her material interests would be better served by complete freedom concerning the types as well as numbers of her warships. Japan's action served to release the U.S. to conduct the tunnel project in the open rather than as a covert project.

By the late 1930s any reservations held by the Roosevelt administration about the strengthening of the Philippine defenses had been fairly well erased by the Japanese military activities in China and rumors of their program of fortifying the Japanese Mandates (which proved unfounded). Continued uncertainty remained within the federal government over the future of American long-term involvement in the Philippines. That uncertainty resulted in a continuance of the practice of benign neglect where improvements to the defenses were concerned. Allocations for Corps of Engineers maintenance and construction in the harbor defenses did not exceed $39,000 per year during the three years preceding the outbreak of World War II in 1939. Despite the hesitancy of the government to enhance the defenses with more modern armament, a desultory program of improvements to the Malinta Tunnel project was continued through the late 1930s and into the 1940s, with the addition of a large number of additional laterals being excavated and lined with concrete. Many of these laterals were reserved for use as quartermaster and ordnance storage, while others were planned as bombproof command and office spaces.

The Malinta tunnel system was expanded still further in 1937 upon the initial project's completion, when a 12-foot wide and 10-foot high, 553-foot-long north-south tunnel between the main tunnel and an exterior entrance that opened on Malinta Hill's north face. This addition was built during Brig. Gen. John W. Gulick's tenure. Gulick had been a staunch advocate of the tunnel while serving as chief of coast artillery in the early 1930s and succeeded Kilbourne in command of the harbor defenses in November 1935. The proposed project of excavating tunnels below the existing post hospital for a wartime hospital in the 1920s was abandoned and the decision made to place the hospital under Malinta Hill, connected to the main tunnel complex. This hospital complex consisted of an additional 12 laterals that branched at right angles off the north-south tunnel, six to each side. These laterals were 162-feet-long, eight feet wide, and 10 feet high. A northern exit from the complex was built along with a doglegged access tunnel that opened onto magazine road skirting Malinta's northern slope. Airflow through this part of the complex was enhanced by 200-foot-long ventilation passages that paralleled the north-south tunnel at the rear of each lateral in the tunnel complex's north section. Both ventilation passages were connected by a ventilation shaft to the outside of the hill. One was 65 feet long and the other 105 feet long. This second phase complex was constructed at a cost of $39,394.06. In 1937 a latrine lateral 10 feet long and eight feet wide with a 15-foot crown was added to the complex. By February 1938 the Malinta complex was essentially complete with the exception of the hospital section.

The island's trolley line was extended through the central lateral of the tunnel to continue eastward as far as the Kindley stop by the quarters complex (but not as far as the airfield itself, despite the name). Originally this was planned as just a single-line track. However, the tunnel was later double tracked, and clear evidence of that can still be seen in the tunnel today. As the storage function of the complex grew in importance, the ability to shuttle freight cars to one side without interfering with normal passenger service was no doubt useful.

Still another expansion of the Malinta storage system south of the main tunnel was projected under Malinta Hill's south slopes. It was expected to add an additional 256,000 cubic feet of storage at an estimated cost of $100,000. Known as the "South Complex," work was begun in 1938 and was initially projected to consist of 65 laterals when completed. Construction continued into late 1941, when work was halted by the war and

West entry to Malinta Tunnel as completed. Smith Collection.

1940 photograph showing storage of what are probably 155 mm projectiles double-stacked on both sides of one of the finished ordnance storage laterals. Life Magazine

the need to use the remaining construction resources on other projects. When work was halted, only 11 laterals had been completed. All branched at right angles from the connecting north-south tunnel. Four laterals branched off to the west from the north-south tunnel and seven others branched to the east.[444]

The important gas proofing of the army tunnels at Malinta Hill was delayed. In 1940, a board of officers reviewed and revamped an existing plan for the gas proofing and improvement of the gun and mortar batteries of the seaward defenses as well as Malinta Tunnel, and $528,000 was allotted in 1941. Soon after his arrival on Corregidor in February 1941, Brig. Gen. George F. Moore, who succeeded General Wilson as harbor defense commander, directed the post engineer to complete the Malinta Hospital complex and install the necessary gas proofing as originally planned. When funding was provided, work was resumed on the hospital tunnels in July 1941. Some 450 feet of additional excavation was required to complete the hospital in accordance with the original plans. Large blowers were installed throughout the hospital laterals to provide forced air ventilation. Although authorized and funded, the blowers for the tunnel's gas proofing system as well as the CWS canisters, collective protectors, and headers for the air lock entries to the hospital failed to arrive before war came and the gas proofing project implemented was a temporary one.[445]

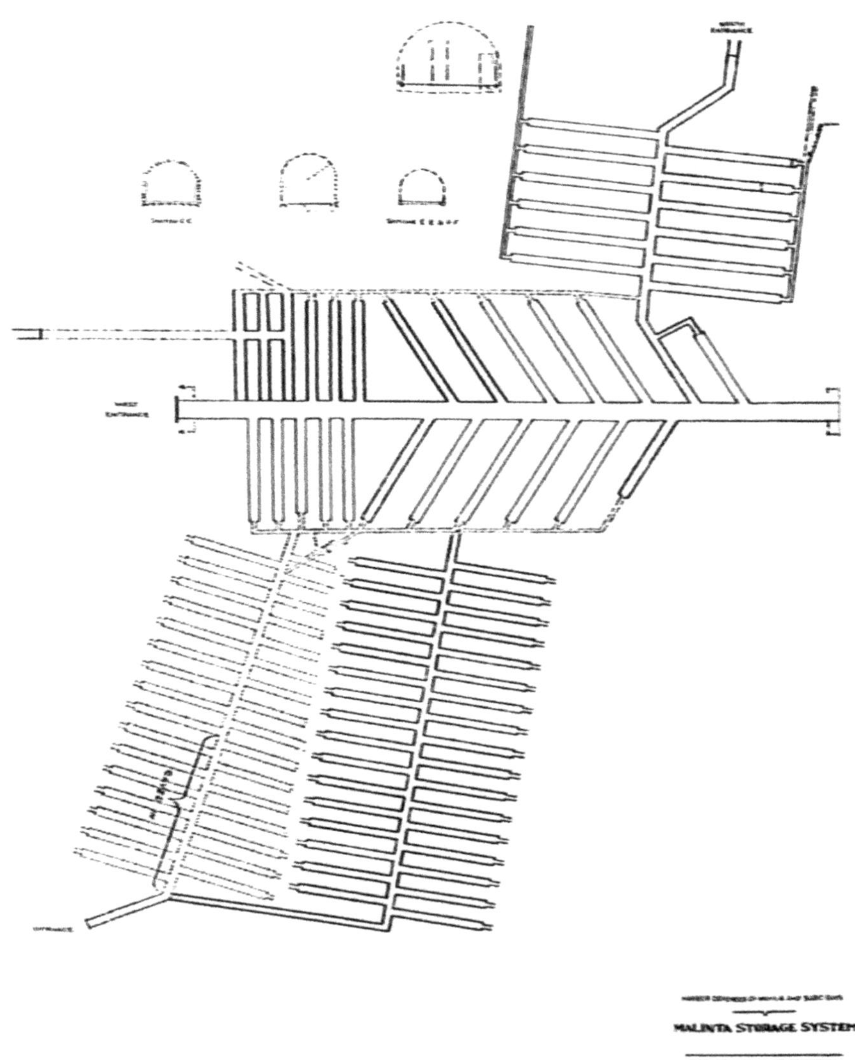

Progress plan for Malinta Tunnel in 1940. The main storage system is complete, as are the northern hospital laterals. Construction of the new naval storage tunnels is still underway. This plan clearly reveals the collapsed condition of the first attempt of the storage complex to the south of the main lateral, and its re-location further east. NARA.

The Navy Mariveles Tunnels

In the mid-1930s the navy approached the army in an effort to establish an emergency radio station on Corregidor or Caballo, but the army did not initially approve. By the late 1930s the 16th Naval District commander, impressed with the Malinta Tunnel project, sought to have a similar bombproof command post on Corregidor in the event Cavite Navy Yard was evacuated. Eventually several construction projects were approved by the War Department to accommodate navy requirements.[446]

One of the five navy storage tunnels (this one for fuel) under construction in October 1941 at the Mariveles site. NARA

Under the contract and agreement for construction of the navy's seaplane base on Sangley Point at Cavite, the Bechtel Corporation, one of eight members of a consortium known as Contractors, Pacific Naval Air Bases, also developed a small base for the inshore patrol and an ammunition depot at the navy's Mariveles Section Base on the tip of the Bataan Peninsula. In addition to boring several tunnels for the storage of munitions and other supplies, this project called for 47 structures, including storage for mine and cartridge cases, ammunition overhaul shops, a general garage, a generating plant, distribution systems for electricity and water, telephone and fire-alarm service, quarters for military personnel and civilian workers, as well as walks, roads, and necessary drainage. As part of this project, five tunnels were driven into the hills around Mariveles for the storage of supplies and food which the navy began moving from Manila and Cavite around December 14, 1941. Some of the tunnels would end up being used to house part of the crew and the machine shops from USS *Canopus* after the submarine tender was bombed. Bechtel continued work on the seaplane base and the Mariveles projects until Christmas Eve of 1941, when Manila was declared an open city. Emergency defense work was continued at Mariveles by civilian workers until April 8, when Bataan was surrendered to the Japanese.[447]

The Navy Radio Intercept Station

Beginning in 1924 the U.S. Navy began collecting radio intelligence in the Far East. Initially it used listening stations for radio intercepts in Shanghai, Guam, and the Philippines. Eventually all the activity was concentrated in the Philippines, though over time its facilities shifted from Olongapo to Mariveles to Cavite and eventually to Corregidor. At the beginning the work was simply "listening in" to foreign (mostly Japanese) transmission, but later actual decryption was begun, and then in 1936 radio-direction finding capability was added. In 1934 it was proposed to relocate the station and antennas to either Corregidor or Caballo Island. The navy's desire was to locate the facilities within the Manila Bay defensive area, but still be near adequate facilities for personnel. At first the army demurred the mixing of navy radio personnel with its own (less well-paid) people, but finally in late 1938 the two service secretaries agreed to authorize the construction of a new facility at Monkey Point on Corregidor.

By August 31, 1939, the following projects were identified: Project AFIRM, the radio intelligence tunnel, and BAKER, the direction finder sites on East Point (the DY direction finder site was about halfway between the DT high frequency direction finder (HF/DF) site and the intercept tunnel). In addition, a model DT-1 direction finder was to be calibrated and placed in storage on Corregidor and a model DP intermediate frequency direction finder (IFDF) was scheduled to be installed. Under Project CAST, quarters for Station "C" personnel were constructed near the tunnel. They consisted of several double sets of quarters for the officers and chief petty officers and two-story barracks for the remaining enlisted men, all wood-frame construction. [448]

The navy came up with the construction funds for Project AFIRM, but the local army engineer office supervised the work. A labor force of Bilibids arrived at the construction site in February 1939 and by spring excavation and drilling was well underway on a concrete bombproof tunnel. By October 1940 work was basically completed, but work would continue through much of 1941 when the finer details such as steel blast doors, improved lighting, emergency air vents, machinery spare parts, and noise suppression measures for the diesel generator would be installed. Final completion came in December 1941.[449]

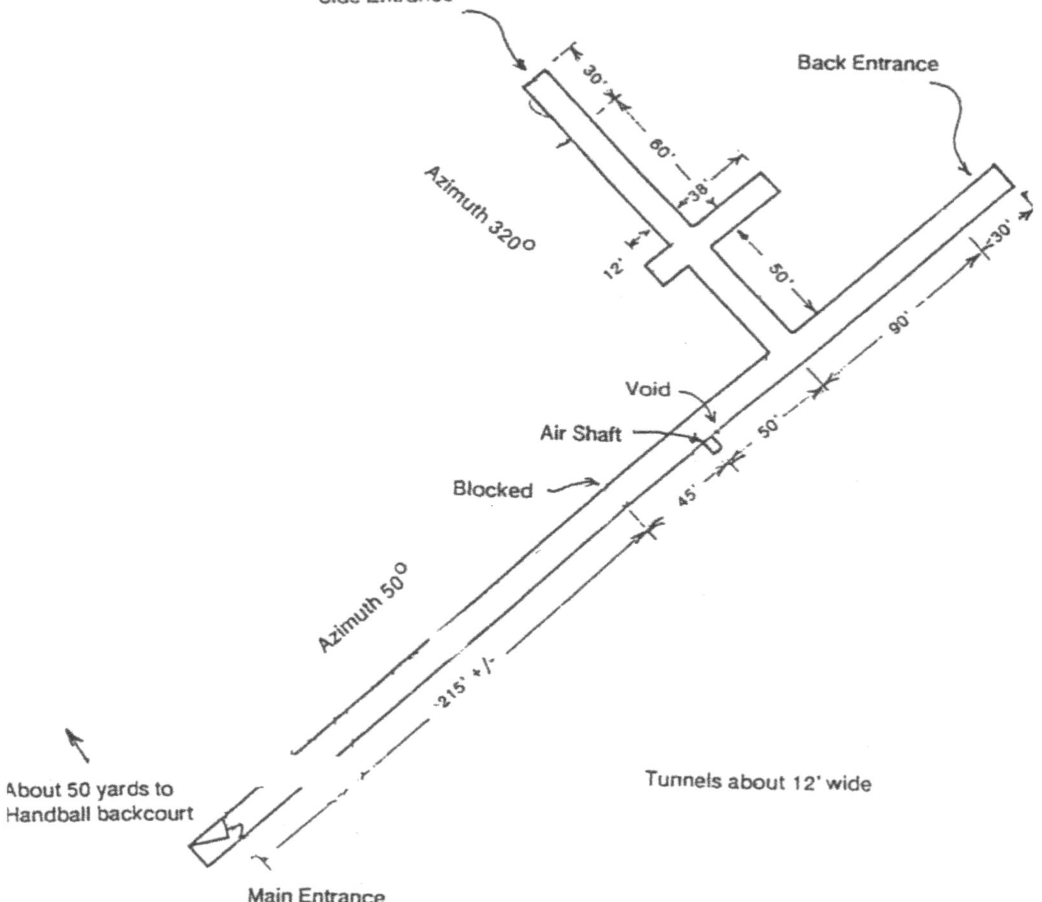

Plan of the Navy Intercept Tunnel on Corregidor. The navy tunnel to house the intercept and code-breaking detail of the 16th Naval District was built in 1939-1941, with navy funding, army engineer supervision, and Bilibid prisoner labor. It was occupied in December 1940 though still lacking some details. Plan courtesy Jim Black.

Although initially designated as the "Navy Emergency Radio Station," its real purpose was that of intercepting and decoding Japanese diplomatic and naval codes. The navy's Fleet Radio Unit for the 16th Naval District radio station, Radio Cavite, call sign "NPO," provided part of the personnel assigned to the radio intelligence station known as "Station C." Its main facility was the first of the navy's several tunnel projects undertaken on Corregidor. In October 1939, the navy transferred an advanced party of Cavite's Station C personnel to Corregidor, where they briefly set up in a part of Battery Geary before moving into the newly completed AFIRM Tunnel. The tunnel complex at Monkey Point was completed in December 1940 and placed in operation during 1941.

The tunnel was about 100 feet long, its main shaft laid out northeast-southwest with its main portal at the southwest end. At the main tunnel's northeast end, there was an emergency exit and a 100-step stairway that led up to the surface. A lateral some 40 feet long branched off the main tunnel at its midpoint. It too had an emergency exit that accessed the ground level. This branch lateral had two more laterals that opened off the branch. Back-up generators, fuel and water tanks, sanitary facilities, and the above ground rhombic antenna field were in place.[450]

Duane Whitlock, who served as a Radioman First Class (RM1) at Station C, described the underground intercept station: [451]

> The tunnel went back under a hillside with a maximum of about sixty feet of earth above it. The first fifty or sixty feet of the tunnel was used for emergency stores and for sleeping space after the war started. At the inner end of this space were the diesels for the auxiliary power supply, and they were closed off from the main operating tunnel by a doorway partition. Just inside that doorway and to the left was a lateral tunnel about forty feet long that housed the Officer in Charge, his yeoman, four traffic analysts, and four or five language officers. At the far end of this lateral and to the right was another short lateral that served as the crypto center. To the left of the entrance to that center was a door and a steep flight of steps leading upward to an emergency exit. The operations tunnel itself was perhaps seventy feet long, and at the far end was a door and another steep flight of steps leading to the second emergency exit. This areaway served also as the antenna trunk for the whole tunnel, an engineering nightmare in which some brilliant designer had specified the use of lead shielded cable. The operations space was separated into two sections by a simple parted curtain draped so that the bottom hung a foot or two off the deck. The area on the front or office side of the curtain, which took up about a third of the operations area, was occupied by general service communicators (NPO) who had been bombed out of the Navy Yard at Cavite.

AFIRM tunnel had an air lock system for gas proofing and was air-conditioned. In addition, a model DT-1 radio direction finder station designated Project BAKER was also positioned to determine the bearings of the Japanese radio signals. This was in an unprotected set of foxholes at the old cemetery on Corregidor's East Point. The HFDF section was eventually quartered in a shack at the DF site.[452]

Navy Tunnel Projects at Malinta Hill

Work had scarcely commenced on the Station C Tunnel when the 16th Naval District staff concluded that it too needed a bombproof command post on Corregidor and later in 1939, the U.S. Navy undertook the planning of several additional tunnels in Malinta Hill. These tunnels were to serve as alternate command and storage facilities for the navy in the event Cavite Navy Yard had to be abandoned. The sum of $500,000 was transferred from the navy to the army, who undertook the actual excavation and construction of five concrete-lined waterproof tunnel projects that were designated "Dog," "Roger," "Queen," "Sugar," and "Tare" in May 1939. As these tunnel projects neared completion in the spring of 1941, they were requiring 66% of the army's supervising engineer's time and utilizing some 80% of the civilian engineering personnel on Corregidor. Construction continued until December 1941 and all were generally completed except for Roger Tunnel. Queen Tunnel, the largest navy tunnel at Malinta Hill, was used as the headquarters of Rear Admiral Francis

W. Rockwell's 16th Naval District. Sugar and Tare Tunnels served as offices, storage facilities, and quarters for the naval staff personnel. Dog Tunnel that branched off the Queen tunnel about 100 feet inside Queen's outside entrance on the hill's south side was converted into a massive vault for the storage of the Philippine Commonwealth's gold and silver bullion reserves estimated to be worth of about $500,000. The navy tunnels were connected to the army's main tunnel complex in Malinta Hill by a low unfinished and unlined passage to the southern quartermaster storage tunnels, and thence to the main tunnel complex. Exits from the navy tunnels were provided on the south side of the hill. The rough finished Roger Tunnel was used for torpedo storage for Asiatic Fleet submarines after the Cavite Navy Yard was abandoned. A narrow-gauge tramway was laid from Roger Tunnel to the South Mine Wharf to facilitate the transfer of torpedoes to the submarines.[453]

Fort William McKinley Gets a Tunnel

The seeming "tunnel fever" of the immediate pre-war period was not unique to the army or even army and navy facilities immediately proximate to the Manila Bay harbor defenses. Even the army's main headquarters at Fort William McKinley in the Manila southern suburbs had its equivalent project. On March 7, 1941, the War Department provided the first $100,000 to construct a new Philippine Department headquarters shelter under the surface of Fort McKinley. It was to contain offices, a map storage vault, dispensary, power room, and temporary personnel shelter. Work started in June and most of the actual main tunnel and laterals were dug but only partially lined when war stopped further work at year's end.

Fort Wint Is Reactivated

Subsequent to the American decision to grant independence to the Philippine Commonwealth, measures were taken to assist the Commonwealth to develop its own army. In 1938 as a part of this program, the War Department leased Fort Wint to the Philippine Commonwealth for use as a Philippine Army Coast Artillery Training Center. Three officers from the 60th C.A., accompanied by about two dozen Philippine Scouts from the 91st and 92nd C.A., provided the initial training cadre for the center. The Commonwealth government remodeled buildings to serve as barracks, officers' quarters, hospital, and administration building. By July 1, 1938, there were 12 to 15 Philippine Army officers and about 250 enlisted trainees at Fort Wint.[454]

Battery D, 92nd C.A., arrived in January 1939, and test fired 155 mm guns before returning to Fort Mills to man Battery Sunset's 155 mm guns. Maj. Delbert Ausmus assumed command of the Coast Artillery Training Center in the early summer of 1939. Upon completion of some basic training, the trainees received instruction in the operation and firing of Batteries Warwick and Jewell. In early June 1941, Battery D, 92nd C.A., commanded by Capt. Alfred D'Arezzo, returned to Fort Wint and began placing the armament back in service and preparing the island fort for war.[455]

Improving the Defenses 1940-1941

Japanese expansionist policies in Asia in the early 1930s and its alliance with Nazi Germany in 1936 increased the threat to U.S. interests in the Far East. The Roosevelt administration and the Congress finally began to alter their positions on reinforcing the U.S. forces in the Philippine islands. By 1940, the administration had reversed the government policies of the previous two decades and began taking action to militarily defend the Philippines. By maintaining possession of the Philippine Archipelago, the U.S. naval and air bases on Luzon would be placed on the flank of any southward movements by the Japanese toward Indo China, Malaya, and the oil-rich Dutch East Indies. Manila and Manila Bay became increasingly important in America's revised strategy and maintaining the Harbor Defenses of Manila and Subic Bays was key to the control of Manila Bay.[456]

The 1940 Philippine Defense Project prepared in the last weeks of 1940 was forwarded to the War Department on May 1, 1941. While considerable military equipment and personnel were finally earmarked to bolster the military and naval forces in the Philippines, and some of it was actually forwarded to the islands, the modernization of the defenses on the fortified islands of Manila Bay proved to be a matter of too little, too late. Although funding to upgrade the defenses had been inadequate for nearly two decades, the various army commanders in the Philippines had not been lax in planning the necessary upgrades for the harbor forts. Therefore, when authorization and funding for improvements finally began coming in 1940, the harbor defense command was ready. In many cases, it simply required taking an already prepared and approved study off the shelf, dusting it off, and resubmitting it to the War Department. In the spring of 1940, a board of officers was convened to prepare plans and estimates for continuing to gas-proof the seacoast batteries and various underground installations and utilities structures. The board simply double-checked its previously submitted plan that was already approved by both the harbor defense command and the Philippine Department and forwarded it to the War Department for approval. The War Department duly approved the plans and estimates, and in June 1941 $528,000 was allotted to gas proof the installations.[457]

Additional Efforts to Add Bombproofing

The "Sandbag Board" which submitted a request for $70,000 for sandbags and miscellaneous items addressed the immediate need for temporary protection of the fortifications. These funds were also allotted in 1941. An expedited program of bombproofing numerous elements of the harbor defense's command and control system was undertaken, and new tunnels were commenced at several locations on the "Rock." Chief among these was the harbor defense command post tunnel near the post administration building at Topside and the seaward defense command post tunnel at the C_1 station above Searchlight Point. A personnel bombproof tunnel was planned for Battery Monja, forming a branch off the existing magazine tunnel of the casemated 155 mm gun emplacement. Personnel bombproofs were also planned and began to serve Batteries Guy B.G. Hanna, Sunset, and Rock Point. Construction of these four tunnel complexes were commenced in November 1941 and work would continue on all four into 1942. The old HDCP tunnel commenced in 1920 but abandoned in an unfinished state to comply with the Washington Treaty was resumed near Battery Wheeler and made serviceable as a personnel shelter.[458]

Reinforcement of the Harbor Defenses

The first of any meaningful coast artillery personnel reinforcements did not begin arriving until the late 1930s. This increase, coupled with the reduction in the overseas tours of duty for coast artillery officers from three to two years, increased the demands on the Army Transport Service. USAT *U.S. Grant*, that had been making a round trip between San Francisco and Manila about once every three months for over a decade, reduced the time span between trips to just under two months as the flow of officers and their families grew and the trickle of enlisted replacements and recruits coming to the Philippines after 1935 increased. By September 1936, USAT *Meigs*, a cargo vessel, had been added to the schedule on an irregular basis and even the navy's transports were being used to carry army personnel between the U.S. and the Philippines. Although the frequency of transport arrivals increased, the majority of the passengers continued to be officers and their families either arriving or departing. The numbers of enlisted personnel arriving in the harbor defenses were scarcely sufficient to enable the batteries of the 59th and 60th C.A. regiments to maintain the status quo. The outbreak of war in Europe in 1939, however, resulted in a slight increase in the number of enlisted men arriving on Corregidor, a flow that would continue to grow into 1941.[459]

In addition to the movement of personnel, the flow of military equipment and supplies increased markedly in 1940. Transportation of dependents, household goods, and private automobiles to overseas stations was a perennial peacetime problem for the Army Transport Service, as officers changed from one overseas station to another, or returned to the United States with their dependents and household goods, and increasingly by the 1930s their private automobiles following. The average army transport could carry only a limited number of cars and the remainder had to be shipped on freight transports. By December 1940, the Philippine Department had issued instructions for the departure, beginning in February 1941, of all military dependents in the territory. By early 1941 the unsettled international situation and the increasing pressure for shipping space combined to eliminate altogether the troublesome shipping of household goods to overseas stations. Families returning to the U.S. were permitted to bring back their household items. An adjutant general's letter of February 18, 1941, directed that dependents of officers and enlisted men ordered to the Philippine Department should remain in the continental United States.[460]

USAT *U.S. Grant* arrived February 15, 1941, bringing Brig. Gen. George F. Moore to take command of the harbor defenses and Colonels Paul D. Bunker and Theodore M. Chase to assume command of the 59th and 60th C.A., respectively. On the transport's return trip to the U.S. in March, she took on board a large number of wives and dependents. More than half the remaining dependents departed on USAT *Republic* that was scheduled to leave Manila's Pier 7 on April 16. Nearly all of the remainder departed aboard USAT *Washington*. They took with them a large assortment of items acquired while on foreign service: Chinese and other Oriental rugs, Tinio plates, furniture, and linens to name just a few.[461]

Fort Mills rapidly became a "bachelor post," as the families began departing on the transports that were now bringing reinforcements in larger numbers. With the departure of USAT *President Taft* down the Boca Chica Channel on July 16, 1941, the last of Corregidor's remaining dependents were gone. While many of the 3,478 male civilians remained on Corregidor, all non-military females in the Philippines, mostly dependents of Philippine Department personnel, were gone by August 1, 1941. War preparations were extended to the evacuation of Oriental civilians including some Filipinos from Corregidor that began in March 1941. During the extensive construction programs instituted by the engineers in 1940 and 1941, some 1,100 Bilibids provided labor at the harbor forts. Between early September and the end of November, this number was gradu-

Bringing the harbor defense units closer to their authorized complement meant the sudden need for more quarters immediately prior to the Second World War. Many new wooden barracks were added in 1940-1941, like this one at Fort Mills. NARA.

ally reduced to some 800 convicts, the minimum number required to effectively advance the various defense projects. On December 9, 1941, the last of the Bilibids were returned to the central prison in Manila.[462]

As relations between Japan and the United States became increasingly strained, strengthening the harbor defenses took on an increased sense of urgency that soon approached a state of full mobilization. Upon his arrival on Corregidor, General Moore assumed command of the harbor defenses, relieving Brig. Gen. Walter K. Wilson. Moore's command was redesignated the Philippine Coast Artillery Command on August 1, 1941, and he was promoted to major general soon thereafter. He wasted little time in taking action to improve the defenses. One of his first acts was to have two Panama mounts constructed for a battery of 155 mm guns at Fort Hughes. These guns were located on the east end of the island to fire into the waters of Manila Bay and that of the Cavite mainland in the vicinity of Ternate. This battery was known initially as "Battery Hooker," as it also covered the Hooker Point area of Corregidor.[463]

Concurrent with the freeing up of funds for the improvement of the Manila Bay defenses in 1940, measures were also taken to strengthen the garrison in the Philippines. The Selective Service Act and the federalizing of the National Guard in September 1940 permitted a significant augmentation of the forces in the Philippines. In 1940, the 59th C.A. received a net gain of four officers and 149 enlisted men, bringing its strength up to 30 officers and 1,209 men. The 60th C.A.'s 33 officers and 661 enlisted men received an additional 15 officers and 93 enlisted men, bringing its numbers up to 48 officers and 754 enlisted personnel. By the beginning of 1941, there were 4,135 officers and men in the Harbor Defenses of Manila and Subic Bays, about half of whom were Philippine Scouts.

Prior to the buildup that began in the spring of 1941, new recruits for the 59th and 60th C.A. had been assigned to the regimental casual company. There they received "basic" training. Upon completion of basic, they were assigned to a specific battery where their training continued. Numerous reserve officers, newly recruited enlistees, and draftees began arriving by the hundreds aboard the transports in 1941. Although there was a smattering of NCOs and experienced enlisted specialists aboard these vessels, the majority of the enlisted men arriving aboard USAT *U.S. Grant, Meigs, Republic, Washington, President Pierce*, and *President Taft* were raw recruits and would be assigned to fill out the ranks of various army units in the Philippines.

When the American regiments began receiving large increases in their ranks in April 1941, recruit training for both regiments was carried out at a newly established recruit camp on Corregidor's tail. Upon arrival at Manila the men assigned to the coast artillery were transported to Fort Mills aboard the quartermaster harbor boats. From the wharf they were marched to the newly established recruit training center adjacent to the old seaplane ramps and Kindley Field. There the troops lived under canvas and received a rudimentary exposure to military life over some 11 weeks before being assigned to the seacoast and antiaircraft gun batteries for more specialized coast artillery training. As then Private John Perkowski recalled: "We learned small arms, and how to march. We spent a lot of time marching on the tarmac down there. There was an old seaplane base there, this big tarmac, and we just marched, and marched, and marched. It was very hot down there."[464]

On May 8, 1941, USAT *Washington* arrived in Manila with another shipment of military personnel for the Philippines. From this shipment the harbor defenses were augmented by one officer and 1,427 enlisted men. The officer and 374 enlisted men were assigned to the 59th C.A., while the remaining 1,053 men allotted to the harbor defenses went to the 60th C.A. These additional personnel were barely adequate to bring the existing units up to near wartime strength, even when the War Department authorized the 59th and 60th C.A.s' reinforcement with a total of 1,465 recruits. The newly arrived troops enabled the 59th C.A. to activate Batteries I, and K, cadres for these newly activated batteries were provided from the regiment's active batteries and the ranks were filled out with the recruits.[465]

Not until May 31, 1941, did the 60th C.A. finally receive sufficient numbers of personnel from the recruit training center to activate Batteries G, H, I, and K. Also activated were Headquarters and Headquarters Batteries, 60th C.A.'s 2nd and 3rd Battalions. Battery H, 59th C.A., was activated in early June 1941 and assigned to Battery Geary's 12-inch M1890M1 mortars for training. This freed up Battery I to join Battery G in making Fort Hughes ready for active service. By the end of July 1941, the peacetime harbor defense garrison had grown to 5,360, of which the 60th C.A. numbered 41 officers and 1,855 enlisted men. Both American regiments received some additional personnel during the last months of 1941, but these augmentations did not offset the number of enlisted men who were reassigned to other organizations, or who rotated back to the United States as their enlistments expired. By November 30, 1941, the 60th C.A.'s strength had actually declined to 72 officers and 1,693 enlisted personnel, reflecting a loss of some 162 enlisted men, many of them experienced NCOs. The terms of overseas duty for these troops having ended, they departed on what would be the last transport to sail for the U.S. During 1941, a substantial number of officers and enlisted men of the 59th C.A. completed their tours of duty in the Philippines, but the regimental ranks experienced a slight net increase. By November 1941 the 59th C.A. had sixty-four officers and 1,264 enlisted personnel assigned; a negligible increase over the previous year. Not all the new arrivals were coast artillery. Quartermaster, signal, ordnance, and medical personnel were also shipped out to Corregidor. These elements of the garrison also had similar gains and losses. While additional troops would continue to arrive until just before the war, most of them would be assigned elsewhere in the Philippines.[466]

To house the newly arrived enlisted men, five two-story temporary wood-frame barracks with wood siding and floors and galvanized iron roofs were authorized for Fort Mills and one for Fort Hughes. Construction was done by Bilibid and civilian labor commencing in late March 1941 and brought to completion October 11, 1941, under the supervision the Quartermaster Corps. Each building had two wings and could accommodate 100 men. These barracks were built at various locations on Corregidor depending upon the type troops who would occupy them. A sixth, smaller, two-story barracks to house 60 men of the Quartermaster Corps was built at Middleside.[467]

Capt. George Steiger arrived on Corregidor for duty with the 59th C.A. in Mid-September 1941. He noted in his diary while a prisoner of war:[468]

> The Island of Corregidor, which is known as the rock, attains a height of 600 ft and is divided into three zones know[n] as Topside, Middleside and Bottomside. The native village at the bottom is called a barrio. The commanding general, Brigadier General Moore, lives at Topside. All intermediate persons live at an elevation corresponding to their rank. All field officers and Captains live Topside. Some lieutenants also live Topside but would have to move if higher ranking officers wanted their quarters. I am living Topside with Capt Bull and 1st Lieutenant Melvin Moore. Since all women have gone home, we are assigned to what would normally be quarters for a family. It contains 3 bedrooms, 2 baths, living room, dining room, kitchen, and servant quarters. My room is 20' X 20'. All ceilings are high, 11', and also 1/3 of the wall space is windows. The curtain rods are 6' from the floor, which leaves 2' above them so that you can pull the curtains and still have the windows open. They do not use glass out here and the window panes are made of 3-inch squares of shell, which is translucent. Hence the windows are kept open except when the wind blows, which is does often with sufficient force to break glass. Upon arrival, I was assigned to Quarters 27, a set of family quarters, with Captain Harcourt G. Bull of Pasadena and Lt. George Melvin Moore, III, of Arcadia. Next day I received my assignment to command I Battery of the 59th Coast Artillery. Commanding officer of the 59th was Colonel Paul D. Bunker, who had been my unit instructor in Los Angeles while I was with the 519th. Col. Bunker died in Japan towards the end of prison life. My executive officer for the battery was 1st Lt. Stockton D. Bruns. All newcomers to the Rock were fascinated by the values. I had several sets of clothing tailored. A complete set of tailor-made khaki cost $2.75, white uniform $7, tuxedo coat $2.50, tux trousers $6.00, mess jacket $2.35, sharkskin suit $7.00, and so on. All were excellent material and beautifully tailored. Due to post regulations which required all units to be operational on a 24-hour schedule, I was able to go to Manila only every third weekend. I would arrive at three in the afternoon and return on the three PM boat Sunday.

Augmenting and Improving Corregidor's Antiaircraft Defenses

After nearly a decade of recommending, requisitioning, and campaigning for adequate upgrading of the antiaircraft defenses, the Philippine Defense Project was revised to provide a total of 36 M3 3-inch AA guns. To join the 12 guns on hand in 1940, four more were slated for delivery in October 1940 and 20 more in

January 1941. Twelve more M4 directors and 21 sound locators were also to be delivered by January 1941. Thirty-two mobile 60-inch AA searchlights were to be delivered in September 1941 and more AA equipment was projected for delivery in the summer of 1942.[469]

Although the 60th was still several hundred men below its authorized peacetime strength in November 1941, the AA defenses in the Philippines had virtually doubled in size with the arrival of the 200th Coast Artillery (AA) Regiment from the United States on September 26, 1941. The 200th C.A., a former New Mexico National Guard unit, consisting of seventy-seven officers and 1,732 enlisted men, was initially posted to Fort Stotsenburg to provide AA defenses for that post and the adjacent Clark Army Air Field, but it would soon find itself a part of the air defenses in support of the field forces on the Bataan Peninsula and the harbor defenses in Manila Bay. After the commencement of hostilities, the 200th C.A. organized a provisional antiaircraft regiment, later designated the 515th Coast Artillery (AA) Regiment. This was made possible by using vehicles and guns recently arrived for the intended purpose of organizing a new AA regiment with Philippine troops. While the troops never got trained, the excess equipment was fortuitously available for the need at hand. The 515th C.A. was assigned to the Manila port area and Nichols Field. Both of these units were ultimately relocated to Bataan for airfield defense. Their positions were also useful in extending Corregidor's northern antiaircraft defense perimeter.[470]

It was discovered that many antiaircraft observation posts (AAOP) sites were unsatisfactory because of a lack of line-of-sight positions for their radios. Observation details equipped with 15-20 mile-range walkie-talkies were finally placed on Pico De Loro, Tagaytay Ridge, on the water tower at Cavite Navy Yard, on Signal Hill north of the Mariveles Mountains, and on Barbari Hill on Bataan. In addition, the AA defenses were able to interconnect with the large system of observation stations operated by the Seaward Defenses. Very early warning of enemy aircraft activity at times could be provided from Japanese radio communications emanating from Formosa that were intercepted by the Navy Intercept Station at Monkey Point. Additional early warning was attainable from the long-range radar sets. All of these information sources were connected with the antiaircraft operations room and command post located in old Battery Way. That command post was moved from Battery Way to lateral 9 in Malinta Tunnel shortly after the war began.[471]

Deliveries of AA matériel proved more expeditious than expected. By late November the 60th C.A. had received 16 of the 24 promised M3 3-inch guns. This enabled the regiment to equip Battery I, 59th C.A., as an AA battery at Fort Hughes and Battery E, 91st C.A., at Fort Frank with the M3 AA guns, replacing the M1918 trailer mounted 3-inch AA guns. Shortly before the war, Batteries A and E, the 60th C.A.'s two searchlight batteries were each reequipped with 15 new M1 60-inch Sperry portable searchlights, their portable GE power plants, and M1 sound detectors, replacing the less powerful 36-inch mobile lights. When the war began,

A trailer mounted M1 aircraft sound locator of Battery A, 60th CA (AA). In the days before widespread use of radar, sound locators were an acceptable method for detecting incoming aircraft flights. Schmidt Collection.

Batteries A and E could each only employ about nine of the 60-inch Sperry lights, as there were insufficient personnel, or locations for that matter, where the excess lights could be used. This left 12 M1 lights and about a dozen older model 36-inch lights in reserve, as replacements, or to provide spare parts when necessary. In prewar defense planning, some of these lights had been slated for emplacement on the south side of Manila Bay in the Calumpan Military Reservation, but the rapid Japanese advances coupled with the lack of adequate Filamerican infantry to provide security precluded American use of that territory. Loss of this large military reservation contributed to the reduced warning of enemy planes approaching from the southeast.[472]

As the 60th C.A.'s strength was augmented, action was also being taken to improve the regiment's battle positions. During the last 10 months before war came, the antiaircraft defenses were steadily improved. Nine new antiaircraft machine gun towers were built, and the original five strengthened; antiaircraft machine guns were also emplaced in sandbagged positions near the seacoast batteries for local defense against low flying enemy aircraft; AA gun positions were strengthened and camouflaged; and as new antiaircraft matériel was procured it was issued to the 60th C.A.'s batteries. During the siege of Corregidor, additional protection for the gun emplacements, height finder, and gun director positions from shrapnel and shell fragments was achieved by filling empty barrels and powder cans with earth and stacking them up end on end around the positions as revetments. The trenches dug for the gun's outriggers were made deeper and served as personnel shelters.[473]

Seaward Defenses Prepare for War

To the officers serving in the Philippines during the years that immediately preceded World War II, war with Japan and a surprise attack on Corregidor was considered a distinct probability. Consequently, war planning included dual assignments for all harbor defense troops. In addition to their primary assignment to their organic armament, a second assignment included emergency beach defense in the event of a surprise landing by the Japanese prior to a formal declaration of war.

In addition to its vulnerability to surprise attack by Japanese task forces, an immediate situation at Corregidor that, while seemingly innocent, constituted a real threat to the garrison. Any night from Topside on Corregidor looking out toward Manila, a hundred or more vessels of the Japanese fishing fleet could be seen drifting about within 1500 or 2000 yards of the Corregidor shore. Each of these boats was capable of carrying 100 men. The thought of what might happen some dark night if these boats fully loaded with armed Japanese

United States Army Transport *U.S. Grant* entering Manila Bay on May 11, 1938. This ship, the former German *Koenig Wilhelm II*, had been taken over in World War I. As *U.S. Grant,* she served for most of the 1920s-30s as one of the regular transports from San Francisco to Hawaii and the Philippines. Williford Collection.

made a dash for the Corregidor shore while the garrison was quietly sleeping was an unpleasant one. Such a surprise rush on Corregidor beaches from the fishing fleet, combined with an air attack, might well have been launched without warning and unless the garrison was on the alert would have had a good chance of success. [474]

General Embick had heightened the general state of readiness in the harbor defenses. In 1934 one antiaircraft battery and a skeleton beach defense force had been maintained on 24-hour alert. In 1940, training was intensified among the four coast artillery regiments on Corregidor, and one seaward defense battery as well as one AA gun battery and one AA machine gun platoon was maintained on alert around the clock, the battery personnel sleeping at their alert positions. This alert duty was rotated every 24 hours and continued until the early spring of 1941, when General Moore ordered an increased state of alert, placing about one-third of the garrison on 24-hour alert at their primary defense positions on a rotating basis. Additional beach defense alerts were also held, the machine guns and 75 mm guns were manned, and the guard reserve was quartered in Malinta Tunnel to be readily available for beach defense support in the vulnerable Bottomside dock area. Splinter-proof protection was provided both men and equipment at the 155 mm gun positions. Ammunition was earmarked for the various batteries and ready for issue immediately in the event of an emergency. Where necessary, fields of fire were cleared and at the islands' various beaches, barbed wire entanglements were placed in front of final defense positions. On November 28, 1941, the entire command went on full alert and occupied their battle positions.[475]

While from seaward most of the gun and mortar batteries in the seaward defenses were generally concealed, from the air and the heights of the Bataan Peninsula, they were clearly visible in the years leading up to World War II. As war clouds darkened in the late 1930s, measures were undertaken to camouflage the batteries and other defense elements in the harbor forts, although the locations of the massive concrete seacoast batteries were no secret to the Japanese.

Army harbor boat *Ledyard*. With several thousand men spread over four major island reservations, the army maintained a small fleet of light vessels to maintain a semblance of a regular supply system. This shows *Ledyard* approaching the dock at Fort Frank. Schmidt Collection.

In February 1941, specific recommendations were prepared in the Office of the Chief of Engineers for the concealment of the defenses. Natural growth was to be encouraged as close to the fixed seacoast batteries as possible without interfering with the guns operation and placed atop the traverse magazines as well. Tone-down painting of the batteries concrete surfaces and painting them in dark green or black blotches to simulate the surrounding terrain was recommended. The use of garnished camouflage nets to cover tunnel entrances and the loading platforms, blast aprons, and the rear portions of the gun batteries and their armament was considered vital. The guns and other metal surfaces were to be painted a dark flat olive drab color. Concrete portions of the Panama mounts were also to be toned-down and covered with nets.[476]

Curiously, the four mortar batteries that would figure so prominently as counter-battery elements during the siege of the harbor forts were considered obsolescent and of such minor importance by the camouflage planners that they were given short shrift and recommended that they be treated as "dummies" to draw hostile fire away from the important installations. Their concrete work should be "lightly toned down to make the enemy believe that is an important installation on which camouflage was attempted, but poorly done."[477]

Post buildings also received the camouflage board's attention. They were to be painted a dark green or brown with no trim showing. Lawns and shrubs were to be planted irregularly; roads were to be darkened by oiling or with cinders, and grass encouraged to grow between the ties on the post trolley lines. Cuts through trees and undergrowth for roads and trails were to be as narrow as possible. The rail branch lines leading to battery position were to be covered with netting.[478]

During the summer of 1941 the harbor defenses received additional M3 3-inch AA guns that enabled the 60th C.A. to replace all of its M1918 trailer mounted AA guns. Battery I was assigned tactically to the AA command, although it remained an element of the 59th C.A. administratively. By early November a battery detachment went over to Caballo Island to establish AA positions on the island's east end for the four M3 guns, a T8-E3 gun director, T-2 height finder, and a power plant. The remainder of the battery and the battery equipment joined the detachment on Caballo on November 30, when the all-out alert went into effect. At Fort Hughes, the new barracks built for Battery I was still undergoing finish work.[479]

The Loss of the Harbor Boat *San Pedro*

The quartermaster harbor boat *San Pedro* plied the waters of Manila Bay between the fortified islands and Manila, and between Fort Wint and Corregidor for a quarter century. On the morning of August 14, 1941, it was en route to Corregidor from Fort Wint, with 28 passengers and crew. The old vessel was about 10 miles south of Subic Bay when she was hit by two successive large swells and took a roll from which she could not recover. *San Pedro* was swamped and sank within a few minutes. Fortunately, all but one crew member survived and were rescued on the morning of August 15, after a 12-hour search by Air Corps planes and army and navy vessels.[480]

Submarine Mine Defenses Are Upgraded and Planted

Over time the size and scope of the submarine mine defenses was expanded. The waters of the bay that in some places attained depths of 100 feet presented special problems not encountered in most U.S. harbors. The submarine mine project for Manila Bay underwent regular revision between 1911 and 1939. The project was nearly 50% complete at the end of June 1939. New equipment in the form of a single-conductor mine system was also being manufactured and assembled for the mine casemate at James Ravine. In March 1940, experiments were carried out by the coast artillery and the navy in which a submarine of the U.S. Navy Asiatic Fleet, USS *S-40*, was able to successfully pass under or around two lines of planted mines without being detected by the mine casemate or striking a mine or cable, thus opening a discussion regarding the minefield's effectiveness. By 1941 a large concentration of buoyant controlled mines had been planted across the Boca Chica entrance of Manila Bay and buoyant contact mines in the Boca Grande entrance were planned. To prevent submarines from being able to pass under or between the controlled mines, the mines were connected by ropes initially, and by late 1941 wire cables. When these wire cables were snagged by vessels passing between the mines, the cable would become taut and tip the adjacent mine(s) more than 25° causing them to detonate when set in contact mode.[481]

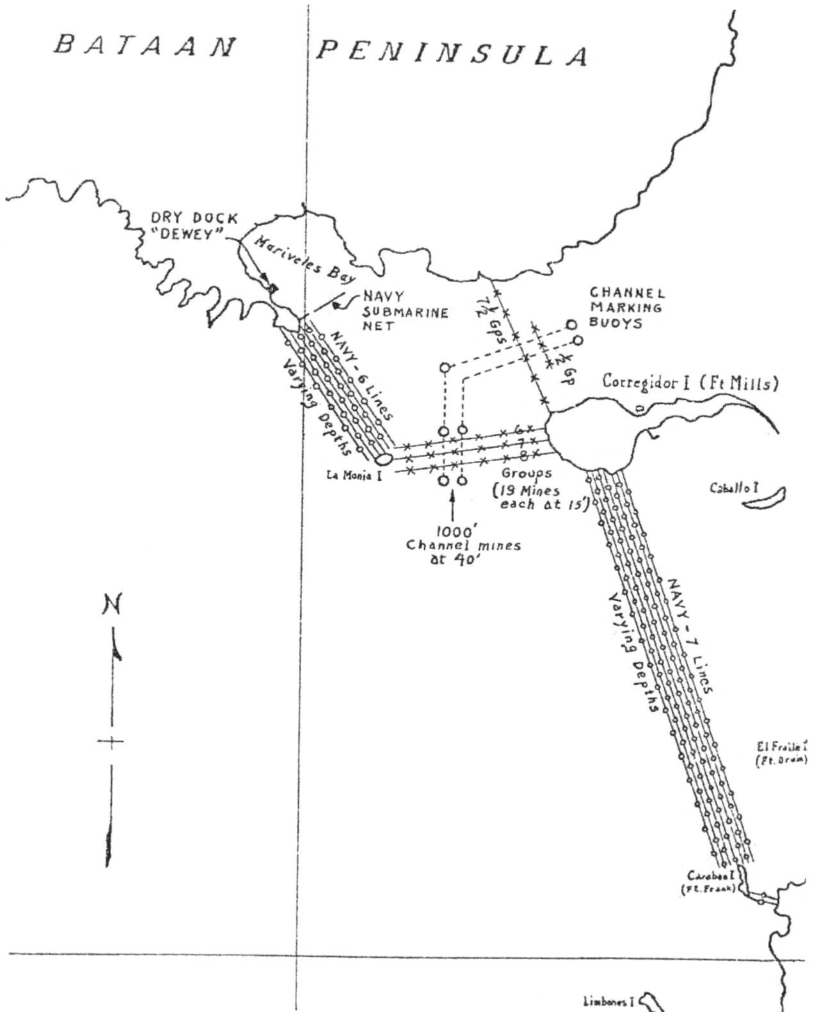

With war tensions increasing with Japan, the defensive minefield was deployed. Starting in July 1941, the army planted its controlled mines and the navy did the same for its contact fields. This shows the major fields in late 1941, though some subsequent shifting did occur up until the final campaign. NARA.

Boca Chica Minefields

Increased concerns that the Japanese might employ fishing boats or disguised merchant vessels to carry out a surprise attack on Corregidor caused General Moore, the harbor defense commander, to urge the Philippine Department to request on February 25, 1941, that the electrical switchboards and 110-volt 60-cycle electrical systems required to implement the revised mine project be forwarded from the Mine Depot at Fort Monroe and that the two sets of diesel-electric generators built in 1940 by the Witte Engine Works in Kansas City, Missouri, also be forwarded to Fort Mills with dispatch. Orders were subsequently issued for their priority transfer to San Francisco for further shipment to Manila on the first available transport. The generators were delivered to the San Francisco Port of Embarkation at Fort Mason where they were placed aboard USAT *Republic* that sailed on March 31, 1941.

The controlled submarine mines were set to function in the following modes:

Safe: All power "off" on channel mines, and out of channel mines on "Supervisory."

Supervisory: Mines on a 110-volt system did not detonate on contact but alerted the mine casemate and enabled observation fire on the target vessel to be plotted by the mine fire control stations, and an appropriate mine electrically fired when observation indicated the target was within the kill zone for that mine. (The casemate manning detachment upon hearing the bell and seeing the signal light indicating a specific mine had been tipped to wait several seconds, and then throw the firing switch for that mine's group into "fire" position, thus detonating the mine).

Contact: A group of mines set so that any mine in the group would detonate on contact as soon as touched or tipped by a ship.

Delayed Contact Fire: This enabled the mine to be manually switched into contact firing status a certain number of seconds after it signaled it had been touched or tipped. Delayed contact fire was preferred because if the mine could be underneath the target and then fired with a few seconds' delay, it had a chance to explode beneath the target's less well-protected bottom.

A joint army-navy local committee restudied the controlled mine fields and determined that alterations in the Boca Chica (North) minefields were necessary. In March 1941, a change in the layout of the fields of ground mines was recommended. Each of the four lines of ground mines in the Rock Point Groups were to have six grand groups and a gap of 1,000 feet was to be created by lowering the mines in that gap to a depth of 45-feet to facilitate the passage of deep draft shipping. A ship-tended antisubmarine net to be operated by the navy was also proposed for installation across an opening into Caballo Bay through the field of contact mines in the Boca Grande minefield. Although the navy was able to install an antisubmarine net at Mariveles Harbor it was unable to provide a net for the proposed opening through Boca Grande's contact mines. The Morrison Point Mine Groups (sometimes termed the North groups) were to be arranged in one continuous line of 7½ grand groups with a back-up second line to be planted at a depth of 45 feet, 500 feet east of the new passage through the Morrison Point Groups. The board also recommended installation of an anti-torpedo net southeast of Corregidor and installation of the sono-radio buoys and listening loop for underwater detection of vessels in the 10-mile area west of Corregidor.[482

General Moore next asked for authorization to close Boca Chica Channel by planting one or more lines of mines as a "protective preparedness measure." The chief of coast artillery concurred with this request, noting that there was sufficient submarine mine material on hand at Fort Mills to plant six grand groups of controlled mines in the Boca Chica Channel (about 25% of the complete project for Manila Bay) and would require six to 10 days to complete the project's partial planting. On March 21, 1941, the adjutant general granted permission for closure of the Boca Chica Channel. On March 24, 1941 planting commenced.[483]

In accordance with the established project, the Boca Chica Channel mine defenses would also consist of an outer field of 320 navy contact mines laid in six lines, with mines at various depths between Los Cochinos Island just off Cochinos Point on the Bataan Peninsula and Monja Island. The lines of contact mines were to be 400 yards apart and the interval between the mines set at 100 yards. One row of seven mines was planted at various depths among the Los Cochinos Rocks.

Shortly before the loss of the quartermaster harbor boat *San Pedro* that had served as a sometimes mine planter, the army leased the civilian harbor boat *Neptune* and pressed her into service as a junior mine planter. In March 1941, USAMP *Colonel George F.E. Harrison,* assisted by *Neptune,* began planting two controlled fields of M3 buoyant mines, consisting of 26 grand groups, each group consisting of 19 mines, and one partial group of nine mines. The outer minefield, designated the Rock Point Group, consisted of 19 groups of controlled mines in three parallel lines extending from Rock Point at Corregidor's west end to Monja Island. The outer line would consist of eight groups of controlled mines; the middle line was composed of seven groups, and the inner line of six groups. With the exception of a 1,000-foot-wide channel where the mines were planted at a depth of 45 feet, the Rock Point minefields were at a depth of 15 feet. An inner field of controlled mines designated the Morrison Point Group was composed of seven and a half groups in one line with a second and much shorter line of a half-group of nine mines that extended north from the vicinity of James Ravine on Corregidor to Lasisi Point on Bataan. These two lines were planted 1,000 feet apart at a depth of 15 feet, with a 1,000-foot break in their center where the mines were also planted at a depth of 45 feet. Both mine fields were fully planted in August. When new mine matériel was received in the last months of 1941, the mine fields were replanted.[484]

The minefields functioned well under the oversight of Lt. Col. Edward Carl Englehart, who had served on the G-2 staff of the Philippine Department prior to his arrival on Corregidor. Because of his familiarity with the harbor defense's minefields, he was assigned with the 91st C.A. to command the mine defense of Boca Chica Channel.[485]

The need for additional mine planters was well recognized as early as 1939, but no action was taken until January 13, 1941, when the Supply Division, G-4, agreed that eight, with an option on four or possibly eight additional boats, should be procured. The new type that emerged was a trim 188-foot all-welded-steel craft which was larger and had more power than any earlier vessel employed. The first of this new class of mine planters, USAMP *General Henry Knox,* was originally intended for use in the Philippines to supplement *Harrison.* Although launched November 4, 1941, and completed in January 1942, it was not commissioned until June 4, 1942, and consequently was never sent to the Philippines, being assigned instead to the Harbor Defenses of Chesapeake Bay.[486]

In April 1941 the army authorized quartermaster funding to lease and outfit a local tug and a barge for a year to aid in minelaying duties. Meanwhile, new boats and yawls were being completed. Right before the Pearl Harbor attack two new 26-foot mine yawls were loaded onto army transport USAT *Ludington* at Honolulu, consigned to the Harbor Defenses of Manila Bay. That vessel was scheduled to stop and unload supplies at one of the new island air ferry bases prior to a final destination of Manila, tentatively scheduled for January 10, 1942. The attack of December 7th intervened, and the ship turned back for the safety of the West Coast with her yawls and other submarine mining equipment.[487]

USAMP *General F.E. George Harrison* and the junior mine planter *Neptune* maintained the Boca Chica minefields into 1942. By February, the diminishing supply of fuel oil began to limit the operations of both army and navy mine craft. A lengthy search for additional sources of fuel oil was successfully concluded when a substantial amount of oil was found in the bunkers of the grounded SS *Don Jose.* This enabled the navy's minesweepers as well as *Harrison* to continue full operations into May 1942.[488]

Boca Grande Minefields

In the Boca Grande, or South Channel, the navy field planned for 736 contact mines laid in six lines was expanded in 1941 to a total of 870 contact mines laid in seven lines from Topside's south shore to Carabao Island, with 400-yard intervals between the lines and individual mines spaced 100 yards apart. Three more lines of contact mines for a total of 42 mines were to be laid between Carabao and Calumpan Point on the Cavite shore. Two minesweepers of the Asiatic Fleet, USS *Tanager* and USS *Whippoorwill,* were pressed into service as minelayers. They laid the initial narrow Boca Grande field of contact mines from Caballo Island eastward in the direction of Carabao island. *Tanager* and *Whippoorwill* then proceeded to Subic Bay, where they laid another minefield by following a line of can buoys put down as a guide. After the minelayers completed the field, a smaller vessel followed along the track of the buoys and sank each buoy. From October through December, USS *Napa* and USS *Tanager* participated in installing an antisubmarine net across Mariveles Bay, Bataan. This difficult operation was accomplished despite the fact that there were no specialized net-laying craft in the Philippines.[489]

USS *Asheville* (PG-21). This ship and her sister USS *Tulsa* had served as station ships in the navy's Asiatic Fleet for many years. While she got away from Manila following the outbreak of hostilities, she was soon lost in the East Indies. NHC.

China river gunboat USS *Luzon* (PR-7), after a last-minute voyage from Hong Kong to Manila, served as a minefield guard ship after the commencement of hostilities. The boat was lost in the final days of the campaign in the waters just off Corregidor. NHC.

CHAPTER 13
WAR COMES TO THE PHILIPPINES

Alert

In the late afternoon of November 28, 1941, the War Department's November 27, 1941, war warning message was received at General Douglas MacArthur's Manila headquarters. MacArthur passed word to General Moore in the harbor defenses to "take such measures as [Moore]... saw fit to ensure the readiness of the command to meet any eventually." When this information was passed along to the general, the state of alert in the harbor defenses was increased to a full alert and all troops began moving into their battle positions.[490]

The succeeding days were filled with intense activity as the garrison moved into its battle positions. Field kitchens were set up at the gun and mortar batteries, camouflage was inspected, and supplies were brought in and stored in battery storerooms.

The 59th C.A. Deploys

The 59th C.A. was responsible for manning most of the major-caliber seacoast armament in the HD of Manila and Subic Bays and for nearly all of the primary seacoast armament on Corregidor. The regiment moved out of its Topside barracks and occupied the seaward defense batteries shortly after 1900 on November 28, 1941, and began assuming its battle positions. Colonel Bunker's command post (C_1 Station) south of Battery Wheeler at the cliff's edge above Searchlight Point, was occupied by details from the regimental headquarters battery. 1st Battalion, commanded by Lt. Col. Norman B. Simmonds, operated the large-caliber Gun Group 1 (G_1), Batteries Smith, Hearn, Wheeler, Cheney, Crockett, Geary, and later Battery Way, when that battery was returned to service.[491]

Lt. Col. Valentine P. Foster was transferred from the 91st C.A. to the 59th C.A. when Lt. Col. Ausmus was transferred from the 59th C.A. to the harbor defense staff as commander of the beach defense artillery. Foster acted briefly as regimental executive until he was placed in command of Fort Hughes but for most of the campaign the position of regimental executive was filled by Major, later Lieutenant Colonel, Dwight D. Edison.

Lt. Col. Lewis S. Kirkpatrick, commanding 2nd Battalion, 59th C.A., moved to Fort Drum upon the outbreak of war, where Battery E, 59th C.A., constituted the garrison. Kirkpatrick was accompanied to the "Concrete Battleship" by a small detachment of the battalion headquarters. In time, a detail from the 60th C.A.

Open air kitchen facilities near a battery position. Cornwell Collection, USAMHI.

would arrive with a portable 60-inch AA searchlight and a 10-man detachment of marines would be assigned to "beach defense" at Fort Drum.[492]

Maj. Armand Hopkins, commanding 3rd Battalion, 59th C.A., was assigned to command Fort Hughes on August 8, 1941. Hopkins was promoted to Lieutenant Colonel December 24, 1941, and continued in command at Fort Hughes until Colonel Bunker sent Lt. Col. Foster in late February 1942. Promoted to full colonel, Foster assumed the command.[493]

The 91st C.A. Deploys

While the 59th manned the heavy-caliber seacoast armament, the 38 officers and 764 enlisted men of the 91st C.A., commanded by Col. Willis Shippam, had primary responsibility for the submarine mine defenses. The regiment manned a considerable number of the semi-mobile 155 mm GPF armament on Corregidor as well as about half the 6-inch medium-caliber and 3-inch rapid-fire fixed seacoast armament. As it became increasingly likely the U.S. would get involved in a war with Japan, training had intensified in 1939. Proficiency by the regimental firing batteries was high, with four of its seven batteries being rated excellent in the annual service practices in 1940. The 91st had two battalions. The 1st Battalion was the mine group, consisting of Batteries A and G. The 2nd Battalion was the gun battalion, Batteries B, C, D, E, and F. By early 1941, a modest increase in the number of Philippine Scouts had been authorized by Congress.[494]

With the additional personnel authorized and the impending arrival of additional AA armament, the decision was made to reorganize the regiment with most of the 2nd Battalion formed into an AA Battalion. Initially, Battery B was slated as the AA searchlight battery. Batteries C, D, and E became antiaircraft batteries, each manning four M1918 3-inch AA guns. This decision was partially rescinded when Battery D turned in its antiaircraft guns and then briefly manned Battery Stockade (four 155 mm GPF guns) in the summer of 1941. Consequently, only Batteries C and E would actually man AA guns when war came to the Philippines.[495]

Between August 1940 and October 1941, there was substantial turnover among the officers and their numbers increased to 41. Headquarters Battery, 91st C.A., operated Gun Group 4 (G_4) from its command post on Way Hill. Later in 1941, Lt. Col. Joseph Kohn, who had joined the regiment as a major in October 1940, was promoted to lieutenant colonel and rose to regimental command from battalion commander, succeeding Colonel Shippam, who rotated back to the United States. Soon after the war began, Colonel Kohn moved his G_4 command post to the vicinity of Battery Hanna, where a tunnel complex was dug into the cliffs.[496]

Shortly after the establishment of the Philippine Army coast artillery training center's training program at Fort Wint, a similar program was undertaken at Fort Mills. There, 428 Filipinos were undergoing coast artillery instruction when war came. With the declaration of war, this group of trainees was organized into the 1st Coast Artillery Regiment, Philippine Army, with a headquarters battery of 28 men and four lettered firing batteries, A-D, each with 100 men. These batteries were assigned to components of the 91st and 92nd C.A. serving at Fort Mills.[497]

The 92nd C.A. Deploys

Lt. Col. James B. Crawford commanded the 92nd C.A. from March 30, 1939, until his departure for the United States on the February 1940 transport. In early 1940 the 1st Battalion (less Battery A at Fort Wint) under Maj. William Braly, the regimental executive, participated in Philippine Department maneuvers. Batteries B, C, and D took their 155 mm GPF guns from Corregidor for the exercises and upon their return commenced their annual service practices, which wound up March 15, 1940. Soon afterward, Braly was reassigned to harbor defenses headquarters as inspector, and shortly thereafter as the Harbor Defense S-3.

Col. Joseph F. Cottrell arrived from the Fort Monroe mine depot in February 1940, relieving Colonel Crawford in command of the 92nd. During Colonel Cottrell's relatively brief tenure, the pace of training increased. Battery officers and troop officers' schools were in full swing and gunners' schools were held almost continuously as the army prepared for war. As the rainy season merged into the typhoon season, training shifted indoors to gunners' instruction and examinations, basic subjects, secrecy discipline, and special schools for NCOs and specialists. Cottrell was detailed in early summer 1940 to the Harbor Defense Headquarters as Assistant Executive and Harbor Defense Inspector. As the typhoon season waned and the rainy weather cleared, the 92nd C.A. resumed beach-defense training and exercises, including target practice with 37 mm and 75 mm mobile beach-defense armament, as well as AA machine guns.

Maj. Napoleon Boudreau had arrived aboard USAT *Grant* on June 20, 1940, and briefly served as 2nd Battalion commander, as well as the regiment's plans and training officer before being reassigned to the temporary command of the 59th C.A. In August 1940, Boudreau was promoted to Lt. Col. and continued in command until the arrival of Col. Paul D. Bunker in February 1941. In October 1941, Boudreau was assigned command of the 92nd C.A. in addition to that of Fort Wint and the training of the 2nd Coast Artillery Regiment, Philippine Army. With Boudreau on detached service at Fort Wint, actual command of the 92nd Regiment devolved upon Lt. Col. DeCarre.

During the summer of 1941 the regiment underwent an expansion and a partial reorganization to a three-battalion regiment. While the intent was to increase the size of the regiment and organize a new 2nd Battalion as an AA unit with two additional firing batteries, the war intervened and the organization of the new 2nd Battalion was never completed and its headquarters battery was never formed. Batteries A, B, C, and D were however, reorganized as the 1st Battalion and the Guard Battalion (Batteries E, and F) became part of the 3rd Battalion. Batteries E and F were reorganized and continued to perform guard duties until December 9, when the remaining convicts were returned to Bilibid Prison in Manila and Batteries E and F resumed full-time soldiering. Tunnel construction labor in the future was by hired miners from the mountain provinces of northern Luzon and drafted refugees from Bataan.

With nearly half its elements detached to other stations in the harbor defense command, the units of the 92nd remaining on Corregidor probably numbered only about 200 officers and men when the war began. Lieutenant Colonel Boudreau remained the 92nd C.A.'s commanding officer only until his return to Corregidor after the evacuation of Fort Wint on Christmas Eve 1941. He was subsequently reassigned to command Fort Frank.

Antiaircraft Defenses Deploy

Col. Theodore M. Chase arrived in the Philippines in February 1941 and assumed his duties commanding the 60th C.A. and the AA defenses for the Harbor Defenses of Manila and Subic Bays. Initially Chase maintained his wartime command post at Battery Way (still armed with its four 12-inch mortars, the battery had been out of service for several years). The AA command post was operated by headquarters staff and headquarters battery of the 60th C.A. His AA command consisted of the 60th C.A. and Batteries C and E, 91st C.A., Battery I of the 59th C.A., and the AA detachment of Battery E, 59th C.A. at Fort Drum. These batteries were positioned throughout the harbor defenses. During the evening of November 28, 1941, the 60th C.A. was ordered to move into the field in full force and take up their prepared firing positions.[498]

The harbor defense AA searchlights were directed by Maj. Arthur C. Peterson, the regimental searchlight officer, from his command post in a newly excavated tunnel near the summit of Malinta Hill. His command consisted of Battery A (ALBANY) equipped with nine 60-inch Sperry mobile AA searchlights and nine sound locators, at various locations throughout the fortified islands. Five of Battery A's 60-inch portable searchlights and sound locators as well as two SCR-268 search radars were on Corregidor. Fort Frank's AA Battery E (ERMITA), 91st C.A.; Fort Hughes' Battery I (IDAHO), 59th C.A.; and Fort Drum's Battery E (ERIE), also of the 59th C.A., each had a 60-inch portable AA searchlight manned by a detail from Battery A throughout the siege. Fort Wint had five AA searchlights manned by a detachment of the 91st C.A. Battery E (ERIE), 60th

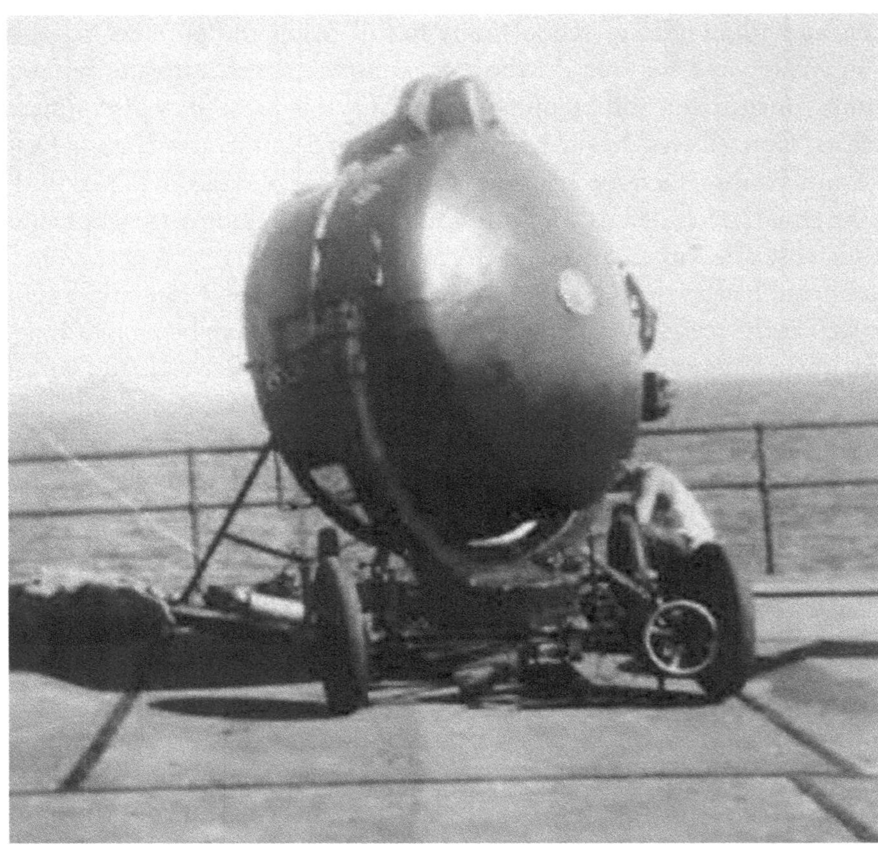

60-inch M1 searchlight at Fort Drum manned by a detachment of Battery A, 60th Coast Artillery. Zink Collection.

C.A., commanded by Capt. William E. Massello, was equipped with nine 60-inch Sperry mobile searchlights, nine sound locators, and two SCR-268 search radars at various locations around Mariveles at the foot of the Bataan Peninsula.[499]

Corregidor Goes to War

Word of the opening of hostilities and the Japanese air raid on Pearl Harbor first reached Corregidor in the early morning hours of December 8, 1941, when operators in the navy's top secret radio intercept Station "C" received messages sent out by NPM, the Naval Radio station at Pearl Harbor Naval Base, "Air raid on Pearl Harbor. This is no drill." This message was soon followed up with: "Hostilities commenced with air raids on Pearl." Lt. Rudolph J. Fabian, USN, the navy intercept station officer in charge, was awakened and he immediately called direct to Major General Moore to report this shocking, but not entirely unexpected sneak attack by the Japanese. While Moore dressed, his aide called Col. William C. Braly, who had the duty in the harbor defense command post ("H" Station) Topside. Braly noted the time as he picked up the phone. It was 0340 when the message texts from Pearl Harbor were relayed to the Headquarters of Gen. Douglas MacArthur, commanding U.S. Army Forces in the Far East (USAFFE) in Manila.[500]

Corregidor's first sighting of Japanese aircraft came at 1026, when a large flight of medium bombers was sighted coming from a raid on Manila's Neilson Field but did not come within range of Corregidor's AA batteries. At 1315 three Japanese medium bombers flying at about 8,000 feet passed within range of the AA batteries on Corregidor's tail and Fort Hughes. The AA gunners of Battery D, 60th C.A., on Corregidor manning 3-inch AA guns responded quickly and opened fire on the Japanese planes. Battery I at Fort Hughes opened fire at 1318 with its four guns. The two AA batteries fired about 35 rounds, of which at least one high explosive round from Battery I managed to hit one plane and it was seen falling into Manila Bay. The remaining two planes turned back. This was the first action against the Japanese taken by the harbor defenses.[501]

By late afternoon, the decision was made to extinguish the lights at the lighthouses on Caballo, Corregidor, and Monja Islands. As darkness fell on December 8, plans of the defense project were being implemented to reinforce the AA defenses of Manila. Initially the formation of a provisional AA machine gun battalion for the defense of the airfields around Manila and the port area had been planned but the war came before the plan could be implemented and Battery M, 60th C.A., commanded by Capt. Harold B. Wright, initially positioned near Kindley Field, was designated to provide these AA machine gun elements. The battery boarded the harbor boat *Mambukal* about 1715 and proceeded to the Port of Manila. A portion of the battery took up positions in the port area and oil storage fields while other sections were assigned to Nichols and Nielson airfields and other important installations to furnish AA defense against low flying enemy aircraft. With the departure of Battery M, measures were also taken to extend the AA defenses. The Japanese, flying out of fields on Formosa, intended to conduct air raids on Manila, its port facilities, and airfields. Battery M took up positions near the Malacañang Palace in Manila for a brief period until Manila was evacuated and declared an open city. Battery M returned to Fort Mills by way of Bataan and reoccupied its position around Kindley Field in early January 1942. Captain Wright and his executive, 1st Lt. K.W. Ramsey, were relieved by Capt. James R. Holmes and 1st Lt. Thomas H. Hackett on January 19, 1942.[502]

Battery B, 92nd C.A., commanded by Capt. Robert J. Lawlor, moved away from Ordnance Point with its 155 mm guns and equipment and boarded the quartermaster boat *McConville* for passage to Cabcaben on Bataan. From Cabcaben the battery traveled by road to Bagac on Bataan's west coast. There it established itself in positions that covered the approaches to Subic Bay and functioned in a beach defense mode as well. This position would later become the left anchor of USAFFE' main line of resistance on Bataan. Battery B was eventually attached to II Corps Artillery.[503]

Manila and Cavite Are Bombed

From December 9 to 29, 1941, the Japanese focus was directed at subduing Manila and the military and naval facilities there and in central Luzon with a heavy aerial bombing campaign as well as bombing the numerous ships anchored in Manila Bay. Manila's Port area and the army and naval installations on Luzon were repeatedly bombed and soon reduced to ruins. On December 10, the Cavite Navy Yard was heavily bombed. The densely packed navy yard's buildings of wood and sheet metal were soon ablaze and rapidly spreading fire threatening the highly volatile fuel facilities, ammunition, and torpedoes stored in the yard. Many vessels moored to the wharves were immobile, undergoing major repairs. The Japanese air raid on the Cavite Navy Yard lasted from about 1330 to 1500 and when it ended the yard was a total wreck. By about 1800 the massive fires that had swept the yard were out, but one restarted in a lumber yard threatened to spread to Fort San Felipe, now serving as the navy's ammunition depot. Amazingly, the old Spanish fort had not yet been set afire or blown up in the bombing. That fire continued to spread and by 2100 Adm. Francis W. Rockwell ordered the yard abandoned. Raging fires at the Cavite Navy Yard could be seen across the bay, the radio towers and buildings clearly silhouetted by the flames. Adm. Thomas C. Hart and the major units of the fleet were already destined for the Dutch East Indies by existing war plans, but the loss of the Cavite base accelerated the transfer of remaining assets in Manila Bay.

Left in the Philippines were the submarine tender USS *Canopus* to service the submarines that continued to operate out of Manila Bay and the handful of river gunboats, PT-boats, minesweepers, tugs, and launches that were incorporated into the Inshore Patrol. Plans were implemented to transfer all remaining navy equipment, supplies, and food stuffs stored in Manila and Cavite to Mariveles and Corregidor as quickly as possible. Navy and Marine Corps personnel and activities would then be transferred to Corregidor and Bataan. Manila was declared an "open city" on Christmas Day 1941. The American and Filipino forces were withdrawing into the Bataan Peninsula, when Rear Admiral Rockwell and his staff boarded the minesweeper USS *Tanager* to the "Rock." There they would occupy the tunnel complex inside Malinta Hill.[504]

On December 10, the first of several Japanese landings was made at Aparri in Northern Luzon. This landing was swiftly followed by additional landings at Vigan, Legaspi, and Naga. Other landings were reported later that day at various locations on Luzon, as well as other islands in the archipelago. The fortified islands of Manila Bay were essentially ignored during this period although when the Japanese planes ventured close enough to be fired upon, the AA guns opened up, resulting in the forts in the bay receiving a wide berth.

General Moore's command took advantage of this calm before the storm to improve their battle positions. Bombproof shelters were dug, the move from the barracks to the battle positions was completed, and field kitchens were established. On Corregidor, the troops continued to live under canvas and their pyramid tents dotted the landscape. The scouts of the 91st C.A.'s Batteries E and F, and the 92nd C.A.'s Battery D occupied the tunnels of Carabao Island, while on Caballo Island the men of Batteries G and I, 59th C.A., were improving their battle positions and making room to accommodate additional troops in their bombproof spaces. At Fort Drum, the deck was cleared of the peacetime temporary barracks by shoving it over the side and Battery E moved into the below-decks dormitories in the concrete battleship.[505]

Fort Drum's cage mast containing fire control instruments and searchlights created a dead space to the rear of the turrets. It was not removed initially, but as the siege continued the mast became heavily battered, its fire control instrumentation and searchlights wrecked and if it had fallen, it might have blocked Battery Marshall's traverse. Further, the structure served as an aiming point for Japanese artillery and the decision was made to dismantle it.[506]

Promotions of officers in the harbor defenses ranging from first lieutenant through lieutenant colonel were made in January, June, and October 1941. Soon after the opening of hostilities, another round of promotions for those not previously promoted in the harbor defenses was made. On December 19, and December 24, 1941, many officers were advanced one grade. A similar round of promotions was carried out in January 1942 and again in March 1942. In June 1942, many officers and enlisted POWs captured on Corregidor were advanced one grade.

Harbor Defenses Adjust to Japanese Aerial Bombardment

Soon after the declaration of war, Fort Mills prepared to receive General MacArthur's headquarters and the Philippine Commonwealth government if it became necessary to evacuate Manila. The process of moving

Japanese Mitsubishi Ki-21, Type 97 twin-engine heavy bombers known as *SALLY* to the allies.
This was the principal bomber used by the enemy forces in bombing Fort Mills and the other fortified islands. NARA.

huge amounts of supplies and foodstuffs from Manila and Cavite to Corregidor and Bataan increased. Much of the material sent to Bataan and all of that sent to Corregidor was moved by small and medium-size ships and barges. Ship traffic was extensive both day and night as the navy moved what was salvageable from Cavite and the army moved large amounts of material from their warehouses in the Manila Port Area to Corregidor and Mariveles. The quartermaster troops on Corregidor managed, because of a still undamaged trolley line, to move 28,800 tons of food from the wharves into wartime storage during the two-week respite before the bombing of Corregidor began. Responsibility for the movement and secure storage of the many tons of supplies and food shipped to Corregidor in 1941 was assigned to the 295 American and Philippine Scout officers, enlisted men, and civilian employees of the Quartermaster Corps, commanded by Col. Chester H. Elmes. The harbor boats *San Pedro*, *Miley*, and *General John McE. Hyde*, the 90-foot Class-A launches *Mitchell*, *Ledyard*, *McConville*, *J.M. Jewell*, and *Geary;* the 65-foot Class-B launches *Adams*, *Forby*, and *Tilly*, and the two Class-C launches *Maxwell* and *Pelican* along with the nine lorchas (sailing vessels having a Chinese junk rig on a European style hull capable of carrying between 125 and 160 tons of cargo) of the Quartermaster Corps performed splendidly. Those vessels and 13 scows (flat bottomed barge-like vessels), each of which could carry 212 tons of cargo, and two scows each capable of transporting 252 tons of cargo or 320 troops, were kept busy shuttling matériel and personnel between Manila's port and the Fort Mills wharves. In addition, several naval vessels were utilized to move both army and naval stores to Corregidor and Mariveles. Quartermaster troops continued to operate the Fort Mills trolley system and the post's central power plant.[507]

At first the Japanese concentrated on bombing the Manila port facilities and the vessels anchored in the bay near the port area, but by Christmas Eve they had expanded their area of coverage to include the entire bay. In so doing, they caught the freighter SS *Don Jose* in the Boca Chica Channel, and set the vessel afire. *Don Jose* managed to run herself aground near Corregidor's Hooker Point. The next day the Japanese bombed the collection of vessels concentrated in Mariveles Harbor, where they sank the SS *Si Kiang*, a former Vichy French vessel that had been seized by the U.S. loaded with gasoline and 2½ million tons of flour. The navy dry dock USS *Dewey*, another target of the bombers, was not hit. This particular flight then streaked over Topside strafing.[508]

The Japanese bombers having dropped their bombs on Manila or Cavite would frequently fly over and past Corregidor en route to their bases on Formosa. The 60th C.A.'s gun batteries regularly engaged these formations, but the Japanese usually flew out range of the 3-inch AA guns. The AA gun batteries were supplied with 3-inch MK IX AA ammunition with Scovill 111 powder-train fuzes, which enabled an effective altitude of

Personnel entering Malinta Tunnel during a Japanese air raid. While the tunnel proved invulnerable to both aerial bombs and artillery shelling, it brought with it tradeoffs for morale and less than optimal human comfort. MacArthur Memorial.

about 8,300 yards (24,900 feet). Local meteorological conditions allowed a slightly higher muzzle velocity to permit an increased altitude of about 8,450 yards (25,350 feet). At the war's start there were only about 1,500 rounds of mechanical fuzes in the Philippines. The mechanical fuzes enabled effective altitudes up to 9,100 yards (27,300 feet) or a maximum of 10,666 yards (32,000 feet). On December 10, 1941, the decision was made to allot all of these fuzes to Battery B, 60th C.A., whose battle position was Topside near Battery Wheeler, commanding the China Sea approaches considered the logical avenue of approach for Japanese aircraft.[509]

Despite the reverses experienced by the Filamerican forces in the field and their resultant withdrawal toward Bataan, Corregidor and the other fortified islands remained untouched until December 29. The engineers rushed several tunnel projects to a state where they could be pressed into service although lacking their "finishing work."

The Fort Mills Hospital had been evacuated to the north complex of Malinta tunnel. By December 14, the Japanese aerial campaign convinced General Moore that it would be necessary to move the harbor defense command post (HDCP) at Topside down to Lateral No. 2 in Malinta Tunnel. The navy abandoned the wreckage of their Cavite base on December 10 and 16th Naval District Headquarters moved into their newly completed tunnels under Malinta's south slopes on December 21.[510]

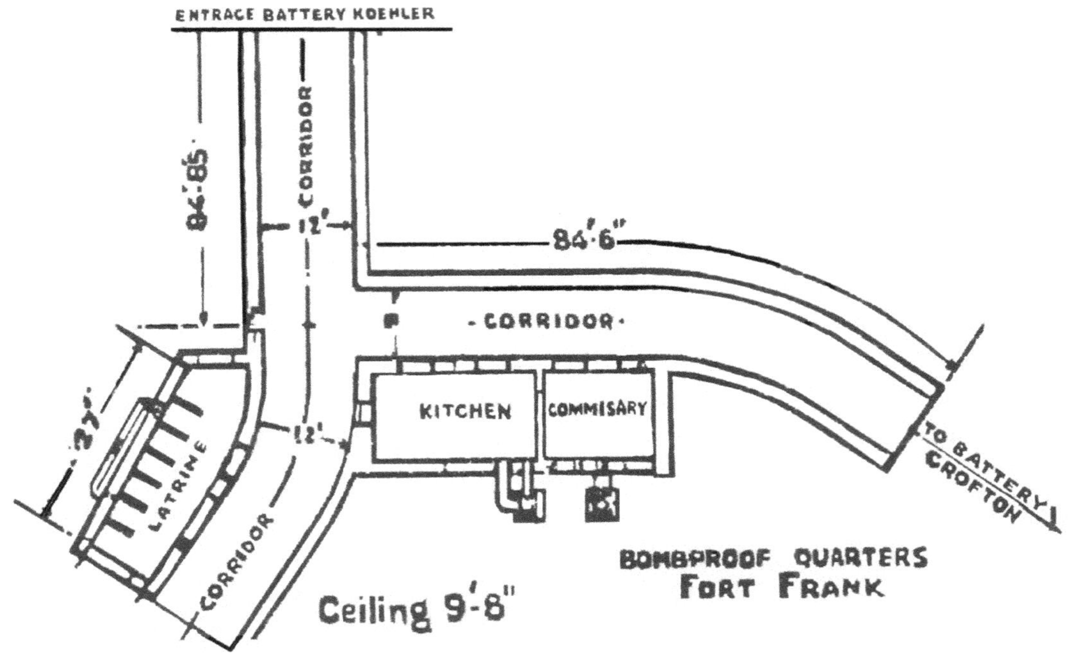

Bombproof quarters in the tunnels at Fort Frank. With the expectation that Carabao Island might be bombarded from the Ternate Shore, provision was made to hang bunks and quarter personnel in some of the long access tunnels connecting the major batteries at Fort Frank. NARA.

Reactivating the Corregidor Lighthouse

Early in the war, torpedoes and spare parts stored in the Cavite Navy Yard's warehouses had been loaded aboard barges and lightered out to Corregidor, for storage in Roger Tunnel. Other torpedoes were sent to the Mariveles section base. In the early days of the war Asiatic Fleet submarines as well as some Pacific fleet submarines operating from as far away as Pearl Harbor replenished their torpedoes and fuel from stocks at Mariveles and Corregidor. Corregidor's lighthouse, extinguished since December 8, was ordered relit on December 16. The light was to operate in conjunction with a navy schedule to facilitate safe passage of submarines into the bay. Corregidor Light would show a white light on a specified fixed azimuth on a secret schedule for each submarine entry for the first 10 minutes of each half hour. During passage of submarines through the controlled mine fields the mines would be placed on "safe" by the mine command and the marking buoys illuminated by the 59th C.A.'s seacoast searchlights. The navy inshore patrol maintained a "Control Ship" inside the bay near the entrance to the minefield channel. They and the proper harbor defense stations coordinated each passage.[511]

Typically, a submarine would enter the bay before dawn, lay submerged in the bay during the day until darkness, then surface and moor alongside *Canopus* in Mariveles Harbor to replenish their torpedoes. Later on, the subs would moor at Corregidor's South Wharf and take on a fresh supply of torpedoes from those stored in the navy's rough-finished Roger Tunnel and then exit the bay before dawn.[512]

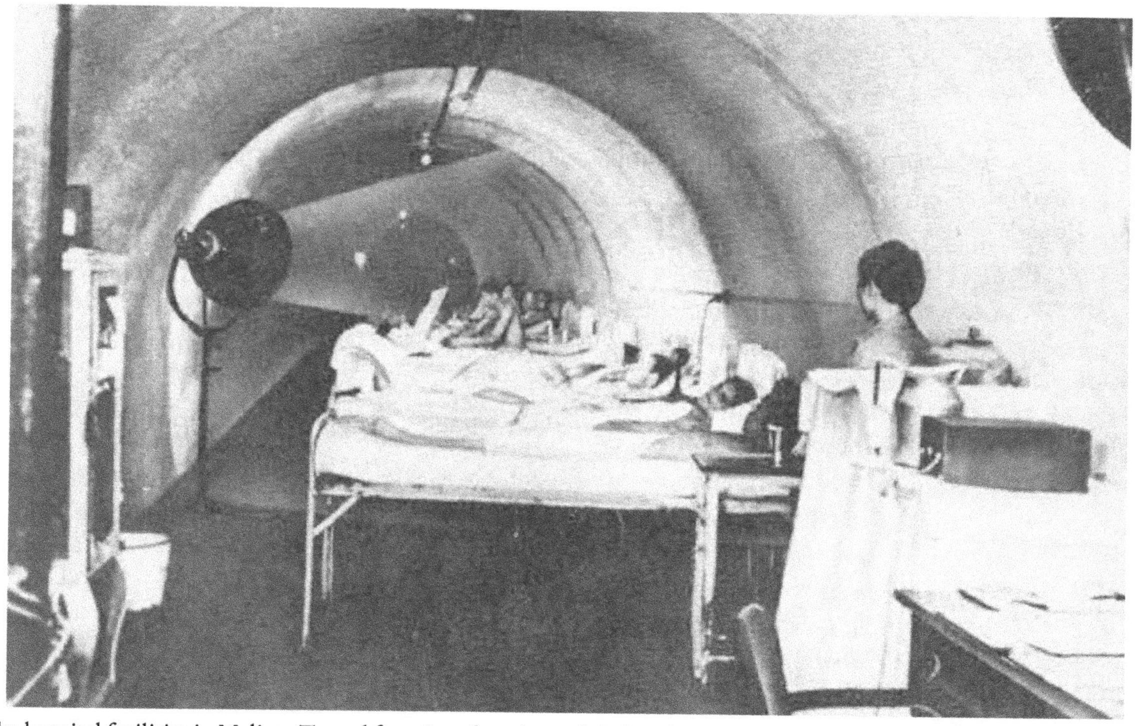

The hospital facilities in Malinta Tunnel functioned as planned during the siege, but the general overcrowding of the entire tunnel system put tremendous strain on the ability of the hospital to properly serve. NARA.

Inshore Patrol

With the laying of the mines in the channels leading into Manila Bay, a guard vessel was positioned to halt ships attempting to enter the bay. Entrance and egress to Manila Bay through the Boca Chica controlled minefield was coordinated by the navy's inshore patrol and the seaward defenses. This duty was performed by vessels of the U.S. Navy Inshore Patrol, which took station to seaward of the minefields to prevent vessels from blundering into the mines and to provide pilots through the fields. Prior to the war, the guard ship function was carried out by the gunboats USS *Asheville* and USS *Tulsa* and minesweeper USS *Whippoorwill.* After war broke out those vessels were assigned other duties and guard ship responsibility was turned over to the six patrol torpedo boats of Lt. John D. Bulkeley's PT Squadron No. 3 and eventually to three river gunboats: USS *Luzon*, *Mindanao*, and *Oahu* that had arrived from China. *Luzon* and *Oahu* moved to Manila just prior to the war, while *Mindanao* reached Cavite late in the morning of December 10, 1941, just prior to the Japanese air raid on Cavite. The minesweepers USS *Quail*, *Tanager*, and *Finch*, and the tugs *Napa*, *Genesee*, and *Vega* also functioned as part of the inshore patrol. These vessels operated from the Mariveles Naval Station after the evacuation of the Cavite Navy Yard and conducted operations in Manila Bay until early April 1942, when they moved over to San Jose Bay off Corregidor.[513]

During the daylight hours of December 9 and 10, many commercial vessels of all types entered and left the harbor through the controlled mine field, usually with coordination between the navy inshore patrol and the seaward defense command, while numerous naval vessels departed for the southern Philippines. On more than one occasion civilian captains attempted to take their vessels through the minefields without authorization, much to the consternation of the army and navy and causing the minefields to be place on "safe."

Widespread damage at the Cavite Navy Station following the devastating attack of December 10, 1941. NARA.

SS *Corregidor* Sinks in the Minefield

Apolinar Calvo, the experienced captain of *Compania Maritima's* inter-island steamer *Corregidor,* had reason for concern on the afternoon of December 16, 1941, as he watched his ship being boarded by hundreds of passengers. Japanese air raids that struck the numerous airfields scattered across Luzon during the past week had practically obliterated the Army Air Corps in the Philippines. Similar air raids had demolished the U.S. Navy base at Cavite on December 10. On Saturday, December 13, Japanese planes attacked shipping in Manila Bay and the bombing of Manila itself was expected at any time. Earlier in the day the army had loaded 16 2.95-inch mountain guns and a large amount of ammunition, equipment, and supplies for the 81st and 101st Field Artillery Regiments, and other units of the fledgling Philippine army in the Visayan-Mindanao area in the ship's forward hold. The military cargo was accompanied by some 150 Filipino soldiers, all destined for the Filamerican Forces in the Southern Islands. Following the commencement of hostilities with Japan on December 8, the schools and colleges in Manila had closed and anxious parents in the Southern Philippines were urging their children to return home as soon as possible. Businessmen and Commonwealth legislators were also seeking transportation back to their homes in Cebu, Mindanao, and Iloilo.

SS *Corregidor* was scheduled to depart Manila Harbor for its weekly trip to and from the Visayan and Mindanao Islands in the south. The steamer had arrived from the south on Sunday, December 14, and although the vessel was usually scheduled to leave at 1500 on Tuesday, this regularly scheduled time of departure came and went. The *Compania Maritima* had oversold the tickets due to the "irresistible pleadings" of people wanting to get away from Manila. Only 326 passengers were listed on the ships manifest when it sailed, although some 800 tickets had been sold and apparently several hundred more passengers had gotten aboard prior to *Corregidor's* departure.[514]

Having delayed getting underway past his authorized and scheduled time of departure, Captain Calvo had to decide when to sail. If he waited for daylight, he would be able to pass through the minefield in good visibility. But a daytime departure would also leave his ship subject to the Japanese air attacks. Rather than risk his already overcrowded ship by waiting for a daytime sailing, Calvo decided to get underway after darkness fell, before even more people made their way on board. As an added precaution, Calvo ordered the ship darkened although at the time there were no orders for such precautions from either the military or port authorities. Calvo took in *Corregidor's* lines at 2200.[515]

As *Corregidor* stood down Manila Bay toward the fortified islands and the minefields at the bay's entrance that moonless night, she was intercepted by USS *Mindanao* of the inshore patrol and her captain, Cmdr. Alan R. McCracken, ordered the steamer to stop, an order Captain Calvo ignored. The river gunboat was apparently engaged in moving army personnel and material from the Cavite-Manila area to Corregidor. It is believed that the gunboat reported the presence of *Corregidor* to the inshore patrol at Mariveles.[516]

Drawing nearer to the Island of Corregidor, SS *Corregidor* was spotted by the east primary mine observation station (M') near Battery James. On receiving the report of the sighting of *Corregidor,* the lieutenant on watch in the mine casemate called his superior, who in turn, called the seaward defense commander, Colonel Bunker, requesting information as to whether he should de-activate the mines in the channel. With a lifetime of experience with the Filipinos, going back to the '98 war and the subsequent insurrection, Colonel Bunker said "No!"

Soon after encountering *Mindanao,* Calvo spotted the two flashing buoys marking the entrance to the channel through the Morrison Point (north) group of mines laid between Alasisin Point, Bataan, and the Corregidor shore about midway between James Ravine and Rock Point. Having traversed the minefields numerous times in the past several months, those passages had been made during daylight hours with the escort of a guard ship. Calvo therefore was generally familiar with the process. He was probably not aware, however, that the minefields planted the previous July and August with their 1,000 foot wide channels had been replanted using newly arrived submarine mine matériel in late November and early December and that the channel width in the Morrison Point group (north minefield) had been reduced to 300 feet and to 600 feet in the Rock Point Group that had been planted between Corregidor and Monja Islands. [517]

Although Captain Calvo managed to traverse the North Group of mines successfully he was far from safe. Calvo's next way point was a buoy with a dim steady light marking the position at which he was to alter course to port and proceed on a southerly course to pass through the large Rock Point minefield. As *Corregidor* approached the midpoint buoy, she was met by *PT-41,* commanded by Ens. George E. Cox Jr., who ordered *Corregidor* to stop. This order was also ignored by Calvo, although he sent the recognition signal to the PT

Inter-island steamer SS *Corregidor.* The ship, under army contract for stores to be taken to the Visayas and overloaded with Filipino passengers trying to join families to the south, was lost with a tragically high loss of life on an American defensive mine in December 1941. Gaines Collection.

boat. At the lighted buoy Calvo altered course to port and took up a heading of 180° that Cox provided once he realized that Calvo was not stopping and would take his ship through the Rock Point groups of mines. *Corregidor* steamed southward through the black night toward the inner channel buoys that were to be illuminated by Searchlight No. 3 to mark the passage through the Rock Point-Monja Island minefield. As the passage of the *Corregidor* was not authorized, the mines were not placed on safe and the searchlights were not ordered active. *PT-41* took up a position in advance of *Corregidor* and led the vessel into the minefield channel.[518]

At this point a combination of factors occurred that ultimately resulted in catastrophe. Captain Calvo, not being aware that the width of the minefield channel had been reduced to 600 feet, nearly half its former width, was unaware his ship was already dangerously close to the west side of the channel. Because of the low visibility Calvo may not have realized that as he steamed south, he was also being swept to the west and as he was already in the righthand side of the channel to begin with, his situation was becoming even more perilous. He most certainly was not aware that cables had been strung between the mines to snare vessels attempting to pass between or below the mines. In any event, as SS *Corregidor* neared the southern edge of the minefield at about 0100, she suddenly altered course to starboard taking the vessel even closer to the channel edge. The reason for the altered course will probably never be known; all who were aware of that course change went down with the ship. There was no reason for Calvo to alter course to starboard (west). The proper course for *Corregidor*, even if there were no mines, was to continue on course of 180° as his destination was the southern islands. Ens. Cox's efforts to stop *Corregidor* were to no avail. Among the possibilities for the abrupt course change are a steering engine failure that caused the rudder to become inoperable, loss of main propulsion that left the ship drifting for a few moments, or seizing up of one of the three propellers on a connecting cable between the deeper planted channel mines and those in the minefield proper that were anchored only 15 feet below the surface. In so doing, the overloaded ship already drawing more water and being in a dangerous position in the minefield, probably snared the cable between the No. 1 and No. 2 mines in Mine Group 6 in the minefield proper. Once *Corregidor* had snared the inter-mine cable and caused one of the mines to tip the requisite 25°, detonation was the next event. If set on delayed contact, the No. 2 mine (noted in the James Ravine mine casemate as the one that detonated) would have been drawn closer to the ship and down the ships starboard side until it was about at the amidship point when it exploded. Survivors described the explosion on the starboard side of the vessel.[519]

Of the few Americans on board *Corregidor,* Jack Fee and his wife occupied one of the portside cabins. Fee, the manager of Standard Vacuum Oil Co., recalled hearing the engines stop briefly and then restart. Almost immediately the vessel was wracked by the exploding mine. *PT-41,* then in position close aboard on *Corregidor's* port hand, was nearly capsized by the mine's detonation. Once Ens. Cox had ascertained that there was no material damage to his boat the PT crew began rescuing the few survivors of the sinking. The massive explosion of the mine near the keel probably broke the back of the SS *Corregidor,* which began sinking immediately. Following the explosion, the mines were placed on safe by the mine casemate. By the time harbor defense Searchlights 3 and 4 on Corregidor went into action a few minutes after the blast, only the forward section of the ship was still visible, sticking straight up. A minute or so later *Corregidor* was gone. Lt. John D. Bulkeley, commander of PT-Boat Squadron 3, saw the massive explosion and the ensuing searchlights sweeping the area of the blast from his base in Sisiman Cove and dispatched three of his PT boats as well as the Philippine Q-Boats to aid the survivors, who were taken to Corregidor for treatment in Malinta Hospital and to SS *Si kiang* in Mariveles Harbor. Of the more than 1200 persons on board only about 280 persons were picked up by the rescue boats.[520]

Capt. George Steiger, commanding Battery Cheney, recalled: "My first knowledge of this affair came when my duty watch called me at 12:55 a.m. The *Corregidor* had struck one of our mines and in the four or five minutes it took to reach my battery command post, the vessel had sunk. The 260 or so who survived came on the Rock. Thereafter, we had no trouble with unauthorized Filipino boats attempting to traverse the channel."[521]

Headquarters USAFFE Moves to Corregidor

The failure of the Filamerican Army to stop and defeat the Japanese in central Luzon prompted Gen. MacArthur to reluctantly implement War Plan Orange 3 on December 23 and order the American and Philippine forces to withdraw into the Bataan Peninsula to await a relief force and the U.S. Pacific Fleet. Christmas Eve also marked the USAFFE Headquarters's evacuation from Manila to Corregidor. General Moore's headquarters was notified at 0200 on December 24 that General MacArthur, U.S. High Commissioner Francis B. Sayre, and Commonwealth President Manuel Quezon and their staffs would leave Manila that evening

American torpedo boat *PT-41* on stateside trials. One of six PT boats delivered to the navy in the Philippines in 1941, it was flagship of Motor Torpedo Boat Squadron 3. This particular boat picked up General Douglas MacArthur and his family on the night of March 12, 1942, at Corregidor and carried him on his first leg to a new command in Australia. MacArthur Memorial.

General and Mrs. Douglas MacArthur moved from Manila to Corregidor on December 24, 1941. Soon they took up residence within the Malinta Tunnel. Here they appear just outside the east entrance. MacArthur Memorial.

to conduct the bombardment made ready to fire. Geary fired about a dozen salvos while Greer sent 16 rounds into the Japanese beachhead. When final approval to open fire came about midnight Battery Geary opened up using the 670-pound HE land-attack shells with "super quick" fuzes which proved most effective, "in this first firing by major caliber coast artillery at an enemy since the Civil War." After firing about 16 salvos, the firing was ordered stopped for the night. On the morning of January 27, Batteries Geary and Hearn conducted a second fire mission. This time the objective was to root out the Japanese dug into the caves on the point. To accomplish this, the batteries fired 24 more 12-inch rounds of HE deck-piercing shells with.05-second delay fuzes that enabled them to burrow into the ground before exploding. The results were considered excellent.

One of Battery Smith's 12-inch long-range M1895M2 guns firing. In general, the guns of Smith and Hearn were not heavily used in the siege, the defenders hoping to conserve them and avoid counter-battery fire in case they were needed to engage naval targets. McGarraugh Collection.

Battery Geary's Pit B with four Model 1908 12-inch mortars was used to fire on various Japanese land positions throughout the campaign, until May 2, 1942. This photo is of a pre-war practice shoot. Alfonte Collection, USAMHI.

A major fire was started, and shell fragments flew some 500 yards from point of impact, inflicting major casualties among the Japanese troops. When asked what affect the artillery fire had on the Japanese force, one wounded Japanese prisoner replied: "We were terrified. We could not know where the big shells or bombs were coming from; they seemed to be falling from the sky. Before I was wounded, my head was going round and round, and I did not know what to do. Some of my companions jumped off the cliff to escape the terrible fire." The fire from Batteries Geary and Hearn was so effective that 24 more rounds were fired on January 29.[548]

Colonel Bunker (who was at this point, at least, a rather caustic observer) was less than impressed with the performance of Battery Geary. He noted in his diary that night:[549]

> As an example of shooting a mortar, it was the worst I have ever seen - as a glance at the time schedule will show. Several reports of "Lanyard broken" and "primer misfire" were received. As we were firing in Zone 10 (extreme range) the powder completely filled the chamber and, in one instance, could not be forced into the chamber. For speed and efficiency it was a terribly humiliating experience-even though most of the firing non-coms had been killed in the bombing of 6 Jan.

In addition to the problems at Battery Geary, the telephone communications between Lt. Col. Norman B. Simmonds, the G-1 commander and Lieutenant Fulmer on Cochinos Point had to be run through three exchanges in order to relay spotting data, and Simmonds had to scream in order to be heard over the poor telephone connection.[550]

One outcome of the Longoskawayan Point bombardment was that Captain King commanding Battery Geary was relieved by Bunker, who was convinced that King had not adequately trained his men which resulted in the "failures" of Battery Geary during the shoot. Bunker promoted 1st Lt. Thomas W. Davis of Battery F to captain and assigned him to command Battery H manning Battery Geary. On January 28 Colonel Bunker ordered the transfer of Captain King to Fort Drum as battery commander of Headquarters Battery, 2nd Battalion, and vice commander of that fort. It is unlikely that any other officer could have performed any better than King, given that most of Battery Geary's personnel had less than nine months service and little more than a week before, a tunnel collapsed by a bomb had buried and killed 31 men of the battery, including the battery's principle firing NCOs.[551]

Battery Marshall, Fort Drum, fires a salvo. McGarraugh Collection.

CHAPTER 14
THE CAMPAIGN SETTLES INTO A DEADLY PATTERN

A Brief Respite for the American Forces

As the American forces withdrew into the Bataan Peninsula in January 1942, the Japanese High Command was planning to take nearly half of General Homma's *Fourteenth Army* from the Philippines for the push into the Netherlands East Indies. This involved redeploying the *48th Division* and the *5th Air Group,* leaving only the *65th Brigade, 16th Division,* and various smaller units under the *Fourteenth Army*. These departures left only the less than combat-ready *65th Brigade* to carry on the campaign against the Filamerican Forces on Bataan. Because of this hasty and radical reorganization, the Japanese army and navy commanders in the Philippines were forced to continue the Bataan operations and the occupation of the Philippine Islands with reduced forces. Japanese combat strength, like that of the Filamerican forces, was also seriously degraded by disease in the Bataan theatre.

General Homma Masaharu. NARA.

General Homma on February 8 ordered a temporary suspension of offensive operations on Bataan in order to reorganize his forces. To compensate for the loss of the redeployed forces, the *65th Brigade* was augmented with selected elements of the *16th Division*; and to replace the *5th Air Group,* the *10th Independent Air Unit* was organized at Clark Field. The latter consolidated all the air strength that was not scheduled for redeployment. At the *16th Division* front east of Bagac, it remained necessary to extricate the pocketed and desperately fighting *3rd Battalion, 20th Infantry*. The *16th Division's* frontline units fought forward to assist in piercing the enemy encirclement of their comrades, while feint attacks were launched in other sectors line to keep the U.S. forces off balance. At the cost of further casualties, the remnants of the *3rd Battalion* — a meager 378 officers and men with the regimental commander — were finally extricated on February 15. The next day, General Homma re-ordered the cessation of aggressive operations and notified *Southern Army* that the attack could not be continued.[552]

On February 22, the *Fourteenth Army* line was withdrawn a few miles to the north, the Filamerican forces following up and re-occupying positions evacuated by the enemy. The fighting on Bataan now entered a protracted lull, during which the Japanese Army and Navy concentrated primarily on tightening the blockade of Manila Bay and continued the artillery bombardment of Corregidor.

The stalemate in the Philippines was in marked contrast to the rapid and decisive victories won by Japanese arms on every other front of the Pacific War. Though embarrassing to the *Fourteenth Army*, the failure to quickly eliminate Filamerican resistance on Bataan at first aroused no particular concerns at *Imperial General Headquarters* and *Southern Army* command, who were jubilant over the overall success of the initial operations in Southeast Asia. However, as reports from General Homma's headquarters became increasingly pessimistic in early February, the *Imperial General Headquarters* began to realize the gravity of Homma's situation and recognized that special measures were necessary to bolster the *Fourteenth Army*.[553]

To provide General Homma with a fresh nucleus of infantry strength for a renewed assault on Bataan, *Imperial General Headquarters* ordered the *4th Division's* deployment from Shanghai to the Philippines on February 10, where it would come under *Fourteenth Army* command. It was further recognized that heavy siege artillery, a lack of which had contributed to the failure to breach the American main line of resistance, would be necessary to assure success. Such units particularly in Hong Kong and Malaya were ordered to the Philippines. Air forces were also to be replenished by pulling back army and navy air units from the southern area.

Throughout the latter part of February and March, *Southern Army* and *Fourteenth Army* staffs shuttled back and forth between Manila and Saigon and between Saigon and Tokyo, planning and implementing the reinforcement operation. It was estimated that the concentration and emplacement of large-caliber artillery from China and Southeast Asia would be completed by early April, at which time the offensive could be renewed. The substantial number of heavy artillery units sent to the Philippines would soon make themselves felt on Corregidor.[554]

The Outpost Fortifications

Beyond minor attention from Japanese aircraft during the early weeks of the war, the outpost fortifications in Manila Bay saw little action. Beyond some sporadic AA fire at passing Japanese planes, the guns of the outpost forts remained silent for a lack of targets until early in 1942.

Fort Hughes

Maj. Armand Hopkins on December 3, 1941, was assigned command of the 3rd Battalion, 59th C.A., and appointed Fort Hughes commander. Battery G manned the fort's primary armament: the 14-inch disappearing guns of Batteries Gillespie and Woodruff as well as the 12-inch mortars of Battery Craighill. Battery Leach's 6-inch guns and Battery Fuger's 3-inch guns, the two, later three, 155 mm GPF guns of Batteries Williams and Hooker as well as the four 75 mm M1917 beach defense guns were secondary assignments for Battery G. Batteries Fuger, Leach, Gillespie, Craighill, and Woodruff were all in good operating condition. Battery Woodruff, however, had been taken out of service prior to the war as it was considered unsafe to fire because of faulty concrete.

Following the annual inspection of the harbor defenses in May 1941, the decision was made to investigate the matter of Battery Woodruff's condition and apply corrective measures as soon as funding was available. In spite of this concern, when hostilities broke out, the decision was made to return Battery Woodruff to service as its field of fire covered parts of Cavite where enemy batteries were located. Battery Gillespie on the other hand had no useful field of fire and could not be used for counter-battery missions. Also, the traversing mechanism of Battery Gillespie was badly damaged by enemy artillery fire early in the siege, further reducing the 14-inch gun's usefulness. During the siege, Gillespie was cannibalized for parts as necessary to keep Battery Woodruff in action.[555]

Antiaircraft Battery I of the 59th C.A. initially had additional duties of helping man Batteries Craighill, Leach, and Fuger of the seacoast armament as well as the 75 mm guns of the beach defense. When it appeared that the Japanese were planning to launch amphibious attacks on some of the harbor forts, a substantial portion of the composite naval battalion at Mariveles was transferred to Corregidor and Fort Hughes. While most of the battalion went to Fort Mills for beach defense duty, the aviation company and the headquarters company of the battalion went to Fort Hughes. These reinforcements enabled Battery I to focus on AA defense alone. About that same time, the Fort Hughes garrison was augmented with a detachment of marines under Maj. Stuart W. King that took over the beach defenses as well as augmenting the AA machine gun defenses of the island. The Japanese artillery on Cavite that opened fire on the island February 6, 1942, inflicted no casualties or serious damage on Fort Hughes. While Fort Hughes was bombed sporadically beginning April 10, the aerial bombardment had no serious effect on the island's defenses. Not until April 12, 1942, when Japanese artillery on Bataan opened fire on Fort Hughes would the first casualties be inflicted in Battery I.[556]

During the course of the siege, Fort Hughes was bombarded by Japanese artillery at times but did not receive the severe pasting given to Corregidor. One mortar pit of Battery Craighill was badly chewed up by fragments. Eventually, all four mortars could be fired but one could not be returned to the loading position. After the fall of Bataan, the crews of the gunboats USS *Luzon, Oahu*, and *Mindanao* were transferred to Fort Hughes, where *Luzon's* crew manned Battery Gillespie and in all probability the 155 mm gun of Battery Hooker. *Oahu's* crew manned Battery Fuger and Battery Williams, the pair of 155 mm guns at the island's eastern end. *Mindanao's* crew provided a manning detachment for one of Battery Craighill's mortar pits and augmented the beach defenses. The crew of the minesweeper USS *Finch* was also sent ashore at Fort Hughes.[557]

Fort Frank

Shortly after the opening of hostilities with Japan, Maj. Will K. Stinnis arrived to assume command of Fort Frank. Stinnis was advanced to lieutenant colonel in January 1942. With the abandonment of Fort Wint at Subic Bay, its commander, Col. Napoleon Boudreau, 92nd C.A., was reassigned to relieve Stinnis in command of Fort Frank about December 31, 1941, and would command there until the surrender. Battery F, 91st C.A., manned the island's seacoast batteries: Battery Koehler's 12-inch mortars, Crofton and Greer's one 14-inch gun each, Battery Frank's four 155 mm GPF guns, and three 75 mm field guns for beach defense. [558]

Fort Frank came under enemy aerial attack in early January 1942, but little damage was done by the Japanese bombs. Battery E, 91st C.A., frequently fired on Japanese aircraft that were conducting raids on the other fortified islands. Another minor attack by two enemy medium bombers came on March 2, but again no

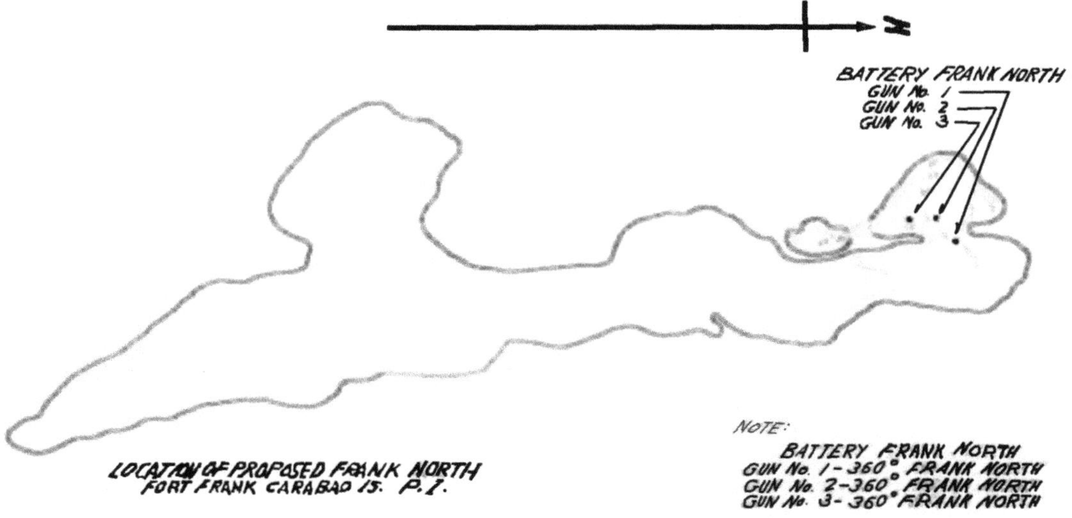

Plan of Fort Frank showing the location on the island's northern end of Battery Frank North for 155 mm guns on Panama mounts. NARA.

damage was suffered and Battery E claimed a hit on one plane. The greatest threat to Fort Frank would come not from Japanese bombs, but from the enemy's artillery hidden in the Cavite hills. On January 31, 1942, Battery Koehler's mortars fired 30 rounds at an enemy concentration near Ternate in Cavite and an additional 36 rounds of 155 mm were fired by Battery Frank (North) in an attempt to disrupt Japanese operations.

Fort Frank suffered only slight damage from the Japanese bombardment until mid-March, when the enemy began using 240 mm howitzers in their bombardment. Heavy Japanese fire on March 15 fell on Fort Frank's AA battery, knocking out all four 3-inch AA guns, and the altimeter received a direct hit. Two guns were permanently destroyed but the other two were repaired and placed back in service, although without adequate direction. Battery Frank also received disabling fire from Cavite that wrecked the Panama mounts, reducing the 155 mm battery's effectiveness to a single gun. On March 16 a 240 mm projectile hit at the junction of the vertical wall and emplacement floor at Battery Koehler, penetrated 18 inches of concrete, passed under a six-foot concrete slab and exploded under the powder room. The floor was broken up and 60 cans of powder overturned but none was set off. By the next day, Koehler's mortars were back in action bombarding enemy positions on the Cavite mainland.

On March 21, the Japanese bombardment of Fort Frank intensified when several hundred 240 mm and 105 mm shells struck Carabao Island in an attempt to silence Batteries Koehler and Crofton. While no guns were hit, there were a number of hits within the emplacements. One 240 mm round penetrated the roof of the Crofton tunnel where the earth cover was only three feet thick. A large number of Philippine Army enlisted men were awaiting inoculations outside the dispensary, 28 men were killed outright, six more would die of their wounds, and an additional 40 were wounded. The hole in the roof was soon repaired.[559]

Fort Frank continued to receive heavy bombardment from Cavite in March and April and Colonel Bunker, concerned the island might succumb to the Japanese onslaught, recommended removal of the breechblocks from Batteries Greer and Crofton as both batteries could in Japanese hands be used to fire on the other fortified islands. Nothing came from this recommendation fortunately, as Battery Crofton's 14-inch gun was the only seacoast gun to engage a blockading Japanese warship. Battery Greer was out of action, having had an elevating rack broken by Japanese artillery when a pair of Japanese destroyers came within range of Fort Frank in late April 1942, Battery Crofton fired, bracketing them with the first two rounds, and the destroyers quickly moved out of range.[560]

Fort Drum

In the final days before war broke out, a detachment of Headquarters Battery, 2nd Battalion, 59th C.A., and Battery E, also of the 59th C.A., constituted the 240-man garrison of Fort Drum. Capt. Lewis S. Kirkpatrick was promoted to major in January 31, 1941, and the following month assigned command of the 2nd Battalion and placed in command of Fort Drum in June 1941. Upon the outbreak of hostilities Kirkpatrick oversaw clearing the fort's upper deck for war. The wooden barracks occupied by the garrison in peacetime was emptied of the soldier's possessions, dismantled, and pushed over the side, and the troops moved inside the concrete battleship. On December 19, Kirkpatrick was promoted to lieutenant colonel.[561]

That the fort had a dead zone in its rear was common knowledge to nearly everyone, including the Japanese who, after occupying Manila, seized a large number of harbor boats and barges in Manila Bay. The fort's vulnerability to an attack from the rear became a serious concern and measures were taken to resolve the situation. In January 1942, an M1903 3-inch gun of Fort Frank's Battery Eli D. Hoyle in storage at Fort Mills was moved to Fort Drum, where the gun and its pedestal mount were emplaced on the fort's "stern" to cover its rear approaches. As it happened, mounting the gun came none too soon. On January 13, 1942, a double-decked inter-island steamer commandeered by the Japanese was spotted traveling down the bay from Manila in the direction of Ternate on the Cavite shore. Unaware of the fort's newest addition, it had drawn as close as 9,000 yards by 1430 when the gun's manning detachment opened fire with the 3-inch gun, installation

Casemates for two 6-inch Model 1908 guns of Battery Roberts on the flank side of Fort Drum. On the opposite side of the fort was a similar dual emplacement of Battery McCrea. Bolling Smith Collection.

which had been completed only that morning. The first six rounds were off the target but caused the vessel to adopt a rapid reversal of its course. Rounds 7 and 8 were close enough to throw water on the steamer's decks. Round nine struck the vessel's stern on its lower deck and the final round fired fell just short of its target as the Japanese vessel rapidly opened the range.[562]

Japanese Artillery Bombards the Fortified Islands from Cavite

Although aerial bombing paused by the end of January 1942, the next Japanese threat came from a new direction. Enemy operations between the barrios of Ternate and Sapang were reported by American civilians formerly employed at the Cavite navy station. This activity consisted of artillery positions of the *Kondo Detachment,* commanded by Maj. Toshinori Kondo and made up of four 105 mm and two 150 mm guns of the *22nd Field Artillery,* supported by troops of the *16th Division* near Ternate. This concentration of artillery was designed to interdict communications between Corregidor and Southern Luzon. The enemy was in fact preparing artillery positions from which they would begin a bombardment of the fortified islands. This news prompted General Moore to authorize bombardment of the suspected positions. Colonel Boudreau at Fort Frank was directed to open fire on the Japanese preparations at Ternate. Beginning at about 1715 Battery Koehler opened fire with its 12-inch mortars using 670-pound HE shells. Over the span of an hour, Battery Koehler dropped some 16 rounds into the barrio area before shifting fire to a hill where the Japanese were suspected of digging a tunnel, expending an additional 14 rounds.

In addition to the mortar fire, Battery Frank's four 155 mm guns also entered the fray, initially firing shrapnel but shifting to high explosive after several rounds fell short. Thirty-six rounds of 155 mm were expended which combined with the mortar fire "seemed to raise hell," in Colonel Bunker's opinion, around Ternate. Hindered by the ravines and hills that defiladed the Japanese positions, and coupled with an absence of effective spotting data, Fort Frank's fire was frequently considered less effective than desired. Nevertheless, by February 3, the combined mortar and GPF fire from Fort Frank had caused the Japanese to largely evacuate Ternate and the neighboring Sapang Barrio. During the ensuing weeks the GPFs of Battery Frank (North) at Fort Frank fired on the Ternate area as well as the eminence known as "Tunnel Hill."[563]

While results were somewhat mixed, the counter-bombardment seemed to disrupt the Japanese operations at least temporarily. Fort Frank's counter-bombardment notwithstanding, the Japanese artillery was not silenced and continued to shell Fort Frank with their 105 mm guns. Their bombardments began as the sun was rising, hindering the American fire control observers' ability to spot the flash of the enemy guns. Thick haze over much of Cavite also inhibited observation of Japanese positions.[564]

Prior to February 6, 1942, no enemy action was taken against Fort Drum. On that date however, the bombardment of Fort Drum by the *Kondo Detachment* from Cavite commenced with their 105 mm and 150 mm guns. From near Ternate they began blasting away at Fort Drum at 0820 on February 6. Lieutenant Colonel Kirkpatrick at Fort Drum ordered a response with Battery Hoyle's 3-inch gun. When Bunker heard Drum was shooting back, he queried Kirkpatrick as to his authority for firing. Kirkpatrick replied, "Why, some son of a bitch is firing at *me*!"[565]

Counter-battery fire was returned by Batteries Koehler and Frank (North) on targets in and around Ternate; all without any known results. One of Koehler's 12-inch mortar shells exploded as it left the muzzle in the forenoon of February 6 seriously wounding Capt. Robert J. White, the commander of Battery F and killing one and wounding seven other scouts. Later in the day, Kirkpatrick received official permission to return fire with the 6-inch guns of Battery Roberts on suspected enemy positions in the hills behind Restinga Point. The effectiveness of Battery Roberts counter-battery fire was adversely affected by its inability to raise its sights to the necessary elevation as the guns had been mounted for firing only on water targets. Additionally, its armor piercing projectiles were unsuitable for land targets. After firing 20 rounds, this counter-battery fire was cancelled. Damage to Fort Drum was minimal beyond the damage to the cage mast that rendered its depression position finder useless, and the destruction of its pair of fixed 3-inch AA guns.[566]

The next day the Japanese shifted their fire to Fort Frank, beginning a daily bombardment from Cavite to which Fort Frank's armament would answer throughout the campaign. While the initial shelling was without visible effect, there were losses. On February 18, a Japanese shell landed in a powder pit of Battery Frank (North) and exploded, wounding seven gun-crew members. The shelling of Fort Hughes on February 6 did little or no damage. Thereafter for many weeks, those seacoast batteries that could fire on the south mainland were in action almost daily, especially those at Forts Frank, Drum, and Hughes.[567]

Major Kondo's detachment in Cavite Province was increased in Mid-February by two Type 96 150 mm howitzers of the *21st Field Heavy Artillery Battalion.* All were emplaced in defiladed positions that were very difficult to locate and the seaward defenses were never sure that they were actually hitting the Japanese guns. In an effort to obtain better intelligence regarding the Japanese batteries' location and to provide spotting data for the seaward defenses, Capt. Richard G. Ivey, from the 60th C.A.'s Intelligence Service, along with a small group of four volunteers, one sergeant and one corporal and two Philippine Scouts, crossed over to the Cavite shore. There they established an observation post on the high ground along Cavite's south coast. When the Japanese batteries fired, Ivey provided data by walkie-talkie to the seaward defenses as to the battery's probable location and provided corrections to the counter-battery fire from the harbor forts. A photoreconnaissance flight by one of the few remaining P-40s coupled with Ivey's radio reports furnished good data at times for the counter-battery fire. Captain Ivey's band of volunteers was driven out of Cavite in the late afternoon of February 12, but on February 13, Ivey was back on the mainland near Batangas to continue spotting for the gun batteries.[568]

The action on February 15 was typical of many in the last half of February 1942. Colonel Braly's diary of operations noted:[569]

3:40 PM-Enemy opened fire on Corregidor from Cavite. Shells falling in vicinity of south dock.

3:52 PM-Batteries Hearn (12" gun) and Hamilton (155 mm guns) on Corregidor and Frank North opened counter-battery.

4:10 PM-Enemy firing ceased.

4:23PM-Captain Ivey (observer on Cavite mainland) reports salvos hitting right in area of enemy gun flashes. He recommends 155s sweep the area. Battery Frank North starting to "sweep."

4:28 PM-Fort Frank under enemy fire.

4:35 PM-Corregidor under fire.

4:55 PM-Enemy ceased firing.

5:15 PM-Enemy firing on Fort Hughes: broke water pipe at Battery Leach 6".

7:00 PM-Battery Frank North completed 139 rounds.

7:11 PM-Fort Hughes again under harassing fire.

9:08 PM-Corregidor under harassing fire.

9:15 PM-Firing ceased.

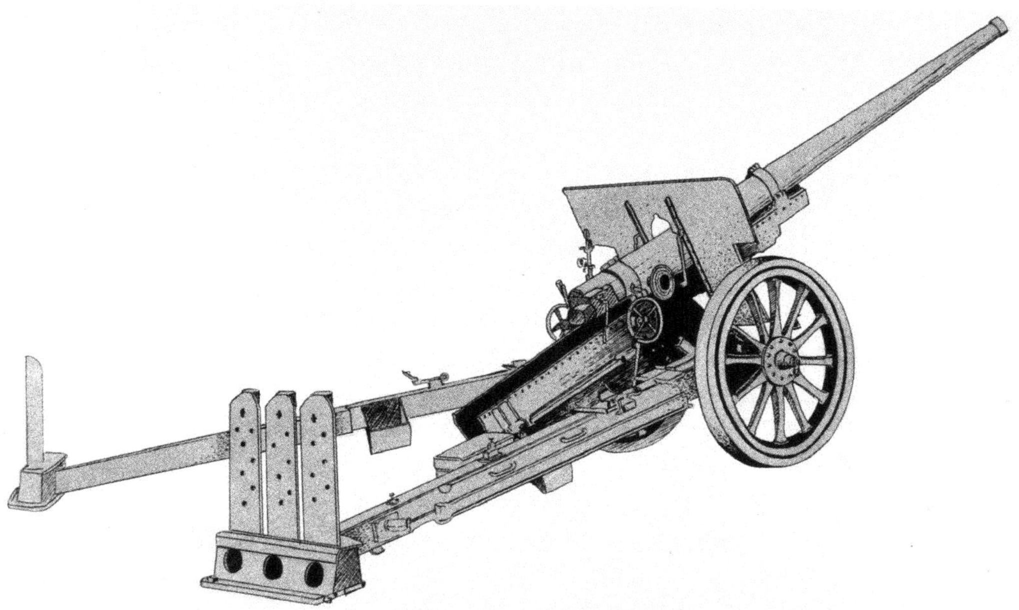

Japanese Type 92 105 mm field gun. First employed in February 1942 against Forts Frank and Drum from the Ternate Shore, this modern piece had a range of 20,000-yards but a shell that was a little light for use against concrete fortifications. NARA.

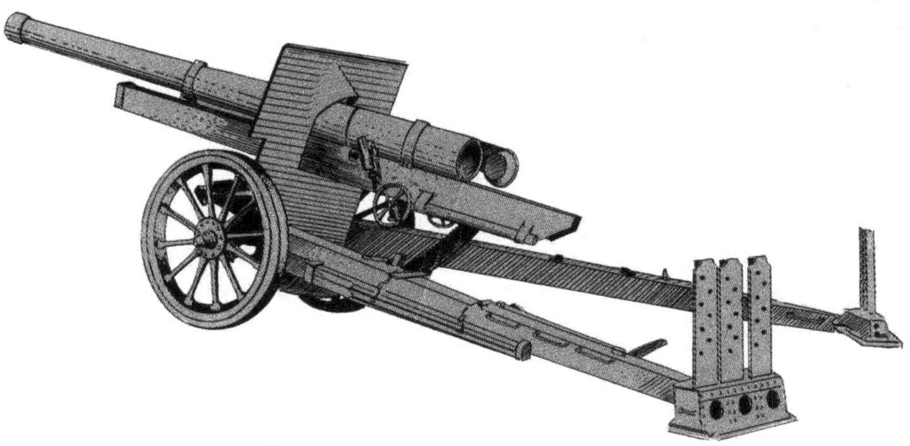

Japanese Type 96 150 mm field howitzer. Used from both the Cavite and Bataan shore, this heavy gun supplied the bulk of the firing on the fortified islands. It fired a 31 kg shell almost 13,000 yards. NARA.

Ivey's assistance to seaward defense command was in Bunker's estimate only marginal, and on February 15, Ivey's small party was attacked by a Japanese patrol. The corporal was killed and a sergeant captured. Ivey and the remaining two scouts managed to escape to Fort Frank. After the fall of Corregidor it was discovered that in many instances on both Cavite and Bataan American counter-battery fire had proven more effective than initially thought.[570]

During the first two weeks of March, the Japanese artillery force was strongly reinforced by the arrival of the *1st Heavy Artillery Regiment* (240 mm howitzers), the *2nd Independent Heavy Artillery Battery* (two 240 mm howitzers) and the *3rd Tractor Unit* with prime movers for the howitzers. The first round fired at Fort Mills that actually hit the island landed in front of Battery Wheeler and was followed by many others. These rounds fired by newly emplaced 150 mm guns would wreak havoc in the days and weeks that followed and the Japanese artillery fire would gradually tear up much of Corregidor. Because the seaward defenses had great difficulty in locating the Japanese batteries in Cavite, in an attempt to counter the Japanese artillery, Colonel Bunker's "Retaliation Fire" was adopted, using selected batteries to open when the enemy guns began firing. By February 13, the "Retaliation Fire" plan had been approved and the first firing was scheduled for 1700. This first retaliatory firing on the Japanese on Cavite, while less than perfect, from the timing aspect, was otherwise generally satisfactory. Whenever the Japanese batteries opened, the seaward defenses would automatically respond: the 155 mm guns of Battery Frank would respond with a single salvo from all four guns and one mortar round from one of Battery Koehler's mortars firing on the battery area at Sapang, and Battery E would fire a salvo of shrapnel from Fort Frank's four 3-inch AA guns of Battery ERMITA at the Japanese positions on Cavite's Restinga Ridge. On Corregidor, Battery South (later renamed Battery Hamilton) would fire a two-gun salvo on Restinga Ridge and Battery Hearn would fire a single round at Naic.[571]

Sometime after midnight February 20 the leased harbor boat *Neptune,* employed as a junior mine planter and harbor defenses supply ship, was approaching the Fort Frank wharf to deliver supplies when enemy fire began landing nearby causing the vessel to withdraw. Later, about 0335 *Neptune* again approached the wharf and Japanese fire resumed. This time a Japanese shell struck on her forward deck that was loaded with gasoline drums and 500 powder charges for Battery Frank's 155 mm guns. The gasoline, some of which was needed to operate the searchlight power plants, was set afire and the powder exploded quickly, turning *Neptune* into an inferno that resulted in her total loss. Burning powder was thrown all over Carabao Island, starting numerous small fires. No casualties resulted as the crew jumped overboard and swam to Carabao.[572]

Lt. Col. Valentine P. Foster, the 59th C.A.'s regimental executive, having experienced sound ranging in France in World War I, suggested to Colonel Bunker that a similar flash and sound ranging system be developed to locate the Japanese batteries in Cavite. Although the system was not precise, in Foster's view it was the best that they could get in the situation. Maj. Harry Julian, the 59th C.A.'s regimental supply officer, was given the task of setting up an experimental flash and sound ranging system based on a horizontal fire control system to calculate distance between the "flash" and the "bang" when a Japanese gun was fired. Julian established one of his stations aboard the wrecked inter-island steamer *San Jose* grounded on Hooker Point at the end of Corregidor's tail. The second station was located at Battery Wheeler. After Japanese batteries were positioned on Bataan, additional stations were established on Morrison Hill and in the mine command observation post on Malinta Hill in an attempt to locate enemy batteries on Bataan.[573]

Most of the Japanese artillery fire from Cavite was directed at Forts Drum and Frank, with Fort Hughes and Fort Mills being subjected principally to harassing fire. Fort Frank received an increase in its garrison when Battery D, 2nd Philippine Coast Artillery, with four officers and 86 enlisted men, was sent to Carabao Island on February 12 and its personnel attached to Batteries E and F, 91st C.A.

When the Japanese destroyed the water line supplying Fort Frank on the afternoon of February 16, Colonel Boudreau ordered the water distillation plant put in operation and a plan was developed to repair the water line. On the morning of February 19, Boudreau sent a 15-man volunteer work detail across to Calumpan Barrio on the Cavite mainland to repair the fort's freshwater pipeline. While the party was working on

Japanese Type 45 240 mm howitzer. Ten of these monsters were used by two heavy Japanese artillery units to bombard the forts first from the Cavite shore (February and March 1942) and then from Bataan after its fall in early April 1942. NARA.

the pipeline, they were attacked by a Japanese patrol numbering between25 and 30. With the aid of 75 mm beach defense guns on Fort Frank, the work party managed to kill all the Japanese and suffered only one man wounded. The pipeline was cut again and repaired yet again in early March until finally the flow of water was ultimately stopped. Still, for several weeks the fort's garrison had substantially eased the water problem.[574]

As the result of wholesale promotions in the 59th and 60th C.A. in December 1941 and January 1942 (nearly all officers were advanced one grade), an oversupply of colonels resulted on Corregidor. Colonel Foster, the regimental executive of the 59th C.A. was sent to Caballo to take command at Fort Hughes. Tactical command and control of Fort Hughes batteries was directed from Corregidor. On February 22, Col. Armand Hopkins reported the newly constructed battery of two 155 mm guns on the island's east end near Battery Leach completed and ready for action. This battery was named Battery Williams, in honor of 1st Lt. George L. Williams, killed in action in Abucay, Bataan. A third emplacement for a 155 mm gun designated Battery Hughes was begun on Caballo's hogback ridge near Battery Gillespie shortly after the commencement of hostilities.[575]

Initially Fort Drum had been taken under fire by the 105 mm guns on Cavite with virtually no effect beyond damage to the cage mast and the AA battery. By mid-March, the Japanese began using the 240 mm howitzers of the *1st Heavy Artillery Regiment* and *2nd Independent Heavy Artillery Battery* to bombard Drum and the other island forts. These howitzer shells had a really "wicked burst." Lieutenant Colonel Kirkpatrick, commanding Drum, noted that when a howitzer shell struck, the whole fort rocked. On March 17, a round from a howitzer hit near the No. 1 casemate of Battery Roberts and broke through into the casemate, knocking out the gun and taking the entire battery out of commission temporarily.[576]

Throughout March and April 1942, Bunker's seaward defenses increased their counter-battery fire on the Japanese in Cavite using Battery Woodruff's 14-inch gun at Fort Hughes, Battery Hearn's 12-inch long-range gun at Fort Mills, and Battery Frank (North)'s 155 mm GPF guns. An experimental firing on the Japanese at Cavite was carried out by Battery Craighill at Fort Hughes using AA fuzes on the 700 pound 12-inch mortar shells without any visible results. A second experiment proved to be a bit more effective. By removing the.05-second delay pellet from the base fuzes of the mortar shells, an instantaneous detonation could be attained. This conversion increased the number of projectiles that could be used against land targets.[577]

8-inch Gun Is Emplaced

In February of 1941 General MacArthur initiated the Inland Seas Project to defend and seal-off various straits separating the central islands of the Philippine Archipelago with guns, searchlights, and mines. It was to depend on Philippine Army troops operating equipment secured from the U.S. under deferred purchase. Twenty-four 155 mm GPF guns and seven 8-inch Model 1888 coast defense tubes on top carriages Model 1918 were supplied for this project in June 1941. The soldiers began training at both Fort Mills and Fort Wint, and the sites were surveyed, but there was not time for much else.[578]

An American 8-inch Model 1888 gun on Model 1918 top carriage for railway mount emplaced in a fixed barbette carriage. This gun was mounted on Oahu, but a similar emplacement was built at road junction 43 (RJ-43) at Fort Mills. Unfortunately, no photos of the Corregidor gun are known to exist. Williford Collection.

At the start of the war the 155 mm guns were gladly taken over as additional field artillery. The 8-inch guns, supplied with a sort of upper carriage barbette that had originated as railway artillery, were not very mobile or immediately useful. Five were destroyed during the retreat to Bataan, but two survived. One was emplaced at Saysain Point on the western Bataan shore and actually saw a little action before being destroyed prior to Bataan's surrender in April. The seventh and final gun made it to southern Bataan in December. It was decided to emplace it in a new, open concrete pad at Fort Mills.

By late February 1942, the construction of a barbette emplacement just east of Malinta Hill was underway. This gun, an M1888MIIA1 and its M1918 barbette carriage, was shipped by barge to Corregidor, where it was landed on the north mine wharf in February 1941. The gun and its carriage were moved to a position east of Malinta Hill and emplaced early in March near Road Junction 43 (hence its informal name of Battery RJ-43). The gun had a range of 24,000 yards, placing both Bataan and Cavite within its field of fire. The gun was proof fired by ordnance personnel March 4, but the gun was never placed in service as no manning detachment was assigned. The emplacement was covered with a camouflage net and left to await a manning detail that was to be provided from among the forces projected for evacuation from Bataan.[579]

Attempts to Resupply the Harbor Defenses

As early as January 1942, measures were taken to get food and medical supplies from Australia and the Netherlands East Indies to Bataan and Corregidor. Running the Japanese blockade of Manila Bay proved almost impossible. Nevertheless, the army embarked on a significant effort to acquire several acceptable cargo vessels and crews in Australia and Netherlands East Indies to carry supplies to the Philippines. The first of these vessels, SS *Coast Farmer*, was loaded and readied for sea by February 10. Before the end of the month seven more vessels were either en route or scheduled to sail within days for either the Philippines or to staging points in the Netherland East Indies. On February 19, two vessels were discovered by the Japanese and bombed. The MV *Don Isidro* was left a disabled hulk and SS *Florence D* was sunk. Only the original freighter *Coast Farmer* and the coasters *Dona Nati* and *Anhui* managed to make the voyage to the Philippines, arriving at Mindanao or Cebu in late February or early March 1942. All other efforts to resupply the Philippines by surface ship from Australia failed.[580]

Some success was achieved using small inter-island vessels transporting relatively small cargos from the army's large quartermaster depot at Cebu to Corregidor. The 1,000-ton inter-island steamer *Legaspi* was the first of these small vessels to make the trip safely from Panay, arriving at Corregidor on January 22, 1942. She made a second journey in February and had embarked upon a third voyage with supplies for Corregidor when she was sunk off the north coast of Mindoro by a Japanese gunboat. In February, the inter-island steamer *Princessa* made the voyage to Corregidor with about 700 tons of food. *Coast Farmer's* cargo was transferred to the *Elcano* and *Lepus* at Mindanao. *Elcano* managed to make the trip to Manila Bay safely, but *Lepus* was captured off Palawan February 28. Ultimately, all the vessels were sunk, captured, or scuttled by their crews to avoid capture. The navy's submarines and the army's aircraft would carry out any further success with resupply.[581]

Submarine Operations in Support of the Harbor Defenses

Concerned by inadequate stockpiles of food and ammunition on Corregidor as early as January 1942, General MacArthur requested that U.S. submarines be employed to run the Japanese blockade of Manila Bay to bring in supplies for his faltering defense of Bataan and Corregidor. Despite the misgivings of both Admiral Hart and Capt. John Wilkes, the Asiatic Fleet Submarine Force commander, for whom the highest priority remained stemming the Japanese advance southward, a number of submarine relief missions were agreed to, if only as a morale-boosting gesture.

USS *Seawolf* undertook the first of these relief missions. Carrying only eight torpedoes in her tubes, *Seawolf* arrived at Corregidor on January 27 with 700 boxes of .50-caliber machine-gun ammunition and 72 3-inch antiaircraft shells. Upon being guided in through the defensive minefields by a PT boat, *Seawolf* off-loaded her cargo of ammunition. For the return trip, the sub took onboard 16 torpedoes from the stocks in storage in the navy's Roger Tunnel at Malinta along with a quantity of submarine spare parts from the submarine tender *Canopus*. Twenty-five passengers slated for evacuation, equally divided between navy and army personnel, were embarked aboard *Seawolf*. She then set her course southward to Surabaya, where the torpedoes and spare parts were made available to U.S. submarines based there.[582]

The most urgent supplies initially requested by the Filamerican forces were ammunition types in critically short supply. Among them were .50-caliber machine gun and 3-inch antiaircraft rounds and particularly the mechanical fuzes for the latter. Also requested at the end of January were one complete M4 antiaircraft director and a long list of parts and cables to repair and allow other directors to continue to function. Towards the end of the campaign the requests ominously changed to foodstuffs and key medical supplies. Precious little of anything managed to make it through.

A second submarine, USS *Trout*, reached Corregidor February 3 after traveling from Pearl Harbor with 2,700 rounds of 3-inch HE antiaircraft ammunition provided with mechanical fuzes and 400 more rounds with powder-train fuzes. After the munitions had been unloaded, 10 torpedoes were taken onboard. The sub was still too light to be trimmed adequately and 25 tons of ballast was requested. Two tons of gold bars and 18 tons of silver coins from the Philippine gold and silver reserves valued at $10,000,000 were taken aboard as ballast along with about 100 bags of securities, mail, and dispatches. *Trout* departed the south wharf around 0230 February 4, and lay on the bottom of Manila Bay until that night when she again surfaced to take on additional securities and mail from a launch. The sub was then escorted through the Boca Chica minefields into the open waters of the South China Sea and departed for Pearl Harbor. The mechanical fuzes were an important improvement over the older style with which the AA batteries were equipped, giving the guns an ability to reach 32,000 feet as compared with the powder-train fuzes that allowed only an altitude of 24,900-27,000 feet. The mechanically fuzed AA rounds were distributed to Batteries B and C of the 60th C.A., whose guns were emplaced on the heights of Topside.[583]

The next submarine to reach "the Rock," USS *Seadragon,* arrived off Corregidor the day after *Trout* departed and entered Mariveles Harbor. That night under enemy artillery fire, working parties took on one and one-half tons of cryptographic matériel, from the navy's Monkey Point intercept facility. Then, 25 passengers, 19 of them cryptographic personnel, were embarked, and *Seadragon* departed for Surabaya, arriving there on February 13.[584]

The next two Corregidor missions, two visits in quick succession by *Swordfish*, were also primarily for the evacuation of personnel, but this time at the highest official level. *Swordfish* picked her way through the minefields on February 19 and entered Mariveles Bay, rearmed with 13 torpedoes, and took on 44,900 gallons of diesel oil from a fuel barge. She then lay at the bottom until darkness on February 20 when she surfaced and moved to Corregidor. After mooring to the south mine wharf, *Swordfish* embarked Philippine President Manual L. Quezon, his wife, son, and two daughters; Vice President Osmena; Chief Justice Santos; and Philippine Army General Valdes, Colonel Nieto, and Chaplain Captain Ortiz. Departing that night, the Quezon party was safely transferred to a motor launch on February 22 at the still-unoccupied island of Panay, 300 miles south, from which they completed their escape. On February 24, *Swordfish* returned to Corregidor and while lying to at the turning buoy, rendezvoused with a launch and embarked High Commissioner Sayre and a party of 12, plus a handful of navy code breakers from Station C. *Swordfish* successfully transported this group to Fremantle, Australia, arriving there March 9.[585]

When the Netherlands East Indies were lost to the Japanese, the U.S. high command ordered General MacArthur out of the Philippines, and the original mission plan to retrieve him was assigned to USS *Permit*, ordered north to Corregidor from the Java Sea on February 22. At the last moment, however, the evacuation of MacArthur's party was entrusted to four PT boats, which left the "Rock" on March 11. *Permit* was ordered to rendezvous with the PT flotilla at Panay on the March 13 but found on arrival there that the general had already moved on to Mindanao, from whence he made his final escape to Australia by air. Seven survivors from one of the "MacArthur" PT boats, which had broken down at Panay were taken aboard *Permit*.

Because of the danger of compromising the extraordinary intelligence source should the enemy capture the Cryptologic unit on Corregidor, the U.S. high command placed a top priority on evacuating Station C personnel from the Philippines when the loss of the islands became a matter of time. This became the primary mission of *Permit* when she arrived off Corregidor on March 15. The sub off-loaded all the spare ammunition she had on board, and embarked 47 passengers, including 36 cryptographers and linguists. Including her own crew, *Permit* had 111 people on board the night after leaving Corregidor, when she was overtaken by a column of three Japanese destroyers that *Permit* lost no time in attacking – unsuccessfully – with two torpedoes. To escape the resulting depth-charge attacks, *Permit* was forced to stay down for 22 hours – putting a severe strain on the boat's oxygen supply – but on April 7, *Permit* with her grateful passengers arrived safely in Fremantle, Australia.[586]

At the end of March, USS *Snapper* and *Seadragon*, both on patrols from Fremantle, were ordered into still uncaptured Cebu to pick up loads of food and ammunition for Corregidor. *Snapper* arrived in Manila Bay on the night of April 6 with 46 tons of food and stores on board. USS *Pigeon* rendezvoused with fleet submarine *Snapper* in the Boca Grande channel off Corregidor under the enemy guns where she hurried to offload the supplies *Snapper* had brought before the start of that night's bombing raids. However, the Japanese advances on Bataan were so threatening that the sub was ordered away after unloading less than a quarter of her cargo. Nonetheless, 27 personnel, including the last of the navy's Station C Cryptologic unit, were embarked before *Snapper* put back to sea. Similarly, when *Seadragon* arrived three days later, only seven tons of her 20-ton cargo of food could be transferred to a small boat, before she was ordered away. But 27 evacuees were crammed onboard before she departed. The last submarine to reach the island, USS *Spearfish*, had surfaced in Mariveles Bay to be met by a small boat bearing the last to be evacuated – 26 personnel, including 12 army and navy nurses and two stowaways. In taking *Spearfish* back to sea through the approaches to Manila Bay, the sub was forced to spend nearly a day submerged, dodging enemy ships. *Spearfish* arrived back in Fremantle on May 20.[587]

When Bataan fell on April 9, two additional submarine relief missions had already departed Fremantle for Corregidor: USS *Swordfish* on April 1 and USS *Searaven* on April 2. Because of the extraordinary risk involved in running the Japanese gauntlet and the relatively little benefit they could have provided, both attempts were aborted on April 10.[588]

Antiaircraft Operations January 7 to March 23, 1942

After the initial aerial onslaught on Corregidor by the Japanese, the island fortress generally received a respite from the bombing between January 7 and March 23. While there were some 48 air raid alerts during this period, most raids were against Bataan; only on two occasions, January 14 and March 2, did the Japanese actually conduct aerial operations of any importance against the harbor forts. This break in the action enabled the garrison to further improve its defenses, digging in and preparing for a renewal of Japanese attacks.[589]

One of the improvements made came in late January 1942 when a water-cooled navy "pom-pom" gun, a 1.1-inch quadruple automatic weapon, was emplaced atop Malinta Hill. Recently an older model 1.1-inch mount had been replaced on USS *Houston*, and was available for the use of local forces. Surviving the attack of December 10, this spare mount had been brought on December 17th by lighter, first to Mariveles and then to Corregidor, where it was turned over to the army to augment the island's low-altitude AA defenses. Fortunately, it came with 25,000 rounds of ammunition of a tracer type that could provide at least some semblance of fire direction. A salvaged Crosley automobile engine powered a small boat pump that ran the rapid-fire AA gun's improvised water-cooling system. A detachment from Battery M, 60th C.A., commanded by 1st Lt. Stanley O. Friedline and trained by a navy gunner, was assigned to man the quad-mount.[590] While the gun was not yet operational for the late December bombing, it was in action for the first time on February 11, 1942. It was only fired a few times but filled in nicely at ranges between 3000-5000 feet. The gun was knocked out late in the campaign and was apparently scrapped by the Japanese during their occupation.

A shipboard navy 1.1-inch quadruple antiaircraft mount. Just beginning to be installed on American warships in 1941, a spare mount was found at Cavite in late 1941 and made available for mounting at the top of Malinta Hill, Fort Mills. NARA.

The wrecked 1.1-inch naval AA mount as found by the Japanese immediately after the campaign. Gasei, Philippine Expeditionary Force.

On March 6, a Japanese plane flew over Fort Frank several times and Battery E, 91st C.A., opened fire and believed they shot it down. During the Japanese shelling of Fort Frank on March 15, all four 3-inch AA guns manned by Battery E were damaged, two beyond repair. With the fort's AA defenses so reduced, the battery was no longer able to adequately cope with any further air raids. Fortunately, the January 14 air raid was the last aerial attack the Japanese made on Fort Frank. However Japanese artillery emplaced on Restinga Point on the Cavite mainland would continue to prove very troublesome to Colonel Boudreau's command on Fort Frank.[591]

During the lull in the bombing in January, February, and March, the machine gun batteries used the respite to improve their positions. Battery I's 12 .50-caliber machine guns had established their positions on Morrison Hill and at Battery Cheney on November 29, 1941. The battery command post and a two-gun section were located in front of the G_4 command post on Way Hill, adjacent to two of the abandoned AA towers. A second section was set up near Wheeler tunnel, a third section at Battery James, a fourth section near the towers at the rifle range, a fifth section near towers at Battery Morrison, and a sixth section in front of Battery Grubbs. Another section initially posted at Ordnance Point on the island's tail was moved to Wilson Park Ridge in support of Battery D, 60th C.A. A platoon of the 4th Marines with six .50-caliber machine guns on tripod mounts was attached to Battery I. Four of the guns were deployed to the position occupied by Battery F at Battery Cheney and the nearby peacetime AA firing point; the other two .50-caliber machine guns were positioned at the east end of the Topside parade near the baseball grandstand. Battery I improved their positions at Topside by building tunnels at Rock Point, Battery James, and Battery Wheeler for their equipment, supplies, and personnel. Those units located close to the AA magazines built in the early 1920s made good use of those reinforced concrete underground bombproof structures.[592]

When Battery L went into the field on November 29, it established its command post at Geary Point. On January 2, 1942, the battery command post received a direct bomb hit during an air raid, killing Captain

Hamilton and three enlisted men. (Battery South, a 155 mm battery on the island's south shore was renamed Battery Hamilton in his honor). A new command post was established in a cave at Sea Shore Cliff on Breakwater Point by 1st Lt. Charles S. Dronenburger, the battery executive. New tunnels were constructed at the top of Ramsay Ravine near the first road bend on Ramsay Trail and HQ moved from Breakwater Point into Ramsay Ravine Tunnel. The battery's .50-caliber machine gun sections were located at Battery Geary, Lubang Point, above Geary Point, and above Ordnance Point. Another section was attached to Battery H near Battery Ramsay.[593]

Upon its return from Manila via Bataan in early January 1942, Battery M of the 60th C.A. took up its prewar positions on the tail. The 1st Platoon was positioned on Malinta Hill with one section on the hill's summit and the other section on the south side of the hill in an old field gun emplacement. The 2nd Platoon was positioned at its peacetime alert position on the ridge at the west end of Kindley Field and the 3rd Platoon took up positions on the low ridge that extended along the southeast side of field. The battery headquarters and mess moved from east of the navy quarters of Station C to a position just north of the center of Kindley Field in a heavily wooded area. Battery M also underwent changes in its commanding officer and battery executive on January 19, 1942, when Capt. James R. Holmes and 1st Lt. Thomas H. Hackett relieved Capt. Harold B. Wright and 1st Lt. Kenneth W. Ramsay.[594]

Antiaircraft Operations March 24 to April 9, 1942

Beginning on March 24, the Japanese renewed their aerial bombardment of Corregidor. Air raids came from all directions, morning and afternoon, and nearly every night as well. These were delivered by the *60th* and *62nd Army Air Regiments*, a total of six bomber squadrons. They were supplemented with two squadrons of land-based Japanese Navy bombers. Usually two or three squadrons of the *60th Air Regiment* and one Japanese naval squadron conducted its raids from dawn to 1100. A second squadron of naval air continued the raids in the afternoon until about 1500 when the *62nd Air Regiment* took up the bombing as well as conducting the nightly raids that were usually carried out with about three planes. The raids were initially supported by artillery fire from Cavite and by early April, from Bataan as well. Corregidor was the focus of the raids although Mariveles was also bombed regularly until the fall of Bataan. The Japanese planes rarely attacked Forts Hughes and Frank.[595]

On March 24, four raids consisting of 60 planes attacked Fort Mills. "About 0900 observers on Bataan reported heavy bomber formations approaching Corregidor from all points of the compass." Many raids came at 31,000 feet and instead of flying a straight route over the island as in the earlier raids, they maneuvered to avoid the AA fire. The Japanese flights each numbered between 12 and 27 planes. Batteries B and C, 60th C.A., the only AA batteries equipped with mechanical fuzes, did most of the firing at the high-flying Japanese bombers. A bomb dropped on an ordnance magazine on Morrison Hill destroyed the magazine: "Ammunition exploded rapidly showering the vicinity with HE shells (many exploding in air) shrapnel, fragments, even until evening." The personnel of Battery C were required to remain in their bombproofs as the exploding munitions rained down on their battery area. With the coming of nightfall the first night raids began.[596]

The first of these night bombings came about 2200 on March 24, when three heavy bombers came in at 27,000 feet. Searchlight Nos. 7, 9, and 10 of Battery E, 60th C.A., on Bataan picked up the Japanese bombers and Searchlight Nos. 1, 3, and 5 carried them in where they were taken over by Battery A's lights on Corregidor. Three light bombs were dropped near Cheney Ravine while the remaining bombs fell in the water. Later that night a few more bombs were dropped on Bottomside. Over the next 10 nights, the Japanese sent in about three or four raids a night beginning about 2200 or 2230 and ending about 0300.[597]

On March 26, Battery C on Morrison Hill was bombed for first time. Bombs came down all around the director and height-finder positions, but no damage was done to the instruments. The battery's oil shed, an ordnance magazine, a tractor shed, and tractor were all demolished. Communications were cut and Battery C was put out of action for about 30 minutes before communications were restored, enabling the height-finder to again function. In subsequent raids, an ammunition trench was hit and 25 HE shells destroyed. That same day an AA machine gun position of Battery I emplaced at Wheeler Tunnel was struck, killing two men. Out at Kindley Field Battery D also suffered losses when the No. 4 3-inch AA gun was put out of action by a bomb hit that also wounded five men. The gun was repaired that night and placed back in service before midnight.[598]

On March 28 Battery C was bombed again. The meat house and a Ford truck were destroyed. Numerous hits inside the gun square put the battery out of action for four hours. That same day Battery C was also shelled for the first time from Cavite. Eight 105 mm rounds landed within 25 yards of No. 4 gun, and the battery's barracks at Middleside were burned out during the night by incendiary bombs. Battery C claimed it shot down one plane and damaged another.

In the remaining days of March, as many as 27 to 65 planes a day came over at altitudes of 25,500 to 27,900 ft. In addition, as April approached, the sound of battle on Bataan got louder as American forces were pushed back toward the foot of the peninsula. The Japanese changed their tactics at the end of March by sending three-plane flights of Type 97 heavy bombers at altitudes of 28,000 to 30,000 feet and three-plane flights of medium bombers at altitudes varying between 20,000 and 23,000 feet. The day and night bombing soon began to wear down the men on Corregidor.[599]

At about 1600 on March 30, after some five daylight raids, Battery F spotted two twin-engine Japanese heavy bombers coming in quite low about 5,700 yards (17,100 ft.) altitude. Data was called over the battalion data net until all batteries reported on target. Battery F opened fire first quickly followed by Batteries B, H, and C, then everyone opened fire. Both planes were hit. Of the first 10 bursts, one chopped the right wing off one bomber, which burst into flames. It made quite a noise as it fell like a meteor from the sky, a twisting ball of fire, and splashed into the Boca Chica Channel. Hardly a trace remained. The second plane disintegrated in the air in plain view of the gun crews. It fell into Manila Bay off Cabcaben. The 1st Battalion, 60th C.A., received credit for the two planes that may have been carrying some important personages, as the Japanese radio traffic increased immediately after the two bombers were shot down.[600]

The night air raids were conducted between March 25 and April 2. During those nine nights, 21 air raids were carried out. In only six of these raids were any bombs dropped on Corregidor, the powerful searchlight beams of Batteries A and E frustrated the remaining attempts. "The effect of searchlight illumination on these night attackers seemed to be very great. It was seldom that the bombs dropped even hit Corregidor, let alone hitting any specific target. On several occasions the bombers appeared to be greatly upset by being blinded by the searchlight beams, and on one occasion three bombers appeared to be on the verge of collision in mid-air due to being blinded by the intense beams."[601]

Although bombed frequently and heavily in the last days of March, Colonel Bunker's seaward defenses received relatively little damage. Battery Monja, manned by a detachment of Battery B, 91st C.A., was the recipient of at least one stick of bombs that failed to inflict any damage except to deposit a lot of dirt on the tramway of Searchlight No. 4 on Wheeler Point. Another detachment of the same unit manning the 155 mm guns of Rock Point Battery was also heavily bombed with only minor damage suffered on March 29 and 30. The bombing during the siege had managed to set many fires on the island and nearly every wooden building had been burned to the ground along with the gutting of many other more permanent structures such as the Topside and Middleside Barracks, the Topside Cine and the Corregidor Club. Beginning about April 1 and lasting through April 8, the Japanese aerial bombardment was generally confined to Bataan as "wave after wave of light and heavy bombers were operating over the entire peninsula...." Searchlight sections of Battery E, 60th C.A., on Bataan were frequent targets of Japanese planes and while communications lines were frequently cut, they were quickly repaired. On April 4, two flights of nine bombers dropped bombs in the area of Hospital No. 1 on Bataan with some bombs landing within 50 to 75 yards of some of Battery E's, searchlight positions and one landing in the battery motor pool.[602]

An unfortunate casualty during the late March bombings was the storage plant in power plant ravine. A bomb hit on March 28 broke some ammonia pipes in the refrigeration unit. The loss of cooling endangered a large quantity of frozen carabao meat. A special forced issue of 250 quarters was authorized for the Bataan garrison. Unfortunately, damage to wharves and barges needed for the transfer, along with the necessity to operate only during hours of darkness proved too much. Despite best efforts, the delay resulted in the spoilage of much of the precious meat supply. Eventually the cold storage plant was at least partially repaired, though other major breaks in the pipes occurred in mid-April 1942. This same story could be told during the campaign of much of Corregidor's infrastructure — damage due to bombing or shell fire, temporary repairs and partially restored service. At the end the supply of food, water, electrical power, and communications were still functioning, if precariously.[603]

Elements of the Harbor Defenses Return to Corregidor

The men on Corregidor heard the sound of ground action grow nearer in early April as the Filamerican forces were gradually forced back toward the foot of the Bataan Peninsula and their supply base at Mariveles. Maj. Gen. Edward P. King's Filamerican Forces ability to hold back the Japanese advances on Bataan seemed increasingly unlikely as 1942 progressed. In late January 1942 General MacArthur had advised General Moore that when the line on Bataan became untenable it was his intent to withdraw the troops of the Philippine Division on Bataan to Corregidor. Moore was directed to make plans for the employment of the division bolstering Colonel Howard's marines in the beach defenses. He was further instructed to maintain food stocks for 20,000 men on half rations on Corregidor sufficient to last until June 30, 1942. The army and navy watercraft were soon busily employed delivering "mountains of supplies from the Mariveles storehouses" to the Bottomside wharves and hundreds of men from the seaward defenses, many from the 59th C.A., were detailed every night to handle and store the supplies as they arrived at Bottomside.[604]

With the end of the Bataan campaign looming in early April, the planned withdrawal of the American troops to Corregidor was ordered. Battery Hearn began firing road interdiction on Bataan to delay the Japanese advance at 1810 on April 8 and continued this mission until 0500 the next day. On April 8, the Filamerican Forces on Bataan made their last effort to throw back the Japanese invaders. The last of the reserves were committed, but even this augmentation was not enough to stem the Japanese onslaught. By the night of April 8, the Japanese were breaking through the defenses and General King decided to enter into negotiations with the Japanese on the morning of April 9. As the greater part of the Philippine Division was fully committed in action with the Japanese right up to the end, virtually no organized division components could be evacuated to Corregidor. Consequently, it was surrendered with the rest of the Bataan force on April 9. Defending the Corregidor beaches would for the most part fall to the 4th Marines, augmented with a miscellaneous collection of American and Philippine Army coast artillery units, Air Corps, and U.S. Navy personnel, on the island.[605]

At 1600, on April 8, Lt. Col. Howard E. Breitung, commanding the 2nd Battalion, 60th C.A., on Bataan, advised the battery commanders of Batteries E, and G and Battery C, 91st C.A., that their personnel would be used as infantry to establish a new line of resistance that night. However, just as the batteries were preparing to take the field as infantry at 1730, Fort Mills ordered Battery E to be ready to provide illumination that night as usual. At 1830, Colonel Chase called Battery E from his Antiaircraft Command Post in Malinta Tunnel and ordered Maj. William Massello (promoted to major on April 5) to deliver five complete searchlight units to the Cabcaben dock for shipment to Corregidor by 2100. All available battery personnel were placed on this task. At 2330 April 8, all Corregidor units on Bataan were ordered to proceed to the quarantine station dock at Mariveles where water transportation was to be provided to take them to Corregidor. The battery positions were demolished and burned and battery personnel with only a few exceptions made their way through personnel clogged roads into Mariveles.[606]

The truck loaded with the remaining personnel of Battery E arrived at the navy's Mariveles tunnels about 0330 April 9, just as the navy began blowing up their subterranean storage facilities. The truck fell into a large crater in the dark and to make matters more chaotic, a major earthquake began rocking both Bataan and Corregidor. In the midst of the natural and man-made chaos, the men of Battery E ended up walking into Mariveles as the Japanese long-range artillery began shelling the area. The battery personnel finally boarded a vessel at the dock. Upon reaching Corregidor's north wharf about 0600, the battery (about 90 men) was directed by Lt. Col. Robert S. Barr, regimental executive, to go up to the Middleside bombproof tunnel and await orders. There they were given some rest and later in the day a hot meal.[607]

Battery G received word at 2015 on April 8, to evacuate to Corregidor and was instructed to take all range section equipment and ammo, but to leave the guns. Four guns belonging to the 200th C.A. were to be taken instead. At midnight Battery G received orders to destroy their SCR-268 radar, leave all other material behind, and move out immediately. Upon arriving at Mariveles the range finders, supplies, ammunition, and kitchen were placed on the inter-island steamer *Ilocano* along with all personnel except the battery commander and 25 enlisted men. *Ilocano* left for Corregidor at 0500 on April 9. Major Massello and his detachment loaded two of Battery G's guns, a prime mover, and a tractor on a barge, the 200th C.A.'s AA guns having been left at Little Baguio. The barge departed Mariveles at 0610 as day was breaking and arrived at Corregidor at 0700 where Lieutenant Colonel Barr met them. The enemy air raids came as the guns and equipment were being unloaded by Massello's detachment. After being unloaded, the two guns were placed in a concealed position. Battery G personnel spent the greater part of the night of April 9 unloading the cargo and supplies from the *Ilocano* that had been anchored between Corregidor and Caballo Islands after disembarking the battery personnel. Battery G moved into the section of Middleside barracks formerly occupied by Battery K.[608]

Its "stevedoring" duties completed; Battery G was advised by regimental headquarters that its personnel would be distributed among various other AA batteries on Corregidor. Battery G's four-gun sections were temporally assigned to Batteries B, D, F, and H until a new firing position for Battery G could be established near the golf course. The range section was assigned to Battery C. The machine gun and communication sections and cooks were apportioned among the batteries. One small detachment of Battery G was posted in the beach defenses briefly (3-5 days) at Cavalry Point.[609]

During the evening of April 7, Lieutenant Colonel Breitung instructed Capt. John Gulick to have Battery C, 91st C.A., standby as reserve reinforcements for the front while continuing to function as an AA unit. By the evening of April 8, Breitung telephoned to advise Gulick that attempts to stem the tide of retreating troops was hopeless; the break-through had become a rout. At 2100 the battalion commander called again to announce that Headquarters Battery, 2nd Battalion, and batteries E and G were to be evacuated to Corregidor. Gulick was advised that Battery C of the 91st C.A. was to destroy its armament before daylight and obtain the 37 mm and 3-inch AA armament belonging to the 200th. Captain Gulick alerted his battery, explained the situation, and prepared to destroy the equipment. About this time, ammunition dumps in the area began to detonate. The sky flashed oddly with explosions and the air resounded spasmodically with erratic trajectories of exploded particles. An earthquake of medium severity shook the ground for about 10 minutes. About this time, the ammunition dump at Little Baguio was blown up and the navy blew up its tunnels at Mariveles. Gulick learned that a barge at Mariveles was reserved for the 2nd Battalion, 60th C.A., to which Battery C had been attached while on Bataan. Major Massello had informed Gulick that if his battery were to represent itself as part of the 2nd Battalion, it could be evacuated to Corregidor provided it was able to be at Mariveles within two hours. Captain Gulick decided to evacuate what he could and not delay equipment destruction.[610]

Lieutenant A.W. Balfonz Jr. (An Air Corps officer attached to Battery C from the 17th Pursuit Squadron) took the .50-caliber machine guns and crews and the outpost personnel to Mariveles while the remainder of the battery personnel destroyed equipment. The director and other instruments were smashed; the guns were fired minus oil with all parts removed. The small arms were set on fire, the 3-inch ammunition in the tunnels was blown up. By 0600 the battery personnel, some 150 men, had collected on the cut-off awaiting transportation. At length the battery range officer arrived in a passenger car to report that the barge for Corregidor was about to pull out and could wait no longer. No trucks being available Battery C marched to Mariveles as dawn was breaking on April.[611]

Upon arrival at Mariveles the battery found that the barge reserved for the 60th had already departed and only a small launch working for an engineer demolition squad remained. First Lt. Morris L. Shoss, the battery executive, prevailed upon the launch captain to tow an empty barge at anchor in Mariveles Harbor over to Corregidor. Soon the battery, with 202 officers and men along with a miscellaneous collection of other troops, made that last trip, reaching Corregidor just in time for a bombing. Three men had been lost in the evacuation it was discovered when roll was called.[612]

Within a few days Battery C was reassigned to Battery Morrison's pair of 6-inch disappearing guns. This assignment lasted only one day. As soon as the guns opened fire on Bataan, the Japanese unleashed a furious counter-battery fire on Morrison Hill that collapsed a tunnel shelter dug into the hillside behind Battery James, burying 70 Philippine Army personnel that had sought shelter there. Battery Morrison was battered out of action and beyond repair. Battery C then moved to Battery Grubbs. Its two 10-inch guns opened on the Japanese batteries and Grubbs received a drubbing similar to that laid on Battery Morrison. By the end of the day, Battery Grubbs had also been reduced to ruins, its guns no longer serviceable.

From their positions on Morrison Hill, the men of Battery C could see the Japanese breakthrough on Bataan and the resultant evacuation and rearguard actions on April 8, and had seen the last P-40s fly out as ammunition dumps were blown up during the night. The 3-inch guns of Battery James at the foot of Morrison Hill and all the 155 mm guns in positions at the stockade level and on Corregidor's tail that could be brought to bear on Bataan's east coast highway began firing in an effort to interdict the Japanese advance down the Bataan Peninsula. The ominous display of fireworks that could be seen from Kindley Field was spectacular, as the ord-

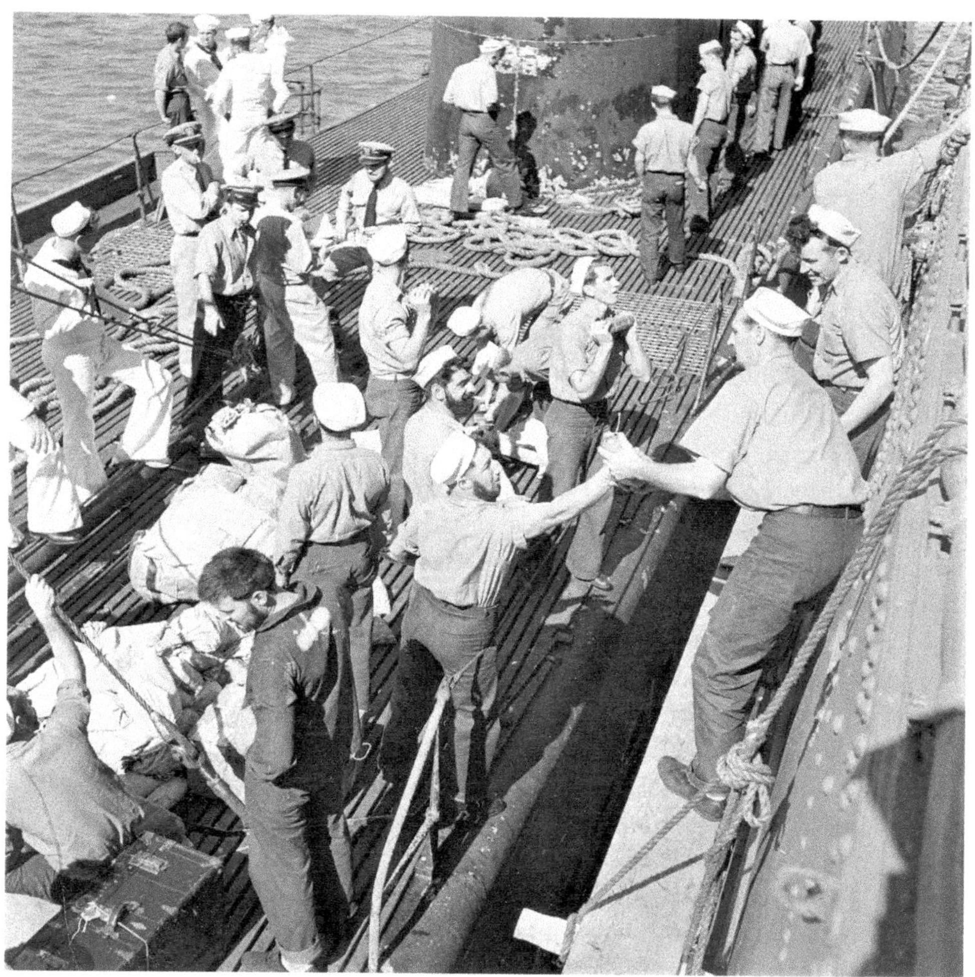

Gold bullion and other currency were transferred from the Philippine Commonwealth to the submarine USS *Trout* at Corregidor on the night of February 3-4, 1942. This navy photograph shows the subsequent transfer to the cruiser USS *Detroit* at Pearl Harbor. NARA.

nance magazine near Little Baguio was blown up. The soon to be surrendered Filamerican troops congregating at the foot of the Bataan Peninsula were clearly visible to men of the 60th C.A. on Kindley Ridge.[613]

Japanese aerial bombardment on Corregidor slackened with the impending collapse of the Filamerican forces on Bataan. The artillery bombardment by the Japanese from Cavite offered little respite to the seaward defenses who continued to counter the fire of the Japanese guns. In addition, as the Japanese pressed forward with their push down the Bataan Peninsula, they finally came within range of Batteries Smith and Hearn's 12-inch guns. At about 2200 on April 8, the two 12-inch guns began laying down interdiction fire on the Japanese advancing along the Limay Road on Bataan, each battery firing about 32 670-pound HE rounds during the night. These rounds were provided with base mounted fuzes from which the .05-second pellets had been removed, giving them an almost instantaneous explosion.[614]

As the boats and barges bearing the various elements of the Fort Mills-based commands continued their evacuation to Corregidor, Battery C, 60th C.A., with its damaged height finder repaired and placed back in service, stood by at its AA positions on Morrison Hill to protect the evacuation fleet crossing from Bataan. However, Japanese planes failed to attack the motley collection of vessels transporting the evacuees to the island.[615]

Anticipating the fall of Bataan, measures were undertaken early in 1942 to preserve as many of the remaining aircraft as possible. An expansion of Kindley Field to accommodate the remnants of the Army Air Corps in the Philippines was started in March by Company A, 803rd Engineer (Aviation) Battalion. This involved grading and leveling of one end of the field and building revetments for the few remaining planes, most of which were P-40s. In light of these improvements, it was necessary to adjust the locations of a searchlight section of Battery A, 60th C.A., and one of Battery M's machine gun sections to accommodate the engineers' expansion of the field.[616]

In addition to the authorized elements of the 60th and 91st C.A. serving on Bataan who were evacuated, an additional 2,000 American and Filipino troops were actually able to cross over to the "Rock" in relative safety. Among these refugees were the 680th and 681st Ordnance Companies, about 80 Philippine Constabulary troops, around 300 U.S. Navy personnel, 900 miscellaneous American and Philippine troops, and 800 civilians who were able to make their way to Corregidor.[617]

In addition to units and foodstuffs, it was planned to transfer certain key weapons to Corregidor from Bataan. An order of April 8 authorized movement of 56 75 mm M1917 field guns, four 155 mm GPF guns, all remaining 37 mm guns available, and all M1 semi-automatic rifles. And ammunition too, of course. As mentioned above, four 3-inch AA guns and one battery of 37 mm AA guns were also desired. Understandably in the resulting chaos of 8-9 April, no conclusive inventory of precisely what made it has survived.[618]

At about 0700 April 9, three Philippine PT-Boats and a motor launch were observed threading the minefield in an attempt to flee Bataan. Believing them to be deserting, Colonel Bunker ordered Battery Guy B.G. Hanna to fire several 3-inch rounds across the bows of the fleeing boats, but they escaped into the South China Sea. Later in the morning, firing was heard to seaward. Japanese fighters and a destroyer had engaged the "deserting" craft and caused the Philippine *Agusan* (Q-113) to return to Corregidor. The four craft had constituted the off-shore patrol during the campaign and its commander Capt. Alberto Naverrette, had planned this escape in the event the forces on Bataan were forced to surrender. Naverette's intention was to flee into the Southern Philippines to continue the fight. The two British-built Thornycroft PT boats *Luzon*, (Q-111) and *Abra*, (Q-112) and the motor launch *Baler* were caught by the Japanese south of Manila Bay and either scuttled or run aground later in the day. Some of the boats' crews eventually managed to join up with guerrilla organizations on Luzon.[619]

The Japanese wasted little time in emplacing artillery on southern Bataan to engage the seacoast batteries on Corregidor. Batteries Rock Point and Hanna fired at eight enemy barges entering Mariveles Harbor, and Battery Rock Point was credited with sinking two. At about 1600 on April 9, a Japanese battery of Type 41 75 mm guns was rushed forward and took up a position on the beach near Cabcaben to bombard Corregidor.

Philippine navy PT boat Q-1 (later renamed as Q-111, or *Luzon*) on trials in Manila Bay on March 13, 1939. The Philippines had an extensive program to acquire a fleet of PT boats for offshore patrol, but only three were obtained prior to combat. MacArthur Memorial.

These Japanese guns opened up on Batteries Kysor, Maxwell Keys, Morrison, James, and Guy B.G. Hanna. The Japanese battery being in plain sight, Battery Kysor's 155 mm guns returned fire, quickly destroying it. Thereafter, the Japanese placed their batteries in defiladed positions not readily visible to the observers on Corregidor. The Corregidor batteries that returned fire in turn received very heavy counter-battery fire from Cabcaben that inflicted considerable damage on the American batteries. The detachment of Battery B, 91st C.A., manning Battery Rock Point on the western end of Corregidor was also taken under fire during the morning from Bataan but suffered no material damage. On the afternoon of April 9, however, a heavier bombardment put the battery's No. 2 155 mm GPF out of action and generally damaged the fortifications and area.[620]

Navy's Inshore Patrol Moves to Corregidor

While the navy's 16th Naval District headquarters was established in its tunnels at Malinta Hill, the majority of the inshore patrol vessels had remained based at Mariveles. In January 1942, several of these formerly based at Mariveles moved to Caballo Bay where they had anchored under the increased protection of Corregidor's AA defenses. While there, they continued to be frequently subjected to inaccurate bombing by the Japanese air forces. When the more accurate artillery bombardment of the islands from the Cavite mainland began, many of the ships in Caballo Bay moved into Corregidor Bay on the Bataan side of Corregidor.

With the fall of Bataan, the gunboats, mine warfare craft, and other vessels that formed the inshore patrol, as well as various other vessels based in Mariveles Harbor, returned to Corregidor Bay where they joined the collection of watercraft that had sought refuge under Fort Mills's guns. After running out of fuel in March, minesweeper USS *Finch* had been anchored in the shallow waters of Caballo Bay and most of her crew taken ashore to man beach defense positions. On April 9, 1942, while moored at the western end of Caballo, *Finch* was damaged by the near miss of a Japanese bomb that opened her seams and pierced her hull with bomb fragments. The remainder of her crew was landed safely and assigned to the beach defenses. USS *Finch* was abandoned to sink the next day. The damaged submarine tender USS *Canopus* was gotten underway and steamed out into Mariveles Bay where she was scuttled. About 0130 on April 9, the scuttling of the tug USS *Napa* was ordered. Most of the crew, with provisions, personal belongings and small arms, were transported, via small boats, to Corregidor Island. *Napa* was then towed 500 yards out from the beach. Her commanding officer and a skeleton crew opened the magazine flood valves and made three openings through the hull in the fire and engine room. At 0500 *Napa* was abandoned. The crew proceeded to Corregidor, from which place they watched their ship remain afloat throughout the remainder of the day and then, finally after nightfall, sink into Manila Bay.[621]

As the waters of Corregidor Bay and the north wharf became subject to direct artillery fire from the newly emplaced enemy batteries on Bataan in April, the minesweeper USS *Quail* swept a channel through the navy contact minefield to provide access around Corregidor's Hooker Point to Caballo and San Jose Bays. She was followed around Corregidor's tail by the river gunboats USS *Luzon, Oahu*, *Mindanao*, the submarine rescue vessel *Pigeon*, the minesweeper *Tanager,* the harbor tug *Trabajado,* the quartermaster's harbor boat *Miley*, and USAMP *Harrison.* These vessels anchored in the waters between Caballo and Corregidor. Most of their crews then went ashore where they were assigned to the 4th Marines to serve in the beach defenses. *Miley* was sunk by Japanese light bombers on April 25, but *Harrison* continued to operate until May 2, when the planter was hit along with other vessels in San Jose Bay about 0915 and set afire. Her master, Chief Warrant Officer James Murray, was killed in the attack.[622]

The two primary harbor defense commanders during the 1941-42 campaign. General George Moore, Commanding General, Harbor Defenses of Manila and Subic Bay (left) and Colonel Paul Bunker, Commander, Seaward Defenses (right). U.S. Army, Pacific, http://www.usarpac.army.mil/history/cgbios/cg_moore.asp and https://www.wikitree.com/photo/jpg/Bunker-1264-1

CHAPTER 15
THE HARBOR DEFENSES UNDER SIEGE

The Bombardment Begins

As Filamerican troops were being evacuated from Bataan, Japanese bombers ranged over both Bataan and Corregidor dropping bombs on various targets. Many bombs intended for land targets landed in the waters off Corregidor, but the numerous boats and small ships moving personnel from Bataan to Corregidor were generally ignored. The gunners of the 60th C.A. rarely fired as the Japanese planes continued to fly at altitudes placing them out of range of the 3-inch AA guns.

At about 1100 on April 9, Battery C, 60th C.A., on Morrison Hill was taken under fire by a Japanese 105 mm gun battery located at Cabcaben. Soon afterward Japanese heavy bombers turned to the congested traffic in the harbor, and after being bombed and set afire the freighter SS *Usang* loaded with 1,500 tons of bombs blew up in a blinding flash. The vessel simply vanished in massive cloud of debris and smoke. The increased artillery fire and bombing made it necessary to move Battery C's kitchen into the battery tunnel. The battery's score for the day was a claim of one plane shot down and another damaged.[623]

That afternoon the enemy batteries in Cavite began firing on Corregidor and Battery Woodruff countered with its 14-inch gun. This caused the Japanese to shift its fire to Fort Hughes and Battery Woodruff. The enemy fire was so accurate that it forced Woodruff's manning detachment to seek cover in the battery bomb-proofs.[624]

On April 11, Battery Morrison opened fire on the enemy batteries on Bataan and promptly received heavy counter-battery fire. Nearby AA Battery C received numerous hits from rounds fired by Japanese at Battery Morrison. Wounded personnel at Battery Morrison's battery command station were taken to Malinta hospital. [625]

By April 11 the remainder of Major Massello's Battery E, 60th C.A., had, with the exception of about seven or eight men, managed to make their way from Bataan and rejoin the battery. Massello sent five of his searchlight sections to operate with Battery A. Knowing that Battery Way's 12-inch mortars were out of service and unmanned, he sought out Colonel Bunker to let him use the remainder of his battery to reactivate the

A 3-inch M3 antiaircraft gun emplacement on Corregidor in January 1942. While an otherwise adequate weapon, there were neither the numbers nor an effective high-altitude fuse available to the defenders. USAMHI.

battery. General Moore approved and over Colonel Chase's objections, the majority of Battery E, 60th C.A., was attached to the seaward defenses with the task of renovating and reactivating Battery Way. A heavy layer of brush grown up around the emplacement had to be removed first. While work was ongoing to make the battery ready for action, the battery personnel begin drilling at Battery Geary under the supervision of that battery's gun crew. On April 23, Battery E moved into Battery Way. The battery kitchen was maintained in Middleside Barracks until space was found in the old radio station near Battery Way.[626]

Battery Way's single pit was armed with four 12-inch, 1890M1 mortars on M1896MII mortar carriages, one of which had been seriously damaged in the December 29, 1941, aerial bombardment and had never been repaired. Battery E's diary notes:[627]

> The powder magazine had been emptied when the Battery was being used as the AACP, but had been refilled by us after manning. The projectile rooms were filled with 700 lb. DP, 824 lb. DP, 1046 lb. DP, and 690 lb. personnel projectiles. Battery Way is located almost in the geographical center of the large part of the island of Corregidor, and therefore was one large bulls-eye of the target in all aerial Bombardments. Over the magazines and projectile rooms was some 10' to 18' of reinforced concrete, covered by anywhere from 6' to 10' of hard earth, with small trees and bushes growing on top. Even this amount of overhead cover did not constitute a bombproof, however, for on December 29, 1941, during the heavy bombing of that day a heavy caliber bomb penetrated the dirt covering and enough of the concrete to crack the ceiling in one of the powder magazines. Nevertheless, it was excellent protection against bombs and against all types of artillery fire. The plotting room and officers' quarters, however, had only a cover of about one foot of reinforced concrete with no dirt covering. Living quarters at Battery Way were of necessity crowded and men slept in every available space in the projectile rooms as well as in a concrete covered draining canal which ran under the railroad tracks nearby but which was dry and airy at this time of year. As a matter of fact, practically the whole battery slept out in the open gun pit on most nights until heavy artillery shelling made this practice too dangerous. An unused searchlight power plant furnished us with electric lights and with power to run the ventilating fans which we installed at the back of each projectile room at the entrances to the ventilating shafts, in order to assure fresh air at all times to the sleeping men. Inasmuch as all the permanent observation stations were already manned by personnel of the Seaward Defense Command and since we were to operate directly under their command, it was decided that observation and spotting would be furnished for our battery by C-l. Our plotting board was prepared with a coordinate grid map of the Bataan-Corregidor area and our targets designated by grid coordinates, thereby making it a simple problem to compute firing data. All firing data was by Case III.

In Ramsay Ravine, the command post of Battery L, 60th C.A., was shelled out by Japanese fire from Bataan. This was the third time the battery's command post was forced to relocate because of Japanese bombing or artillery bombardment.[628]

Once they had taken possession of Bataan the Japanese lost little time in preparing for their long-planned landings on Corregidor. Their first requirement was to bring landing craft from their staging point in Subic Bay. This required passing around the Bataan Peninsula, through Boca Chica Channel, and into Manila Bay, an act that would place them directly under the guns of Corregidor during their passage. At 1730 on April 11, a Japanese destroyer was observed near Hornos Point, Bataan, escorting eight 41-foot armored landing craft and shortly thereafter five of these craft rounded Hornos Point making for Mariveles Harbor. Colonel Bunker ordered Batteries Rock Point, Guy B.G. Hanna, and Sunset to open fire on the barges. Although the group was slow to commence firing, three barges were probably sunk. Battery Rock Point was credited with two of them. Battery Sunset alone fired 32 155 mm rounds; the remaining barges turned around and retreated behind Hornos Point.[629]

General Wainwright issued orders to the batteries on Corregidor not to fire on Bataan after the surrender of Filamerican forces for fear of inflicting additional suffering on the prisoners of war. Once the prisoners were gone from Bataan, the orders halting fire were rescinded on April 12. Battery Geary opened fire on a Japanese concentration near Bataan's Lokanin Point, destroying two enemy batteries there as well as an adjacent ammunition dump and a tank park, setting them afire. Japanese counter-battery fire with 75 mm, 105 mm, and

150 mm guns was ferocious. Bunker ordered the 6-inch and 155 mm medium-caliber batteries to counter the Japanese fire that continued all day long. Considerable enemy fire was concentrated on the James and Power Plant Ravines, two projected Japanese landing areas. Battery Kysor's 155 mm guns were a special thorn in the side of the Japanese, who heavily bombarded that battery, killing two men and wounding one officer. Battery Sunset's one remaining 155 mm gun that could bear on Bataan was knocked out of action in the bombardment. Attempts to use the mortars of Battery Craighill at Fort Hughes against the wharf and boats in Mariveles Harbor were only marginally successful. That only served to incite the enemy batteries on the Cavite mainland to open on both Fort Hughes and Corregidor. Two men were killed at Fort Hughes.

Battery Rock Point, manned by a detachment of Battery B, 91st C.A., fired 105 rounds of 155 mm counter-battery fire that day. The Battery Rock Point detachment of Battery B, 91st C.A., was moderately damaged by Japanese bombardment during the day on April 14, and at 2000, the Japanese "suddenly engaged it with furious shelling catching many of the personnel atop the fortifications and exposed all about." Two men were killed, and Capt. William H. Owen and three enlisted scouts were wounded. After a particularly heavy bombardment, the decision was made to move No. 1 GPF to a less exposed location at the Topside Rifle Range. On April 21, that gun was fired for the first time from its new position at the rifle range, expending just nine rounds before it received a barrage that completely wrecked the gun. The second gun at Rock Point was knocked out for a week by a direct hit in a bombardment that also destroyed the command station and telephone dugout.[630]

The AA batteries were also on the receiving end of the Japanese bombardments. The 60th C.A.'s Battery C was augmented on April 12 with 14 men from the 200th and 515th C.A., who had been evacuated from Bataan. At 1100, shells destroyed the kitchen and communications shacks and communication lines were cut up, briefly taking the battery out of action. The battery also received bombardment from 105 mm guns on Bataan from 1050 to 1830 and was shelled out again at 1600. This time the command post was destroyed with 13 casualties including Capt. Godfrey R. Ames, who was wounded. The battery area looked like a WW I no man's land. All artificial camouflage had been ruined. Leaves and branches were blown off trees and others had been reduced to stumps. Throughout April Battery C was unable to fire due to the high altitudes from which the Japanese planes bombed Corregidor.[631]

Crew manning an antiaircraft gun director of the 60th C.A. Regiment on Corregidor, probably dating from January 1942. Gaines Collection.

During the night of April 12, Battery F received a heavy bombardment that set fires, wrecked some personnel shelters and AA machine gun positions, and threatened to set the gasoline reserves and sleeping accommodations on fire as well. In an effort to increase the AA fire at Topside, a new AA battery of three 3-inch guns was established with the two guns that had been brought from Bataan by Battery G and a third supplied by Battery F. These three guns were to be emplaced on the golf course between the Corregidor Club and Battery Geary. They were to be manned by Battery G that was to be reassembled for that purpose. The various detachments of Battery G were brought together on April 15. On the afternoon of April 22, Battery G engaged its first target from the new position near Batteries Wheeler and Geary on Corregidor: a flight of enemy light bombers in the afternoon.[632]

The Japanese bombardment from Bataan continued to take a toll throughout April. The experiences of Battery C on Morrison Hill were typical for the exposed AA battery positions on Topside. On April 13, Battery C was shelled again. Its No. 1 3-inch AA gun was destroyed by a direct hit. The batteries on Corregidor were so clearly visible from Bataan and so accurately zeroed in by the Japanese that whenever the American AA guns were elevated above the edges of their pits the Japanese guns would open fire on the battery. On April 14, Battery C, equipped with mechanical fuzes, was ordered to only fire at planes at high altitudes. Any movement in the Battery C area detected by the Japanese during daylight hours from April 14 to May 6 resulted in a barrage of artillery from Bataan. Personnel had to crawl around to avoid being seen. At night, trenches were dug between gun pits, a new command post, and a director position. The battery was shelled every day. When it

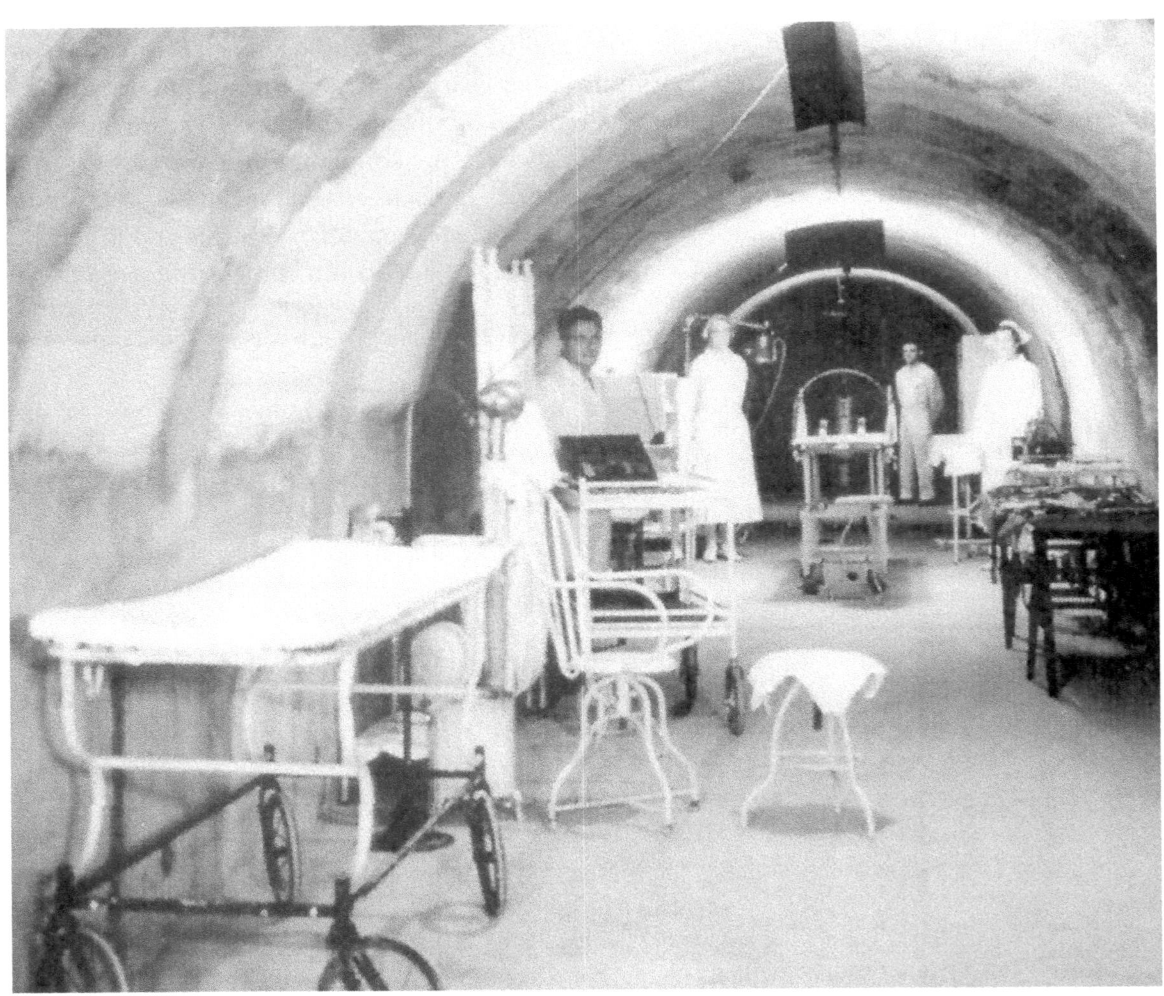

Hospital lateral in the Malinta Tunnel, probably dating from late 1941. NARA.

fired, it brought down an immediate Japanese counter-battery firing with 100 rounds of 150 mm fire mostly and later some 240 mm howitzer fire from Bataan. Sometimes the shelling lasted for four to eight hours. As the month of May approached Battery C made preparations for the coming invasion; fields of fire for the battery's machine guns, Browning Automatic Rifles, and rifles were cleared. Finally, seven .30-caliber machine guns were put in place and foxholes and trenches dug. The battery's tunnel was enlarged.[633]

The area around the 60th C.A.'s Battery F and Battery Cheney had always been a bit bare of vegetation, so the position was easily seen by Japanese observers on Mount Bataan and Signal Hill. As with other AA batteries, the mere elevation of the gun tubes to fire was a signal for the 150 mm guns on Bataan to open on previously registered gun pits. "Hence targets were tracked in azimuth only until the fuze clocks...indicated the time to fire. Then the guns were elevated, fired until the target was out of range and the crew took cover in the outrigger slots." Battery F personnel supplemented Battery Cheney's manning detachment when Cheney fired at targets in the Mariveles area and both batteries messed together. As soon, however, as Battery Cheney opened on Mariveles, the Japanese moved to counter this threat. A battery of Japanese 240 mm howitzers was moved into position behind Sisimán Bay and in concert with a battery of 150 mm guns commenced counter-battery fire. This position enabled the Japanese battery to also target Batteries Monja and Wheeler, as well as Battery F's AA guns with only minor alterations in azimuth. Consequently, all of these batteries were frequently subjected to heavy bombardment throughout the siege.[634]

The AA position adjacent to Battery Ramsay at Middleside was so exposed to Japanese observation that all of its camouflage was blown away and any attempt made to fire invited a furious Japanese barrage. Enemy bombers were usually too high to hit with the powder-train fuzed ammunition with which Battery H's guns were equipped. After each day's bombardment, the men rebuilt the positions' earthen and sandbag walls and added sandbag protection to the entries to Ramsay's magazine galleries that were also in the direct line of sight from Bataan. On April 16, artillery fire from Bataan cut the halyards of the battle flag flying above Topside. Capt. Arthur E. Huff and three enlisted men of the 60th C.A. went to the flagpole and raised the colors back to full staff.[635]

Various administrative functions had to continue to function while quartered inside Malinta Tunnel during the siege. Here finance section personnel work in Lateral 12. NARA.

On Corregidor's tail, the Japanese onslaught was as severe as it was on Topside. There the 60th C.A.'s Battery D continued to receive an almost continuous pasting by the enemy batteries on Bataan. On April 13, a Japanese shell killed 1st Lieutenant George E. Levagood. Losses continued to mount and on April 24 the battery received a debilitating blow from which it would not recover. John H. Brady, who on that day in a battlefield promotion had been promoted from first sergeant to second Lieutenant, and Corporal Rogers were killed when an enemy shell struck the battery observation post atop the Kindley Field water tanks. Morale of the battery plummeted and never recovered. Even assigning a new battery commander failed to rekindle the spark that had been extinguished.[636]

The troublesome fire from the Japanese high-trajectory Type 45 240 mm howitzers that had been bombarding the fortified islands from Cavite slackened around the middle of April, only to return with renewed intensity on April 18 when several batteries of these howitzers opened from Bataan. This fire coupled with artillery of lesser caliber would do far more damage than the months of aerial bombardment.

During the last days of April, the AA batteries on Corregidor were constantly knocked out of action by the artillery on Bataan as the communications lines between the director, height-finder, and guns were being continuously cut. All camouflage had long been obliterated, leaving the AA batteries clearly visible to the Japanese observers on Bataan. Casualties continued to mount. Although repeatedly put out of action, the batteries were repeatedly repaired and returned to action with as little delay as possible. The guns continued to knock down Japanese planes. Light bombers now attacking Corregidor proved to be very inaccurate. However, the enemy planes attacking out of the sun continued to present a major disadvantage to the AA batteries. Picking up aerial targets had become increasing difficult due to intense heat glare and haze adversely affecting vision. Cod liver oil and boric acid obtained from Malinta Hospital was only marginally effective in alleviating the problem.[637]

Gutted interior of the Topside Cine. USAMHI.

Adoption of Roving Batteries

Nearly all of Corregidor was clearly visible to the Japanese on Mariveles Heights, and the American batteries on Topside were being taken out of action at a rapid rate. Colonel Braly suggested that some of the still undamaged 155 mm GPF guns be moved into positions defiladed from Bataan to provide counter-battery fire. General Moore approved the recommendation and defiladed positions were selected for this mission. The guns then could be moved at night between selected positions from which they could engage in counter-battery fire. Three "roving" batteries were formed about April 20. One, made up of a pair of 155 mm GPF guns manned by a detachment of Philippine Scouts of Battery D, 91st C.A., commanded by Capt. John M. Wright Jr., took up position on Topside; one gun at the ordnance machine shop where the north mortar station for Batteries Geary and Way were located and the other at the commissary storehouses south of the lighthouse and signal station. A second battery commanded by Capt. Fred E. Rose, 92nd C.A., had one 155 mm gun that was initially at Bottomside, but later moved to Herring Field at Middleside. Capt. John Gulick, Battery C, 91st C.A., with a pair of 155 mm guns that were initially near the ordnance machine shop, commanded the third of the roving batteries. Gulick's battery was reduced to one piece, however, when one of the guns blew up the first time it was fired. Gulick used General Moore's quarters for his observation post. These roving 155 mm guns soon became the main counter-battery force against the Bataan batteries. In addition to the roving guns, a pair of portable 60-inch AA searchlights was obtained from Battery A, 60th C.A., along with a manning detachment from Battery E of the same unit. These lights were used to illuminate the waters off Corregidor and at daylight were removed to a bombproof shelter.[638]

The Japanese continued their attempts to bring landing craft and barges into Manila Bay. At about 2200 on April 20, an "invasion barge" was observed coming out from behind Hornos Point on Bataan towing two more landing craft. Gun Group 4 observers spotted them in the moonlight. Two searchlights that might have been used to illuminate the enemy barges failed to accomplish that task as No. 3 light had no power and No. 4 light was too slow coming around to cover the target area. As Colonel Bunker recorded:[639]

The Fort Mills Ordnance Machine Shop. One of the original protected buildings on the island, the facility provided a full range of ordnance repair and maintenance capabilities. Roving Battery Wright with 155 mm guns positioned near the shop was one of the final batteries still engaged against the Japanese invasion on May 6, 1942. NARA.

> They headed toward us, passed through the rocks at Cochinos Pt. followed Mariveles boom barrier and, unscathed, entered through our North channel and proceeded towards Manila! Scandalous! I dashed up to C-1-OP and tried like hell to get Kohn's Group 4 to do something about it but they seemed unable to do so. Finally Btry Monja got off a few shots very slowly but the shooting was very poor. Btry Sunset also fired about 3 but they also were wild. The barges finally disappeared around the corner and that was that!

Part of the problem was that the on-carriage sights of the 155 mm GPF guns of Battery Sunset were inadequate for the task as the gun pointers could not see the small targets at night and simply fired at the searchlight beam intersections. Battery Monja had simply fired at Hornos Point with the two rounds that it got off. Battery Grubbs could not see the targets and the enemy craft were outside Battery Hanna's field of fire. All in all, the entire affair was, Bunker recorded, "a great fiasco."[640]

On April 22, an observer at Fort Frank was able to spot a group of enemy landing craft moored to a rock 300 yards southwest of Longoskawayan Point. Once the firing data was verified, Battery Geary fired two salvos of three shots each which Colonel Bunker hoped had dissuaded the Japanese from attempting another run past Corregidor that night. Bunker's bombardment, however, unleashed an enemy counter-bombardment that in turn prompted a retaliation shoot from the harbor forts. The 14-inch turret guns of Fort Drum fired 10 rounds on Cabcaben while Battery Geary loosed four rounds at one battery and six more at another battery on Bataan. Battery Craighill at Fort Hughes dropped 10 rounds on a Japanese position south of Cabcaben while two roving 155 mm gun batteries fired about 100 rounds at an enemy battery on Bataan's south end. With the seacoast searchlights back in action covering Hornos Point, no effort was made by the Japanese to run their barges past Corregidor on the night and early morning of April 22-23.[641]

Artillery Duels

During the early evening of April 23, after an afternoon of bombing by the Japanese, the seaward defenses carried out a substantial fire mission against the enemy batteries and supply dumps on Bataan in an effort to disrupt the Japanese invasion timetable. Battery Monja fired 40 rounds into the Mariveles' quarantine wharf area; Battery Cheney fired six rounds at Mariveles. Battery Wright's roving 155 mm gun expended 14 rounds

Emplacement No. 1 of Battery Crockett. The four heavy disappearing gun batteries on the western side of Topside were all subjected to intensive artillery bombardment during the siege of 1942. On April 24, 1942, Battery Crockett was subjected to heavy enemy 240 mm fire, knocking out the hoists, damaging the guns, and starting a powder fire. USAMHI.

against an enemy position on a road north of Cabcaben. The 155 mm gun of roving Battery Farris (Rose's Battery of the 92nd C.A.) fired 15 rounds on a location on the Cabcaben Road south of that town.[642]

On April 24, a particularly intensive enemy bombardment that included recently emplaced enemy 240 mm howitzers rained down on Battery Crockett, causing several casualties. One 240 mm round struck under the overhang at the rear of No. 1 Emplacement and penetrated the emplacement's rear wall. The hit set the battery office, the storeroom/personnel shelter, and the passageway outside the No. 1 Powder Magazine afire. Fortunately, the fire was extinguished before it could reach the magazines. Other shells penetrated the service platform. The rear of the battery was heavily damaged. The bombardment left the battery a wreck with its No. 1 gun ruined and its elevation arm broken off. The battery's other gun was also inoperable because the ammunition service hoists and trolleys were heavily damaged.[643]

On the morning of April 26, 1942, Battery Way was given its first firing mission. The target was an enemy gun position 10,500 yards away on Bataan. Battery E was instructed to use 700 lb. projectiles with the .05-second delay pellet removed — making the fuzes instantaneous. The battery's three serviceable mortars (Mortar No. 1 had been out of service since December 29 when it was struck by an aerial bomb) were fired and the C_1 station reported that they were on target and ordered four more salvos that destroyed the enemy battery. However, the sudden firing of Battery Way brought forth a massive response from the Japanese, who covered Battery Way with a heavy shelling. Over the next several days, Battery Way continued to fire missions. [644]

The waning days of the siege became increasingly hazardous to the coast artillerymen on Corregidor. As the artillery degraded the AA defenses, the Japanese bombers began flying at lower altitudes, dropping 500 kg bombs, the heaviest so far in the campaign. Batteries B, C, F, and H, 60th C.A., received heavy shelling. As the shelling from Bataan intensified, more AA battery guns, directors, and height-finders were damaged, and it became increasingly necessary to obtain altitude data by telephone from other batteries with still operable equipment. Battery C, 60th C.A., continued to shoot down enemy planes. On April 29 Battery B received a terrific artillery barrage on its positions. Three 240 mm shells hit the director bombproof. The height-finder was put out of action, a power plant was hit, cables were cut, and the No. 1 Gun received a hit on the muzzle, damaging the tube. Several men were wounded. During the night of April 29, new positions were dug for the director and height-finder and the director and a height finder from Battery F was moved to the newly dug in positions in an attempt to keep Battery B firing. Battery H had to be taken out of action on several occasions due to damage and one 105 mm shell exploded above the No. 1 gun pit, mortally wounding one man and seriously wounding two others. Communications and cables were broken numerous times.[645]

Reorganized and reequipped with one of Battery F's guns and two others brought from Bataan, Battery G, now rearmed with three 3-inch AA guns, was emplaced on the Topside golf course. It engaged its first target over Corregidor from the new position near Batteries Wheeler and Geary on the afternoon of April 22 when it fired on a flight of light bombers. At its exposed position it quickly suffered serious damage from both artillery fire and bombing which hit the power plant pit and a communications trench, wounding two men who had sought cover in it. Other personnel who were on the trail between the battery and Geary on the way to their evening meal were also seriously wounded. Several dumps of 75 mm ammunition located along Geary Trail were ignited by the bombs. Battery personnel were instrumental is extinguishing the worst fires. On April 30, the battery suffered still more casualties on Geary Trail as men headed for Battery Geary's bombproofs after finishing their shifts at the AA guns about 0815. Again, bombs set off more ammunition dumps and created several major fires. Eleven more men on the trail were killed in connection with this bombing.[646]

Battery C was even more exposed on Morrison Hill and during the last half of April would be subjected to almost continuous devastating enemy fire that created casualties and regularly knocked out the battery's ability to fire as fire control and communication cables were cut. By April 19, an officer and 15 enlisted men of the 1st Signal Service Company (PA) to help repair the cables, and medical personnel from the 12th Medical Regiment to treat the wounded, were attached. Battery C was back in service on April 20, but the next day Morrison ill wa on the recieving end of a heavby shelling and the battery was knowcked out action again Hill was again heavily shelled and the battery again knocked out of action. The height-finder position received a direct hit badly damaging the instrument. The various positions occupied by the AA battery were torn up and the night-time hours were spent making repairs. The Japanese 105 mm howitzers continued their barrage the following day as the men of Battery C continued to make repairs to equipment and their dug in positions.[647]

Sufficient repairs made during the night of April 22 enabled Battery C to put its three remaining guns back in action despite very heavy shelling by 105 mm and 150 mm guns. Altitudes of the enemy planes frequently had to be obtained by telephone from other batteries as the height-finder was still in the repair shop. On April 25 intensive shelling by the 150 mm guns on the No. 3 and No. 4 Gun Positions inflicted heavy damage and the No. 3 Gun's splinter proof was nearly destroyed. A three-hour-long barrage of Corregidor came during the afternoon of April 27, Batteries C, F, H, and B receiving heavy shelling. Japanese bombers increasingly emboldened by the diminished fire of the AA batteries began flying at altitudes as low as 25,000 feet. Battery C managed to shoot down one of these Japanese bombers.[648]

On April 28, perhaps in retribution for the loss of one of their planes, the Japanese opened a terrific artillery barrage on Battery C. First Lt. Herbert E. Pace Jr., the assistant battery executive, was struck by a 105 mm shell as he was hastened the last of his men into a bombproof. The damage to the battery position was now almost impossible to repair and as the shelling continued on April 29, Capt. Godfrey Ames was instructed to seek a new position. He found a location near Concepcion Barrio where the terrain masked observation from Bataan. On April 30, Capt. Paul R. Cornwell was relieved from Battery C and reassigned to D in an effort to restore efficiency to the demoralized battery on the tail. Battery C continued working to get its guns back into action as they awaited orders to move to the new position. On May 2, 1st Lt. Thomas H. Fortney was transferred from Battery E to Battery C to serve as assistant battery executive. As with so many others assigned to the Morrison Hill AA position, his arrival was greeted by another heavy barrage from Bataan.[649]

By the end of April, it was apparent that it was only a matter of time before the Japanese would make their invasion attempt. The 59th C.A.'s regimental executive, Col. Dorsey J. Rutherford, was appointed to command the Corregidor Provisional Regiment composed of coast artillery and other personnel to be assigned as beach defense infantry in the event of an invasion. This force was largely made up of men from the batteries of the 59th and 60th C.A. serving on Topside. Beginning on May 1, Battery F, 60th C.A., was ordered to prepare to move out to the beach defenses each night as infantry, if and when called upon. As the coast artillery batteries on Topside were among the lowest priority units to be called out for beach defense duty, the officers and men of Battery F knew an invasion was expected soon. On April 25 the marine machine-gun platoon and their .50-caliber AA machine guns that had been attached to Battery F, 60th C.A., were shifted from their position at the AA firing point near Battery Cheney to Battery Hearn.[650]

As April neared an end, Battery H, 60th C.A., was taken out of action on several occasions as communications cables were broken, and in one instance, a 105 mm shell exploded above the No. 1 Gun Pit, mortally wounding one man and seriously wounding two others. On April 29, the director and height-finder positions were moved from Battery Ramsay to a new location behind the quartermaster stables at Middleside. The height-finder was knocked out of action but repaired on two occasions. Altitudes of enemy planes were obtained from other batteries so no action was missed.[651]

In an effort to reach the enemy batteries back of Sisimán Bay and elsewhere on Bataan that were inflicting widespread damage, and to interdict the Japanese supply line, Colonel Bunker had Batteries Byrne and Rose, two roving 155 mm batteries, open up on the Arno River Bridge and the truck traffic along the Cabcaben road. When a Japanese plane showed up to determine where the firing was coming from, the American batteries ceased firing and prepared for another firing mission that afternoon. This time when Battery Byrne opened on a battery it quickly received a three-shell salvo from a Japanese battery at Gorda Point. The Japanese got a quick response from Batteries Monja and Cheney. The enemy battery also received a thorough going over from Battery Way's three serviceable mortars. This action drew an intensified Japanese counter-battery fire on Battery Way. Later in the day, Battery Rose again began placing interdicting fire on truck traffic in Cabcaben and still later, it took the former Philippine Revenue Cutter *Apo* under fire hitting it several times and setting her alight.[652]

Meanwhile on Corregidor's tail, per orders of Lt. Col. H.E.C. Breitung, Capt. Paul R. Cornwell assumed command of Battery D, 60 C.A., relieving Capt. Benson Guyton. Battery D, like Battery C, had suffered heavily from the Japanese bombardment and was instructed to relocate to a new battery site on the south side of Kindley Field Ridge, away from Bataan's artillery fire. Cornwell was directed to leave two guns on Kindley Ridge and take the other pair of guns to the new position. The gun director and height-finder were, however, to remain in place until further orders. It was also necessary to almost totally reorganize the battery. Morale had declined following the death of battery executive 1st Lt. George E. Levagood and 2nd Lt. John H. Brady (the battery's former first sergeant), and other casualties sustained as the Japanese bombardment from Bataan registered on the battery position. Cornwell appointed a new first sergeant and strongly reminded the section leaders and NCOs of their duties and obligations.[653]

Although Fort Mills was being plastered by Japanese artillery from Bataan and to a lesser extent from Cavite, Fort Hughes suffered somewhat less. After the AA battery at Fort Drum had been blasted from the concrete battleship's deck, Battery I, 59th C.A., manning Fort Hughes's AA battery, obtained Fort Drum's M1 Height Finder to replace its obsolescent T-2 instrument along with Fort Drum's AA power plant. This augmentation of the Fort Hughes AA battery on April 13, 1942, was greatly welcomed.

Despite the nearly continuous Japanese bombardment from the air and shelling from Bataan, Corregidor was still far from defeated. Its seacoast batteries were still firing and when enemy planes came within range of its AA guns, there were hits and the Japanese frequently dropped their bomb loads in the waters off the island. The Japanese were throwing everything they had into the attack by May 1942. Three Japanese Navy light bombers began making attacks beginning May 1. The damage inflicted on the harbor defenses by the enemy bombers up to the end of April, while somewhat serious, had not measurably diminished the overall state of the defenses as they faced the enemy landing.[654]

One of the most troublesome batteries on Corregidor to the Japanese was Battery Geary and its eight 12-inch mortars. It had proven its effectiveness in the bombardment of the Japanese on Longoskawayan Point earlier in the year. As soon as their batteries were emplaced on Bataan, the Japanese targeted Battery Geary with a nearly continuous bombardment from 240 mm howitzers. The batteries of the seaward defenses that could be brought to bear on the Japanese positions on Bataan delivered a heavy barrage early in the morning of May 2, 1942, to which the Japanese replied with a vengeance. Finally, at 1627 during an intensive bombardment, a 240 mm projectile penetrated the central traverse magazine of Battery Geary and exploded; blowing up the entire center and right sections of the battery that contained the shot and powder magazines, completely demolishing the battery. The whole island shook when Geary blew up. A column of black smoke and acrid dust rose 3,000 feet above Corregidor. To Cpl. Albert Corn on Fort Drum it looked as if the top of the island had blown off. When Battery Geary blew up, 1,600 62-pound full-section powder charges exploded, blowing huge chunks of concrete hundreds of yards in all directions. The massive explosion collapsed the traverse retaining walls and demolished both mortar pits.

Several of the mortars were blown out of their pits. One 13-ton mortar was sent high in the sky before descending, others landed between Batteries Geary and Crockett and some were blasted through the walls of the left traverse magazines. Casualties might have been greater if the battery commander had not ordered most of the men out of the battery prior to the destructive hit. Perhaps as many as 27 men of Battery H were killed with many more injured. As one observer noted, all that was left of Geary was a "huge gaping hole in the ground." This proved to be an exaggeration; although the battery had been obliterated, substantial ruins remained of the left traverse.[655]

The damage was not restricted to Battery Geary. When the Japanese shell hit the battery's powder magazine, "pieces of concrete, reinforcing, and 12-inch mortar shells" fell around the antiaircraft guns of AA Battery B destroying one machine gun position. A piece of concrete fell on the old 1920s T-1 height finder brought to

Battery Geary as found in 1945. The mortar battery was subjected to heavy fire by Japanese 240 mm howitzers. One round finally penetrated the central traverse on May 2, 1942. The entire battery was wrecked, with heavy casualties. NARA.

the battery as a backup for Battery B's own height finder which was undergoing repairs. First Lt. Thomas H. Forney of Battery E had scarcely arrived at his battery position on Morrison Hill when he was greeted by the heavy Japanese artillery barrage that demolished Battery Geary on the island's opposite side. One enlisted man of the 60th C.A.'s Battery C was killed by falling debris. A chunk of concrete from Battery Geary, about the size of a small dining room table, had been blown some 350 yards before landing right on Battery F's height finder. Concrete chunks and 12-inch projectiles rained down on Battery G's golf course position. Fragments from the explosion destroyed one AA gun on the golf course, one man was killed, and 27 wounded in their open gun pits by the debris raining down on them. The battery's No. 2 Gun was placed out of action when a 12-inch mortar projectile landed on it. Battery H, 60th C.A., also felt the damage of falling concrete. One 500-pound chunk landed on a foxhole, mortally injuring its occupant. Another piece weighing about 10 tons landed between the director and the height finder.[656]

Spurred on by the havoc they had wrought, the Japanese bombardment continued and intensified, covering Topside in a massive cloud of black smoke and dust that towered hundreds of feet into the air. The Japanese fire was enhanced by one of the two captive "sausage" balloons of the *1st Balloon Company* that was raised some 40 to 60 feet above Cabcaben to spot the very accurate artillery fire. With the destruction of Battery Geary, the surviving personnel of the battery were reassigned to other batteries. Only the three serviceable mortars at Battery Way, the 12-inch guns of Batteries Smith and Hearn at Fort Mills, the 14-inch guns of Fort Drum, and the mortars of Battery Craighill at Fort Hughes remained in action to lay effective large-caliber fire on Bataan from Corregidor.[657]

Battery Way was hit hard as well. The severe Japanese counter-bombardment in late April destroyed Mortar Nos. 3 and 4; both were struck by direct hits on their muzzles and the tubes cracked clear through and the bores pushed in 2 to 3 inches. By early May, Mortar No. 1 was the only operable mortar. The gun crew "immediately set about taking parts off the damaged guns to patch up No. 2 Gun," rendered inoperable in the air raid of December 29, 1941, "but it was a job which required much time and our men had had no experience in that kind of work," as Major Massello recalled.[658]

During the nights, the batteries attempted to repair the damage sustained during the now almost continuous artillery barrages and bombings. The armament was shifted around as necessary as more AA guns and fire control instruments were destroyed by the Japanese artillery. A 3-inch gun obtained from Battery F a few days before was emplaced in one of Battery G's golf course positions. Because Battery C was essentially all but de-

15-9 Mortar Battery Way was more fortunate than Battery Geary. Not reactivated until late April and manned by antiaircraft personnel formerly of Battery E, 60th CA (AA), the battery fired until just a single mortar was firing until the island's surrender. USAMHI.

stroyed in its exposed position on Morrison Hill, the director and ammunition with the 30-second mechanical fuzes was exchanged with that of Battery G and plans were made to relocate the battery from Morrison Hill. Eight men from the USAMP *Harrison* were sent to Battery G on the golf course to augment the personnel of the gun sections depleted by the Battery Geary explosion.[659]

On May 3, 1942, more Japanese batteries opened on Corregidor from Bataan positions extending from Lamao to Mariveles. Seaward defense batteries on Topside were unable to silence the Japanese guns for as soon as they opened on an enemy battery, other enemy batteries would shift their fire to the battery on Corregidor that was firing. Consequently, increased reliance had to be made upon the 14-inch turret-mounted guns of Batteries Wilson and Marshall at Fort Drum and the roving batteries of 155 mm guns that did good service firing several rounds and then quickly moving to a new location before the Japanese counter-bombardment. Using spotting data provided from an observation post on Malinta Hill, the four 14-inch guns of Fort Drum were especially effective in countering the Japanese batteries on Bataan by working over the large concentrations of enemy troops in the assembly area north of Cabcaben. Japanese guns on the Cavite mainland placed a heavy volume of fire on the concrete battleship and eventually the ability of Battery Marshall's turret to traverse was reduced by a hit on the base ring beneath the turret. Battery Wilson, however, continued to do good work against the Japanese on Bataan. Battery Craighill's mortars at Fort Hughes also fired against enemy batteries in and around Mariveles. Enemy planes became increasingly active at both high and low altitudes as the AA defenses were degraded and communications lines were cut.[660]

Although the Japanese had focused much of their attention on the Topside area of Corregidor throughout much of the siege, by May 1 the bombardment of Corregidor's tail and the Bottomside area was also intensified. The enemy bombing and shelling continued with unrelenting ferocity. Between April 28 and May 5, Japanese aircraft flew 618 missions, dropping more than 2,700 bombs. At the same time nine 240 mm howitzers, 34 150 mm howitzers, and 32 other artillery pieces of lesser caliber pounded Corregidor day and night. Nearly all the Japanese artillery was on Bataan, although one reinforced artillery battalion, the *20th Independent Mountain Artillery Battalion* armed with 75 mm (pack) artillery and a battery of the *21st Heavy Artillery Battalion* equipped with 150 mm guns continued to fire from Cavite Province. Battery D of the 60th C.A., then in the process of moving into a new position partially shielded by Kindley Ridge, received much of the Japanese bombardment from Cavite. By early May, the *2nd Independent Heavy Artillery Battery (Motorized)* equipped with two Type 96 240 mm howitzers and two Type 96 150 mm guns also arrived in Cavite, adding even more destructive power to the bombardment.[661]

On May 4 the AA director of Battery D was demolished by a 240 mm shell. The remaining guns were ordered to continue firing at the Japanese planes even without adequate fire control. With this in mind the battery personnel continued to improve their position.[662]

Beach Defenses

In the years between the two world wars, Corregidor's defense planning had called for the army to make an infantry force available for what became termed the "beach defenses" of the fortified islands. The Philippine Division, constituted in October 1921, was designated to provide the fortified islands' defense force in the event it became necessary for the Commonwealth government to retire to Corregidor as a result of an invasion or civil insurrection. From the mid-1920s until 1941 the four coast artillery regiments had, in addition to their seacoast and AA defense missions, a beach defense role serving either as a reserve force of infantry, or as field artillery at Fort Mills or one of the harbor defense outposts. Seven of the 25 firing batteries of coast artillery were deployed to garrison the outposts, leaving 18 batteries on Corregidor to defend the beaches in the event of an invasion. Tactical beach defense exercises were conducted by the coast artillery garrison frequently as the probability of war increased in 1940 and 1941.

By 1941 the Philippine Division was fully engaged in training the fledgling Philippine Army and by year's end in opposing the invading Japanese Army. Pre-war plans to employ the division's 31st U.S. Infantry Regiment for beach defense on Corregidor had been superseded by the need for that regiment in Bataan's defense. The 4th Marines arrival from China earlier in 1941 presented a new option for providing a beach defense force and the marines were sent to Corregidor soon after the outbreak of hostilities. General MacArthur's plan to bring the Philippine Division to Corregidor in the event the lines on Bataan could no longer be held were overtaken by events, as noted above, and could not be implemented.

Col. Samuel McCullough served as General Moore's executive for beach defense, and Col. Delbert Ausmus served as beach defense artillery officer. They continued in these capacities when the marines assumed overall command of the beach defenses. The marines, supported by naval and Air Corps personnel and army stragglers, provided the infantry force. Artillery in support of Corregidor's three beach defense sectors was provided by elements of the 91st and 92nd C.A. Philippine Scout Regiments. Altogether the beach defense forces had at their disposal one 155 mm GPF gun (at Battery Stockade), 22 75 mm field pieces (Model 1917 type), four 37 mm ex-caliber guns for 155 mm GPFs mounted on .50-caliber AA mounts, three 3-pounder ex-navy guns on pedestal mounts, and two 3-inch navy Mark XI landing guns. Ten of the 75 mm guns were positioned on Corregidor's tail. Some of this armament was emplaced in prepared concrete splinter proof positions. The score of semi-permanent prepared positions for 75 mm armament were frequently arranged to receive a pair of artillery pieces; however most, if armed at all, were provided with only a single gun.

Col. Samuel Howard and Lt. Col. John Anderson of the 4th Marines with Maj. Gen. George Moore, commander of the harbor defenses in March 1942. Upon arrival on Corregidor the Marine Corps picked up primary responsibility for beach defense of the post. NARA.

At the outposts, Fort Hughes had three 155 mm guns, one on the top of Caballo's ridge designated Battery Hughes, the other two in Battery Williams, on the island's lower portion near Battery Leach and the AA battery. Fort Frank had the four 155 mm GPFs of Battery Frank (North), and four 75 mm field pieces. Beach defense of Fort Drum was limited to machine gun and small arms. By the time the invasion on Corregidor began, the 3-inch gun on Fort Drum's stern as well as its pair of M1917 3-inch AA guns had been wrecked by enemy fire.[663]

Only one 60-inch searchlight, a portable one emplaced at Breakwater Point, operated primarily as part of the beach defenses. Eleven 18, 24, and 36-inch searchlights were also dedicated to illuminating the landing beaches. One 18-inch light and two 36-inch lights were operated from prewar tunnel searchlight shelters dug into the slopes of Malinta Hill.[664]

The Marines Arrive on Corregidor

The 4th Marines, long stationed in China, arrived in the Philippines aboard SS *President Madison* and *President Harrison* on November 30 and December 1. When war came these marines were assigned to guard the naval stations at Olongapo and Mariveles. In the early days of the war, the two battalions comprising the 4th Marines were placed under army tactical control. They were considered to be of less value tactically on Bataan than the 31st U.S. Infantry. The marines of the 4th were, however, assigned to take over the 31st Infantry's beach defense mission on Corregidor.

On December 21, 1941, the 1st Separate Battalion, U.S. Marines, under Lt. Col. John P. Adams that had been formed from the old contingent at the Marine Barracks Cavite, arrived at the small Mariveles Section Base. There it joined the 1st Battalion, 4th Marines, that had arrived from Olongapo on December 8. A small detachment of the Separate Battalion remained at Cavite until Christmas Day to complete the destruction of the base facilities and was then transferred to Corregidor. The marines at Mariveles numbered about 900 officers and enlisted men. The 2nd Battalion, 4th Marines, began evacuating the naval station at Olongapo Christmas Eve night and moved to Mariveles joining the other contingents.[665]

> At 10:00 a.m., on December 26, the 4th Marines began its move to Corregidor. More than 400 marines of the 1st Separate Marine Battalion were loaded on lighters and taken across the channel. They were then transported by narrow-gauge railway to Middleside Barracks. The forward echelon of the Headquarters and Service Companies and the 2nd Battalion loaded on a minesweeper and lighters just after darkness the following day. Shortly after midnight on 27 December, the 336 marines and their equipment were completely unloaded on Corregidor. Two days later at 2010, the 1st Battalion and the remainder of the regiment completed the transfer

Marines outside their protective cave on Corregidor. The marines had arrived on Corregidor on December 26 and 27 and immediately took over responsibility for beach defense. USMC HC.

by an organized unit. The two reserve companies used a tank trap dug across Bottomside to cross the artillery-swept burnt-out barrio to Malinta's west entrance.[687]

Major Schaeffer alerted his two companies which formed the regimental reserve and sent Turner's Filipino cadet platoon in advance to Malinta Tunnel. Shortly before midnight, he moved the rest of his men to the tunnel. The marines pulled on their bandoliers of ammunition, fastened grenades to their cartridge belts, and as Private First-Class Melvin Sheya remembered, said to each other, "Well, here goes nothing." The two companies moved along the South Shore Road under Japanese artillery fire but lost only a few men before reaching the tunnel.

At 0100, Major Schaeffer gave his company and platoon commanders orders to counterattack and drive the Japanese off the tail of Corregidor. During the next hour the marines and the Filipino cadets attempted to drive the Japanese from their positions at the water tanks on Denver Hill. Companies O, and P became separated, and the Japanese machine guns pinned both down.

Before midnight, Colonel Howard alerted his 4th Battalion at Government Ravine to be ready to move to Malinta Tunnel and replace the regimental reserve should more men be needed. Major Williams had already alerted his battalion based on his view of the situation. By midnight, extra ammunition was issued, and all companies were ready to move out. At 0130, Colonel Howard's order came to move to the tunnel. Marching in two columns the battalion advanced in the darkness from Government Ravine along the South Shore Road, spread out to minimize casualties from Japanese artillery fire. Although delayed by a 20-minute artillery barrage the battalion suffered few casualties. By 0230, the 4th Battalion was in Malinta Tunnel awaiting orders. At 0430 Colonel Howard committed the marines, sailors, and soldiers of this reserve that now numbered 500 men that had long been ready to move. As they moved out of the severely congested and stuffy tunnel, Lieutenant Charles R. Brook, USN, remembered, "It was hot, terribly hot, and the ventilation was so bad that we could hardly breathe."[688]

As soon as the battalion emerged from the tunnel, it was subjected to severe shelling and casualties began to mount even before the last company left the tunnel. Reformed under fire, the battalion moved forward. Then another barrage struck, causing still more casualties and confusion. Again reorganized, the advance continued. At 200 yards behind the 1st Battalion's line, Major Williams ordered Companies Q and R to deploy in a skirmish line and guide to the left of the line. Company T repeated the orders, formed on the right of Company R, and guided to the right. Company S formed the reserve.[689]

The battalion formation proved prudent, as the main line of resistance was badly in need of reinforcement. The deployment into skirmish formation in the moonlight was difficult, but was eventually accomplished. Contact with the 1st Battalion was spotty at best and Company R found no marines in their front. Scattered parties of Japanese soldiers, however, had been infiltrating behind the marine positions throughout the night and their sniping proved worrisome to the inexperienced sailors. Both Companies Q and R were receiving fire from both ahead and behind as they moved into position.[690]

At 0530, three green flares signaled the successful landing of still another battalion of Japanese troops. The *3rd Battalion, 61st Infantry*, along with engineers and light artillery, had arrived with at least 880 men to join the battle. This force had originally been scheduled to arrive at 0230, but the losses of landing craft during the initial landings delayed their arrival on Corregidor and prevented them from bringing five tanks and most of the field artillery. They did not, however, land unopposed:[691]

> In the confusion, two sailors, Signalman First Class Maurice C. Havey and Signalman First Class Frank H. Bigelow, became separated from their command and came upon an unmanned twin .50-caliber machine gun overlooking the beach area. They manned the gun and opened fire on the Japanese on the coastline for 30 minutes. Havey fired until the barrels burned out and Bigelow then replaced them. Suddenly, Havey dropped from the gun, turned and said, "I'm hit." He staggered to the rear toward Malinta Tunnel while Bigelow stayed with the gun. Havey had traveled only 100 yards when he was killed by seven machine gun bullets across the chest.

The company commanders of 4th Battalion attempted to put their men into position between 0530 and 0600 but were hampered by the darkness, lack of familiarity with the terrain, and the 1st Battalion's scattered state. In one instance, the 4th Battalion formed a line behind the 1st Battalion positions with no knowledge of the marines in their front. Luckily, the Japanese artillery was strangely silent. When Major Schaeffer came off the firing line to confer with Major Williams on the placement of reinforcements, Schaeffer indicating the neediest area was the gap between his two companies. Company S moved out to fill the breach.[692]

Major Williams and the 4th Battalion headquarters staff armed themselves with rifles and hand grenades and moved into the front lines where the fighting was the heaviest. This reduced coordination, as the company commanders often would have little idea how to contact Williams. The 4th Battalion eventually managed to extend its flanks to cover the island from shore to shore. By this time, the battalion was down to about 400 men.[693]

As dawn broke, Williams ordered the battalion to counterattack. All companies were alerted and moved out at 0615. The order, "Charge!" came down the line and the marines, sailors, and soldiers attacked with fixed bayonets, "yelling and screaming... cursing and howling..." Gunner Ferrell tried to use the 1st Battalion's old World War I Stokes mortars to support the attack, but the rounds were too inaccurate to use. While Companies Q and R gained ground on the left front, Company S was halted by heavy machine gunfire after advancing only 100 yards. Company T also failed to gain ground. Williams's counterattack was met with a heavy 10-minute Japanese artillery barrage from Bataan. When the barrage ended Company T again moved out toward the Japanese position on Denver Hill in the face of Japanese machine gunfire that soon halted their advance. A machine gun position on the north road was knocked out, but at heavy cost.

Major Schaeffer was pinned down in his command post by a machine gun on the North Shore Road and another on Denver Hill and lost contact with his men. When the machine guns were finally destroyed, Schaeffer, slightly wounded and out of contact with much of his battalion, tried to reorganize his men and explain to Williams what had happened. Major Williams had Schaeffer cared for and calmly took control of the action. Contact was lost between the two left companies, Q and R, and the two companies on the right, S and T. The companies on the left having outdistanced those on the right by 200 yards, Williams halted Companies Q and R, ordering them to regain contact with the stalled companies and try to break into the Japanese flank on Denver. Two boatloads of Japanese soldiers that were left drifting, became grounded offshore, and were destroyed by the sailors in Company Q. At 0630 Williams began to shift men to the right, which was hard-pressed.

Quartermaster Clerk Frank W. Ferguson, who had succeeded to command of Company O, attacked two machine guns covering the beach road by the flank. "Ferguson, with six men, moved down the road covered for some distance by the road embankment. Unfortunately, two new machine-guns opened on the party and they were bracketed by knee mortars. By the time Ferguson was abreast of the first guns, he had only one man left, Cpl. Alvin E. Stewart of the 803d Engineer Battalion. The two gave up the enterprise and moved to the south side of the road to place rifle fire on the offending machine guns." The Japanese on top of the hill evidently thought a larger party of men was flanking them and a reinforced platoon began to advance to counter Ferguson's move. The Japanese were entirely in silhouette against the skyline and the two Americans by the road had perfect targets. Ferguson later wrote, "There wasn't a chance to miss them — we were too close for that." Within seconds, 20 Japanese soldiers were killed or wounded. The Americans were so intent on firing that they did not notice a Japanese rifleman coming up behind them. A glancing bullet in the face hit Ferguson, leaving blood streaming from his nose and cheek. Stewart was able to pull him back to the marine battle line without further wounds.[694]

The marine advance on both the right and the left was halted by enemy machine guns at the Battery Denver positions near the water towers. From Denver Hill the guns could hit any movement from the north coast to the south. Various attempts to permanently silence the machine guns were unsuccessful and caused major losses in the 4th Battalion. By 0900 the battalion was stalled and Williams requested reinforcements and artillery support to resume the attack. Neither was available.

The Japanese holding Denver Hill were clearly visible from the island's south shore. There 1st Lt. Mason F. Chronister, commanding a platoon of Company B, organized an attack against the hill. The platoon, augmented with volunteers from the intercept station's communications tunnel and AA Battery M, moved in concert with the 4th Battalion's attack. As they moved up the hill, they were intercepted by elements of the *3rd Battalion, 61st Infantry,* that had just landed. Lieutenant Chronister, and his men withdrew and moved to join Williams's line at the water tanks.

Additional support for the marines on Corregidor's tail came from Battery I, 59th C.A. Manning 3-inch AA guns on Fort Hughes, Battery I received orders on the morning of May 6, to open fire on the Japanese on Corregidor's tail. Colonel Foster at Fort Hughes had previously registered his artillery to fire on potential locations on and around Corregidor so as soon as visibility permitted, two of the battery's 3-inch AA guns were placed horizontal, opened up at 0520, and continued to fire until 0615, expending about 210 rounds (70 HE and 140 shrapnel) that inflicted heavy casualties on Japanese forces. The battery and Fort Hughes were intermittently shelled and bombed the rest of day and evening and at 2330 underwent a heavy artillery bombardment, just before the Japanese landed on Corregidor at midnight.

At 0900 on May 6, a detachment of soldiers that had been manning Battery Crockett reinforced the marines and sailors on the tail with 60 members from the battery. Major Williams placed the soldiers on the north shore beaches to his left where heavy losses had whittled away at his strength. With the reinforcements some advance was made, but against strong enemy resistance. Nevertheless, much fighting was done with the bayonet, as the Japanese were running short of ammunition. The tide was beginning to turn against the Japanese. As Lt. Gen. Masaharu Homma reflected one year after the surrender, "If the enemy had stood their ground 12 hours longer, events might not have transpired as smoothly as they did."[695]

By mid-morning, the Japanese were beginning to run out of ammunition. Each of the Japanese rifleman had come came ashore with 120 rounds of ammunition and two hand grenades.[696]

The machine gun sections brought only two cases totaling 720 rounds of ammunition and three to six grenades. The knee mortar sections had only 36 heavy grenades and three light grenades. A large quantity of additional ammunition had been loaded on the landing craft due to the expected problems in resupplying the force. However, the ammunition crates had been hurriedly dumped overboard by the crews of the landing craft as they grounded on Corregidor and now few boxes could be recovered in the murky water. By morning most of the Japanese on Denver Hill were either out of ammunition or very close to it. Many Japanese soldiers were now fighting with the bayonet and even threw rocks at the marines to hold the hill.

The shortage in munitions was offset largely by the arrival of Japanese tanks. Three tanks, two Japanese Type 97 tanks and a captured American M3, were landed on the beach below Cavalry Point. Two more tanks were lost when only 50 yards offshore during the landing with the *2nd Battalion, 61st Infantry.* Because of the steep cliffs and beach debris left behind by the advancing infantry, the three surviving tanks became stranded on the beach. After an hour of work, the tank crews and engineers managed to work a path up to the foot of the cliffs. There they found the inclines too steep for the tanks and were again stalled. Upon being alerted to the presence of tanks, the marines sent Gunner Ferrell to Cavalry Point to investigate and found the vehicles apparently hopelessly stalled.[697]

By daylight the Japanese managed to cut a road to Cavalry Beach and the more powerful M3 finally negotiated the cliff and towed the Japanese tanks up the from the beach. By 0830, all three tanks were on the North Shore Road and moving inland. At 0900, Gunnery Sergeant Mercurio reported the presence of enemy armor to Malinta Tunnel.[698]

At 1000 marines on the north beaches watched as the Japanese began an attack with their tanks, which moved in concert with light artillery support. Private First Class Silas K. Barnes fired on the tanks with his machine gun to no effect. He watched helplessly as they began to take out the American positions. He remembered the Japanese tanks' guns "looked like mirrors flashing where they were going out and wiping out pockets of resistance where the marines were." The Marines still had nothing in operation heavier than automatic rifles to deal with the enemy tanks. Word of the enemy armor caused initial panic, but the remaining marine, Navy and Army officers soon halted the confusion.

While the Japanese continued to land men on the tail's north shore, they were preparing to assault the Bottomside docks as well as Cheney and James Ravines. At 0400, Fort Drum opened fire on the Cabcaben dock area with the 14-inch guns of Batteries Marshall and Wilson. When dawn broke about 20 minutes later, a wave of landing boats could be seen approaching Corregidor's north dock area. Fort Drum then changed target to those boats that were also being effectively taken under fire by roving 155 mm Batteries Wright and Gulick. About half of these barges were sunk and the remainder changed course and headed for Mariveles. This concentration of artillery fire broke up what was believed to be a landing attack destined for Bottomside and Power Plant Ravine.[699]

At sunrise, effective Japanese artillery fire from Bataan was brought to bear on the remaining elements of the beach defense reserve battalion and Batteries B and C of the 59th C.A. on the tail, while light bombers in large numbers strafed them mercilessly. Some men were driven back into Malinta Tunnel while all others were pinned to the ground.[700]

One problem on the rapidly diminishing sector east of Malinta Hill was the steady accumulation of wounded who could not be evacuated. With only four corpsmen available, and no first aid packets, or even a tourniquet, the walking wounded tried to get to the rear on their own. However, the heavy artillery bombardment prevented any move to Malinta Tunnel, and no personnel could be spared from the line to take the wounded to the rear. By 1030 the pressure from the Japanese on what was left of the American lines was too great and men began to fall back from the firing line despite the efforts of Major Williams and other offices who tried to halt them. The Japanese tanks moving along the North Road fired on American positions, knocking them out one by one. Finally, Williams ordered his men to withdraw to the prewar Infantry Trench system just east of Malinta Hill.[701]

With the withdrawal of the 4th and 1st Battalions, the Japanese sent up a green flare as a signal to the Bataan artillery which redoubled its fire, and all organization of the two battalions ceased. Men made their way to the rear in small groups and began to fill the concrete trenches at Malinta Hill. The Japanese guns swept the area from the hill to Battery Denver and then back again several times. In 30 minutes only 150 men were left to hold the line.

Topside and Middleside Prepare for the End

As dawn broke on the morning of May 6, the defense of Corregidor became increasingly scattered as small bands of American soldiers, sailors, marines, and Filipino troops prepared to confront the Japanese when they landed at Cheney and James Ravines and at Bottomside. At Topside, preparations to augment the beach defenses by taking troops from the fixed batteries for the coming onslaught had been underway since May 1. By May 5, the defenses on Morrison Hill had been practically battered into oblivion. Battery Morrison's 6-inch disappearing guns, manned briefly by Battery E of the 60th C.A., after their arrival from Bataan, were totally out of action and had been abandoned in favor of Battery Grubbs 10-inch disappearing guns which were also shelled out of action almost as soon as they opened fire on Bataan. Battery E had then consolidated its personnel at Battery Way.

Morrison Hill's AA Battery C was under fire almost all day long with its personnel working on the trench system and field fortifications at night. The chaplain of the 60th C.A. held confession during the evening and said mass at midnight, when "Lunch" was served. At about 0015 on May 6, word came that the Japanese had landed and the battery was ordered to stand by for service in local defenses. Equipment and ammo were checked and a double ration of breakfast was served at 0400. The battery was subsequently ordered to man the local defenses. A terrific artillery barrage began at daybreak, falling directly on their foxholes and causing many casualties.[702]

Although James Ravine below Morrison Hill was an expected Japanese landing site, all action on May 6 was still east of Malinta Hill. The Japanese barrage had cut communications between Battery C and its command post in Malinta Tunnel before 0100. With its guns and fire control instruments wrecked, Battery C retired from the foxhole line into shelters and stood by for orders about 0630, sustaining numerous casualties from the artillery barrage during the evacuation. The battery remained under cover until 1100, when 1st Battalion informed them of the impending surrender, and that enemy artillery would cease at noon. Demolition of equipment prior to that time was ordered. The intact battery property that remained was reduced to scrap, class C (canned) rations were issued and the men marched to Middleside Tunnel, where the wounded were given care.[703]

At 2200 on May 5, Battery D of the 59th C.A., manning Battery Cheney, was ordered to move out to beach defense stations. Battery F from the 60th was standing by with their machine guns awaiting similar orders. At 0100 on May 6 they were ordered to move to Middleside Tunnel and report to west sector commanding officer to act as beach defense reserve. The battery moved out in three platoons, two rifle platoons and one machine gun platoon in "approach march" formation with five-minute intervals between platoons. En route, they passed the ruins of the Corregidor Ciné and Topside Barracks, moved down the "Golden Staircase," and up Middleside's back road to Middleside Tunnel. Battery F found the unfinished tunnel already crowded with several hundred Filipinos (some of whom were Philippine Army Air Corps troops) and a company of marines that was quartered in the tunnel. All were being held in reserve to oppose landings at James and Cheney Ravines. The tunnel's blower system was barely able to keep the air breathable. Widely spaced light bulbs provided the only illumination of Middleside Tunnel and its cross-laterals. After arriving at the tunnel, Battery F sent a detail back up to Topside to gather more .30-caliber ammunition from Wheeler Tunnel, Battery Cheney, and from the Battery B, and Battery F AA positions. At 1115 on May 6, the order came down to destroy all equipment prior to the noontime surrender. Shelling and bombing continued throughout the afternoon and into the evening.[704]

Battery B of the 60th C.A. near Battery Wheeler also received orders during the evening of May 5 to prepare for its beach defense mission. The battery soon thereafter moved to Wheeler Tunnel and prepared to reinforce the marines rear defense positions at Cheney Ravine. They received word at their position near Battery Wheeler soon after daybreak on May 6 that all limits on targets and restrictions on volume of fire had been removed. Japanese bombing raids on Corregidor's tail continued throughout the morning of May 6. The defenders managed to break up some of the aerial attacks. At 1100 orders for destruction of equipment began to spread among the remaining AA batteries. Battery B's director and height-finder were "blown to bits." Power plants were blown up, the guns drained of oil and fired. Fire control clocks were smashed and the gun pits set on fire to destroy ammunition. Once the battery equipment was destroyed, the battery personnel assembled at various pre-assigned points.[705]

In its position on Fort Mill's golf course, AA Battery G also suffered from the heavy barrage of artillery fire from Bataan in the afternoon of May 5 just after firing on a flight of nine heavy bombers. A second flight was picked up at 1500, and just as the battery began to fire, a concentrated barrage of artillery fire swept back and forth over the battery position that lasted for an hour and a half. Although no casualties were received, the Japanese fire neutralized the battery. During the night battery personnel heard the massive pre-invasion bombardment of the Kindley Field area. At daybreak, they again began firing against the light bombers working over Corregidor, alternating with Battery B. Topside was again racked with 240 mm fire from Bataan and about 2200 word came that the long-awaited invasion had begun. At 2300 Battery G was told to prepare to move out as infantry reserves.[706]

Surrender of Corregidor

At 1020, on May 6, word reached Malinta Tunnel that enemy tanks had landed on the island and were assembling near Kindley Field. General Wainwright informed General Moore:[707]

> ...that in view of the situation and what might be expected to occur during the ensuing night, and in order to prevent the further useless sacrifice of lives, he had decided to surrender the fortified islands to the Japanese at noon. He was going to have a message to that effect broadcast at once. He further directed that the armament be destroyed in accordance with secret instructions already issued to regimental and fort commanders, this to be accomplished by noon; that the command would lay down arms at noon at which time the Corregidor flag would be lowered and burned and a white flag displayed. These instructions were relayed to all concerned as fast and insofar as disrupted communications permitted. All units received the orders in time to comply with instructions except Fort Hughes.

The Japanese followed the American retreat aggressively and were soon within 300 yards of the line with tanks moving around the American right flank. At 1130, Major Williams entered the tunnel and reported to Colonel Howard that his men could hold no longer. He asked for reinforcements and antitank weapons.[708]

Colonel Howard replied that General Wainwright had decided to surrender at 1200. Wainwright agonized over his decision and later wrote, "It was the terror vested in a tank that was the deciding factor. I thought of the havoc that even one of these beasts could wreak if it nosed into the tunnel." Williams was ordered to hold the Japanese until noon when a surrender could be arranged.

Colonel Braly recalled how the surrender was carried out:[709]

> A flag of truce was carried out by Captain Golland H. Clark, USMC, accompanied by First Lieutenant Allan S. Manning, USMC. They proceeded eastward from Malinta Hill until they contacted the enemy and were taken to the senior Japanese officer on the spot. Neither nationality could speak the other's language but the difficulty was overcome when it was found that Lieutenant Manning and a Jap officer could manage a few words of French to each other. About an hour later the marine officers returned with the word that General Wainwright should come out to the Japanese commander if he desired to discuss terms. Accordingly, General Wainwright, accompanied by General Moore and their respective aides, Lieutenant Colonel Johnnie Pugh and Major Tom Dooley, and Major Bob Brown, proceeded by car, under a white flag, to the foot of Kindley Field Water Tank Hill where they got out and walked up the hill to meet the Jap commander. Dead and dying were on every hand, the proportion being about three Japs to one American. At the conference with the Japanese officials arrangements were made for General Wainwright to be taken to Bataan to meet General Homma, their supreme commander in the Philippines. After some delay this was accomplished by means of a Jap boat from North Point to Cabcaben, Major Dooley accompanying the General. Meanwhile General Moore and the others returned to our headquarters, traversing en route an area being swept by artillery fire from Bataan and strafing planes. The white flag flying meant nothing to our antagonists. Around 4:00 PM the Japanese moved in and took charge and we were no longer free agents... The final gallant defense of the Philippines had ended.

Meanwhile at Hooker Point, First Lieutenant Lawrence's command was cut off from the rest of the island after the Japanese landed at North Point and were among the last to surrender. They had finished off the Japanese survivors of the *2nd Battalion, 61st Infantry*, in the daylight hours and faced little opposition for the rest of the day. By the afternoon Forts Hughes and Drum fell silent and as evening approached, they heard the Japanese firing on Corregidor diminish. Lieutenant Lawrence and his second in command assembled their men together at 1700, and marched to Kindley Field under a bed sheet symbolizing a flag of truce. There the marines found some Japanese soldiers, who took their surrender.

At about 1045 Lieutenant Colonel Breitung, the AA gun defense commander, called Capt. Aaron Abston of Battery G at his golf course battery position on Topside and told him that he "had refused an order to lower the national colors." At 1100, Abston was informed that the garrison battle flag would be lowered at noon, adding that he was to destroy the battery material. Colonel Bunker, whose command post was not very far from the flagpole, was given the task of taking down the national colors and raising the flag of surrender. A few minutes before noon Abston saw the white flag being raised over Topside:[710]

> Col. Bunker, Lt. Col. Simmonds, Lt. Col. Edison and Captain Cooper (Adjutant 59th) were there along with Pvts. Welch (Col. Bunker's orderly and driver) and Derr (Regimental Driver) several other enlisted men (I cannot remember their names) and myself. The flag was slowly lowered while we all stood at a salute, taken off the rope without it touching the ground and placed in a small bonfire started for this purpose. When the flag was completely burned, a white sheet was raised in its place.

By the morning of May 6, the kitchen and food stores of Battery H had been destroyed. Its communication and data transmission cables had been cut several times during the morning, repeatedly putting the battery out of action. The battery assumed a beach defense mode as well as continuing a reduced AA mission. A portion of the battery personnel reported to the marines commanded by Maj. Andrew J. Matheson and at 1130 orders came from Colonel Breitung to destroy the battery position and all equipment before 1200. The battery remained at the Battery Ramsay position until late afternoon, when it began moving in small groups to Middleside tunnel.[711]

At 0300 on May 7, the Japanese landed unopposed at James and Power Plant Ravines. Other Japanese forces arrived at the C_1G_1 tunnel before dawn and advised Colonel Bunker that American troops were to be off Topside by 0700. As dawn broke on the morning of May 7 the troops in Middleside Tunnel received orders to proceed to Bottomside. "The first group of Japs (encountered) was bivouacked at Middleside Parade Ground." Upon reaching Bottomside, they were herded to the entrance of Queen Tunnel. After leaving Battery Way, Battery E, 60th C.A., spent the night at Battery Hearn and at 0500 on May 7 left and began the march down to Bottomside to surrender. On May 9, some canned food was brought out of Queen and eaten cold and then

American POWs on Corregidor. Apparently being marched under light guard to either an encampment or perhaps embarkation. NARA.

the officers were ordered to assemble at the east entrance of Malinta Tunnel at 1330. All enlisted troops were herded to the 92nd C.A.'s regimental garage area, where the Americans were separated from the Filipinos. Later on, all personnel on Corregidor were concentrated in the garage area, but officers and enlisted men were kept separated. Thus command of the enlisted prisoners fell upon the senior NCOs.[712]

On the morning of May 7, Malinta's main tunnel as well as its various laterals were choked with the remnants of the 4th Marines that were driven back to the tunnel from the tail, hundreds of refugees from numerous other army and navy units, as well as the numerous headquarters and medical personnel that numbered in the thousands by some estimates. Another thousand sick and wounded lay in bunks stacked three high in the hospital laterals. The air in the overcrowded tunnel was foul. When the Japanese arrived in the late afternoon they had the American occupants prepare to exit the tunnel. After a long file of Japanese infantry had passed through the tunnel's west entrance at Bottomside, Brig. Gen. Charles Drake, the senior officer remaining in the tunnel, had the Americans and Filipinos follow the Japanese out to Bottomside. For some time after the surrender, the garrison's senior officers and their immediate staffs were allowed to remain in the tunnel.

Surrender of the Outposts

Telephone communications between Fort Hughes and Fort Mills remained uninterrupted until the end of March 1942, but beginning in April, the cables connecting the islands was intermittently cut. Although fully restored during the night of May 4, communications were lost entirely early in the morning on May 5 because of cables again being repeatedly cut on Corregidor, but Colonel Foster on Caballo could reach the Harbor Defense Headquarters occasionally by radio.

When Japanese aircraft bombed Fort Hughes in the mid-afternoon of May 5, their bombs deposited considerable concrete debris and dirt in Battery Craighill's mortar pits, wounding six men. During the early morning hours of May 6, Colonel Foster ordered the mortars to fire on the waters about 100 yards offshore from Corregidor's tail in an effort to disrupt the Japanese landings. Anticipating that the Japanese would attempt a landing on Corregidor, Colonel Foster had pre-prepared barrage points over the North Channel at a range of 6000 yards for the 155 mm, 75 mm and 3-inch AA guns in mid-April 1942. As soon as there was sufficient visibility at about 0500 on May 6, Colonel Foster issued orders to open fire on the enemy troops landing on Corregidor's tail. He ordered two of his 75 mm beach defense guns to fire on Japanese landings on North Point and for two of his 3-inch AA guns to fire shrapnel over Kindley Field. This fire was continued until 0600.[713]

Around 1000, on May 6, an observation post at Fort Hughes reported a white flag flying at Corregidor. Colonel Foster pulled out the Harbor Defense letter of April 10 that contained the instructions for the demolition of equipment but specified that this would be carried out only on specific orders from the Harbor Defense Commander. Unable to reach Fort Mills by telephone or radio directly about 1030 Foster requested instructions as to the surrender and carrying out demolitions, by radio to a navy station, where it had to be relayed once to reach Malinta tunnel. He received no reply until about 1400, when a message was received confirming the surrender and directing him to take no action concerning demolitions. No demolitions were carried out.[714]

The Japanese forces were so consumed with handling of the surrender of the troops on Corregidor, however, that it was not until 2330 on May 6 that the first Japanese set foot on Caballo Island. Colonel Foster had sent an officer by boat to meet the Japanese and lead them through the submarine minefield to Fort Hughes. The captured Fort Hughes garrison was transferred to the 92nd C.A. Garage concentration camp on May 8.

Not until the afternoon of May 7 did the Japanese get around to landing on Carabao and Fort Drum. Colonel Boudreau, commanding Fort Frank, recalled:[715]

> Before noon 6 May I had received a message which read in part as follows: "Destroy equipment, raise white flag at noon and notify Forts Drum and Hughes." The decoded message was telephoned in full to Lt. Col. Kirkpatrick of Fort Drum....Repeated efforts to reach Fort Hughes failed.

> There was no time to permit firing those batteries with empty recoil cylinders before 1200 6 May so that the breech blocks were removed and together with tools and loose spare parts thrown into the sea. Men broke off all parts possible with sledge hammers and battered the pistons in. About half the powder was burned. A number of shells from Cavite hit in the pits of Btry Koehler but the eight mortars were all in operation at the surrender. Prior to noon of this day all guns were rendered inoperative. The firing mechanisms and parts of the breech block that could be removed were thrown over the cliff into the ocean. The pistons were hammered with a sledge hammer and all other possible parts broken off with the hammer. About half the powder was burned. Btry Frank North, four 155 mm guns on Panama mounts, manned by Btry C, 92nd and by Btry B, 92nd was often shelled. Two of them were destroyed prior to the surrender. By the surrender the two remaining guns were fired with empty recoil cylinders. The firing mechanisms, breech block, fuzes, tools and spare parts were thrown into the sea. All powder charges were burned. Btry A, 91st, manned a 3-inch AA battery at Fort Frank. Two of the four guns were destroyed by artillery fire prior to the surrender. At the surrender the remaining two guns were fired with empty recoil cylinders. The breech blocks, tools, spare parts, and all ammunition were thrown into the sea. In addition to the demolitions describe above, the 3-inch mortars and the 75 mm field guns were partially stripped and pushed over the cliff into the sea. All small arms and small arms ammunition, tools, and loose spare parts, telephones, observing instruments, telephone switchboards, field glasses and similar items were thrown into the sea, being first smashed when practical. The 60-inch seacoast and AA searchlights and smaller beach defense searchlights were smashed when practical. Emplacement books, maps, correspondence, typewriters, etc., were destroyed. The cable ways and dock crane were destroyed. All power plants, except one 25 KW set which was kept running for our own benefit, were smashed. All water reservoirs had previously been destroyed by shell fire except three 10,000 gallon tanks which were at each end of the three major batteries. These were kept intact for our benefit.

During the trip from Corregidor to Manila May 23-24, 1942, Colonel Boudreau talked to Lt. Col. Kirkpatrick, commander of Fort Drum. Kilpatrick told Boudreau that:[716]

> ... he emptied all recoil cylinders of all guns, placed sandbags in the muzzles and fired them with full charges. The muzzle of one of the 14-inch guns was split and another 14-inch jumped from its carriage with the breech resting against the rear of the turret. He flooded the powder magazines with salt water and threw everything the men could handle into the sea except rations and medical supplies.

American military personnel from Fort Drum of approximately 224 men and the Fort Frank garrison of 56 Americans and 395 Filipinos were taken prisoners by the Japanese and shipped by Japanese fishing boats to Wawa Barrio, the port of Nasugbu in Batangas Province some 20 miles south of Manila Bay. There they were unloaded on what had formerly been a deep sea pier that had been wrecked by American forces prior to evacuation in December 1941. There the prisoners were stripped of all possessions, including hats, canteens and mess gear, and a Japanese colonel commanding the Japanese Military District made a short speech during which he announced that the Japanese would fight for one hundred years - until the last American was exterminated, and told us that they were to be severely punished by the Japanese. The Japanese began working the POWs for three successive days, 24 hours each day. For two days they received no water at all, and at the end of this period nearly all were unconscious or very ill. The American prisoners were then formed into a line similar to bucket brigades and required to pass rocks in this manner with great rapidity. These lines were paced by Filipino citizens working under Japanese bayonets, and these Filipinos were relieved every 50 minutes to keep fresh Filipinos working all the time. Every time an American dropped a rock or slowed down, a Japanese guard would come up and club the man to the ground with a rifle. The only rest they received during the three days consisted of two one-hour breaks during the night. Even during these breaks, they were not allowed to lie down and any American who so much as touched his elbow to the ground was struck with a bayonet or clubbed into unconsciousness. Filipino citizens by the hundreds were herded by Japanese soldiers who forced the Filipinos to witness this brutality at bayonet point. Capt. Ben King recalled: [717]

A motion picture camera was brought up and while the Japanese announcer taunted and jeered at us the Japanese took motion pictures of us at work. They announced to us and to the Filipinos that this picture would be titled "America learns to work." This punishment continued for approximately seven days, and at the end of that time the men from Forts Drum and Frank were marched to Nasugbu and forced to publicly put on a review for the Japanese. They were practically naked and were never allowed to put any covering on their heads at all.

As a result, very few of these Americans survived the first year of imprisonment, their resistance had been so lowered. Fort Drum's commanding officer Lt. Col. Lewis Kirkpatrick never completely recovered from his exposure and beating and died the following April of pneumonia. This entire course of treatment and public exhibition was administered under the direction of the Japanese District Commander. The troops at Fort Drum and Fort Frank were brought to Corregidor for evacuation to Manila about May 23.[718]

Concentrating the Garrison at the 92nd Garage

With the surrender of the Harbor Defenses of Manila and Subic Bays, the Japanese began assembling some 13,000 Americans and Filipinos. All but the patients and hospital staff and the American commanders were herded into the 92nd C.A.garage area on Corregidor's tail where they were left for several days with only what food they had managed to bring with them into captivity. A single faucet supplied the only source of water. Those who could, crafted shelters using wreckage from the old hangers, but most were simply left out on the concrete apron exposed to the elements at the beginning of the monsoon season.[719]

Many staff and general officers who had been quartered in Malinta tunnel were moved to Bottomside after a few days, concentrated at the old Filipino market. The American officers and enlisted men were eventually separated from the Filipinos in the 92nd C.A. Garage area. Work parties of prisoners of war were formed by the Japanese to collect the bodies of the dead from the battlefield for cremation. At irregular intervals small disbursements of food were made by the Japanese but never in sufficient quantities to meet the needs of the many thousands of concentrated prisoners. On May 21 the majority of the American and Filipino prisoners

Crowded conditions at the 92nd Garage Area (the old seaplane beach), where the island's POWs were initially concentrated. Gasei, Philippine Expeditionary Force.

Another view of the tent city that arose in the garage area.
Note the abundance of shelter halves being used mostly for protection from the sun. USAMHI.

began moving in groups to Bottomside, where they were loaded aboard three small transports and every inch of deck and space below was jammed with people. Each transport, designed to normally accommodate 120 passengers, was loaded with 4,000 men. There were no toilets and 50% of the men had come down with dysentery. The transports remained at Corregidor until May 24, before finally departing for Manila. When they arrived off Manila, the prisoners were loaded onto landing boats that brought them closer to the beach, where the American POWs had to jump out into waist deep water and make their way ashore. Many had to swim ashore because they were dropped off in even deeper water. They were then paraded through the streets of Manila on the way to prison camps. While there were casualties among the harbor defense POWs, at least there was no repeat on the scale of the infamous death march endured by the Bataan POWs. The officers held in Bottomside were grouped with the officers from Forts Frank and Drum and most were also transported to Manila on May 24 and then moved into prisoner of war camps.[720]

About 130 American officers and enlisted men were retained on Corregidor to work on clean up and salvage details. Much of this matériel had been demolished and proved difficult to move. Also collected were small arms, fire control equipment, both AA and seacoast, all badly wrecked. The Japanese had them collect all 3-inch AA, 75 mm and 155 mm guns, as well as other moveable metal for scrap. The junk was loaded aboard a transport and shipped to Japan as scrap. All of the ammunition found was stored in the tunnels or placed in the battery magazines. What quartermaster matériel remained was also collected and prepared for shipping. In June 1942 a detail of about 73 American prisoners under Lt. Col. Lewis S. Kirkpatrick was returned to Corregidor from the POW camps at Cabanatuan to join the contingent previously left there. Twelve of these were returned to Cabanatuan because of illness. Of the others, some were retained for more than a year in an attempt to return a few of the seacoast batteries to serviceability. Compared to most other POW experiences, these detachments were well treated. Their food allotment was regular and good, they had medical attention, and they were even paid and allowed to use the funds for additional small purchases of food and toiletries. [721]

Japanese sentry stands guard at the Malinta Tunnel. Apparently, the frame for a bunk bed is being removed by prisoners. USAMHI.

Japanese Type 97 medium tank. The Japanese managed to land two of these tanks on Corregidor, but initially they were stranded on the beach. By the morning of the 6th they had managed to surmount the short cliff and were advancing slowing inland. Gasei, Philippine Expeditionary Force.

Japanese sketch showing the surrender negotiations with General Jonathan Wainwright (on right, preparing to stand), United States Forces in the Philippines on May 6, 1942. NARA.

The new Japanese owners inspect the 12-inch gun of Battery Hearn. The "fortress" of Corregidor appears to have become somewhat of a tourist attraction to Japanese officers and friendly foreign journalists. NARA.

CHAPTER 16
THE JAPANESE OCCUPATION AND AMERICAN RECONQUEST

Initial Japanese Occupation

The Japanese concentrated on three matters following the capitulation of the fortified islands. First was the need to contain, sustain, and relocate the prisoners that surrendered. Next there was an interest in studying both the fortifications and weapons found on the islands — although apparently as much for propaganda and demonstration of Japanese prowess as a real desire to learn from a defeated enemy. And then finally the forts and their supplies were exploited for their material value, primarily as high-value scrap.

Over the next two years, though dwindling in size with transfers to the mainland, an American POW contingent assisted in the clean-up on the fortified islands. Capt. John M. Wright has left us an interesting account of their activities in his book, *Captured on Corregidor*. Initially much time was spent in sorting and salvaging remaining ammunition, though the Americans proved purposely inept at its salvage. They claim to have destroyed or reported damaged over half of what they processed. Damaged shells were thrown into the sea and powder was burned. Brass shell casings were deemed valuable by the enemy and saved for scrapping. Some 155 mm GPF guns found their way to Japanese units, but the 75 mm and many of the 3-inch guns were scrapped. The Japanese seemed interested in trying to salvage much of the fire control system — plotting boards, observing instruments, radios, and telephones. In June of 1943 most of the Americans were sent away, being replaced with Filipinos. A small group of American ordnance technicians under Capt. J.J. Coughlin, Ordnance Department, remained to assist on technical issues.[722]

Interest in the fortifications and the supporting military technology was expressed by the conquerors. Following the same pattern that was shown in Singapore and a host of smaller conquests, the enemy catalogued facilities and inventoried captured weapons. Items deemed worthy of technical scrutiny proved few. The American coast defenses did not possess much in the way of technically-advanced breakthroughs; it appears that only some radio and radar components and what was salvageable from the code-breaking machinery in the naval intercept tunnel were taken back to Japan for technical examination. Interviews were conducted with most captured officers in order to learn from their combat experience. The Japanese were convinced that a tunnel connected Corregidor and Bataan and were highly frustrated when officer after officer denied that such a link existed.

Large quantities of infantry-type accoutrements and personal gear had already been captured on Bataan, and there was little interest in the military re-use of that obtained on the fortified islands. Of course, food stocks, medical supplies, engineer, and quartermaster supplies were readily appropriated by the local Japanese command and units stationed on Corregidor. There was also wide-spread looting by Japanese soldiers of personal items found in trunks, quarters, and on the POWs themselves.

Japanese Propaganda Usage

Being the scene of a major Japanese triumph, the island also held value from a propaganda standpoint. More than a few Japanese reports, newspaper articles, movie theatre newsreels, and even books were published on the subject of Corregidor's conquest. Naturally the stronger the fortress was described, the more magnificent its fall seemed. A German correspondent from the *Deutsche Allgemeine Zeitung* was allowed to tour the fortress and ran an article in Germany on January 7, 1943. Wilhelm Schulze described Corregidor as the strongest fortress in the Far East, the Americans not bragging about the site unlike their British counterparts for Singapore. According to him the Japanese had learned about the fortification by calculating the use of concrete sold to the Americans from Japan during construction. The tunnel system was acknowledged as "impenetrable," and no doubt built in contravention of the disarmament treaties then in force. Much was made of the supposed poor treatment of the Filipinos by the Americans. (Not that the Axis regimes were known for their tolerance!).[723]

It did not take long for the Japanese to show interest in the large amount of metal scrap available. The first shipment of scrap from Corregidor left on a boat with the majority of captured prisoners as soon as May 24 — just 18 days after the surrender. Materials of interest seemed to have been steel (or iron) and copper alloys — bronze and brass. Little lead other than counterweights for disappearing guns was available, and it was one metal the Japanese had in relative abundance. Due to the haphazard distribution of scrap metal on the island following the campaign, at one point the Japanese organized a complete sweep by POWs starting at the tail of the island working westward to collect all scrap of value.[724]

Japanese Re-Use of Buildings and Repair of Gun Batteries

Japanese made only minimal attempts to repair or recondition the various post structures captured on the island. They originally did not intend to garrison the island beyond what was required to obtain salvage. Even with the majority of buildings extensively damaged, there were more than enough rooms, tunnels, and other structurally sound places to use as quarters, shops, and administrative offices. During the 1945 reoccupation, Americans found clear evidence of use of several senior officer's quarters and living spaces. Offices complete with re-used American filing cabinets were in several large American buildings around Topside. Topside barracks had quantities of fabric, clothing, and even alcohol, attesting to its use as a large warehouse. Middleside Barracks was less damaged than Topside and was re-used for some Japanese garrison troops. Malinta tunnel, the navy intercept tunnel, and some former fixed antiaircraft emplacements of the early 1920s were used to store explosives and fixed munitions. At least one hospital wing was repaired and utilized by the Japanese for the same function. The commissary storehouse was also repaired and used as a barracks for Filipino laborers.[725]

Repairs to buildings almost appeared casual, with no thought given to any extensive re-use. A bad typhoon hit the island in October 1942, adding to the war damage many of the buildings already exhibited. Many roads were abandoned and allowed to become overgrown. Some attempt was made early on to repair a section of the trolley line from Bottomside to Morrison Hill. That work stopped in June 1943 and eventually most of the trolley rail was torn up and shipped out as scrap, leaving the rail beds as an alternate road system. The reservoirs and water purification system were only modestly repaired; the small Japanese garrison envisioned in 1942 was adequately served by the small springs and wells on the island. Corregidor's diesel power plant remained in operation at the time of surrender and continued to function for the Japanese.

Starting in late 1942 an effort was made to at least preserve, if not repair and restore, the least damaged guns. More than a few were cleaned of dirt and rust, repainted and oiled. According to American POW reports and some surviving Japanese records, several large guns were at least nominally repaired for use. Sometimes it required combining damaged parts from two guns or carriages to make a functioning one. One gun each was reported repaired at the 12-inch batteries on Corregidor. Battery Cheney Gun No. 1 was repaired, and Battery Crockett No. 2 was completely disassembled, restored, painted and put back into commission. At Battery Wheeler the Japanese used civilian American POW labor (former Pacific Naval Air Base personnel) to dismount the usable gun from Emplacement No. 1, drag it across the traverse, and drop it onto the loading platform of Emplacement No. 2 ready for mounting. However, the project was suspended and the gun was never lifted onto the repaired carriage.[726]

Apparently, this was not the first time the Japanese were disadvantaged by their lack of heavy hoisting gear, which probably helped insure the historical survival of the big gun tubes and carriages. An interesting story involved the attempts to scrap the mortars. Being much shorter and thus lighter, the mortar tubes on Corregidor were just barely within the weight limitations of the available equipment. After the war three mortars were found missing — two M1890M1s from Battery Geary Pit A, and a spare tube of the same model. Apparently all three were removed by the Japanese. One of these tubes was found on the banks of the Pasig River in Manila in 1945, apparently as far as it got on its way to scrapping. A second is simply unaccounted for. The third was lost while trying to get it on a barge at Corregidor. Following the war, Staff Sergeant Woznniak described the attempt to move this tube: "As a part of their metal salvaging operations the Japs took two tractors and a detail of POWs and after two days of arduous work had finally dragged it down to the dock for shipment. During the loading out process, when the crane had the big cannon in midair, something suddenly snapped and down went the old mortar to a watery grave. The Japs were so astounded they were speechless, then gave way to a kind of sickly smile. The Americans smiled too, not so sickly."[727]

In addition to the disappearing guns, one of the 12-inch long-range BCLR guns was repaired. Battery Hearn was patched back together using the spare tube already at the battery and parts from similarly armed Battery Smith not far away. Prisoners straightened the piston rods using a salvaged hydraulic jack. Battery Ramsay was newly painted and repaired using rollers moved from Battery Morrison. Light batteries Maxwell Keys and Alonzo H. Cushing were put back into service. The Japanese also emplaced three 3-inch M1903 guns on their pedestal carriages in new "cave" emplacements on Malinta Hill. These were guns probably relocated from the other forts in the bay. Despite these reports, during the landing at Mariveles and naval bombardment of Corregidor (or the other islands for that matter), no heavy enemy gunfire was reported. There was some activity from lighter guns (three to five-inch estimated), and some hits; but no 12-inch gunfire was ever encountered. Whether they were being saved for later action, whether the attack came just too suddenly, or whether the "repaired" status was greatly exaggerated is not known.[728]

Some of the American vessels lost or scuttled at the end of the campaign were salvaged by the Japanese. Mine planter *Harrison* was repaired and put into service as a cable layer in October 1942, renamed *Harushima Maru.* Tug USS *Genesee* became *Patrol Boat 107* in April 1944 but was lost the following November. Navy minesweeper USS *Finch* was repaired in April 1943 and served the enemy as *Patrol Boat 103.* In that guise she was lost in January 1945. Finally, river gunboat USS *Luzon* became the gunboat *Karatsu.* Not only scuttled by the Americans, in Japanese service she was again scuttled in Manila Bay in February 1945.

The occupiers also tried to make the underwater mine defense operable again. Mines were planted again in 1943 and the mine casemate in James Ravine was repaired and used to control the mines in the northern channel. Another interesting re-use occurred at the unique casemated emplacement of Battery Monja at Wheeler point. The protected structure which had formerly held a 155 mm gun was used for a Japanese-built seacoast radar set. In March 1945 the captured set was of considerable interest to American inspectors.[729]

The Japanese Garrison

Serious Japanese attempts to provide Corregidor with an effective military garrison did not materialize until the fall of 1944. In August of that year the Japanese Army sent two more companies to its meager garrison, raising its Corregidor force to about 500 men. Subsequently an additional 300 army personnel were added to the garrison. In September the Imperial Japanese Navy began to assume a much more active role. It dispatched its *31st Special Base Force* commanded by Capt. Akira Itagaki, IJN, to the island. These were naval infantrymen, somewhat analogous to the U.S. Marine Corps. From Manila came a number of light AA guns and other captured weapons. The *333rd Construction Party* was assigned to Corregidor in later October 1944, augmenting what had up to that time been a largely civilian group of construction personnel on the island. Along with army units they set out to build seven gun emplacements armed with 14 cm guns from a Japanese warship sunk in Manila Bay. That same month 10 150 mm seacoast guns and two batteries of 120 mm dual-purpose guns were sent, along with 318 men of four fortress batteries under navy Lieutenant Endo. Some of the 120 mm guns were sent to Caballo and Carabao Islands, the others were emplaced on Corregidor at Middleside at the old stockade compound. The concrete structure there is the only permanent building on the fortified islands that can be credited to the Japanese during the occupation.[730]

The *332nd Construction Party* joined the *333rd* about the middle of November and they were combined as the "*Yoshida Party,*" under Colonel Yoshida. Dual-purpose batteries Nos. 1, 2, and 3 were built from Rock Point in an easterly direction towards James Ravine. The other four batteries were built from Wheeler Point in a westerly direction. They successfully test fired the guns on January 10, 1945.

Another interesting Japanese naval unit occupied Corregidor. In mid-October 1944 a squadron of *Shinyo* attack boats under LCDR Shoichi Koyamoda, IJN, was assigned. There were seven "units," each hosting about 15 boats supported by a total of about 200 naval personnel. These vessels were relatively light, inexpensive wooden boats loaded with a 500 lb. explosive charge. *Shinyo* boat crews were supposed to steer their boats at American warships or landing craft and set them for explosion. The crews would either jump out at the last moment for subsequent rescue, or ride them all the way in. This same October had seen the first large-scale use of Japanese airplane Kamikaze tactics in the war. Numerous caves were dug out along the Corregidor shoreline, particularly between Infantry and Engineer Points, to store and protect the motorboats. Thirty boats were expended against the American amphibious landing at Mariveles, but another 19 intact boats were discovered on the south shore near Ramsay Ravine later in the month while mopping up. Apparently they were being held for future invasion attempts, but their use was interrupted by the speed of the American aerial and amphibious landing of February 16.[731]

By January 31, 1945, 5,062 men were reported on Corregidor. This was by far the largest garrison location for the defense unit. Mariveles had 160 men, Caballo Island 373, Carabao Island about 400, and El Fraile had 65 sailors. Interestingly enough, the latter were recent survivors from sunken super-battleship *Musashi*. The collective unit was designated the *Manila Bay Entrance Force* and placed under Capt. Akira Itagaki, IJN.[732]

Tunnel on Corregidor dug by the Japanese to house *Shinyo* attack boats. These were expendable wooden boats packed with explosive designed to be steered towards enemy ships or landing craft and detonated. Some of the boats did have success against some American small craft prior to the reconquest of February 1945. NARA.

The Japanese used casemated Battery Monja as a site for a radar. Whether the set was operational or in use during the retaking is not known, but the electronics for it were found in the battery's tunnel by the Americans later. USAMHI.

Another Japanese inspection, this one of Battery Wheeler's disappearing gun. From several photographs and even evidence remaining today, the widespread claim that all the breechblocks had been removed or destroyed was not completely true. Schmidt Collection.

Japanese Use of the Outer Fortified Islands

Even less use was made by the Japanese of the other fortified islands in Manila and Subic Bay. Fort Wint in Subic Bay was not even occupied until January 10, 1942. There is no evidence that anything more than cursory salvage efforts was ever undertaken here. In Manila Bay, after the outlying islands were occupied on May 7, small teams of POWs and Japanese guards stayed for just a couple of weeks on each island to salvage the most valuable undamaged material. Later parties were occasionally sent from Corregidor to work on each island several days to reclaim usable equipment, preserve good ammunition, and obtain scrap metal. It does not appear that there was ever a permanent Japanese defense force on any of the islands until the last-minute preparations in late 1944.

At Fort Hughes on Caballo Island there were attempts made to care for and restore some coast defense batteries. In the first campaign the island had never been heavily bombed, and while it did receive some shellfire, this was not nearly as intensive as at Fort Mills. Also due to the communications confusion at the campaign's end, the Americans were not able to demolish the defenses. Even today the breechblocks of both 14-inch disappearing guns and the mortars at Battery Craighill are still intact. U.S. Army reports state that the Japanese were able to restore Battery Gillespie to firing condition, though like the Corregidor batteries, it was never fired against the returning Americans. The 3-inch guns of Battery Fuger were removed by the Japanese, and likely were among those re-emplaced in tunnel defenses on Corregidor. The emplacement itself was subsequently buried and graded over by the Japanese.

The island's 6-inch disappearing guns at Battery Leach were also virtually intact at the time of the American surrender. However, during the intensive American bombing campaign in early 1945, the emplacement's magazine was hit and violently exploded. Both guns were tossed from their carriages, and concrete chunks spread over quite an area. The exact date of this hit (probably from B-24 bombings by the 5th Air Force) is unknown, but from aerial photographs it must have occurred before January 27, 1945. Also, late in 1944 the island received a 120 mm gun battery; three or four guns of this type were emplaced on the slopes above Battery Woodruff. When the island was retaken the Japanese garrison numbered about 300-400 men.[733]

Fort Drum was a significant curiosity to the Japanese and was frequently toured by military brass. There was an attempt to salvage the large ammunition stocks of the 14-inch guns. While some of the powder charges had been purposely water-damaged at the time of surrender, the POWs working at the fort convinced their overseers that most of the powder was unusable and gladly helped dispose of it by dumping it in the sea. The 14-inch turret guns had been successfully damaged at the time of surrender. The crew had placed loaded sandbags in the muzzles and fired the guns. At Battery Wilson the left gun had its muzzle jacket split, and the right gun jumped back off its carriage cradle into the turret. Similarly, at Battery Marshall the right gun was also put out of action. Further damage was done by an American 2000 lb. bomb on January 27, 1945. The right-hand gun was broken off 15 feet from the muzzle and even the wire-wrapped tube came loose. The left gun was holed and left bulged. There was evidence that the Japanese were able to still traverse at least one turret, but with inoperable guns that was pointless.[734]

The fort's diesel power plant was still operating at the surrender and continued to be utilized by the Japanese garrison. Except for the damage to Battery Marshall mentioned above, the saturation bombings of 1944-45 by the Americans did little damage to the fort. The September 1945 American damage survey found three large bomb craters on the deck some 30 feet in diameter and three feet deep. Besides the cosmetic effect, these hits did not damage to the structural integrity of Fort Drum. The Japanese used POW labor to remove the 3-inch gun on the fantail. It was probably relocated to Corregidor along with Fort Hughes's Battery Fuger guns to arm the Japanese defensive positions on Malinta Hill.[735]

Even less is known about the Japanese use of Fort Frank on Carabao Island. The Americans had managed to execute a fairly thorough demolition of the facilities prior to the surrender. All armament was rendered useless, many of the firing mechanisms being thrown over the cliffs into the ocean. Fire control observation and radio equipment was removed and destroyed. Some salvage operations were attempted by the Japanese, but apparently a lack of heavy equipment and boats prevented completion. Battery Crofton in some reports was considered repaired by the Japanese, but like the "restored" Corregidor batteries, there is no evidence that is was subsequently used. Three damaged 155 mm GPF guns and carriages from Battery Frank North were found in 1945, still on the wharf awaiting transport. There was evidence that the Japanese used the Battery Crofton Tunnel as quarters for the small garrison detachment stationed on the island.[736]

Retaking the Fortified Islands

The strategic decision to return to the Philippines was not an easy one for the Americans. Despite the country's history with the island chain, there were military advantages to occupying Formosa as an alternative. It was less heavily garrisoned by the enemy (implying fewer casualties in taking), and its airfields were close enough to Japan to substantially aid the strategic bombing effort. The navy, particularly Adm. Ernest J. King, strongly advocated that Formosa should be the target of the Pacific war efforts in the last half of 1944. General MacArthur, perhaps understandably with his strong emotional affinity to the Philippines, thought there was a moral obligation to return and liberate the Philippines instead.

In late July 1944 President Roosevelt invited his two primary Pacific commanders — General MacArthur and Adm. Chester Nimitz — to a conference in Honolulu to present their points and facilitate a decision. On July 29, the president and a few close aides listened to Nimitz present the navy's case. After just a few clarification questions, the general rose for his turn. MacArthur always had a reputation for being a persuasive orator, and apparently on this date and place he was at his best. Even though not specifically prepared prior to the meeting, the arguments for a Philippine return for both military and ethical reasons won the day. After only a 92-minute meeting, the president was convinced; the Philippines would be the shared army and navy objective for the fall.[737]

Helping facilitate this decision was an emerging appreciation of Japanese weakness, particularly in the air. Admiral Halsey had delivered massive (and heavily one-sided with regard to airplane losses) carrier air attacks on the central Philippines between September 9 and 11, 1944. Almost 500 Japanese aircraft were accounted for, and a similar tally was racked up 10 days later during attacks on Luzon. Halsey thought the timetable for the invasion of Leyte could be moved up, and so did the chiefs of staff. Just a month later, on October 20, MacArthur's Sixth Army landed at Leyte. Combat was fierce, and a subsequent Japanese naval attack resulted in the war's largest naval engagement in Leyte Gulf. Still, that battle was a major U.S. victory, and American progress was steady. In mid-December the army returned to lightly-defended Mindoro Island, and on January 9, 1945, the major assault on Luzon began with an amphibious invasion at Lingayen — the very beaches the Japanese had used just three years earlier.[738]

The first ex-coast artillery fort to be reclaimed was Fort Wint, on Grande Island in Subic Bay. The Japanese had never attempted to fortify or otherwise prepare defenses on the island. But there were fears that the island might have been fortified and would oppose the planned landings in Subic Bay. Consequently, it had been subject to extensive aerial bombing by the 5th Air Force in January, and naval shelling just prior to the amphibious assault. Apparently, this bombardment resulted in the destruction of 6-inch Battery Hall. The emplacement was reported intact by a January 27 aerial survey. But on reoccupation it was found that the magazine between the guns had exploded, making a crater 100 feet wide and 15 feet deep. Both gun carriages were heavily damaged, with Gun No. 1 half retracted and still with a projectile in its chamber. The island was occupied by 2nd Battalion, 151st Infantry Regiment, 38th Infantry Division, on January 30, 1945. There were no enemy on the island — they had departed two weeks earlier, and thus there were no American casualties.[739]

For some reason the late war survivability of the old 6-inch disappearing batteries seems peculiarly poor. Of the five such batteries in the harbor defenses of Manila and Subic Bay (Batteries Morrison, Ramsay, Leach, Hall, and Woodruff), four were destroyed in 1945 by either American bombing/shelling or accidental explosion. Along with Battery Hall at Fort Wint, sister Battery Woodruff was not to last long. The battery was undamaged during the early 1945 reoccupation. However, in August 1945 a group of navy sightseers visited the emplacement. They entered the powder magazine, and a wayward match or cigarette got away. A slight explosion was soon followed by a full detonation of the magazine's contents. Fortunately, this sequence allowed the visitors to safely escape. The explosion leveled the emplacement's central traverse and scattered concrete blocks for quite a distance. The guns were knocked off their carriages.[740]

Serious planning for the clearing of Manila Bay began in Lt. Gen. Walter Kruger's 6th Army headquarters in early February. Immediately following an expected successful amphibious assault on Mariveles, Corregidor was to be retaken with a daring combined amphibious/airborne attack. MacArthur approved the plan on February 5, and a target date of February 12 selected. Strong Japanese resistance at Zig-Zag pass slowed the operations to isolate the Bataan peninsula, and forced the postponement of the Corregidor assault to February 16.[741]

It was found necessary to secure the small port of Mariveles on the southern tip of the peninsula. This was accomplished by an amphibious assault launched from Subic Bay on D-1. The following day this port would in turn launch an amphibious attack on Corregidor. The attack was carried out as scheduled with a flotilla of vessels under Adm. Russell Berkey. The assault troops were the 151st Regimental Combat Team, 38th Infantry Division. Mariveles also played host to a small American flotilla of mine craft and light gunboats. Early on the morning of February 16, these were attacked by the Corregidor-based Shinyo boats. Initially about 30 were dispatched, but 18 quickly dropped out. Twelve boats attacked the American landing flotilla and six exploded successfully, sinking three LCS (L) landing craft gunboats and damaging another. Luckily this proved to be one of the very few successes for this type of weapon.[742]

The Assault Plan

Corregidor was subjected to an unusually heavy bombardment prior to the assault. The plentiful airfields in the Philippines and large naval forces made it easy to assign a very heavy bombardment schedule. In particular the B-24s and A-20s of the 5th Air Force enjoyed working the island over. One notable victim of this preparation was Battery Ramsay. When the Americans occupied the island in mid-February, they found the battery freshly destroyed. A huge crater 25 feet deep was located where the former traverse magazine had been between Guns 2 and 3. Only the two far sides of the three-gun battery still existed, and even there the guns

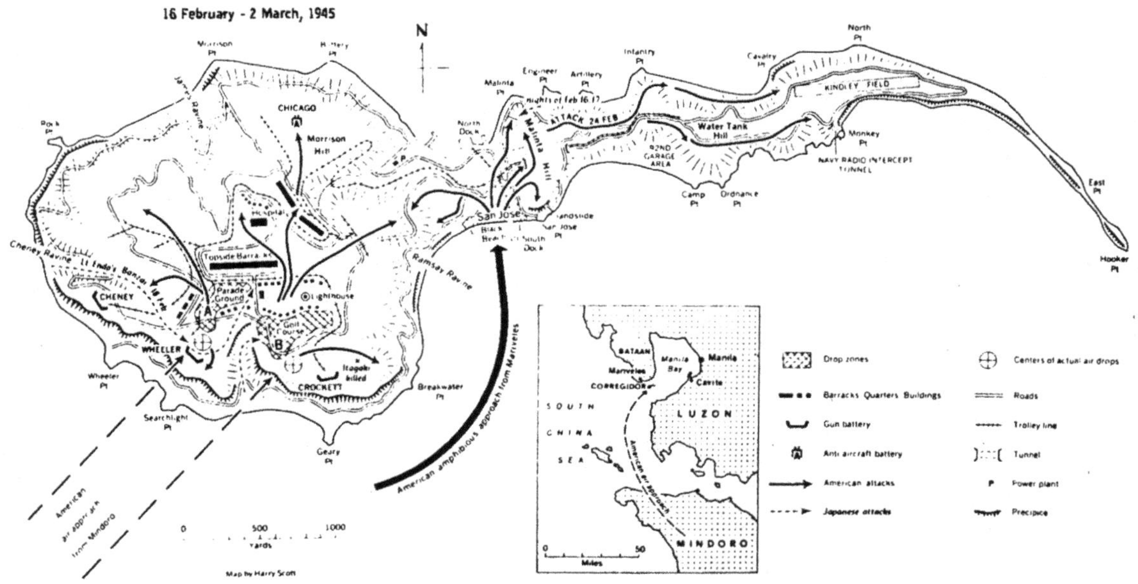

Map showing the American planned parachute air drop approach and the selected landing craft assault beach of the February 16, 1945, attack. From Flanagan, *Corregidor; The Rock Assault Force.*

were tilted askew from what must have been a devastating explosion. No Japanese accounts of this incident, or a record of their casualties has been found.[743]

For planning the Americans fully utilized not only aerial photographs, but pre-war plans of the topography and structures. Interviews with former residents were also undertaken. Plans were crafted to carry out a two-phased assault. The 503rd Parachute Infantry Regiment (Reinforced) would make an aerial jump on Topside. Two tiny landing zones were selected — basically the old parade ground bordered by Topside barracks, officers' quarters, and administration buildings, and the other on the old 9-hole golf course adjacent to the Corregidor Club ruins. One battalion would jump initially on both zones. Subsequently the transport planes would return to base (southern Mindoro Island), and the second battalion would load and drop on the same zones. There was much concern about the condition of the landing zones. As mentioned above they were very small — each about 1000 feet long and 430 feet wide. They were not clear; while relatively flat they were punctured with craters and strewn with concrete and metal debris from surrounding buildings. Also, the customary high winds at the island and surrounding cliffs suggested that parachutes might be blown beyond the landing zones onto the cliff sides or even in the water, a 500-foot drop from Topside. To lessen the danger, the drop would be made from just 500-foot altitude, barely giving paratroopers time to open their chutes and slow to safe landing speeds.[744]

With the Japanese garrison supposedly preoccupied with the paratroopers on Topside, a reinforced 3rd Battalion, 34th U.S. Infantry Regiment, 24th Division, would make an amphibious landing on Black Beach, just west of the South Dock. This unit would board its landing craft in Mariveles, and time its landing for 1030. After landing it was to take the summit of Malinta Hill and prevent the Japanese forces on the island's tail from reinforcing Topside. Finally, on D+1 the 3rd Battalion 503rd U.S. Parachute Infantry Regiment would jump and reinforce the troops on Topside. In one of biggest surprises in the Pacific Theatre, the Americans grossly underestimated the enemy's strength. Approximately 600-800 Japanese troops were assumed for the defense. In truth, about 6,000 were present, a mix of army and naval personnel. Captain Itagaki was himself headquartered on Topside. The Japanese did have a number of guns in cave emplacements, from about 3-inch to 5-inch size. Light field artillery, machine guns, mortars, and small arms with ammunition were plentiful.[745]

The Rock Force Paratroop Drop

The American attack force — dubbed the "Rock Force" — was commanded by Col. George M. Jones, the commander of the largest unit, the 503rd Parachute Regiment. The task force had just been constituted as a combined arms team for this operation and consisted of the three parachute battalions of the 503rd Parachute Infantry Regiment, the 462nd Parachute Field Artillery Battalion, and one company of the 161st Parachute Engineer Battalion. The amphibious infantry assault unit – 3rd Battalion, 34th Infantry Regiment, reinforced with an additional company and attached small units of medical, signal, antiaircraft, tanks, and anti-tank troops, completed the task force. In all the American assault force was to total about 3,000 officers and men.[746]

At 0700 on February 16, Colonel Jones and 3rd Battalion took off from Mindoro in a fleet of C-47s of the 317th Troop Carrier Group. Fifteen minutes later navy cruisers and destroyers started bombarding and coordinating B-24s dropping fragmentation bombs. The paratroopers arrived and began their descent. Initially the Japanese were quiet. Itagaki had been warned of a paratroop attack, but personally thought the terrain was too difficult and had dismissed this as an option. Thus, not only were the bulk of the enemy forces deployed near the shoreline, but the Japanese were fortunately caught looking the wrong direction. For the first wave of troopers, coming in at 0833 enemy fire was light. However as predicted, landing difficulties were encountered. Many troopers suffered injuries from hard landings, and several others were blown into the trees of cliffs south and west of Topside. Several hundred of the first 1,000 Americans to land in this wave were at least temporarily put out of action by accident. When Colonel Jones landed, he quickly was able to establish a headquarters and aid station in the bombed-out remains of Topside barracks.

View of the actual parachute drop in February 1945. Note how barren and pock-marked from bombs the landscape looks on Corregidor. On the right center edge can barely be seen the No. 2 Emplacement of Battery Wheeler. NARA.

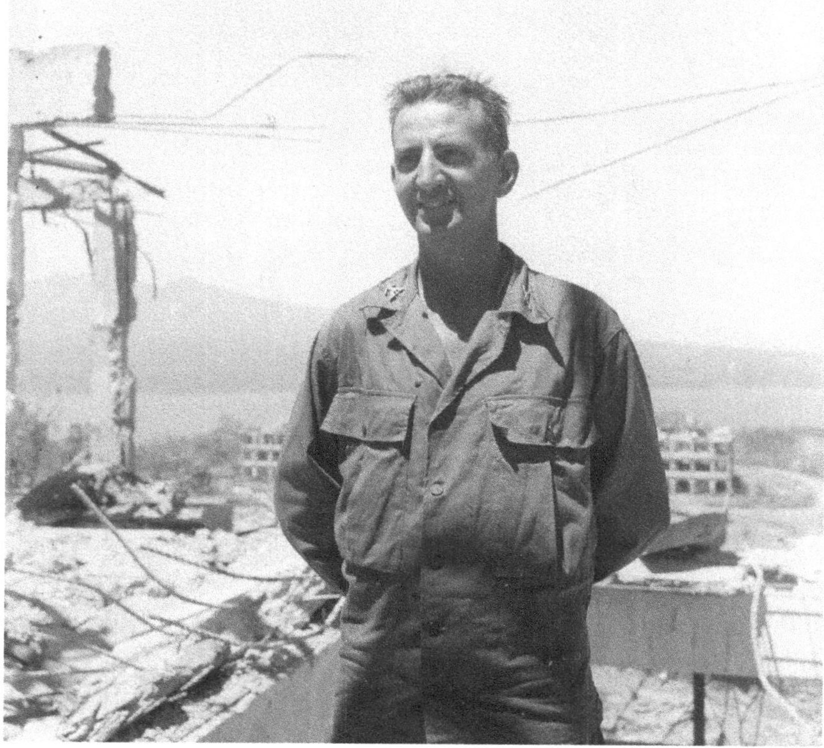

Col. Jones of 503rd RCT on Corregidor, March 1942, USAMHI.

February 16, 1945, the 503rd RCT lands on Corregidor. USAMHI.

Parachutes descend directly behind the old swimming pool of the Corregidor Club on February 16, 1945. One chute appears draped over the edge of the pool itself and others are hung in the adjacent trees. NARA.

One particular small group was blown off-target and landed on the cliff tops. They surprised a Japanese contingent and killed all of them, using small arms and grenades. Captain Itagaki was found among the dead. He had left his command post to watch for the anticipated approaching amphibious landing craft. Less than an hour after the start of combat, the enemy was left without its leadership. The exact location is difficult to pinpoint using the surviving descriptions; positions ranging from Breakwater Point to Geary and Wheeler Point have been suggested. Adding to Japanese woes was also the early capture of the old protected switchboard room, which had continued to operate as the enemy's communications hub. Between the loss of their commander and the ability to communicate between dispersed forces, the Japanese were unable to coordinate major defensive moves.[747]

Landing at Black Beach

A little flotilla of 25 LCMs of the 592nd Engineer Boat and Shore Regiment delivered the reinforced battalion of the 34th Infantry Regiment to Black Beach at 1028. Commanding officer Lt. Col. Edward M. Postlethwait led his troops ashore. While there were two bands of landmines to negotiate, just like the paratroopers, the first craft encountered only sporadic rifle fire. Companies K and L pushed a couple of hundred yards across the ruins of Barrio San Jose, and then turned to ascend Malinta Hill. Even though carrying full packs, they quickly scrambled up the road and trails to the hill's summit, fortunately without any casualties. Unknown to them, they were soon sitting on top of a tunnel system that held something like 2,000 enemy soldiers and tons of munitions. The subsequent waves of LCMs gradually encountered heavier opposition. Machine guns and mortars from Ramsay Ravine and Breakwater Point took an increasing toll of troops landing on the beach. Land mines near the beach accounted for more than a few vehicles, including several tanks.[748]

Landing craft of the water-borne section of the assault on Black Beach. This was the old south beach not far from the South Mining Wharf. This shot was taken from the south coast road around Malinta Hill on February 17, 1945. Schmidt Collection.

The second aerial drop was made during the early afternoon. By this time the Japanese were thoroughly alerted, and the antiaircraft fire was more intense. Numerous paratroopers and transport planes were hit. The drop height was further reduced to a bare 350 feet. Upon landing this battalion quickly helped consolidate the landing zones, and the combined forces began to branch out into the surrounding wrecked buildings during the afternoon. With the casualties taken on this last jump, it was decided to land the last paratroop battalion on the next day by seaborne landing craft like the 34th rather than risk another drop. During this first night there were sporadic encounters on the landing zone perimeters, though most were just probing attacks. There were, however, major enemy counterattacks on the army positions on Malinta Hill. Two outpost hills flanking Malinta Point were heavily attacked and overrun with many casualties inflicted. The soldiers actually on Malinta Hill repulsed several heavy attacks staged by Japanese troops quartered underneath them within Malinta Tunnel.

Soldiers man a 37 mm M3 antitank gun near the South Dock on Corregidor. Although enemy tanks were not encountered on the island, the gun was useful in clearing Japanese strongpoints and cave positions. NARA.

Battery Wheeler photographed after the end of the war in September 1945. The Japanese defensive forces managed to infiltrate into and through the battery during the most intense phases of the island's retaking. USAMHI.

Subsequent Days

The second day of the attack, February 17, saw further expansion of the American position, but opposition was still fierce. The Japanese resisted from a multitude of caves, ravines, and tunnels. While few attacks were coordinated, it proved very difficult to take out the individual positions. The pattern of the attack had left almost 2,000 enemy troops near the cliffs and shore to the west and south of Topside, and at least as many still in the huge Malinta Tunnel complex. Classic Pacific War tactics of position isolation, grenades, satchel charges, flamethrowers, and pointblank artillery and bazooka fire were necessary. Corregidor never had a complete interior defense system — but the large number of old but still substantial concrete buildings, plus the ease of tunneling in the soft volcanic rock made up for it. Most of the fire control stations on the island were used by the Japanese as pillboxes. The damage to the wrecked ruins of most of these that can still be seen today date from the American demolitions of February 1945 rather than from the earlier campaign.[749]

Over the next several days, battles raged in and around several former battery sites. Battery Geary, Cheney, and Smith all saw significant combat. The most stubborn position of all proved to be old Battery Wheeler. While neither of the 12-inch guns was operable, the battery's interior magazines, air spaces, and passages to the gun wells proved to be attractive enemy hideouts. On February 16, the Japanese used the battery's BC station as a pillbox for a machine gun. Two companies of the 503rd tried sequentially to take the position the next day. After a furious firefight they were repulsed. It seemed that after every attempt to sweep the position of enemy soldiers, it soon became repopulated from mysterious underground sources (the magazines and spaces mentioned above). Early on the morning of February 18, about 0300, the battery's magazine was ignited causing a large explosion and fire. Casualties were heavy on both sides. As late as February 27 and 28, the battery had to be repeatedly cleared of enemy soldiers.[750]

Also, this second day saw additional heavy fighting to clear the road between Bottomside and Topside—the Japanese used to their advantage the old antiaircraft gun magazines near Middleside and numerous caves on the eastern side of Topside. Night fighting was still heavy atop Malinta with yet more furiously aggressive Japanese attacks.

A soldier wields a BAR in combat on Corregidor on February 20, 1945, four days after the initial assault. Combat operations continued until the island was declared secure on February 28. USAMHI.

Day three degenerated into numerous small unit hunt and search for hidden enemy positions and the paratroopers continued to expand their perimeter. That evening the remaining Japanese forces around Topside launched a major "banzai" attack. Two columns totaling perhaps 1,800-2,000 men left caves in Cheney and Grubbs Ravines to attack the American forces. While most were eliminated as they approached the perimeter, several small groups of the enemy broke through to positions on Topside. Even the headquarters and medical station in the old Mile-Long Barracks were reached. Colonel Jones, his staff, and many hastily armed, wounded patients were needed to finally eliminate the attackers. Almost all the enemy soldiers in the attack were killed. On February 19, the old engineer reservation and combined cold storage and power plant were cleared with heavy fighting. That same day James ravine was cleared, but only after hard fighting around the old mine casemate (still being used for that purpose by the enemy) and infantry tunnel. The force atop Malinta Hill had stayed in place. Two days later the Japanese inside the tunnel attempted to detonate large explosive charges to clear the blocked entrances and stage another attack. Unfortunately for them the explosion's force mostly rebounded inside the tunnel, killing perhaps 600 waiting Japanese soldiers while burying half a dozen Americans outside.[751]

Starting on February 24, troops began their push east from Malinta Hill towards Monkey Point and the tail. Up to this point an estimated 2,500 enemy had been killed, and there were not thought to be many left. Mopping up was still actively in progress on Topside, and there was still concern over enemy troops left in the Malinta Tunnels. However, early in the morning of February 24, a final series of seven explosions rocked the hill. The remaining tunnel garrison had detonated more munitions, killing themselves. The tail assault bogged down near Water Tank Hill, famous from the battle three years earlier. A night "banzai" attack by about 300 Japanese was quickly eliminated by the paratroop battalions. However enemy mortar fire hit the battalion command post and inflicted numerous casualties.[752]

In 1945 American found a collection of guns the Japanese had apparently gathered as scrap in a jumble near the north dock. Included were even some old Spanish guns that had been retained on the island since 1898 as Spanish-American War trophies. NARA.

The following day the assault continued, clearing Water Tank Hill. Progress was not fast, but steady, and the troopers had reached the vicinity of the old Station C intercept tunnel near Monkey Point. About 11:00 on the morning of February 26, just as the Americans were swarming around the tunnel and its entrances, a truly massive explosion occurred. Whether it was set off by a high-explosive round fired by a nearby supporting Sherman tank or by Japanese detonation is unknown. Apparently, the Japanese had been using the tunnel for munitions storage. All the Japanese inside the tunnel perished, and unlike the previous explosions at Malinta Tunnel, Americans were caught in proximity and also took heavy casualties. The tank near the entrance was tossed about and all but one of its crew killed. American casualties totaled 196, 52 of which were killed. Only an estimate of the Japanese deaths, placed at 150-200, was possible. Still, despite periodic setbacks, by the end of day on February 28, organized enemy resistance had ended.[753]

Small actions and mopping-up continued for several weeks, but no more large encounters were experienced. Total counted Japanese deaths were 4,506; maybe 20 prisoners were taken. Estimating that about 1,500 enemy troops were sealed in caves and tunnels, drowned while trying to escape the island, or lost in major explosions, perhaps 6,000 Japanese defenders had been accounted for. Rock Force reported 210 killed, 5 missing, 450 wounded, and 340 injured (mostly jump injuries). Total American casualties vary by source. The numbers quoted from Smith and Devlin puts them at 455 killed and 1005 wounded, up until end of organized resistance (several more occurred after that date). Belote and Belote states 197 killed and 1022 wounded.

The colors were raised once again on Corregidor on March 2, 1945. Interestingly, the old flagpole still survived and was used once again. NARA.

General Macarthur Returns

On March 2 General MacArthur returned to the Rock. With his usual flair for historical imagery, the general returned the same way he left — on a naval PT boat. He brought along surviving staff members that had been here with him three years earlier. Visits were made to a number of familiar locations, including Topside Barracks and Malinta Tunnel. After a carefully arranged tour and flag-raising at the former Fort Mills parade ground, he announced: "Gentlemen, Corregidor is living proof that the day of the fixed fortress is over."[754]

Retaking Fort Hughes

Following the Corregidor operation, on March 23, a Sixth Army field order was prepared for the reoccupation of Caballo (Fort Hughes), El Fraile (Fort Drum), and Carabao Islands (Fort Frank). Preceding the actual assaults, all three islands were thoroughly saturated by bombing, naval bombardment, and in the case of Caballo Island, artillery fire from Corregidor. On March 27, elements of the 151st U.S. Infantry, 38th Division, made an amphibious assault by 8 LCMs on Caballo. The initial landing at 0859 on the island's eastern lowlands was relatively quiet. The island's crest was secured by the early afternoon. However, it was soon found that the bulk of the garrison was holding out in old mortar Battery Craighill. Taking advantage of the unique topography, the Japanese garrison fought back hard with machine guns and small arms. Several tanks were brought in on the third, although one threw its tread, and another bogged down in a hole in the rocks near the beach. (The latter still exist on the beach). But the slope around the mortars was too steep to use the tanks, and artillery fire could not reach deep into the pits. The presence of the protected former magazines made it easy for the defenders to simply take cover when attacks with grenades or satchel charges were attempted. A sort of standoff developed which lasted for six days.[755]

Next in line was Fort Hughes on Caballo Island. A landing was made by infantry of the 151st Regiment, 37th Division, on March 27, 1945. Here troops try to ascend the steep hogback from the beach during the invasion; a most difficult way to attempt it. NARA.

Retaking Fort Hughes, March 1945, looking down on 14-inch Battery Woodruff. NARA.

On the night of April 3, the Japanese tried a "banzai" attack from their positions around the mortar battery; about 80 attackers were killed without effect on the Americans. Finally, on April 5, 2,400 gallons of a diesel-gasoline mix were pumped into the eastern pit, and then ignited. The fire burned for two hours but did not totally eliminate the enemy. Returning the next day, 3,000 gallons of flammable mixture was pumped in the other pit, which also burned furiously. On April 7, 6,000 gallons were pumped into both and detonated simultaneously with TNT bundles placed in the vent shafts. A fourth and final dousing on April 8, finally managed to do the trick. When the attackers were finally able to enter the mortar battery on April 13, they found 50 bodies and just one survivor to kill. There persists today remains of Japanese writing on some of the mortar battery walls indicating that at least one survivor held out until early 1946.[756]

Retaking Forts Drum and Frank

Fort Drum was heavily worked over by a naval gunnery task force prior to the attempt at retaking it. In particular the light cruiser USS *Phoenix* (CL-46) raked the 6-inch gun casemates at almost pointblank range, penetrating the armor of Battery Roberts. On April 13 the 151st Infantry supplied a reinforced company for the assault on Fort Drum. This time the army incorporated the burning technique from the beginning. A

Heavy fighting took place around Battery Craighill at Fort Hughes. Eventually it took pumping fuel into the battery and then igniting it to clear the defenders out. USAMHI.

American airstrike on Fort Drum, February 21, 1945. NARA.

specially rigged LSM with a swing ramp brought the infantrymen and elements of the 113th Engineer Combat Battalion to the concrete battleship deck. Outside of periodic small arms fire, there was no sign of the estimated 70 Japanese defenders. Over 2,200 gallons of fuel mixture were pumped into deck ventilator shafts before being detonated with a 600 lb. TNT charge. The first explosion proved deceptively disappointing, but it was soon followed by a massive blast. A 12-foot-square armored plate over the 6-inch casemate at Battery McCrae flew hundreds of feet into the air before crashing back down on the deck. It took days for the interior to cool enough for an exploratory team to enter. The soldiers found eight dead Japanese on the second floor and 60 more down on the third level. Only three Americans had been slightly injured in the entire operation.[757]

Retaking Fort Drum. None of the armament was still in use, but a Japanese garrison still occupied its interior. From *16th Division History*.

At Fort Drum American troops assault the fortification from an adjacent landing craft rigged with a special ramp. Subsequently 2200 gallons of gasoline was pumped inside and detonated with 600 lb. of TNT. NARA.

After backing off, explosive charges were detonated on Drum. There were no Japanese survivors. NARA.

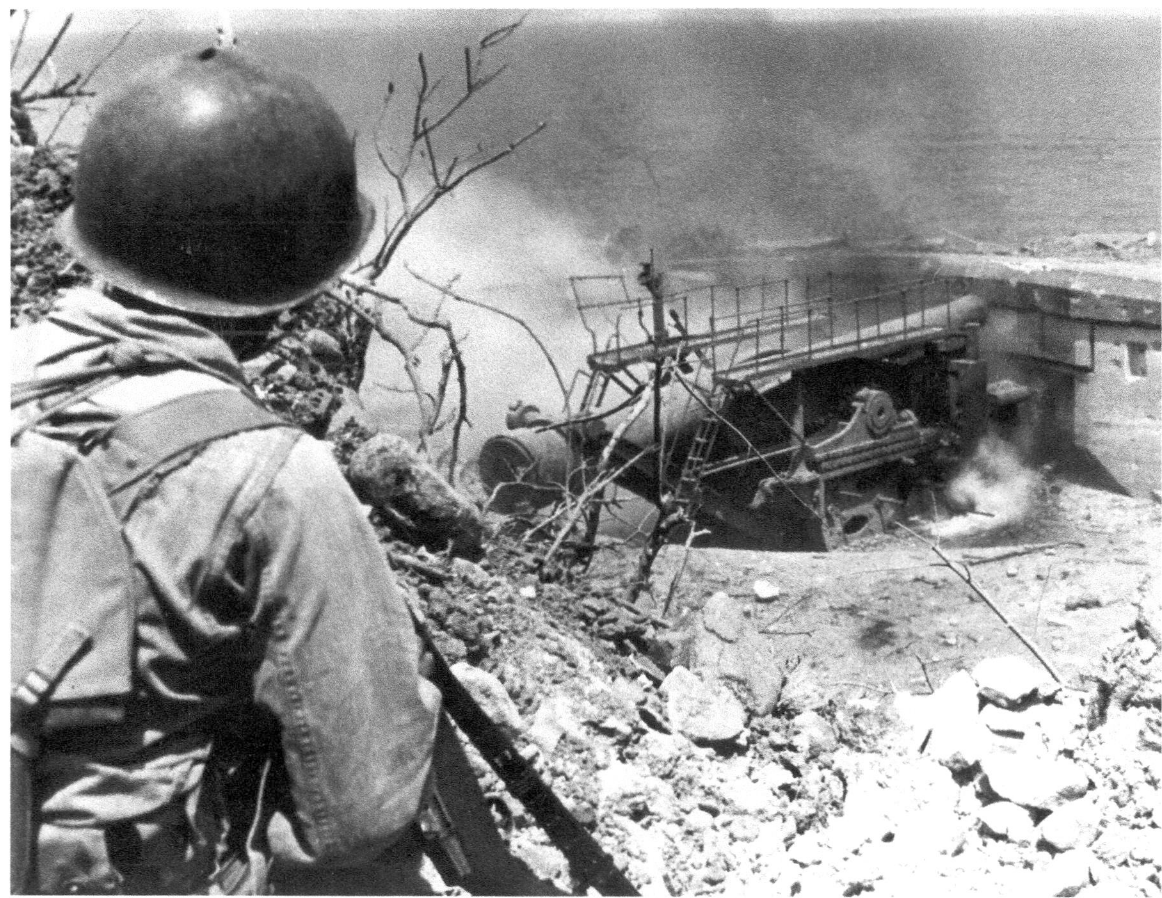

Fort Frank was attacked on April 6 by the 1st Battalion, 151st Infantry. Fortunately, the Japanese had already evacuated the island, and no combat occurred. Here a soldier looks over one of the fort's 14-inch gun batteries at that time. NARA.

On April 16, following another intense bombardment, the 1st Battalion, 151st Infantry, landed on Fort Frank. LCMs were used to transport these troops and two platoons of the 113th Engineers. Fortunately, the island had been recently evacuated. The Japanese garrison of about 350 soldiers had left to join the defensive forces at Cavite in early February. The only American casualties were caused by a mine the enemy had left behind.

Battery Koehler at Fort Frank after its return to American troops. The damage is an accumulation of 1942, 1944, and 1945 bombardment by both the Japanese and Americans - there was never any infantry combat on the island during either campaign. USAMHI.

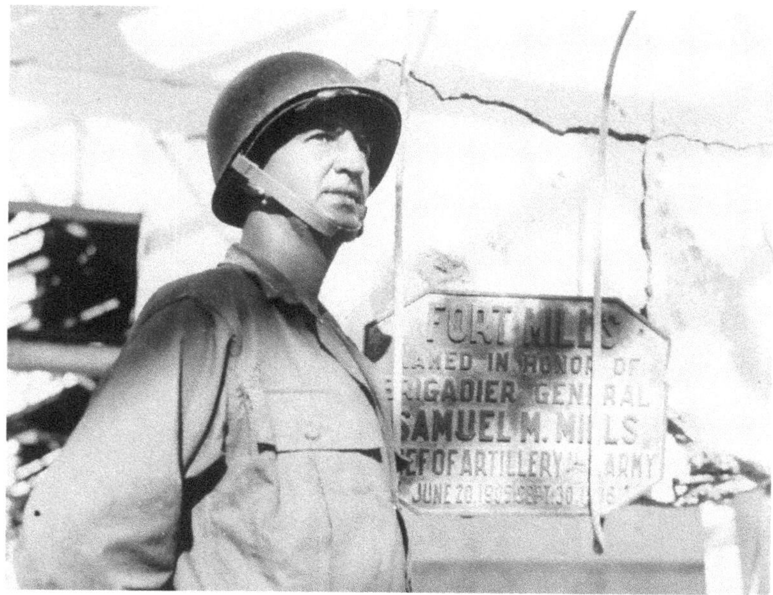

Colonel George Jones, commanding officer of the 503rd Parachute Infantry Regiment posing with the original Fort Mills plaque on March 6, 1945. NARA.

EPILOGUE

While mopping up continued for several months, the Americans made no military use of the retaken fortified islands. Graves registration companies with a protecting infantry company were the only occupants following the withdrawal of combat forces. Every now and then an enemy soldier would be found. There was quite a surprise when a soldier encountered 20 Japanese soldiers led by a lieutenant wanting to surrender on January 1, 1946. They had found an old newspaper mentioning the end of the war and decided it was time to quit. In September of 1945 a special survey of the fortifications was made by an army board. Known as the Case or Melberg Board, the report commented mostly on the condition or survivability of the defensive structures as found at combat's end. Needless to say, they found the harbor defenses damaged beyond any further use. The report and its testimony today provide a useful historical accounting of aspects of the campaigns and enemy occupation not obtainable elsewhere.[758]

Following the war, a small garrison of Philippine Scouts was stationed on Corregidor and generally small-scale training for the Philippine Army was conducted here. At a formal ceremony on October 12, 1947, the US officially transferred Corregidor to the Philippine Republic. General Moore returned to the island to provide a historical perspective. He is reported to have said "With it go the warmest wishes of all Americans, that

All the former American harbor defense islands were transferred from U.S. to Philippine ownership in a ceremony on October 12, 1947. Here the Philippine flag is being raised for the first time on the Corregidor flagpole. NARA.

until the end of history no other flag than that of the Philippine Republic shall fly over the hallowed ground of Corregidor." The small local garrison, located in temporary structures on Bottomside, occasionally escorted official visitors and tried to prevent destruction of remaining metalwork by scrappers.[759]

By the early 1960s a fairly regular, though small, tourist trade was established to see the battlefield ruins. A small, private inn opened to serve occasional overnight stays of adventure-seekers and returning veterans. Well into the 1960s the Philippine armed forces still used the island periodically for training exercises, at times quite extensive. Small units were occasionally quartered on the island. In recent years a claim has been made about the training and subsequent massacre of a unit of Muslim commando soldiers on the island in 1967. The actual facts about this event have never been collaborated, and there is an indication that the entire account, subsequently known as the "Jabidah Massacre," is a fabrication.

In 1962 the U.S. Congress passed legislation to aid in the establishment of a battlefield park on Corregidor Island. That in turn resulted in an appropriation two years later to share in the funding of a Pacific War Memorial. Work was undertaken fairly promptly, and an impressive rotunda, peace sculpture and museum were completed in 1968 with both Philippine and American funding. The cost of these facilities on the Topside cantonment's east end was about $1.2 million. Unfortunately, the memorial became neglected by the 1980s. The markers and memorials became cracked and overgrown, and maintenance was not kept up. Scrappers continued to hunt for scrap metal to sell. The otherwise unprotected islands of Carabao and El Fraile were particularly hard hit. All the guns and carriages and many metallic fixtures have been gutted from Carabao, including the rails of the tram lines and even the outer layers of rebar just beneath concrete walls and ceilings, were cut and removed by scrappers along with steel doors, railings, and fixtures. Fortunately, the Filipino Navy at Fort Hughes and the U.S. Navy at Fort Wint prevented this scale of destruction on those islands. Fort Mills itself was also generally protected, but several batteries and structures were at least partially scavenged during night raids by opportunistic scrappers.[760]

After the war, there has been a consistent flow of American, Filipino, and Japanese visitors to the "Rock" of Corregidor. Emplacements, like Battery Way pictured here in 2006, have been kept relatively clean of debris and made accessible by cleared trails. Mark Berhow collection.

In 1986 jurisdiction of the shrine moved from the Department of National Defense to the Department of Tourism (although legal ownership still resides with the Philippine military). At the same time the Corregidor Foundation, Inc. (C.F.I.) was created as a private, non-profit foundation with the mission of conserving Corregidor's relics as well as to further develop the island's tourism potential. Thereafter extensive investments were made to build a new inn, repair the docks, and build a replica church and administration buildings on Bottomside. Regular tour boat service was contracted to Sun Cruisers in the early 1990s and a brisk, regular tourist trade developed (including a number of Japanese tourists, many of whom came to pay their respects to ancestors who had died on the island).[761]

Grande Island in Subic Bay remained in U.S. Navy hands following the war and was gradually developed into a low-key rest and recreation site for naval crews during the Vietnam War. Through the effort of a few motivated, historically aware individuals, some of the abandoned armament at Fort Wint was relocated to the American mainland in the 1960s. The two 10-inch disappearing guns at Battery Warwick and four smaller guns (the two 3-inch M1903 guns at Battery Flake, and one 3-inch M1903 and one ex-naval 3-inch, which had been mounted in 1941 as a training weapon at Battery Jewell) were dismounted and transported to Washington State. While it took several years, these guns were eventually cleaned and prepared for mounting at batteries at Fort Casey and Fort Flagler State Parks in Washington, where they remain. Grande Island went to

In the late 1960s an investment was made to create a national war shrine on Corregidor, with a museum and peace memorial. Eventually the island became managed by the Corregidor Foundation and continues today to serve visitors and historians. Williford Collection.

Philippine hands following the U.S. Navy's closure of Subic Bay Naval Station and the Cubi Point Naval Air Station. In the mid-1990s it was developed further as a resort with a private hotel and recreational facilities. The old gun battery sites and some surviving concrete buildings are still on the island. The two 6-inch guns and carriages at Battery Hall still exist, fortunately saved from scrappers by the military's long presence on the island.

Caballo Island was occupied by the Philippine Navy soon after the property's postwar transfer to that nation. Never developed into a major facility, it appears that the island's main use was for munitions storage. New earth-covered magazines were built on the lowlands on the island's eastern side, and some garrison quarters near the wharf. It remains an ammunitions storage facility, and visitation is not encouraged. Due to the continuous occupancy by the navy, the island's remaining ordnance has been protected from scrappers. The guns for Batteries Gillespie, Woodruff, Craighill, and Leach remain in place, though unpreserved and unprotected from the elements. Even remains of the Japanese 120 mm dual-purpose battery and a Sherman tank hull on the beach still exist. Caballo made news in 2011, when 4,000 pieces of vintage explosives and ammunition were safely removed from the Naval Arsenal and brought to Crow Valley gunnery range in Capas, Tarlac, to be safely detonated.

Two other islands in Manila Bay are totally neglected. Nominally El Fraile and Carabao Island are administered by the Philippine Marines, but both are unoccupied. These islands are difficult to access by boat; there are no serviceable wharves or beaches. At abandoned Fort Drum the remote navigational aid on the deck is the site's only remaining function. Most of Fort Drum's internal turret structures, casemates, engine room, and even ammunition were removed by scrappers. The turrets themselves proved too large to cut and move, but lengths of the barrels were sawed off and taken away.

Inevitably the historian is drawn to questions concerning the effectiveness of the coast defenses in the Philippines. The Harbor Defenses of Manila and Subic Bay was but one of several dozen defenses built by the United States. However, it was the only one to be subjected to a significant combat test during the modern period. In both 1942 and 1945 these forts witnessed warfare of a type and scale never envisioned by their constructors. What conclusions as to the suitability of the design concepts and tactical employment can be reached?

To begin with the mission of the American fortifications changed, often subtly, over time. In the initial construction phases the work was aimed solely at providing seacoast defense for the two strategically important harbors in the Philippines - Manila and Subic Bays. These defenses were built to satisfy the army's responsibility to protect the navy bases and create refuges for the small Asiatic Fleet to take cover from a potentially superior enemy until an American fleet could arrive from home. The defenses followed conventional engineer practices of the time, though the weapons were of a more advanced design and the tactical structures utilized plans of the most current type. This initial network of large disappearing guns, high-angle mortars, and numerous submarine mines was certainly adequate to the task assigned to it. Local geography worked both ways for the designers. The high elevations available on the island forts certainly offered excellent perches for battery location, and in the days of flat trajectories, impressive protection from enemy gunfire. On the other hand, the close shorelines in Subic Bay and on both the northern and southern shores of Manila Bay did not interfere with the seacoast role, but did make it much more difficult to carry out the mission if the surrounding land defenses fell.

The expansion of the role of the defenses (evolving about 1910-1915) tried to manage this dilemma. The existing defenses could still adequately cope with a "raid," a potential enemy attempting to quickly attack Manila Bay and its city, navy base, or sheltering Asiatic Fleet. But a sustained attack could not be resisted solely by the peacetime American-Filipino forces stationed in the territory. Eventually adopted as military policy in the Orange Plan, in the 1920s and 1930s, the Harbor Defenses were an integral part an expanded military plan. They were to be an important part of a defensive cordon or rampart surrounding the City of Manila and the Bataan Peninsula. Forces were to hold out for up to a year, simultaneously preserving the harbor of Manila and its naval base while depriving an enemy of the same, until a relieving fleet could reach the islands. To accomplish this role, attention was paid to protecting the gun emplacements and garrison from land bombardment (the bombproofing effort), to preventing enemy local forces from landing on the island forts (the land defense program), and stockpiling supplies for the siege.

When put to the test, how did the American plans and technology cope? The seacoast role was implemented well. Never did the Japanese even attempt to directly sail into Manila Bay with fleet units. Eventually they moved barges and small craft (mostly at night) along the Bataan shore from points north to load at Mariveles for the invasion of Corregidor, but even late in the campaign regular naval ships were too vulnerable to be risked to the defenders. The vulnerable design of disappearing and barbette guns and mortars became clear during the siege. However, the seacoast defenses were never fully eliminated, though some batteries were. The almost impregnable design of Fort Drum and judicious husbanding of batteries Smith and Hearn preserved the most important (and long-ranged) guns of the seacoast defenses intact. Moreover, they still had ammunition, functioning fire control, and trained personnel to operate them effectively. The seacoast defenses delivered successfully on their responsibility.

The experience resisting the siege of 1941-42 was less successful. More than a few writers have attempted to describe the successful Asian sieges by the Japanese of defensive fortifications (Port Arthur, Tsingtao, Singapore, Manila Bay) as an example of poor planning by the defenders; as if they were totally unanticipating a land siege. At least for Manila Bay that is mostly untrue. The Americans were very aware of the dangers of land bombardment from both the Bataan and Cavite shores. They conducted tactical shoots and built or increased bombproof protection for garrison and magazines. It was well known that the defenses were vulnerable to sustained bombardment by heavy howitzers. Attempts to mitigate that damage were taken, but only so much could be done. Likewise, the possibility of physical invasion (really only attempted on Corregidor) was considered. Land and beach defenses were built, fields of fire cleared, and necessary supplies stockpiled. Being aware of a danger and being unable to prevent it are difference challenges. The Japanese effort was simply overwhelming, and any significant reinforcement unavailable for the defenders. It is worth noting that the defenses did manage to hold out for five of the six months they were tasked to prepare for. And of course, it would take two and one-half year for the Americans to return, for which no plausible scenario could foresee.

Tactically the defenders could have improved on their situation. Do remember, however, that no changed decision or presence of any particular item would have made any significant change in the outcome. Once the war started, it was inevitable that the Filamerican forces, including the Harbor Defenses, would fall, maybe on a different date, maybe inflicting more delay or casualties on the enemy, but the final outcome was never in doubt. From the beginning of the defenders' isolation the defenses were below-strength for certain supplies and authorized personnel. Some corrections were made in late 1941, but not nearly enough. Ammunition supplies proved to be tight but adequate. Certain types were critically lacking, such as higher-altitude 3-inch AA fuzes. Even better would have been more 12-inch high-explosive rounds (especially for the mortars) to help the defenders improve battery counterfire.

Though understrength, the garrison seems to have been adequate for the task at hand and the batteries were well served. As trying as the siege must have been, there are no indications of any widespread problems with the morale of the defenders. The faith in the Philippine Scout ranks was fully justified, both in the coast artillery as well as the infantry in the Regular Army they turned out to be outstanding soldiers — unlike some of their counterparts in other colonial forces in the theatre. At Corregidor there were stories of problems with some of the administrative troops isolated mostly in Malinta Tunnel during the siege. Morale there was at times poor, and instances of malingering, food hoarding, and avoidance of outside jobs frequent. The officer ranks of the coast artillery units performed their duties well. The top leadership by Moore, Bunker, and other senior officers seems in retrospect to have been adequate, if not particularly innovative or anticipatory.

There did seem to be an issue with the beach defense force. By the time of the war there were no longer dedicated infantry units on the islands to provide beach defense, rather it was to be left with either detachments from the coast artillery regiments or opportunistically from other troops available. A scheme to transport at least some of the professional Philippine Division to Fort Mills before surrender of the Bataan force could not be implemented. Fortunately, the 4th Marine Regiment was already on the island in early April and available to take on the task of beach/invasion defense. However, the 4th had its own issues with morale and had been supplemented with marines and sailors otherwise unattached to fill out its battalions. At best its professionalism was uneven. The performance of some of the static defense positions on the island's tail during the night enemy landing was outstanding, inflicting terrific casualties. The follow-on attempts to clear the enemy the following day was less successful and eventually entirely bogged down.

Overall, the defenses of Manila Bay performed their intended service well. They prevented the Japanese entrance and occupancy of Manila Bay, they kept enemy aerial bombardment to a manageable level, and finally engaged an enemy landing when the time came. While some of the technical elements were obsolete by 1941 standards, they functioned adequately enough when the moment of need came. Even if the strategic goal to protect and safeguard the Philippine harbor for six months in the face of no practical assistance was overly optimistic or maybe even misguided, the defenders valiantly tried and nearly succeeded. The 1945 campaign was significantly different. Even though just three years later, the strategic situation and technology of warfare had changed to the point that the remains of the harbor defense were useful only as concrete caves. The age of fixed fortifications had ended, but the Harbor Defenses of Manila and Subic Bay will hopefully live on through accounts of its history.

Regimental crests of the four primary Coast Artillery units of the 1942 campaign (left to right)— the 59th (Harbor Defense), the 60th (Antiaircraft), the 91st (Harbor Defense, Philippine Scouts), and the 92nd (Tractor Drawn, Philippine Scouts) Greg Hagge Collection.

The Coat of Arms for the Coast Defenses of Manila and Subic Bays
The motto is *Corregidor omnia vigilat* (Corregidor guards all)

The design of the coat of arms was based on a modified version of the coast of arms of the Philippine Islands, although different meanings were attached to the devices used. The shield consisted of an upper blue half and a lower red half, separated by a wavy line, the heraldic way of indicating water, which, in this case, consisted of the two bays defended. The seahorse in the upper half represents the island of Caballo, on which Fort Hughes was located. The castle below represents Corregidor, or Fort Mills, the principal fortification, and it is placed between two croziers of gold, symbolizing the monk (El Fraile, Fort Drum) and the nun (La Monja) of the legend, familiar to those that served in Manila. The crest is a carabao's head, full face in the natural colors, and represents Fort Frank on Carabao Island.

APPENDIX I
CORPS OF ENGINEER CONSTRUCTION DATES AND COSTS

One of the more valuable source documents for major tactical structures (gun batteries, mine buildings, switchboards, power plants, fire control structures, searchlights, etc.) is a form generated by the U.S. Army Corps of Engineers at the completion of construction. It is known as the "Report of Completed Works." This was essentially a dated form of one or more pages. It contained a formatted report of the actual work done: name, dates, construction material, etc. Usually on a second page was a drawing of the structure. These are now filed at the National Archives, College Park, MD, in Record Group 77, Records of the Chief of Engineers, Entry 1007. While they are extremely valuable as an historical accounting of each structure (sometimes virtually the only document about the building that survives), it is necessary to understand the context of some of the information contained. Specifically, in this work you will see mention of the following items sourced from these documents:

Dates

Routinely the Reports of Completed Works list a beginning or start date for a structure and then a subsequent date of transfer. Often it might also contain a "completion" date—however this is usually just the day before transfer was made, and does not represent an actual, physical completion date. The start date is usually accurate for when physical work began, not a planning, designing, or authorizing date. The transfer date refers to the day the engineers turned over the structure to the tactical organization which would operate the structure. Usually for these posts that meant the Coast Artillery, but could also be the engineers, ordnance, signal, or medical detachments of the post. In fact, this date could be many months, even years after the physical completion of the structure. It had as much to do with how prepared the Coast Artillery Corps was for the structure and how much the structure was fully equipped as to when it was "done." Thus, for some batteries there might be a span of up to four years in time between dates. This should not imply that physical construction took four years. Even the largest batteries or buildings were usually built during just several months of a building season or contract, though equipping and furnishing might take just as long as construction.

Costs

The engineers listed on these forms what it cost their department to do its portion of the work on a structure. Usually that was what was paid directly for the contracted labor, materials, departmental overhead, and contingencies. The figure is useful for comparison purposes, but does not in fact represent the entire expense of getting a battery prepared for service, Not included is any cost of the original land or reservation, for non-engineering equipment (like fire control devices, furniture, stores, communications), for the armament itself, or the ammunition. In very general terms the construction cost for most batteries was only one-third of the overall costs. Even beyond that the supporting fire control stations, switchboard and communications buildings, power plants, and quarters for the crew were accounted for elsewhere. Thus the "cost" figures used in this narrative should always be considered just a fraction of the total expenditures.

APPENDIX II
ORDNANCE DEPLOYED IN FIXED, NAMED BATTERIES, SERIAL NUMBERS OF GUNS AND CARRIAGES HARBOR DEFENSES OF MANILA AND SUBIC BAYS 1907-1942

FORT AND BATTERY	INITIAL ARMAMENT 1907 – 1919	FINAL ARMAMENT DECEMBER 8, 1941
FORT WINT		
BATTERY WARWICK	2x10-in M1895M1 &M1901 DC No. 27/ No. 13 (replaced with No. 26 by April 1909 after damage in proofing) No. 28/ No. 15	2 x 10-in M1895M1 & M1901 DC No. 26/ No. 13 No. 28/ No. 15
BATTERY HALL	2 x 6-in M1905 & M1905 DC No. 6/ No. 6 No. 7/ No. 7	2 x 6-in M1905 & M1905 DC No. 6/ No. 6 No. 7/ No. 7
BATTERY WOODRUFF	2 x 6-in M1905 & M1905 DC No. 5/ No. 1 No. 8/ No. 8	2 x 6-in M1905 & M1905 DC No. 5/ No. 1 No. 8/ No. 8
BATTERY FLAKE	4 x 3-in M1903 guns & pedestal No. 11/ No. 6 No. 12/ No. 7 No. 14/ No. 8 No. 15/ No. 9	2 x 3-in M1903 guns & pedestal No. 11/ No. 6 No. 12/ No. 7
BATTERY JEWELL	4 x 3-in M1903 guns & pedestal No. 17/ No. 10 No. 18/ No. 11 No. 29/ No. 12 No. 33/ No. 13	2 x 3-in M1903 guns & pedestal No. 17/ No. 10 No. 18/ No. 11 1 x 3-in navy MkVI & pedestal MkII No. 4954 1 x 6-pdr navy MkII & pedestal No. 899

FORT MILLS		
BATTERY HEARN	1 x 12-in M1895M1A2/ M1917 BCLR No. 44 Watervliet/ No. 31	1 x 12-in M1895M1A2/ M1917 BCLR No. 8 Watervliet/ No. 31
BATTERY SMITH	1 x 12-in M1895M1A2/ M1917 BCLR No. 47 Watervliet/ No. 30	1 x 12-in M1895M1A2/ M1917 BCLR No. 1 Watervliet/ No. 30
BATTERY CHENEY	2 x 12-in M1895M1/M1901 DC No. 3 Bethlehem/ No. 16 No. 11 Bethlehem/ No. 17	2 x 12-in M1895/ M1901 DC No. 37 Watervliet/ No. 16 No. 12 Watervliet/ No. 17
BATTERY CROCKETT	2 x 12-in M1895M1/ M1901 DC No. 15 Bethlehem/ No. 14 No. 9 Bethlehem/ No. 15	2 x 12-in M1895M1/ M1901 DC No. 13 Bethlehem/ No. 14 No. 27 Watervliet/ No. 15
BATTERY WHEELER	2 x 12-in M1895M1/ M1901 DC No. 8 Bethlehem/ No. 13 No. 7 Bethlehem/ No. 12	2 x 12-in M1895M1/ M1901 DC No. 7 Bethlehem/ No. 13 No. 36 Watervliet/ No. 12
BATTERY WAY	4 x 12-in mortars M1890M1/ M1896 mortar carriage No. 173/ No. 158 No. 174/ No. 151 No. 170/ No. 241 No. 172/ No. 150	4 x 12-in mortars M1890M1/ M1896 mortar carriage No. 173/ No. 158 No. 174/ No. 151 No. 170/ No. 241 No. 172/ No. 150
BATTERY GEARY	4 x 12-in mortars M1890M1/ M1896 mortar carriage No. 31/ No. 104 No. 32/ No. 116 No. 33/ No. 210 No. 40/ No. 294 4 x 12-in mortars M1908/ M1908 mortar carriage No. 2/ No. 17 No. 12/ No. 18 No. 13/ No. 19 No. 22/ No. 20	4 x 12-in mortars M1890M1/ M1896 mortar carriage No. 31/ No. 104 No. 32/ No. 116 No. 33/ No. 210 No. 40/ No. 294 4 x 12-in mortars M1908/ M1908 mortar carriage No. 2/ No. 17 No. 12/ No. 18 No. 13/ No. 19 No. 22/ No. 20
BATTERY GRUBBS	2 x 10-in M1895M1 & M1901 DC No. 25/ No. 14 No. 22/ No. 16	2 x 10-in M1895M1 & M1901 DC No. 25/ No. 14 No. 22/ No. 16
BATTERY MORRISON	2 x 6-in M1905 & M1905M1 DC No. 31/ No. 12 No. 32/ No. 13	2 x 6-in M1905 & M1905M1 DC No. 31/ No. 12 No. 32/ No. 13

BATTERY RAMSAY	3 x 6-in M1905 & M1905 DC No. 4/ No. 10 No. 2/ No. 9 No. 33/ No. 11 M1905M1	3 x 6-in M1905 & M1905 DC No. 4/ No. 10 No. 2/ No. 9 No. 33/ No. 11 M1905M1
BATTERY JAMES	4 x 3-in M1903 guns & pedestal No. 2/ No. 2 No. 3/ No. 3 No. 4*/ No. 4 No. 5/ No. 5 *Gun No. 4 damaged in proofing on 3/04/1908, replaced with M1903 No. 8	4 x 3-in M1903 guns & pedestal No. 28/ No. 13 No. 58/ No. 103 No. 41/ No. 4 No. 39/ No. 5
BATTERY MAXWELL KEYS	2 x 3-in M1903 guns & pedestal No. 101/ No. 100 No. 102/ No. 101	2 x 3-in M1903 guns & pedestal No. 101/ No. 100 No. 102/ No. 101
BATTERY ALONZO H. CUSHING	2 x 3-in M1903 guns & pedestal No. 15/ No. 9 No. 14/ No. 8	2 x 3-in M1903 guns & pedestal No. 50/ No. 9 No. 7/ No. 8
BATTERY GUY B. G. HANNA	2 x 3-in M1903 guns & pedestal No. 2/ No. 3 No. 3/ No. 2	2 x 3-in M1903 guns & pedestal No. 2/ No. 3* No. 3/ No. 2 *Probably; gun No.2 here is unconfirmed
FORT FRANK		
BATTERY CROFTON	1 x 14-in M1907M1/ M1907 DC No. 4/ No. 4	1 x 14-in M1907M1/ M1907 DC No. 4/ No. 4
BATTERY GREER	1 x 14-in M1907M1/ M1907 DC No. 2/ No. 3	1 x 14-in M1907M1/ M1907 DC No. 2/ No. 3
BATTERY KOEHLER	8 x 12-in mortars M1908/ M1908 mortar carriage No. 8 / No. 1 No. 21/ No. 9 No. 9/ No. 2 No. 23/ No. 10 No. 10/ No. 3 No. 24/ No. 11 No. 11/ No. 4 No. 25/ No. 12	8 x 12-in mortars M1908/ M1908 mortar carriage No. 8 / No. 1 No. 21/ No. 9 No. 9/ No. 2 No. 23/ No. 10 No. 10/ No. 3 No. 24/ No. 11 No. 11/ No. 4 No. 25/ No. 12
BATTERY HOYLE	2 x 3-in M1903 guns & pedestal No. 33/ No. 13 No. 29/ No. 12	2 x 3-in M1903 guns & pedestal* No. 33/ No. 13 No. 29/ No. 12 One gun and carriage moved to Fort Drum and mounted 1/12/1942

FORT DRUM		
BATTERY MARSHALL	2 x 14-in turret gun M1909 No. 1 No. 2	2 x 14-in turret gun M1909 No. 1 No. 2
BATTERY WILSON	2 x 14-in turret gun M1909 No. 3 No. 4	2 x 14-in turret gun M1909 No. 3 No. 4
BATTERY MCCREA	2 x 6-in M1908MII & M1910 ped No. 1/ No. 1 No. 3/ No. 2	2 x 6-in M1908MII & M1910 ped No. 1/ No. 1 No. 3/ No. 2
BATTERY ROBERTS	2 x 6-in M1908MII & M1910 ped No. 4/ No. 3 No. 2/ No. 4	2 x 6-in M1908MII & M1910 ped No. 4/ No. 3 No. 2/ No. 4
FORT HUGHES		
BATTERY GILLESPIE	1 x 14-in M1910M1/ M1907M1 DC No. 15/ No. 20	1 x 14-in M1910M1/ M1907M1 DC No. 15/ No. 20
BATTERY WOODRUFF	1 x 14-in M1910/ M1907M1 DC No. 8/ No. 17	1 x 14-in M1910/ M1907M1 DC No. 8/ No. 17
BATTERY CRAIGHILL	4 x 12-in mortars M1912/ M1896MIII mortar carriages No. 40/ No. 41 No. 39/ No. 40 No. 41/ No. 38 No. 38/ No. 39	4 x 12-in mortars M1912/ M1896MIII mortar carriages No. 40/ No. 41 No. 39/ No. 40 No. 41/ No. 38 No. 38/ No. 39
BATTERY LEACH	2 x 6-in M1908 & M1905MII DC No. 5/ No. 20 No. 6/ No. 21	2 x 6-in M1908 & M1905MII DC No. 5/ No. 20 No. 6/ No. 21
BATTERY FUGER	2 x 3-in M1903 guns & ped No. 99/ No. 98 No. 100 / No. 99	2 x 3-in M1903 guns & ped No. 99/ No. 98 No. 100 / No. 99

APPENDIX III
MAJOR AMERICAN GUN TYPE CHARACTERISTICS HARBOR DEFENSES OF MANILA AND SUBIC BAYS

GUN SIZE AND MODEL	USUAL MISSION	CARRIAGE TYPE AND MODEL	MAXIMUM ELEVATION	PROJECTILE WEIGHT	MAXIMUM RANGE (YDS)
3-inch M1903	Seacoast	M1903 Pedestal	16 degrees	15 pounds	8,771 yards
6-inch Armstrong	Emergency Seacoast	Armstrong 6-inch gun and pedestal	16 degrees	106 pounds	10,185 yards
6-inch M1905	Seacoast	M1905 and M1908 Disappearing	15 degrees	108 pounds	11,800 yards
6-inch M1908MII	Seacoast	M1910 Casemate	12 degrees	108 pounds	9,930 yards
155 mm M1917 and M1918	Seacoast	M1917 and M1918 Carriage	35 degrees	96 pounds	17,400 yards
8-inch M1888	Seacoast	M1918 Railway Top Carriage	42 degrees	200 pounds	21,000 yards
10-inch M1895	Seacoast	M1901 Disappearing	12 degrees	617 pounds	12,259yards
12-inch M1895	Seacoast	M1901 Disappearing	10 degrees	900 – 1070 pounds	11,636 yards
12-inch M1895	Seacoast	M1901 Disappearing modified for increased elevation.	15 degrees	900 – 1070 pounds	17,300 yards
12-inch M1895	Seacoast	M1917 Long-range Barbette	35 degrees	900 – 1070 pounds	29,300 yards
12-inch M1890M1	Seacoast Mortar	M1896MII Mortar Carriage	65 degrees	700 – 1046 pounds	15,291 yards
12-inch M1908	Seacoast Mortar	M1908 Mortar Carriage	65 degrees	700 – 1046 pounds	15,291 yards
12-inch M1912	Seacoast Mortar	M1896MIII Mortar Carriage	65 degrees	700 – 1046 pounds	19,319 yards
14-inch M1907M1	Seacoast	M1907 Disappearing	15 degrees	1560 – 1660 pounds	16,867 yards
14-inch M1907M1	Seacoast	M1907 Disappearing modified for increased elevation.	20 degrees	1560 – 1660 pounds	20,000 yards
14-inchM1910	Seacoast	M1907M1 Disappearing	15 degrees	1560 – 1660 pounds	19,244 yards
14-inch M1910	Seacoast	M1907M1 Disappearing modified for increased elevation.	20 degrees	1560 – 1660 pounds	24,000 yards
14-inch M1909	Seacoast	M1909 Turret Mount	15 degrees	1560 – 1660 pounds	19,244 yards

37 mm M1916	Beach Defense	M1916 carriage	21 degrees	1.2 pounds	3,500 yards
6-pounder M1898 and M1900	Land Defense	M1898 and 1900 parapet mounts	12 degrees	6 pounds	6,241 yards
75 mm M1917	Beach and Land Defense	M1917 carriage	16 degrees	13.6 – 16 pounds	6,500 yards
3.2-inch M1897	Beach and Land Defense	M1892 carriage	20 degrees	13.5 pounds	6,343 yards
5-inch M1890 and M1898 Siege Gun	Land Defense	M1890 and M1898 carriages	20 degrees	45 pounds	8,000 yards
7-inch M1890 and M1898 Siege Howitzer	Land Defense	M1890 and M1898 carriages	40 degrees	105 pounds	8,062 yards
3-inch M1918	Antiaircraft	M1918 Trailer Carriage	85 degrees	15 pounds	8,539 yards ceiling
3-inch M1917	Antiaircraft	M1917 Pedestal	85 degrees	15 pounds	9,843 yards ceiling
3-inch M2	Antiaircraft	M2 Pedestal	80 degrees	15 pounds	9,300 yards ceiling

Source: 1918 and 1924 editions of Ordnance Department's *Table of United States Army Cannon and Projectiles.*

APPENDIX IV
HARBOR DEFENSES OF MANILA AND SUBIC BAYS
BATTERY NAMING CITATIONS

BATTERY CHENEY (Fort Mills)
Named in War Department General Orders, (G.O.) No. 77, May 12, 1908, to honor 1st Lt. Ward Cheney, Company C, 4th US Infantry Regiment. Ward Cheney initially enlisted as a private in Company G, 1st Connecticut Volunteers, May 10, 1898, but was promoted to second lieutenant, 4th US Infantry, on July 9, 1898. He attained the rank of first lieutenant November 21, 1899, but was killed in action at Puente Julien near Imus, PI, on January 7, 1900, during an engagement with Philippine insurrectionists.

BATTERY CRAIGHILL (Fort Hughes)
Named in War Department G.O. No. 15, April 25, 1916, to honor Brig. Gen. William Price Craighill. An 1853 graduate USMA, he was appointed a brevet second lieutenant in the Corps of Engineers. In March 1855 he was promoted to second lieutenant, to first lieutenant in July 1859, and captain in March 1863. He was advanced to major in November 1865 and received the brevet rank of lieutenant colonel in March 1865 for faithful and meritorious service during the Civil War, particularly for his work in the defense of Cumberland Gap in Tennessee. He was advanced to the permanent rank of lieutenant colonel in January 1881 and to colonel in January 1887. On May 10, 1895, Craighill was promoted to brigadier general and appointed chief of engineers, a position he held until February 1, 1897, when he retired. General Craighill died January 18, 1909, at age 76, at Charles Town, WV.

BATTERY CROCKETT (Fort Mills)
Named in War Department G.O. No. 77, May 12, 1908, to honor 2nd Lt. Allen Taylor Crockett. Crockett entered the army as a sergeant in Company G, 3rd Georgia Volunteers, on July 12, 1898. He was promoted to drum major and battalion sergeant major, US Volunteer Infantry, on July 25, 1899, and on July 3, 1900, he was appointed second lieutenant, 27th Infantry, US Volunteers. On February 2, 1901, he was appointed second lieutenant, 21st US Infantry Regiment. On September 24, 1901, he was killed in action at Candelaria, near Nayabubu, PI, during an engagement with Philippine insurrectionists.

BATTERY CROFTON (Fort Frank)
Named in War Department G.O. No. 15, January 28, 1909, to honor Capt. William Moore Crofton, 1st US Infantry, appointed October 7, 1891, from civilian life as a second lieutenant in the 1st Infantry Regiment, promoted to first lieutenant April 26, 1898, and captain February 2, 1901. He died June 7, 1907, at the New York Arsenal at age 63.

BATTERY ALONZO H. CUSHING (Fort Mills)
Named March 27, 1922, to honor 1st Lt. and Bvt. Lt. Col. Alonzo Hersford Cushing. Cushing was an 1861 graduate of USMA who served with Battery A, 4th US Artillery Regiment, during the Civil War. Cushing was brevetted lieutenant colonel on July 1, 1863, for conspicuous gallantry on July 1, 1863, at Gettysburg, PA. He was killed in action at Gettysburg, July 3, 1863.

BATTERY FLAKE (Fort Wint)
Named in War Department G.O. No. 77, May 12, 1908, to honor 2nd Lt. Campbell W. Flake, 22nd US Infantry Regiment. Flake commenced his military career as first sergeant of Company I, 3rd Infantry Regiment, USV, June 7, 1898. He was appointed second lieutenant in the 27th US Infantry Regiment, February 2, 1901, and transferred to the 22nd Infantry Regiment on December 2, 1901. Lieutenant Flake was killed in action against Philippine insurgents near Marahui, Mindanao, PI, on January 22, 1904.

BATTERY FUGER (Fort Hughes)
Named in War Department G.O. No. 63, September 2, 1914, to honor Lt. Col. Frederick Fuger, a native of Germany who served as an enlisted man in the 4th US Artillery Regiment from 1856 to November 1863. While serving as first sergeant of Battery A, 4th Artillery Regiment, at the Battle of Gettysburg, Pennsylvania, July 3, 1863, he succeeded to command of the battery when all of its officers were killed or wounded and five of its guns disabled during Pickett's assault. First Sergeant Fuger continued the fight with his remaining guns until the battery was ordered withdrawn. He was subsequently appointed second lieutenant in October 1863. Following actions in Virginia in 1864, Lt. Fuger received brevet promotions to first lieutenant and captain for gallant and meritorious service at the Battles of Yellow Tavern and Dinwiddie Court House, Virginia. Following the war, he was awarded the Medal of Honor for distinguished gallantry during the Battle of Gettysburg. Fuger attained the rank of captain in 1887 and major in 1899. He retired with the rank of lieutenant colonel June 18, 1900, after forty-four years of service. Colonel Fuger died October 13, 1913.

BATTERY GEARY (Fort Mills)
Named in War Department G.O. No. 77, May 12, 1908, to honor Capt. Woodbridge Geary, 13th US Infantry Regiment, an 1882 graduate of the USMA. He served in the 19th US Infantry Regiment until promoted to captain, when he was reassigned to the 13th Infantry Regiment, January 1, 1899. Captain Geary was mortally wounded during an engagement with Philippine insurgents near Buena Vista, Luzon, PI, while in command of the 3rd Battalion, 13th Infantry Regiment, and died October 11, 1899, at San Francisco de Malabon, Luzon.

BATTERY GILLESPIE (Fort Hughes)
Named in War Department G.O. No. 63, September 2, 1914, to honor Brig. Gen. and Chief of Engineers George Lewis Gillespie Jr. Gillespie entered the USMA in July 1858 and upon graduation was commissioned a second lieutenant of engineers in June 1862. In 1864, 1st Lt. Gillespie passed through Confederate lines Near Bethesda Church, Virginia, during the Civil War, to contact General Sheridan, but was captured by Confederate troops. He escaped and reached Sheridan's headquarters and quickly returned to Gen. George Gordon Meade's headquarters with the information sought by Meade. For this, he was awarded the Medal of Honor in October 1897. Gillespie was brevetted major and lieutenant colonel for his service in the campaigns before Richmond and from Winchester to Appomattox Court House, Virginia, in 1864 and 1865. Gillespie was promoted to captain in April 1864, to major in September 1871, lieutenant colonel in October 1886, and colonel in October 1895. He was appointed a brigadier general of USV, May 27, 1898, and discharged from USV October 31, 1898. On May 3, 1901, Gillespie was promoted to chief of engineers with the rank of brigadier general and to major general January 23, 1904. General Gillespie retired June 15, 1905, with over 40 years of service. General Gillespie died at Saratoga Springs, New York, September 27, 1913, at age 72.

BATTERY GREER (Fort Frank)
Named in War Department G.O. No. 15, January 28, 1909, to honor Col. John Edwin Greer, Ordnance Department. An 1863 USMA graduate, Greer served as an ordnance officer, rising to the rank of colonel prior to his death while commanding the New York Arsenal, September 19, 1907.

BATTERY GRUBBS (Fort Mills)

Named in War Department G.O. No. 77, May 12, 1908, to honor 1st Lt. Hayden Young Grubbs, 6th US Infantry Regiment. Lieutenant Grubbs was an 1896 graduate of USMA appointed to the 18th US Infantry Regiment on June 12, 1896. He was appointed lieutenant colonel of the 2nd US Volunteer Regiment, June 25, 1898, honorably mustered out on June 22, 1899, and reassigned to the 6th US Infantry Regiment as a first lieutenant on January 1, 1899. At age 27, Lieutenant Grubbs was killed in action on October 1, 1899, at Tabuan, Negros Island, PI, during an engagement with Philippine insurrectionists.

BATTERY HALL (Fort Wint)

Named in War Department G.O. No. 77, May 12, 1908, to honor 2nd Lt. Joseph Hines Hall, 17th US Infantry Regiment. A native of Alabama, Hall enlisted in Company F, 1st Colorado Volunteer Infantry Regiment, on June 18, 1898, and served in that unit until July 14, 1899, when he transferred to the 18th US Infantry Regiment. Early in the 1900s he served in the 5th and 18th Field Artillery Batteries of the Artillery Corps, advancing to the rank of sergeant. On October 17, 1902, Hall was appointed a second lieutenant in the 17th US Infantry Regiment serving in the Southern Philippines. Lieutenant Hall was killed in action at Simitan, Mindanao, PI, on May 8, 1904.

BATTERY GUY B. G. HANNA (Fort Mills)

Named in War Department G.O. No. 13, March 27, 1922, to honor Capt. Guy Ben Gad Hanna, 78th Co., CAC. Captain Hanna served as a private in the 12th Minnesota Infantry Regiment during the Spanish American War until November 1898 and in the 19th and 11th US Infantry Regiment from March to September 1899. He served with the Porto Rico Regiment as a sergeant September 1899 to June 1901 and was appointed a Second Lieutenant in the Artillery Corps June 30, 1901. Advancing to captain, he was commanding the 78th Company, CAC, at Fort Moultrie, SC, when he was mortally wounded during a night service target practice at Battery Lord, May 22, 1913, when the gun misfired. The firing pin was still protruding through the face of the breechblock of a 3-inch gun when it was slammed shut, striking the base of the shell casing and blowing out the breechblock. Captain Hanna died of his injuries on May 23, 1913.

BATTERY HEARN (Fort Mills)

Batteries Smith No. 1 and No. 2 were formally separated October 29, 1937, when the latter was renamed in AGO letter dated September 17, 1937, to honor the late Brig. Gen. Clint Calvin Hearn, who as a major in 1909 had been the first coast artillery field officer assigned to command Fort Mills. Hearn was an 1890 graduate of USMA and was appointed an additional second lieutenant in the 4th US Artillery Regiment. He was advanced to First Lieutenant in the 7th US Artillery Regiment. From April 10 to August 29, 1900, he served with the Siege Battery O, 7th Artillery Regiment. Appointed captain in the Artillery Corps, February 28, 1901, and posted at Fort Barrancas, Fort Monroe, and Fort Adams from February 1902 to July 1906. Promoted to major May 1908 and on February 17, 1909, departed for the Philippines, arriving there April 22, 1909. Hearn commanded the Coast Artillery District of Manila Bay to Feb. 4, 1911. Hearn was promoted to lieutenant colonel, CAC, January 24, 1914. On January 3, 1916, Colonel Hearn again served as post commander at Fort Mills, PI, until February 1, 1917, when he assumed command of the Coast Artillery garrison, Coast Defenses of Manila and Subic Bays, February 2 to August 3, 1917. He was promoted to Brigadier General, NA, August 5, 1917. He was returned to the US and commanded the 153rd Field Artillery Brigade, June 14, 1918, to May 15, 1919. Hearn was returned to the permanent rank of colonel, CAC, on June 16, 1919, while on duty at Washington, D.C., in the office of the chief of coast artillery, where he served until August 20, 1919. After a variety of coast artillery postings, including the 4th Coast Artillery District, he retired May 31, 1927, for "disability incident to the service." Colonel Hearn died February 11, 1928. He was posthumously promoted to brigadier general by Act of June 21, 1930, to date from February 11, 1928.

BATTERY ELI D. HOYLE (Fort Mills)

Named in War Department G.O. No. 13, March 27, 1922, to honor Brig. Gen. Eli DuBose Hoyle. Hoyle was an 1875 graduate of USMA appointed second lieutenant in the 2nd US Artillery Regiment, June 16, 1875. He was promoted to first lieutenant October 28, 1883, and to major, USV, July 18, 1898. Hoyle was promoted to captain, 1st US Artillery Regiment, in the Regular Army September 18, 1898, and participated in the campaigns in Puerto Rico. On May 12, 1899, he was discharged from the USV and resumed his Regular Army rank as captain with his regiment. Captain Hoyle served as a field artillery officer in the Artillery Corps after 1901, was promoted to major in the Artillery Corps August 10, 1903, to lieutenant colonel January 25, 1907, and was assigned to the 6th Field Artillery Regiment June 6, 1907. He was placed in command of the regiment June 15, 1908. Hoyle was promoted to colonel March 3, 1911, and commanded the 6th Field Artillery Regiment at San Antonio, Texas, and Fort Riley, Kansas, until appointed to command the Central Department at Chicago, Illinois. Colonel Hoyle was promoted brigadier general September 24, 1913, and assigned to the Philippine Department. He commanded the District of Luzon, Philippine Department, December 11, 1913, to April 30, 1914, and the post of Fort McKinley May 6, to December 15, 1914. General Hoyle was retired with more than forty years of service with the rank of brigadier general January 19, 1915. During World War I, General Hoyle was recalled to active duty and commanded the Eastern Department, Headquartered at Fort Jay, Governors Island, New York, from August 1917 to January 15, 1918. General Hoyle died July 27, 1921, at Washington, D.C.

BATTERY JAMES (Fort Mills)

Named in War Department G.O. No. 77, May 12, 1908, to honor 1st Lt. John F. James, 8th US Infantry Regiment. James enlisted as a sergeant in Company A, 3rd Virginia Volunteers, May 12, 1898. He was commissioned first lieutenant in the 7th US Volunteer Infantry Regiment, July 19, 1898, and was honorably mustered out February 28, 1899. He joined the Regular Army as a second lieutenant in the 8th US Infantry Regiment on April 10, 1899, and was promoted to first lieutenant on February 2, 1901. Lieutenant James was killed in action against Philippine insurgents near Julita, Leyte, PI, on August 9, 1906.

BATTERY JEWELL (Fort Wint)

Named in War Department G.O. No. 77, May 12, 1908, to honor 2nd Lt. James McDonald Jewell, 14th US Cavalry. Jewell entered service April 26, 1898, in Co. M, 1st Illinois Volunteer Cavalry, in which he served until October 11, 1898, when he was transferred to the 8th US Cavalry, where he served as a private, corporal, and quartermaster sergeant in Troops C and H until May 7, 1901. He was appointed a second lieutenant in the 14th US Cavalry February 2, 1901, and served in the 14th Cavalry in the Philippines. Lieutenant Jewell died January 8, 1905, of wounds incurred in action at Usaps Cotta on Jolo Island in the Southern Philippines on January 7, 1905.

BATTERY KOEHLER (Fort Frank)

Named in War Department G.O. No. 15, January 28, 1909, to honor 1st Lt. Edgar Frederick Koehler, 9th US Infantry. Koehler entered service as a private in the 8th US Infantry November 8, 1891, and on October 31, 1894, was appointed second lieutenant in the 11th US Infantry. He was promoted to first lieutenant and transferred to the 14th US Infantry before returning to the 9th US Infantry September 16, 1898. He was killed in action at Barrio Tinuba, PI, on March 4, 1900.

BATTERY LEACH (Fort Hughes)

Named in War Department G.O. No. 63, September 2, 1914, to honor Col. Smith Stallard Leach, CE. Colonel Leach rose in rank in the Corps of Engineers following his graduation from the USMA in 1875 as he carried out civil and fortification construction assignments, including the construction of the fortifications at the entrance to Long Island Sound as a major 1896 to 1902. He was promoted to colonel of engineers and served as assistant to the chief of engineers from August 1907 until his death at the age of 58, October 16, 1909.

BATTERY WILLIAM L. MARSHALL (Fort Drum)

Named in War Department G.O. No. 13, March 27, 1922, to honor Brig. Gen. William Louis Marshall who entered military service as a private in the 10th Kentucky Cavalry (Union) August 16, 1862. He was discharged in September 1863, entered the USMA July 1, 1864, and graduated as a brevet second lieutenant of engineers, June 15, 1868. Marshall served on various exploration expeditions and river and harbor improvements, attaining the rank of major in 1895 and colonel in 1907. Colonel Marshall was promoted to brigadier general and chief of engineers July 2, 1908, and was instrumental in planning Fort Drum as well as the Panama Canal defenses. General Marshall retired June 11, 1910, and died July 2, 1920, at Washington, D.C.

BATTERY TULLY B. McCREA (Fort Drum)

Named in War Department G.O. No. 13, March 27, 1922, to honor Brig. Gen. Tully McCrea who entered the USMA in 1858 and graduated in June 1862 as a second lieutenant, 1st US Artillery Regiment. McCrea served with gallantry in the Civil War, receiving brevets for his service at Antietam, Maryland, September 17, 1862, at Gettysburg, Pennsylvania, and at Olustee, Florida, where he was severely wounded February 30, 1864. Returning to duty in October 1864, he served as an assistant professor of geography, history, and ethics at USMA until 1866. He briefly returned to the 1st Artillery Regiment as a captain and brevet major before transferring to the 42nd Infantry Regiment until 1868. He was reassigned to the 1st Artillery Regiment in 1868 and served with that regiment until promoted to major in the 5th US Artillery Regiment in December 1888. He was advanced to lieutenant colonel of the 5th Artillery Regiment in March 1898, and to colonel of the 6th US Artillery Regiment in July 1900. McCrea was promoted to brigadier general on February 21, 1903, and retired at his own request with over 40 years of service on February 22, 1903. General McCrea died at West Point, New York, on September 5, 1918, at age 79.

BATTERY MAXWELL KEYS (Fort Mills)

Named in War Department G.O. No. 15, April 25, 1916, to honor 2nd Lt. Maxwell Keys. Keys entered service as a private in the 10th US Infantry Regiment, February 19, 1895, serving in that capacity until February 18, 1898. He was appointed second lieutenant in the 1st US Volunteer Cavalry Regiment on May 6, 1898, and was promoted to first lieutenant on August 11 of that same year. He was honorably mustered out of the USV on September 15, 1898. He resumed his career with an appointment as a second lieutenant in the Regular Army and was assigned to the 3rd US Infantry Regular on June 1, 1899. On November 24, 1899, Lieutenant Keys was killed while Companies I, J, and K, of the 3rd Infantry Regiment, and Battery G, 3rd US Artillery Regiment, were engaging Philippine Insurrectionists at San Ildefonso, PI.

BATTERY MORRISON (Fort Mills)

Named in War Department G.O. No. 77, May 12, 1908, to honor 1st Lt. John Morrison Jr. A native of Iowa, Morrison was an 1896 graduate of the USMA and was appointed an additional second lieutenant of cavalry, assigned to the 2nd US Cavalry Regiment, June 12, 1896. He was appointed second lieutenant, 3rd US Cavalry Regiment, September 9, 1896, and was transferred to the 1st Cavalry Regiment as a first lieutenant December 13, 1899. On February 23, 1900, he was assigned to the 4th Cavalry Regiment. While engaged with Philippine insurrectionists January 18, 1901, on the Rio Corona near Gapan, PI, he was killed in action.

BATTERY RAMSAY (Fort Mills)
Named in War Department G.O. No. 77, May 12, 1908, to honor 1st Lt. Charles Rufus Ramsay, who entered service in the 3rd Maryland Infantry Regiment, April 25, 1898. He was appointed second lieutenant, 21st Infantry Regiment, July 9, 1898, and transferred to the 10th Infantry Regiment and promoted to first lieutenant September 16, 1899. Ramsay was transferred back to the 21st Infantry Regiment, March 26, 1900. He was mortally wounded in action June 10, 1901, at Lipa, Batangas Province, PI, and died on July 13, 1901.

BATTERY BENJAMIN K. ROBERTS (Fort Drum)
Named in War Department G.O. No. 13, March 27, 1922, to honor Brig. Gen. Benjamin Kearney Roberts, who entered military service as a second lieutenant in the 7th Iowa Cavalry Regiment in July 1863. He served through the Civil War and was awarded the brevet rank of major in the US Volunteers. He was mustered out of the volunteers July 1, 1866. Roberts was then appointed second lieutenant in the 5th US Artillery Regiment, April 1, 1866. He was transferred to the 2nd Artillery Regiment as a major in October 1899 and in September 1901 to lieutenant colonel of the newly organized Artillery Corps. He was advanced to colonel and then to brigadier general before his retirement. General Roberts died July 16, 1921.

BATTERY FRANK G. SMITH (Fort Mills)
Named in War Department G.O. No. 13, March 27, 1922, to honor Brig. Gen. Frank Guest Smith, who entered service as a lieutenant of the 4th US Artillery Regiment in August 1861. He was brevetted captain for gallantry and meritorious service at the Battle of Stones River, Tennessee, and to brevet major for gallantry and meritorious service at the Battle of Chickamauga during the Civil War. He was promoted to captain in the Regular Army in 1867 and continued to serve with the 4th Artillery Regiment until 1891, when he was promoted to major and reassigned to the 2nd Artillery Regiment. He was appointed colonel of the 6th US Artillery Regiment, March 8, 1898. On the eve of his retirement, Colonel Smith was promoted to brigadier general, retired, June 20, 1905, and died October 7, 1912.

BATTERY WARWICK (Fort Wint)
Named in War Department G.O. No. 77, May 12, 1908, to honor Capt. Oliver B. Warwick, who attended the USMA from September 1868 to February 1873. Upon graduation, he was appointed second lieutenant on October 1, 1873, and assigned to the 18th US Infantry. On February 20, 1882, Warwick was promoted to first lieutenant and again to captain on November 30, 1892. Captain Warwick was killed in action November 26, 1899, during an engagement between elements of the 18th Infantry Regiment and Philippine insurrectionists at Passi, Luzon, PI.

BATTERY WAY (Fort Mills)
Named in War Department G.O. No. 77, May 12, 1908, to honor 2nd Lt. Henry Newell Way, an 1899 graduate of USMA He was appointed second lieutenant, in the 4th US Infantry Regiment on February 15, 1899. He was assigned to Company F, 4th US Infantry Regiment and died August 28, 1900, of wounds incurred in action against insurrectionists at Villavieja near Catbalogan, PI, on August 27, 1900.

BATTERY WHEELER (Fort Mills)
Named in War Department G.O. No. 77, May 12, 1908, to honor Capt. David P Wheeler, 22nd US Infantry Regiment. Wheeler, an 1898 graduate of the USMA, served as a second lieutenant in the 23rd Infantry Regiment from April 26, 1898, until transferring to the 22nd Infantry Regiment on March 2, 1899. He was promoted to captain in the 26th Infantry Regiment on January 27, 1903, and transferred back to the 22nd Infantry Regiment on April 7, 1903. He was mortally wounded April 11, 1904, during an engagement with Philippine insurrectionists at Taraca, Mindanao, PI, and died April 14, 1904.

BATTERY JOHN M. WILSON (Fort Drum)

Named in War Department G.O. No. 13, March 27, 1922, to honor Brig. Gen. John Moulder Wilson, who graduated from the USMA in 1860 and was assigned as a brevet second lieutenant in the 1st US Artillery Regiment. He transferred as first lieutenant to the 2nd US Artillery Regiment in 1861 and to the Topographical Engineers in July 1862. He was brevetted captain for his service at Gaines Mill and major for gallantry at Malvern Hill during the Richmond Campaign of 1862, for which he was awarded the Medal of Honor while serving as first lieutenant of engineers with Batteries B and L, 2nd US Artillery Regiment, at Malvern Hill. He was brevetted colonel for his service at Spanish Fort and Blakely and Mobile, Alabama, in 1865. He advanced through the ranks in the post-Civil War era and attained the rank of brigadier general and chief of engineers, February 1, 1897. General Wilson retired April 30, 1901, and died February 1, 1919, at Washington, D.C.

BATTERY WOODRUFF (Fort Wint)

Named in War Department G.O. No. 77, May 12, 1908, to honor 1st Lt. Harry Adsit Woodruff, 17th US Infantry Regiment. Like many junior officers who served in the regiments that fought the insurgents led by General Emilio Aguinaldo, Woodruff had been appointed from civilian life and assigned initially to the 13th US Infantry Regiment. He transferred to the 17th Infantry Regiment on June 8, 1899, and was promoted to first lieutenant February 2, 1901. He was killed in action at Simitan, Mindanao, PI, on May 8, 1904.

BATTERY WOODRUFF (Fort Hughes)

Named in War Department G.O. No. 63, September 2, 1914, to honor Brig. Gen. Carle Augustus Woodruff, whose military career began with his appointment as a second lieutenant in the 2nd US Artillery Regiment, October 22, 1861. He was promoted to first lieutenant July 24, 1862, and brevetted captain for gallant and meritorious service at the Battle of Gettysburg, Pennsylvania, July 3, 1863. In an action at Newby's Cross-roads, Virginia, he served with distinction and gallantry while commanding a horse artillery section of Battery M, 2nd Artillery Regiment, for which he was awarded the Medal of Honor in September 1893. He received the brevet rank of major for his service at the Battle of Trevilian Station, Virginia, and lieutenant colonel for his good conduct and gallant service in the Civil War. Following the Civil War, Woodruff was promoted to Regular Army captain in May 1869, to major in March 1894, lieutenant colonel, 7th US Artillery Regiment in February 1899, and to colonel, Artillery Corps, May 8, 1901. He was promoted to brigadier general upon his retirement, and died July 20, 1913.

APPENDIX V
COMMANDING OFFICERS OF THE COAST AND HARBOR DEFENSES OF MANILA AND SUBIC BAYS AND COAST ARTILLERY REGIMENTS

Artillery District of Manila Bay

Captain Charles E. Kilbourne	May 7, 1907 - April ? 1909
Major C.C. Hearn	April ? 1909 - February ? 1911
Colonel J.A. Lundeen	March ? 1911 - February ?1912
Colonel J.W. Ruckman	May 7, 1912 - December 15, 1913
Brigadier General Charles J. Bailey	November ? 1914
Colonel H.C. Davis	January 6, 1914 - May 15, 1915

Artillery District of Subic Bay

Captain R.E. Wylie	September 4, 1907 - April ? 1909
Major D.W. Ketcham	April ? 1909 - April 2, 1911
Lieutenant Colonel S. C. Schumm	April 3, 1911 - April 19, 1911
Major J.F. Brady	July 5, 1912 - September 12, 1913
Major T.W. Winston	September ? 1913 - November ? 1913
Colonel C. L. Phillips	October ? 1913

Coast Defenses of Manila and Subic Bay

Colonel C. L. Phillips	October ? 1913 - October ? 1914
Brigadier General Charles J. Bailey	November 3, 1914 - April 15, 1917
Lieutenant Colonel James M. Williams	April 16, 1917 - August 3, 1917
Brigadier General Clarence P. Townsley	August 3, 1917 - August 11, 1917
Brigadier General C.C. Hearn, NA	August 11, 1917 - September 14,1917
Lieutenant Colonel James M. Williams	September 14, 1917 - December 5, 1917
Lieutenant Colonel William R. Doores	December 5,1917 - December 23, 1917
Colonel James M. Williams	December 23, 1917 - April 20, 1918
Colonel William R. Doores	April 20, 1918 - August 10, 1918
Colonel Samuel E. Smiley, Inf	August 10, 1918 - February 16, 1919
Colonel Samuel E. Allen	February 16, 1919 - May 16, 1919
Colonel Richmond P. Davis	May 16, 1919 - March 14,1921
Lieutenant Colonel Ernest R. Tilton	March 14, 1921 - April 3, 1921
Colonel Charles H. Barth	April 3, 1921 - August 13, 1921
Brigadier General Henry D. Todd	August 13, 1921 - July 2, 1923
Colonel Andrew Hero Jr.	July 2, 1923 - November 18, 1923
Brigadier General Malin Craig	November 18, 1923 - July 10, 1924
Colonel Andrew Hero Jr.	July 10, 1924 - October 4, 1924
Colonel Earle D'A. Pearce	October 4, 1924 - August 26, 1924
Brigadier General Campbell King	August 26, 1924 - April 24, 1925
Colonel William R. Doores	April 24, 1925 - July 16, 1925

Brigadier General Frank M. Caldwell	July 16, 1925 - November 18, 1927
Lieutenant Colonel Avery J. Cooper	November 18, 1927 - December 1, 1927
Brigadier General Henry J. Hatch	December 1, 1927 - September 14, 1929
Colonel William H. Monroe	September 14, 1929 - October 4, 1929
Brigadier General Charles E. Kilbourne Jr.	October 28, 1929 - June 17, 1932
Brigadier General Stanley D. Embick	June 18, 1932 - February 20, 1935
Colonel William S. Bowen	February 20, 1935 - March 19, 1935
Brigadier General Charles E. Kilbourne Jr.	March 19, 1935 - November 14, 1935
Brigadier General John W. Gulick	November 14, 1935 - November 6, 1936
Brigadier General Percy P. Bishop	November 6, 1936 - February 25, 1937
Brigadier General Walter K. Wilson	February 26, 1937 - November 1940
Brigadier General George S. Moore	November 1940 - 13 May 1942

Commanders, Coast Artillery Regiments

59th Coast Artillery (HD) Regiment

Colonel Sydney Grant	December 29, 1917 - June 8, 1918
Colonel James M. Wheeler	June 8, 1918 - July ? 1918
Colonel Richard K. Cravens	December ? 1918 - January ? 1919
Colonel Harry P. Wilbur	January, 1920 - July 30, 1920
Major Arthur H. Doig	July 30, 1920 - October 3, 1920
Lieutenant Colonel Harry P. Wilbur	October 3, 1920 - December 15, 1920
Colonel Earle D'A. Pearce	December 15, 1920 - July 13, 1921
Major Edgar H. Thompson	July 13, 1921- September 26, 1921
Lieutenant Colonel John L. Roberts	September 26, 1921 - November 1922
Major Edgar H. Thompson	November 1922 - January 14, 1923
Lieutenant Colonel Frank S. Long	January 14, 1923 - July 14, 1923
Colonel Percy P. Bishop	July 14, 1923 - January 1, 1924
Lieutenant Colonel Frank S. Long	January 1, 1924 - June 30, 1924
Colonel Stanley Embick	June 30, 1924 - February 27, 1926
Colonel Samuel C. Vestal	February 27, 1926 - October 1, 1926
Colonel Harry C. Barnes	October 1, 1926 - August 26, 1927
Major Raymond E. Fenner	August 26, 1927 - September 20, 1927
Lieutenant Colonel Clarence G. Bunker	September 20, 1927 - May 2, 1928
Major John P. McCaskey Jr.	May 10, 1928 - June 15, 1928
Major Harry L. King	June 15, 1928 - July 2, 1928
Lieutenant Colonel Earl Biscoe	July 2, 1928 - October 4, 1929
Colonel Earle D'A. Pearce	October 4, 1929 - November 13, 1931
Lieutenant Colonel James B. Taylor	November 13, 1931 - September 6, 1933
Lieutenant Colonel Matthew A. Cross	September 6, 1933 - October 10, 1934
Major La Rhett L. Stuart	October 10, 1934 - December 1, 1934
Colonel Allen Kimberly	December 1, 1934 - April 15, 1935
Colonel Paul D. Bunker	April 15, 1935 - April 5, 1937
Lieutenant Colonel Edward W. Turner	April 5, 1937 - July 3, 1937
Colonel George Ruhlen	July 3, 1937 - July 19, 1939
Colonel Robert P. Glassburn	July 19, 1939 - June 20, 1940
Lieutenant Colonel Napoleon Boudreau	June 20, 1940 - February 28, 1941
Colonel Paul D. Bunker	February 28, 1941 - May 13, 1942

60th Coast Artillery (AA) Regiment

Major Stewart O. Elting	October 31, 1922 - June 1, 1924
Major John T.H. O'Rear	June 30, 1924 - July 14, 1925
Major Charles B. Meyer	July 14, 1925 - July 7, 1928
Captain Donald L. Dutton	July 7, 1928 - October 21, 1928
Lieutenant Colonel Franc Lecocoq	October 21, 1928 - March 4, 1930
Colonel George T. Perkins	March 4, 1930 - April 27, 1932
Major Robert M. Perkins	April 27, 1932 - June 17, 1932
Lieutenant Colonel Benjamin Booth	June 17, 1932 - October 15, 1932
Colonel Frederick L. Dengler	October 15, 1932 - July 31, 1933
Lieutenant Colonel Benjamin Booth	July 31, 1933 - September 29, 1933
Lieutenant Colonel Howard K. Loughry	September 29, 1933 - April 15, 1935
Colonel Allen Kimberly	April 15, 1935 - December 2, 1936
Lieutenant Colonel Franklin Kemble	December 2, 1936 - April 15, 1937
Captain William L. Richardson	April 15, 1937 - May 1, 1937
Colonel James H. Cunningham	May 1, 1937 - September 19, 1938
Major John H. Harrington	September 19, 1938 - November 4, 1938
Colonel William C. Koenig	November 4, 1938 - November 1940
Colonel John L. Holcombe	November 1940 - March 1, 1941
Colonel Theodore M. Chase	March 1, 1941 - May 6, 1942

91st Coast Artillery Regiment (PS)

Colonel Andrew Hero Jr.	1 July 1924 - 2 March 1925
Colonel William R. Doores	April 2, 1925 - December 2, 1925
Lieutenant Colonel James L. Long	March 2, 1925 - April 2, 1925
Lieutenant Colonel William H. Raymond	December 2, 1925 - November 23, 1926
Colonel Frederick W. Stopford	November 23, 1926 - October 26, 1928
Colonel William H. Monroe	October 26, 1928 - June 27, 1930
Lieutenant Colonel Franc Leccoq	June 27, 1930 - October 9, 1930
Lieutenant Colonel Forrest E. Williford	October 9, 1930 - September 8, 1932
Colonel Clarence B. Ross	September 8, 1932 - October 5, 1934
Lieutenant Colonel Hollis L. Muller	October 7, 1934 - January 26, 1935
Lieutenant Colonel Clair W. Baird	January 26, 1935 - November 6, 1936
Colonel James H. Cunningham	November 6, 1936 - April 30, 1937
Lieutenant Colonel Richard S. Dodson	May 1, 1937 - October 5, 1937
Captain Arthur L. Lavery	October 5, 1937 - October 13, 1937
Major Benjamin Bowering	October 13, 1937 - October 29, 1937
Colonel William C. Koenig	October 29, 1937 - November 4, 1938
Colonel Frederic A. Price	November 4, 1938 - March 23, 1939
Colonel Willis Shippam	March 23, 1939 - February 28, 1941
Colonel John L. Holcombe	March 1, 1941 - October 31, 1941
Colonel Joseph P. Kohn	November 1, 1941 - May 13, 1942

92nd Coast Artillery Regiment (PS)

Colonel William R. Doores	July 1, 1924 - November 9, 1924
Colonel Samuel C. Vestal	November 9, 1924 - February 26, 1926
Colonel Harrison S. Kerrick	February 26, 1926 - September 13, 1927
Colonel George O. Hubbard	September 14, 1927 - October 20, 1928
Major Edward W. Turner	October 20, 1928 - March 11, 1930
Major Robert E. Phillips	March 11, 1930 - August 30, 1930
Major Estaban B. Dalao	August 30, 1930 - October 2, 1930
Major Eli E. Bennett	October 2, 1930 - July 5, 1932
Lieutenant Colonel Albert L. Loustalot	July 5, 1932 - October 2, 1934
Lieutenant Colonel Reinold Melberg	October 2, 1934 - February 25, 1937
Lieutenant Colonel Albert H. Warren	February 25, 1937 - March 30, 1939
Lieutenant Colonel James B. Crawford	March 30, 1939 - January 27, 1940
Colonel Joseph F. Cottrell	January 27, 1940 - July 1940
Colonel Octave DeCarre	July 1940 - May 6, 1942

? -- Actual dates(s) of command are approximate

APPENDIX VI
1935 DETAIL MAPS OF THE FORTS OF THE HARBOR DEFENSES OF MANILA AND SUBIC BAYS

Another valuable set of source documents for major tactical structures (gun batteries, mine buildings, switchboards, power plants, fire control structures, searchlights, etc.) are the "confidential blueprint" series of maps generated by the U.S. Army Corps of Engineers from various dates after construction. These maps were updated periodically through out the periods of construction. This appendix consists of a set of maps dated 1935 that show the layout of the forts approaching the war years.

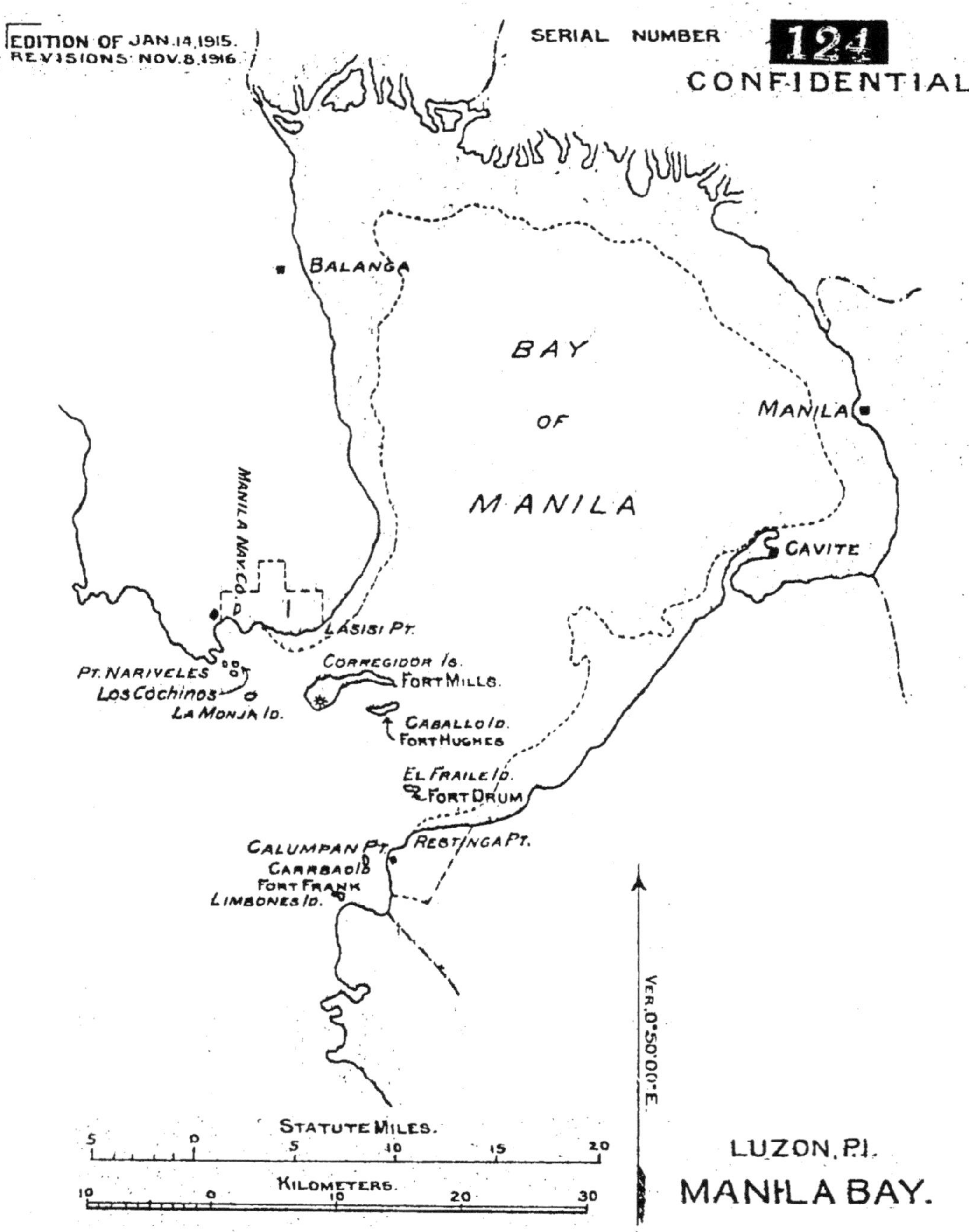

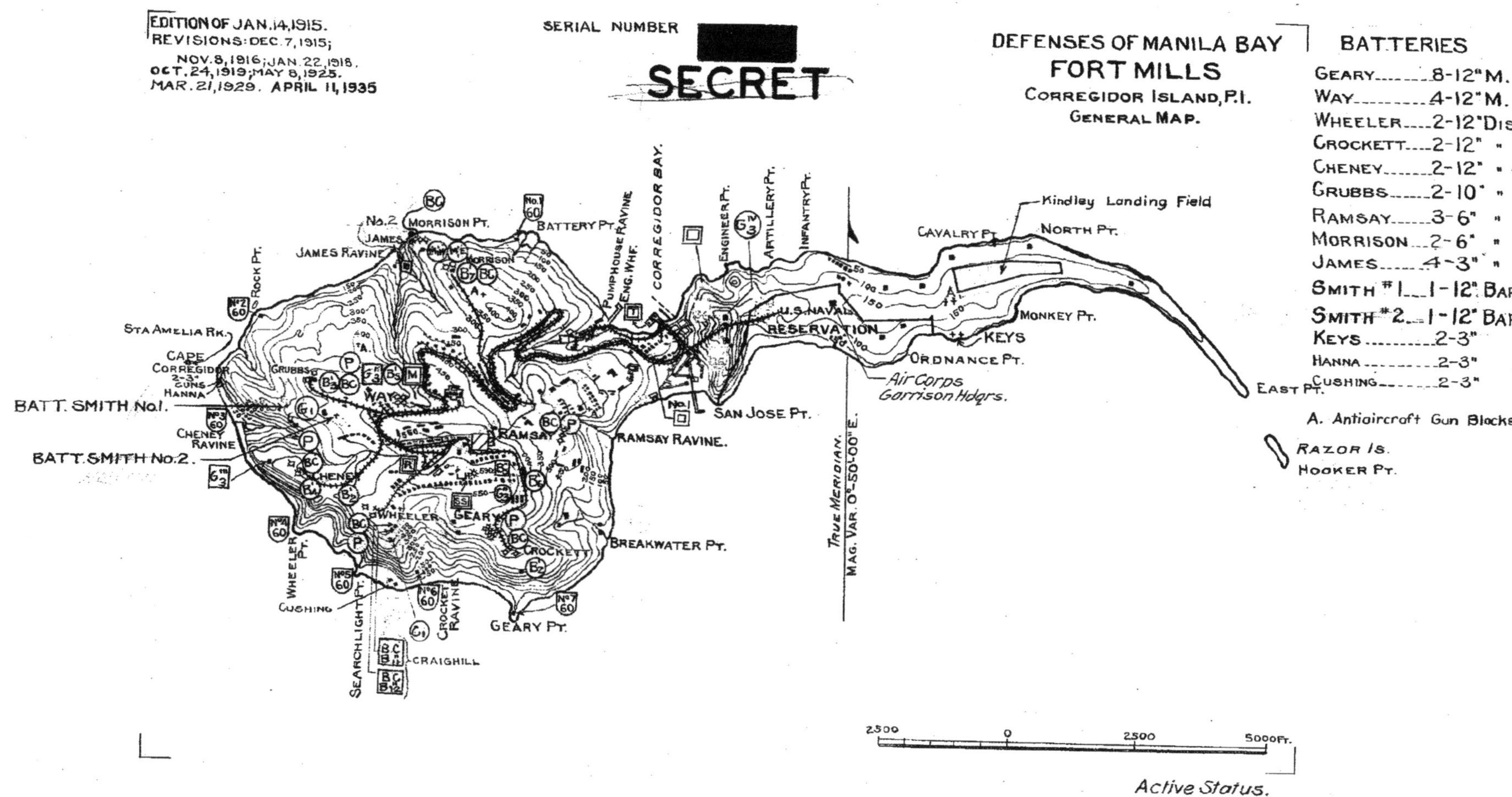
EDITION OF JAN. 14, 1915.
REVISIONS: DEC. 7, 1915;
NOV. 8, 1916; JAN. 22, 1918.
OCT. 24, 1919; MAY 8, 1925.
MAR. 21, 1929. APRIL 11, 1935
SERIAL NUMBER
SECRET
DEFENSES OF MANILA BAY
FORT MILLS
CORREGIDOR ISLAND, P.I.
GENERAL MAP.
BATTERIES
GEARY 8-12" M.
WAY 4-12" M.
WHEELER 2-12" DIS.
CROCKETT 2-12" "
CHENEY 2-12" "
GRUBBS 2-10" "
RAMSAY 3-6" "
MORRISON 2-6" "
JAMES 4-3" "
SMITH #1 1-12" BAR
SMITH #2 1-12" BAR
KEYS 2-3"
HANNA 2-3"
CUSHING 2-3"
A. Antiaircraft Gun Blocks
RAZOR IS.
HOOKER PT.
EAST PT.
Kindley Landing Field
CAVALRY PT.
NORTH PT.
MONKEY PT.
KEYS
ORDNANCE PT.
Air Corps
Garrison Hdqrs.
U.S. NAVAL RESERVATION
SAN JOSE PT.
RAMSAY RAVINE.
BREAKWATER PT.
INFANTRY PT.
ARTILLERY PT.
ENGINEER PT.
CORREGIDOR BAY.
ENG. WHF.
PUMPHOUSE RAVINE
BATTERY PT.
MORRISON PT.
JAMES RAVINE
ROCK PT.
STA AMELIA RK.
CAPE CORREGIDOR 2-3" GUNS HANNA
BATT. SMITH No. 1.
CHENEY RAVINE
BATT. SMITH No. 2.
WHEELER PT.
CUSHING
SEARCHLIGHT PT.
CROCKET RAVINE
CRAIGHILL
GEARY PT.
TRUE MERIDIAN.
MAG. VAR. 0°-50'-00" E.
2500 0 2500 5000 FT.
Active Status.

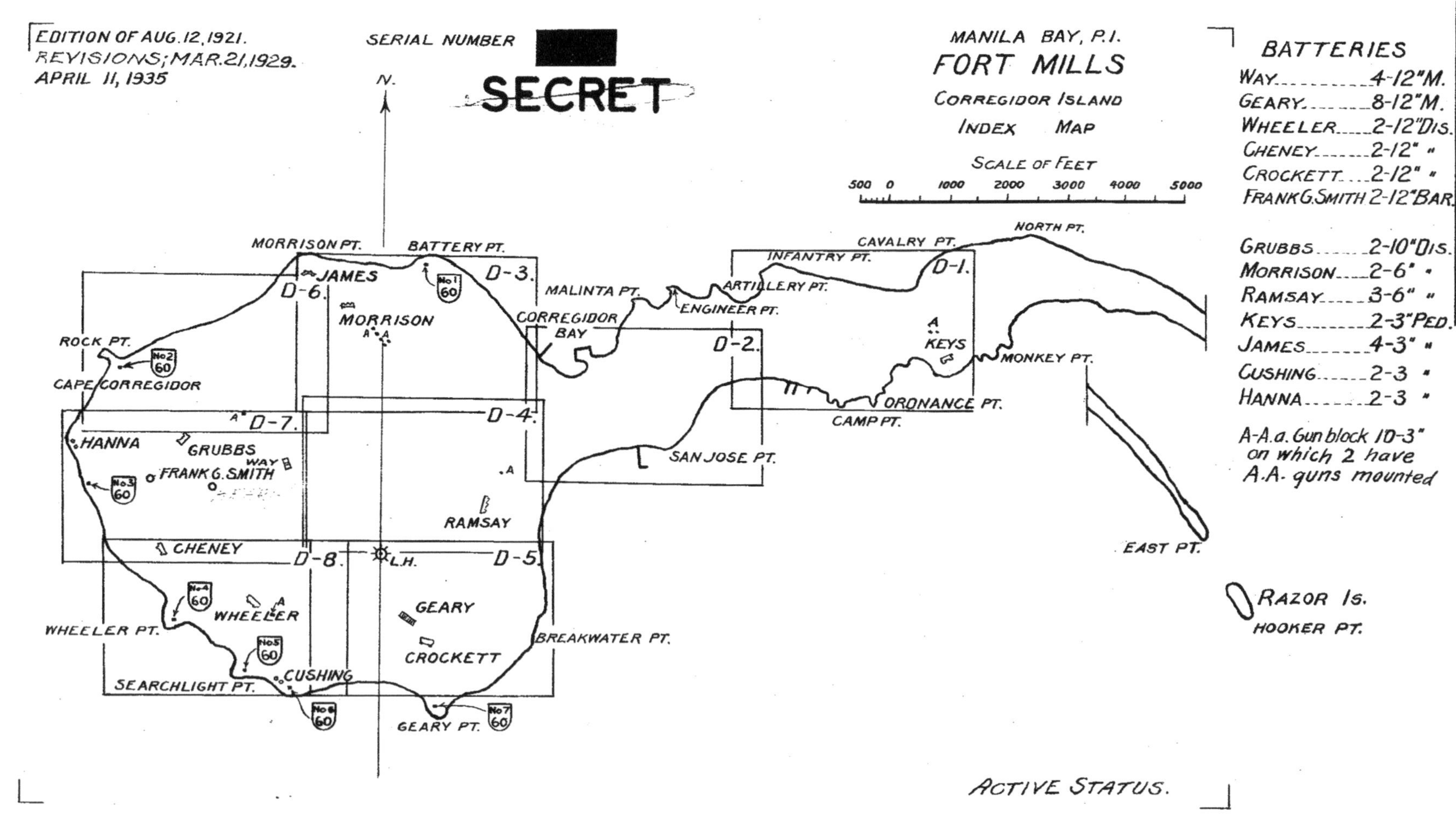
EDITION OF AUG. 12, 1921.
REVISIONS; MAR. 21, 1929.
APRIL 11, 1935
SERIAL NUMBER
SECRET
N.
MANILA BAY, P.I.
FORT MILLS
CORREGIDOR ISLAND
INDEX MAP
SCALE OF FEET
500 0 1000 2000 3000 4000 5000
BATTERIES
WAY 4-12" M.
GEARY 8-12" M.
WHEELER 2-12" DIS.
CHENEY 2-12" "
CROCKETT 2-12" "
FRANK G. SMITH 2-12" BAR.
GRUBBS 2-10" DIS.
MORRISON 2-6" "
RAMSAY 3-6" "
KEYS 2-3" PED.
JAMES 4-3" "
CUSHING 2-3 "
HANNA 2-3 "
A-A.a. Gun block 10-3" on which 2 have A.A. guns mounted
MORRISON PT.
BATTERY PT.
JAMES
D-3.
D-6.
MORRISON
MALINTA PT.
CORREGIDOR BAY
ENGINEER PT.
ARTILLERY PT.
INFANTRY PT.
CAVALRY PT.
NORTH PT.
D-1.
KEYS
MONKEY PT.
D-2.
ORONANCE PT.
CAMP PT.
ROCK PT.
CAPE CORREGIDOR
D-7.
D-4.
HANNA
GRUBBS
WAY
FRANK G. SMITH
SAN JOSE PT.
RAMSAY
CHENEY
D-8.
L.H.
D-5.
EAST PT.
RAZOR IS.
HOOKER PT.
WHEELER
GEARY
WHEELER PT.
BREAKWATER PT.
CROCKETT
CUSHING
SEARCHLIGHT PT.
GEARY PT.
ACTIVE STATUS.

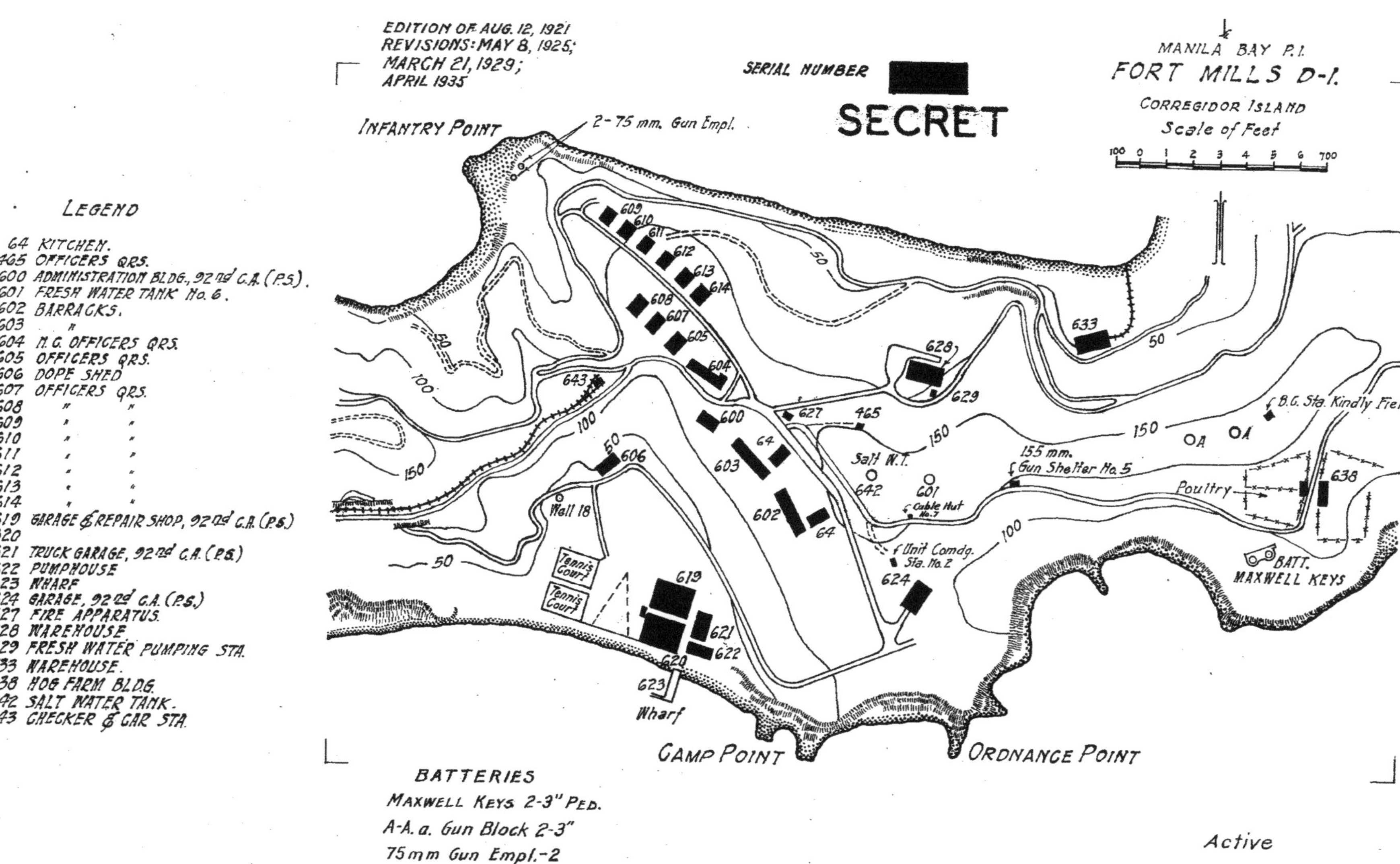
EDITION OF AUG. 12, 1921
REVISIONS: MAY 8, 1925; MARCH 21, 1929; APRIL 1935
SERIAL NUMBER
SECRET
MANILA BAY P.I.
FORT MILLS D-1.
CORREGIDOR ISLAND
Scale of Feet
INFANTRY POINT
2-75 mm. Gun Empl.
LEGEND
64 KITCHEN.
465 OFFICERS QRS.
600 ADMINISTRATION BLDG., 92nd C.A. (P.S.).
601 FRESH WATER TANK No. 6.
602 BARRACKS.
603 "
604 N.C. OFFICERS QRS.
605 OFFICERS QRS.
606 DOPE SHED
607 OFFICERS QRS.
608 " "
609 " "
610 " "
611 " "
612 " "
613 " "
614 " "
619 GARAGE & REPAIR SHOP, 92nd C.A. (P.S.)
620
621 TRUCK GARAGE, 92nd C.A. (P.S.)
622 PUMPHOUSE
623 WHARF
624 GARAGE, 92nd C.A. (P.S.)
627 FIRE APPARATUS.
628 WAREHOUSE
629 FRESH WATER PUMPING STA.
633 WAREHOUSE.
638 HOG FARM BLDG.
642 SALT WATER TANK.
643 CHECKER & CAR STA.
Salt W.T.
Cable Hut No. 1
Unit Comdg. Sta. No. 2
155 mm. Gun Shelter No. 5
B.C. Sta. Kindly Field
Poultry
BATT. MAXWELL KEYS
Well 18
Tennis Court
Tennis Court
Wharf
CAMP POINT
ORDNANCE POINT
BATTERIES
MAXWELL KEYS 2-3" PED.
A-A. a. Gun Block 2-3"
75mm Gun Empl.-2
Active

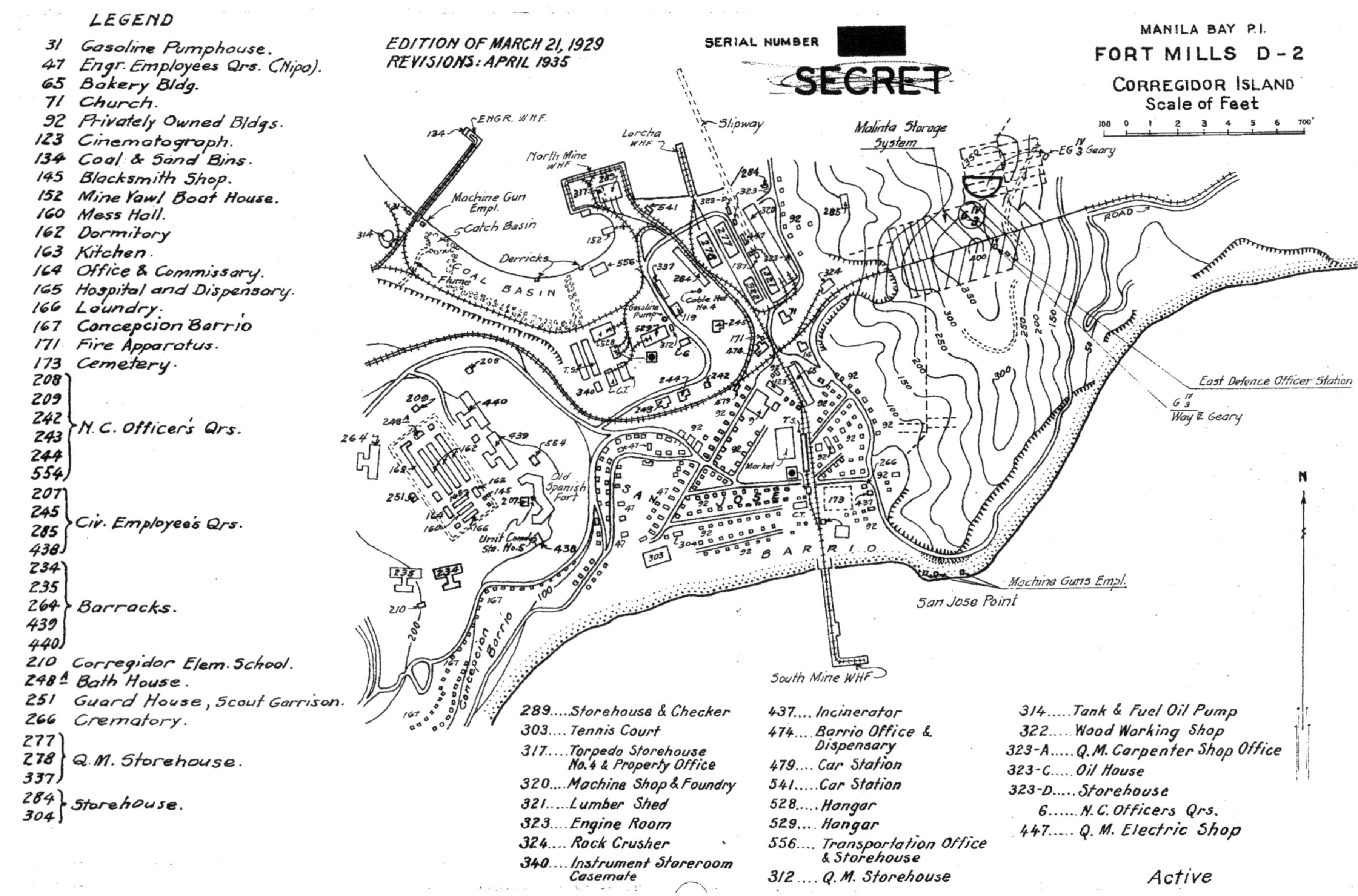
LEGEND
31 Gasoline Pumphouse.
47 Engr. Employees Qrs. (Nipo).
65 Bakery Bldg.
71 Church.
92 Privately Owned Bldgs.
123 Cinematograph.
134 Coal & Sand Bins.
145 Blacksmith Shop.
152 Mine Yawl Boat House.
160 Mess Hall.
162 Dormitory
163 Kitchen.
164 Office & Commissary.
165 Hospital and Dispensary.
166 Laundry.
167 Concepcion Barrio
171 Fire Apparatus.
173 Cemetery.
208, 209, 242, 243, 244, 554 N. C. Officer's Qrs.
207, 245, 285, 438 Civ. Employee's Qrs.
234, 235, 264, 439, 440 Barracks.
210 Corregidor Elem. School.
248A Bath House.
251 Guard House, Scout Garrison.
266 Crematory.
277, 278, 337 Q.M. Storehouse.
284, 304 Storehouse.
EDITION OF MARCH 21, 1929
REVISIONS: APRIL 1935
SERIAL NUMBER
SECRET
MANILA BAY P.I.
FORT MILLS D-2
CORREGIDOR ISLAND
Scale of Feet
100 0 1 2 3 4 5 6 700'
ENGR. WHF.
North Mine WHF
Lorcha WHF
Slipway
Malinta Storage System
Machine Gun Empl.
Catch Basin
Derricks
COAL BASIN
Flume
Gasoline Pump
Cable Hut No. 4
Old Spanish Fort
Unit Comdg. Sta. No. 5
Market
SAN JOSE
BARRIO
Concepcion Barrio
ROAD
East Defence Officer Station
Way & Geary
Machine Guns Empl.
San Jose Point
South Mine WHF
N
289....Storehouse & Checker
303....Tennis Court
317....Torpedo Storehouse No. 4 & Property Office
320....Machine Shop & Foundry
321....Lumber Shed
323....Engine Room
324....Rock Crusher
340....Instrument Storeroom Casemate
437....Incinerator
474....Barrio Office & Dispensary
479....Car Station
541....Car Station
528....Hangar
529....Hangar
556....Transportation Office & Storehouse
312....Q.M. Storehouse
314....Tank & Fuel Oil Pump
322....Wood Working Shop
323-A....Q.M. Carpenter Shop Office
323-C....Oil House
323-D....Storehouse
6....N.C. Officers Qrs.
447....Q. M. Electric Shop
Active

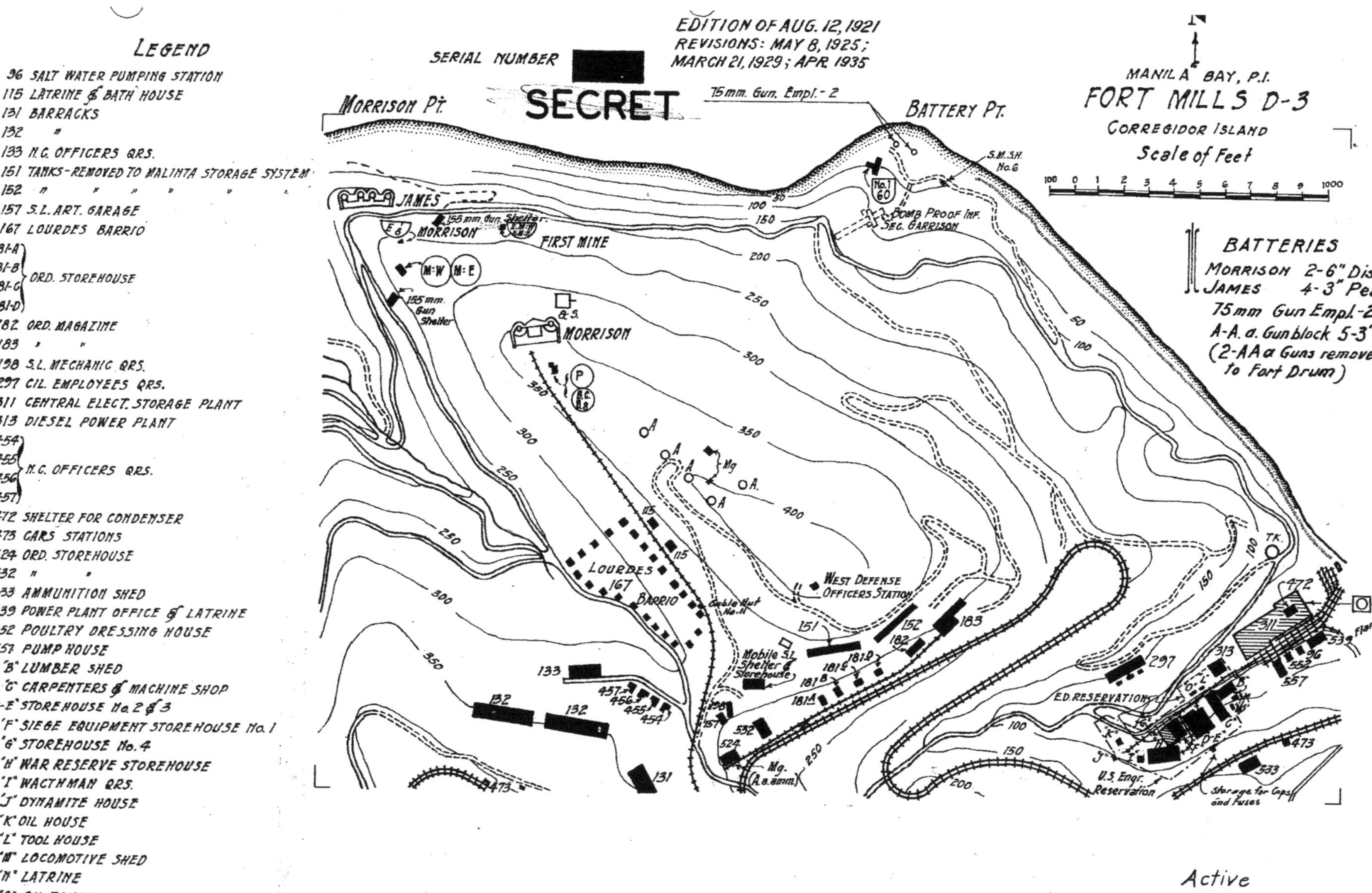
LEGEND
36 SALT WATER PUMPING STATION
115 LATRINE & BATH HOUSE
131 BARRACKS
132 "
133 N.C. OFFICERS QRS.
151 TANKS-REMOVED TO MALINTA STORAGE SYSTEM
152 " " " " " "
157 S.L. ART. GARAGE
167 LOURDES BARRIO
181-A 181-B 181-C 181-D ORD. STOREHOUSE
182 ORD. MAGAZINE
183 " "
198 S.L. MECHANIC QRS.
297 CIL. EMPLOYEES QRS.
311 CENTRAL ELECT. STORAGE PLANT
313 DIESEL POWER PLANT
454 455 456 457 N.C. OFFICERS QRS.
472 SHELTER FOR CONDENSER
473 CARS STATIONS
524 ORD. STOREHOUSE
532 " "
533 AMMUNITION SHED
539 POWER PLANT OFFICE & LATRINE
552 POULTRY DRESSING HOUSE
557 PUMP HOUSE
"B" LUMBER SHED
"C" CARPENTERS & MACHINE SHOP
"D-E" STOREHOUSE No. 2 & 3
"F" SIEGE EQUIPMENT STOREHOUSE No. 1
"G" STOREHOUSE No. 4
"H" WAR RESERVE STOREHOUSE
"I" WACTHMAN QRS.
"J" DYNAMITE HOUSE
"K" OIL HOUSE
"L" TOOL HOUSE
"M" LOCOMOTIVE SHED
"N" LATRINE
"O" OIL TANKS
SERIAL NUMBER
SECRET
EDITION OF AUG. 12, 1921
REVISIONS: MAY 8, 1925;
MARCH 21, 1929; APR 1935
75mm. Gun. Empl.-2
MORRISON PT.
BATTERY PT.
MANILA BAY, P.I.
FORT MILLS D-3
CORREGIDOR ISLAND
Scale of Feet
BATTERIES
MORRISON 2-6" Dis.
JAMES 4-3" Ped.
75mm Gun Empl.-2
A-A.a. Gunblock 5-3"
(2-AAa Guns removed to Fort Drum)
JAMES
MORRISON
FIRST MINE
BOMB PROOF INF. SEC. GARRISON
S.M.SH. No. 6
155mm Gun Shelter
MORRISON
LOURDES BARRIO
WEST DEFENSE OFFICERS STATION
Mobile S.L. Shelter & Storehouse
Cable Hut No. 11
E.D. RESERVATIONS
U.S. Engr. Reservation
Storage for Caps and Fuses
Flame
Active

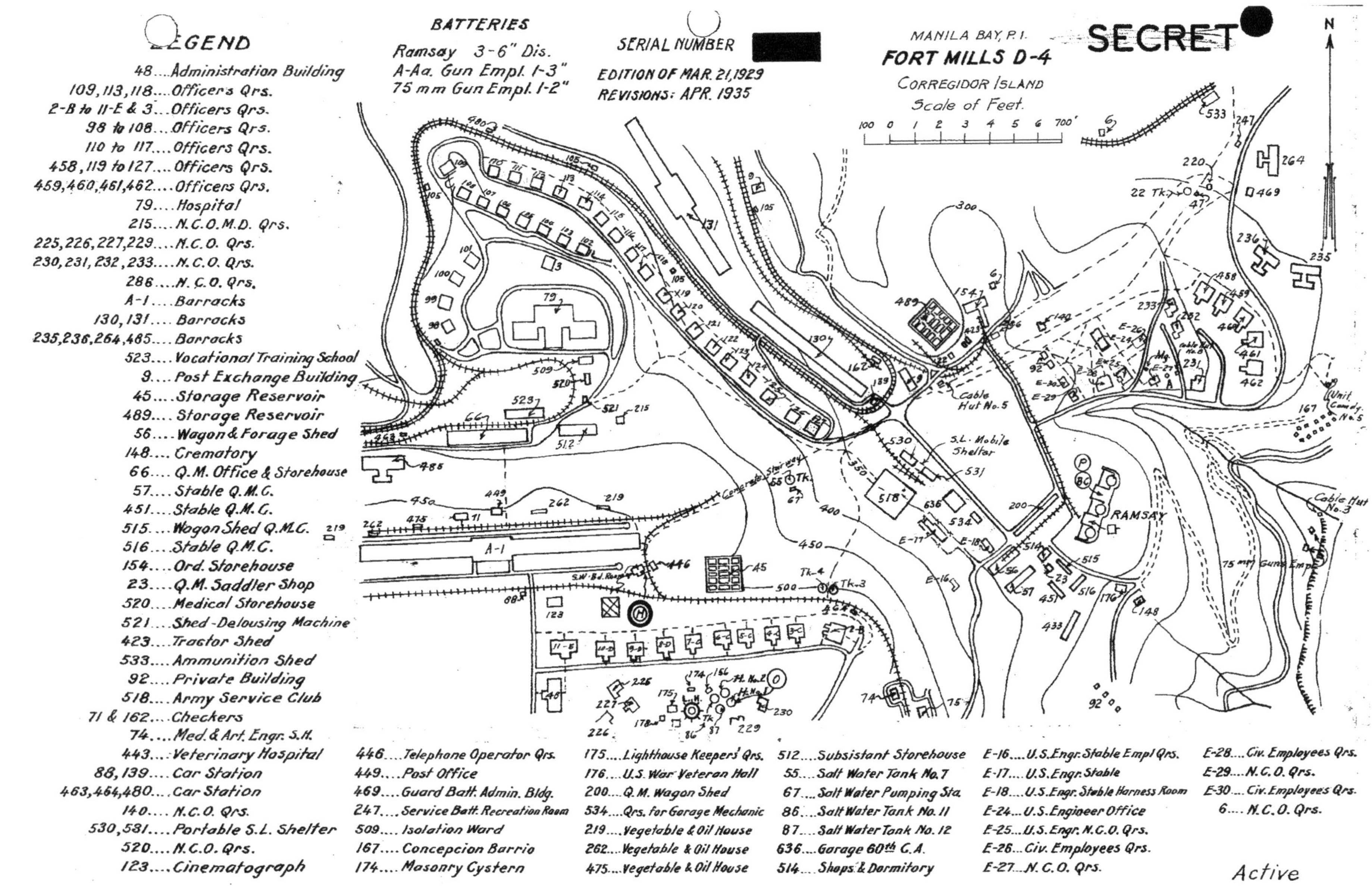
LEGEND
48....Administration Building
109,113,118....Officers Qrs.
2-B to 11-E & 3....Officers Qrs.
98 to 108....Officers Qrs.
110 to 117....Officers Qrs.
458,119 to 127....Officers Qrs.
459,460,461,462....Officers Qrs.
79....Hospital
215....N.C.O.M.D. Qrs.
225,226,227,229....N.C.O. Qrs.
230,231,232,233....N.C.O. Qrs.
286....N.C.O. Qrs.
A-1....Barracks
130,131....Barracks
235,236,264,485....Barracks
523....Vocational Training School
9....Post Exchange Building
45....Storage Reservoir
489....Storage Reservoir
56....Wagon & Forage Shed
148....Crematory
66....Q.M. Office & Storehouse
57....Stable Q.M.C.
451....Stable Q.M.C.
515....Wagon Shed Q.M.C.
516....Stable Q.M.C.
154....Ord. Storehouse
23....Q.M. Saddler Shop
520....Medical Storehouse
521....Shed-Delousing Machine
423....Tractor Shed
533....Ammunition Shed
92....Private Building
518....Army Service Club
71 & 162....Checkers
74....Med. & Art. Engr. S.H.
443....Veterinary Hospital
88,139....Car Station
463,464,480....Car Station
140....N.C.O. Qrs.
530,531....Portable S.L. Shelter
520....N.C.O. Qrs.
123....Cinematograph
BATTERIES
Ramsay 3-6" Dis.
A-Aa. Gun Empl. 1-3"
75 mm Gun Empl. 1-2"
SERIAL NUMBER
EDITION OF MAR. 21,1929
REVISIONS: APR. 1935
MANILA BAY, P.I.
FORT MILLS D-4
CORREGIDOR ISLAND
Scale of Feet.
100 0 1 2 3 4 5 6 700'
SECRET
N
RAMSAY
Cable Hut No. 5
Cable Hut No. 3
S.L. Mobile Shelter
Concrete Stairway
75 mm Guns Empl.
Unit Comdy. No. 5
446....Telephone Operator Qrs.
449....Post Office
469....Guard Batt. Admin. Bldg.
247....Service Batt. Recreation Room
509....Isolation Ward
167....Concepcion Barrio
174....Masonry Cystern
175....Lighthouse Keepers' Qrs.
176....U.S. War Veteran Hall
200....Q.M. Wagon Shed
534....Qrs. for Garage Mechanic
219....Vegetable & Oil House
262....Vegetable & Oil House
475....Vegetable & Oil House
512....Subsistant Storehouse
55....Salt Water Tank No. 7
67....Salt Water Pumping Sta.
86....Salt Water Tank No. 11
87....Salt Water Tank No. 12
636....Garage 60th C.A.
514....Shops & Dormitory
E-16....U.S. Engr. Stable Empl Qrs.
E-17....U.S. Engr. Stable
E-18....U.S. Engr. Stable Harness Room
E-24....U.S. Engineer Office
E-25....U.S. Engr. N.C.O. Qrs.
E-26....Civ. Employees Qrs.
E-27....N.C.O. Qrs.
E-28....Civ. Employees Qrs.
E-29....N.C.O. Qrs.
E-30....Civ. Employees Qrs.
6....N.C.O. Qrs.
Active

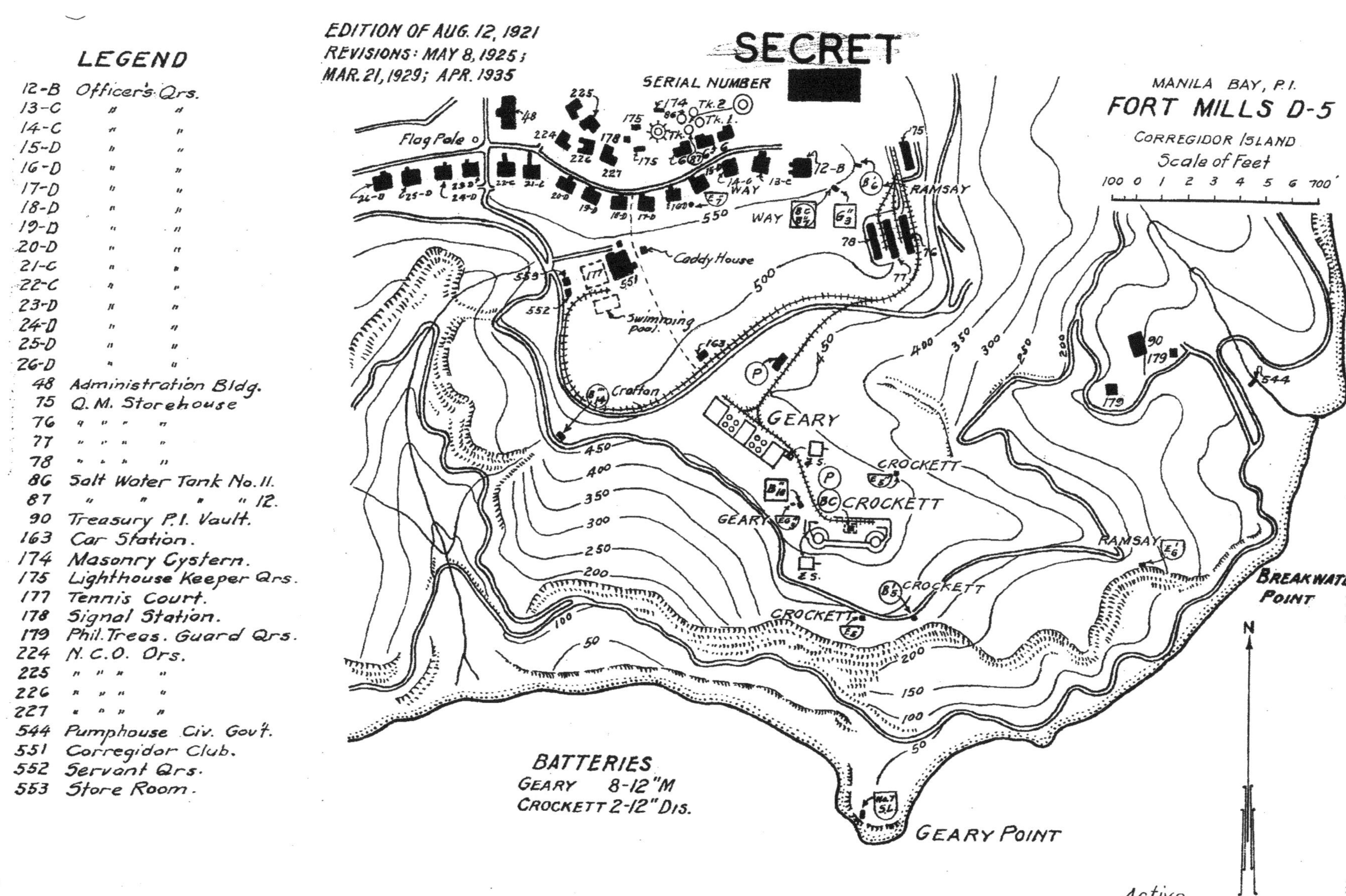
EDITION OF AUG. 12, 1921
REVISIONS: MAY 8, 1925;
MAR. 21, 1929; APR. 1935
SECRET
SERIAL NUMBER
MANILA BAY, P.I.
FORT MILLS D-5
CORREGIDOR ISLAND
Scale of Feet
100 0 1 2 3 4 5 6 700'
Flag Pole
Caddy House
Swimming pool.
Grafton
WAY
RAMSAY
GEARY
CROCKETT
BREAKWATER POINT
GEARY POINT
N
BATTERIES
GEARY 8-12"M
CROCKETT 2-12" DIS.
Active
LEGEND
12-B Officer's Qrs.
13-C " "
14-C " "
15-D " "
16-D " "
17-D " "
18-D " "
19-D " "
20-D " "
21-C " "
22-C " "
23-D " "
24-D " "
25-D " "
26-D " "
48 Administration Bldg.
75 Q.M. Storehouse
76 " " "
77 " " "
78 " " "
86 Salt Water Tank No. 11.
87 " " " " 12.
90 Treasury P.I. Vault.
163 Car Station.
174 Masonry Cystern.
175 Lighthouse Keeper Qrs.
177 Tennis Court.
178 Signal Station.
179 Phil. Treas. Guard Qrs.
224 N.C.O. Qrs.
225 " " "
226 " " "
227 " " "
544 Pumphouse Civ. Gov't.
551 Corregidor Club.
552 Servant Qrs.
553 Store Room.

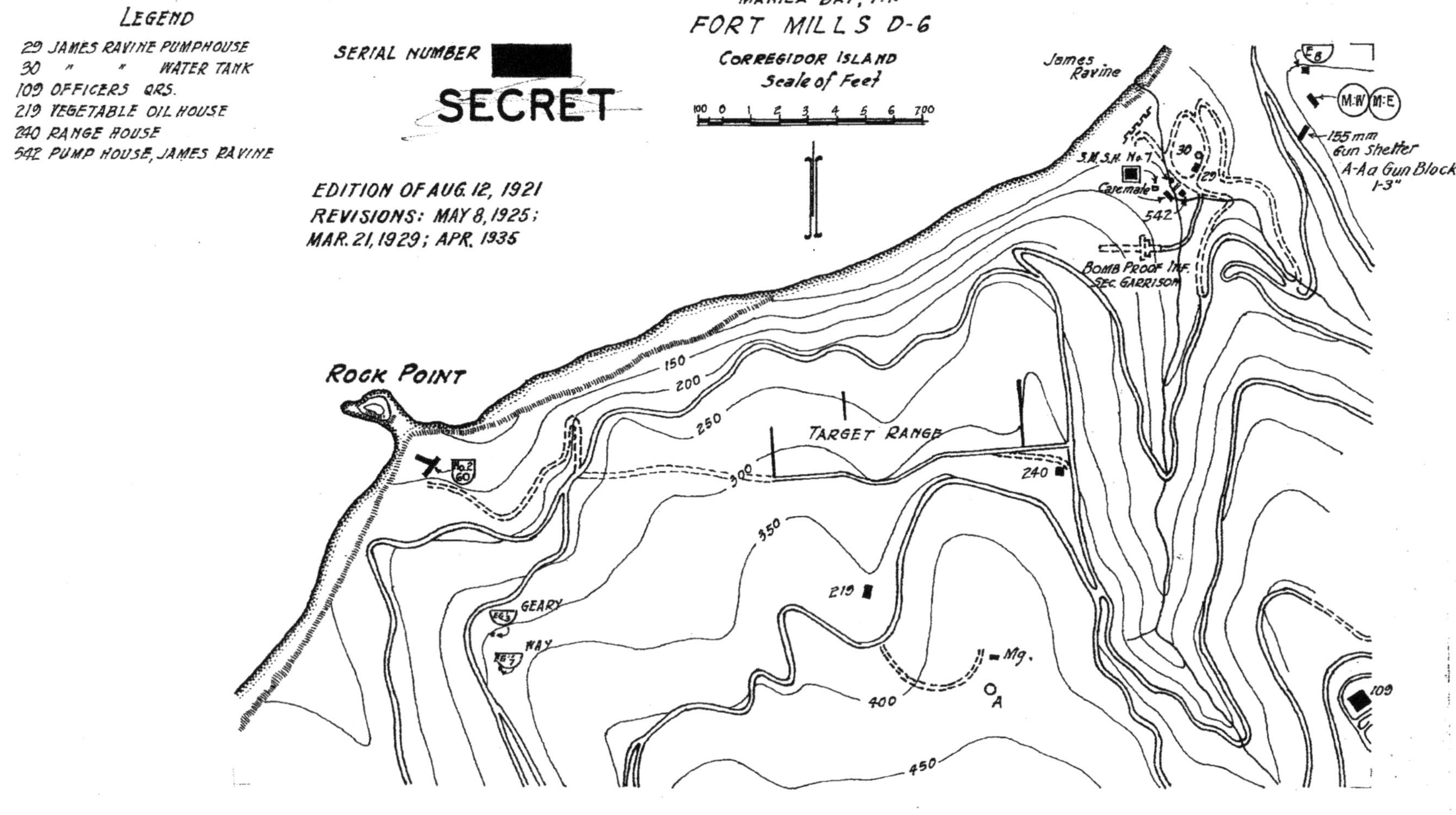
LEGEND
29 JAMES RAVINE PUMPHOUSE
30 " " WATER TANK
109 OFFICERS QRS.
219 VEGETABLE OIL HOUSE
240 RANGE HOUSE
542 PUMP HOUSE, JAMES RAVINE
SERIAL NUMBER
SECRET
MANILA BAY, P.I.
FORT MILLS D-6
CORREGIDOR ISLAND
Scale of Feet
EDITION OF AUG. 12, 1921
REVISIONS: MAY 8, 1925;
MAR. 21, 1929; APR. 1935
James Ravine
S.M.S.H. No. 7
Casemate
BOMB PROOF INF. SEC. GARRISON
155 mm Gun Shelter
A-Aa Gun Block 1-3"
ROCK POINT
TARGET RANGE
GEARY
WAY
Mg.
150
200
250
300
350
400
450
Active

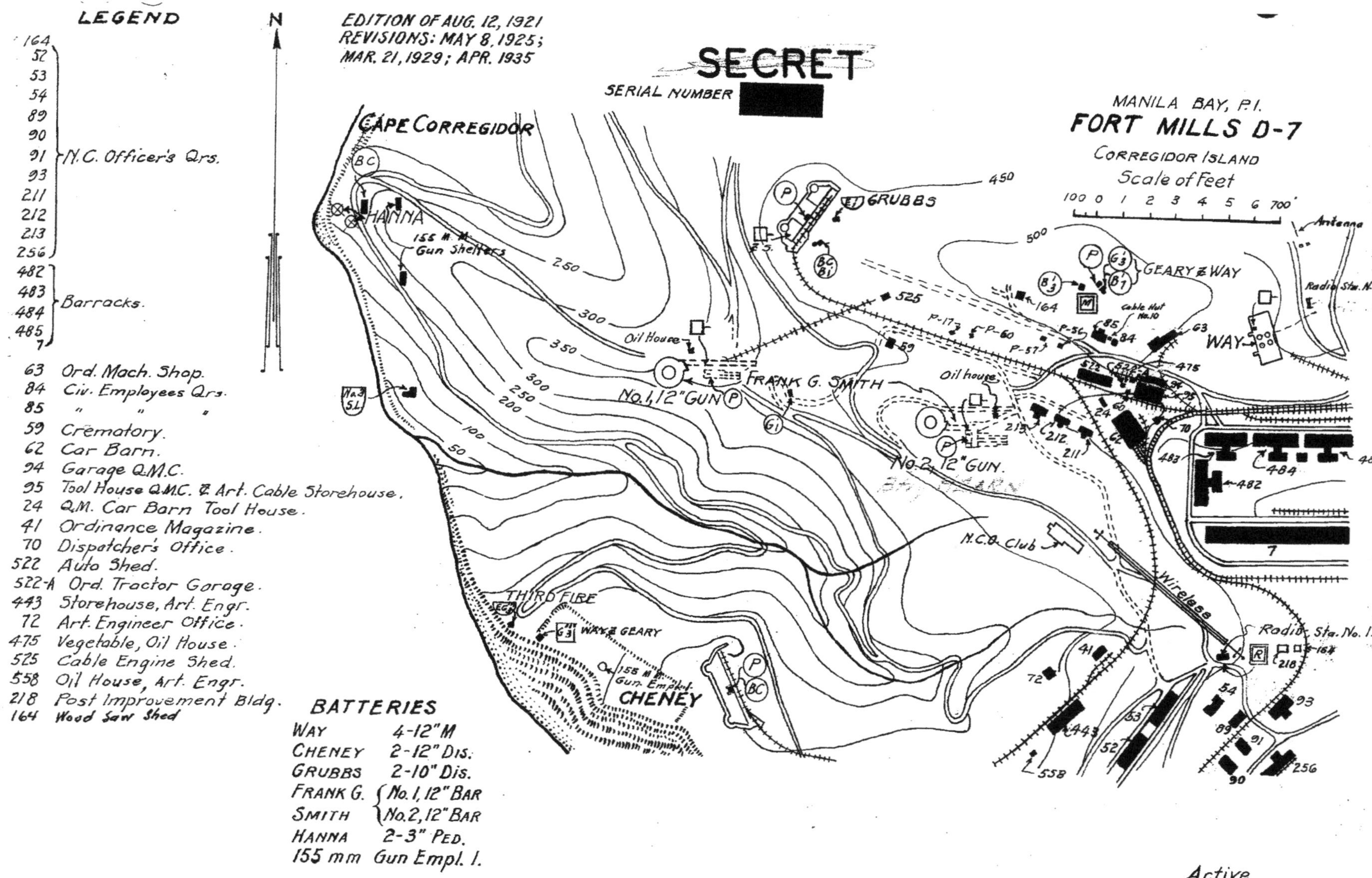
SECRET
SERIAL NUMBER
MANILA BAY, P.I.
FORT MILLS D-7
CORREGIDOR ISLAND
Scale of Feet
100 0 1 2 3 4 5 6 700'
EDITION OF AUG. 12, 1921
REVISIONS: MAY 8, 1925;
MAR. 21, 1929; APR. 1935
N
LEGEND
164, 52, 53, 54, 89, 90, 91, 93, 211, 212, 213, 256 N.C. Officer's Qrs.
482, 483, 484, 485, 7 Barracks.
63 Ord. Mach. Shop.
84 Civ. Employees Qrs.
85 " "
59 Crematory.
62 Car Barn.
94 Garage Q.M.C.
95 Tool House Q.M.C. & Art. Cable Storehouse.
24 Q.M. Car Barn Tool House.
41 Ordinance Magazine.
70 Dispatcher's Office.
522 Auto Shed.
522-A Ord. Tractor Garage.
443 Storehouse, Art. Engr.
72 Art. Engineer Office.
475 Vegetable, Oil House.
525 Cable Engine Shed.
558 Oil House, Art. Engr.
218 Post Improvement Bldg.
164 Wood Saw Shed
BATTERIES
WAY 4-12" M
CHENEY 2-12" Dis.
GRUBBS 2-10" Dis.
FRANK G. SMITH No. 1, 12" BAR / No. 2, 12" BAR
HANNA 2-3" PED.
155 mm Gun Empl. I.
CAPE CORREGIDOR
HANNA
155 M.M. Gun Shelters
GRUBBS
FRANK G. SMITH
No. 1, 12" GUN
No. 2, 12" GUN
Oil House
Oil house
GEARY & WAY
WAY
Cable Hut No. 10
Antenna
Radio Sta. No. 2
Radio Sta. No. 1
N.C.O. Club
Wireless
THIRD FIRE
WAY & GEARY
155 M.M. Gun Empl.
CHENEY
250
300
350
450
500
200
100
50
Active

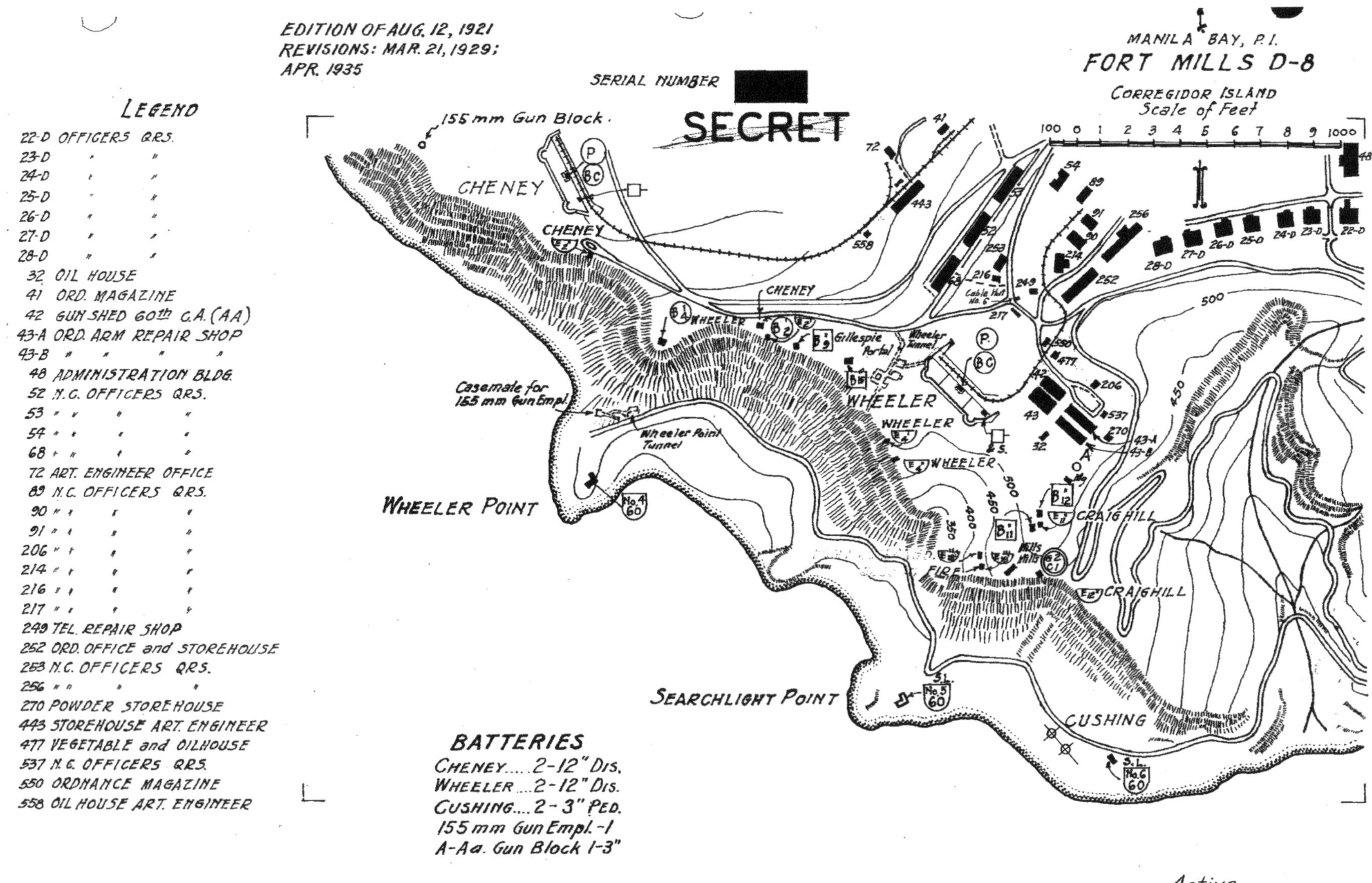
MANILA BAY, P.I.
FORT MILLS D-8
CORREGIDOR ISLAND
Scale of Feet
100 0 1 2 3 4 5 6 7 8 9 1000
EDITION OF AUG. 12, 1921
REVISIONS: MAR. 21, 1929;
APR. 1935
SERIAL NUMBER
SECRET
LEGEND
22-D OFFICERS QRS.
23-D " "
24-D " "
25-D " "
26-D " "
27-D " "
28-D " "
32 OIL HOUSE
41 ORD. MAGAZINE
42 GUN SHED 60th C.A. (AA)
43-A ORD. ARM REPAIR SHOP
43-B " " " "
48 ADMINISTRATION BLDG.
52 N.C. OFFICERS QRS.
53 " " " "
54 " " " "
68 " " " "
72 ART. ENGINEER OFFICE
89 N.C. OFFICERS QRS.
90 " " " "
91 " " " "
206 " " " "
214 " " " "
216 " " " "
217 " " " "
249 TEL. REPAIR SHOP
252 ORD. OFFICE and STOREHOUSE
253 N.C. OFFICERS QRS.
256 " " " "
270 POWDER STOREHOUSE
443 STOREHOUSE ART. ENGINEER
477 VEGETABLE and OILHOUSE
537 N.C. OFFICERS QRS.
550 ORDNANCE MAGAZINE
558 OIL HOUSE ART. ENGINEER
155 mm Gun Block.
CHENEY
CHENEY
CHENEY
WHEELER
WHEELER
WHEELER
WHEELER
Gillespie Portal
Wheeler Tunnel
Cable Hut No. 6
Casemate for 155 mm Gun Empl.
Wheeler Point Tunnel
WHEELER POINT
CRAIGHILL
CRAIGHILL
FIRE
CUSHING
SEARCHLIGHT POINT
500
450
400
350
BATTERIES
CHENEY.....2-12" DIS.
WHEELER.....2-12" DIS.
CUSHING.....2-3" PED.
155 mm Gun Empl.-1
A-Aa. Gun Block 1-3"
Active

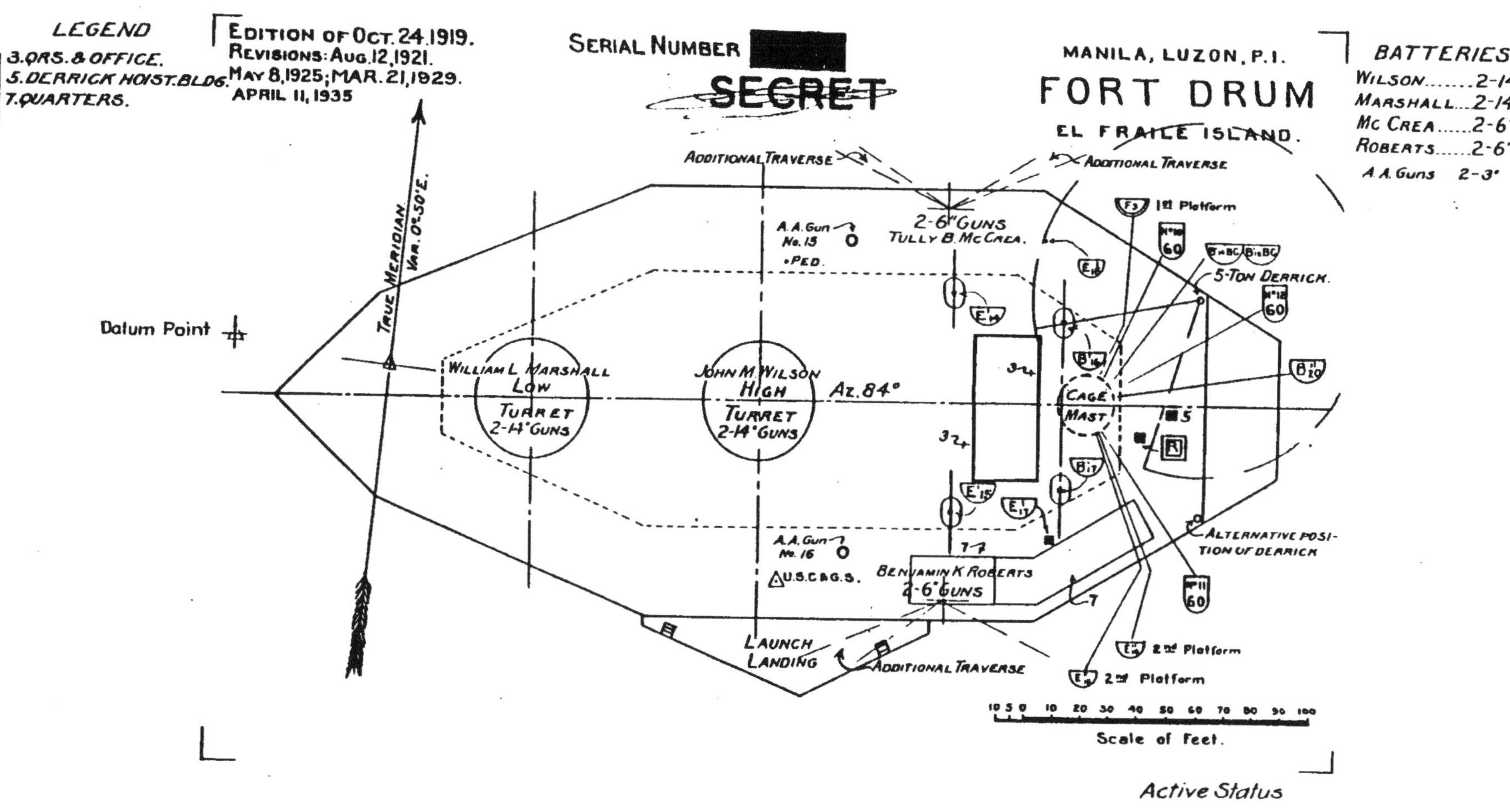
LEGEND
3. QRS. & OFFICE.
5. DERRICK HOIST. BLDG.
7. QUARTERS.
EDITION OF OCT. 24. 1919.
REVISIONS: AUG. 12, 1921.
MAY 8, 1925; MAR. 21, 1929.
APRIL 11, 1935
SERIAL NUMBER
SECRET
MANILA, LUZON, P.I.
FORT DRUM
EL FRAILE ISLAND.
BATTERIES
WILSON.......2-14"
MARSHALL...2-14"
Mc CREA.....2-6"P
ROBERTS.....2-6"P
A.A. Guns 2-3"
TRUE MERIDIAN
VAR. 0°50'E.
Datum Point
ADDITIONAL TRAVERSE
ADDITIONAL TRAVERSE
2-6" GUNS
TULLY B. McCREA.
A.A. Gun No. 15
PED.
1st Platform
5-TON DERRICK.
WILLIAM L. MARSHALL
LOW
TURRET
2-14" GUNS
JOHN M. WILSON
HIGH
TURRET
2-14" GUNS
Az. 84°
CAGE
MAST
ALTERNATIVE POSITION OF DERRICK
A.A. Gun No. 16
U.S.C.&G.S.
BENJAMIN K. ROBERTS
2-6" GUNS
LAUNCH
LANDING
ADDITIONAL TRAVERSE
2nd Platform
2nd Platform
Scale of Feet.
Active Status

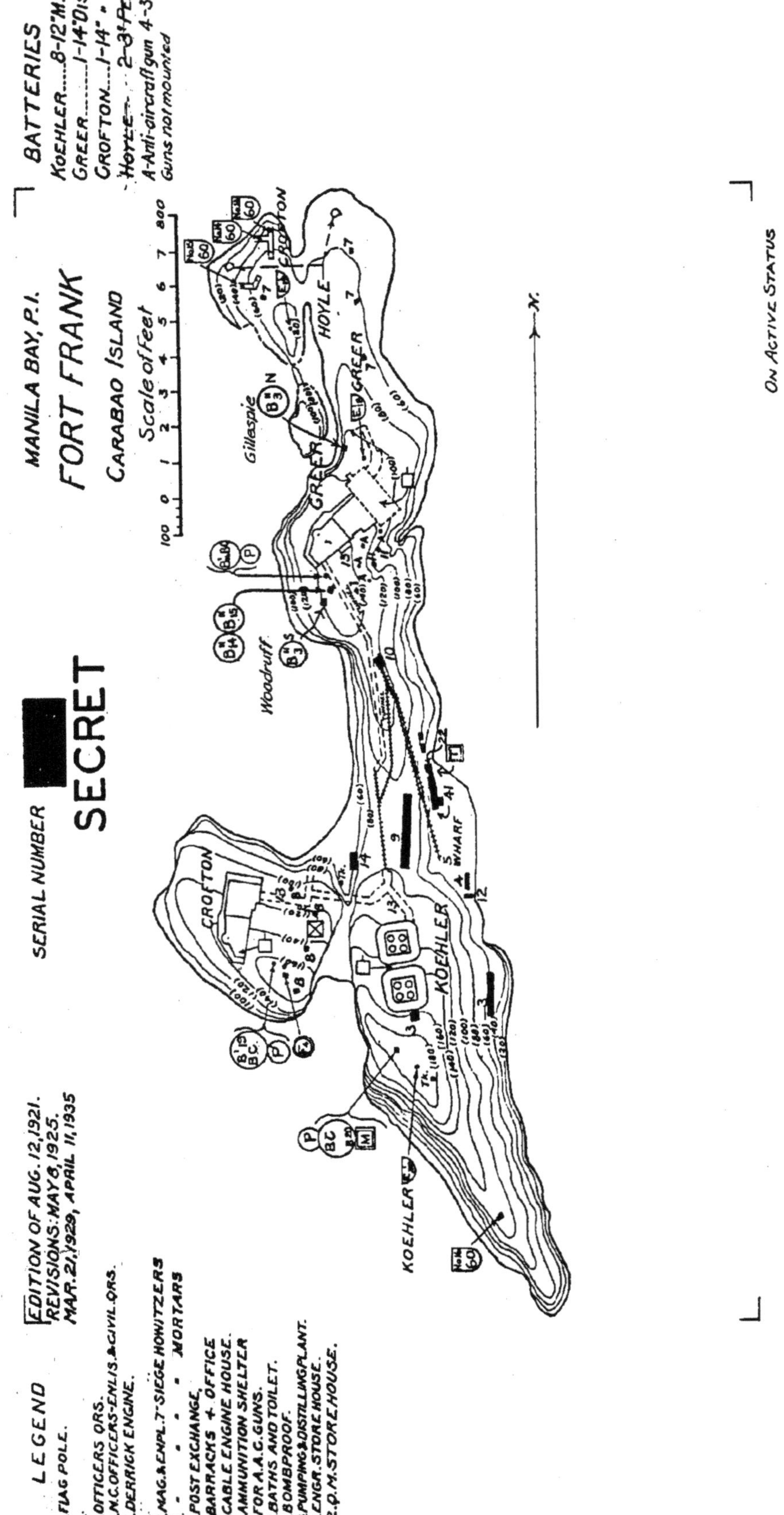
LEGEND
1. FLAG POLE.
2.
3. OFFICERS QRS.
4. N.C. OFFICERS-ENLIS. & CIVIL. QRS.
5. DERRICK ENGINE.
6.
7. MAG. & EMPL. 7" SIEGE HOWITZERS
8. - " " " MORTARS
9. POST EXCHANGE, BARRACKS + OFFICE
0. CABLE ENGINE HOUSE.
1. AMMUNITION SHELTER FOR A.A.C. GUNS.
2. BATHS AND TOILET.
3. BOMBPROOF.
4. PUMPING & DISTILLING PLANT.
1. ENGR. STORE HOUSE.
2. Q.M. STOREHOUSE.
EDITION OF AUG. 12, 1921.
REVISIONS: MAY 8, 1925.
MAR. 21, 1929, APRIL 11, 1935
SERIAL NUMBER
SECRET
MANILA BAY, P.I.
FORT FRANK
CARABAO ISLAND
Scale of Feet
100 0 1 2 3 4 5 6 7 800
BATTERIES
KOEHLER.....8-12" M.
GREER.........1-14" DIS.
GROFTON.....1-14" "
HOYLE...... 2-3" PED
A-Anti-aircraft gun 4-3"
Guns not mounted
CROFTON
KOEHLER
Woodruff
Gillespie
GREER
HOYLE
WHARF
N.
ON ACTIVE STATUS

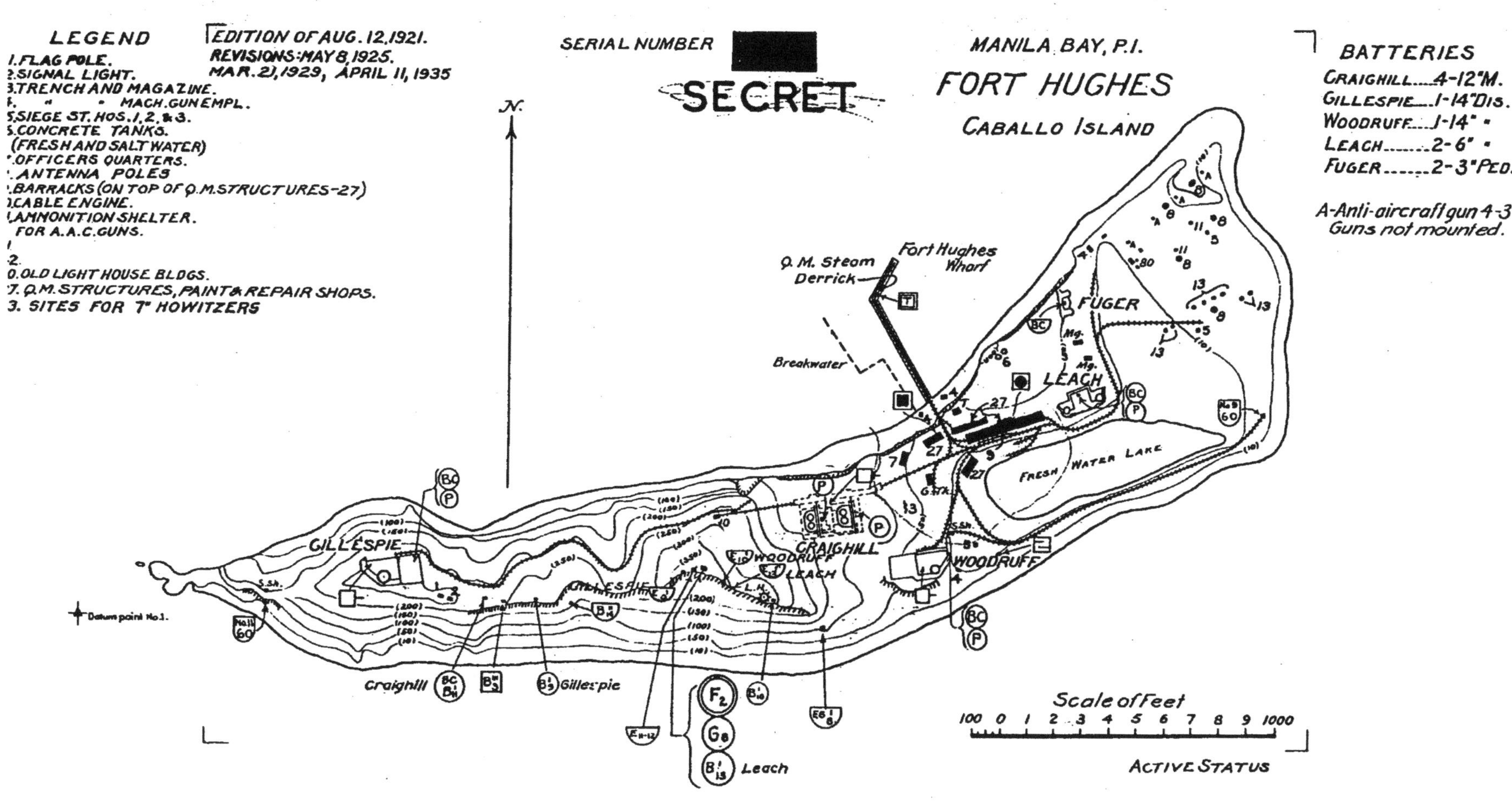
LEGEND
1. FLAG POLE.
2. SIGNAL LIGHT.
3. TRENCH AND MAGAZINE.
" " MACH. GUN EMPL.
SIEGE ST. NOS. 1, 2, & 3.
CONCRETE TANKS.
(FRESH AND SALT WATER)
OFFICERS QUARTERS.
ANTENNA POLES
BARRACKS (ON TOP OF Q.M. STRUCTURES-27)
CABLE ENGINE.
AMMUNITION SHELTER.
FOR A.A.C. GUNS.
OLD LIGHT HOUSE BLDGS.
Q.M. STRUCTURES, PAINT & REPAIR SHOPS.
SITES FOR 7" HOWITZERS
EDITION OF AUG. 12, 1921.
REVISIONS: MAY 8, 1925.
MAR. 21, 1929, APRIL 11, 1935
SERIAL NUMBER
SECRET
MANILA BAY, P.I.
FORT HUGHES
CABALLO ISLAND
BATTERIES
CRAIGHILL.....4-12"M.
GILLESPIE.....1-14"DIS.
WOODRUFF.....1-14" "
LEACH.........2-6" "
FUGER.........2-3"PED.
A-Anti-aircraft gun 4-3"
Guns not mounted.
N
Q.M. Steam Derrick
Fort Hughes Wharf
Breakwater
FUGER
LEACH
FRESH WATER LAKE
GILLESPIE
CRAIGHILL
WOODRUFF
Craighill
Gillespie
Leach
Datum point No. 1.
Scale of Feet
100 0 1 2 3 4 5 6 7 8 9 1000
ACTIVE STATUS

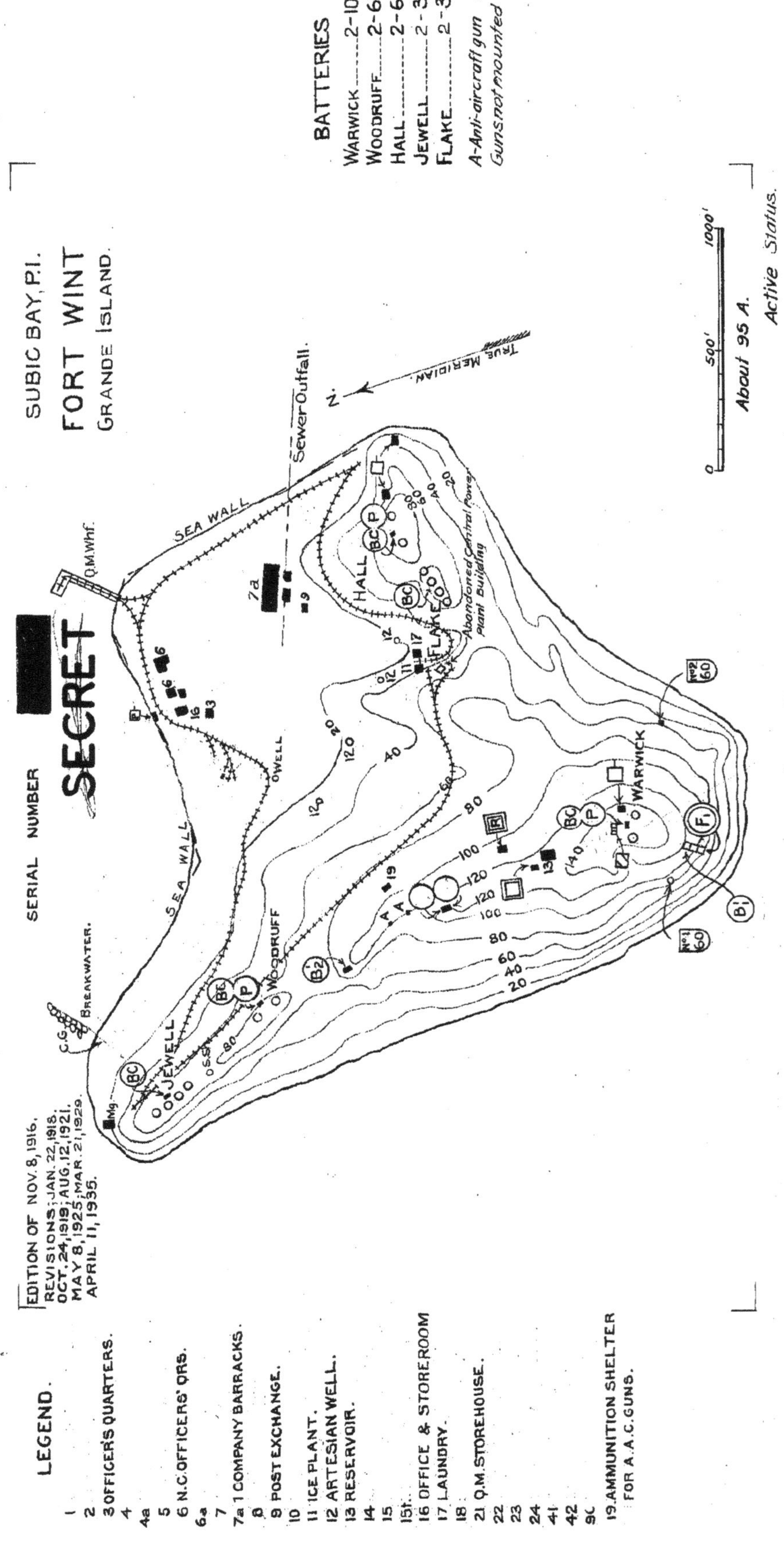
LEGEND.
1
2
3 OFFICER'S QUARTERS.
4
4a
5
6 N.C.OFFICERS' QRS.
6a
7
7a 1 COMPANY BARRACKS.
8
9 POST EXCHANGE.
10
11 ICE PLANT.
12 ARTESIAN WELL.
13 RESERVOIR.
14
15
15t.
16 OFFICE & STOREROOM
17 LAUNDRY.
18
21 Q.M.STOREHOUSE.
22
23
24
41
42
90
19.AMMUNITION SHELTER FOR A.A.C.GUNS.
EDITION OF NOV.8,1916.
REVISIONS; JAN. 22,1918.
OCT. 24,1919; AUG.12,1921.
MAY 8,1925; MAR. 21,1929.
APRIL 11, 1935.
SERIAL NUMBER
SECRET
SUBIC BAY, P.I.
FORT WINT
GRANDE ISLAND.
C.G.
BREAKWATER.
Q.M.Whf.
SEA WALL
SEA WALL
JEWELL
WOODRUFF
WELL
HALL
FLAKE
WARWICK
Sewer Outfall.
Abandoned Central Power Plant Building
N.
TRUE MERIDIAN.
BATTERIES
WARWICK 2-10"DIS.
WOODRUFF 2-6" "
HALL 2-6" "
JEWELL 2-3"PED.
FLAKE 2-3" "
A-Anti-aircraft gun 2-3"
Guns not mounted
0 500' 1000'
About 95 A.
Active Status.

NOTES TO SOURCES

While much has been written and published about the World War II events on Corregidor and the other fortified islands of Manila Bay, very little has been available covering the development of these defenses. Beyond articles appearing in the army's professional journals, little else has been available outside the official records of the U.S. Army. For the period 1900-1941, the author has principally relied upon archival records and professional literature of the US Army, coupled with the personal diaries and accounts of persons stationed in the harbor defenses. In recounting the events associated with the defense of fortified islands in Manila and Subic Bays in the early months of World War II and of their retaking by the U.S. Army in February 1945, the author has relied upon the official post-war reports of the siege and the numerous first-hand accounts published in monographs and periodical articles.

Archival Sources

National Archives I, Washington D.C.

The National Archives facility in downtown Washington D.C. in general contains the textual records for the army covering activities up and through the First World War. In practice a judgment call was made to split some larger record groups based on date and integrity of holdings or to keep the entire group intact to facilitate research. In the case of the Harbor Defenses of Manila and Subic Bay, records for engineer, ordnance, signal corps, and the Adjutant General are split, while those for the Coast Artillery and its commands are entirely housed at Archives II. The major holdings consulted for this study at National Archives I were:

RG-77 Records of the Chief of Engineers.
- Entry 103, General Correspondence, 1894-1923. Files arranged by topics and enumerated with an assigned index number. Contains copies of "Reports of Completed Batteries." These were summary reports completed each year listing all coast defense tactical structures built under Corps of Engineer supervision with date of transfer, cost, details of armament, and equipment. Consulted were versions for 1908, 1911, 1913 and 1914.
- Entry 220, Coast Defense Fortification File 1898-1920. Contains summary sheets of individual engineer works by harbor defense.
- Entry 225, Correspondence, blueprints, and reports relating to defense.

RG-92 Records of the Quartermaster General
- Entry 89, Correspondence of the Office of the Quartermaster General, 1890-1914.

RG-94 Records of the Adjutant General
- Entry 25, Adjutant General Document File, 1890-1917.

RG-111 Records of the Office of the Chief Signal Officer
- Entry 44, General Correspondence, 1889-1917.

RG-156 Records of the Chief of Ordnance
- Entry 28, Correspondence of the Chief of Ordnance, 1894-1913.
- Entry 29, Correspondence of the Chief of Ordnance, 1910-1915.

RG-165 Records of War Department General and Special Staffs.
- Entry 281, War Plans Division correspondence.
- Entry 518 Record of Proceeding of the Board to Revise the Report of the Endicott Board, 1905-06.

National Archives II, College Park, MD

National Archives II in College Park, Maryland, holds the major army textual records for the technical and administrative services (engineers, ordnance, quartermaster, transportation, adjutant general) for the interwar and Second World War period. In addition, all the records for the Coast Artillery Corps are held here. Also, the College Park facility holds all cartographic, still, and motion picture archives, regardless of date. Major holdings consulted were:

RG-77 Records of the Chief of Engineers.

Entry 393, Historical Records of Buildings at Active Army Posts. 1905-1942. Contains by post a large number of sheets for individual post structures and buildings, mostly garrison structures rather than batteries or emplacements. Often known as the "Quartermaster Building File," these pages with photos are often the only surviving record of individual barracks, quarters, storehouses, etc.

Entry 1006, Correspondence of the Chief of Engineers, 1915-1942, Harbor Defense Files.

Entry 1007, Correspondence of the Chief of Engineers, 1915-1942, Geographical Files, Harbor Defenses, (classified). Contents arranged by the War Department decimal system. File No. 600.914 contains sets of "Reports of Completed Works" or simply "RCWs." These successors to the Reports of Completed Batteries date from 1919-1945. They are forms filled out for each tactical structure (gun batteries, searchlights, power plants, switchboards, cable huts, mining structures, etc.). Usually they are accompanied by a one-page drawing and occasionally photographs.

Entry 1009, Correspondence of the Chief of Engineers, Geographical Files (unclassified).

RG-156 Records of the Chief of Ordnance

Entry 36, Correspondence of the Chief of Ordnance, 1915-1941.

RG-177 Records of the Chief of Arms, Office of the Chief of Coast Artillery.

Entry 4, General Correspondence 1907-1918.

Entry 8, General Correspondence 1918-1942.

Entry 19, Proceedings of the Coast Artillery Board, 1905-1919.

RG-407 Records of the Adjutant General

Entry 20, The Philippine Archives Collection.

Contains a full copy of the "Wainwright Papers" (See below under USAMHI).

Entry 360, General Correspondence, 1918-1945.

Entry 365, Plans for the defense of the United States and possessions, 1920-1948.

RG-496 Records of the General Headquarters, Southwest Pacific Area.

Entry 540 Records of the Far Eastern Army Command and United States Army Forces, Pacific.

The Military Personnel Records Section, National Personnel Records Center, St. Louis, MO.

This facility is the repository for organizational and personnel records of the US Armed Forces. The Organizational Records Unit contains microfilm files of the Morning Reports as well as Historical Data Sheets and Station Lists for Regular Army units. This latter material is also housed at The U.S. Army Center of Military History, Fort Leslie J. McNair.

United States Army Military History Institute, Carlisle Barracks, PA.

This facility has several pertinent collections held in the Special Collections Archives.
Most useful are the records in the following collections:

- Belote Papers
- Brady Papers
- Homer Case Papers (contains the personal copy of General Case's "Proceedings of a Board of Officers Appointed to Evaluate War Damage to the Harbor Defenses of Manila and Subic Bay," Headquarters 14th Antiaircraft Command, 6 October 1945. Subsequently referred to as the "Case Report").
- Moore Papers (contains an original copy of the "Report of Operations on the Harbor Defenses of Manila and Subic Bay 14 February 1941 – 6 May 1942," which in turn is one of the eighteen annexes in the Wainwright Papers – see below)
- Morton Papers contain a copy of the entire "Wainwright Papers." This report is formally designated "Report of Operations of USAFFE and USFIP in the Philippine Islands 1941 – 1942. Copies also exist in the National Archives and were published postwar in a compendium of four volumes edited by Celedonio A. Ancheta, Quezon City, Philippines, New Day Publishers, 1980. Volume 2: pages 1-104 is often referred to as the "Moore Report."
- Several collections of period photographs of various aspects of the Harbor Defenses of Manila and Subic Bay were sourced from the following Photographic Archive Collections:
  - Alfonte Collection
  - Ashton Collectiion
  - Charles Coffin Collection
  - Cornwell Collection
  - Douglas Collection
  - McCrary Collection
  - Ruhlen Collecctin
  - Sherr Collection
  - Winslett Collection

The MacArthur Memorial Archives, Norfolk, VA.

Most of the unique holdings relative to the 1941-1942 campaign in the Philippines are in the Douglas MacArthur Papers. Most usefull regarding the Philippine campaign are those in RG-2, Records of Headquarters, USAFFE 1941-1942, available on Microfilm Reel 4-21.

PUBLISHED WORKS

Books

Adjutant General's Office. *Army List and Directory of Officers of the Army of the United States.* Washington D.C.: GPO editions of 1909, 1910, 1915, 1920 and 1921.

Allen, Francis J. *The Concrete Battleship: Fort Drum, El Fraile Island, Manila Bay.* Missoula, MT: Pictorial Histories Publishing Co., 1989.

Aluit, Alfonso J. *Corregidor. Manila*: Galleon Publications, 1995.

Annual Report of the Chief of Coast Artillery. Washington D.C.: GPO, editions for 1908-1927.

Barlow, Keith A. (U.S.A. ret), ed. *Bunker's War: The World War II Diary of Colonel Paul D. Bunker.* Novato, CA: Presidio Press, 1996.

Bartsch, William H. *Doomed at the Start: American Pursuit Pilots in the Philippines, 1941–1942.* College Station: Texas A&M University Press, 1992.

Belote, James H., and William M. Belote. *Corregidor: The Saga of a Fortress.* New York: Harper and Row, 1967.

Bogart, Charles H. *Controlled Mines: A History of their Use by the United States,* Bennington Vt: Weapons and Warfare Press, 1985.

Braisted, Williams Reynolds. *The United States Navy in the Pacific, 1909-1922.* University of Texas Press, Austin, Texas, 1971.

Braly, William C. (U.S.A. ret.). *The Hard Way Home.* Washington D.C.: Infantry Journal Press, 1947.

Breuer, William B. *Retaking the Philippines.* New York: St. Martin's Press, 1986.

Bulkley, Captain Robert J., Jr. (ret.). *At Close Quarters: PT Boats in the United States Navy.* Washington, D.C.: Naval History Division, U.S. Navy, 1962.

Call, Lewis W. *United States Military Reservations, National Cemeteries and Military Parks, Title, Jurisdiction,* Etc. Washington DC: GPO, 1907.

Carlisle, Sheila, ed. *U.S. Naval Cryptographic Activities in the Philippines Prior to World War II.* Laguna Hills, CA: Aegean Park Press, 1982.

Cave, Dorothy. *Beyond Courage: One Regiment Against Japan, 1941–1945.* Las Cruces, NM: Yucca Tree Press, 1992.

Chamberlain, William. *Coast Artillery War Game, 4th Ed.* Washington, D.C.: GPO, 1916.

Clay, Lt. Col. (Ret.) Steven C. *U.S. Army Order of Battle 1919-1941, Vol. I, the Arms: Major Commands Infantry,* US Army Combined Arms Center Fort Leavenworth, KS: Combat Studies Institute Press.

_____. *U.S. Army Order of Battle 1919-1941, Vol. II, the Arms: Cavalry, Field Artillery and Coast Artillery.* US Army Combined Arms Center Fort Leavenworth, KS: Combat Studies Institute Press.

_____. *U.S. Army Order of Battle 1919-1941, Vol. III, the Services: Air Services, Engineers and Special Troops Organizations,* US Army Combined Arms Center, Fort Leavenworth, KS: Combat Studies Institute Press.

Coletta, Paolo E., ed. *United States Navy and Marine Corps Bases, Overseas.* Westport, CT: Greenwood Press, 1985.

Craven, Wesley Frank, and James Lea Cate, eds. *The Army Air Forces in World War II. vol. 1, Plans and Early Operations: January 1939 to August 1942.* Chicago: University of Chicago Press, 1948.

Cullum, George Washington. *Biographical Register of the Officers and Graduates of the U.S. Military Academy at West Point, NY.* Saginaw, MI: Seemann and Peters, 1910.

De Morga, Antonio. *History of the Philippine Islands.* Cleveland: The Arthur H. Clark Co., 1907.

Devlin, Gerard M. *Back to Corregidor: America Retakes the Rock.* New York: St. Martin's Press, 1992.

Dupuy, Earnest R. and Trevor N. *The Encyclopedia of Military History From 3500 B.C. to the Present.* New York: Harper and Row, 1970.

Dyess, Lt. Col. William E. *The Dyess Story.* New York: G.P. Putnam's Sons, 1944.

Edmonds, Walter D. *They Fought with What They Had: The Story of the Army Air Forces in the Southwest Pacific, 1941–1942.* Washington, D.C.: Zenger Publishing Co., 1982.

Flanagan, Lt. Gen. Edward M. Jr. (U.S.A. ret). *Corregidor: The Rock Force Assault.* New York: Jove Books, 1989.

Gasei, Watari. *Philippine Expeditionary Force.* Tokyo: Group Information Department Publication, Manila, 1943.

General Headquarters, Far East Command, Military History Section. *Philippines Air Operations Record, Phase I. Japanese Monograph No. 11.* Fort Leavenworth, KS: 1952.

Gordon, John. *Fighting for MacArthur The Navy and Marine Corps's Desperate Defense of the Philippines.* Naval Institute Press, Annapolis, MD, 2011.

Heitman, Francis B. *Historical Register and Dictionary of the United States Army from its Organization September 29, 1787 to March 2, 1903.* Washington D.C.: GPO 1903.

Hough, Lt. Col. Frank O., Maj. Verle E. Ludwig, and Henry I. Shaw Jr. *History of U.S. Marine Corps Operations in World War II. Vol. 1, Pearl Harbor to Guadalcanal.* Washington, D.C.: Historical Branch, G-3 Division, Headquarters, U.S. Marine Corps.

James, D. Clayton. *The Years of MacArthur. Vol. 1, 1880–1941.* Boston: Houghton Mifflin Company, 1970.

Jose, Ricardo Trota. *The Philippine Army, 1935–1942.* Manila: Ateneo de Manila University Press, 1992.

Kreuger, General Walter. *From Down Under to Nippon: The Story of Sixth Army in World War II.* Washington, D.C.: Zenger Publishing, 1953.

Kwiecinski, Stephen A. *Honor Courage Faith; A Corregidor Story.* Mandaluyong City, Philippines: Anvil Publishing Inc., 2014.

Larson, Harold. *Water Transportation for the United States Army 1939-1942.* Office of the Chief of Transportation, Army Service Forces, 1944.

Linn, Brian McAllister. *Guardians of Empire; The U.S. Army and the Pacific 1902-1940.* Chapel Hill, NC: The University of North Carolina Press, 1997.

Leutze, James. *A Different Kind of Victory: A Biography of Admiral Thomas C. Hart.* Annapolis: Naval Institute Press, 1981.

Lockwood, Charles A. *Sink 'Em All: Submarine Warfare in the Pacific.* New York: P. Dutton, 1951.

Mallonée, Richard C., II, ed. *The Naked Flagpole: Battle for Bataan.* San Rafael, CA: Presidio Press, 1980.

Manchester, William. *American Caesar: Douglas MacArthur, 1880–1964.* Boston: Little, Brown and Co., 1978.

McGovern, Terrance C., and Mark A. Berhow. *American Defenses of Corregidor and Manila Bay 1898-1945.* Oxford, UK: Osprey Pub., 2003.

Mellnik, General Stephen. *Philippine Diary, 1939–1945.* New York: Van Nostrand Reinhold Co., 1969.

Messimer, Dwight R. *In the Hands of Fate: The Story of Patrol Wing Ten, 8 December 1941–11 May 1942.* Annapolis: Naval Institute Press, 1985.

Miller, Colonel E. B. *Bataan Uncensored.* Little Falls, MN: Military Historical Society of Minnesota, 1991.

Miller, Edward S. *War Plan Orange: The U.S. Strategy to Defeat Japan, 1897– 1945.* Annapolis: Naval Institute Press, 1991.

Miller, J. Michael. *From Shanghai to Corregidor: Marines in the Defense of the Philippines.* Washington, D.C.: Marine Corps Historical Center, 1997.

Moore, Major General George. "Report of Operations on the Harbor Defenses of Manila and Subic Bays 14 February 1941 – 5 May 1942." *Wainwright Papers: Historical Documents of World War II in the Philippines*, edited by Celedonio A. Ancheta. Quezon City, Philippines: New Day Publishers, 1980.

Morris, Eric. *Corregidor: The End of the Line*. New York: Stein and Day, 1981.

Morton, Louis. *The Fall of the Philippines*. United States Army in World War II. Washington, D.C.: Office of the Chief of Military History, United States Army, 1953.

———. *Strategy and Command: The First Two Years*. United States Army in World War II. Washington, D.C.: Office of the Chief of Military History, Department of the Army, 1962.

Pearl Harbor Attack: Hearings before the Joint Committee on the Investigation of the Pearl Harbor Attack. Washington, D.C.: GPO, 1946.

Prange, Gordon W. *At Dawn We Slept: The Untold Story of Pearl Harbor*. New York: Penguin Books, 1982.

Report of the National Coast Defense Board Appointed by the President of the United States by Executive Order January 31, 1905. Washington D.C.: GPO, 1906.

Reports of General MacArthur, Japanese Operations in the Southwest Pacific Area, Vol, II Part 1. Washington D.C.: GPO, 1966.

Small, Charles P. *Rails to Doomsday: The U.S. Army's Corregidor and Manila Bay Railroads.* Greenwich, CT.: Railroad Monographs, 1980.

Smith, Robert Ross. *Triumph in the Philippines.* United States Army in World War II. Washington, D.C.: Office of the Chief of Military History, Department of the Army, 1963.

Sullivan, Charles J. (Comp.) *Army Posts and Towns: The Baedeker of the Army*. Plattsburg Barracks, NY: 1926.

Underbrink, Robert I. *Destination Corregidor*. Annapolis: Naval Institute Press, 1971.

U.S. Army War College, *Order of Battle of the United States Land Forces in the World War (1917-1919), Zone of the Interior*, Vol. III. Washington, D.C.: GPO, 1949.

Uno, Kazumaro. *Corregidor: Isle of Delusion*. Shanghai, the Mercury Press, 1942.

Wainwright, Gen. Jonathan M. *General Wainwright's Story*. Westport, CT: Greenwood Press, 1970.

Whitman, Lt. Col. John W. (ret.). *Bataan, Our Last Ditch*. New York: Hippocrene Books, 1990.

Williford Glen. *Racing the Sunrise: Reinforcing America's Pacific Outposts 1941-42*. Annapolis: Naval Institute Press, 2010.

Winslow, Col. Eben Eveleth. *Notes on Seacoast Fortification Construction*. Occasional Papers No. 61 of the Engineer School United States Army. Washington D.C.: GPO, 1920.

Winslow, Capt. W.G. (ret.). *The Fleet the Gods Forgot: The U.S. Asiatic Fleet in World War II*. Annapolis: Naval Institute Press, 1982.

Wright, John M. Jr. *Captured on Corregidor: Diary of an American P.O.W. in World War II*. Jefferson. NC: McFarland & Co. Inc., 1988.

Young, Donald J. *The Battle of Bataan*. Jefferson, NC: McFarland & Co. Inc., 1992.

Articles

Allen, W. I., "Notes from the Philippines," *Coast Artillery Journal,* Vol. 76 (Nov.-Dec. 1933): 444-446.

Barnes, H.C., "A Regimental Organization for the Coast Artillery Corps," *Coast Artillery Journal,* Vol. 60 (April 1924): 293-299.

Birkhimer, William E., "Land Defenses of Manila Bay, May 1, 1898". *Journal of the United States Artillery,* Vol. 15, No. 1 (January-February 1901): 16-21.

Bocksel, Arnold A. "The USAMP General George Harrison in the Harbor Defenses of Manila and Subic Bay." *Coast Artillery Journal,* Vol. 89, No. 6 (Nov. – Dec. 1946): 54.

Bogart, Charles H. "Fort Hughes: Outpost Duty Between Wars" *Periodical: The Journal of the Council on America's Military Past,* Vol. XV, No. 3 (Oct. 1987): 25-40.

_______ "Radar in the Philippines 1941-1942." *Periodical: Journal of America's Military Past* Vol. XXVI, No. 2 (Fall 1999): 27-35.

_______ "Subic Bay and Fort Wint: Keys to Manila." *Periodical: The Journal of the Council on America's Military Past,* Vol. XI (Spring 1979): 26-37.

_______ "The Concrete Battleship—Fort Drum." *Periodical: The Journal of the Council on America's Military Past,* Vol. IX, No. 3 (Winter 1977-78): 13-15.

Braly, William C. (U.S.A. ret.). "Corregidor: A Name, A Symbol, A Tradition." *Coast Artillery Journal,* Vol. 90, No. 4 (Jul.-Aug. 1947).

Brown, Burton R. "Corregidor." *Coast Artillery Journal* Vol. 84 No. 4 (Jul. – Aug. 1941), and Vol. 84, No. 5 (Sept. – Oct. 1941).

Case, Colonel Homer. "War Damage to Corregidor." *Coast Artillery Journal,* Vol. 90, No. 5 (May – June 1947): 36-42.

Ellicott, John M. "Corregidor in 1898," *Proceedings of the United States Naval Institute*, Vol. 68 (May 1942), 638-641.

_____ " Defenses of Manila Bay," *Proceedings of the United States Naval Institute,* No. 94 (1900): 279-286.

_____ "The Naval Battle of Manila," *Proceedings of the United States Naval Institute,* No. 95, (1900): 489-514.

Feredo, Tony. "The Corregidor Railway System." *Historical Corregidor Society*, 1-2.

Gaines, William C. "240 mm Howitzers on Oahu, 1922-1944." *Coast Defense Journal,* Vol. 16, No. 4 (Nov. 2002): 4-27.

_______ "92nd Coast Artillery Regiment (Philippine Scouts)." *Coast Defense Journal,* Vol. 20, No. 1 (Feb. 2006): 11-33.

_______ "Antiaircraft Defenses in the Harbor Defenses of Manila and Subic Bays 1921-1940," *Coast Defense Study Group Journal,* Vol. 14, No, 1 (February 2000): 21-43.

_____ "Corregidor the Early Years." *Coast Defense Journal,* Vol. 21, No. 3 (Aug; 2007): 4-23.

Gibson, R. T. "Bilibid's Guard Battalion," *Coast Artillery Journal,* Vol. 80 No. 6 (Nov.-December 1937): 488-491.

Goldblith, Samuel A. "The 803d engineers in the Philippine Defense." *The Military Engineer* (Aug. 1946): 323–325.

Green, Fred M. "Coast Artillery Life in the Philippines" *Coast Artillery Journal,* Vol. 58, No. 5 (May 1922): 444-452.

Hagge, Gregory J. "What Happened to the Mortars of Corregidor?," *CDSG Journal,* Vol. 9, No. 2 (May 1995): 21-27.

Heaney, G.F. Jr. "Machine Gun Towers." *Coast Artillery Journal,* Vol. 77, No. 1 (Jul.-Aug.), 1934): 275-276.

_______ "Present Conditions at Corregidor." *Coast Artillery Journal,* Vol. 74, No. 7 (Nov.-Dec. 1931): 542-543.

Himmler, Charles. "The C.A.C. with the Japanese Relief Expedition," *Coast Artillery Journal,* Vol. 61, No. 3 (Sept. 1923), 265-266.

Jewell, Henry C. "History of the Corps of Engineers to 1915." *The Military Engineer,* Vol. 14, (1922): 306.

Kingman, Brig. Gen. John J. "The Genesis of Fort Drum, Manila Bay." *The Military Engineer,* Vol. 37, No. 234 (Apr. 1945): 128-130.

Landreth, Earl. "The British Capture of Manila—1762." *Coast Artillery Journal,* Vol. 78, No. 6 (Nov.-Dec. 1935): 446-450.

Lawry, Nelson H. "Another Five Degrees: WWI Alterations to the Disappearing Carriage." *Coast Defense Study Group Journal,* Vol. 10, No. 2 (May 1996): 4-12.

Lawry, Nelson H. and Glen M. Williford. "The Coast Artillery 14-inch Gun 1907-1918" *Coast Defense Study Group Journal,* Vol. 12, No. 3 (Aug. 1998): 4-31.

Malone, Daniel. "Artillery Weapons at Fort Drum." *Coast Defense Study Group News,* Vol. 5, No. 3 (Aug. 1991): 19-34.

Markland, Herbert F., with Shawn A. Welch. "A Coast Artilleryman's Experiences at Fort Mills (Pt. 1)." *CDSG Journal,* Vol. IX, No. 1 (Feb. 1995): 4-15.

Meixsel, Richard. "The Philippine Scout Mutiny of 1924." *Southeast Asia Research,* Vol. 10, No. 3: 333-359.

Mellnik, Gen. Stephen. "How the Japanese Took Corregidor." *Coast Artillery Journal,* Vol. 88, No. 2 (Mar.-Apr. 1946): 2-11, 17.

_____ "The Life and Death of the 200th Coast Artillery (AA)." *Coast Artillery Journal,* Vol. 90, No. 2 (Mar. – Apr. 1947): 2-7.

Morton, Louis. "Military and Naval Preparations for the Defense of the Philippines during the War Scare of 1907." *Military Affairs,* Vol. 13 (Summer 1949): 95-104.

"Night Practice at Fort Mills, P.I." *Journal of United States Artillery,* Vol. 35. No. 3 (Nov. – Dec. 1911): 334-336.

Philips, R.E. "Corregidor." *Coast Artillery Journal,* Vol. 82, No. 6 (Nov. – Dec. 1939): 592.

Postlethwait, E.M. "Corregidor Coordination." *The Infantry Journal,* Vol. 57 (Aug. 1945): 16-19.

Rutherford, Andrew. "Reminiscences of Corregidor." *Periodical: Journal of American Military Past,* Vol. XXIV, No. 3 (Fall 1997): 31-40.

Smith, J.H. "Calibrating the Guns of the 59th Artillery," *Coast Artillery Journal,* Vol. 60, No. 3 (Mar. 1924): 198-211.

Strong, Col. Paschal N. Jr. "The Lean Years." *The Military Engineer,* Vol. 41, (May-June 1949): 179-181.

Tabaniag, Antonio. "The Pre-War Philippine Scouts," *University of Manila Journal of East Asiatic Studies,* Vol. IX, No. 4 (Oct. 1960): 7-26.

Warner, Oscar C. "Corregidor Newsletter." *Coast Artillery Journal,* Vol. 80, No.1 (Jan -Feb 1937): 70-71 and Vol. 80, No.2 (Mar.-Apr. 1937): 167-168.

Waters, K.L. "The Army Mine Planter Service." *Warship International,* Vol. 22, No. 4 (1985): 400-411.

Williford, Glen, "At the Southern Extreme: Fire Control on Limbones Island." *Coast Defense Journal,* Vol. XIV, No. 3 (Aug. 2000): 85-90.

_______ "Land Defense for the Coast Defense of Manila Bay." *Coast Defense Journal,* Vol. 16, No. 2 (May 2002): 4-28.

_______ "On Occasion They Did Make Mistakes: Engineer Construction Errors during the Taft Era." *Coast Defense Journal,* Vol. 24, No. 2 (May 2010): 35-49.

Manuscripts

Abston, Aaron A. "Diary of Battery G, 60th Coast Artillery June 1, 1941-May 6, 1942." USAMHI, Carlisle Barracks, PA.

Alcaraz, Ramon A. "Journal of Commodore Ramon A. Alcaraz, December 1941," 20, 26. http://www.oocities.org/comralcaraz/ diary.html.

Ames, Godfrey R. "Narrative Report of Action during War, October 20, 1943." [Battery C, 60th Coast Artillery] http://corregidor.org/ca/btty_chicago/chicago_1.htm

Barr, Earl L. "Diary, " RG 407, Archives II.

_____. "History of Battery M, 60th CA (AA)," Center of Military History, Washington, D.C.

"Battery F History," Organizational Records Unit, Military Personnel Records Section, National Personnel Records Center, St. Louis, MO.

Bruns, Stockton, "History of Battery I, 59th Coast Artillery," Folder 59th Coast Artillery Antiaircraft. Roster of officers Reminiscences and letters Corregidor Box, William and James Belote Collection, Archives, USAMHI, Carlisle Barracks, PA.

Cornwall, Paul R., "War History, Battery D, 60th CA (AA) Regiment," Organizational Records Unit, Military Personnel Records Section, National Personnel Records Center, St. Louis, MO.

"Diary of Battery E, [60th CA (AA)]," RG 407, Archives II.

"Diary of Battery L, 60th Coast Artillery (AA)," Organizational Records Unit, Military Personnel Records Section, National Personnel Records Center, St. Louis, MO.

Lowe, Karl H., "America's Foreign Legion: The 31st Infantry Regiment at War and Peace," 31st US Infantry Association. Chapter 1, 1-3. http://www. 31stinfantry. org/

Shiley, E.M. "History of Battery I, 60th CA (AA) 1917-," RG 407, Archives II.

"Siege of Corregidor, " Coast Artillery Training Bulletin, Vol. 3, No. 1 (Feb 1944).

Starr, Warren A. Battery Commander's Narrative Report of Battery Hartford's Action during the War Period from November 29, 1941 to the Surrender of Corregidor May 6, 1942, Organizational Records Unit, Military Personnel Records Section, National Personnel Records Center, St. Louis, MO.

______"My Years with the Military," http://corregidor.org/chs_starr/starr_01.htm

Wooten, William P. "The Provisional Battalion of Engineers in the Philippines." Occasional Paper No. 42, Engineer School Washington Barracks (1910): 34.

Youngberg, G. A. "History of Engineer Troops in the United States Army 1775-1901". Occasional Paper No. 37, Engineer School Washington Barracks (1910): 32-33.

ENDNOTES

NARA Record Groups

RG 77: Records of the Office of the Chief of Engineers.
RG 80: General Records of the Department of the Navy.
RG 92: Records of the Office of the Quartermaster General.
RG 94: Records of the Adjutant General's Office.
RG 111: Records of the Office of the Chief Signal Officer.
RG 112: Records of the Office of the Surgeon General.
RG 156: Records of the Office of the Chief of Ordnance.
RG 165: Records of the War Department General and Special Staffs.
RG 407: Records of the Adjutant General's Office.
RG 177: Records of the Chiefs of Branches, 1878-1942, Records of the Chief of Coast Artillery.

[1] Antonio de Morga, "History of the Philippine Islands," http://www.bohol.ph/.

[2] William R. Nayler, "A Brief History of Fort Mills, Philippine Islands," March 21, 1925, Historical File, HD Manila and Subic Bays, RG 177, Archives II. Hereafter: Nayler, "Brief History of Fort Mills."

[3] Ibid.

[4] John M. Ellicott, "The Defenses of Manila Bay," *Proceedings of the United States Naval Institute*, Vol. 26, No. 94 (1900), 279-285. Hereafter: Ellicott, "The Defenses of Manila Bay." As a naval lieutenant John M. Ellicott served as the intelligence officer on USS *Baltimore* during the Battle of Manila Bay.

[5] Earl Landreth, "The British Capture of Manila — 1762," *Coast Artillery Journal (CAJ)*, Vol. 78, No. 6 (Nov.-Dec. 1935), 446-450.

[6] "A Brief History of Sangley Point," http://web2.iadfw.net/lrs/sangley.html.

[7] "The Olongapo Story," *Bamboo Breeze,* Vol. 6, No. 3 (July 28, 1953).

[8] Ibid.

[9] Ellicott, "The Defenses of Manila Bay." "The Olongapo Story," *Bamboo Breeze*, Vol. 6, No. 3 (July 28, 1953).

[10] Ellicott, "The Defenses of Manila Bay."

[11] Ibid.

[12] Corregidor Light remained in use until the outbreak of World War II, during which it was heavily damaged. Following that war, the lighthouse was rebuilt in accordance with the 1897 specifications.

[13] Patricio Montojo y Pasaron, "The Official Report of Spanish Admiral Montojo on the Battle of Manila Bay," http://www.spanamwar.com /mtreport.htm Hereafter: Montojo, "Official Report."

[14] Matheson's shutter-apparatus electrically controlled mine was designed about 1870 by Quartermaster Sergeant Mathession, Royal Engineers. John Townsend Bucknill, *Submarine Mines and Torpedoes as Applied to Harbour Defence* (New York: John Wiley and Sons, 1889), 122-123, 134-135. Montojo, "Official Report."

[15] Ellicott, "The Defenses of Manila Bay." William E. Birkhimer, "Land Defenses of Manila Bay, May 1, 1898," *Journal of the United States Artillery* (*JUSA*), Vol. 15, No. 1 (Jan.-Feb. 1901), 16-21. Hereafter: Birkhimer, "Land Defenses of Manila Bay, May 1, 1898," Nayler, "A Brief History of Fort Mills." Herbert Wrigley Wilson, *The Downfall of Spain: The Naval History of the Spanish American War* (London: Samson, Low, Marston and Co. Ltd., 1900), 125, 158-159. Hereafter: Wilson, *Downfall of Spain.*

[16] Ellicott, "The Defenses of Manila Bay."

[17] Montojo, "Official Report."

[18] The work that in later years would become known as Spanish Fort was begun in April 1898 and consisted of a simple earthen épaulement behind which the armament was emplaced. The terms "Bottomside," "Middleside," and "Topside" were derived from the pidgin English used by the Filipino workers during the American construction period in the early 1900s to define the three major areas of the island west of Malinta Hill. A fourth area that encompassed the area of the island east of Malinta Hill was simply referred to as the "tail." William R. Nayler, "A Brief History of Fort Mills, Philippine Islands." "Story of Simon de los Reyes, Policeman of the Barrio de San Jose de Corregidor," Statement of de Los Reyes to Maj. J.C. Johnson,

CAC, August 26, 1914, Historical File, Artillery District of Manila Bay, RG 177, Archives II. Hereafter: "Story of Simon de los Reyes." Herbert Wrigley Wilson, *The Downfall of Spain*, 126.

[19] Nayler, "Brief History of Fort Mills." Ellicott, "The Defenses of Manila Bay."

[20] Nayler, "Brief History of Fort Mills."

[21] Ordonez Guns were seacoast artillery pieces, developed by Spanish Capt. Salvador Diaz Ordonez in 1880, used to defend Spanish harbors, military installations, and overseas possessions.

[22] Ellicott, "The Defenses of Manila Bay." Charles H. Bogart, "Subic Bay and Fort Wint: Keys to Manila," *Periodical: The Journal of the Council on American's Military Past*, Vol. 11, (Spring 1979), 26-37. Hereafter: Bogart, *"Subic Bay and Fort Wint."*

[23] Ellicott, "The Defenses of Manila Bay." "Story of Simon de los Reyes."

[24] Birkhimer, "Land Defenses." Ellicott, "The Defenses of Manila Bay." "Story of Simon de los Reyes."

[25] A considerable number of the smaller artillery pieces also eventually made their way into the hand of the insurgents. "Story of Simon de los Reyes."

[26] "Memorandum for the Chief of Staff on the Evolution and Present Status of Defenses on Corregidor Island, September 25," 1914, RG 177, Entry 4, Archives II.

[27] Letter to Chief of Engineers Brig. Gen. John Wilson from Chief of Ordnance Brig. Gen. Daniel Flagler, May 20, 1898, NARA, Washington, D.C., RG 77, Entry 103, File 26742.

[28] War Department, *Annual Report of Surgeon General, 1899*, 99-100 (first quotation), 110, and *1900*, 105, 111, 115-16. *Annual Report of Secretary of War, 1900*, l (Pt. 3), 124-25, *1903*, Pt 3, 196. William O. Owen, "Some of the Trials and Tribulations of a Medical Officer of the United States Army," 388-89, 392 (second quotation). War Department, *Correspondence Relating to the War with Spain*, 2, 847, 1014. Flexner and Barker, "Prevalent Diseases," 523.

[29] "Official History of the Operations of the Tenth Pennsylvania Infantry, U.S. Volunteers, in the Campaign in the Philippine Islands," http://www. paroots. com/westmoreland/data/10painfantry.html

[30] "Memorandum for the Chief of Staff on the Evolution and Present Status of Defense on Corregidor Island," September 25, 1914, RG 177, Entry 4, Archives II. Ellicott, "The Defenses of Manila Bay."

[31] *Annual Report of Secretary of War, 1903*, Pt. 3, 196. "Story of Simon de los Reyes." Nayler, "Brief History of Fort Mills."

[32] NARA, Washington, D.C., RG 77, Entry 103, File 95308-1, September 19, 1914.

[33] NARA, Washington, D.C., RG 77, Entry 103, File 26742-3, July 27, 1904.

[34] Ibid, 1-2, 13-16.

[35] Louis Morton, "Military and Naval Preparations for the Defense of the Philippines During the War Scare of 1907," *Military Affairs*, Summer 1949. NARA, Washington, D.C., RG 80, Entry 25, General Board File No. 408.

[36] "Report of the Commander in Chief U.S. Naval Forces on Asiatic Station," Annex Q, in *Annual Report of the Secretary of Navy, 1903*, NARA, Washington, D.C., RG 80, Entry 25, General Board File No. 408.

[37] Ibid.

[38] NARA, RG 94, Entry 25, File 1416707, February 8, 1910.

[39] NARA, Washington, D.C., RG 77, Entry 103, File 29530-31, January 14, 1902, and 29530-118, August 4, 1902. George Cullum, *Biographical Register of the Officers and Graduates of the U.S. Military Academy at West Point* (Saginaw, MI: Seemann and Peters, 1910 and 1920), Vol. V, 128, Hereafter "Cullum."

[40] NARA, Washington, D.C., RG 77, Entry 103, File 95308-1, September 19, 1914. Lewis W. Call, *United States Military Reservations, National Cemeteries and Military Parks Title Jurisdiction, Etc.* (Washington DC: GPO, 1907), 410. Hereafter: Call, "Military Reservations."

[41] NARA, Washington, D.C., RG 77, Entry 103, File 29530-349, December 14, 1903.

[42] For its first ten years in American hands, Subic Bay was frequently referred to even in official correspondence as "Subig Bay." Only from the 1920s did the term "Subic" emerge as dominant.

[43] NARA, Washington, D.C., RG 77, Entry 103, File 29530-31, January 14, 1902.

[44] Ibid.

[45] *Report of the National Coast Defense Board Appointed by the President of the United States by Executive Order, January 31, 1905* (Washington D.C.: GPO, 1906), 12, 24, 26-27. Hereafter: *Report of the National Coast Defense Board.* "Memorandum for

the Chief of Staff on the Evolution and Present Status of the Defense on Corregidor Island," September 25, 1914, RG 177, Entry 4, Archives II.

[46] *Report of the National Coast Defense Board*, 26.

[47] Mark Henkiel, "Battery Warwick: General History, Data and Performance," Unpublished essay, October 1, 1995. Bogart, "Subic Bay and Fort Wint," 26-37.

[48] "Proceedings of a Board of Officers Convened by Headquarters, Philippine Department, January 11, 1915, to Report on Various Questions Affecting the Coast Defenses of Manila Bay and the Mobile Forces in the Philippine Islands," RG 177, Entry 4, Archives II.

[49] Call, *Military Reservations*, 410, 412. For a discussion of the American decision to use Subic and the subsequent decision to move the US naval base to Cavite, see Brian McAllister Linn, *Guardians of Empire: The U.S. Army and the Pacific 1902-1940* (Chapel Hill, NC: University of North Carolina Press, 1997), 82-97, passim.

[50] Cullum, Vol. V, Pt. 2, 314; Pt. 3, 481-82, 499; Pt. 5, 716.

[51] "Report of Completed Works, Engineer Structures, February 1907, Grande Isle, Subic Bay, P.I.," RG 77, Entry 1007, Geographical File, Archives II. Hereafter "RCW."

[52] Glen Williford, "Fort Wint," unpub. Memorandum. Matthew L. Adams, (comp.) *Designating US Seacoast Fortifications: War Department General Orders and Letters from the Adjutant General 1809-1950* (Peoria, IL, 2000), 90. Hereafter: Adams, *Designating US Seacoast Fortifications*. Francis Heitman, *Historical Register and Dictionary of the United States Army from its Organization September 29, 1787 to March 2, 1903,* (Washington D.C.: GPO, 1903), Vol. I, 489, 1051, 1058. Hereafter: Heitman, "Historical Register." Cullum, Vol. V, 482, 749, 776.

[53] "RCW Battery Hall," corrected to January 1, 1920." "RCW, Battery Woodruff, corrected to January 1, 1920."

[54] *Report of the Adjutant General, October 28, 1908*, 380-381, RG 94, Archives II. The Adjutant Generals Office, *Army List and Directory Officers of the Army of the United States,* December 20, 1907 (Washington, D.C.: GPO, 1907). Hereafter: *Army List and Directory* and date.

[55] "RCW Battery Warwick, corrected to January 1, 1920." Williford, "Fort Wint." Adams, *Designating US Fortifications*, 90. Heitman, *Historical Register*, Vol. I, 1004, Vol. II, 456. Mark Henkiel, "Battery Warwick: General History, Data and Performance," unpublished essay, October 1 1995.

[56] Adams, *Designating US Fortifications,* 90. Heitman, *Historical Register*, Vol. I, 424, 573.

[57] "RCW, Cable Tank,"; "Mine Storehouse"; "Mine Loading Room"; "Gun Cotton Magazine"; "Mine Wharf"; "Tramway"; "Mine Casemate"; "Double Primary Mine Observation Station and Plotting Room"; "Primary Stations for Batteries Warwick and Woodruff"; "Battle Commander and Fire Commander Station"; "Protected Switchboard Room"; "Wireless Station"; "Protected Shelters for 60-inch Searchlights"; and "Post Power Plant"; Fort Wint, Coast Defenses of Subic Bay, corrected to January 1, 1920.

[58] "Fire Control, Subic Bay Ledger," Fortification Notebook, RG 77, Entry 20, NARA, Washington, D.C. Hereafter: "Battery Journal," Fortification Notebook. Report of Completed Batteries, Fort Wint, Subic Bay, PI, RG 77, Entry 103, File 66629, NARA, Washington, D.C., December 31, 1914. (Hereafer "RCB," which contains CD of both Manila and Subic Bays.)

[59] Cablegram Ainsworth to Wood, August 17, 1907; Extract from Cablegram Wood to TAG, Washington, D.C., August 20, 1907, RG 94, Entry 411, Archives II.

[60] Memorandum by Chief of Engineers Brigadier General Alexander MacKenzie, June 13, 1904, RG 77, Entry 103, file 51145-6, NARA, Washington, D.C.

[61] "Memorandum for the Chief of Staff on the Evolution and Present Status of Defense on Corregidor Island," NARA, Washington, D.C., RG-77, Entry 1003, file 95308-1, September 19, 1904. Stanley D. Embick, "Memorandum for the Chief of Coast Artillery, February 24, 1915, RG 177, Entry 4, Archives II.

[62] These numerous changes are all documented in a long series of letters between the chief of engineers and the Manila office. See for example: NARA, Washington, D.C., RG 77, Entry 103, Files 51145-143, March 29, 1906; 51145-159, April 27, 1906; 51145-447, December 4, 1907; and 51145-462, January 23, 1908.

[63] Corregidor Island, Manila Bay Site Map, 1908, Drawer 111, Sheet 110-2, Cartographic Section, RG 77, Archives II.

[64] Ibid. Charles S. Small, *Rails to Doomsday: the U.S. Army's Corregidor and Manila Bay Railroads* (Greenwich, CT: Railroad Monographs, 1980), 7-8. Tony Feredo, "The Corregidor Railway System," Historic Corregidor Society, 1-2.

[65] The Carcel y Presidio Correccional de Bilibid was the official designation of Manila's Bilibid Prison. Munro was an 1897 USMA graduate who first served in the cavalry and while serving as a captain, 3rd U.S. Cavalry Regiment, was detailed to the Philippine Scouts as a major and placed in command of the 2nd Battalion, Philippine Scouts. The battalion was sent to Corregidor, January 30, 1908, to establish a garrison on the island. Munro continued to command Camp Avery until November 1909. Cullum, Vol. V, 588-89; Vol. VIa, Pt. 5, 797-98.

[66] General Orders No. 36, July 1, 1908, HQ Philippine Division. E.R. Stuart to TAG, Philippine Division, December 1, 1908, RG 77, Entry 1226, Miscellaneous Histories and letters, NARA, East Point, GA.

[67] G.O. 77, War Department, May 12, 1908. Adams, *Designating US Seacoast Fortifications*, 90. Heitman, *Historical Register*, Vol. I, 714. Cullum, Vol. III, 56; Vol. IV, 155-56; Vol. V, 124-25.

[68] *Mindanao*, a former steel-hulled Spanish unarmored gunboat built at Cavite was captured by the US Army May 1, 1898, and acquired by the US Navy January 17, 1899. The cost of preparing her for sea duty was too high and she was stricken from the *Navy List* February 11, 1905, and sold to the army for use by army engineers. E.R. Stuart to TAG, Philippine Division, December 1, 1908, RG 77, Entry 1226, Miscellaneous Histories and letters, NARA, East Point, GA.

[69] Charles E. Kilbourne to Stanley D. Embick, December 9, 1908, RG 177, Entry 4, Archives II. Completion Reports for Post Buildings, Fort Mills, RG 77, Entry 393, Archives II.

[70] Charles E. Kilbourne to Stanley D. Embick, December 9, 1908, RG 177, Entry 4, Archives II.

[71] "Memorandum for the Chief of Staff on the Evolution and Present Status of Defense on Corregidor Island, September 25, 1914." "Proceedings of a Board of Officers Convened by Headquarters, Philippine Department, January 11, 1915, to Report on Various Questions Affecting the Coast Defenses of Manila Bay and the Mobile Forces in the Philippine Islands," RG 177, Entry 4, Archives II.

[72] NARA, Washington, D.C., RG 165, Entry 281, File 4853-64, October 12, 1916. "Proceedings of a Board of Officers Convened by Headquarters, Philippine Department, January 11, 1915, To Report on Various Questions Affecting the Coast Defenses of Manila Bay and the Mobile Forces in the Philippine Islands," RG 177, Entry 4, Archives II.

[73] Archives II, RG 407, Entry 360, File 660.2, Philippine Department, 1932.

[74] NARA, Washington, D.C., RG 77, Entry 103, File 51145-77, July 12, 1904.

[75] NARA, Washington, D.C, RG 77, Entry 103, File 51145-462, January 23, 1908.

[76] Heitman, *Historical Register*, Vol. I, 1023.

[77] Charles E. Kilbourne to Stanley D. Embick, May 25, 1908, RG 177, Entry 4, Archives II. Glen Williford, "Modern Defenses of Manila, Fort Mills," Undated and Unpublished essay. Hereafter: Williford, "Fort Mills." Lieutenant Johnson, CE, to Alexander Mackenzie, chief of engineers, September 30, 1907, RG 77, Archives II. Heitman, *Historical Register*, 1023. "Report of Completed Works – Seacoast Fortifications (Gun and Mortar Batteries) Coast Defenses of Manila and Subic Bays, Fort Mills, Corregidor Island, Battery Wheeler," corrected to February 17, 1936, RG 77, Entry 1007, Archives II.

[78] NARA, Washington, D.C., RG 77, Entry 103, File 51145-77, July 12, 1904.

[79] "Battery Journal," Fortification Notebook. Charles E. Kilbourne to Stanley D. Embick, June 19, 1908, RG 177, Entry 4, Archives II. William Chamberlaine, "Annual Report of Artillery Officer, Philippine Division, July 9, 1908," RG 177, Entry 4, Archives II.

[80] Charles E. Kilbourne to Stanley D. Embick, June 19, 1908; August 7, 1908, RG 177, Entry 4, Archives II.

[81] William Chamberlaine to Stanley D. Embick, August 29, 1908; Charles E. Kilbourne to Stanley D. Embick, December 9, 1908, RG 177, Entry 4, Archives II.

[82] Charles E. Kilbourne to Stanley D. Embick, December 9, 1908; William Chamberlaine to Stanley D. Embick, January 22, 1909; Charles E. Kilbourne to Stanley D. Embick, January 29, 1909, RG 177, Entry 4, Archives II.

[83] "RCW, Battery Wheeler, January 1, 1920."

[84] Modifications to the 12-inch carriages were only in relative elevation. At the battery sites ordnance personnel changed out the elevating band, elevating arm, and elevating disk, and that part of the elevating gear sufficient to shift the maximum elevation from 10° to 15°. In so doing they shifted the lower limit from -5° to 0°. The added 5 degrees in elevation extended the gun range from 13,200 to 17,300 yards when firing the half-ton, long-point projectile. Nelson H. Lawry "Another Five Degrees: WW I Alterations to the Disappearing Carriage," *Coast Defense Study Group Journal*, Vol. 10, No. 2 (May 1996), 4-10.

[85] Armament Officer, Philippine Armament District, to Ordnance Officer, Field Service Maintenance Division, Washington D.C., 1st Indorsement, November 23, 1919, RG 177, Entry 4, Archives II.

[86] Charles E. Kilbourne to Stanley D. Embick, May 25, 1908; William Chamberlaine to Stanley D. Embick, January 22, 1909, RG 177, Entry 4, Archives II.

[87] William Chamberlaine to Stanley D. Embick, January 22, 1909; "Statement of Artillery Officer, Philippine Division, showing completion of fortifications at Forts Mills and Wint, P.I., to include March 1, 1909," March 8, 1909; William Chamberlaine to Colonel Bailey, March 9, 1909; P.R. Ward to the adjutant, Ft. Mills, February 20, 1911, RG 177, Entry 4, Archives II.

[88] William Chamberlaine to Stanley D. Embick, January 22, 1909, RG 177, Entry 4, Archives II. "RCW, Battery Way, Corrected to January 1, 1920." "Battery Journal," Fortification Notebook. Heitman, *Historical Register,* Vol. I, 1010, Vol. II, 462. Glen Williford, "Fort Mills." Adams, *Designating US Fortifications*, 90.

[89] W.H. Bixby, Chief of Engineers, to the Adjutant General January 19, 1911, RG 177, Entry 4, Archives II. "RCW Battery Geary, corrected to January 1, 1920"; "RCW, Battery Way, corrected to January 1, 1920."

[90] NARA, RG 156, Entry 28A, File 34348-106, July 29, 1907.

[91] William Chamberlaine, "Annual Report of the Artillery Officer, Philippine Division, July 9, 1908," RG 177, Entry 4, Archives II. "Battery Journal," Fortification Notebook. "RCW Battery Cheney," corrected to January 25, 1938. Heitman, *Historical Register,* Vol. I, 298, Vol. II, 457.

[92] "Battery Journal," Fortification Notebook. "RCW Battery Cheney, corrected to January 25, 1938." Charles E. Kilbourne to Stanley D. Embick, January 29, 1909; December 9, 1908; William Chamberlaine to Stanley D. Embick, January 22, 1909; William Chamberlaine to Lt. Col. C.J Bailey, March 9, 1909; RG 177, Entry 4, Archives II.

[93] "RCW Battery Crockett, corrected to January 1, 1920." Heitman, *Historical Register*, Vol. I, 339. Vol. II, 470. Adams, *Designating US Fortifications*, 90.

[94] William Chamberlaine, "Annual Report of Artillery Officer, Philippine Division, July 9, 1908," RG 177, Entry 4, Archives II. "Battery Journal," Fortification Notebook.

[95] "Statement of Artillery Officer, Philippine Division, showing completion of fortifications at Forts Mills and Wint, P.I., to include March 1, 1909," March 8, 1909, 1st Indorsement, November 23, 1909; Armament Officer, Philippine Armament District, to Ordnance Officer, Field Service Maintenance Division, Washington D.C., RG 177, Entry 4, Archives II.

[96] William Chamberlaine, "Annual Report of Artillery Officer Philippine Division, July 9, 1908"; "Statement of Artillery officer, Philippine Division, showing completion of fortifications at Forts Mills and Wint, P.I. to include March 1, 1909," March 8, 1909, RG 177, Entry 4, Archives II.

[97] Heitman, *Historical Register*, Vol. I, 813. Adams, *Designating US Seacoast Fortifications*, 90. "Battery Journal," Fortifications Notebook.

[98] Glen Williford, "On Occasion They Did Make Mistakes: Engineer Construction Errors during the Taft Era," *Coast Defense Journal*, Vol. 24, No. 2 (May 2010), 35-49, Hereafter Williford, "They Did Make Mistakes."

[99] Charles E. Kilbourne to Stanley D. Embick, May 25, 1908, RG 177, Entry 4, Archives II. "Battery Journal," Fortification Notebook. Williford, "They Did Make Mistakes," 35-49. "RCW Battery Grubbs, corrected to January 1, 1920." Heitman, *Historical Register*, Vol. I, 483, Vol. II, 454.

[100] Williford, "They Did Make Mistakes," 35-49.

[101] Charles E. Kilbourne to Stanley D. Embick, May 25, 1908; June 19, 1908; "Statement of Artillery Officer, Philippine Division, showing completion of fortifications at Forts Mills and Wint, P.I., to include March 1, 1909," March 8, 1909, RG 177, Entry 4, Archives II. "RCW Battery Grubbs, corrected to January 1, 1920." "Battery Journal," Fortification Notebook.

[102] Stanley D. Embick to the chief of coast artillery, February 24, 1915, RG 177, Entry 4, Archives II. "Battery Journal," Fortification Notebook. "Memorandum for the Chief of Staff on the Evolution and Present Status of Defense on Corregidor Island," September 25, 1914, Archives II, RG 177, Entry 4, Archives II. "RCW Battery Morrison, corrected to January 1, 1920." Heitman, *Historical Register*, Vol. I, 729, Vol. II, 465. Adams, *Designating US Fortifications*, 90. Williford, "Fort Mills."

[103] Stanley D. Embick to C.C. Hearn, May 6, 1910; William Chamberlaine, "Annual Report of Artillery Officer, Philippine Division, July 9, 1908," RG 177, Entry 4, Archives II, NARA. "RCW Battery Geary, corrected to January 1, 1920." Cullum, Vol. IV, 365. Heitman, *Historical Register*, Vol. I, 450. Adams, *Designating US Fortifications*, 90.

[104] Battery Frank Whitman at Fort Andrews in the CD of Boston was undergoing reconstruction. The battery was originally armed with 12-inch Model 1890M1 mortars on model 1896M1 carriages. In mid-1910 Washington decided to emplace four of the new-type mortars (not actually produced yet but funded and scheduled for production) in one of the pits of Battery

Whitman. In turn Fort Andrews was to ship four of its most modern M1890M1 mortars with steel top carriages to Fort Mills for use in Battery Geary. Regarding the placing of M1908 mortars at Battery Whitman, "While the correspondence never directly stated the rationale, it is presumed that this was to facilitate training and access to the newest type of mortar in the continental United States," Williford, "They Did Make Mistakes," 35-49. Henry P. McCain TAG to Commanding General, Department of the East, August 12, 1910, RG 94, Archives II. "RCW Battery Geary, corrected to January 1, 1920." "Battery Journal," Fortification Notebook.

[105] W.H. Bixby, Chief of Engineers, to the Adjutant General January 19, 1911, RG 177, Entry 4, Archives II. "RCW Battery Geary, corrected to January 1, 1920."

[106] "RCW Battery James, corrected to January 1, 1920." Heitman, *Historical Register*, Vol. I, 571. Adams, *Designating US Fortifications*, 90.

[107] William Chamberlaine, "Annual Report of Artillery Officer, Philippine Division, July 9, 1908," RG 177, Entry 4, Archives II. "RCW Battery James, corrected to January 1, 1920." Heitman, *Historical Register*, Vol. I, 571. Adams, *Designating US Fortifications*, 90. Williford, "Fort Mills." "Battery Journal," Fortification Notebook.

[108] NARA, RG 94, Entry 25, File No. 1416707, September 27, 1911.

[109] NARA, RG 156, Entry 28, File 35396-114, November 3, 1909. "Statement Showing Reserve Ammunition Now Provided for Armament in Insular Possessions," NARA, RG 156, Entry 28A, File 35396-168, April 11, 1911. "RCW, Storehouse, January 1, 1920."

[110] Cablegram, Ainsworth to Wood, August 17, 1907; Wood to Ainsworth, August 20, 1907; RG 177, Entry 4, Archives II. "Annual Report of the Chief of Coast Artillery, October 3, 1908," *War Department Annual Report*, 1908 (Washington, D.C.: GPO, 1908), 241-42.

[111] Charles E. Kilbourne to Stanley D. Embick, May 25, 1908; June 19, 1908, RG 177, Entry 4, Archives II.

[112] Charles E. Kilbourne to Stanley D. Embick, August 7, 1908, RG 177, Entry 4, Archives II.

[113] NARA, RG 94, Entry 25, File 1416707, October 12, 1914.

[114] Charles E. Kilbourne to Stanley D. Embick, December 9, 1908; William Chamberlaine to Col. Bailey, January 29, 1909, RG 177, Entry 4, Archives II. "Annual Report of the Chief of Coast Artillery, October 30, 1912," *War Department Annual Report*, 1912 (Washington, D.C.: GPO, 1912), 1000.

[115] Charles E. Kilbourne to Stanley D. Embick, January 29, 1909; C.C. Hearn to C.J. Bailey, March 27, 1910, RG 177, Entry 4, Archives II.

[116] War Department GO 81, May 4, 1910. C.C. Hearn to C.J. Bailey, March 27, 1910; C.C. Hearn to Stanley D. Embick, July 13, 1910, RG 177, Entry 4, Archives II.

[117] C.C. Hearn to C.J. Bailey, March 27, 1910, RG 177, Entry 4, Archives II.

[118] Stanley D. Embick to C.C. Hearn, May 6, 1910, RG 177, Entry 4, Archives II.

[119] C.C. Hearn to Edward Carpenter, August 14, 1910, RG 177, Entry 4, Archives II.

[120] Artillery Barracks Buildings 1-A-F Fort Mills, Corregidor, P.I., Historical Records of Buildings, RG 77, Entry 393, Archives II. Hereafter: Building name and Historical Record of Buildings.

[121] Field and company grade officers' quarters, Historical Record of Buildings.

[122] Johnson Hagood to E.M. Weaver, December 14, 1913, RG 177, Entry 4, Archives II. Middleside Barracks, Historical Record of buildings.

[123] Middleside Coast Artillery and Infantry Barracks, Historical Record of Buildings.

[124] Stockade Structures, Historical Record of buildings.

[125] Quartermasters Storage Buildings and Barracks, Historical Record of Buildings.

[126] Barracks, Philippine Scouts, Historical Record of Buildings.

[127] G.F. Heaney Jr., "Corregidor: An Estimate of the Situation, A Revision of Data contained in Lieutenant Buntings Circular Published Several Years Ago by the Chief's Office," *CAJ*, Vol. 75, No. 4 (Jul.-Aug. 1932), 285-87. Fred M. Green, "Coast Artillery Life in the Philippines," *CAJ*, Vol. 56, No. 5 (May 1922), 444-52.

[128] These structures were based upon an experimental fire control station suggested by Capt. John S. Sewell of the engineers and built about 1905 in the Harbor Defenses of Portland, Maine, by Maj. William M. Black. This type of construction proved so satisfactory that Sewell type construction was incorporated into many other kinds of structures. The original Sewell buildings

consisted of metal laths nailed to a timber stud frame, and this lathwork was covered with cement plaster, with a tin roof laid on a sheath and frame of timber. However, the noise from rain on the tin roofs soon resulted in their replacement with tar and gravel. This construction, known as "Sewell-type," became standard for numerous functions reasonably distant from gun or mortar batteries. Structures closer to batteries were more commonly built of concrete to better survive the blast of the guns. Engineer Mimeograph No. 71, "Type of Thin Reinforced Concrete Construction for Fire Control Stations, etc.," RG 77, NARA, Washington D.C. Green, "Coast Artillery Life in the Philippines," 444-52. Selma Harrison Calmes, "Lost Corregidor: The Home Front Life before World War II," Part II, Corregidor Historical Society.

[129] Green, "Coast Artillery Life in the Philippines," 444-52.

[130] Annual Estimate F.Y. 1942, Supporting Data.

[131] Ibid.

[132] William Braisted, *The United States Navy in the Pacific, 1909-1922* (Austin, Texas: University of Texas Press, 1971), 125-40.

[133] George T. Davis, *A Navy Second to None* (New York: Harcourt Brace & Co., 1940), 191.

[134] "Memorandum for the Chief of Coast Artillery prepared by Captain Stanley D. Embick, February 24, 1915," RG 177, Entry 4, Archives II.

[135] William Chamberlaine to Stanley Embick, August 29, 1908, RG 177, Entry 4, Archives II. Cullum, Vol. VI, 205. Arthur Murray, "Remarks of the Chief of Coast Artillery on Confidential Report of Fortifications Board, Philippine Division, November 22, 1909, relative to land defenses Corregidor Island in Extract of Proceedings of the Fortification Board, November 22, 1909," RG 177, Entry 4, NARA, Archives II.

[136] William Chamberlaine to Stanley Embick, August 29, 1908, RG 177, Entry 4, Archives II.

[137] General Story retired June 19, 1905, and was promoted to major general upon retirement but continued to serve on the NCDB. "Memorandum for the Chief of Staff: Evolution and Present status of Defenses on Corregidor Island, September 25, 1914." "Memorandum for the Chief of Coast Artillery, February 24, 1915," RG 177, Entry 4, Archives II.

[138] Charles E. Kilbourne to Stanley D. Embick, December 9, 1908; William Chamberlaine to Stanley D. Embick, January 22, 1909, RG 177, Entry 4, Archives II.

[139] Nelson H. Lawry and Glen M. Williford, "The Coast Artillery 14-inch Gun, 1907-1918," *Coast Defense Study Group Journal (CDSG Journal)*, Vol. 12, No. 3 (Aug. 1998), 4-31.

[140] Cullum, Vol. 5, 716, 775; Vol. VI, 1275. Erasmus Weaver, *Annual Report to the War Department for 1913*, RG 177, Entry 4, Archives II.

[141] "Proceedings of a Board of Officers Convened by Headquarters, Philippine Department, January 11, 1915, to Report on Various Questions Affecting the Coast Defenses of Manila Bay and the Mobile Forces in the Philippine Islands," RG 177, Entry 4, Archives II.

[142] Cullum, Vol. III, 83-84; Vol. IV, 166; Vol. V, 135-36. Adams, *Designating US Seacoast Fortifications*, 94.

[143] "Battery Journal," Fortification Notebook. Cullum, Vol. V, 716. Adams, *Designating US Seacoast Fortifications*, 94. Bolling W. Smith, "1912 Type or 'Panama' Fourteen-Inch Disappearing Gun Batteries," *CDSG Journal*, Vol. 7, No. 2 (May 1993), 33-48. Nelson H. Lawry, "Another Five Degrees: World War Alterations to the Disappearing Carriage," *CDSG Journal*, Vol. 10, No. 2 (May 1996), 4-10. Glen M. Williford and Nelson H. Lawry, "The Coast Artillery 14-inch Gun, 1907-1918," *CDSG Journal*, Vol. 12 No. 3 (Aug. 1998), 4-31. Bolling W. Smith, "Seacoast Guns and Carriages," Vol. 12, No. 4 (November 1998), 73-118.

[144] "Battery Journal," Fortification Notebook. Adams, *Designating US Seacoast Fortifications*, 94. Bolling W. Smith, "1912 Type or 'Panama' Fourteen-Inch Disappearing Gun Batteries," *CDSG Journal*, Vol. 7, No. 2 (May 1993), 33-48. Nelson H. Lawry, "Another Five Degrees: World War Alterations to the Disappearing Carriage," *CDSG Journal*, Vol. 10, No. 2 (May 1996), 4-10. Glen M. Williford and Nelson H. Lawry, "The Coast Artillery 14-inch Gun, 1907-1918," *CDSG Journal*, Vol. 12, No. 3 (Aug. 1998), 4-31. Bolling W. Smith, "Seacoast Guns and Carriages," *CDSG Journal*, Vol. 12, No. 4 (Nov. 1998), 73-118.

[145] Col. Eben Eveleth Winslow, *Notes on Seacoast Fortification Construction,* Occasional Papers No. 61 of the Engineer School, United States Army (Washington D.C.: GPO, 1920), 130-36. "Battery Memoranda," Fortification Notebook. "RCW, Battery Greer, corrected to January 1, 1920"; "RCW Battery Crofton, corrected to January 1, 1920."

[146] "RCW, Battery Koehler, corrected to January 1, 1920."

[147] Heitman, *Historical Register*, Vol. I, 339, 433-34, 476, 608. Adams, *Designating US Seacoast Fortifications*, 94.

[148] Cullum, Vol. II, 707-08; Vol. IV, 111; Vol. V, 92. Adams, *Designating US Seacoast Fortifications*, 93.

[149] "Proceedings of a Board of Officers Convened by Headquarters, Philippine Department, January 11, 1915, to Report on Various Questions Affecting the Coast Defenses of Manila Bay and the Mobile Forces in the Philippine Islands," RG 177, Entry 4, Archives II.

[150] Ibid.

[151] Ibid. Glen Williford, "Land Defense for the Coast Defenses of Manila Bay," *Coast Defense Journal*, Vol. 16, No. 2 (May 2002), 4-28.

[152] "Report of a Committee of the Defense Board Relative to the Protection of the Seacoast Batteries on Carabao Island," NARA, Washington, D.C., RG 77, Entry 103, File 68090-123, November 27, 1912.

[153] Fort Frank Structures, Historical Record of Buildings.

[154] Completion Report, Construction of a double set of caretakers' quarters at the Calumpan Military Reservation, June 22, 1932, RG 77, Archives II. W.I. Allen, "Activities at Fort Mills," *CAJ*, Vol. 77, No. 4 (Jul.-Aug. 1934), 297-98. Call, *Military Reservations* (Washington D.C.: GPO, 1907), 410.

[155] NARA, RG 77, Entry 103, File 75208-8, December 20, 1910.

[156] Adams, *Designating US Seacoast Fortifications*, 96. Heitman, *Historical Register*, Vol. I, 552-53. Charles H. Bogart, "Fort Hughes: Outpost Duty Between the Wars," *Periodical: The Journal of the Council on America's Military Past*, Vol. XV, No. 3 (Oct. 1987), 25-40. Hereafter: Bogart, "Fort Hughes." Adams, *Designating US Seacoast Fortifications*, 96.

[157] Cullum, Vol. VI, 652, 1409.

[158] "Battery Journal," Fortification Notebook. "RCW Battery Gillespie, corrected to January 1, 1920." Cullum, Vol. VI, 652, 1409. "Annual Report of the Chief of Coast Artillery, September 1, 1910," *War Department Annual Report*, 1910 (Washington, D.C.: GPO, 1910), 3.

[159] "Battery Journal," Fortification Notebook. "RCW, Battery Gillespie, corrected to January 1, 1920."

[160] "Battery Journal," Fortification Notebook. Cullum, Vol. II, 844-46, Vol. IV, 134, Vol. VI, 99. Adams, *Designating US Fortifications*, 105.

[161] "Battery Journal," Fortification Notebook. "RCW, Battery Woodruff, corrected to January 1, 1920."

[162] Winslow, *Notes on Seacoast Fortification*, 108. "RCW, Battery Gillespie, corrected to January 1, 1920"; "RCW, Battery Woodruff, corrected to January 1, 1920. Bogart, "Fort Hughes," 38. Interview with Lt. Col. Clifton Chamberlain, October 4, 1962, Folder Corregidor 1941-1942, 59th Coast Artillery, Antiaircraft Roster of officers, Reminiscences and letters, Corregidor Box, William and James Belote Collection, Archives, US Army Military History Institute (USAMHI), Carlisle Barracks, PA.

[163] "Battery Journal," Fortification Notebook. "RCW Battery Leach, corrected to January 1, 1920."

[164] Winslow, *Notes on Seacoast Fortification*, 114. "RCW Battery Leach, corrected to January 1, 1920."

[165] "RCW Battery Craighill, corrected to January 1, 1920." Winslow, *Notes on Seacoast Fortification*, 214.

[166] "Battery Journal," Fortification Notebook. "RCW Battery Craighill, corrected to January 1, 1920." Cullum, Vol. II, 520-21, Vol. IV, 88. Heitman, *Historical Register*, Vol. I, 334. Adams, *Designating US Fortifications*, 108.

[167] Williford, "Land Defense," 4-28.

[168] Fort Hughes Structures, Historical Record of Buildings. Adams, *Designating US Fortifications*, 105.

[169] Charles H. Bogart, "The Concrete Battleship — Fort Drum," *Periodical: The Journal of the Council on Abandoned Military Posts*, Vol. IX, (Winter 1977-1978), 13-15.

[170] "Manila Bay, Condition of Defenses, October 31, 1907,", RG 177, Entry 4, File 5635, Archives II.

[171] One plan considered by Kingman in 1908 called for two turrets, each armed with a single 14-inch gun. Charles E. Kilbourne to Stanley D. Embick, May 25, 1908, RG 177, Entry 4, Archives II. John J. Kingman, "The Genesis of Fort Drum, Manila Bay," *The Military Engineer*, Vol. XXXVII, Whole No. 234 (Apr. 1945), 128-30. Cullum, Vol. VI, 1073.

[172] "The Turret in the Coast Defense System of the United States," *JUSA*, Vol. 44, No. 1, (Jul.-Aug. 1915), 116-17.

[173] Ibid. "Battery Journal," Fortification Notebook. "RCW, El Fraile Island, corrected to January 1, 1920." Francis J. Allen, *The Concrete Battleship: Fort Drum, El Fraile Island, Manila Bay* (Missoula, Montana: Pictorial Histories Publishing Co., 1999), 5-6.

[174] Heitman, *Historical Register*, Vol. I, 384. Adams, *Designating US Seacoast Fortifications*, 96.

[175] "Annual Report of the Chief of Coast Artillery," September 27, 1909, *War Department Annual Report*, 1909 (Washington, D.C.: GPO, 1909), 287.

[176] "RCW, Fort Drum, El Fraile Island, corrected to January 1, 1920." "The Turret in the Coast Defense System of the United States," *JUSA*, Vol. 44, No. 1, (Jul.-Aug. 1915), 116-17. Glen Williford, "Fort Drum," unpub. Memorandum.

[177] Office of the Inspector of Ordnance to Harry Whitley, June 11, 1915, NARA, RG-156, Entry 28, File 34348-710.

[178] While similar in overall design to contemporary barbette carriages such as the M1900MI, the pedestal was more heavily built as it accommodated a more extensive shield. The shield of the M1910 casemate carriage was circular and wrapped almost completely around the tube, recoil mechanism, gun pointer, and trainer platforms, leaving only a narrow 35-inch-wide horizontal gap at the rear through which the breech and recoil mechanism projected within the casemate. The front of the shield was pierced in its center only with a narrow (approximately 30-inch vertical by 18-inch-wide) slit to accommodate elevation of the barrel and a 6½-inch sighting hole, on the left side to accommodate the gunner's sight. This shield had a uniform thickness of 5.3 inches and was 40 inches from top to bottom. For a comprehensive discussion of Fort Drum's armament, see Danny Malone, "Artillery Weapons of Fort Drum," *CDSG News*, Vol. 5, No. 3 (Aug. 1991), 19-34

[179] "Battery Journal," Fortification Notebook.

[180] Adams, *Designating US Seacoast Fortifications*, 123-24.

[181] NARA, Washington, D.C., RG 77, Entry 103, File 67966, November 3, 1910.

[182] "RCW, Fort Drum, corrected to January 1, 1920."

[183] NARA, Washington, D.C., RG 77, Entry 103, File 67966-2904, January 31, 1917. "RCW Fort Drum Awnings, El Fraile Island, corrected to January 1, 1920."

[184] "Project for Fire Control Installations for the Defenses of Fort Mills, Corregidor, and Caballo Islands, Philippine Islands," Archives II, RG 177, Entry 4, File 4392, June 25, 1908.

[185] "Memorandum on the Fire Control Project for the Artillery District of Manila Bay," NARA, Washington, D.C., RG 77, Entry 103, File 53743-70, February 10, 1909.

[186] Archives II, RG 177, Entry 4, File 6244, February 10, 1909.

[187] Charles E. Kilbourne to Stanley D. Embick, May 25, 1908; June 19, 1908, RG 177, Entry 4, Archives II.

[188] Charles E. Kilbourne to Stanley D. Embick, June 19, 1908; August 7, 1908, RG 177, Entry 4, Archives II. Kilbourne and Chamberlaine refer to firing over the batteries' battery commander stations. In 1904 the engineers had approved battery designs featuring this station as a separate structure on the flank of a battery, and the three 12-inch batteries were so begun. However very soon in mid-1908 it was decided to build a combined plotting room and BCS immediately behind the central traverse of each battery. The three batteries actually entered service with these new structures, but for a short time while being evaluated, the battery commander stations were actually with the primary stations in front and on the flank of the gun positions.

[189] Charles E. Kilbourne to Stanley D. Embick, August 7, 1908; William Chamberlaine to Stanley D. Embick, August 29, 1908; Charles E. Kilbourne to Stanley D. Embick, December 9, 1908, RG 177, Entry 4, NARA, Archives II.

[190] William Chamberlaine to the Adjutant General, Philippine Division, January 19, 1909, RG 177, Entry 4, Archives II.

[191] "RCB, Fort Wint," December 1913, NARA, Washington, D.C., RG 77, Entry 103, File 66629.

[192] C.C. Hearn to C.J. Bailey, January 14, 1910, RG 177, Entry 4, Archives II.

[193] McKinstry to Chief of Engineers, November 26, 1909, RG 177, Entry 4, November 26, 1909, Archives II. Williford, "They Did Make Mistakes."

[194] Archives II, RG 177, File 6244-4E, November 16, 1909, and RG 77, Entry 103, File 51145-792, March 10, 1911. "RCB," Fire Control Stations, December 31, 1908. "RCW F' B' (Geary and Way) 360° M1911."

[195] "RCB, Ft. Wint," corrected to December 1913, RG 77, Entry 103, File 66629, NARA, Washington, D.C.

[196] Charles De F. Chandler to Commanding General, Philippine Department, August 12, 1915; G.W. Cocheu to Commanding Officer, Coast Artillery Garrison, March 2, 1917, RG 177, Entry 4, Archives II.

[197] Archives II, RG 177, Entry 4, File 6244, February 10, 1909. Glen Williford, "At the Southern Extreme, Fire Control on Limbones Island," *Coast Defense Journal*, Vol. XIV, No. 3 (Aug. 2000), 85-90.

[198] Winslow, *Notes on Seacoast Fortification*, Occasional Papers No. 61 of the Engineer School United States Army (Washington D.C.: GPO, 1920), 274-81.

[199] "Electrical Installation Journal," Fortifications Notebook. C.C. Hearn to Stanley D. Embick, July 13, 1910, RG 177, Entry 4, Archives II. Cable Power House, Historical Record of Buildings.

[200] C.C. Hearn to Stanley D. Embick, July 13, 1910, RG 177, Entry 4, Archives II. C.C. Hearn to C.J. Bailey, March 27, 1910, RG 177, Entry 4, Archives II. "Memorandum for the Chief of Staff on the Evolution and Present Status of Defense on Corregidor Island," September 25, 1914, Archives II.

[201] "Memorandum for the Chief of Staff on the Evolution and Present Status of Defense on Corregidor Island," September 25, 1914, Archives II. Central Power Plant and Cold Storage Plant, Historical Record of Buildings, RG 77.

[202] Central Power Plant and Cold Storage Plant, Historical Record of Buildings.

[203] Completion Report, Construction of a Diesel Engine Power Plant and Fuel Oil Storage System, Fort Mills, P.I., Diesel-generator plant, House, Historical Record of Buildings.

[204] Usually referred to by the Aboriginal name Jarrah, Eucalyptus marginata is one of the most common species of Eucalyptus trees in the southwest of Western Australia. "Memorandum for the Chief of Staff on the Evolution and Present Status of Defense on Corregidor Island," September 25, 1914, Archives II. Charles S. Small, *Rails to Doomsday: the U.S. Army's Corregidor and Manila Bay Railroads* (Greenwich, CT: Railroad Monographs, 1980), 7-8. Tony Feredo, "The Corregidor Railway System," 1-2. Andrew Rutherford, "Reminiscences of Corregidor," *Periodical: Journal of America's Military Past*, Vol. XXIV, No. 3 (Fall 1997), 31-40.

[205] C.C. Hearn to Stanley D. Embick, July 13, 1910; C.C. Hearn to C.J. Bailey, March 27, 1910, RG 177, Entry 4, Archives II.

[206] "Memorandum for the Chief of Staff on the Evolution and Present Status of Defense on Corregidor Island," September 25, 1914, Archives II. Charles S. Small, *Rails to Doomsday: the U.S. Army's Corregidor and Manila Bay Railroads*, 7-8. Col. Valentine P. Foster to William and James Belote, October 23, 1963. "Statement on the Street Car Accident 1925," William and James Belote Collection, USAMI, Carlisle, PA.

[207] Nayler, "A Brief History of Fort Mills."

[208] Bolling W. Smith and William C. Gaines, "Coast Artillery Organization: A Brief Review," in Mark A. Berhow, *American Seacoast Defenses: A Reference Guide,* 417-71.

[209] Interview of Maj. Gen. Charles E. Kilbourne, July 3, 1962, by William M. Belote and James H. Belote, Belote Papers, USAMI, Carlisle, PA.

[210] Ibid.

[211] Lieutenant Kingman had arrived on Corregidor in August 1907 and had been assigned to fortification construction in Manila Bay. He would continue that duty until September 26, 1910, except for March 15 to June 12, 1909, when he was on leave of absence. Cullum, Vol. 1A, 1073.

[212] Charles E. Kilbourne to Stanley D. Embick, May 25, 1908, RG 177, Entry 4, Archives II.

[213] Ibid.

[214] "Annual Report of the Chief of Coast Artillery," October 3, 1908, *War Department Annual Report, 1908* (Washington, D.C.: GPO, 1908) 241-42.

[215] "Annual Report of the Chief of Coast Artillery," September 27, 1909, *War Department Annual Report*, 1909 (Washington, D.C.: GPO, 1908), 300-01. *Army List and Directory Officers of the Army of the United States*, June 20, 1909 (Washington, D.C.: GPO, 1908).

[216] *Army List and Directory Officers of the Army of the United States* October 20, 1909 (Washington, D.C.: GPO, 1909). "Annual Report of the Chief of Coast Artillery," October 3, 1908, *War Department Annual Report*, 1908 (Washington, D.C.: GPO, 1908), 241-42.

[217] William Chamberlaine to C.J Bailey, March 9, 1909; C.C. Hearn to C.J. Bailey, January 14, 1910; C.C. Hearn to C.J. Bailey, March 27, 1910; C.C. Hearn to Stanley D. Embick, July 13, 1910, RG 177, Entry 4, Archives II. War Department G.O. 81, May 4, 1910. "Crack Gunners for Manila," *New York Times*, May 2, 1910, 8.

[218] Stanley D. Embick to C.C. Hearn May 6, 1910, RG 177, Entry 4, Archives II.

[219] "Memorandum for the Secretary of War on the Defense of Corregidor," July 29, 1915, RG 177, Entry 4, Archives II.

[220] Regan Barracks was established January 23, 1900, by Brig. Gen. William Kobbe, "History of the 15th US Infantry Regiment," www.geocities.com/Eureka/Plaza/7750/15thinf02.htm. Antonio Tabaniag, "The Pre-war Philippine Scouts," *University of Manila Journal of East Asiatic Studies*, Vol. IX, No. 4 (Oct. 1960,) 7-26. Karl H. Lowe, "America's Foreign Legion: The 31st Infantry Regiment at War and Peace," 31st US Infantry Association, Chapter 1, 1-3., Chapter II, 1-2, http://www.31st infantry.org/.

[221] Memorandum for the Chief of Staff, "Evolution and Present Status of Defenses on Corregidor Island, September 25, 1914," RG 177, Entry 4, Archives II.

[222] Ibid. NARA, RG 94, Entry 25, File 1416707, November 22, 1911. Charles H. Bogart, *Controlled Mines: A History of their Use by the United States* (Bennington Vermont, Weapons and Warfare Press, 1985), 8.

[223] Memorandum for the Chief of Staff, "Evolution and Present Status of Defenses on Corregidor Island, September 25, 1914," RG 177, Entry 4, Archives II. "Torpedo Defense Journal," Fortification Notebook.

[224] William Chamberlaine, "Annual Report of the Artillery Officer, Philippine Division," July 9, 1908," RG 177, Entry 4, Archives II. William Chamberlaine to Stanley D. Embick, August 29, 1908, RG 177, Entry 4, Archives II.

[225] "Torpedo Defense Journal," Fortification Notebook. "RCB," June 30, 1908.

[226] "Mine Practice Reports, First Mine Command, Artillery District of Manila Bay," RG 177, Entry 4, Archives II.

[227] "Torpedo Defense Journal," Fortification Notebook.

[228] "Annual Report of the Chief of Coast Artillery," October 3, 1908, *War Department Annual Report*, 1909 (Washington, D.C.: GPO, 1908), 243. "Annual Report of the Chief of Coast Artillery," September 27, 1909, *War Department Annual Report*, 1909 (Washington, D.C.: GPO, 1909), 308. Appendix I, "List of Coast Guard Cutters, Harbor Service and Artillery Boats and Lighthouse Tenders," in William Chamberlaine, *Coast Artillery War Game* 4th Ed. (Washington D.C.: GPO, 1916), 85-89. Harold Larson, *Water Transportation for the United States Army, 1939-1942*, Office of the Chief of Water Transportation, Army Service forces, 1944, 125.

[229] *Army List and Directory*, October 20, 1909 (Washington D.C.: GPO, 1909), 30. "Annual Report of the Chief of Coast Artillery," September 27, 1909, *War Department Annual Report*, 1909 (Washington, D.C.: GPO, 1909), 305, 308. K.L. Waters, "The Army Mine Planter Service," *Warship International*, Vol. 22, No. 4 (1985), 401.

[230] William Chamberlaine to C.J. Bailey, March 9, 1909, RG 177, Entry 4, Archives II.

[231] "Searchlight Journal," Fortification Notebook. Hereafter "Searchlight Journal." "RCB" December 1913, RG 77, NARA, Washington, D.C.

[232] William Chamberlaine to C.J. Bailey, March 9, 1909; C.C. Hearn to C.J. Bailey, January 14, 1910, RG 177, Entry 4, Archives II.

[233] C.C. Hearn to C.J. Bailey, March 27, 1910, RG 177, Entry 4, Archives II.

[234] Stanley D. Embick to C.C. Hearn, May 6, 1910, RG 177, Entry 4, Archives II.

[235] "Searchlight Journal," Fortification Notebook.

[236] Ibid. "RCB, Ft. Wint," December 1913, NARA, Washington, D.C., RG 77, Entry 103, File 66629. "RCW, Searchlight No.1 corrected to January 2, 1922."

[237] Architectural drawings for searchlights, 1-7 May 10, 1912, RG 77, Entry 103, File 68612-385, Archives II. "Searchlight Journal," Fortification Notebook.

[238] "RCW, Searchlight No. 13 and No. 14 corrected to January 2, 1922."

[239] William Chamberlaine to Stanley D. Embick, January 22, 1909, RG 177, Entry 4, Archives II. "Searchlight ledger," Fortification Notebook. "RCW, 36-inch Portable Searchlights, corrected to November 1, 1920."

[240] "RCW, Searchlight Nos. 8 and No. 12."

[241] Annual Estimate F.Y.1942 in Harbor Defense Project 1940, Archives II**,** RG 165, Entry 281, file 4525.

[242] The Philippine Division was the army's administrative headquarters in the Philippines and in 1911 was redesignated the Philippine Department. A tactical unit, the Philippine Division, was constituted in June 1921, composed of both American troops and Philippine Scouts. Extract of Proceedings of the Fortification Board, November 22, 1909, RG 177, Entry 4, Archives II.

[243] "Proceedings of the Defense Board," NARA, RG 94, Entry 25, File 1416707, October 2, 1912.

[244] George T. Davis, *A Navy Second to None* (New York: Harcourt Brace & Co., 1940), 199.

[245] Memorandum for the Chief of Staff, September 25, 1914," RG 177, Entry 4, Archives II. Cullum, Vol. VI, 545, 1224, 1340.

[246] "Report of the Fortification Board on the Land Defense of Corregidor," Archives II, RG 77, Entry 103, File 73729-22, November 22, 1909.

[247] There were at Olongapo in 1909 twenty 6-inch guns as well as four 4.7-inch and four 4-inch naval guns. At Cavite Navy

Base, there were an additional ten 4-inch, three 3-inch field guns, and numerous smaller-caliber weapons. "Memorandum for the Chief of Staff, September 25, 1914, Proceedings of the Fortification Board," Archives I, RG-77, Entry 103, file 95308, November 22, 1909. C.C. Hearn to C.J. Bailey, January 14, 1910, Archives II, RG 177, Entry 4. "Land Defense Memorandum," Fortification Notebook.

[248] C.C. Hearn to C.J. Bailey, March 27, 1910; C.C. Hearn to C.J. Bailey, March 27, 1910; C.C. Hearn to Stanley D. Embick, July 13, 1910, Archives II, RG 177, Entry 4. "Proceedings of a Board of Officers Convened by Headquarters Philippine Department January 11, 1915 To Report on Various Questions Affecting the Coast Defenses of Manila Bay and the Mobile Forces in the Philippine Islands," Archives II, RG 177, Entry 4. "Land Defense Memorandum," Fortification Notebook.

[249] Cullum, Vol. VI, 1340 "Memorandum for the Chief of Staff on the Evolution and Present Status of Defense on Corregidor Island, September 25, 1914," Archives II, RG 177, Entry 4. "Proceedings of a Board of Officers Convened by Headquarters, Philippine Department, January 11, 1915, to Report on Various Questions Affecting the Coast Defenses of Manila Bay and the Mobile Forces in the Philippine Islands," Archives II, RG 177, Entry 4.

[250] NARA, RG 94, Entry 25, File 1416707, August 12, 1911, September 5, 1911, and June 25, 1913.

[251] The "Benet-Mercie machine rifle, caliber .30" firing the 30-06 cartridge was adopted by the U.S. in 1909 as the M1909 machine gun. The name comes from the two main designers, Lawrence Benet and Henri Mercie, and the U.S. designation system at the time, which labeled arms with "Model of Year." Lawrence Benet was related to retired Brig. Gen. Stephen Vincent Benet, former chief of the US Army Ordnance Department. "Memorandum for the Chief of Staff on the Evolution and Present Status of Defense on Corregidor Island, September 25, 1914," Archives II, RG 177, Entry 4. "Proceedings of a Board of Officers Convened by Headquarters, Philippine Department, January 11, 1915, to Report on Various Questions Affecting the Coast Defenses of Manila Bay and the Mobile Forces in the Philippine Islands," Archives II, RG 177, Entry 4. "Land Defense Memorandum," Fortification Notebook.

[252] John McA. Palmer to the Commanding General, Coast defense of Manila and Subic Bays, Ft. Mills, Corregidor Island, March 23, 1915, in "Proceedings of a Board of Officers Convened by Headquarters, Philippine Department, January 11, 1915, to Report on Various Questions Affecting the Coast Defenses of Manila Bay and the Mobile Forces in the Philippine Islands," Archives II, RG 177, Entry 4. Cullum, Vol. VI-A, 382, 717.

[253] Williford, "Land Defense," 4-28.

[254] John McA. Palmer to the Commanding General, Coast defense of Manila and Subic Bays, Ft. Mills, Corregidor Island, March 23, 1915, in "Proceedings of a Board of Officers Convened by Headquarters, Philippine Department, January 11, 1915, to Report on Various Questions Affecting the Coast Defenses of Manila Bay and the Mobile Forces in the Philippine Islands," Archives II, RG 177, Entry 4.

[255] "Report of the Fortification Board," NARA, Washington, D.C., RG 77, Entry 103, File 73729-50, September 6, 1910.

[256] NARA, Washington, D.C., RG 77, Entry 103, File 66637-336, May 17, 1911.

[257] John McA. Palmer to the Commanding General, Coast defense of Manila and Subic Bays, Ft. Mills, Corregidor Island, March 23, 1915, in "Proceedings of a Board of Officers Convened by Headquarters, Philippine Department, January 11, 1915, to Report on Various Questions Affecting the Coast Defenses of Manila Bay and the Mobile Forces in the Philippine Islands," Archives II, RG 177, Entry 4. "Land Defense Memoranda," Fortification Notebook. S.E. Allen to the Adjutant General, May 15, 1919, Archives II, RG 177, Entry 4.

[258] The Power Plant Ravine Tunnel was resumed in 1941 and later known as the "Engineer Tunnel," as it was used for the storage of engineer supplies and as the offices of the Post Engineer. Defenses in the form of tunnels and other extemporaneous bombproofs would be built around Cheney Ravine in 1941-1942, but not in accord with the original plans, NARA, Washington, D.C., RG 77, Entry 103, File 73729-261, December 10, 1916.

[259] "RCW, Bombproofs for Infantry Sector Garrisons, Battery Point and James Ravine, corrected to March 8, 1921." It is doubtful that any work was ever begun on the other infantry bombproofs projected.

[260] The squadron, during the period in Texas was most probably a flight-training unit. Steven C. Clay, *U.S. Army Order of Battle 1919-1941*, Vol. III, *The Services: Air Services, Engineers and Special Troops Organizations*, 1367-68.

[261] "Proceedings of a Board of Officers Convened by Headquarters, Philippine Department, January 11, 1915, to Report on Various Questions Affecting the Coast Defenses of Manila Bay and the Mobile Forces in the Philippine Islands," Archives II, RG 177, Entry 4.

[262] Ibid.

[263] Ibid.

[264] Ibid.

[265] Ibid.

[266] Ibid.

[267] U.S. Congress House Documents, 64th Congress, 1st Session, *Report of the Board of Review of the War Department, November 26, 1915, on the Coast Defense of the United States, the Panama Canal and the Insular Possessions* (Washington D.C.: GPO, 1916).

[268] *Army List and Directory Officers of the Army of the United States,* December 20, 1910 (Washington D.C., GPO, 1910). "Crack Gunners for Manila," *New York Times*, May 2, 1910, 8. "Night Practice at Fort Mills, P.I.," *JUSA*, Vol. 36, No. 3 (Nov.-Dec. 1911), 334-36.

[269] Effective October 1, 1915, the tours of duty for officers and enlisted men was set at two years, although both could be permitted to serve in the Philippines for a longer period. War Department G.O. No. 36, June 9, 1915.

[270] U.S. Army War College, *Order of Battle of the United States Land Forces in the World War (1917-1919),* "Zone of the Interior," Vol. III, Pt. 2, 1209-12 (Washington, D.C., GPO).

[271] Ibid.

[272] R. Earnest Dupuy and Trevor N. Dupuy, *The Encyclopedia of Military History From 3500 B.C. to the Present* (New York: Harper and Row, 1970), 944-45.

[273] S.E. Allen to The Adjutant General, May 15, 1919, RG 177, Entry 4, Archives II.

[274] NARA, Washington, D.C., RG 77, Entry 103, File 77340-357, March 1, 1917. U.S. Army War College, *Order of Battle of the United States Land Forces in the World War (1917-1919)*, "Zone of the Interior," Vol. III, Pt. 2, 1209-12.

[275] U.S. Army War College, *Order of Battle of the United States Land Forces in the World War (1917-1919)*, "Zone of the Interior," Vol. III, Pt. 2, 1209-12.

[276] "Proceedings of a Board of Officers Convened by Headquarters, Philippine Department, January 11, 1915, to Report on Various Questions Affecting the Coast Defenses of Manila Bay and the Mobile Forces in the Philippine Islands," Archives II, RG 177, Entry 4.

[277] "Torpedo Defense Journal," Fortification Notebook.

[278] P.C. March to the Secretary of War, January 6, 1920, "Revision of Submarine Mine Project and Defensive Sea Area, Archives II, RG 177, Entry 4. "Manila Bay to be Closed at Night," *New York Times,* April 8, 1917. Samuel R. Kimble to TAG Sept. 15, 1918, Signal Corps Inspection Files, Archives II, RG 177, Entry 4, 1st Endorsement, September 23, 1918. Appendix I, *List of Coast Guard Cutters, Harbor Service and Artillery Boats and Lighthouse Tenders*, in William Chamberlaine, *Coast Artillery War Game,* 4th Ed. (Washington D.C.: GPO, 1916), 85-89.

[279] U.S. Army War College, *Order of Battle of the United States Land Forces in the World War (1917-1919)*, "Zone of the Interior," Vol. III, Pt. 2, 1209-12.

[280] Ibid.

[281] Ibid., Adjutant General's Memorandum for the Chief Clerk, Office of the Chief of Coast Artillery, May 6, 1938, Archives II, RG 177, Entry 4.

[282] U.S. Army War College, *Order of Battle of the United States Land Forces in the World War (1917-1919),* "Zone of the Interior," Vol. III, Pt. 2, 1209-12.

[283] In 1911, the 15th Infantry's regimental headquarters and 2nd and 3rd Battalions (less Company G of the 2nd Battalion) departed the US for China, while the 1st Battalion and Company G of the 2nd Battalion were sent to the Philippine Islands. There the 1st Battalion became part of the Manila garrison. During the World War, the 1st Battalion and Company G of the 2nd Battalion were retained in the Philippines and elements were posted on Corregidor. In 1922, the 1st battalion was assigned to the Philippine Division, while Company G was inactivated. Signal Corps Inspection Files, Archives II, RG 177, Entry 4, "History of the 15th US Infantry Regiment." www.geocities.com/Eureka/Plaza /7750/15thinf02.htm. The 31st Infantry was activated in 1916 at Fort William McKinley, U.S. Army War College, *Order of Battle of the United States Land Forces in the World War (1917-1919)*, "Zone of the Interior," Vol. III, Pt. 2, 1209-12. Karl H. Lowe, "History of the 31st United States Infantry Regiment," 31st US Infantry Association.

[284] Cullum, Vol. VIa, 289-90, 545, 313.

[285] U.S. Army War College, *Order of Battle of the United States Land Forces in the World War (1917-1919)*, "Zone of the Interior," Vol. III, Pt. 1, 631. "Annual Report of the Coast Defense Commander," May 15, 1919, 1st Indorsement, September 23, 1918, Samuel R. Kimble to TAG September 15, 1918. Signal Corps Inspection Files, 2nd Indorsement, September 23, 1918,

Archives II, RG 177, Entry 4. Cullum, Vol. VIa, 403-05. S.E. Allen to the Adjutant General, May 15, 1919, Archives II, RG 177, Entry 4.

[286] "Record of Annual Tactical Inspection (1925) of Coast Defenses of Manila & Subic Bays," Archives II, RG 77.

[287] "Battery Journal," Fortification Notebook. "RCW Battery Fuger, corrected to January 1, 1920." Winslow, *Notes on Seacoast Fortification,* 108. Adams, *Designating US Fortifications,* 105.

[288] Adams, *Designating US Fortifications*, 108. Heitman, *Historical Register*, Vol. I, 596, Vol. II, 456.

[289] "Seacoast Guns and Carriages Record Cards," Archives II, RG 156, Entry 712. Hereafter "Ordnance Card File."

[290] "Land Defense Memorandum," Fortification Notebook. Two guns each from Battery James, Flake, and Jewell were removed earlier in the First World War for use on military transports, and while not used as such, remained dismounted and in storage and thus "available" for an alternate use.

[291] "RCW Battery Guy Ben Gad Hanna, corrected to January 1, 1920 and May 22, 1922." G.A. Taylor, "Captain Guy B.G. Hanna," *CAJ*, Vol. 57, No. 2 (July 1922) 87-88. Heitman, *Historical Register*, Vol. I, 497. Adams, *Designating US Seacoast Fortifications*, 124.

[292] "RCW Battery Alonzo H. Cushing, corrected to June 1, 1920, and November 1, 1934." Heitman, *Historical Register*, Vol. I, 347. Adams, *Designating US Seacoast Fortifications*, 124.

[293] Adams, *Designating US Seacoast Fortifications*, 124.

[294] U.S. Congress House Documents, 64th Congress 1st Session, *Report of the Board of Review of the War Department, November 26, 1915, on the Coast Defense of the United States, the Panama Canal and the Insular Possessions* (Washington D.C.: GPO, 1916).

[295] "RCW Battery Smith, corrected to November 1, 1921."

[296] Winslow, *Notes on Seacoast Fortification*, 152. "RCW Battery Smith, corrected to November 1, 1921."

[297] "Tactical Inspection of the Coast Defenses of Manila and Subic Bays," February 28, 1922, 1st Indorsement, Chief of Coast Artillery to the Adjutant General, December 13, 1922; "Tactical Inspection Report," May 8, 1924, RG 177, Entry 4, Archives II.

[298] Adams, *Designating US Seacoast Fortifications*, 124.

[299] Archives II, Cartographic Files, Plan No. 111-195-15, November 6, 1919

[300] Williford, "At the Southern Extreme," 85-90, Addendum to: "At the Southern Extreme, Fire Control Stations on Limbones Island in Manila Bay," *CDJ*, Vol. 15, No. 2 (May 2001), 90-91.

[301] Archives II, RG 77, Entry 1009, File 665(MAN) F79-1, December 21, 1921.

[302] Williford, "At the Southern Extreme," 85-90.

[303] Archives II, RG 77, Entry 1009, File 665(MAN) F79-1, December 21, 1921.

[304] Herbert F. Markland and Shawn Welch, "A Coast Artilleryman's Experience on Fort Mills," Pt. 2, *CDSG Journal*, Vol. IX, No. 2 (May 1995.), 4-15. Keith Barlow, ed., *Bunker's War: The World War II Diary of Colonel Paul D. Bunker* (Novato, CA: Presidio Press, 1996), 32, 80. Hereafter Barlow, *Bunker's War.*

[305] NARA, Washington, D.C., RG 77, Entry 103, File 53743-401, February 12, 1918.

[306] NARA, Washington, D.C., RG 77, Entry 103, File 53743-401 February 12, 1918. RCW files for individual structures, Corrected to January 18, 1921.

[307] NARA, Washington, D.C., RG 77, Entry 103, File 53743-280, February 8, 1915.

[308] "Technical Inspection of CD Manila and Subic Bays, April 3, 1920," RG 177, Archives II.

[309] *Army List and Directory,* January 1, 1920.

[310] Ibid.

[311] Memorandum for the Chief of Staff, May 3, 1921; Memorandum for the Assistant Chief of staff G-4, May 3, 1921, RG 177, Archives II.

[312] Memorandum for the Director, Supply Division, General Staff, February 5, 1921, RG 177, Archives II.

[313] NARA, Washington, D.C., RG 77, Entry 103, File 99735-276, April 8, 1917.

[314] "RCW, AA Batteries, A, B, C, and D, corrected to January 1, 1920."

[315] Memorandum for the Assistant Chief of Staff G-4, May 3, 1921, 2nd Indorsement, Maj. Gen. F. Coe to the Adjutant General, August 30, 1921; A.A. Maybach to G.M. Barnes, January 27, 1927, RG 177, Archives II. "RCW Seacoast Fortifications Coast Defense of Manila and Subic Bays, Fort Mills, Antiaircraft Batteries, A, B, C, and D, corrected to January 1, 1920."

[316] "RCW, AA Battery No. 7, Ft. Drum, corrected to October 15, 1936." "RCW Batteries, A, B, C, and D," corrected to January 1, 1920."

[317] "Annual Report of the Coast Defense Commander, May 15, 1919," RG 177, Entry 4, Archives II.

[318] Mine Defense Commander to Commanding Officer, Coast Defenses of Manila and Subic Bays, Semi-Annual Report of Mining Operations, January 10, 1922, RG 177, Entry 4, Archives II.

[319] P.C. March to the Secretary of War, January 6, 1920, revision of Submarine Mine Project and Defensive Sea Area, RG 177, Entry 4, Archives II. Technical Inspection of CD Manila and Subic Bays, April 3, 1920, RG 177, Entry 4, Archives II. Joint Army-Navy Board No. 353, June 9, 1921, RG 409, Archives II. "RCB," December 1913, RG 77, Entry 103, NARA, Washington, D.C.

[320] Quartermaster Corps List of Temporary Buildings, Fort Mills, Corregidor, P.I. August 18, 1922, Site Map, Fort Mills Corregidor Island, Manila Bay, Edition of August 12, 1921. RG 92, Entry 391, Archives II.

[321] Completion Report, Air Service Projects Construction Projects carried on during 1919-1921, February 26, 1922, RG 92, Archives II.

[322] Ibid., Pope to the chief of engineers, July 25, 1922, RG 77, Archives II.

[323] Steven C. Clay, *U.S. Army Order of Battle 1919-1941*, Vol. III, *the Services: Air Services, Engineers and Special Troops Organizations*, 1367-68.

[324] Kindley Field at Fort Mills on Corregidor Island in the Philippines was named in honor of Capt. Field Eugene Kindley, Air Service. Kindley was a motion picture operator in Coffeyville, Kansas, when he joined the Kansas National Guard in May 1917. Transferring to the U.S. Army Signal Corps, he attended the School of Military Aeronautics at the University of Illinois before going to England for advanced flight training at Oxford. To gain combat experience he was assigned to RAF 65 Squadron on the Western Front on May 22, 1918. Flying the Sopwith Camel, Kindley scored his first victory on June 26, 1918, shooting down a Pfalz D.III flown by the commanding officer of Jasta 5, Wilhelm Lehmann. Reassigned to the 148th Aero Squadron as a flight commander, Kindley's patrol engaged Jasta 11 on August 13, 1918. That day he scored his fourth victory, shooting down a Fokker D.VII possibly flown by Lothar von Richthofen who was wounded in the battle. Promoted to Captain on February 24, 1919, Kindley assumed command of the 94th Aero Squadron at Kelly Field in Texas in January 1920. Less than a month later, in preparation for a visit by Gen. John J. Pershing, he was severely injured and badly burned during a practice flight when a control cable broke and the S.E.5a he was flying crashed. He died that evening at the post hospital. On January 1, 1946, Kindley Field in Bermuda was named for Captain Kindley. Aerodrome: Aces and aircraft of World War I.com.

[325] The 28th Aero Squadron was organized June 22, 1917, and demobilized on June 16, 1919, but reconstituted, and consolidated on January 9, 1922, with 28th Squadron (Bombardment) that had been constituted August 30, 1921, and organized on September 20, 1921. The squadron was inactivated June 28, 1922, but reactivated September 1, 1922. On January 25, 1923, the 28th Squadron was redesignated the 28th Bombardment Squadron.

[326] F.L. Dingler, "Report on Tactical Inspection, C.D. Manila and Subic Bays, May 8, 1924," RG 177, Entry 4, Archives II.

[327] I.H. Edwards, and G.H. Burgess, "Air Service Operations in Coast Artillery Service Practice," *CAJ*, Vol. 59, No. 4 (Oct. 1923), 312-22. Steven C. Clay, *U.S. Army Order of Battle 1919-1941*, Vol. III, *The Services: Air Services, Engineers and Special Troops Organizations,* 1394.

[328] *Army List and Directory*, October 1, 1920; October 1, 1921. Steven C. Clay, *U.S. Army Order of Battle 1919-1941*, Vol. III, *The Services: Air Services, Engineers and Special Troops Organizations*, 1569, 1573-74.

[329] Details of various tanks, pump houses, and reservoirs generally from Quartermaster Form 177s, NARA RG 92, Entry 391, Archives II, for the various Manila and Subic Bay forts.

[330] "Annual Report, Department Surgeon, Philippine Department, to Surgeon General, U.S. Army, February 11, 1927," Archives I, RG-112, Entry 31F.

[331] "Completion Report, Drilling of Well No. 26, Fort Mills, P.I.", Quartermaster Form 177 from RG 92, Entry 391, Archives II. Wilhelm Schutze, "Flying Tour through Occupied East Asia, No. 7, Through Corregidor in MacArthur's Auto," *Deutsche Allgemeine Zeitung*, Berlin, January 7, 1943, Belote Papers, USAMHI, Carlisle Barracks, PA.

[332] Archives II, RG 177, Entry 4, File 5834-38, February 17, 1918, Quartermaster Form 177s from NARA RG 92, Entry 391. *Siege of Corregidor, Coast Artillery Training Bulletin*, Vol. 3, No. 1 (Feb. 1944), Coast Artillery School, Fort Monroe, VA, 11.

[333] Quartermaster Form 177s from NARA RG 92, Entry 391. James Belote and William Belote, *Corregidor: The Saga of a Fortress* (New York: Harper and Row, 1967), 88-89.

[334] "Annual Reports, Department Surgeon, Philippine Department, to Surgeon General, U.S. Army, January 31, 1921, and February 11, 1927," Archives I, RG 112, Entry 31F.

[335] Ibid.

[336] Notes on Major Philippine Supply Shipments, Records of the Chief of Ordnance, RG 156, Entries 36A and B, Archives II.

[337] Janice E. McKinney, *Air Defense Artillery* [Army Lineage Series] (Washington, D.C., 1985), 277. The 155 mm GPF gun was designed during World War I by Colonel L.J.F. Filloux to meet France's urgent need for modern heavy artillery. Translated, GPF means "high powered Filloux gun." The 155 mm GPF models 1917 and 1918 became the standard mobile medium caliber seacoast gun of the US Army into World War II. "Annual Report, Chief of Coast Artillery, September 8,1924," RG 177, Entry 8, Archives II. "Annual Report, Chief of Coast Artillery, September 14, 1923," RG 177, Entry 8. RG 156, Entry 36A, Archives II. War Department, *Seacoast Artillery Weapons*, TM 4-210 (Ft. Monroe, VA: Coast Artillery School, 1944), 135, 138.

[338] Janice E. McKinney, *Air Defense Artillery* [Army Lineage Series] (Washington, D.C., 1985), 277.

[339] Green, "Coast Artillery Life in the Philippines," 444, 446-447.

[340] Unit Files, 59th CA (TD) Regiment, US Army Center of Military History, Ft. Leslie McNair.

[341] Kuehn, John T., *Agents of Innovation: The General Board and the Design of the Fleet That Defeated the Japanese Navy*, (Annapolis: Naval Institute Press, 2008), 187.

[342] Archives II, RG 156, Entry 36A, File 400.356, File 5539, March 28, 1922.

[343] Ibid.

[344] For a discussion of the role of the 240 mm howitzers on Oahu, see William C. Gaines, "240 mm Howitzers on Oahu 1922-1944," *Coast Defense Journal*, Vol. 16, No. 4 (Nov. 2002), 4-27. Letter, March 8, 1922, RG 156, Entry 36A, File 400.356-55539, Archives II. William C. Addleman, *History of the United States Army in Hawaii 1849-1939,* Schofield Barracks, T.H., 1939, 33.

[345] NARA, RG 165, Entry 281, File 4270, February 17, 1922.

[346] Signal Corps Inspection Files, RG 177, Entry 4, Archives II, R.J. Woods, "Corregidor Doings," *CAJ*, Vol. 77 (Sept.-Oct. 1934), 374-75.

[347] "Signal Corps Inspection Files," RG 177, Entry 4, Archives II. Antonio Tabaniag, "The Pre-War Philippine Scouts," *University of Manila Journal of East Asiatic Studies*, Vol. IX, No. 1 (Oct. 1960):7-26.

[348] A.G.O. G.O. No. 21, May 13, 1922. RG 94, NARA, Washington, D.C., Unit Files, 91st and 92nd CA (TD) Regiments (PS), US Army, Center of Military History, Ft. Leslie McNair.

[349] War Department G.O. No. 21, May 18, 1922.

[350] *Army List and Directory* October 1, 1922, 19.

[351] "Tactical Inspection of the C.D. of Manila and Subic Bays March 15-27, 1924, & May 8, 1924," RG 177, Entry 8, Archives II. War Department G.O. No. 8, February 1924. Unit Files, 91st and 92nd CA (TD) Regiments (PS), US Army Center of Military History, Ft. Leslie McNair.

[352] J.H. Smith, "Calibrating the Guns of the 59th Artillery," *CAJ,* Vol. 60, No. 3 (March 1924), 198-211.

[353] Charles Himmler, "The C.A.C. with the Japanese Relief Expedition," *CAJ*, Vol. 61, No. 3 (Sept. 1923), 265-66.

[354] *Army List and Directory, January 1, 1924*, 8.

[355] "Tactical Inspection of the C.D. of Manila and Subic Bays March 15-27, 1924, May 8, 1924, RG 177, Entry 8, Archives II.

[356] War Department G.O. No. 8, February 27, 1924, RG 94, Archives I, NARA, Washington, D.C.

[357] *Historical Summaries and Station Lists, 91st and 92nd CA Regiments (PS),* US Army Center of Military History, Ft. Leslie McNair.

[358] Richard Meixsel, "The Philippine Scout Mutiny of 1924," *Southeast Asia Research*, Vol. 10, No. 3, 333-59.

[359] "Annual Report, Chief of Coast Artillery," September 8, 1924, RG 177, Entry 8, Archives II.

[360] *Army List and Directory, January 1, 1925*, 8; *September 1, 1927,* 8.

[361] George Munson, "91st Coast Artillery: A Short History," Corregidor Then and Now web site.

[362] R.T. Gibson, "Bilibid's Guard Battalion," *CAJ*, Vol. 80, No. 6 (Nov.-Dec. 1937), 488-91. Steven C. Clay, *U.S. Army Order of Battle 1919-1941,* Vol. II, *The Arms: Cavalry, Field Artillery and Coast Artillery 1919-1941,* 1099-1100

[363] Gibson, "Bilibid's Guard Battalion," 488-91. Recollections of Mrs. Fredrick C. Amos, [2nd Lieutenant, 1st Lieutenant, Captain, 92nd CA (PS)], Reminiscences, Recommendations and letters, 60th Coast Artillery Regiment, William and James Belote Collection, USAMHI, Carlisle Barracks, PA.

[364] Gibson, "Bilibid's Guard Battalion," 488-91.

[365] Ibid., Conversation with Jules D. Yates, March 15, 1982, Folder 92nd Coast Artillery Reminiscence of Surrender of Corregidor, Corregidor Box William and James Beloit Collection, USAMHI, Carlisle Barracks, PA.

[366] "Record of Annual Tactical Inspection (1925) of Coast Defenses of Manila & Subic Bays," RG 77, Archives II.

[367] "Annual Report of the Chief of Coast Artillery, August 13, 1929"; "Annual Report of the Chief of Coast Artillery, July 14, 1932, RG 177, Entry 8, Archives II; July 9, 1935, RG 177, Entry 8, Archives II.

[368] *Army List and Directory, May 1, 1924*, 8. Waters, "The Army Mine Planter Service," 400-11. Steven C. Clay, *U.S. Army Order of Battle 1919-1941,* Vol. II, *The Arms: Cavalry, Field Artillery and Coast Artillery 1919-1941*, 1183-84.

[369] G.F. Heaney Jr. "Corregidor: An Estimate of the Situation, A Revision of Data contained in Lieutenant Buntings Circular Published Several Years Ago by the Chief's Office," *CAJ*, Vol. 75, No. 4 (Jul.-Aug. 1932), 285-87.

[370] In Spanish, the colonial language of the Philippines, *despidida* is an expression of farewell, a formal ceremony usually conducted the night before a transport sailed away with those returning to the U.S. Mainland.

[371] Charles J. Sullivan, (Comp.) *Army Posts and Towns: The Baedeker of the Army* (Plattsburg Barracks, NY: Burlington Free Press Printing Co., 1926) 35-36.

[372] G.F. Heaney Jr. "Corregidor: An Estimate of the Situation, A Revision of Data contained in Lieutenant Buntings Circular Published Several Years Ago by the Chief's Office," *CAJ*, Vol. 75, No. 4 (Jul.-Aug. 1932), 285-87.

[373] Completion Reports for Post Buildings, Fort Mills, RG 77, Entry 391, Archives II.

[374] "Corregidor," *CAJ*, Vol. 75, No. 3 (May-June 1932), 227-28. "Corregidor Newsletter," *CAJ,* Vol. 78, No. 2, (Mar.-Apr. 1935), 142-43. Army Service Club, Historical Record of buildings.

[375] W.I. Allen, "Notes from the Philippines," *CAJ*, Vol. 76, No. 6 (Nov.-Dec. 1933), 444. Oscar C. Warner, "Corregidor News Letter," *CAJ*, Vol. 79, No. 6 (Nov.-Dec. 1936), 460

[376] Oscar C. Warner, "Corregidor News Letter," *CAJ*, Vol. 80, No.1 (Jan.-Feb. 1937, 70-71; Vol. 80, No. 2 (Mar.-Apr. 1937), 167-68.

[377] Oscar C. Warner, "Corregidor News Letter," *CAJ*, Vol. 80, No. 2 (Mar.-Apr. 1937), 170.

[378] Sullivan, (Comp.) *Army Posts and Towns: The Baedeker of the Army.*

[379] G.F. Heaney Jr. "Corregidor: An Estimate of the Situation, A Revision of Data contained in Lieutenant Buntings Circular Published Several Years Ago by the Chief's Office," *CAJ*, Vol.75, No.4 (Jul.-Aug. 1932), 285-87.

[380] Rutherford, "Reminiscences of Corregidor," 31-40. R.J. Wood, "Corregidor Doings: Renovation of the Cine," *CAJ*, Vol. 77, No. 2 (Sept.-Oct. 1934), 374-75.

[381] Sullivan, (Comp.) *Army Posts and Towns the Baedeker of the Army,* 31-33. "Corregidor Notes," *CAJ*, Vol. 77, No. 2 (Mar.-Apr. 1934), 133.

[382] G.P. Heaney, "Present Conditions at Corregidor," *CAJ*, Vol. 74, No. 7 (Nov.-Dec. 1931), 542-43.

[383] Bogart, "Fort Hughes: Outpost Duty between the Wars," *Periodical, Journal of the Council on America's Military Past,* Vol. XV, No. 3 (Oct. 1987), 25-40.

[384] On October 26, 1922, the War Department authorized the constitution of the 60th Artillery (AA) Battalion, CAC, as an antiaircraft unit, organized from the 127th and 128th Companies at Fort Crockett in the Coast Defenses of Galveston, Texas. They would form the nucleus of the battalion. The 127*th* Company was redesignated Headquarters Detachment and Combat Train of the 60th Battalion (Antiaircraft), and the 128th Company was redesignated as Battery "A" of that battalion. Two additional companies of Coast Artillery were transferred to Fort Crockett to help form the battalion. The 77th and 80th Companies, CAC, arrived from the Coast Defenses of Key West and were redesignated as Batteries "B" and "C," respectively. On November 21, 1936, the 60th Artillery, CAC, organized in 1917, was reconstituted and consolidated with the 60th CA (AA) Regiment. "Regimental History, Sixtieth Coast Artillery, August 4, 1938," RG 177, Entry 8, Archives II. "The 60th Coast

Artillery (Antiaircraft)," *CAJ*, Vol. 67 (Aug. 1927), 167-68. For a history of the 60th CA (AA) Regiment prior to its arrival in the Philippines, see William C. Gaines, "Antiaircraft Defenses in the Harbor Defense of Manila and Subic Bays 1921-1942," *CDSG Journal*, Vol. 14, No. 1 (Feb. 2000), 21-43.

[385] The M1923-E[xperimental] 3-inch AA gun was developed following World War I and was standardized as the M3 AA gun in 1927. This was a major improvement over both the M1917 and the M1918 AA guns. This new M3 gun mounted on the semi-mobile M2A2 "spider-mount" carriage had a higher rate of fire and was built with removable, and therefore, replaceable liners for the gun tubes. E.E. Booth to the Adjutant General, November 22, 1932, RG 407, Archives II. M.A. Elliot Jr. to the Commanding General, Philippine Department, March 10, 1935, RG 407, Archives II.

[386] Gwinn U. Porter, "Antiaircraft Defense of Corregidor," Regular Course Monograph, Command and General Staff College, Fort Leavenworth, KS, US Army Military History Institute. Hereafter: Porter, "AA Defense of Corregidor."

[387] The Adjutant General to the Commanding General, Philippine Department, March 10, 1933, RG 407, Archives II. Walter K. Wilson to the Commanding General, Philippine Department, March 28, 1939, RG 77, Archives II.

[388] G.F. Heaney Jr., "Machine Gun Towers," *CAJ*, Vol. 77 No. 1 (Jul.-Aug. 1934), 275-76. "RCW Two Machine gun Towers Morrison Hill, August 9, 1936."

[389] Walter K. Wilson to the Commanding General, Philippine Department, March 28, 1939, RG 77, Archives II.

[390] The Adjutant General to Commanding General, Philippine Department, August 13, 1940. RG 407, Archives II.

[391] "Corregidor," *CAJ*, Vol. 75, No. 3 (May-June 1932), 227-28.

[392] "Kilbourne Sent to Manila," *New York Times*, July 8, 1928. G.F. Heaney, "Present Condition at Corregidor," *CAJ*, Vol. 74, No. 6 (Nov.-Dec. 1931), 542-43.

[393] "Contributions Requested for Swimming Pool at Corregidor," *CAJ*, Vol. 73, No. 6 (Dec. 1930), 575-76. "Harbor Defense of Manila and Subic Bays," *CAJ*, Vol. 74, No. 3 (May-June 1931) 306-07. Rutherford, "Reminiscences of Corregidor," 31-40.

[394] "Harbor Defense of Manila and Subic Bays," *CAJ*, Vol. 74, No. 3 (May-June 1931) 306-07. W.I. Allen, "Activities at Fort Mills," *CAJ*, Vol. 77, No. 4 (Jul.-Aug. 1934), 297-98. "Contributions Requested for Swimming Pool at Corregidor," *CAJ*, Vol. 73, No. 6 (Dec. 1930), 575-76. "Harbor Defenses of Manila and Subic Bays News Letter," *CAJ*, Vol. 78, No. 1 (Jan.-Feb. 1935), 67.

[395] "Harbor Defenses of Manila and Subic Bays," *CAJ*, Vol. 74, No. 5 (Jul.–Aug. 1931), 386-91.

[396] Completion Report of Repairs, North Mine Wharf, Lorcha Wharf, July 12, 1927; Completion Report, Shoreline Pier, July 26, 1930; Completion Report of Repairs, Reconstruction of Railroad System at Fort Mills, June 30, 1930. RG 77, Entry 391, Archives II. "Harbor Defense of Manila and Subic Bays," *CAJ*, Vol. 74, No. 5 (Jul.-Aug. 1931), 386-91. Heaney, "Present Conditions at Corregidor," *CAJ*, Vol. 74, No. 6 (Nov.-Dec. 1931, 542-43. "Corregidor News Letter," *CAJ*, Vol. 78, No. 1 (Jul.-Aug. 1935), 302-03.

[397] C.D.Y. Ostrum, "An Observers' School at Fort Mills," *CAJ*, Vol. 70, No. 2 (Feb. 1928), 155-56.

[398] W.I. Allen, "Notes from the Philippines," *CAJ*, 76 (Nov.-Dec. 1933), 444-46. "Corregidor," *CAJ*, Vol. 75, No. 3 (May-June 1932), 227-28.

[399] Herbert F. Markland with Shawn A. Welch, "A Coast Artilleryman's Experiences at Fort Mills (Pt. 1)," *CDSG Journal*, Vol. IX, No. 1 (Feb. 1995), 9.

[400] Oscar C. Warner, "Corregidor Newsletter," *CAJ*, Vol. 80, No. 2 (Mar.-Apr. 1937), 167-70.

[401] "Training Directive for Coast Artillery," *CAJ*, Vol. 78, (Jul.-Aug. 1935), 308-09. Steven C. Clay, *U.S. Army Order of Battle 1919-1941,* Vol. II, *The Arms: Cavalry, Field Artillery and Coast Artillery 1919-1941*, 1099-1100.

[402] "Annual Report of the Chief of Coast Artillery, August 1, 1931," RG 177, Entry 8, Archives II. "Corregidor Newsletter," *CAJ*, Vol. 79, No. 2 (Mar.-Apr. 1936), 145-46. Walter K. Wilson to the Adjutant General, "Annual Report of Training, February 8, 1940," RG 337, Entry 80, Archives II.

[403] Walter K. Wilson to the Adjutant General, "Annual Report of Training, February 8, 1940," RG 337, Entry 80, Archives II. "Corregidor News Letter," *CAJ*, Vol. 79, No. 2 (Mar.-Apr. 1936), 145-46. Oscar C. Warner, "Corregidor Newsletter," *CAJ*, Vol. 80, No. 2 (Mar.-Apr. 1937), 167-70; Vol. 80, No. 3 (May-June 1936), 259-61.

[404] "Annual Report of the Chief of Coast Artillery, July 14, 1932," *War Department Annual Report, 1932*, 3; "Annual Report of the Chief of Coast Artillery, July 14, 1935," 1. "Corregidor News Letter," *CAJ*, Vol. 78, No. 2 (Mar.-Apr 1935), 142-43.

[405] Walter K. Wilson to the Adjutant General, "Annual Report of Training, February 8, 1940," RG 337, Entry 80, Archives II.

[406] Harrison, "Espionage," Corregidor, Then and Now, http://corregidor.org/crypto/chs_crypto1/sting1.htm

[407] Interview with Col. Valentine P. Foster, by William and James Belote, November 29, 1963, Folder on 59th CA, Corregidor Box, William and James Belote Collection, USAMHI, Carlisle Barracks, PA.

[408] Harrison, "Espionage," Corregidor, Then and Now, http://corregidor.org/crypto/chs_crypto1/sting1.htm. Cullum,Vol. 9, 667.

[409] Other colors were assigned to Canada (Crimson), Mexico (Green), Great Britain (Red), Italy (Gray) Germany (Black), to name only a few.

[410] Adam M. Cannon, "Scylla and Charybdis: The Army's Development of War Plan Orange," Fort Leavenworth, KS, U.S. Army Command and General Staff College, 2012, 14.

[411] Ibid., 14, 20.

[412] Ibid., 17.

[413] Ibid., 43-44, 51,53.

[414] "Annual Inspection Report and Correspondence, June 6, 1938," RG 177, Archives II. Engineer Annex, 1940, Philippine Defense Project, Annual Estimates F.Y. 1942, RG 407, Entry 365, Archives II.

[415] Archives II, RG 407, Entry 360, File 472.3, January 27. 1932. Ordnance Department, *Handbook of Ordnance Data*, November 15, 1918 (Washington DC: GPO, 1919), 26.

[416] Report of Completed Batteries, Harbor Defenses of Manila Bay, December 31, 1913, RG 77, Entry 103, NARA, Washington, D.C. "Ordnance Card File."

[417] Archives II, RG 165, Entry 281, file 3610, August 10, 1933.

[418] Williford, "Fort Mills," "Ordnance Card File."

[419] Archives II, RG 77, Entry 1009, File 662B (Manila) 45/9 of August 26, 1930.

[420] "RCW Battery Monja, March 9, 1937." "Exhibit E, Engineer Annex," in Moore, "Report of Operations, HD M&SB," 60.Interview of Lt. Col. Emil Ulanowicz by William M. Belote, October 2, 1963, in 92nd Coast Artillery Folder, Reminiscences of Surrender of Corregidor, William and James Belote Collection, USAMHI, Carlisle Barracks, PA.

[421] Interview of Lt. Col. Emil Ulanowicz by William M. Belote October 2, 1963, in 92nd Coast Artillery Folder, Reminiscences of Surrender of Corregidor, William and James Belote Collection, USAMHI, Carlisle Barracks, PA.

[422] Commanding General, Harbor Defenses of Manila and Subic Bays, to Commanding General, Philippine Department, Extracts covering Secret matters pertaining to 1941 Annual Inspection of Harbor Defenses of Manila and Subic Bays, May 8, 1941, RG 77, Archives II.

[423] "Engineer Annex, Report of Operations HD M&SB," 57-59. Philippine Department Engineer Office, Corregidor Island, Coast Defenses of Manila Bay March 31, 1936, RG 77, Archives II.

[424] Ben E. King, "Report of Operations on Fort Drum," 31 August 1945, in Moore, "Report of Operations, HD M&SB," 109-10. In Report of Operations of USAFFE and USFIP in the Philippine Islands 1941-1942, Office of the Chief of Military History, Washington D.C. Hereafter: Moore, "Report of Operations, HD M&SB." William C. Braly (USA Ret.), "Corregidor: A Name, A subject, A Tradition," *CAJ*, Vol. 90, No. 4 (Jul.-Aug. 1947), 8. Hereafter Braly, "Corregidor."

[425] Engineer Annex, 1940 Philippine Defense Project, Exhibit E, Engineer Annex, Report of Operations, HD M&SB, 58, RG 407, Entry 365, Archives II.

[426] Ibid.

[427] Philippine Department Engineer Office, Corregidor Island, Coast Defenses of Manila Bay, March 31, 1936, Map Scale 1-inch: 200 feet, RG 77, Archives II.

[428] Adams, *Designating US Seacoast Fortifications,* 192.

[429] The unfinished HDCP Tunnel or "Middleside Tunnel" as it would later be termed, was improved, partially finished, and placed in service during the early months of World War II.

[430] Harbor Defense Annex 1932 to the 1931 Philippine Defense Project, RG 407, Entry 365, Archives II.

[431] Ibid.

[432] Ibid.

[433] Ibid.

[434] Annual Estimate F.Y.1942 in Harbor Defense Project 1940, Archives II, RG 165, Entry 281, file 4525,"Exhibit E, Engineer Annex," in Moore, "Report of Operations, HD M&SB," 60.

[435] W.A. Danielson to Colonel Eltinge, May 26, 1921, RG 177, Archives II.

[436] Pashael N. Strong, "The Lean Years," Military Engineer, Vol. 41 (May-June 1949), 179-81.

[437] "RCW, Engineer Department Structure [Malinta Storage System], Ft. Mills HD Manila and Subic Bays, corrected to June 30, 1934." Cullum, Vol. VIII, Pt. 4, 500.

[438] Interview of Maj. Gen. Charles E. Kilbourne, July 3, 1962, by William M. Belote and James H. Belote, Belote Collection, USAMHI, Carlisle, PA.

[439] Strong, "Lean Years."

[440] Ibid.

[441] Ibid., Interview of Maj. Gen. Charles E. Kilbourne, July 3, 1962, by William M. Belote and James H. Belote, Belote Collection, USAMHI, Carlisle, PA.

[442] "RCW, Engineer Department Structure [Malinta Storage System], Ft. Mills HD Manila and Subic Bays, corrected to June 30, 1934." Strong, "Lean Years." Ralph Forty, "The Corregddor Tramway," *Modern Tramway,* Vol. 32, (1969).

[443] "RCW, Engineer Department Structure [Malinta Storage System], Ft. Mills, HD Manila and Subic Bays Corrected to June 30, 1934."

[444] Progress drawing of Malinta Storage System as of June 30, 1934, Archives II, Cartographics, RG-77, Map 115-28A-15. "Annual Inspection Report, HD Manila and Subic Bays, October 18, 1938," RG 177, Archives II. "Engineer Annex, in George F. Moore," Report of Operations Harbor Defenses of Manila and Subic Bays," 58.

[445] "Engineer Annex," Report of Operations on the Harbor Defenses of Manila and Subic Bays, February 14, 1941 – 6 May 1942, 62, in Celedonio A. Ancheta, *The Wainwright Papers*, Vol. II, (Quezon City, Philippines: New Day Publishers, 1980), Hereafter: "Engineer Annex, Report of Operations, HD M&SB." "RCW, Engineer Department Structure [Malinta Storage System], Ft. Mills HD Manila and Subic Bays, corrected to May 26, 1937." "RCW, Engineer Department Structure [Malinta Storage System], Ft. Mills HD Manila and Subic Bays, corrected to June 30, 1937.".

[446] "Corregidor the Beginnings," in Graydon A. Lewis, (ed.), *Corregidor in Naval Intercept Station "C": from Olongapo through the Evacuation of Corregidor*, 16 (Denver, CO: Naval Cryptologic Veterans Association, n.d). Hereafter: Lewis, *Intercept Station "C".*

[447] Department of the Navy, Bureau of Yards and Docks, "Building the Navy's Bases in World War II: History of the Bureau of Yards and Docks and the Civil Engineer Corps 1940-1946," 392, http://www.ibiblio.org/ hyperwar/USN/ Building Bases/ bases-29.html. John Gordon, *Fighting for MacArthur: The Navy and Marine Corps' Desperate Defense of the Philippines*, (Annapolis, MD: Naval Institute Press, 2011), 8-9, 68, 117-18. Hereafter Gordon, *Fighting for MacArthur.*

[448] Timothy J. Mucklow, "The Naval Tunnel Station C: Tip of the Lance," *Federal History,* 2011, 51-65

[449] Sheila Carlisle (ed.), *U.S. Naval Cryptographic Activities in the Philippines Prior to World War II, SRH-180,* (Laguna Hills, CA, Aegean Park Press, 1982).

[450] Timothy J. Mucklow, "The Naval Tunnel Station C: Tip of the Lance," *Federal History*, 2011, 51-65.

[451] Duane Whitlock, "Station Charlie," in Lewis, *Intercept Station "C",* 63-67.

[452] "Engineer Annex, "Report of Operations, HD M&SB," 57-58.

[453] Ibid.

[454] "Philippine Army Coast Artillery," *CAJ*, Vol. 81, No. 4, (Jul.-Aug. 1938), 310.

[455] Moore, "Report of Operations, HD M&SB, Exhibit K, Personnel Annex," 92. Interview with Col. Alfred D'Arezzo, USA, by William M. Belote, October 7, 1963, William and James Belote Collection, USAMHI. George Munson, "A Short History of Fort Wint."

[456] Brian McAllister Linn, *Guardians of Empire: The U.S. Army and the Pacific 1902-1940* (Chapel Hill, NC: The University of North Carolina Press, 1997), 244-45.

[457] "Engineer Annex, "Report of Operations, HD M&SB," 62. Engineer Annex, 1940 Philippine Defense Project, RG 407, Entry 365, Archives II.

[458] Ibid., 58-60.

[459] "Corregidor News Letter," *CAJ*, Vol. 78, No. 2 (Mar.-Apr. 1935), 142. R.E. Phillips, "Corregidor," *CAJ*, Vol. 82, No. 6 (Nov.-Dec. 1939), 592.

[460] Harold Larson, *Water Transportation for the United States Army 1939-1942*, Office of the Chief of Transportation, Army Service Forces, 1944, 25, 46, 82-86.

[461] S. McCullough, "Corregidor," *CAJ*, Vol. 84, No. 3 (May-June 1941) 291. Burton B. Brown, "Corregidor,", *CAJ*, Vol. 84, No. 4 (Jul.-Aug. 1941), 385.

[462] USAT *President Taft* of the American President Line was purchased by the army June 17, 1941, and renamed USAT *Willard H. Holbrook* in September 1941. When she left Manila in July 1941, she still wore her civilian colors but was referred to as Army Transport *President Taft*. "ExceReports from Colonel Bowler's Diary edited by Col. V.P. Foster, in his Notebook," Corregidor Files, Archives, USAMHI, Carlisle Barracks, PA. Burton R. Brown, "Corregidor," CAJ, Vol. 84, No. 4 (Jul.-Aug. 1941), 385; Vol. 84, No. 5 (Sept.-Oct. 1941), 502. "Exhibit K, Personnel Annex, Report of Operations, HD M&SB," 91, 94. "Engineer Annex, PDP 1940 Revision, 1."

In 1940 the prisoners, equipment, and facilities at Bilibid Prison were transferred to a new prison in Muntinlupa, Rizal Province, called "The New Bilibid Prison." The old facility was retained in use as the Manila City Jail. The convicts from Corregidor were sent to the "new" prison.

[463] "Engineer Annex, PDP 1940 Revision 3." Braly, "Corregidor", 37.

[464] Commanding General, Harbor Defenses of Manila and Subic Bays, to Commanding General, Philippine Department, Extracts covering Secret matters pertaining to 1941 Annual Inspection of Harbor Defenses of Manila and Subic Bays, May 8, 1941, RG 77, Archives II. Ray LeClaire Makepeace, "Account of Personal and Military Life," unpub. memoir in Gaines' collection. Transcript of interview of Val Gavito by Bob Brown, September 2002, Branson, MO. Interview with Corporal John Perkowski, Corregidor Box, William and James Belote Collection, Archives, US Army Military History Institute (US-AMHI), Carlisle Barracks, PA.

[465] "Annual Inspection of the Harbor Defenses, May 8, 1941," RG 177, Archives II.

[466] "Exhibit K, Personnel Annex, Report of Operations, HD M&SB," 91- 94. Historical Data Sheet and Station List, 60th Coast Artillery (AA) Regiment, ORS, MPRU, NPRC, St. Louis, MO. Louis Morton, *The Fall of the Philippines*, (Washington D.C.: GPO, 1953), 24, 40-41, 478. Hereafter Morton, *The Fall of the Philippines*. Belote and Belote, *Corregidor*, 29.

[467] Harbor Defense Quartermaster, "Completion Report, General Housing Project, October 22, 1941."

[468] Capt. George Steiger, "A POW Diary." Gaines' collection. Lt. Harcourt G. Bull served as the Fort Mills Post Exchange Officer and 1st Lt. George Melvin Moore III was assigned to Headquarters Battery, 59th CA.

[469] The Adjutant General to Commanding General, Philippine Department, August 13, 1940, RG 407, Archives II.

[470] "Report of Operations of the Provisional Coast Artillery Brigade (AA) (PCAB)(AA) in the Philippines," Records of the Philippine Division, MPRU, NPRC, St. Louis, MO. Stephen M. Mellnik, "The Life and Death of the 200th Coast Artillery (AA)," CAJ, Vol. 90 No. 2 (March-April), 1947, 2-7. Dorothy Cave, *Beyond Courage: One Regiment Against Japan, 1941-1945* (Las Cruces, NM: Yucca Tree Press, 1992), 391-93.

[471] Porter, "AA Defense of Corregidor."

[472] "Operations Report, AA Defense Command," Records of the Philippine Division, ORS, MPRU, NPRC, St. Louis, MO.

[473] "Engineer Annex, Report of Operations, HD M&SB," 12. "Operations Report, AA Defense Command, Report of Operations on the HD Manila and Subic Bays, 14 February-6 May 1942," Records of the Philippine Division, ORS, MPRU, NPRC, St. Louis, MO.

[474] Moore, "Report of Operations, HD M&SB," 11.

[475] "Annual Inspection of the Harbor Defenses, April 25, 1933," RG 177, Archives II. Commanding General, Harbor Defenses of Manila and Subic Bays, to Commanding General, Philippine Department, Extracts covering Secret matters pertaining to 1941 Annual Inspection of Harbor Defenses of Manila and Subic Bays, May 8, 1941, RG 77, Archives II. Moore, "Report of Operations, HD M&SB," 15.

[476] "Philippine Department, Harbor Defenses of Manila [and] Subic Bay[s], Addenda to Introduction to report "Camouflage of Seacoast Fortifications, March 12, 1942, RG 77.

[477] Ibid.

[478] Ibid.

[479] Stockton Bruns, "Battery I, 59th Coast Artillery."

[480] Burton R. Brown, "Corregidor," *CAJ*, Vol,84, No. 6, (Nov.-Dec. 1941), 622-23.

[481] "Annual Report of the Chief of Coast Artillery, August 13, 1930"; Walter K. Wilson to J.A. Green, April 4, 1940; K.T. Blood to Commanding Officer, Submarine Mine Depot, Fort Monroe, June 7, 1940; K.T. Blood to Walter K. Wilson, May 17, 1940, RG 177, Entry 8, Archives II.

[482] George Grunert to Chief of Staff and Chief of Naval Operations December 21, 1940; Proceedings of a Meeting of a Local Army-Navy Committee on Controlled Minefields, March 22, 1941, RG 177, Archives II.

[483] Radiogram dated March 10, 1941; J.A. Green to the Assistant Chief of Staff, War Plans Division, March 14, 1941, Radiogram dated March 24, 1941; Grunert to Adjutant General's Office, January 25, 1941; Cablegram from K.T. Blood to C.O. Submarine Depot, January 29, 1941, and endorsements; Radio Gram, Grunert to the Adjutant General, March 10, 1941; Memorandum from J.A. Green to the Assistant Chief of Staff, War Plans Division, Re: Submarine Mine Project HD Manila and Subic Bays, March 14, 1941; Adjutant General to the Commanding General, Philippine Department, March 21, 1941; RG 177, Entry 8, Archives II,

[484] Defensive Coastal Area Limits and Underwater Defense Project for Manila Bay, December 21, 1940, Records of RG 177, Entry 8, Archives II. Moore, "Report of Operations, HD M&SB," 13-14.

[485] Braly, Corregidor," 6. Moore, "Report of Operations, HD M&SB, 193-194." Belote and Belote, *Corregidor,* 43-44.

[486] Henry L. Jones, "Increase in the CAC's Navy," *CAJ*, Vol. 84, No. 6, (Nov.-Dec. 1941), 589-92. K.L. Waters, "The Army Mine Planter Service," *Warship International*, Vol., 22, No. 4, (1985), 400-11. Harold Larson, *Water Transportation for the United States Army, 1939 -1942*, Office of the Chief of Transportation, Army Service Forces, August 1944, 144.

[487] Glen Williford, *Racing the Sunrise: Reinforcing America's Pacific Outposts 1941-42* (Annapolis: Naval Institute Press, 2010), 177.

[488] Arnold A. Bocksel, CAC, "The USAMP *General George Harrison* in the Harbor Defenses of Manila and Subic Bay," *CAJ*, Vol. 89, No. 6 (Nov.-Dec. 1946), 54.

[489] "Defensive Coastal Area Limits and Underwater Defense Project, Manila Bay, June 16, 1938," revised to December 16, 1940, Philippine Defense Project, 1940 revision, RG 407, Entry 365, Archives II,

[490] Moore, "Report of Operations, HD M&SB," 15, Braly, "Corregidor," 3.

[491] Moore, "Report of Operations, HD M&SB," 15.

[492] Barlow, *Bunker's War*, 47.

[493] Cullum, Vol. VII, Pt. 11, 1940; Vol. VIII, Pt. 5, 635; Vol. IX, Pt. 5, 485.

[494] R.E. Philips, "Corregidor," *CAJ*, Vol. 82, No. 3 (May-June 1939), 272. "Annual Report, Training for 1939," Headquarters, HD Manila and Subic Bays, February 8, 1940, Enclosure 3, RG 337, Entry 80, File 65, Archives II, NARA . Valentine P. Foster, "91st Coast Artillery (PS)," in S. McCullough, "Corregidor," *CAJ*, Vol. 83, No. 4 (Jul.-Aug. 1940), 374.

[495] George Munson, "The Best of The Best, (91st Coast Artillery, Philippine Scouts," Corregidor Historical Society.

[496] Barlow, *Bunker's War*, 84.

[497] Moore, "Report of Operations, HD M&SB, Exhibit K, Personnel Annex," 92.

[498] Cullum, Vol. IX, 136. "Exhibit of the Antiaircraft Defenses Command, Harbor Defense of Manila and Subic Bays," in Moore, "Report of Operations, HD M&SB," 72.

[499] "Exhibit F, Antiaircraft Defense Command, Harbor Defenses of Manila and Subic Bays," in Moore, "Report of Operations, HD M&SB." Bob Hudson, "Testimony of Major Arthur Peterson, 60th CA Prisoner of War." Cullum, Vol. IX, Pt. 6, 649.

[500] Braly, "Corregidor," 3. Moore, "Report of Operations, HD M&SB," 15.

[501] Braly, "Corregidor," 3. Stockton Bruns, "History of Battery I, 59th Coast Artillery," Folder, 59th Coast Artillery (Antiaircraft), Roster of officers, Reminicesences[sic] and letters, Corregidor Box, William and James Belote Collection, Archives, USAMHI, Carlisle Barracks, PA. Moore, "Report of Operations, HD M&SB," 16. Braly, "Corregidor," 3.

[502] Earl L. Barr, "History of Battery 'M,' 60th CA (AA)," Center of Military History, Washington, D.C. Charles Reel, Biographical Sketch, Gaines Collection.

[503] Braly, "Corregidor," 5-6. Moore, "Report of Operations, HD M&SB," 16. Belote and Belote, *Corregidor*, 102. By March 1942, Lawlor was delirious with malaria and only four of about 100 enlisted scouts had the strength to lift the 98-pound shells for the 155 mm guns. Lieutenant Edward Kalbfleish, the battery executive, had to act as gunner as no one else was physically able to do so. On April 8, 1942, Battery "B," 92nd CA, surrendered with the rest of the Bataan Forces.

[504] Moore, "Report of Operations, HD M&SB," 16-17. Braly, "Corregidor," 4. Gordon, *Fighting for MacArthur*, 46-64, 89-90.

[505] Moore, "Report of Operations, HD M&SB," 16-17, 55-56.

[506] "Report of Operations on Fort Drum, 31 August 1945," in Moore, "Report of Operations," 115.

[507] "Exhibit H, Quartermaster Appendix, Philippine Department Philippine Defense Project, 1938 Revision, RG 407, Entry 365, Archives II.

[508] The SS *Don Jose* put into Manila on December 12, 1941, with a cargo of 212 motor vehicles, including fifty-seven Universal (Bren Gun) Carriers for the two Canadian motorized infantry battalions, the Royal Rifles of Canada and the Winnipeg Grenadiers, posted in the Hong Kong garrison. *Don Jose* was held in Manila as there was little prospect of her cargo ever being made available to Hong Kong's garrison; a request by Washington was granted by Canada, for the use of the equipment by Provisional Tank Group on Bataan, where they were manned by a force of grounded air corps personnel and some Filipinos. "Canadian Participation in the Defence of Hong Kong," December 1941, Report No 163, Historical Section, Canadian Military Headquarters, 31. Moore, "Report of Operations, HD M&SB," 18. Aaron A. Abston, "Diary of Battery G, 60th Coast Artillery, June 1, 1941-May 6, 1942." Jas. R.N. Weaver, "Report of Operations of the Provisional Tank Group, USAFFE, 1941-1942," 8. Belote and Belote, *Corregidor*, 42-43.

[509] Warren Starr, "My Years with the Military," http://corregidor. org/chs_starr/starr_01.htm Godfrey R. Ames, "Narrative Report of Action during War "

[510] Moore, "Report of Operations, HD M&SB," 17. Braly, "Corregidor," 5.

[511] Ibid.

[512] Moore, "Report of Operations, HD M&SB," 17, 18, 193. E.L. Sackett, USS Canopus History."

[513] USS *Asheville, Tulsa, Luzon, Mindanao, Quail, Tanager, Finch, Napa, Vega, Genesee, in Dictionary of American Naval Fighting Ships.*

[514] SS *Corregidor* was a 316-foot-long 1617 gross tonnage steamer laid down in 1910 and launched September 23, 1911, as the SS *Engadine* and placed in service as a cross channel ferry between Folkestone, England, and Boulogne, France. She was taken over by the Royal Navy in 1914 and modified, with cranes and a hangar aft of the funnels, so that she could carry four Short 184 seaplanes. After service in WW I, *Engadine* was sold back to her original owners, the South Eastern and Chatham Railway in December 1919 and reentered the ferry service until 1933, when the ship was sold to a Philippine shipping company and placed in service as the inter-island passenger and cargo steamer SS *Corregidor*. SS *Corregidor* operated between Manila and the Southern Islands of the Philippines. http://www.ibiblio. org/hyperwar/USN/USN-Chron/USN-Chron-1941.html. A.V.H. Hartendorp, "The Sinking of the SS Corregidor, December 17, 1941," *The American Chamber of Commerce Journal* (Manila). Vol. 29 (Sept. 1953), 350-52. "Journal of Alcaraz," 20, 26. http://www.oocities.org/comralcaraz/ diary.html.http:// www.oocities.org/comralcaraz/diary.html. Hereafter "Journal of Alcaraz." Gordon, *Fighting for MacArthur*, 75. The original plan had been to allocate 16 ex-navy 3-inch landing guns as artillery to the Visayan defense. However subsequent correspondence cancelled that transfer and substituted the 2.95-inch mountain guns. That confusion has led some published accounts to mistakenly assert that the 3-inch guns were lost with SS *Corregidor*.

[515] A.V.H. Hartendorp, "The Sinking of the SS Corregidor, December 17, 1941," *The American Chamber of Commerce Journal* (Manila). Vol. 29 (Sept. 1953), 350-52.

[516] USS *Mindanao* did not begin its duties as mine field guard ship until December 21. "Sinking of the USS *Mindanao* (PR-8) and Captivity of the Crew," http://www.navsource.org/ archives/12/1208d.htm

[517] Moore, "Report of Operations, HD M&SB," 13-14.

[518] "Journal of Alcaraz," 26.

[519] A.V.H. Hartendorp, "The Sinking of the SS *Corregidor*, December 17, 1941," *The American Chamber of Commerce Journal* (Manila), Vol. 29 (Sept. 1953), 350-52. "Journal of Alcaraz," 20.

[520] A.V.H. Hartendorp, "The Sinking of the SS *Corregidor*, December 17, 1941," *The American Chamber of Commerce Journal* (Manila), Vol. 29 (Sept. 1953), 350-52. "Journal of Alcaraz," 20, 26.

[521] George Steiger, "A POW Diary," http://www.fsteiger. com/ gsteipow. Html.

[522] Moore, "Report of Operations, HD M&SB," 18-19. Braly, "*Corregidor*," 6. Belote and Belote, *Corregidor*, 42-43. The *Cassandra*, an oil-burning yacht, was built in 1908, acquired by oil tycoon Edward L. Doheny and renamed the Casiana, after his first major oil well in Mexico. In 1936, the Commonwealth government acquired it for $50,000, and the ship arrived in Manila on November 25 of the same year. The name was changed to *Banahaw*, and it was made part of the Coast Guard service, although, primarily, it was reserved for use of the President and his family. On December 29, 1941, it was sunk off the Fort Mills Engineering Wharf, Corregidor, by Japanese bombing.

[523] Moore, "Report of Operations, HD M&SB," 21.

[524] Porter, "AA Defense of Corregidor." Statement of Captain Wimer, Signal Corps, in Headquarters, 14th Antiaircraft Command, "Report on War Damage to the Harbor Defenses of Manila and Subic Bays, 6 October 1945, Appendix E, 16-17." C.J. Wimer, "History of Signal Corps Radar Units in the Philippine Islands, August 1, 1941–May 6, 1942," RG 111, Entry 200, Archives II. For a discussion of the use of radar in the Philippines early in World War II, see Charles H. Bogart, "Radar in the Philippines, 1941-1942," *Journal of America's Military Past*, Vol. XXVI, No. 2 (Fall 1999), 27-35. Moore, "Report of Operations, HD M&SB," 19.

[525] Patrol Wing Ten, commissioned December 16, 1940, at Cavite Navy Base, Capt. Frank D. Wagner, USN commanding, had two squadrons of PBY-4 Catalina flying boats, VP-101 (redesignated from VP-21) and VP-102. Four seaplane tenders supported the wing: USS *Langley*, *Childs*, *William Preston*, and *Heron*. The Wing lost many of its forty-three aircraft in the early days of the war and on December 14, 1941, the Wing was ordered to Australia via the Netherlands East Indies.

[526] Moore, "Report of Operations, HD M&SB," 17-19. Interview with Col. Alfred D'Arezzo, USA, by William M. Belote, October 7, 1963, William and James Belote Collection, USAMHI. George Munson, "A Short History of Fort Wint," unpublished essay in Gaines's collection. Braly, "Corregidor," 6. J.Michael Miller, *From Shanghai to Corregidor: Marines in the Defense of the Philippines* (Washington D.C.: Marine Corps Historical Center, 1997), 30. Hereafter Miller, *From Shanghai to Corregidor*, 14-15.

[527] Moore, "Report of Operations, HD M&SB," 17-19. Interview with Col. Alfred D'Arezzo, USA, by William M. Belote, October 7, 1963, William and James Belote Collection, USAMHI. Braly, "Corregidor," 6.

[528] Japanese Monograph No. 11, General Headquarters, Far East Command, Military History Section Japanese Research Division, "Philippines Air Operations Record, Phase I," Japanese Monograph No. 11, 1 February 1952, Archives, Fort Leavenworth, KS, 28-30.

[529] Arthur E. Huff, "History of Battery B, 60th CA (AA) Regiment. Moore, "Report of Operations, HD M&SB," 20. Belote and Belote, *Corregidor*, 49. Braly, "Corregidor," 6. General Headquarters, Far East Command, Military History Section Japanese Research Division, "Philippines Air Operations Record, Phase I," Japanese Monograph No. 11, 1 February 1952, Archives, Fort Leavenworth, KS, 10.

[530] Robert D. Glassburn, "History of Battery F, 60th CA (AA)." E.M. Shiley, "History of Battery I, 60th CA (AA)."

[531] Godfrey R. Ames, "Narrative Report of Action during War, October 20, 1943." E.M. Shiley, "History of Battery I, 60th CA (AA)."

[532] Paul R. Cornwell, "War History of Battery D, 60th CA (AA)."

[533] Warren Starr, "Battery Commander's Narrative Report of Battery Hartford's Action during the War Period from November 29, 1941, to the Surrender of Corregidor, May 6, 1942."

[534] Colonel Braly was the operations officer for the Harbor Defenses and Colonel Bowler was the harbor defense adjutant and personnel officer. Statements of Col. Delbert Ausmus, 59th CA, and 1st Lieutenant, Balogona, 91st CA (PS), in Headquarters, 14th Antiaircraft Command, "Report on War Damage to The Harbor Defenses Of Manila and Subic Bays, 6 October 1945, Appendix E," 6. Braly, "Corregidor," 6-7. Moore, "Report of Operations, HD M&SB," 20. Morton, *The Fall of the Philippines*, 479-81. Coast Artillery School, "The Siege of Corregidor," Coast Artillery Training Bulletin Vol. 3, No. 1 (Feb. 1944), 5. The Japanese Navy land-based bombers that struck Corregidor were based on Palau and Formosa. General Headquarters, Far East Command, Military History Section, Japanese Research Division, "Philippines Air Operations Record, Phase I," Japanese Monograph No. 11. 1 February 1952, Archives, Fort Leavenworth, KS, 27.

[535] Statement of 1st Sgt. Francisco Bautista, 92nd CA (PS), "Appendix E, Statement of Witnesses, Report of War Damages to the Harbor Defenses of Manila and Subic Bays 6 October 1945," Headquarters 14th Antiaircraft Command, 2. Morton, *Fall of the Philippines*, 481. Barlow, *Bunker's War*, 13. General Headquarters, Far East Command, Military History Section, Japanese Research Division, "Philippines Air Operations Record, Phase I," Japanese Monograph No. 11. 1 February 1952, Archives, Fort Leavenworth, KS, 25.

[536] On September 1, 1941, the 31st Infantry Regiment was reassigned from the Philippine Department to the Philippine Division, which since 1931 had consisted of only Philippine Scout units. The transfer order was not posted and therefore went unnoticed to men of the regiment who continued to wear the blue and white seahorse patch of the Philippine Department, rather than the red and gold carabao (water buffalo) patch of the Philippine Division. Karl H. Lowe, "America's Foreign Legion: The 31st U.S. Infantry Regiment at War and Peace," (a book in progress), Chapter 5, 9, Chapter 6, 6, 8-10. http:// www.31st Infantry.org /history.htm

[537] Morton, *Fall of The Philippines*, 482. Statement of Lt. Col. Carl E. Englehart in Headquarters, 14th Antiaircraft Command, "Report on War Damage to the Harbor Defenses of Manila and Subic Bays, 6 October 1945, Appendix E, 1," Copy in Gaines' collection. Moore, "Report of Operations, HD M&SB," 21.

[538] Battery South II (three 155 mm guns) was renamed in honor of Captain Hamilton, Battery L, 60th CA (AA). Moore, "Report of Operations, HD M&SB," 22, 23.

[539] Moore, "Report of Operations, HD M&SB," 22.

[540] President Quezon's yacht *Banahaw* was formerly the yacht *Casandra* built in 1908. "Exhibit F, the Antiaircraft Defenses Command, Harbor Defense of Manila and Subic Bays," in Moore, "Report of Operations, HD M&SB," 22-23, 72-73.

[541] General Headquarters, Far East Command, Military History Section, Japanese Research Division, "Philippines Air Operations Record, Phase I," Japanese Monograph No. 11. 1958, Archives, Fort Leavenworth, KS. Estimates compiled by Tony Feredo and related to author in personal correspondence, April 25, 2015.

[542] "Exhibit F, the Antiaircraft Defenses Command, Harbor Defense of Manila and Subic Bays," in Moore, "Report of Operations, HD M&SB," 72.

[543] Moore, "Report of Operations HD M&SB," 23. Barlow, *Bunker's War*, 20-21.

[544] "Exhibit F, the Antiaircraft Defenses Command, Harbor Defense of Manila and Subic Bays," in Moore, "Report of Operations, HD M&SB," 72. Moore, "Report of Operations, HD M&SB," 22.

[545] Barlow, *Bunker's War*, 87.

[546] "Exhibit E, Engineer Annex in Moore, 'Report of Operations, HD M&SB,'" 60. Barlow, *Bunker's War*, 10, 26, 55, 67, 79, 82-83, 85, 88-89, 91-92, 95, 103-104, 108, 118-119, 128.

[547] Barlow, *Bunker's War*, 43-49, passim. Braly, "Corregidor," 8. Morton, *Fall of the Philippines*, 296-308, passim.

[548] Moore, "Report of Operations, HD M&SB," 24, 73. Braly, "Corregidor," 8. Morton, *Fall of the Philippines*, 296-308, passim. Barlow, *Bunker's War*, 43-49, passim. "Perkowski Letters"

[549] Barlow, *Bunker's War*, 44.

[550] Ibid, 44.

[551] Ibid. 45, 47. Moore, "Report of Operations, HD M&SB," 23.

[552] Douglas MacArthur, *MacArthur Reports*, Vol. II (Washington D.C.: Center of Military History, 1966), 110-112, Hereafter: MacArthur, *MacArthur Reports*.

[553] Ibid.

[554] Ibid.

[555] "Extracts from Report of Annual Inspection of the Harbor Defenses of Manila and Subic Bays, Fort Mills, P.I., for the fiscal year 1941, May 8, 1941," RG 177, Archives II. Barlow, *Bunker's War*, 101. Cullum, Vol. IX, Pt. 5, 485. Interview with Lt. Col. Clifton Chamberlain, October 4, 1962, Folder, Corregidor 1941-1942, 59th Coast Artillery (Antiaircraft) Roster of officers, Reminiscences and letters, Corregidor Box, William and James Belote Collection, USAMHI, Carlisle Barracks, PA.

[556] Stockton Bruns, "History of Battery I, 59th Coast Artillery," Folder 59th Coast Artillery (Antiaircraft), Roster of officers Reminiscences and letters Corregidor Box, William and James Belote Collection, USAMHI, Carlisle Barracks, PA. Gordon, *Fighting for MacArthur*, 178.

[557] Interview with Lt. Col. Clifton Chamberlain, n.d.; Interview with Col. Armand Hopkins, n.d., Corregidor, 1941-1942, 59th Coast Artillery Folder, William and James Belote Collection, USAMHI, Carlisle Barracks, PA. Gordon, *Fighting for MacArthur*, 242-43.

[558] Cullum, Vol. IX, Pt. 6, 656. "Perkowski Letters."

[559] "Testimony of Col. Napoleon Boudreau, Exhibit E, Report on War Damage to the Harbor Defenses of Manila and Subic Bays."

[560] Barlow, *Bunker's War,* 107.

[561] Ben E. King, "Report of Operations on Fort Drum, 31 August 1945." in Moore, "Report of Operations, HD M&SB," 109-110. Cullum, Vol. IX, Pt. 4, 454.

[562] Because Battery Hoyle's field of fire was essentially the same as that of Battery Frank (North), its two guns had been dismounted and sent to Corregidor. Ben E. King, "Report of Operations on Fort Drum 31 August 1945," in Moore, "Report of Operations, HD M&SB," 109-110. Braly, "Corregidor," 8.

[563] In 1938, a Panama mount for a 155 mm gun had been built on the south side of Fort Frank and termed Battery Frank (South). In early 1941 the gun at Battery Frank (South) was moved to the island's North end and four Panama mounts built. Upon their completion, three more 155 mm guns were brought from Fort Mills to arm Battery Frank (North). "Extracts

from Report of Annual Inspection of the Harbor Defenses of Manila and Subic Bays, Fort Mills, for the fiscal year 1941 May 8, 1941," RG 177, Entry 8, Archives II. Barlow, *Bunker's War*, 52, 54. Moore, "Report of Operations, HD M&SB," 24-25. Braly, "Corregidor," 8-9. Morton, *Fall of the Philippines*, 485. "Perkowski Letters."

[564] Moore, "Report of Operations, HD M&SB," 24-25. Barlow, *Bunker's War*, 52. Morton, *Fall of the Philippines*, 485.

[565] Barlow, *Bunker's War*, 62. Morton, *Fall of the Philippines*, 485.

[566] Captain White died of his wounds on July 10, 1942, at Cabanatuan POW Camp. Barlow, *Bunker's War*, 62, 192, 196.

[567] Barlow, *Bunker's War*, 62. Moore, "Report of Operations, HD M&SB," 25-26. "Report of Operations on Fort Drum, 31 August 1945," 9-10.

[568] Barlow, *Bunker's War*, 66-69 passim. Braly, "Corregidor," 9. Morton, *Fall of the Philippines*, 486. "Perkowski Papers."

[569] Braly, "Corregidor," 36.

[570] Barlow, *Bunker's War*, 66-69 passim. Braly, "Corregidor," 36.

[571] Barlow, *Bunker's War*, 62, 66-69 passim. Moore, "Report of Operations, HD M&SB," 26-27. MacArthur, *MacArthur Reports*, Vol. II, 110-112. Morton, *Fall of the Philippines*, 486

[572] Moore, "Report of Operations, HD M&SB," 27. Braly, "Corregidor," 36. "Perkowski Letters."

[573] Barlow, *Bunker's War*, 74, 78. Braly, "Corregidor," 39, Interview with Col. Valentine P. Foster, USA (Ret) November 29, 1963, Folder 59th Coast Artillery (Antiaircraft) Roster of officers, reminiscences and letters, Corregidor Box, William and James Belote Collection, USAMHI, Carlisle Barracks, PA.

[574] Moore, "Report of Operations, HD M&SB", 27. Barlow, *Bunker's War*, 74.

[575] Ibid., 79. Interview with Col. Armand Hopkins, n.d. Corregidor 1941-1942, 59th Coast Artillery Folder, William and James Belote Collection, USAMHI, Carlisle Barracks, PA.

[576] Barlow, *Bunker's War*, 103. "Report of Operations of Fort Drum, 31 August 1945," in Moore, "Report of Operations, HD M&SB," 114.

[577] Battery Woodruff had been taken out of service before the war, as its structure was considered unsafe. It was asserted that the concrete had been made using salt water that corroded the steel reinforcement. When fired, chunks of concrete fell inside the battery. Prewar plans to investigate the suspected unsafe condition had been implemented. Despite the "unsafe" condition, Battery Woodruff was placed back in service and was used regularly in counterbattery fire against Cavite. Barlow, *Bunker's War*, 84, 90. Interview with Lt. Col. Clifton Chamberlain, n.d.; Interview with Col. Armand Hopkins, n.d. Corregidor 1941-1942, 59th Coast Artillery Folder, William and James Belote Collection, USAMHI, Carlisle Barracks, PA

[578] Glen Williford, *Racing the Sunrise: Reinforcing America's Pacific Outposts 1941-42* (Annapolis: Naval Institute Press, 2010), 202-04.

[579] This gun was one of many 8-inch M1888 guns removed from fixed emplacements in the US coast defenses early in World War I for remounting on railway carriages. In May 1941, five 8-inch M1888MIA1 guns and two M1888MIIA1 guns with their M1918 barbette carriages along with twenty-four 155 mm M1917-18 GPF guns and their fire control equipment were shipped to the Philippines as part of an Inland Seas Defense Project. The project advanced slowly and war came before the project was practically started. Several 155 mm guns were removed from the Ordnance Depot at Fort Stotsenburg and moved to the depot at Limay on the Bataan Peninsula. These ended up being reallocated to partially equip the 301st Field Artillery (Philippine Army), which withdrew into the Bataan Peninsula with the rest of the Fil-American forces in January 1942. One of the army 8-inch guns was emplaced on Bataan's west coast at Saysain Point, where it was manned by a detachment from the 1st Coast Artillery, Philippine Army, commanded by Capt. Alfred J. D'Arezzo, 92nd CA (PS). For a discussion of the Philippine Inland Seas Defense Project, see Charles H. Bogart, "Philippine Seas Defenses Project," *Periodical: Journal of the Council on America's Military Past*, Vol. XIV, No. 1 (March 1986), 37-44; Vol. XIV, No. 2 (June 1986), 55-56; Vol. XIV, No. 3 (Sept. 1986), 46-47, Vol. XV, No. 1 (Apr. 1987), 55-56. Hereafter: Periodical "Philippine Seas." Barlow, Bunker's War, 87. Braly, "Corregidor," 37. Moore, "Report of Operations, HD M&SB," 29. Interview with Col. Alfred D'Arezzo, USA, by William M. Belote, October 7, 1963, William and James Belote Collection, USAMHI.

[580] Glen Williford, *Racing the Sunrise: Reinforcing America's Pacific Outposts 1941-42*, (Annapolis: Naval Institute Press, 2010), 228-47.

[581] Morton, *The Fall of the Philippines*, 390-403.

[582] Ibid.

[583] An estimated $10,000,000 in gold bullion and silver coinage had been removed from the vaults in Manila at the beginning of the war, relocated to Corregidor, and stored in the Government Vault in the Insular Government Reservation in a ravine southeast of Topside and later in the Navy's "Dog" Tunnel under Malinta Hill. Colonel Chase reported the number of mechanically fused 3-inch AA munitions received as 2,700 rounds while General Moore indicated that 3,500 rounds were received. This discrepancy can perhaps be explained thus: There was an undeclared amount of mechanically fused ammunition on hand at the beginning of the war that was provided to Battery B, 60th CA. This ammunition had been reduced to about 800 rounds when the supplementary ammunition arrived aboard *Trout*, thus providing 3,500 rounds of the mechanically fused munitions on Corregidor, which were then distributed evenly between Batteries B and C. Barlow, *Bunker's War*, 56, 58, and 60. Moore, "Report of Operations, HD M&SB," 25. "Exhibit F, The Antiaircraft Defenses Command in Harbor Defense of Manila and Subic Bays," in Moore, "Report of Operations, HD M&SB," 75. Charles A. Lockwood, *Sink 'Em All, Submarine Warfare in the Pacific* (New York: P. Dutton, 1951), 14. Hereafter Lockwood, *Sink 'Em All*. Morton, *The Fall* of *the Philippines*, 390-403.

[584] Lewis (ed.) "Intercept Station 'C'," 45, 51. Morton, *The Fall of the Philippines*, 390-403.

[585] Lockwood, *Sink 'Em All*, 277. Morton, *The Fall of the Philippines*, 390-403.

[586] Lewis (ed.) Intercept Station "C", 52-53.

[587] Lockwood, Sink 'Em All, 241-43. Morton, *The Fall of the Philippines,* 390-403. Lewis (ed.), *Intercept Station "C",* 58, 60.

[588] Morton, *The Fall of the Philippines*, 390-403.

[589] "Exhibit F, the Antiaircraft Defenses Command, Harbor Defense of Manila and Subic Bays," in Moore, "Report of Operations, HD M&SB," 73.

[590] "Exhibit F, the Antiaircraft Defense Command, Harbor Defense of Manila and Subic Bays," in Moore, "Report of Operations, HD M&SB," 24, 73. Earl L. Barr, "History of Battery 'M,' 60th CA (AA)," Center of Military History, Washington, D.C.

[591] When Fort Frank's two remaining AA guns were finally knocked out of action by Japanese artillery fire from Cavite in late March, the battery's M1 height-finder and power plant were transferred to Fort Hughes for use by Battery I, 59th Coast Artillery, and its M4 director was moved to Corregidor. "Exhibit F, the Antiaircraft Defenses Command, Harbor Defense of Manila and Subic Bays," in Moore, "Report of Operations, HD M&SB," 73-74. Coast Artillery School, "The Siege of Corregidor," Coast Artillery Training Bulletin Vol. 3, No. 1 (February 1944), 7.

[592] "Battery History, Battery I, 60th Coast Artillery (AA)."

[593] "Diary of Battery L, 60th Coast Artillery (AA)," Organizational Records Unit, Military Personnel Records Section, National Personnel Records Center, St. Louis, MO.

[594] E.L. Barr, "History of Battery 'M,' 60th CA (AA)," Center of Military History, Washington, D.C.

[595] "Exhibit F, The Antiaircraft Defenses Command, Harbor Defense of Manila and Subic Bays," in Moore, "Report of Operations HD M&SB." 74. General Headquarters, Far East Command, Military History Section, Japanese Research Division, "Philippines Air Operations Record, Phase I," Japanese Monograph No. 11, 1 February 1952, Archives, Fort Leavenworth, KS, 35.

[596] Arthur E. Huff, "History of Battery B, 60th CA (AA) Regiment." Godfrey R. Ames [Battery C, 60th CA I (AA) Regiment] "Narrative Report of Action during War October 20, 1943." Paul R. Cornwall, "War History, Battery D, 60th CA (AA) Regiment," Organizational Records Unit, Military Personnel Records Section, National Personnel Records Center, St. Louis, MO. "Diary of Battery E, 60th Coast Artillery," RG 407, Archives II. "Exhibit F, The Antiaircraft Defenses Command, Harbor Defense of Manila and Subic Bays," in Moore, "Report of Operations, HD M&SB," 74-75.

[597] "Diary of Battery E, 60th Coast Artillery," Organizational Records Unit, Military Personnel Records Section, National Personnel Records Center, St. Louis, MO. "Exhibit F, the Antiaircraft Defenses Command, Harbor Defense of Manila and Subic Bays," in Moore, "Report of Operations, HD M&SB," 77.

[598] Godfrey R. Ames, "Narrative Report of Action during War, October 20, 1943" [Battery C, 60th Coast Artillery]. E.M. Shiley, "History of Battery I, 60th CA (AA)," 1917- RG 407, Archives II, NARA. Paul R. Cornwall, "War History, Battery D, 60th CA (AA) Regiment," Organizational Records Unit, Military Personnel Records Section, National Personnel Records Center, St. Louis, MO.

[599] Arthur E. Huff, "History of Battery B, 60th CA (AA) Regiment." Charles L. Kasler, "History of Battery D, 60th Coast Artillery (AA)."

[600] Arthur E. Huff, "History of Battery B, 60th CA (AA) Regiment." Godfrey R. Ames, "Narrative Report of Action during War, October 20, 1943" [Battery C, 60th Coast Artillery]. Paul R. Cornwall, "War History, Battery D, 60th CA (AA) Regiment";

"Battery F [60th CA] History"; Warren A Starr, "Battery Commander's Narrative, Report of Battery Hartford's Action during the War Period from November 29, 1941, to the Surrender of Corregidor, May 6, 1942," Organizational Records Unit, Military Personnel Records Section, National Personnel Records Center, St. Louis, MO. "Exhibit F, the Antiaircraft Defenses Command, Harbor Defense of Manila and Subic Bays," in Moore, "Report of Operations, HD M&SB," 76.

[601] "Diary of Battery E, RG 407, Archives II. Moore, "Report of Operations, HD M&SB," 35. "Exhibit F, the Antiaircraft Defenses Command, Harbor Defense of Manila and Subic Bays," in Moore, "Report of Operations, HD M&SB," 77-78. General Headquarters, Far East Command, Military History Section, Japanese Research Division, "Philippines Air Operations Record, Phase I," Japanese Monograph No. 11, February 1, 1952, Archives, Fort Leavenworth, KS, 27-28.

[602] Charles L. Kasler, "History of Battery D, 60th Coast Artillery (AA)." "Diary of Battery E," RG 407, Archives II. "Record of Events, Battery B, 91st C.A. (PS), Nov. 28, 1941, to May 7, 1942," RG 407, Archives II. Moore, "Report of Operations, HD M&SB," 35. "Exhibit F, the Antiaircraft Defenses Command, Harbor Defense of Manila and Subic Bays," in Moore, "Report of Operations, HD M&SB," 77.

[603] "Report of Operations of the Quartermaster Corps, U.S. Army," in Wainwright Papers as published in Historical Documents of World War II in the Philippines, Vol. IV, Celedonio A. Ancheta, 77. Morton, *The Fall of the Philippines*, 372.

[604] Barlow, *Bunker's War*. Moore, "Report of Operations, HD M&SB," 25.

[605] Moore, "Report of Operations, HD M&SB," 36.

[606] "Diary of Battery E," RG 407, Archives II. Aaron A. Abston, "Diary of Battery G, 60th Coast Artillery, June 1, 1941-May 6, 1942."

[607] "Diary of Battery E," RG 407, Archives II, NARA

[608] Aaron A. Abston, "Diary of Battery G, 60th Coast Artillery June 1, 1941-May 6, 1942."

[609] Ibid. Interview with Walter A. Kulinski, October 14, 1963, Folder, 60th Coast Artillery Regiment, Reminiscences and letters, Corregidor (5-inch Box), William and James Belote Collection, USAMHI, Carlisle Barracks, PA. Arthur E. Huff, "History of Battery B, 60th CA (AA) Regiment."

[610] John Gulick, "Cebu, the Combat History of Battery C, 91st Coast Artillery (Philippine Scouts)," Corregidor Historical Society.

[611] Ibid.

[612] Ibid.

[613] Little Baguio was located on the slopes of Mariveles Mountain about halfway between Cabcaben and Mariveles. Kasler, "History of Battery D, 60th Coast Artillery (AA)." Paul R. Cornwall, "War History, Battery D, 60th CA (AA) Regiment," Organizational Records Unit, Military Personnel Records Section, National Personnel Records Center, St. Louis, MO.

[614] Barlow, *Bunker's War*, 120. "Battery F [60th CA] History"; Warren A. Starr, "Battery Commander's Narrative, Report of Battery Hartford's Action during the War Period from November 29, 1941, to the Surrender of Corregidor, May 6, 1942," Organizational Records Unit, Military Personnel Records Section, National Personnel Records Center, St. Louis, MO.

[615] Godfrey R. Ames, "Narrative Report of Action during War, October 20, 1943" [Battery C, 60th Coast Artillery]; Paul R. Cornwall, "War History, Battery D, 60th CA (AA) Regiment," Organizational Records Unit, Military Personnel Records Section, National Personnel Records Center, St. Louis, MO.

[616] The 803rd Engineers (Aviation) Bn (Separate) had arrived in the Philippines on October 23, 1941, assigned to expansion of airfields around Manila and later to construction of airfields and trails on Bataan and Corregidor. Company A, 803rd Bn, had been assigned to Corregidor in January 1942. "Engineer Annex," in Moore, "Report of Operations, HD M&SB," 25, 61. E.L. Barr, "Diary."

[617] Moore, "Report of Operations, HD M&SB," 36.

[618] Archives II, RG 407, Entry 360A, File 470.05, April 8, 1942.

[619] "Records of Events, Battery B, 91st C.A. (PS), Nov. 28, 1941, to May 7, 1942," RG 407, Archives II. Barlow, *Bunker's War*, 125.

[620] Moore, "Report of Operations, HD M&SB," 37. Barlow, *Bunker's War*, 125. Warren A Starr, "Battery Commander's Narrative, Report of Battery Hartford's Action during the War Period from November 29, 1941, to the Surrender of Corregidor, May 6, 1942," Organizational Records Unit, Military Personnel Records Section, National Personnel Records Center, St. Louis, MO. "Records of Events, Battery B, 91st C.A. (PS), Nov. 28, 1941, to May 7, 1942," RG 407, Archives II.

[621] USS *Canopus, Finch, Napa,* in *Dictionary of American Naval Fighting Ships.*

[622] Moore, "Report of Operations, HD M&SB," 37, 41, 44. USS *Luzon*, *Mindanao*, *Pigeon*, *Tanager*, in *Dictionary of American Naval Fighting Ships*. Arnold A. Bocksel, "The USAMP *General George Harrison* in the Harbor Defense of Manila and Subic Bay," *CAJ*, Vol., 89, No. 6, (Nov.-Dec. 1946), 54. Gordon, *Fighting for MacArthur*, 256-59.

[623] Godfrey R. Ames, "Narrative Report of Action during War, October 20, 1943" [Battery C, 60th Coast Artillery], Barlow, *Bunker's War*, 125.

[624] Barlow, *Bunker's War*, 125.

[625] Godfrey R. Ames, "Narrative Report of Action during War, October 20, 1943" [Battery C, 60th Coast Artillery].

[626] "Diary of Battery E," RG 407, Archives II. Battery Way had been put into reduced service in the 1930s. While not abandoned, no active unit had been assigned to the battery and its magazine spaces were shared with other temporary occupants. The armament was kept in place along with its ammunition, but trees and brush had been allowed to grow heavily on the pit slopes. It had not been manned or fired at all during the campaign up until occupancy by Battery E, 60th CA.

[627] Ibid.

[628] "Diary of Battery L, 60th Coast Artillery (AA)," Organizational Records Unit, Military Personnel Records Section, National Personnel Records Center, St. Louis, MO.

[629] Barlow, *Bunker's War*, 128. Moore, "Report of Operations, HD M&SB," 36. Braly, "Corregidor," 41.

[630] "Records of Events, Battery B, 91st C.A. (PS), Nov. 28, 1941, to May 7, 1942," RG 407, Archives II. Barlow, *Bunker's War*, 128-29.

[631] Godfrey R. Ames, "Narrative Report of Action during War, October 20, 1943" [Battery C, 60th Coast Artillery].

[632] Aaron A. Abston, "Diary of Battery G, 60th Coast Artillery June 1, 1941-May 6, 1942."

[633] Godfrey R. Ames, "Narrative Report of Action during War, October 20, 1943" [Battery C, 60th Coast Artillery].

[634] "Battery F, [60th CA] History," Organizational Records Unit, Military Personnel Records Section, National Personnel Records Center, St. Louis, MO.

[635] Arthur E. Huff, "History of Battery B, 60th CA (AA) Regiment."

[636] Paul R. Cornwall, "War History, Battery D, 60th CA (AA) Regiment," Organizational Records Unit, Military Personnel Records Section, National Personnel Records Center, St. Louis, MO.

[637] Godfrey R. Ames, "Narrative Report of Action during War October 20, 1943" [Battery C, 60th Coast Artillery].

[638] Braly, "Corregidor," 41. Moore, "Report of Operations, HD M&SB," 40. Capt. John McM. Gulick, "Battery C, 91st CA (PS)." Capt. John M. Wright, "Battery D, 91st CA (PS)." "Appendix E, Statement of Witnesses, Report of War Damages to the Harbor Defenses of Manila and Subic Bays 6 October 1945," Headquarters 14th Antiaircraft Command.

[639] Barlow, *Bunker's War*, 132-133.

[640] Ibid.

[641] Ibid, 134-35.

[642] Moore, "Report of Operations, HD M&SB," 40.

[643] Barlow, *Bunker's War*, 137-138. Braly, "Corregidor," 41.

[644] "Diary of Battery E," RG 407, Archives II. This report states that Battery Way's Gun No. 1 was the final firing mortar, but personal accounts by battery commander Maj. William Masello and gun commander Sergeant Walter Kwiecinski both contradict that statement, saying that Gun No. 2 (the right-hand, forward gun) was the final firing element. Those eyewitness accounts are judged more reliable. Stephen A. Kwiecinski, *Honor Courage Faith; A Corregidor Story* (Mandaluyong City, Philippines: Anvil Publishing Inc., 2014).

[645] Arthur E. Huff, "History of Battery B, 60th CA (AA) Regiment." Godfrey R. Ames, "Narrative Report of Action during War, October 20, 1943" [Battery C, 60th Coast Artillery]. General Headquarters, Far East Command, Military History Section, Japanese Research Division, "Philippines Air Operations Record, Phase I," Japanese Monograph No. 11, 1 February 1952, Archives, Fort Leavenworth, KS, 28.

[646] Aaron A. Abston, "Diary of Battery G, 60th Coast Artillery June 1, 1941-May 6, 1942."

[647] Godfrey R. Ames, "Narrative Report of Action during War October 20, 1943" [Battery C, 60th Coast Artillery].

[648] Ibid.

[649] Ibid.

[650] "Battery F [60th CA] History," Organizational Records Unit, Military Personnel Records Section, National Personnel Records Center, St. Louis, MO.

[651] Warren A Starr, "Battery Commander's Narrative Report of Battery Hartford's Action during the War Period, from November 29, 1941, to the Surrender of Corregidor, May 6, 1942," Organizational Records Unit, Military Personnel Records Section, National Personnel Records Center, St. Louis, MO.

[652] Barlow, *Bunker's War*, 139-140. "Diary of Battery E," RG 407, Archives II.

[653] Paul R. Cornwall, "War History, Battery D, 60th CA (AA) Regiment," Organizational Records Unit, Military Personnel Records Section, National Personnel Records Center, St. Louis, MO.

[654] Warren A Starr, "Battery Commander's Narrative Report of Battery Hartford's Action during the War Period from November 29, 1941, to the Surrender of Corregidor, May 6, 1942," Organizational Records Unit, Military Personnel Records Section, National Personnel Records Center, St. Louis, MO.

[655] "Diary of Battery E," RG 407, Archives II. Battery F [60th CA] History, Organizational Records Unit, Military Personnel Records Section, National Personnel Records Center, St. Louis, MO. Moore, "Report of Operations, HD M&SB," 45. Capt. Thomas W. Davis, "Appendix E, Statement of Witnesses, Report of War Damages to the Harbor Defenses of Manila and Subic Bays, 6 October 1945," Headquarters 14th Antiaircraft Command. Gregory J. Hagge, "What Happened to the Mortars of Corregidor," *The Coast Defense Study Group Journal*, Vol. 9, No. 3 (Aug. 1995), 21-27.

[656] Arthur E. Huff, "History of Battery B, 60th CA (AA) Regiment." Godfrey R. Ames, "Narrative Report of Action during War October 20, 1943" [Battery C, 60th Coast Artillery]. Aaron A. Abston, "Diary of Battery G, 60th Coast Artillery, June 1, 1941-May 6, 1942." Warren A Starr, "Battery Commander's Narrative Report of Battery Hartford's Action during the War Period from November 29, 1941, to the Surrender of Corregidor, May 6, 1942," Organizational Records Unit, Military Personnel Records Section, National Personnel Records Center, St. Louis, MO. Col. Arnold D. Amoroso, "Appendix E Statement of Witnesses, Report of War Damages to the Harbor Defenses of Manila and Subic Bays, 6 October 1945," Headquarters, 14th Antiaircraft Command. Interview of Albert L. Corn by Dr. W.M. Belote, May 29, 1975, Folder 59th Coast Artillery (Antiaircraft), Roster of officers, Reminicesences [sic] and letters, Corregidor Box, William and James Belote Collection, Archives, USAMHI, Carlisle Barracks, PA.

[657] Godfrey R. Ames, "Narrative Report of Action during War, October 20, 1943" [Battery C, 60th Coast Artillery]. Capt. Thomas W. Davis, "Appendix E, Statement of Witnesses, Report of War Damages to the Harbor Defenses of Manila and Subic Bays 6 October 1945," Headquarters, 14th Antiaircraft Command. Gordon, *Fighting for MacArthur*, 240.

[658] "Diary of Battery E," RG 407, Archives II.

[659] Aaron A. Abston, "Diary of Battery G, 60th Coast Artillery, June 1, 1941-May 6, 1942."

[660] Arthur E. Huff, "History of Battery B, 60th CA (AA) Regiment." Godfrey R. Ames, Narrative Report of Action during War, October 20, 1943," [Battery C, 60th Coast Artillery]. Moore, "Report of Operations, HD M&SB," 42-47.

[661] MacArthur, *MacArthur Reports*, Vol. II, 110-12. Moore, "Report of Operations, HD M&SB," 42-47. Philippine Air Operations Record Phase One, Far East Command, Japanese Monograph #11, 1 Feb. 1952 Document 17807, 11, Archive Section, Fort Leavenworth, KS, Plate 8 following p. 35.

[662] Paul R. Cornwall, "War History, Battery D, 60th CA (AA) Regiment," Organizational Records Unit, Military Personnel Records Section, National Personnel Records Center, St. Louis, MO. Miller, *From Shanghai to Corregidor*, 44.

[663] Col. Delbert Ausmus, "Appendix E, Statement of Witnesses, Report of War Damages to the Harbor Defenses of Manila and Subic Bays 6 October 1945," Headquarters 14th Antiaircraft Command. "Exhibit "G", Beach Defense Artillery Tabulation."

[664] Ibid. Moore, "Report of Operations, HD M&SB," 88-89.

[665] Miller, *From Shanghai to Corregidor*, 30.

[666] Miller, *From Shanghai to Corregidor*, 30-31. Moore, "Report of Operations, HD M&SB," 21.

[667] Ibid, 32.

[668] Miller, *From Shanghai to Corregidor*, 43-44. Moore, "Report of Operations, HD M&SB," "Exhibit K, Personnel Annex," 103.

[669] "Battery F [60th CA] History," Organizational Records Unit, Military Personnel Records Section, National Personnel Records Center, St. Louis, MO.

[670] E.M. Shiley, "History of Battery I, 60th CA (AA)," RG 407, Archives II.

[671] E.L. Sackett, "History of USS *Canopus*." Miller, *From Shanghai to Corregidor*, 4.

[672] Miller, *From Shanghai to Corregidor*, 41-47.

[673] Braly, "Corregidor," 8. Stephen M. Mellnik, "How the Japs Took Corregidor," *CAJ*, Vol. 88, No. 2 (Mar.-Apr. 1946), 10. Col. Delbert Ausmus, "Appendix E, Statement of Witnesses, Report of War Damages to the Harbor Defenses of Manila and Subic Bays 6 October 1945," Headquarters 14th Antiaircraft Command. Moore, "Report of Operations, HD M&SB," 43.

[674] Miller, *From Shanghai to Corregidor*, 27-28. Morton, *Fall of the Philippines*, 552.

[675] Miller, *From Shanghai to Corregidor*, 48.

[676] Ibid.

[677] "Diary of Battery E," [60th CA AA]," RG 407, Archives II.

[678] Miller, *From Shanghai to Corregidor*, 49.

[679] Ibid, 50-51.

[680] Ray G. Lawrence to William Belote, October 3, 1963, Folder 92nd Coast Artillery Regiment, Reminiscences of Surrender of Corregidor, Corregidor Box, William and James Belote Collection, USAMHI, Carlisle Barracks, PA.

[681] Ibid.

[682] Miller, *From Shanghai to Corregidor*, 52.

[683] Miller, *From Shanghai to Corregidor*, 52. Paul R. Cornwall, "War History, Battery D, 60th CA (AA) Regiment," Organizational Records Unit, Military Personnel Records Section, National Personnel Records Center, St. Louis, MO.

[684] Earl L. Barr, "History of Battery "M," 60th CA (AA)," Center of Military History, Washington, D.C.

[685] Miller, *From Shanghai to Corregidor*, 52.

[686] Paul R. Cornwall, "War History, Battery D, 60th CA (AA) Regiment," Organizational Records Unit, Military Personnel Records Section, National Personnel Records Center, St. Louis, MO.

[687] Miller, *From Shanghai to Corregidor*, 55.

[688] Miller, *From Shanghai to Corregidor*, 58. Lt. Col. Frank O. Hough, Maj. Verle E. Ludwig, and Henry I. Shaw Jr., *History of U.S. Marine Corps Operations in World War II*, Vol. 1, *Pearl Harbor to Guadalcanal* (Washington, D.C.: Historical Branch, G-3 Division, Headquarters, U.S. Marine Corps), 195.

[689] Miller, *From Shanghai to Corregidor*.

[690] Ibid.

[691] Ibid., 63.

[692] Ibid., 59.

[693] Ibid., 60.

[694] Ibid., 60-61.

[695] Ibid., 64-65.

[696] Ibid., 64.

[697] Ibid., 65.

[698] Ibid., 65.

[699] Braly, "Corregidor," 21. Coast Artillery School, *Siege of Corregidor,* Coast Artillery Training Bulletin, Vol. 3, No. 1 (Feb 1944), Fort Monroe, VA, 18.

[700] Ibid.

[701] Miller, *From Shanghai to Corregidor*, 66.

[702] Godfrey R. Ames, "Narrative Report of Action during War October 20, 1943" [Battery C, 60th Coast Artillery].

[703] Ibid.

[704] "Battery F History," Organizational Records Unit, Military Personnel Records Section, National Personnel Records Center, St. Louis, MO.

[705] Arthur E. Huff, "History of Battery B, 60th CA (AA) Regiment."

[706] Aaron A. Abston, "Diary of Battery G, 60th Coast Artillery June 1, 1941-May 6, 1942."

[707] Braly, *"Corregidor,"* 43.

[708] Miller, *From Shanghai to Corregidor*, 66.

[709] Braly, "Corregidor," 44.

[710] Aaron A. Abston, "Diary of Battery G, 60th Coast Artillery June 1, 1941-May 6, 1942."

[711] Warren A Starr, "Battery Commander's Narrative Report of Battery Hartford's Action during the War Period from November 29, 1941, to the Surrender of Corregidor, May 6, 1942," Organizational Records Unit, Military Personnel Records Section, National Personnel Records Center, St. Louis, MO.

[712] Godfrey R. Ames, Narrative Report of Action during War October 20, 1943," [Battery C, 60th Coast Artillery], courtesy of Ms. Karol Ames. "Battery F History," Organizational Records Unit, Military Personnel Records Section, National Personnel Records Center, St. Louis, MO. Moore, "Report of Operations, HD M&SB," 52.

[713] Stockton Bruns, History of Battery I, 59th Coast Artillery, Folder 59th Coast Artillery; Interview with Col. Valentine P. Foster, USA (Ret) November 29, 1963, Folder, 59th Coast Artillery (Antiaircraft) Roster of officers, reminiscences and letters, Corregidor 5-inch Box, William and James Belote Collection, Archives, USAMHI, Carlisle Barracks, PA.

[714] Interview with Col. Valentine P. Foster, USA (Ret) November 29, 1963; Interview with Col. Armand Hopkins, Folder 59th Coast Artillery (Antiaircraft), roster of officers, Reminiscences and letters, Corregidor 5-inch Box, William and James Belote Collection, Archives, USAMHI, Carlisle Barracks, PA.

[715] Col. Boudreau, "Testimony Appendix E, Statement of Witnesses, Report of War Damages to the Harbor Defenses of Manila and Subic Bays 6 October 1945", Headquarters 14th Antiaircraft Command.

[716] Ibid.

[717] Ben E. King, "Testimony Before the Judge Advocate General War Crimes Office, War Department," June 6. 1945.

[718] Ibid.

[719] Belote and Belote, *Corregidor*, 182-83.

[720] Barlow, *Bunker's War*, 163-64, 167. "Appendix E, Statement of Witnesses, Report of War Damages to the Harbor Defenses of Manila and Subic Bays 6 October 1945," Headquarters 14th Antiaircraft Command.

[721] "Appendix E, Statement of Witnesses, Report of War Damages to the Harbor Defenses of Manila and Subic Bays, 6 October 1945," Headquarters 14th Antiaircraft Command.

[722] John M. Wright, *Captured on Corregidor; Diary of an American P.O.W. in World War II* (Jefferson, NC: MacFarland & Co., Inc., 1988). Headquarters 14th Antiaircraft Command, "Proceedings of a Board of Officers Appointed to Evaluate War Damage to the Harbor Defenses of Manila and Subic Bay", October 6, 1945. Archives, US Army Military History Institute (USAMHI), Carlisle Barracks, PA., Appendix E, Statements of Lieutenant Ramsey," 11.

[723] Kazumo Uno, *Corregidor: Isle of Delusion* (Shanghai: Press Bureau of the Imperial Japanese Army, General Headquarters in China, 1942). Watari Gasei, *Philippine Expeditionary Force,* (Tokyo: Group Information Department Publication).

[724] Wright, *Captured on Corregidor*, 5-35.

[725] Gerard M. Devlin, *Back to Corregidor: America Retakes the Rock* (New York: St. Martin's Press, 1992), 90-91. Hereafter: Devlin, *Back to Corregidor.*

[726] Belote and Belote, *Corregidor*, 189-190.

[727] William C. Braly, *The Hard Way Home* (Washington D.C.: Infantry Journal Press, 1947), 233.

[728] Case Report, 71-72.

[729] Evidence from photographs, MHI.

[730] Belote and Belote, *Corregidor,* 197.

[731] Lt. Gen. E.M. Flanagan, Jr., *Corregidor: The Rock Force Assault* (New York: Jove Books, 1989), 99. Hereafter: Flanagan, *Corregidor.*

[732] Belote and Belote, *Corregidor*, 197-98.

[733] Case Report, 50, and "Appendix E," 8.

[734] Case Report, 55-82.

[735] Case Report, p. 57.

[736] Case Report, 52-54.

[737] William B. Breuer, *Retaking the Philippines* (New York: St. Martin's Press, 1986), 1-7. Hereafter: Breuer, *Retaking the Philippines.*

[738] M. Hamilin Cannon, *Leyte: The Return to the Philippines,* U.S. Army in World War II (Washington DC: Office of the Chief of Military History, United States Army, 1954), 1-9.

[739] "Amphibian Engineer Operations," Volume IV of *Engineers of the Southwest Pacific 1941-1945,* Office of Chief Engineer, (Washington DC: GPO, 1959), 551-52.

[740] Case Report, 64.

[741] Gen. Walter Krueger, *From Down Under to Nippon: The Story of the Sixth Army in World War II* (Washington D.C.: Zenger Pub., 1953), 262-65.

[742] "Amphibian Engineer Operations," Vol. IV of *Engineers of the Southwest Pacific 1941-1945,* Office of Chief Engineer, (Washington DC: GPO, 1959), 557-58. Belote and Belote, *Corregidor,* 211-12.

[743] Case Report, pp. 17-20.

[744] Flanagan, *Corregidor,* 153-55.

[745] Ibid., 94-100.

[746] Breuer, *Retaking the Philippines,* 180.

[747] Ibid., 199.

[748] "Amphibian Engineer Operations," 559-61.

[749] Breuer, *Retaking the Philippines,* 214-17.

[750] Ibid., 219-20.

[751] Devlin, Back to Corregidor, 219-39.

[752] Breuer, *Retaking the Philippines,* 241.

[753] Devlin, *Back to Corregidor,* 186-89.

[754] Breuer, *Retaking the Philippines,* 255.

[755] 38th Infantry Division, "Avengers of Bataan," Albert Love Enterprises, 1947.

[756] Krueger, *From Down Under to Nippon,* 290.

[757] Robert Ross Smith, *Triumph in the Philippines, United States Army in World War II* (Washington, D.C.: Office of the Chief of Military History, Department of the Army, 1963), 355-56.

[758] Breuer, *Retaking the Philippines,* 262-63.

[759] Belote and Belote, *Corregidor,* 252-56.

[760] Ibid.

[761] Belote and Belote, *Corregidor,* 256. *Corregidor, Island of Value, Peace and International Understanding,* Corregidor Foundation, 1986, 35-46.

Index

Note: *Names of ships are in italics,* for locations and structures specific to Corregidor Island, entries are under Fort Mills.

G

H

I

J

The Coast Defense Study Group, Inc. (CDSG) is a tax-exempt corporation dedicated to study of seacoast fortifications. CDSG's purpose is to promote and encourage the study of coastal defenses, primarily but not exclusively those of the United States of America. The study of coast defenses and fortifications in- cludes their history, architecture, technology, strategic and tactical employment and evolution. The primary goals of the CDSG are the following:

- Educational study of coast defenses
- Technical research and documentation of coast defenses
- Preservation of coast defense sites, equipment and records for current and future generations
- Accurate coast defense site interpretations
- Assistance to groups interested in preservation and interpretation of coast defense sites
- Charitable activities which promote the goals of the CDSG

Membership is open to any person or organization interested in the study or history of the coast defenses and fortifications. Membership in the CDSG will allow you to attend the annual conference, special tours and receive the CDSG's quarterly journal and newsletter. For more information on the CDSG, please visit the CDSG website at cdsg.org or contact us at 24624 W. 96th Street, Lenexa, KS 66227-7285 USA, Attn: Quentin Schillare, Membership.

The CDSG Fund supports the efforts of the Coast Defense Study Group by raising funds for preservation and interpretation of American seacoast defenses. The CDSG Fund is seeking donations for projects sup- porting its goals. Donations are tax-deductible for federal tax purposes as the CDSG is a 501(c)(3) orga- nization, and 100% of your gift will go to project grants. Major contributions are acknowledged annually. The Fund is always seeking proposals for the monetary support of preservation and interpretation projects at former coast defense sites and museums. A one-page proposal briefly describing the site, the organization doing the work, and the proposed work or outcome should be sent to the address below. Successful proposals are usually distinct projects rather than general requests for donations. Upon conclusion of a project a short report suitable for publication in the CDSG Newsletter is requested. The trustees shall re- view such requests and pass their recommendation onto the CDSG Board of Directors for approval. Send donations and grant requests to: CDSG Fund c/o Terry McGovern 1700 Oak Lane McLean, VA 22101- 3326 USA or use your credit card via PayPal on the cdsg.org website.

The CDSG Press

CDSG Books and CDSD Gear ($ domestic / $ International) prices include domestic/international postage $US currency only (cash, check, money order or credit card via PayPal at the cdsg.org store), allow 6-8 weeks for delivery.

- *Notes on Seacoast Fortification Construction* by Col. Eben E. Winslow, 1920, 428 pp. 1994 reprint HC with drawings $45/$60
- *Seacoast Artillery Weapons Technical Manual* (TM) 9-210 by U.S. War Dept. 1944, 202 pp. 1995 reprint PB $25/$35
- *The Service of Coast Artillery* by F. Hines & F. Ward, 1910, 736 pp. 1997 reprint HC $40/$60
- *Permanent Fortifications & Sea-Coast Defences* by U.S. Congress, 1862, 544 pp. 1998 reprint HC
- $30/$45
- *American Coast Artillery Matérial* Ordnance Dept. Doc#2042 by U.S. War Dept., 1922, 528 pp., 2001 reprint HC $45/$65
- *American Seacoast Defenses: A Reference Guide* (3rd Edition) by Mark A. Berhow, (2015) 732 pp. HC $45/$80
- The Endicott & Taft Board Reports, reprint of original reports of 1886 and 1905 by U.S. Congress, 525 pp. 2007 reprint HC $45/$80
- *Artillerists and Engineers: The Beginnings of US Fortifications 1794-1815* by Col. Wade, U.S. Army. PB, 226 pp. $25/$40
- CDSG Logo Hats each $20.00 domestic and $25.00 foreign. CDSG Logo Patches each $ 4.00 domestic & foreign.
- CDSG T-Shirts (XXXL, XXL, XL, L; Red, Khaki, Navy, Black) $18.00 Domestic and $26.00 Foreign.

Send order to: CDSG Press Attn: Terry McGovern 1700 Oak Lane, McLean, VA 22101-3326
Or order via our online store at cdsg.org.

The CDSG Digital Library

The CDSG has digitized an extensive set of historic manuals, reports, records and documents on the harbor defenses of the United States Army.

- The CDSG provides back issues of the CDSG Publications (from 1985) in electronic format.
- The CDSG Documents covers a range of historical material related to seacoast defenses -- most are from the National Archives. Included are the annual reports of the chief of coast artillery and chief of engineers; several board proceedings and reports; army directories; text books; tables of organi- zation and equipment; WWII command histories; drill, field, training manuals and regulations; ordnance department documents; ordnance tables and compilations; and the ordnance gun and carriage cards.
- CDSG Documents related to specific harbor defenses. These PDF documents form the basis of the conference and special tour handouts that have been held at these locations. They include RCBs/RCWs; maps; annexes to defense projects; CD engineer notebooks; quartermaster building records; and aerial photos taken by the signal corps 1920-40. Please consult cdsg.org for more details.

Information on the CDSG ePress items can be obtained from Mark Berhow at berhowma@cdsg.org or by post to PO Box 6124, Peoria, IL 61601 USA, or at cdsg.org.

McGovern Publishing Presents:

McGovern Publishing is comprised of two divisions: Redoubt Press (military titles) and Three Sisters Press (Rebecca, Rachel, and Alana) offering a range of subjects. McGovern Publishing is interested in new titles, especially those dealing with fortifications, please contact Terry McGovern at 703/538-5403 or at tcmcgovern@att.net if you have a title that you are seeking to have published.

Visit our website at www.mcgovernpublising.com, or post to 1700 Oak Lane, McLean, Virginia 22101-3326 USA

Redoubt Press

A Division of McGovern Publishing

A Division of McGovern Publishing

The Chesapeake Bay at War!
The Coastal Defenses of Chesapeake Bay During World War II
by Terrance McGovern

The defense of America's seacoast has been one of key concerns since the earliest years of the Republic. American coastal defenses steadily evolved through the age of muzzle loading cannon, ever larger breech loading weapons, and finally to the culmination of large, long range guns capable of targeting the largest and most heavily armed warships of their age. By the end of World War II, the United States had some of the strongest defenses in the world. Given the importance of the U.S. naval bases around Norfolk, Virginia and the shipyards of Hampton Roads, the seacoast defenses protecting Chesapeake Bay contained the largest collection of firepower in the continental United States as they reached their apex during World War II.

This book tells the story of preparing the coastal defenses of the Chesapeake Bay for the coming of World War II and their operations from 1941 to 1945. Over a hundred rare black & white U.S. Army photographs and plans help document our nation's extensive efforts to defend against naval attacks and raids from Nazi Germany. A collection of over 50 recent color aerial photographs are also included allowing the reader to survey the surviving elements of these mighty defenses. A product of extensive research this book brings together rare images and the little-known military history of the Chesapeake Bay for the first time. Three Sisters Press (Rebecca, Rachel, and Alana) is pleased to offer this 70-page softbound book for $20 plus $5 for domestic shipping or $10 for foreign shipping.

American Defenses of the Panama Canal
By Terrance McGovern.

The end of 20th Century has brought to a close the American involvement in the Panama Canal, a tremendous technological achievement that was started in the early days of the century. The Panama Canal took over 10 years to complete and involved the expenditure of millions of dollars and thousands of worker's lives. The importance of the Panama Canal to commerce and naval forces resulted in fortifications that match its size and cost. While the history of the Panama Canal has been recorded in numerous books and articles, the history of its defenses has not. This book hopes to remedy this situation by exploring the thirty-five years of fortification construction and use in the Panama Canal Zone.

The first part of this book discusses how the various fortification boards decided, with the help of Congress, on what defenses were needed and how evolving threats resuled in changes to these defenses. The second part of the book descibes in detail the construction, service life, and current status o each major battery. Assisting this narrative are many current nd period photographs, along with engineering drawings an site maps detailing the construction of these impressive fofications. All serious students of seacoast defenses and the Pana a Canal should have a copy.

This title was originally published in U.K based ortress Study Group annual journal, *FORT: The International J nal of Fortification and Military Architecture* (Volume 26: 199 This 116-page book is softbound using the same high- qualit aper and printing process as *FORT.* As the most detailed and us-trated article to ever be produced on these defenses, the ok has 45 maps and drawings, 43 historical B&W photogr s, and 40 color photographs (taken in 1993 and 1999 by the thor). This book is offered at a price of $50 plus $5 for dome shipping or $10 for foreign shipping.

The Concrete Battleship
Fort Drum, El Fraile Island, Manila Bay
by Francis J. Allen

Fort Drum on El Fraile Island in the Philippines is unique in the development of United States coastal fortifications. Fort Drum is part of a chain of forts built across the entrance of Manila Bay to defend the Bay from naval attack. The construction of Fort Drum began in 1909 by reducing tiny El Fraile Island to the low water mark. Over the next ten years a multi-deck concrete island was built to mount two twin 14-inch guns in superimposed Army designed armored turrets. The completed work rises 40 feet above sea level, it is 350 feet long and 144 across at its widest point. The exterior walls are up to 28 feet thick and the top deck attains a thickness of 20 feet of re-enforced concrete. The interior of the fort held a large engine room, powder and shell magazines, a mining casemate, storerooms and tankage, a accommodations for 300 personnel. The design of the fort followed a naval pattern with turrets, a cage mast, and secondary armament in side casemates. Due to these characteristics, Fort Drum became known as the "Concrete Battleship."

When completed in 1918, Fort Drum was the most powerful defense work in Manila Bay, but the advances in military technology during World War I already began to make the fort obsolete. The post-World War I reduction in military spending, the re- strictions of the Washington Naval Treaty of 1922, and economic depression of the 1930s resulted in Fort Drum being quickly reduced to caretaker sta- tus until the coming of World

War II. Fort Drum became an important weapon during the Japanese siege of Corregidor and the other island forts during 1942 but only play a minor role during the American retaking of these islands in 1945. The battles of World War II would transform Fort Drum from an American-manned, fully operating fort to a burned-out hulk inhabited by lifeless Japanese sailors.

This revised and enlarged 64-page softbound volume tells the story of The Concrete Battleship in words, diagrams, and photographs from its inception to the present day. Redoubt Press is pleased to offer this book for $20 plus $5 for domestic shipping or $10 for forign shipping.

The Delaware Bay at War!
The Coastl Defenses of Delaware Bay During World War II

by Terrance McGovern

The fense of America's seacoast has been one of the key concerns sir the earliest years of the Republic. American coast defense stily evolved through the age of muzzle loading cannon, ever lar breech loading weapons, and finally to the culmination in larg long range guns capable of targeting the largest and most heavi armed warships of their age. By the end of World War II, the ted States had some of the strongest defenses in the world. Giv the importance of the military- industrial complex along the nks of the Delaware River, including the large Philadelphia N Shipyard, the seacoast defenses protecting Delaware Bay h eclined dramatically since the turn of the century resulting i whole program of modern coast artillery batteries and other nses to be constructed starting in the late 1930's and reaching r reached their apex during the middle of World War II.

This book tells the story of preparing the coastal defenses of e Delaware Bay for the coming of World War Two and their opations from 1941 to 1945. Over a hundred rare black & white J.S. Army photographs and plans help document our nation's xtensive efforts to defend against naval at- tacks and raids from Nazi Germany. A collection of recent color aerial photography is also included allowing the reader to survey the surviving elements of these generally unknown defenses. A product of extensive research this book brings together rare images and the little-known military history of the Delaware Bay for the first time. Three Sisters Press (Rebecca, Rachel, and Alana) is pleased to offer this 65-page softbound book for $20 plus $5 for do- mestic shipping or $10 for foreign shipping.

A Legacy in Brick and Stone – 2nd Edition
American Coastal Defense Forts of the Third System 1816-1867

By John R. Weaver II

The definitive history of the American Third System of Fortifications that defended our coastline for more than half of century, these architectural wonders were built from 1816 through 1867 from Maine through the Florida Keys to New Orleans, with two forts in San Francisco Bay. Most of these 42 masonry forts still stand guard along our shores, and open to the public. *A Legacy in Brick and Stone* provides the background of these famous Civil War forts – why they were built where they are, who built them, and how they functioned – as well as descriptions of each of the forts.

This revised and expanded edition has grown to 340 pages with 400 new photographs and drawings. John Weaver II, a nationally known expert on masonry coastal fortifications, has invested over 30 years of research into *A Legacy in Brick and Stone* to produce the only a full treatment of the magnificent American Third System.

The book begins with a study of the history of the Coastal Fortifications Board, which developed and implemented this massive defense project. It then details the art of fortification of that period and describes the particular architecture components that were key to their design. A description of the development of the system over its 50-year life is followed by an analysis of how well certain forts held up under attack during the American Civil War. Approximately two-thirds of this volume is dedicated to a fort-by-fort description of the system. The overall defense scheme for each harbor is discussed, then each fort in that harbor is analyzed. The author uses unique photographs and drawings to answer many of the questions about of these forts that today's visitors ask. The book also documents the current status of these historic forts, including information about how to visit these forts today.

Redoubt Press is pleased to offer a deluxe hardcover edition with color illustrations $64.95 plus a $5 fee for domestic shipping and $10 for foreign shipping. Paperback edition with black and white ilustrations $39.95 plus a $5 fee for domestic shipping and $10 for foreign shipping.

Seacoast Cannon Coloring Book

By Brian B. Chin

The big seacoast guns thunder once again. From the decorated brass cannon of Spanish New World, to the powerful iron guns in the American Civil War, to the complex disappearing guns of the turn of the century, to the huge guns of steel and armor in World War II, this detailed picture book shows how coast artillery once protected American shores from enemy attack. This second edition brings to life the coast defenses that today remain as empty forts and batteries with our national, state, and local parks. The author, Brian B. Chin, is a well-known author and artist that has produce several works on military fortifications. This coloring book allow a new generation to learn the history of American seacoast defenses while having fun coloring in this 52-page softbound book. It is hoped that book will help generate interest in preserving and interpreting these historic sites for future generations.

Three Sister Press (Rebecca, Rachel, and Alana) are pleased to offer this coloring book for $10 plus $5 for domestic shipping or $10 for foreign shipping.

Lightning Source UK Ltd.
Milton Keynes UK
UKHW030446031220
374527UK00007B/697